Cases on Digital Strategies and Management Issues in Modern Organizations

José Duarte Santos
Instituto Superior Politecnico, Spain

A volume in the Advances in Business Strategy
and Competitive Advantage (ABSCA) Book Series

Published in the United States of America by
IGI Global
Business Science Reference (an imprint of IGI Global)
701 E. Chocolate Avenue
Hershey PA, USA 17033
Tel: 717-533-8845
Fax: 717-533-8661
E-mail: cust@igi-global.com
Web site: http://www.igi-global.com

Copyright © 2022 by IGI Global. All rights reserved. No part of this publication may be reproduced, stored or distributed in any form or by any means, electronic or mechanical, including photocopying, without written permission from the publisher. Product or company names used in this set are for identification purposes only. Inclusion of the names of the products or companies does not indicate a claim of ownership by IGI Global of the trademark or registered trademark.

Library of Congress Cataloging-in-Publication Data

Names: Santos, Jose Duarte, 1966- editor.
Title: Cases on digital strategies and management issues in modern organizations/
   Jose Duarte Santos, editor.
Description: Hershey, PA : Business Science Reference, [2022] | Includes
   bibliographical references and index. | Summary: """This book explores
   the application of strategy conceptual models and theories in the
   current competitive business world"--Provided by publisher"-- Provided
   by publisher.
Identifiers: LCCN 2019032856 (print) | LCCN 2019032857 (ebook) | ISBN
   9781799816300 (hardcover) | ISBN 9781799816317 (paperback) | ISBN
   9781799816324 (ebook)
Subjects: LCSH: Strategic planning--Case studies. | Management--Case
   studies.
Classification: LCC HD30.28 .C4133 2022 (print) | LCC HD30.28 (ebook) |
   DDC 658.4/012--dc23
LC record available at https://lccn.loc.gov/2019032856
LC ebook record available at https://lccn.loc.gov/2019032857

This book is published in the IGI Global book series Advances in Business Strategy and Competitive Advantage (ABSCA) (ISSN: 2327-3429; eISSN: 2327-3437)

British Cataloguing in Publication Data
A Cataloguing in Publication record for this book is available from the British Library.

All work contributed to this book is new, previously-unpublished material. The views expressed in this book are those of the authors, but not necessarily of the publisher.

For electronic access to this publication, please contact: eresources@igi-global.com.

Advances in Business Strategy and Competitive Advantage (ABSCA) Book Series

Patricia Ordóñez de Pablos
Universidad de Oviedo, Spain

ISSN:2327-3429
EISSN:2327-3437

Mission

Business entities are constantly seeking new ways through which to gain advantage over their competitors and strengthen their position within the business environment. With competition at an all-time high due to technological advancements allowing for competition on a global scale, firms continue to seek new ways through which to improve and strengthen their business processes, procedures, and profitability.

The **Advances in Business Strategy and Competitive Advantage (ABSCA) Book Series** is a timely series responding to the high demand for state-of-the-art research on how business strategies are created, implemented and re-designed to meet the demands of globalized competitive markets. With a focus on local and global challenges, business opportunities and the needs of society, the **ABSCA** encourages scientific discourse on doing business and managing information technologies for the creation of sustainable competitive advantage.

Coverage

- Adaptive Enterprise
- Value Creation
- Balanced Scorecard
- Cost Leadership Strategy
- Tacit Knowledge
- Resource-Based Competition
- Ethics and Business Strategy
- Strategic Management
- Innovation Strategy
- Foreign Investment Decision Process

IGI Global is currently accepting manuscripts for publication within this series. To submit a proposal for a volume in this series, please contact our Acquisition Editors at Acquisitions@igi-global.com or visit: http://www.igi-global.com/publish/.

The Advances in Business Strategy and Competitive Advantage (ABSCA) Book Series (ISSN 2327-3429) is published by IGI Global, 701 E. Chocolate Avenue, Hershey, PA 17033-1240, USA, www.igi-global.com. This series is composed of titles available for purchase individually; each title is edited to be contextually exclusive from any other title within the series. For pricing and ordering information please visit http://www.igi-global.com/book-series/advances-business-strategy-competitive-advantage/73672. Postmaster: Send all address changes to above address. Copyright © 2022 IGI Global. All rights, including translation in other languages reserved by the publisher. No part of this series may be reproduced or used in any form or by any means – graphics, electronic, or mechanical, including photocopying, recording, taping, or information and retrieval systems – without written permission from the publisher, except for non commercial, educational use, including classroom teaching purposes. The views expressed in this series are those of the authors, but not necessarily of IGI Global.

Titles in this Series

For a list of additional titles in this series, please visit: http://www.igi-global.com/book-series/advances-business-strategy-competitive-advantage/73672

Handbook of Research on Big Data, Green Growth, and Technology Disruption in Asian Companies and Societies
Patricia Ordóñez de Pablos (The University of Oviedo, Spain) Xi Zhang (Tianjin University, China) Mohammad Nabil Almunawar (Universiti Brunei Darussalam, Brunei) and José Emilio Labra Gayo (University of Oviedo, Spain)
Business Science Reference • © 2022 • 415pp • H/C (ISBN: 9781799885245) • US $295.00

Driving Factors for Venture Creation and Success in Agricultural Entrepreneurship
Mohd Yasir Arafat (Aligarh Muslim University, Aligarh, India) Imran Saleem (Aligarh Muslim University, Aligarh, India) Jabir Ali (Indian Institute of Management, Jammu, India) Adil Khan (O.P. Jindal University, Raigarh, India) and Hamad Hussain Balhareth (Saudi Electronic University, Saudi Arabia)
Business Science Reference • © 2022 • 315pp • H/C (ISBN: 9781668423493) • US $215.00

Handbook of Research on Emerging Business Models and the New World Economic Order
Jose Manuel Saiz-Alvarez (Catholic University of Avila, Spain, & Catholic University of Santiago de Guayaquil, Ecuador)
Business Science Reference • © 2022 • 454pp • H/C (ISBN: 9781799876892) • US $275.00

Cases on Survival and Sustainability Strategies of Social Entrepreneurs
Charles Oham (University of Greenwich, UK)
Business Science Reference • © 2022 • 305pp • H/C (ISBN: 9781799877240) • US $195.00

Digital Transformation and Internationalization Strategies in Organizations
Orkun Yildiz (Izmir Democracy University, Turkey)
Business Science Reference • © 2022 • 326pp • H/C (ISBN: 9781799881698) • US $195.00

Analyzing the Relationship Between Corporate Governance, CSR, and Sustainability
Muddassar Sarfraz (Hohai University, China) and Syed Ghulam Meran Shah (Southwestern University of Finance & Economics, China)
Business Science Reference • © 2022 • 315pp • H/C (ISBN: 9781799842347) • US $215.00

Leadership and Followership in an Organizational Change Context
Sajjad Nawaz Khan (Iqra University, Pakistan)
Business Science Reference • © 2022 • 361pp • H/C (ISBN: 9781799828075) • US $225.00

701 East Chocolate Avenue, Hershey, PA 17033, USA
Tel: 717-533-8845 x100 • Fax: 717-533-8661
E-Mail: cust@igi-global.com • www.igi-global.com

This book is dedicated to the three pillars of my life:

Sílvia Santos

Gabriel Santos

Dinis Santos

Table of Contents

Preface xiii

Chapter 1
Digital Transformation: Is It Part of a Strategic Process or a New Strategic Practice? 1
    Irene Ciccarino, Polytechnic Institute of Leiria, Portugal
    Carla Diniz dos Santos da Silva, IBMEC-RJ, Brazil

Chapter 2
Be Like Amazon: Achieving a Competitive Advantage Based on Digital Footprint Analysis 23
    Anna Tarabasz, Curtin University, UAE

Chapter 3
Digital Value Innovation and Strategic Management Practices of Adyar Ananda Bhavan 51
    Shakti Chaturvedi, REVA Business School, India
    Meenakshi Verma, Symbiosis International University, India
    Sonal Purohit, Chandigarh University, India
    Raghava Reddy Varaprasad, REVA University, India

Chapter 4
Consumer Perception of Brand Repositioning Through Benefit Diversification and Intensity of
Use: The Case of Pedras 77
    Francisca Quintas Rodrigues, Faculty of Economics, University of Porto, Portugal
    Beatriz Casais, School of Economics and Management & CICS.NOVA, University of Minho,
        Braga, Portugal

Chapter 5
Rose-Patisserie and Coffee House: Business Development Alternatives 91
    Paulo Botelho Pires, Porto Business School, Portugal
    António Correia Barros, Instituto Politécnico do Porto, Portugal

Chapter 6
THEIA: Thermal Insulation – A Business Strategy 119
    Paulo Botelho Pires, Porto Business School, Portugal
    António Correia Barros, Politécnico do Porto, Portugal
    José Duarte Santos, Polytechnic Institute of Gaya, Portugal

Chapter 7
The Bonduelle Group's Distribution Strategy: Adding a Branded Retail Store?................................ 150
    Véronique Boulocher-Passet, University of Brighton, UK
    Randall D. Harris, Texas A&M University, USA
    Sabine Ruaud, EDHEC Business School, France

Chapter 8
How to Build a Leading So-Called Neobank and Pursue Its Growth? The Case of the FinTech
Nickel in Europe 177
    Jean Michel Rocchi, Sciences Po Aix, France

Chapter 9
Purpose-Driven Marketing Wars: Dishwashing Detergent Brands' Purpose-Driven Marketing
Campaigns in Turkey 200
    Emrah Gülmez, Anadolu University, Turkey

Chapter 10
SWOT Analysis and a Case Study at Kayseri Airport... 236
    Sabiha Annaç Göv, Gaziantep University, Turkey

Chapter 11
The Adoption of a CRM Strategy Based on the Six-Dimensional Model: A Case Study................ 255
    José Duarte Santos, Polytechnic Institute of Gaya, Portugal
    José Pita Castelo, Universidade de Vigo, Spain

Chapter 12
How Competitive Strategies Affect Organizational Structure: A Research in Technology
Development Zones in Turkey 271
    Muhammed Seyda Akdag, Yıldız Technical University, Turkey
    Yasemin Bal, Yıldız Technical University, Turkey

Chapter 13
The Effects of Real-Time Content Marketing on Consumer Emotions and Behaviors: An Analysis
on COVID-19 Pandemic Period 300
    Hayat Ayar Senturk, Yildiz Technical University, Turkey
    Ece Ozer Cizer, Yildiz Technical University, Turkey
    Tugce Sezer, Yildiz Technical University, Turkey

Compilation of References 330

About the Contributors 359

Index 363

Detailed Table of Contents

Preface xiii

Chapter 1
Digital Transformation: Is It Part of a Strategic Process or a New Strategic Practice? 1
    Irene Ciccarino, Polytechnic Institute of Leiria, Portugal
    Carla Diniz dos Santos da Silva, IBMEC-RJ, Brazil

The COVID-19 pandemic has intensified the digitization of traditional businesses. In the retail sector, e-commerce played a fundamental role and promoted major changes in the consumer pattern. This evolution and its impact can be studied through the digital transformation lens, which is a multidisciplinary and holistic concept that encompasses a new strategy and new ways of strategizing. The present study aims to describe the digital transformation strategy implementation path at a Brazilian pre-digital retail company and discusses the role the COVID-19 pandemic had played. Moreover, the case highlights important strategic issues and provides the opportunity to analyze whether it is a strategic process or a strategic practice. Thus, it can enlighten which theory best supports DTS studies. This study also increases the understanding of the strategic configuration of digital transformation embracing context, process, and outcomes. And it also sheds light on the dilemma between brick-and-mortar stores and digital ones.

Chapter 2
Be Like Amazon: Achieving a Competitive Advantage Based on Digital Footprint Analysis 23
    Anna Tarabasz, Curtin University, UAE

Gaining competitive advantage requires a detailed benchmark of performance against other market players, and profound gap analysis in comparison to the best practice applies to the audit of the digital presence (online footprint analysis), which, based on scripting codes, is done easily on its premises. SEO software and social medial listening tools allow for a comprehensive understanding of the digital performance of the company. Unfortunately, some businesses underestimate the potential dormant in different types of live analytics and performance trackers and being unaware of the analysis capacity to be performed on competitors and market leaders completely off cost. The case presents a study of a digital footprint template analysis performed for Amazon in the United Arab Emirates and shows the comparison with local and global market players like Noon.com, eBay, or Alibaba using software like SEMrush, SimilarWeb, and Brand24 to showcase how to leverage on gathered insights and gain competitive advantage.

Chapter 3
Digital Value Innovation and Strategic Management Practices of Adyar Ananda Bhavan 51
    Shakti Chaturvedi, REVA Business School, India
    Meenakshi Verma, Symbiosis International University, India
    Sonal Purohit, Chandigarh University, India
    Raghava Reddy Varaprasad, REVA University, India

This case focuses on the strategic management practices of Adyar Ananda Bhavan (prevalently known as A2B), a quickly developing contemporary sweet chain of Chennai in South India that is currently proclaiming a target of 900 crores turnover from 2021 onwards with 8,000 employees. The case has a close theoretical association with the famous strategic management models, for instance Michael E. Porter's model, Ansoff Matrix, Blue Ocean Strategy, Balanced Scorecard, and Resource-Based View and explains how an organization can strategically grow its business through digital value-based innovation. Contending sources of data, for example print and electronic media, have been utilized to accumulate and report raw facts and figures. The authors analyzed based on insights gained from various academicians from different universities across India, some mid-level managers from industry, and some unofficial conversations with A2B staff in Bangalore. This case is planned to be utilized in the strategic management subject for both undergraduate and postgraduate courses.

Chapter 4
Consumer Perception of Brand Repositioning Through Benefit Diversification and Intensity of
Use: The Case of Pedras 77
    Francisca Quintas Rodrigues, Faculty of Economics, University of Porto, Portugal
    Beatriz Casais, School of Economics and Management & CICS.NOVA, University of Minho,
      Braga, Portugal

A company's positioning strategy is focused on how the company wants its brand to be perceived in the market. However, the constant change of markets has led many companies to carry on repositioning strategies to deliberately change their strategic positioning, namely by widening its product or service benefits to attract a wider market audience. As product or service positioning is always defined by the consumer, there is the need to understand the extent to which each company is able to communicate its new intended positioning and actually make it perceived. This chapter presents the case of Pedras, a Portuguese brand of naturally sparkling water which ramped up its communication efforts regarding the extension of its product's benefits in order to minimize the potential gap between intended and perceived positioning. Digital communication strategies are discussed to engage young consumers.

Chapter 5
Rose-Patisserie and Coffee House: Business Development Alternatives 91
    Paulo Botelho Pires, Porto Business School, Portugal
    António Correia Barros, Instituto Politécnico do Porto, Portugal

This case traces the life of a new endeavor, starting with a small patisserie and coffeehouse and the subsequent development of the business, considering three alternatives, namely optimizing the concept, expanding through a franchise network, and building a network of company-owned stores. The story of Rui and Joana raises a wide range of issues that managers need to address. After reading and working through the case, students will be able to evaluate the product portfolio, based on actual sales data, and to evaluate and propose strategic options using classical models.

Chapter 6
THEIA: Thermal Insulation – A Business Strategy 119
    Paulo Botelho Pires, Porto Business School, Portugal
    António Correia Barros, Politécnico do Porto, Portugal
    José Duarte Santos, Polytechnic Institute of Gaya, Portugal

THEIA provides technical solutions for the construction industry, specializing in materials for thermal insulation. It is positioned in the middle of the distribution channel, between manufacturers and construction companies, and the profound changes that occurred in the sector had repercussions on the company's activity, forcing it to rethink its business strategy. THEIA repositioning was studied according to a specific methodology, combining analysis techniques to assess organizations' internal capacity and the exploration of external conditioning factors. The strategic plan used financial and commercial information from THEIA and from the sector where it operates, according to the following steps: analysis of THEIA's internal situation, external positioning of THEIA in the national market, definition of strategic objectives, elaboration of scenarios and recommendations.

Chapter 7
The Bonduelle Group's Distribution Strategy: Adding a Branded Retail Store? 150
    Véronique Boulocher-Passet, University of Brighton, UK
    Randall D. Harris, Texas A&M University, USA
    Sabine Ruaud, EDHEC Business School, France

This case study discusses the distribution strategy of the Bonduelle Group and the ability to and value of becoming a retail brand for the world's leading producer and supplier of ready-to-eat processed vegetables. In 2010, the family business opened its first flagship store named 'Bonduelle Bienvenue'. It was entirely dedicated to processed vegetables and offering a big range in the same selling space. The objective of this prototype was not to substitute the company's existing distribution network, or even to hinder it, but to complement it by providing brand visibility and enabling an increase in Bonduelle Group's market share within households. Introducing the reader to the company, the first steps of the concept store back in 2012, and the following other D2C initiatives of the group, this case aims to address the advantages and drawbacks for a food processing brand to engage in selling directly to end consumers.

Chapter 8
How to Build a Leading So-Called Neobank and Pursue Its Growth? The Case of the FinTech
Nickel in Europe 177
    Jean Michel Rocchi, Sciences Po Aix, France

Compte-Nickel, a brand of La Financière des Paiements Electroniques (FPE), is a FinTech founded in 2012 by Ryad Boulanouar and Hugues Le Bret. After an extremely promising start of operations in France in February 2014, the so-called neobank was acquired in 2017 by BNP Paribas, and its integration was successfully achieved thanks to good cooperation with the founders due to the preservation of its independence. Since the beginning, the key factor of its success has been an electronic terminal that allows to open a banking account in a few minutes, which is deployed in a network of partner tobacconists. In 2018, the FinTech became profitable conversely to most of its local competitors. The same year its name was shortened to Nickel, and in accordance with initial plans, development in Europe is being prepared. In December 2020, Nickel opens its doors in Spain. Will the policy of internationalization in Europe undertaken by the parent company BNP Paribas be as successful as in France?

Chapter 9
Purpose-Driven Marketing Wars: Dishwashing Detergent Brands' Purpose-Driven Marketing
Campaigns in Turkey 200
Emrah Gülmez, Anadolu University, Turkey

Purpose is a definitive statement about the difference that a brand is trying to make in the world. It is becoming more and more popular every day, especially because Gen Y and Gen Z are more interested in economic, political, environmental, and social problems in the world. The interest and sensitivity of these issues have also been reflected in marketing and brand communication. In this context, purpose-driven marketing is a marketing perspective and trend that aims to connect brands with their consumers through their brand purpose. The implications of all these in the field of marketing have begun to be seen in Turkey, too. In particular, brands in the dishwashing detergent market have entered a purpose-driven marketing war with each other, so to speak. Finish, Fairy, and Pril have made purpose-driven marketing campaigns in Turkey. So, in this chapter, Water of Tomorrow by Finish, Don't Waste by Fairy, and Together at the Table by Pril campaigns are examined within the scope of purpose-driven marketing as case studies.

Chapter 10
SWOT Analysis and a Case Study at Kayseri Airport 236
Sabiha Annaç Göv, Gaziantep University, Turkey

In this study, Kayseri Airport, which operates under Dhmi in Kayseri, is discussed within the scope of SWOT analysis. As a result, the most powerful aspect of Kayseri Airport is its proximity to the city, and the weakest dimension of Kayseri Airport is the low frequency of flights during the daytime. The outstanding features of Kayseri Airport regarding the opportunities arising from the external environment are tourism potential of the city, transport modes supporting each other, investments around the airport, supporting civil aviation nationwide, development of trade volume of the city. The most important feature of Kayseri Airport regarding the threats arising from the external environment are that it is not seen as a direct departure/destination point for international flights and distorted construction around the airport land.

Chapter 11
The Adoption of a CRM Strategy Based on the Six-Dimensional Model: A Case Study 255
José Duarte Santos, Polytechnic Institute of Gaya, Portugal
José Pita Castelo, Universidade de Vigo, Spain

If the definition of CRM is not consensual, the model for incorporating or analyzing the concept within an organization is also not. In this chapter, considering the 'Six-Dimensional Model CRM Strategy', which integrates 65 critical success factors, the authors analyze how these manifest themselves in an organization. Thus, the case studied is presented and described following the six dimensions (CRM strategy formulation, relational marketing philosophy, best practices, organizational and human resources, CRM processes, CRM technology) and also synthesizes in a table how the company analyzed reacted to critical success factors.

Chapter 12
How Competitive Strategies Affect Organizational Structure: A Research in Technology
Development Zones in Turkey 271
    Muhammed Seyda Akdag, Yıldız Technical University, Turkey
    Yasemin Bal, Yıldız Technical University, Turkey

Organizational structures can change according to the strategy determined by the businesses. The purpose of this chapter is to extend that research by analyzing the relationship between Porter's competitive strategies and Burns and Stalker's structure types. The authors conduct their research on the enterprises in Technology Development Zones in Istanbul, Turkey. One hundred sixty of 5,506 enterprises participated in the research. Then, to search deeper, the authors conducted a qualitative research on the 25 enterprises in Technology Development Zones. Results show that, while the mechanical structure tendency is observed in the enterprises following the cost leadership strategy, the mechanical or organic structure tendency is not observed in the enterprises following the differentiation and focus strategies. Also, according to the interviews, results show that the organizational structures in the enterprises in Technology Development Zones are affected by the size of the organization or the strategic awareness level of the senior managers rather than the competitive strategies.

Chapter 13
The Effects of Real-Time Content Marketing on Consumer Emotions and Behaviors: An Analysis
on COVID-19 Pandemic Period 300
    Hayat Ayar Senturk, Yildiz Technical University, Turkey
    Ece Ozer Cizer, Yildiz Technical University, Turkey
    Tugce Sezer, Yildiz Technical University, Turkey

This study, carried out during the COVID-19 pandemic in Turkey, aimed to provide suggestions for creating a successful real-time content marketing strategy. For this purpose, data were collected from 319 participants using the online questionnaire technique. Outcomes of the analysis indicate that while positive perception toward real-time content marketing campaigns can lead to positive emotions, negative perception toward real-time content marketing campaigns can lead to negative emotions. It was also found as an important result that both positive and negative emotions affect negative consumer behavior during the pandemic period. In addition, negative emotions as a mediator variable strengthen negative consumer behavior. As a result, it can be said that real content marketing campaigns also have negative consequences on consumer behavior during pandemics. Consequently, marketing authorities should continue their real-time content marketing activities with this result in mind.

Compilation of References 330

About the Contributors 359

Index 363

Preface

Editing a book composed of case studies is a project that tends to be quite challenging. The cases should be unique to arouse attention, but they must also have a generic scope that reaches a reasonable number of scholarly readers of the subjects addressed. It is also intended that the cases addressed remain current for the longest period of time, which is increasingly difficult due to the speed of change that focuses on the various sectors of activity and on companies.

The uniqueness of a case can occurs in several areas. However, we can mention some themes that tend to be reflected in the various cases present in the book: strategic management, functional management (financial, marketing, sales, production, procurement, resource humans, IT department, quality), operations management, organizational, technology and processes. There are cases that reflect the anxieties caused by the challenges of digital, others that focus on situations that do not encompass digital, and others that still seek to respond to the needs of integration between the two contexts – digital and non-digital – that seem to be opposite, competing with each other, but that need to be seen and framed in the organization as complementary. Also, the cases presented may be from an organization, a company or a non-profit institution, about an industry or a country.

It is not surprising that a book published in 2021 also has cases addressing COVID19. Strange would be the opposite because the situation forced organizations to adapt, to redesign themselves, to reinvent themselves, which gave researchers new realities, new sources of analysis, the emergence of new best practices, new models, new theories and clear new results that deserve to be presented, analyzed and contribution to the projection of new scenarios. And this book, *Cases on Digital Strategies and Management Issues in Modern Organizations*, is no exception.

In the case presentation structure, we seek the greatest possible uniformity, safeguarding some adaptations that were necessary to safeguard the specificity of the content of the case. The existence of a brief theoretical framework that allows the analysis and better understanding of the case was also an existing concern. Thus, the reader can more easily understand the options taken, the directions chosen and, mainly, can also elaborate their decisions based on their previous knowledge and those acquired with the reading made on the theoretical bases that frame the events and decisions.

The most usual in a case book is to highlight events, in this case in the business universe, in which success existed and constitutes itself as remarkable due to the facts and events presented. This book is no exception. However, we believe that the failure of something that has been planned and has not happened is still important to study, analyze and draw lessons for the future. But to be possible to have these types of cases, it will still be necessary to overcome some mental barriers because the company, the brand where the failure tends not to want to share and many successes do not reach the light of day, do not come to be known, or if they are, the data are scarce. It would also be advantageous, in order to sustain the choice of these cases, considering the impact of the same failure. That is, the failure itself to be valued and framed as a case must have a level of importance for the sector where it is part and not only for the organization. Despite the desire to incorporate cases of failure, this book only presents success cases, following the "normal pattern".

Another challenge of this book was to try to present a reasonable level of multi-nationality to achieve a breadth that allows a more comprehensive view of the different topics addressed. Thus, throughout the book the cases presented transport us to different countries, diverse cultures, specific local realities. The organizational dimension also varies, from small companies to large companies of only national or multinational nature. In all cases it is intended that readers have contact with the solution found for each situation, but it is also intended to present lessons that allow readers to also develop their critical spirit and counter alternatives.

This book, *Cases on Digital Strategies and Management Issues in Modern Organizations*, is a pivotal reference source that provides original case studies designed to explore various issues facing contemporary organizations, evaluate the usefulness of strategy and operational tools and models, and examine how successful and failing companies have faced issues with practical ideas and solutions. While highlighting topics such as business ethics, stakeholder analysis, and corporate governance, this publication demonstrates various ways that different models/tools can be applied in different types of companies for various purposes and from diverse perspectives. This book is ideally designed for managers, executives, managing directors, business strategists, industry professionals, students, researchers, and academicians seeking current research on key business framework strategies.

To help better understand cases and also facilitate their use, we consider that it would be important to incorporate additional resources in each case, namely questions and answers, epilogue and lessons learned list of additional sources. Thus, the arguments for the use of this book in teaching, particularly in undergraduate or graduate degrees, are strengthened. However, the inclusion of this complementary information is also useful for readers from the business area because they allow consolidating the concepts inherent to the case and eventually awakening them to issues, situations they may not have thought about.

To order the thirteen chapters in the book, it was decided to include first the chapters that addressed a specific case and not a sector of activities. The chapters that incorporate the digital theme were also given priority, followed by cases that analyze the company from the point of view of the business and, finally, the cases that focus on a certain area of the company, in a particular specific problem. So, then, we present the chapters that are part of this book synthetically.

The first chapter, "Digital Transformation: Is It Part of Strategic Process or a New Strategic Practice?" aims to describe the digital transformation strategy implementation path at a Brazilian pre-digital retail company and discusses the role the COVID-19 pandemic had played. Moreover, the case highlights important strategic issues and provides the opportunity to analyze whether it is a strategic process or a strategic practice. This study also increases the understanding of the strategic configuration of digital transformation embracing context, process, and outcomes. And it also sheds light on the dilemma between brick-and-mortar stores and digital ones.

Gaining competitive advantage requires a detailed benchmark of own performance against other market players and profound gap analysis in comparison to the best practice applies to the audit of the digital presence (online footprint analysis), which based on scripting codes is done easily on its premises. SEO software and social medial listening tools allow for comprehensive understanding of the digital performance of the own company. The second chapter, "Be Like Amazon: Achieving a Competitive Advantage Based on Digital Footprint Analysis," presents a case study of a digital footprint a template

Preface

analysis performed for Amazon in the United Arab Emirates and shows the comparison with local and global market players like Noon.com, eBay, or Alibaba, using software like SEMrush, SimilarWeb, and Brand24 to showcase how to leverage on gathered insights and gain competitive advantage.

The next chapter, "Digital Value Innovation and Strategic Management Practices of Adyar Ananda Bhavan," has a close theoretical association with the famous strategic management models, for instance, Michael E. Porter's model, Ansoff Matrix, Blue Ocean Strategy, Balanced Scorecard, and Resource-based View, and explains how an organization can strategically grow its business through digital value-based innovation. So, the case focuses on the strategic management practices of Adyar Ananda Bhavan, a quickly developing contemporary sweet chain of Chennai in South India.

The constant change of markets has led many companies to carry on repositioning strategies to deliberately change their strategic positioning, namely by widening its products or services benefits to attract a wider market audience. As product or service positioning is always defined by the consumer, there is the need to understand the extent to which each company is able to communicate its new intended positioning and actually make it perceived. This chapter, "Consumer Perception of Brand Repositioning Through Benefit Diversification: The Case of Pedras," presents the case of Pedras, a Portuguese brand of naturally sparkling water which ramped up its communication efforts regarding the extension of its product's benefits in order to minimize the potential gap between intended and perceived positioning. Digital communication strategies are discussed to engage young consumers.

The next case traces the life of a new endeavor, starting with a small patisserie and coffeehouse and the subsequent development of the business, considering three alternatives, namely, optimizing the concept, expanding through a franchise network, or building a network of company-owned stores. The story of Rui and Joana raises a wide range of issues that managers need to address. After reading and working through the case present in the chapter "Rose-Patisserie and Coffee House: Business Development Alternatives," readers will be able to evaluate the product portfolio, based on actual sales data, and to evaluate and propose strategic options, using classical models.

"THEIA: Thermal Insulation – A Business Strategy" is the chapter that addresses a company that provides technical solutions for the construction industry, specializing in materials for thermal insulation. The organization is positioned in the middle of the distribution channel, between manufacturers and construction companies, and the profound changes that occurred in the sector had repercussions on the company's activity, forcing it to rethink its business strategy. In this case, it is possible to analyze the strategic plan with financial and commercial information from THEIA and from the sector where it operates.

Chapter 7, "The Bonduelle Group's Distribution Strategy: Adding a Branded Retail Store?" discusses the distribution strategy of the Bonduelle Group and the ability to and value of also becoming a retail brand for the world's leading producer and supplier of ready-to-eat processed vegetables. In 2010, the family business opened its first flagship store named 'Bonduelle Bienvenue'. It was entirely dedicated to processed vegetables and offering a big range in the same selling space. The objective of this prototype was not to substitute the company's existing distribution network, or even to hinder it, but to complement it by providing brand visibility and enabling an increase in Bonduelle Group's market share within households. Introducing the reader to the company, the first steps of the concept store back in 2012, and the following other D2C initiatives of the Group, this case aims to address the advantages and drawbacks for a food processing brand to engage in selling directly to end consumers.

"How to Build a Leading So-Called Neobank and Pursue Its Growth? The Case of the FinTech Nickel in Europe" is the following case that seeks to highlight the evolution of a FinTech company with a special focus on its internationalization. Its acquisition by BNP Paribas and its integration being successfully achieved were factors that contributed to the success that is analyzed in this case.

The next chapter, "Purpose-Driven Marketing Wars: Dishwashing Detergent Brands' Purpose-Driven Marketing Campaigns in Turkey," focuses on Generation Y and Generation Z, who are concerned about the economic, political, environmental and social problems in the world. Thus, the case analyzes the brands in the dishwashing detergent market from the perspective of marketing communication for these generations. So, in this chapter, "Water of Tomorrow" by Finish, "Don't Waste" by Fairy, and "Together at the Table" by Pril campaigns are examined within the scope of purpose-driven marketing.

In next case, "SWOT Analysis and a Case Study at Kayseri Airport," the Kayseri Airport is discussed within the scope of SWOT analysis. As a result, the most powerful aspect of Kayseri Airport is its proximity to the city, and the weakest dimension of Kayseri Airport is the low frequency of flights during the daytime. The outstanding features of Kayseri Airport regarding the opportunities arising from the external environment are tourism potential of the city, transport modes supporting each other, investments around the airport, supporting civil aviation nationwide, development of trade volume of the city. The most important feature of Kayseri Airport regarding the threats arising from the external environment are that it is not seen as a direct departure / destination point for international flights and distorted construction around the airport land.

Chapter 11, "The Adoption of a CRM Strategy Based on the Six-Dimensional Model: A Case Study," presents a case study of a company that has changed its way of being in the market and relating to its customers, restructuring the role played by the sales force and betting more on related marketing supported by digital marketing, development of content that strengthened trust and strengthened the relationship with the customer. The entire approach of this company's analysis is based on the CRM Six-Dimensional Model that incorporates CRM strategy formulation, relational marketing philosophy, the application of best practices, organizational and human resources, CRM processes, CRM technology. Each of these dimensions consists of several factors that are identified and analyzed from the perspective of its application in the company.

The purpose of the chapter "How Competitive Strategies Affect Organizational Structure: A Research in Technology Development Zones in Turkey" is to extend that research by analyzing the relationship between Porter's competitive strategies and Burns and Stalker's structure types. The authors conduct their research on the enterprises in Technology Development Zones in Istanbul, Turkey. Results show that, while the mechanical structure tendency is observed in the enterprises following the cost leadership strategy, the mechanical or organic structure tendency is not observed in the enterprises following the differentiation and focus strategies. It was also possible to verify that the organizational structures in the enterprises in Technology Development Zones are affected by the size of the organization or the strategic awareness level of the senior managers rather than the competitive strategies.

In the last chapter, "The Effects of Real-Time Content Marketing on Consumer Emotions and Behaviors: An Analysis of the COVID-19 Pandemic Period," presents a study carried out during the Covid-19 pandemic in Turkey, which aimed to provide suggestions for creating a successful real-time content marketing strategy. This study, across several economic sectors, showed that, during the pandemic, real content marketing campaigns also have negative consequences on consumer behavior.

José Duarte Santos
Polytechnic Institute of Gaya, Portugal

Chapter 1
Digital Transformation:
Is It Part of a Strategic Process or a New Strategic Practice?

Irene Ciccarino
https://orcid.org/0000-0002-6517-4154
Polytechnic Institute of Leiria, Portugal

Carla Diniz dos Santos da Silva
IBMEC-RJ, Brazil

EXECUTIVE SUMMARY

The COVID-19 pandemic has intensified the digitization of traditional businesses. In the retail sector, e-commerce played a fundamental role and promoted major changes in the consumer pattern. This evolution and its impact can be studied through the digital transformation lens, which is a multidisciplinary and holistic concept that encompasses a new strategy and new ways of strategizing. The present study aims to describe the digital transformation strategy implementation path at a Brazilian pre-digital retail company and discusses the role the COVID-19 pandemic had played. Moreover, the case highlights important strategic issues and provides the opportunity to analyze whether it is a strategic process or a strategic practice. Thus, it can enlighten which theory best supports DTS studies. This study also increases the understanding of the strategic configuration of digital transformation embracing context, process, and outcomes. And it also sheds light on the dilemma between brick-and-mortar stores and digital ones.

ORGANIZATION BACKGROUND

The retail sector is central in all economies, and it occupies a privileged position near customers. The trade occurs when a business sells a product or service to an individual consumer for his or her use. Therefore, it can catch firsthand changes in consumer preferences. It is the heart of a complex value chain that includes storage, logistic, legal transactions, advertising, and so on. The retail sector is also very diversified, with many business models, but lately, the central discussion point has been the pros and counts of a brick-and-mortar store and virtual business channels (Reinartz, Wiegand & Imschloss 2019).

DOI: 10.4018/978-1-7998-1630-0.ch001

E-commerce has been a phenomenon that promotes major changes in consumption patterns, that have created real economic giants like Amazon (Baker, 2021; Verhoef, Broekhuizen, Bart, Bhattacharya, Dong, Fabian & Haenlein, 2021). In the strategic arena traditional companies needed to face innovative fast-growing digital-born entrants (Verhoef et al., 2021) for a while. However, this arena has changed again (Baker, 2021). The omnichannel tendency combines the shopping experience in brick-and-mortar stores with a variety of digital channels to increase retailer's differentiation and leverage competitive edge (Sopadjieva, Dholakia & Benjamin, 2017). It hinges on the premise that "Consumers are more likely to trust a brand they have seen in the real world". Because of it, born-digital businesses have started to create brick-and-mortar stores (Baker, 2021, p. 3).

Meanwhile, the COVID-19 pandemic has intensified the digitization of traditional businesses. Thus, the e-commerce giant Amazon continues to grow but lost market shares in 2020. The pandemic has influencing market dynamics, but it didn't change digital evolution paths: "Many of the perceived Covid winners such as e-commerce, videogame and streaming media companies have simply been pulled a few years forward into an inevitable future. Their destiny did not change." (Baker, 2021, p.2).

This evolution can be studied through the digital transformation lens, which is a multidisciplinary and holistic concept that encompasses a new strategy (Verhoef et al., 2021) and new ways of strategizing (Chanias, Myers & Hess, 2019; Correani, De Massis, Frattini, Petruzzelli & Natalicchio, 2020). Although SAP, a renowned technology company, has estimated that 84% of global companies regard digital transformations as a critical issue (Chanias et al., 2019), it is still a new trend with no consensus about what it is in business (Schallmo & Williams, 2018). Moreover, European Union (EU) has assumed the digitalization of the economy as a 2030 agenda goal based on the assumption that it will be the next major growth driver for the region, helping to fulfill integration gaps (Novak et al., 2018).

In this sense, the present study aims to describe a digital transformation strategy, hereinafter called DTS. It tells the story of a Brazilian pre-digital retail company's path to accomplish a digital transformation from the start and discusses the role the COVID-19 pandemic had played. Moreover, the case highlights important strategic issues (Schallmo & Williams, 2018) and provides the opportunity to analyze if it is a strategic process (Correani et al., 2020) or if it is a strategic practice (Chanias et al., 2019). Thus, it can enlighten which theory best supports DTS studies (Jones & Karsten, 2008; Whittington, 1996).

The Uni.Co is the evolution of the Brazilian family-owned decoration and gift company Imaginarium, founded in 1991. The group emerged after its sale to an investment fund in 2012. The investment thesis was based on strong-brand acquisitions and building impeccable and profitable franchise management with a competitive supply chain. In 2018 Uni.Co was composed by the brands Imaginarium, MinD, and Pucket. It has 412 stores in all Brazilian states. The strategy of the Uni.Co group was clearly to increase the value of the business over time based on the safety of a lasting investment thesis. In the first years, the number of franchisees' growth associated with an efficient operation proved a successful business model and management.

The company was growing in value. Investors, however, yearned for more. After 6 years of growth in the number of franchises and observing the movements of the retail market, the investors chose to activate e-commerce and generate growth in sales volume from it. Although Uni.Co had strong experience in innovation and a creative team, it had no experience with digital innovation, and all its business was entirely focused on brick-and-mortar stores and franchises. The former e-commerce recorded less than 1% of net revenue and had a low conversion rate (access to sale). The challenge was to increase growth, despite the lack of know-how and fear due to a strong belief that e-commerce would cannibalize brick-and-mortar sales and undermine the relationship with franchisees (Reinartz et al., 2019). All expansion of the company until then had been made based on the business model of franchises with an excellent reputation. More than 30% of franchisees have been operating Uni.Co's brands for more than 10 years. Over 25 years of existence, they have received more than 35 stamps from the Brazilian Franchise Association (ABF) and several awards in the segment. This study describes the DTS in progress since 2018 that currently represents 12% of sales. In 2020 the group's revenue was from 380 million reais (R$) and has more than 2,4 thousand online consumers.

SETTING THE STAGE

Hitherto, the strategy still evokes an orderly picture of rational decision-making and logical procedures based on systematic analysis and control or a masterpiece from skill and talent (Chanias et al., 2019; Mintzberg, 1987), even with all changes that already happened in the strategic field and the production's heartwood. Production is expected to evolve to an automated, autonomous, and intelligent system (Kumar & Bhatia, 2021) affecting strategic and social relationships that are intertwined with it (Jarzabkowski, 2004). These changes can be studied through DTS (Chanias et al., 2019; Verhoef et al., 2021).

Just like innovation (Fagerberg, 2004), digital technology use or adoption can change organizations, processes, products, services, business models, and the competitive environment (Chanias et al., 2019; Correani et al., 2020;). However, digital technology alone is nothing more than another form of daily life production and reproduction available for social use. But it has assumed a pervasive character in all social spheres (Teubner & Stockhinger, 2020). In the words of Verhoef et al. (2021): "*Digital transformation and resultant business model innovation have fundamentally altered consumers' expectations and behaviors, putting immense pressure on traditional firms, and disrupting numerous markets.*" Therefore, it has a structural and structuring role in complex and interconnected social relationships (Giddens, 1983), and the broad concept of industry 4.0 is intertwined in it as well (Kumar & Bhatia, 2021).

Although technology and the transformations provided by it are ripe topics in social sciences (Jones & Karsten, 2008), digital transformation is a new trend with no consensus about what it is in business (Schallmo & Williams, 2018). Informational system literature is the closest background found (Chanias et al., 2019). It has evolved from a specific goal achievement as management planning and projects (the 70s and 80s decade), passing for a strategic design and competitive positioning standpoint (the 90s and 2000s decade) to be currently deal in an integrative perspective with strategy (Teubner & Stockhinger, 2020) acknowledged as DTS (Schallmo & Williams, 2018).

In the beginning, digital technologies were appealing because they enable cost reduction and create more ways to find, collect and analyze consumer data, increasing sales opportunities and brand awareness (Correani et al., 2020; Schallmo & Williams, 2018). The concept of digital transformation arises from the moment that technology became a strategic issue (Chanias et al., 2019; Correani et al., 2020), as the investment in digital structures and digital skills-building became not just a shortcut to get a competitive advantage but a process to achieve parity (Correani et al., 2020). DTS cannot be anymore dealt with as a simple matter of "reap the maximum advantage and reduce the cost burden" (Correani et al., 2020, p. 41). However, it is not clear if it is part of the strategic process (Correani et al., 2020) or if it is a strategic practice (Chanias et al., 2019). Defining whether DTS is episodic (Correani et al., 2020) or it is a strategic practice (Chanias et al., 2019) can enlighten which theory best supports DTS studies (Jones & Karsten, 2008; Whittington, 1996). As a result, the main contribution of this study is observing the behavior of DTS formulation and implementation case to outline which one of these standpoints raises.

Therefore, this case study deepens the understanding of a complex phenomenon in its context (Ulriksen & Dadalauri, 2016) helping DTS knowledge development (Chanias et al., 2019; Schallmo & Williams, 2018) and linking it to strategic theory. In doing so, this study also increases the understanding of the strategic configuration of digital transformation (Mintzberg, Ahlstrand & Lampel, 2010) embracing context, process, and outcomes filling a theoretical gap (Pettigrew, 2012). Thus, relying on the strategy theory helps to understand the digital phenomenon that is based on change and adaptation (Verhoef et al., 2021). The strategy is fundamental to set the organizational direction and to analyze the right structures to foster efficiency. It also helps a firm's effort convergence and coherence (Mintzberg et al., 2010). Because digital transformation is naturally intensive in technology and innovation, raising it to the level of strategy (Chanias et al., 2019; Teubner & Stockhinger, 2020) is an important step towards ensuring flexibility, adaptability, and business survival (Leonard-Barton, 1992; Zajac, Kraatz & Bresser, 2000).

The Case Study is an appropriate methodology whenever a topic needs a new perspective of analysis because of its flexibility and broad capacity to find and combine theoretical and empirical evidence providing synthesis. It is a way to pave trends for theoretical development (Eisenhardt, 1989) and merge different perspectives (Ghauri, 2004). Secondary data from reports, news, and online data were triangulated with 3 interviews carried out in a semi-structured manner and 2 in-depth (Patton, 2002). The in-depth interviews were conducted with the former CEO and with the Director of Human Resources (CHRO). They oversaw the company in 2018 when the DTS had started. Three semi-structured interviews were done with the current CEO, the Chief Digital Officer (CDO), and the Head of Omnichannel. The interviewees' selection was non-random to ensure the validity of their perspective and the alignment with the research goals (Ulriksen & Dadalauri, 2016). This concern limited the number of interviews in the study, which covered only those involved in the DTS. Data analysis was performed by Pattern-matching, identifying patterns in a recurring and systematic way in the data and the supporting literature to achieve theoretical saturation. This procedure corroborates the selection of the single case to deal in an integrated manner with the quantity and complexity of the information analyzed (Ghauri, 2004; Verschuren, 2003).

CASE DESCRIPTION

The Uni.Co case was project-oriented using the Agile approach and focused on the operational bottom. It happened because of a mature platform business model which aim is to serve two clients: the franchisees and the customers. Initially, the website promoting the brand and virtual sales was incipient. While trying to deal with franchisees' resistance, after visits to business fairs, case studies, and benchmarking, the company chose the omnichannel to integrate physical and digital sales. It solves the problem with franchisees and logistical issues of deliveries far from the company's distribution center.

Digital sales should create a positive experience with customers and increase the direct earnings of the company and franchisees (Baker, 2021; Sopadjieva et al., 2017). Therefore, the company has decided on two purchase models: Model 1) 'pick up on the store', where the customer would buy online but pick it up in the store and Model 2) 'shipment from the store', where brick-and-mortar stores would be transformed into a distribution point, using their stock to fulfill online orders, reducing logistical costs. The DTS started with the first one, then developed the second. The Imaginarium CEO and Director of Uni.Co commented that:

So, there was an executive from a large company who called me and said: I have already spent 3 million reais (R$) on systems, and I cannot evolve, I am far behind you. I said: The problem is not the technology. (...) Before choosing the technology, you need to understand the dynamics of your franchisee.

Therefore, DTS was inspired by the social context in retail practice (Teubner & Stockhinger, 2020). To carry out the DTS, the company formed a dedicated team composed of 2 analysts reporting to the CRHO. The company understood the strong cultural issue to be addressed. The goal was to show the organization that the process was possible and to convince franchisees and employees to join it through the results. Initially, they tried to find a supplier to assist them in the strategy development, as well as a startup that could do it, but nothing worked, so they decided to do it internally. The two analysts were beginners, and the CRHO also had no experience in the subject. To streamline the process and reduce costs, they decided to use the existing Imaginarium website and make changes during the night, when the customer access was low. They understood that this was part of the Agile methodology. The first sale made was a mistake: a week before the first pilot was run, at the end of a night's work, the programmer forgot to put the new system down and a customer purchased by Model 1. The team had to run to guide the store in the delivery procedures and decided to make all communication via WhatsApp.

Everything went well, and they decided to turn on the system for interested franchisees. At this moment, they did not have a defined business model, and they wanted the franchisee to perceive value in going digital because by taking the customer to the store, they could generate new sales. So, they analyzed the minimum viable product (MVP) realizing the need for more investment. Thus, they chose to charge the franchises only 5% for the digital sale, which was much less than the cost they had with maintaining the site and investing in advertising on social media.

In January 2019, they disclosed the modality to franchises. In March, twelve stores have connected to the Model 1. Soon the first internal problems showed up. The customer service team (SAC) did not agree with the salesperson's communication with customers via WhatsApp. The issues ranged from aesthetics to the legality of the process. The new way was completely informal. IT problems also arose: store's calls were now much more to solve issues with equipment and system failures. And they often needed immediate service, as the customer was at the store to pick up the product. There were still flaws involving salespeople and storage workers who had difficulty operating the system, making e-commerce calls, or writing off inventory. Franchisees were not aware of the laws that involved digital sales and the company had also not revised the normative instruments to signal, for instance, what the exchange policy would be for purchases made online. And the DTSteam had assumed the premise to delight the customer and generate new sales through this channel. Thus, the withdrawal of the product in the store and the exchange or return should work flawlessly. The customer must not see any problem no matter the team cost.

We solve everything, at any time. (...) But we said, from the beginning: the only thing we are going to be hyper-strict with is "it cannot affect the end customer". While we are resolving here among us... Among us, we were franchisee, the guy from the distribution center, the guy from e-commerce, the director, the board member. CHRO

Despite all struggles, the achievement of the first results made the project relevant and inspired the Uni.Co's areas to accept the changes that needed to be implemented. The case was used as an example by the management team to support requests to increase staff, to overcome resistance to change some processes, and to change the permissive relationship with some older franchisees. These were internal problems embedded in the culture, that the DTS team has already figured out they would face. For this reason, the DTS was placed under the leadership of the CHRO.

The DTS evolution was generating a feeling that it was possible to carry out, although the change was uncomfortable for the various internal areas and even for the relationship with some franchisees. However, the DTSteam was small and inexperienced which raised confidence issues among stakeholders that hindered its progress.

So, it started to trouble, but in a way that brought good, you know? And those who did not want to either learned or ended up leaving (...) It was contagious. (...) People were doing things differently (...) the customers' response was accelerating discussions and giving answers to questions that perhaps the group would naturally not even want an answer to. CHRO

While internal problems were addressed in a learning-by-doing process, lessons learned were recorded, and the number of stores with the Model 1 was increasing. In June 2019, 85 stores had already adhered to this model. The new problems were not about confidence or fear to change. At this moment, the issues were more technical and required specific knowledge of digital marketing, sales, and omnichannel. In addition, the lack of a well-defined process spurred conflicts with former policies and standards. They must also be reviewed and specified for digital businesses, to enlighten both the Uni.Co team and the franchisees to how to proceed. There was a lack of understanding about what was allowed and what was not. They needed a guideline to move to the next steps.

The DTS' second model started. It consists of the traditional delivery to home plus the convenience of the shortest deadline possible. It would bring logistical gains considering that the company has franchises throughout Brazil, but a single distribution center, in the southern region. This model would reduce delivery time and costs. It takes only one day to achieve any Brazilian city with a franchise, which is a huge gain in a country with continental dimensions. However, the challenge of this model was the new skills required from the franchises and their teams who must perform, in addition to selling, an operation of a distribution center, hiring, and managing delivery services. From June to October 2019, the model started in 19 stores.

With these 19 stores running the Model 2 and with 100 stores in the Model 1, DTS has reached its scale. The lack of structured processes and an overburdened staff prevented the DTS expansion. The DTS team had one more member that is the team has only three dedicated people. They were still green, lacking the knowledge needed to keep going. The DTS had to improve its sustainability while scaling up. Therefore, in the second semester of 2019, the company decided to create a CDO position to hire a professional specialized in DTS. The sales of the digital store, the integration of digital channels, the growth of franchises linked to the omnichannel system, and the responsibility for creating and conducting the digital transformation process in a structured and standardized manner throughout the company were under her management.

So, like that, there was a model very focused on execution. But zero strategy behind it. It was like this: everyone is doing it, I need to have it. I do not know how. (...) In terms of execution, the group is impeccable. It was flawless at the beginning. And that is what left us in a safe position, okay? It performed very well, but the strategy was not designed. CDO

Digital Transformation

The first analysis carried out by CDO regarded the DTS' design and the omnichannel implementation process. The model had a good design, and the execution was impeccable, but it was not economically viable. The fee charged for the service was much lower than the Customer Acquisition Cost (CAC), which includes costs with the electronic platform, staff, and digital marketing. The previous DTS was built as a pilot project, to favor change and to surpass the resistance among franchisees. However, to scale it up it must be adapted, and its costs updated which means to persuade the franchisees that the first cost model had been an investment to enable the project. They decided to show the DTS costs to franchisees explaining the strategy and its goal to leverage sales by omnichannel. They relied on the expected sales impact to build consensus. Furthermore, they also took advantage of the 'shipment from store' model newly implantation to sell the idea that they would increase the conversion rate of the site and so the revenue for the franchises that made the deliveries.

It was possible for CDO to quickly observe that despite having a virtual store, the sales mentality for digital channels was not running. There was no online specific sales target, and the digital and the brick-and-mortar store were running the same way. There was a fear to harm the relationship with franchisees otherwise. Hence, they usually kept an online showcase for 15 days long as they did in the brick-and-mortar store. It is completely inappropriate since the virtual customer can visit the digital store every day if he wants. The online product area had not a detailed description of the releases. It is nonsense since online stores lack brick-and-mortar customer direct contact with the product and with the salesperson. In addition, virtual search engines work based on this product description. Therefore, Search Engine Optimization (SEO) had not worked, preventing digital sales. The DTS required a huge turnaround, and this change crossed several Uni.Co's departments. The new DTS must also be introduced to each of them relying on the top management sponsorship.

And then I effectively started a process of evangelization and digital transformation with the whole company, okay? (...) And then this process of evangelization, it must happen for the whole company, at a level where each one operates, right? And it ... it was really top-down, right? CDO

The first big challenge related to online sales was the Black Friday of 2019, which took place in Brazil on November 29. The digital sales team had not reached the sales target for 18 months and CDO wanted to use this milestone for the turnaround. They achieved 37% of all monthly sales volume through the digital channel, which was an exceptional result. And at this rate, they entered Christmas, when for the first time they managed to extend sales through digital channels until December 23rd, because delivery through stores in one business day now allowed the extension of sales that previously ended around December 15th on that channel. With these measures, the fourth quarter of 2019 closed concerning the third one with a 50% increase in the number of visits to the site and an 88% increase in Gross Merchandise Volume (GMV).

Another improvement done was the way that digital sales would be counted and how this could impact the digital team's targets. Until that moment, sales were measured by each channel: sales performed by brick-and-mortar stores and sales performed by e-commerce. With the advancement of sales integration between physical and digital, it was common to register what came straight from the distribution center to the end customer as a digital sale and what was delivered from stores as a physical sale. But now, the sale could be captured based on the advertisement made on the website, completed on the digital channel. Hence, delivered by the brick-and-mortar store, in the Model 2. The problem was that this sale has kept account as a physical sale damaging the digital sales numbers, discouraging the digital sales team from promoting this model. This issue was preventing the omnichannel goal.

My goal is to sell, it does not matter if I am going to deliver it through the store or the website. Because if I had followed that parameter just from the website, do you think I would be selling via a store? Of course not! So, the transformation is not just outside the company. It must be inside. Because otherwise, you will boycott yourself internally. CDO

In 2020's first quarter, the DTS was re-planned and started. Some franchisees were still joining the omnichannel system until the COVID-19 pandemic broke out. Thus, all DTS implementation rushed. With the movement restrictions measures imposed by the local governments, franchisees saw the integration between brick-and-mortar stores and digital stores as the only way to sell and cover their brick-and-mortar costs, avoiding bankruptcy. Some franchises that had joined the omnichannel before tripled their sales at the beginning of the pandemic breaks out. That was because they have done all the digital sales deliveries for a while.

And then the pandemic came. We just rushed everything. So, the franchisee who had not joined until that time, done, you know, overnight. In two weeks, we put everything else in store. And there it was effectively ... They saw a forced change, right? Then it was a change of chapter for the entire market, right? CDO

To leverage digital sales, Uni.Co became part of some marketplace platforms in Brazil, such as Mercado Livre, B2W, and Rappi. It allowed an increase of 88% in digital sales in the first quarter of 2020, compared to the same period of the previous year. With the learning from this experience, they launched their own marketplace, named "*Nossos Crushes*" in July 2020. Digital sales can still happen in third-party marketplaces and each brand e-commerce. In addition to all Uni.Co's brands, "*Nossos Crushes*" sell other brands as well. The selection was done by an internal curator. As a result, in September 2020, the group recorded 25 million reais (R$) in net revenue through digital channels, an increase of 219% concerning the same period of the previous year. The pandemic momentum can be felt in this narrative:

Where we are today, in March 2021, in terms of adherence to digital penetration, both in sales volume and in numbers of stores integrated into the omnichannel, it was supposed to be reached only in December (...) 100% stores use omnichannel with both models. I have anticipated my digital evolution roadmap here in practically 14 to 18 months. CEO's Imaginarium and Director of the Uni.Co group

At this moment, the CDO had already managed to organize processes and structure to support the digital transformation. She needed a new area dedicated to technological solutions, such as artificial intelligence and data analysis, with experienced people mainly in the digital environment and agile methodology. They also incorporated a digital media agency to speed up decision-making on investments and to manage in a better way the performance engines and the customer profitability. The goal was to improve the customer journey and to increase lifetime value (LTV). The new area, now called Unilabs, had 20 people working in squads in a horizontal structure. The most affected processes were the logistics of the distribution center for franchises and the inventory control, which started to use artificial intelligence and data analysis tools. It helped to forecast the demands by region and aid in decision-making to expedite deliveries.

Digital Transformation

Hence, with the successful implementation of digital solutions to increase sales, a digital transformation movement began to break out across the company. Different organizational areas started to demand the use of technology to improve their routines and digital support. Digitalization demand popped in several aspects mainly operation, decision-making, purchases, price planning, product mix composition, logistics, and the distribution to stores. Therefore, a process for the digital transformation was established, as follows 1) definition of a business partner for digital issues in each business department; 2) digital opportunities' identification; 3) The Unilab and the business partner build up a project and gauge the availability of resources needed to implement it as well the benefits for the overall Uni.Co's business. The projects are presented to the management team that meets weekly. All projects approved make up the digital initiatives roadmap and are ranked in a "priority tower" that defines the implementation deadline for the Unilab team. This selection process enables projects that come from the bottom-up and the top-down directions. Both, executives, and employees have the chance to pose projects. However, projects that came from employees have tended to be implemented more quickly, since they usually are solutions to daily problems.

In the first quarter of 2021, all omnichannel routines were transformed into organizational processes and transferred to business departments. The Unilab team now is focused in develop and implement new projects. There was still some resistance, mainly because the business departments consider the digital transformation routines as a Unilab's job. They took a time to see the new process as part of their routines. Unilab must figure out how to transfer the projects' results to each business department to focus on its real job: digital transformation and digital support. Even past two years, this was a persistent conflict issue. Everybody wants digital transformation to do better, but anyone wants. If Unilab kept all the digital jobs it would lose accuracy, speed, and efficiency. It could prevent important projects to be done, and it also damages the integration goal.

The omnichannel implementation brought the possibility of selling products that franchisees have always wanted but could not because of the store's size constraints for display and stock. Moreover, it allowed the new product department to explore alternatives that were avoided due to the standard size of franchises, such as the sale of electric bicycles. Pumped by this new trend, Uni.Co decided to implement an 'infinite shelf', where the customer could see all products in a digital showcase inside the brick-and-mortar stores and do the purchase right away. The 'infinite shelf' would serve digital sales as well because it would be embedded in both marketplace and each brands' e-commerce. However, the pandemic's restrictions have reduced the customers in person and imposed some stores to close for a while. Thus, the company postponed the 'infinite shelf' implementation. Verhoef et al. (2021) have drawn on extant literature to make a digest of DTS' stages and the assets and capabilities required for a successful accomplishment. Table 1 correlates their work to the case to offer a synthesis framework, showing the strategic imperatives.

Table 1. Uni.Co's Phases of Digital Transformation

Year	Type	Case's analysis	Digital Growth Strategies	Metrics used	Goal	Organizational Structure
Before 2012	Digitization	Status before the case study	Market development	Gross revenue Number of franchises Average ticket Ebitda	Cost savings: More efficient deployment of resources for existing activities	Franchise Stores teams, Corporate departments, 1 (one) distribution center, brand's e-commerce
From 2012 untill 2018 From 2018	Digitalization	Case study start. There was a website promoting the brand and virtual sales were incipient.	[Above] + Platform-based market penetration	Number of franchises benefiting from digital sales; Number of followers in social media Time between order and delivery On-time delivery Gross Revenue of Digital sales Gross Revenue of brick-and-mortar sales	Cost savings & increased revenues: Enhanced customer experience	[Above] + e-commerce team, 'pick up on the store' model
Second half of 2019	Digital Transformation	Omnichannel integration to promote an assets reconfiguration in a new business model.	[Above] + Platform diversification	[Above] + NPS for digital channels Last-mile logistics e-commerce conversion rate Gross Merchandise Volume Customer Acquisition Cost (CAC)	New cost-revenue model: Reconfiguration of assets to develop new business models.	[Above] + 'shipment from the store' model, CDO position, Unilab, third-party marketplaces, "Nossos Crushes" Marketplaces.
Ongoing		Status not fully achieved nor planned during the case study				

Source: Adapted from Verhoef et al. (2021, p. 892).

Strategy as a Process

Even though DTS has led to substantial changes in firm activities, processes, and capabilities changing the business model essential features, for Correani et al. (2020), DTS is a process that happens during a business instance aimed to achieve a specific result. The goal is to find weaknesses and strengths in the business model to enable the best use of new digital assets and available technology.

Pettigrew (2012) studied the knowledge accumulation on strategic management studies exploring the epistemological difficulties to link formulation and implementation. He poses that from 1970th Mintzberg was the precursor in the strategy as a process thinking, considering context and instance into the analysis. Mintzberg et al. (2010) also paid attention to the evolution of strategic thinking. They classified strategy from the top-down design school to the transformation process in the configuration school. Strategy as a process considers the relationship between context and the firm in an instance through the internal and external variables that influence the strategic formulation and implementation. Thus, there are two different and interdependent stages of the same process. The strategic process has inputs and outputs. It has a start and end, therefore the results translated into the performance concept can be evaluated at the end of the process (Correani et al., 2020; Pettigrew, 2012).

The process concept is essentially time-bounded, turning performance sustainability into a temporal issue as well. The past performance tends not to represent or guarantee future performance (Richard et al., 2009) because it is not seen as a continuum but as temporal cycles. The strategy as a process is built upon categories, typologies, and analytical methods (Pettigrew, 2012). It helps to set the organizational direction and to analyze the right structures to fosters efficiency (Mintzberg et al., 2010). To emphasizing the context perspective, one can use the strategic fit concept. It measures how well suited to its context the strategy is. It is usually gauged through a rational analysis of the discrepancy between how something is done and how it should be done, establishing a parameter to what is good or bad in organizational terms (Venkatraman & Prescott, 1990).

Correani et al. (2020), pose that most digital transformation projects fail due to strategic execution problems. It is a matter of fit between DTS and the business model. In this sense, the business model is used as a framework to emphasizes the firm perspective concerning the context. It depicts how firms create value and appropriate it in a context that constraints resources, opportunities, and results. The strategic formulation is the thesis of how to do it, and the implementation is about how to make the job done. The failure usually happens because of the underestimation of change management's important aspects concerning customers, such as brand interaction, and concerning employees such as the way to work, organizational culture, and climate.

The way to take Correani et al. (2020) lens to analyze the DTS as a process is the classification of the type of strategy (Mintzberg & Waters, 1985). It links the capacity to assess the environment and find the best way to take advantage of resources, capabilities, and circumstances (Venkatraman & Prescott, 1990) to the inner perspective of a firm's resources and capacities to influences the context (Leonard-Barton, 1992). The type of strategy is a useful framework analysis that embraces change and allows follow-up progress by comparing what was intended and what was accomplished (Mintzberg & Waters, 1985).

The context constraints and challenges mixed with the firm's strengths, weaknesses, and motivations induce the strategic formulation classified as the intended strategy. It is what was planned. Then, the execution must follow the plan, but the context can influence its performance. Therefore, the deliberate strategy is how much strategy was done as planned, the emergent strategy is the adaptations due to what has emerged from the circumstances, and there is also an unrealized portion of strategy (Mintzberg & Waters, 1985). The capability to identify and carry through the changes needed during the execution is crucial (Pettigrew, 2012).

In this case, the deliberated strategy was using franchised stores as a distribution point, addressing the logistics issue, and meeting the customer's needs by a convenient and fast delivery. Billing the sale to the franchise also has allowed it to enter the digital sales process, capturing value (Mintzberg & Waters, 1985). The changes in the external scenario because of the COVID-19 pandemic brought benefits to the integration strategy between brick-and-mortar store and virtual stores, accelerating the entry of the most resistant franchisees (Baker, 2021; Pettigrew, 2012).

The first emergent strategy happened in the beginning when Omnichannel was chosen to integrate physical and digital sales, without the business cannibalization of franchises. There was also a turning point into specialization after the CDO was hired and started an integration process of top-down and bottom-up demands into a unified strategy (Chanias et al., 2019). This huge adjustment required to scale up and achieve efficiency can figure as an emergent strategy as well. Although the omnichannel implementation had brought the possibility of 'infinite shelf' implementation, it was postponed due to the reduction of customers in person presence as a pandemic consequence. It was an example of unrealized strategy (Mintzberg & Waters, 1985).

Strategy as a Practice

Chanias et al. (2019) pose that digital strategy has spanned the boundaries between business strategy and information systems. The last has been approached like an operational issue or a strategic investment for a long time, but nowadays is too embedded in the structures-agency dialectics of society to be dealt with apart from the strategy. The digital in our lives shape the digital strategy as an indivisible social practice (Teubner & Stockhinger, 2020). Thus, the 20th-century classical strategic canon of design, planning, and the process is less effective to deal with a fuzzy innovation-driven reality. It is necessary to rely on theories that emphasize learning, change, and adaptation while coping with recursiveness (Jarzabkowski, 2004; Mintzberg et al., 2010).

Therefore, "*strategy is not as something a firm has, but something a firm does*" (Jarzabkowski, 2004, p. 529), it is what is going on running a business (Whittington, 1996). That is why it is so difficult to keep a holistic standpoint examining strategy. The Gordian knot is that we can get cross-section insights, but longitudinal data are needed to gouge the big picture. However, as the context changes strategies tend to adapt (Jarzabkowski, 2004). The business theory has not developed based on this premise, always seeking patterns, causalities, and results (Pettigrew, 2012) following the hard science examples (Miller, 1991). But sociology has trends to deal with it. Then we can use the sociological practice lens assuming that business is a truly social practice embedded in social structures and agency relationships (Jarzabkowski, 2004). Strategy as a practice is a way to find new synthesis and finally bring the academy closer to practitioners (Chanias et al., 2019; Whittington, 1996).

The practice is an outcome of agents' relationships embedded in social structures. However, practice influences both the relationships between agents and structures due to their stability over time. It is perceived as the persistence of social order and tends to serve agency until a new power interferes in their balance (Giddens, 1983; Jarzabkowski, 2004). Usually, innovation does it (Fagerberg, 2004), mainly when innovation is already embedded in social agency and structures (Chanias et al., 2019; Teubner & Stockhinger, 2020). The strategic fit concept offers a simplification of the agency-structure dialectic, although it was not conceived to this goal (Venkatraman & Prescott, 1990).

The structure encompasses organizational strengths and weaknesses that can favor or constrain the change. The main stakeholders in line with the change were the investors, who asked for DTS and the management team. Corporate employees were suspicious about the change because of fear to harm the firm's reputation and lack of understanding about the DTS process and outcomes. The main detractor was the franchisees who also compose a core agent in the business model. Some part of DTS was recursive from the start because it took advantage of the digital structure that already existed (Jarzabkowski, 2004). The omnichannel was a natural improvement to integrated business agents and to exploit strong points while dealing with weakness (Mintzberg,1987).

The main need for adaptation came from cultural change and training. Therefore, top-business stakeholders were receptive to DTS, while the franchisees and staff were non-receptive. The overall retail industry pressure favors a receptiveness improvement. Several rivals were struggling to go more digital. However, organizational culture and clear change goals within a coherent policy were challenges (Pettigrew, 2012). The learning by doing DTS practice made the cultural changes needed to create adaptation while coping with recursiveness (Jarzabkowski, 2004; Mintzberg et al., 2010). It is possible to observe that the company has developed its strategy along the execution (Mintzberg & Waters, 1985). Results from implementation shapes the next step in a learning-by doing process (Jarzabkowski, 2004; Mintzberg et al., 2010). The DTS became an essential part of the business reaching some degree of stability. The recursiveness supports the adaptation needs that are still addressed by a project management approach. The Uni.Co's DTS is recent and is still ongoing, therefore it is not possible to assess the efficiency level, nor the specialization level achieved (Jarzabkowski, 2004). The strategy as practice seems to embrace innovations in a flexible way while building competences (Fagerberg, 2004; Leonard-Barton, 1992).

Chanias et al. (2019) found seven phases description of DTS in a pre-digital case. Their contribution is useful because provides parameters to assesses the DTS progress over time. Time is fundamental to appraise background and trends, and it is a way to address the balance between recursiveness and adaptation (Richard et al., 2009), mainly because strategy is not just a matter of change, some degree of stability is needed to achieve efficiency (Jarzabkowski, 2004). And because there is an investment for knowledge accumulation, capacity development, and consequent specialization, which create path dependencies (Leonard-Barton, 1992). It, in turn, block the identification of factors useful for innovation (i.e., lock-in situation), even making it difficult to perceive the need for change or adapting strategies (Fagerberg, 2004; Leonard-Barton, 1992). Fagerberg (2004) adopts an evolutionary logic to suggest that the organization needs to be flexible, in line with the ambidexterity concept (March, 1991) and with modern agility practices (Chanias et al., 2019).

Recognizing the need for digital transformation (phase 0) emerges from strategic directions based on digital reality assessment understanding what is already available at the organization and the issues that need attention (i.e., diagnosis). Then the phase 1 is when opportunities and the job to done are analyzed to determine what is ideal and what is possible (i.e., prognosis). Phase 2 is a synthesis of top-down and bottom-up strategic practices through building blocks. The top-down formulation starts with a development roadmap and a customer-oriented conception that evolves to a minimum value product pivotal analysis. The bottom-up formulation emerges from democratic participation by idea collection and problem-oriented proposals. The match between these strategic formulations is achieved through decision gates in an iterative movement (Chanias et al., 2019).

The top-down formulation focus is digital exploitation strategies to provide guidelines that sustain a holistic development in line with values such as customer-centric thinking to work agile and flexibly, collaboratively, and interdisciplinary, always keeping open-mind settings favoring experimentation. The bottom-up effort aims to digital exploration based on an extensive digital innovation process relying on an idea funnel, inspired by proven, agile procedures from the start-up industry, such as idea pitching or rapid prototyping (Chanias et al., 2019). Therefore, the formulations emulated the ambidexterity concept (March, 1991). Besides, one strategic practice can be more successful than the other (Chanias et al., 2019), perhaps because of organizational structure, culture, and context (March, 1991).

The following phases (3 to 6) are about strategic realization where it is possible to classify which are deliberate, emergent, or unrealized strategies (Mintzberg & Waters, 1985). It is along with the strategic realization that the effect of practice really shows up (Jarzabkowski, 2004; Whittington, 1996). The narratives alleged during the strategic practice enlightens motivations, circumstances, and constraints. There are receptive and non-receptive contexts, and some elements increase the receptiveness such as environmental pressures, a supportive organizational culture, and simple and clear change goals within a coherent policy (Pettigrew, 2012).

Digital Transformation Strategy

It is possible to frame Uni.Co's DTS into the types of strategy and to highlight its strategic fit in terms of the social use of technology, the retail sector tendencies, and the COVID-19 pandemic issues. Even though a time-bounded analysis and the cross-sectional way of case's data collection can induce an episodic perspective favoring the strategy as a process lens (Correani et al., 2020), the difficulty to set an end to the DTS results and to establish inputs and outputs due to its recursiveness turns it difficulty to see it as cycles (Jarzabkowski, 2004).

For Chanias et al. (2019) DTS is a strategic practice because it is a moving target with no foreseeable end in line with the 'becoming' perspective because the agency and social structures are in dynamic movement balancing change and inertia. It is never done until it is overcome. A strategy can be formal or informal but exists as long as the organization endures and changes with it. Furthermore, there is no real separation between what is happening in the context and strategic practice. There is a complex generative practice (Jarzabkowski, 2004). This complexity is what differs strategy as a practice from strategy as a process (Pettigrew, 2012; Whittington, 1996).

The argument about a digital paradigm embedded in the structures-agency dialectics of society is also appealing to strategy as a practice standpoint (Chanias et al., 2019; Teubner & Stockhinger, 2020). It enlightens how to cope with adaptation and recursiveness through learning-by-doing and lessons-learned records (Jarzabkowski, 2004) that fill the gap between strategy and operation (Pettigrew, 2012).

Because acknowledging the strategic types during an instance is another way to reach a tangible basis to gauge the agency-structure dialectic (Jones & Karsten, 2008) it is not possible to achieve a final decision about the best way to approach DTS. The strategy as a process and the strategy as a practice both have pros and cons, mainly concerning the kind of data that better suits each analysis. The analytical standpoint of strategy as a process is better used with cross-sectional data (Correani et al., 2020) like those collected in this case study. However, it is difficult to point out which theoretical standpoint made the case analysis easier, and it was harder to separate the analysis of the strategy as a process from the analysis of the strategy as a practice. Therefore, we propose the complementarity between both.

Moreover, it seems that the strategy as a practice embraces the process analytical standpoint becoming a more complete theoretical perspective, despite it still lacks further theoretical development (Jarzabkowski, 2004). DTS as a new trend socially embedded (Jones & Karsten, 2008) has the potential to boost the new synthesis favored by strategy as a practice perspective (Whittington, 1996) bringing the academy closer to practitioners (Chanias et al., 2019). This standpoint seems to be more suited to face the expected automated, autonomous, and intelligent production evolution (Kumar & Bhatia, 2021) enabling the flexibility needed to make strategy pace with context change. This issue has been discussed by seminal authors in strategy and innovation (Fagerberg, 2004; Leonard-Barton, 1992; March, 1991) but lacked the sociological background concerned in the strategy as practice perspective (Chanias et al., 2019).

The correct strategic practice is what sustains competitive advantage (Jarzabkowski, 2004; Whittington, 1996), and it can explain the transition of digital issues to the strategic level in the firm's decision-making (Teubner & Stockhinger, 2020). And its complex generative practice (Jarzabkowski, 2004) allows studying industry isomorphism, innovation, and evolutions patterns. It also allows pointing out efficiency issues and their tools and techniques, understanding experience and learning curves, and seek best practices (Chanias et al., 2019).

CURRENT CHALLENGES

Uni.Co group has faced some challenges while carrying out DTS implementation. It started with professionals hiring in the technology area, such as developers, programmers, and data analysts. According to the CEO, the group had about 15 vacancies having a hard time to be fulfilled. This people shortage has an impact on project development and the digital transformation scale. For Verhoef et al. (2021), this is a common problem, especially for non-digital companies since the technology specialized workforce prefers to work for digital-native companies. Even though the company has been doing its best to provide training and development for their current employees to fulfill these new competencies, they do not afford to wait for that development.

The pandemic has brought up a lot of constraints which is another challenge. Brazil has been through an economic hard time with a high unemployment rate and a high Covid-19 contagion rate. Apart from all the need for social isolation and movement restrictions to contain the disease spread, the company does not sell products that are considered essential. The Imaginarium brand products are specially sold as gifts for special date celebrations. So, Uni.Co tried to redirect the product development to office decoration goods to overcome this challenge and take advantage of home-office tendencies. In addition, franchisees have been facing a lower revenue stream while paying all the costs for the closed brick-and-mortar stores like rents and labor costs. This hindered the inventory replenishment, damaging the Model 2. On one hand, the pandemic rushed this model implementation and helped to increase the integration in the omnichannel. On the other hand, the costs of the same event are preventing product replenishment in brick-and-mortar stores. Therefore, hindering the model efficiency.

Uni.Co sought to open capital to deal with investment issues and to improve the support offered to franchisees in this difficult moment. It also served as an expansionist strategy with new aims for business acquisition and more omnichannel scale. However, the pandemic worsening in Brazil made them give up. Uni.Co and its investment fund feared a bad IPO evaluation in a bad stock-market moment. But the IPO structuration process caught the attention of investors interested in Uni.Co' acquisition.

In April 2020, 70% of the company was sold to a Brazilian retail giant, Lojas Americanas. Lojas Americanas has been operating in e-commerce since 1999, has great experience in this segment, and has Magazine Luiza and Amazon as its main competitors in Brazil. It was one of the marketplaces used by Uni.Co even after the development of "Nossos Crushes" in July 2020. Therefore, the acquisition is an unexpected turnaround for Uni.Co, probably, maybe because of the disinvestment of its previous fund. The Antitrust Council in Brazil (CADE) is still analyzing the acquisition. Thus, it is impossible to know currently what goes next. This issue also harmed the present research constraining the available interviews.

SOLUTIONS AND RECOMMENDATIONS

This case study sheds light on the DTS process faced by pre-digital companies (Chanias et al., 2019) and points out a COVID-19 pandemic influence in the retail industry (Baker, 2021). It relies on strategy theory emphasizing change, adaptation, and learning while coping with recursiveness helping to fill a theoretical gap (Jarzabkowski, 2004; Mintzberg et al., 2010; Pettigrew, 2012). In this sense this study also provides an example of strategic fit (Venkatraman & Prescott, 1990) and of change receptive and non-receptive elements (Pettigrew, 2012). The pandemic and the retail industry moment (Baker, 2021) have increased the receptiveness even providing an environmental pressure but the organizational culture, and the lack of simple and clear change goals within a coherent policy represented non-receptive elements in the same context. These weaknesses were overcome by the Uni.Co's capability to identify and carry through the changes needed during the execution (Pettigrew, 2012) what can be also interpreted in terms of the ambidexterity discussed by March (1991). Unfortunately, the negative aspects of the pandemic brought the unexpected sale of 70% of Uni.Co. The DTS was important for business development and ensured the survival of the company and its franchises. The successful implementation of DTS increased the business value and made it attractive, enabling its acquisition.

There are several practical implications. The study confirms that the DTS process is business-centered and customer-oriented. Technology is a means to meet the strategy that bounds it, not an end (Teubner & Stockhinger, 2020). In the case of retail, DTS is not only about looking for new customers, but it is also meeting the former customer's needs. The customer started to value brands that demonstrated the ability to provide convenience since buying to the offer of various delivery options and the speed of meeting their demand. Therefore, the presence of e-commerce tends to not extinguish the brick-and-mortar stores. In addition to becoming a place of experience and engagement with the brand, these stores have gained a new function as a distribution center, mainly in a country with continental dimensions such as Brazil. It enables short-term delivery, which consequently increases a positive brand perception (Sopadjieva et al., 2017; Baker, 2021).

The case confirms that DTS needs both top-down and bottom-up formulation processes. In the top-down sense, DTS has the power to create a new strategic vision for the company and address its vision of the future. In the bottom-up sense, DTS brings solution for organization's current problems and boosts productivity gains. The bottom-up strategizing increases the DTS execution speed and accuracy by looping in feed-back and adaptations. It helps to keep DTS on the right track (Chanias et al., 2019; Jarzabkowski, 2004).

It was also possible to identify the DTS phases which have emerged in Chanias et al., (2019) study, increasing the understanding about them by a new empirical example. The DTS was also described through types of strategies perspective (Mintzberg & Waters, 1985) and has fulfilled the elements of the strategy as a practice to comply with recursiveness and adaptation movements (Jarzabkowski, 2004). The strategy as practice seems to embrace innovations in a flexible way while building competences (Fagerberg, 2004; Leonard-Barton, 1992). However, the Uni.Co's DTS is recent and is still ongoing, therefore it is not possible to assess the efficiency level, nor the specialization level achieved (Jarzabkowski, 2004).

It was not possible to establish which strategic theoretical perspective is the best to analyze DTS due to their complementarity. The strategy as a process best suits cross-sectional data and offer useful frameworks to pragmatically analysis what is going on (Correani et al., 2020). The strategy as a practice is more complex (Pettigrew, 2012; Whittington, 1996) but is also better suited to digital transformation context due to its sociological component (Jones & Karsten, 2008; Whittington, 1996). Therefore, this standpoint embraces more theoretical and practical issues (Chanias et al., 2019).

The digital phenomenon is based on change and adaptation (Verhoef et al., 2021). Hence, strategy is fundamental to set the organizational direction and to analyze the right structures to foster efficiency, balancing the firm's effort in a coherent way (Mintzberg et al., 2010). It also helps to identify and carry out the changes needed during the execution (Pettigrew, 2012; Zajac et al., 2000) avoiding rigidities traps (Fagerberg, 2004; Leonard-Barton, 1992) and increasing DTS success chances (Correani et al., 2020). As a result, we reinforce the need for more studies based on the rich and well-developed strategy literature to better understand the phenomenon of digital transformation (Chanias et al., 2019; Correani et al., 2020). At the same time, we believe that digital transformation offers a unique perspective of renewal for this theory (Kumar & Bhatia, 2021; Teubner & Stockhinger, 2020). Studies that include other stakeholders involved in the DTS beyond the strategic level would also be enlightening, as they allow to gouge DTS' effects from another angle.

Future studies can deepen the fusion-view of information systems literature and strategy and search for examples that highlight the differences between DTS and isolated digital development. Due to the single case design the results can be idiosyncratic (Tight, 2010; Verschuren, 2003). Therefore, future research can replicate this study to validate its results by comparison (Ghauri, 2004). It is also worth pointing out that the results can not apply to non-pre-digital organizations (Chanias et al., 2019) and there is an opportunity for diversification and comparison.

REFERENCES

Baker, G. (2021). *Why category leading brick and mortar retailers are likely the biggest long term Covid beneficiaries*. https://gavin-baker.medium.com/

Chanias, S., Myers, M. D., & Hess, T. (2019). Digital transformation strategy making in pre-digital organizations: The case of a financial services provider. *The Journal of Strategic Information Systems*, *28*(1), 17–33. doi:10.1016/j.jsis.2018.11.003

Correani, A., De Massis, A., Frattini, F., Petruzzelli, A. M., & Natalicchio, A. (2020). Implementing a Digital Strategy: Learning from the Experience of Three Digital Transformation Projects. *California Management Review*, *62*(4), 37–56. doi:10.1177/0008125620934864

Eisenhardt, K. M. (1989). Building theories from case study research. *Academy of Management Review*, *14*(4), 532–550. doi:10.5465/amr.1989.4308385

Fagerberg, J. (2004). *Innovation: a guide to the literature*. Georgia Institute of Technology.

Ghauri, P. (2004). Designing and conducting case studies in international business research. Handbook of Qualitative Research Methods for International Business, 1(1), 109–124.

Giddens, A. (1983). Comments on the Theory of Structuration. *Journal for the Theory of Social Behaviour*, *13*(1), 75–80. doi:10.1111/j.1468-5914.1983.tb00463.x

Jarzabkowski, P. (2004). Strategy as practice: Recursiveness, adaptation, and practices-in-use. *Organization Studies*, *25*(4), 529–560. doi:10.1177/0170840604040675

Jones, M. R., & Karsten, H. (2008). Giddens's structuration theory and information systems research. *MIS Quarterly: Management Information Systems*, *32*(1), 127–157. doi:10.2307/25148831

Kumar, S., & Bhatia, M. S. (2021). Environmental dynamism, industry 4.0 and performance. *Industrial Marketing Management*, *95*, 54–64. doi:10.1016/j.indmarman.2021.03.010

Leonard-Barton, D. (1992). Core Capabilities and Core Rigidities: A Paradox in Managing New Product Development. *Strategic Management Journal*, *13*(S1), 111–125. doi:10.1002mj.4250131009

March, J. G. (1991). Exploration and exploitation in organization learning. *Organization Science*, *2*(1), 71–87. doi:10.1287/orsc.2.1.71

Miller, E. S. (1991). Of economic paradigms, puzzles, problems, and policies; or, is the economy too important to be entrusted to the economists? *Journal of Economic Issues*, *25*(4), 993–1004. doi:10.10 80/00213624.1991.11505228

Mintzberg, H. (1987). Crafting strategy. *Harvard Business Review*, 477–486.

Mintzberg, H., Ahlstrand, B., & Lampel, J. (2010). Safari de estratégia: Um roteiro pela selva do planejamento estratégico. *The Bookman*.

Mintzberg, H., & Waters, J. A. (1985). Of strategies, deliberate and emergent. *Strategic Management Journal*, *6*(3), 257–272. doi:10.1002mj.4250060306

Novak, J., Purta, M., Marciniak, T., Ignatowicz, K., Rozenbaum, K., & Yearwood, K. (2018). *The rise of Digital Challengers*. Digital McKinsey. https://www.mckinsey.com/~/media/McKinsey/Featured%20 Insights/Europe/Central%20and%20Eastern%20Europe%20needs%20a%20new%20engine%20for%20 growth/The-rise-of-Digital-Challengers.ashx

Patton, M. Q. (2002). *Qualitative research & Evaluation Methods* (3rd ed.).

Pettigrew, A. M. (2012). Context and Action in the Transformation of the Firm. *Journal of Management Studies*, *49*(7), 1304–1328. doi:10.1111/j.1467-6486.2012.01054.x

Reinartz, W., Wiegand, N., & Imschloss, M. (2019). The impact of digital transformation on the retailing value chain. *International Journal of Research in Marketing*, *36*(3), 350–366. doi:10.1016/j. ijresmar.2018.12.002

Richard, P. J., Devinney, T. M., Yip, G. S., & Johnson, G. (2009). Measuring Organizational Performance. *Journal of Management*, *35*(3), 718–804. doi:10.1177/0149206308330560

Schallmo, D. R., & Williams, C. A. (2018). History of digital transformation. In D. Schallmo & C. Williams (Eds.), *Digital Transformation Now!* (pp. 3–8). Springer. doi:10.1007/978-3-319-72844-5_2

Sopadjieva, E., Dholakia, U. M., & Benjamin, B. (2017). A Study of 46,000 Shoppers Shows That Omnichannel Retailing Works. *Harvard Business Review*. https://hbr.org/2017/01/a-study-of-46000-shoppers-shows-that-omnichannel-retailing-works

Teubner, R. A., & Stockhinger, J. (2020). Understanding information systems strategy in the digital age. *The Journal of Strategic Information Systems*, *29*(4), 101642. doi:10.1016/j.jsis.2020.101642

Ulriksen, M. S., & Dadalauri, N. (2016). Single case studies and theory-testing: The knots and dots of the process-tracing method. *International Journal of Social Research Methodology*, *19*(2), 223–239. doi:10.1080/13645579.2014.979718

Venkatraman, N., & Prescott, J. E. (1990). Environment-strategy coalignment: An empirical test of its performance implications. *Strategic Management Journal*, *11*(1), 1–23. doi:10.1002mj.4250110102

Verhoef, P. C., Broekhuizen, T., Bart, Y., Bhattacharya, A., Dong, J. Q., Fabian, N., & Haenlein, M. (2021). Digital transformation: A multidisciplinary reflection and research agenda. *Journal of Business Research*, *122*, 889–901. doi:10.1016/j.jbusres.2019.09.022

Verschuren, P. J. M. (2003). Case study as a research strategy. *International Journal of Social Research Methodology: Theory and Practice, 6*(2), 121–139. doi:10.1080/13645570110106154

Whittington, R. (1996). Strategy as practice. *Long Range Planning, 29*(5), 731–735. doi:10.1016/0024-6301(96)00068-4

Zajac, E. J., Kraatz, M. S., & Bresser, R. K. F. (2000). Modeling the dynamics of strategic fit. *Strategic Management Journal, 21*(4), 429–453. doi:10.1002/(SICI)1097-0266(200004)21:4<429::AID-SMJ81>3.0.CO;2-#

KEY TERMS AND DEFINITIONS

Digital Transformation: It is a change process to develop digital assets and capabilities to comply with customers' needs and competition challenges. It has three stages according to the complexity of the change and the digital integration in terms of strategies, metrics, and goals.

Digital Transformation Strategy: A digital transformation strategy can be a new strategy part of the strategic process or a strategic practice, depending on how it is designed and implemented.

Omnichannel: The omnichannel combines shopping experience in brick-and-mortar stores with a variety of digital channels to increase retailer's differentiation and leverage competitive edge.

Retail Sector: The retail sector is central in all economies, and it occupies a privileged position near to customers. It is the heart of a complex value chain that includes storage, logistic, legal transactions, advertising, and so on. The retail sector is also very diversified, with many business models.

Strategy: Strategy is what sustain competitive advantage. It is fundamental to set the organizational direction and to analyze the right structures to fosters efficiency. It also helps an efforts convergence and improves coherence, and it is an important factor to ensure flexibility, adaptability, and business survival.

Strategy as a Practice: It consists of what the company does in terms of strategy. The practice is an outcome of agents' relationships embedded in social structures. The structure encompasses organizational strengths and weaknesses that can favor or constrain the change. Therefore, part of the strategy as a practice is about recursiveness allowing competence and efficiency building. And part relies on learning and adaptation.

Strategy as a Process: It considers the relationship between context and the firm in an instance through the internal and external variables that influence the strategic formulation and implementation. Thus, there are two different and interdependent stages of the same process. The strategic process has inputs and outputs. It has a start and end, therefore the results translated into the performance concept can be evaluated at the end of the process.

APPENDIX 1

Questions and Answers

1. What is the overall problem presented in this case?

How a pre-digital retail company formulated and accomplish its digital transformation strategy, also discussing the role the COVID-19 pandemic had played.

2. Describe the main elements of Uni.Co's digital transformation strategy:

There were three important stakeholders in the DTS: 1) Uni.Co and its brands; 2) the investment fund; 3) franchisees of each Uni.Co's brands.

To create value to all stakeholders, the DTS was based on two purchase models: 1) 'pick up on the store' where the customer would buy online but pick it up in the store, and 2) 'shipment from the store' where brick-and-mortar stores would be transformed into a distribution point, using their stock to fulfill online orders, reducing logistical costs. The DTS also relied on omnichannel to combine the shopping experience in brick-and-mortar stores with a variety of digital channels to increase retailer's differentiation and leverage a competitive edge.

The DTS boosted organizational changes in the Uni.Co and in each Franchisee. There were also changes in the franchise rules and logistics.

3. What were the pros and cons of Uni.Co's digital transformation strategy?

The strategy adopted by Uni.Co group has pros and counts. Regarding the pros, they have chosen an in-house development strategy. As they did not adopt a "ready to use" solution, it was necessary to search for tools and best practices that could fit into their business model until they find a way. They followed a learning-by-doing methodology putting more effort in the execution than in strategic planning, and they used their business knowledge to include franchises as a strength. This process allowed the company to be faster in the implementation and find a unique path to build a capability that could turn into a model for digital transformation. The model uniqueness could not be emulated by competitors easily. However, the model did not fit the organizational structure and lacked ways to scale up. Hence, they spent resources and overburdened their team not involving a digital specialist from the start. They also took a lot of time to choose for digital transformation, despite data and market pointing to that way. And they took a while to overcome the fear of harming the relationship with franchisees, and it blurred the decision-making, for instance, charging less than the expenditure.

4. Defend the case analysis from the perspective of strategy as a process.

The strategy as a process best suits cross-sectional data and offer useful frameworks to pragmatically analysis what is going on (Correani et al, 2020). It considers the relationship between context and the firm in an instance through the internal and external variables that influence the strategic formulation

Digital Transformation

and implementation. Thus, there are two different and interdependent stages of the same process that can be analyzed. The strategic process has inputs and outputs that helps the decision-making in an easy causes and consequences framework. It also has a start and end, therefore the results translated into the performance concept can be evaluated at the end of the process.

5. Defend the case analysis from the perspective of strategy as a practice.

It is not possible to establish an end for digital transformation as the digital became a social structure. The structure encompasses organizational strengths and weaknesses that can favor or constrain the change. Therefore, the strategy as a practice can help to assess business factors for recursiveness and adaptation. The first allows competence and efficiency building. The second is essential for learning and survival.

6. Point out alternatives to overcome the challenges of Uni.Co's digital transformation strategy.

Depends on the creativity of those who respond to it and is constrained by technological and theoretical factors at the time the case is applied.

7. How digital transformation can influence strategic theory and practice?

In the case of retail, DTS is not only about looking for new customers, but it is also meeting the former customer's needs. It is a central issue to business model generation and adaptation. The presence of e-commerce tends to not extinguish brick-and-mortar stores. The strategic theory can help to evaluate the pros and counts of a brick-and-mortar store, virtual business channels, and omnichannel. The digital transformation can bring the strategic theory closer to practitioners. It serves as a social structure proxy because DTS is business-centered and customer-oriented. Because the digital phenomenon is based on change and adaptation it provides a way to keep business strategy updated.

Epilogue and Lessons Learned

In the case of retail, DTS is not only about looking for new customers, but it is also meeting the former customer's needs. It is a central issue to business model generation and adaptation. The presence of e-commerce tends to not extinguish brick-and-mortar stores. The strategic theory can help to evaluate the pros and counts of a brick-and-mortar store, virtual business channels, and omnichannel. The digital transformation can bring the strategic theory closer to practitioners. It serves as a social structure proxy because DTS is business-centered and customer-oriented. Because the digital phenomenon is based on change and adaptation it provides a way to keep business strategy updated.
Lessons learned:

1. In the case of retail, DTS is not only about looking for new customers, but it is also meeting the former customer's needs. The customer started to value brands that demonstrated the ability to provide convenience since buying to the offer of various delivery options and the speed of meeting

their demand. Therefore, the presence of e-commerce tends to not extinguish the brick-and-mortar stores.
2. In addition to becoming a place of experience and engagement with the brand, the brick-and-mortar stores have gained a new function as a distribution center, mainly in a country with continental dimensions such as Brazil. It enables short-term delivery, which consequently increases a positive brand perception.
3. The DTS was successful in the value creation to franchises as well. However, the pandemic's downsides hindered the DTS' two purchase models (i.e. 'pick up on the store' and 'shipment from the store') due to franchisees' financial difficulties in buying products to refill their storage.

Chapter 2
Be Like Amazon:
Achieving a Competitive Advantage Based on Digital Footprint Analysis

Anna Tarabasz
https://orcid.org/0000-0002-6819-517X
Curtin University, UAE

EXECUTIVE SUMMARY

Gaining competitive advantage requires a detailed benchmark of performance against other market players, and profound gap analysis in comparison to the best practice applies to the audit of the digital presence (online footprint analysis), which, based on scripting codes, is done easily on its premises. SEO software and social medial listening tools allow for a comprehensive understanding of the digital performance of the company. Unfortunately, some businesses underestimate the potential dormant in different types of live analytics and performance trackers and being unaware of the analysis capacity to be performed on competitors and market leaders completely off cost. The case presents a study of a digital footprint template analysis performed for Amazon in the United Arab Emirates and shows the comparison with local and global market players like Noon.com, eBay, or Alibaba using software like SEMrush, SimilarWeb, and Brand24 to showcase how to leverage on gathered insights and gain competitive advantage.

ORGANIZATION BACKGROUND: UNDERSTANDING THE E-COMMERCE MARKET IN UAE

According to Visa (2021), the eCommerce market in the United Arab Emirates (UAE) is on a path of visible growth, in comparison to other both emerging and mature economies. High internet penetration ratio (Internet World Stats, 2020), reaching 100%, along with eCommerce payments, driven mainly by government-initiated and education-driven transactions, make the country unique. But still in the long run UEA's role among other big eCommerce players (like China, US, UK) is negligible. Comparing the retail eCommerce sales worldwide, predicted for 2021 by eMarketer (2019) as $4.93 trillion, eCom-

DOI: 10.4018/978-1-7998-1630-0.ch002

merce revenue brought locally, according to Statista (2021), the amount totaling to $7.456 million, which seems insignificant. However, one needs to understand that these numbers are generated by a society of 9.5 million inhabitants, with a 66% eCommerce adoption rate (We Are Social, 2021). Moreover, is not only the current status of the market, with expected CAGR of 10.30% for 2021-2025, (resulting in a projected market volume of $11,034million by 2025, with predominant component coming from the Fashion Industry, instead of leading now government-related transactions) and expected average revenue per user (ARPU) with an amount of $1,075.81 (Statista, 2021). Worth noting is as well the fact that for the same period predictions of Euromonitor International (2021) predict the Retail Value RSP in the UAE (2021-2025) for the eCommerce 15% and 18% for mobile eCommerce.

According to Fielding & Armstrong (2020) e-commerce in the UAE represents currently 4.2% of the retail revenue and is estimated to grow by an average of 23% by 2022. What is important, more and more visible becomes the transition from a characteristic offline shopping experience towards digital shopping, online self-service, and everyday e-commerce transactions. Previously preferred CoD (Cash on Delivery) is being replaced with credit card payments and wire transfers. The ease of digital payments starts to play an increasingly important role. This transition has not happened by coincidence but was triggered by pandemic circumstances and "hard lockdown" between March and June 2020, which visibly sped up the digital transformation. Moreover, the same approach was visible everywhere. According to McKinsey (2020), calculating the average share of digital customer interactions in comparison to all exchanges, globally the digital adoption accelerated by 3 years, being the most visible in the Asia-Pacific region, with an average of 4 years. Digitization of almost all industries in the Emirates was therefore inevitable and as per data of Emirates News Agency (2020) in the first five months of 2020, an increase of 300% in consumer demand for e-commerce services was recorded. Moreover, the DED Trader license in Dubai (which supports the growth of UAE e-commerce) noted 943 licenses were issued to new businesses in the first three months of 2020, leading to a 179% YoY increase in comparison to the same period in 2019. With a society willingly "embracing tomorrow and foreseeing the future", the shift towards digital was obvious. Not only on the big scale – like digitization of processes, government transactions but impacted everyday life - work from home, grocery shopping and facilitated digital payments.

SETTING THE STAGE: AMAZON.AE AMONG THE MAIN UAE MARKET PLAYERS

With many businesses struggling for survival during the Covid-19 pandemic and post-pandemic time, the e-commerce market in the UAE is thriving. A set of well-established players like Amazon, eBay, Noon, Namshi, Deliveroo, or Zomato is being followed by more incumbent operators like Aido, Awok, Careem Eats, FarFetch, Mumzworld, Ounas, DesertCart, and many more. But Amazon.ae was not there always. Souq.com (سوق, "market" in Arabic), the largest e-commerce platform in the Arab World, was acquired in March 2017 for $580 million by Amazon. Brands co-existed for a while, but on 1st May 2019 Souq.com in the UAE got rebranded as Amazon.ae. The same process was applied in June 2020 for Souq.com in the Kingdom of Saudi Arabia (nowadays Amazon.sa). The Egyptian version operates under the original name till today.

Figure 1. Amazon.ae competitive domain traffic analytics comparison
Source: SEMrush.com, 2021

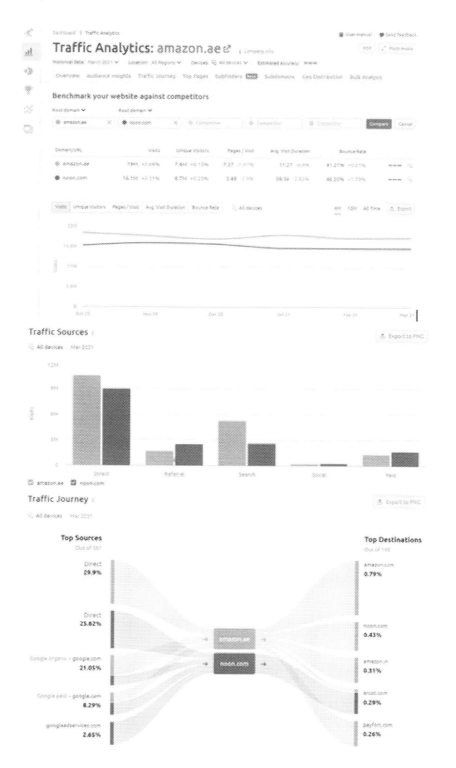

As per section "about us" Amazon.ae (2021), hiring 3600 people, brings together the best of Souq's local know-how and Amazon's global retailing experience, listing in total more than 35 million products. Its 7.4 million users generate traffic to the website of 18.4 million visits, more than 7 pages per visit of an average duration of more than 11 minutes (Cf. Figure 1). With lower traffic rates, its main competitor Noon.com, welcomes 14.6 million visits per month, having almost 4 million less unique visitors monthly. What is interesting, the number of pages per visit is less by half of Amazon's results (4.96 vs. 7.61). Significantly lower is as well the average visit duration with not much higher bounce rate. Performing way better than organic competitors (Carrrefouruea.com) both are significantly way behind global trendsetters like eBay.com or Aliexpress.com. However, when comparing the traffic sources for both UAE-based platforms majority of traffic originates as direct, whereas the second most visible traffic category becomes the search, followed by referral and paid traffic. Therefore, as evident becomes, that Amazon.ae is at the top of mind of the users, who (as further analysis will show) are still searching for Souq.com domain. More detailed analysis of sub-pages and keywords, to be conducted further, and domain analysis with the use of tools like SEMrush, Similar Web, and SEOptimer will prove the same and provide detailed knowledge related to on-page and off-page factors leading to dominating position of Amazon.ae in the United Arab Emirates.

CASE DESCRIPTION: UNDERSTANDING IMPORTANCE OF DIGITAL FOOTPRINT

Unwinding customer experience throughout the omnichannel journey, companies need to understand that having the complete picture of the digital footprint and unbiased assessment is an absolute necessity for contemporary marketers. Presence expressed within well-managed touchpoints like website (along with SEO and SEM), social media, mobile marketing, mail marketing, and display ads is critical. Customer experience across these channels of communication shall be seamless, therefore companies shall align their presence and focus more on omnichannel, than multichannel presence. And as researchers indicate it is so both for individuals (Buettner, 2019; Lambiotte & Kosinski, 2014; Micheli et al., 2018), organizations (Goreglyad, 2019; Olinder et al., 2020; Teng & Maxwell, 2021), and even governments! (Cerina & Duch, 2020). Well-managed digital footprint across omnichannel customer journey can drip the marketing funnel faster and push the customers from undecided to decided more efficiently. However, still, by many this part of presence is underestimated and therefore not done professionally enough.

The skillful analysis becomes therefore priceless and may leverage corporate standing. Unfortunately, usually, marketing managers are standing in front of an information challenge. As said by Cameron (2013) with the data claimed to be more than the new oil, its visualization becomes the new soil and therefore shall be nowadays understood as a cornerstone of building competitive advantage. Moreover, marketers need to reach the relevant sources to generate insights that will be further translated into business decisions. On the one hand, they face the information overload with tools analyzing their performance (Google Analytics, Google AdWords Keyword Planner, and additional dedicated tools for their respective social media channels), on the other they proverbially "face the wall" in terms of business insights on competitors. Questions looking simple at the first glance – "how do we stand against the competition?", "are our actions aligned with the industry standards?", "how to improve our performance and set opponents aside?" remain unanswered due to a lack of source of relevant business insights. As handy come here the solution based on keyword analysis, useful both for Search Engine Optimization (SEMrush,

SimilarWeb, SEOptimer, etc.) and social media mentions (Brand24, KeyHole, Hubspot) useful for social media listening. Subsequent subsections will indicate a simple step-by-step approach to do the same.

Setting priorities and starting from scratch: the Aquarium Framework

Assessment of the digital footprint needs to be conducted continuously, as it is a performance-based cycle of incessant improvements. However, the most often mistake done is based on the lack of understanding, that the footprint shall be perceived from a strategic angle and managed the same way. Therefore, the online presence of the company shall be seen from a birds-eye perspective (to be proven later in the text) and well structured. Ordering the building blocks shall be executed based on the Aquarium Framework of the digital presence (Cf. Figure 2).

Figure 2. Aquarium Framework of digital footprint
Source: Own elaboration, 2021

The creation of a structured digital presence (including an omnichannel campaign) could be compared to the art of setting a decorative fish tank. It is a laborious process, but its crowning achievement pleases the eye of spectators. However, this time ingredients of success will have a slightly different nature. An empty fish tank and four more items (always measuring the required amount of building components) are needed. Commencing, at first, an empty aquarium shall be filled with rocks, till not a single one could be added. Only then one can observe, that still there is a space in between, which could be covered with a smaller substance – gravel, followed by sand. Once all the air pockets seemed to be fully used, water could be added as a final ingredient, ultimately creating a solid, opaque, concrete-resembling cuboid. Assuming, as marked before, that amount of all the components have been previously measured, and then trying to reverse the process: starting with an equal amount of water, followed by sand, gravel, and rocks ultimately will not fit the aquarium. That exactly represents the effort of every marketer. With defined budgets and boundary conditions, he/she can fit nicely all under the rigor of only starting from the cornerstone (rocks), followed by lighter building materials (gravel and sand), and concluded with water, that adjusts to the existing conditions.

As depicted above, rocks reflect the foundation concepts of digital presence – buyer persona, USP (Unique Selling Point) of the business model, and value key proposition delivered to customers. Determined by the same, gravel stands for selected digital marketing channels and tools of marketing communication. Sand in this approach depicts the content, represented by impactful visuals and relevant and appealing text which ultimately attracts the pre-defined buyer persona. Water, being a kind of a binder/adhesive substance, connects all the previously mentioned into a solid construct, and represents all the performed actions leading to the creation of the desired content (searches, phone calls done, emails sent, approvals taken, etc.). Unfortunately, many marketers do the opposite, by not following the proposed framework and the role manner of filling it, but building their aquaria first with water, followed by sand and gravel, and in this regard not leaving enough space for the foundation of solid rock. By doing the same, they fall into the trap of "pathway to hell". Following blindly, without any constructive criticism, the previously established manner of communication creates a vicious circle of mismatched both B2C and B2C communication. This leads to an asymmetry between the proposed offer, non-fulfilled customer expectations, and ultimately prevents the creation of the desired brand perception.

Making the rock right: defining the Digital Buyer Persona

Following properly the depicted Aquarium Framework, companies shall revise strategically their digital marketing foundation by setting rightly their Buyer Persona and USP. In a customer-centric marketing approach, the consumer shall be the focal point of an organization. Standard STP (Segmentation, Targeting, Positioning) approach, indicated by many as a leading one for successful marketing practices (Andaleeb & Hasan, 2016; Rajagopal, 2016; Schlegelmilch, 2016; Weinstein, 2004;) with the dynamic approach to the data drive decisions is still beneficial and effective, though *ad-hoc* decisions often indicate micro-segments and this strategy might be way more effective (Marketing Mania, 2013). With Seth Godin saying rightly "as long as you try to please everyone, you won't please anyone", talking to a broad and unspecified audience seems to be pointless. Zambito (2016) in his research has indicated a strong positive correlation in acknowledgment that goals and goal-directed behaviors were at the heart of buyer persona development. Moreover, Adelle Advella (Vidal-Cabeza, 2015) was indicating that by "combining the Buyer Profile with Buying Insights company will have a clear guidance for the decisions to be made to win the business". And this becomes the *clou* of the concept of the Buyer Persona, defined by Hubspot as "a semi-fictional representation of your ideal customer based on market research and real data about your existing customers". Instead of utilizing the standard sociodemographic criteria, the concept is more focused on psychographic identification of needs, pain points, challenges, frustrations, and behavior triggers, by the answer to 5W+1H (Who?, When? What? Why? How?) ultimate buying questions. Naming Buyer Persona facilitates the task halfway only, as the other task remains to understand how a particular product helps to fulfill the buyer's needs. Furthermore, worth stressing is the fact, that sometimes companies are urged to create them, as customers are not aware that they exist! Moreover, as Ginni Rometty (IBM's CEO) said "Big Data will spell the death of customer segmentation and force the marketer to understand each customer as an individual within 18 months or risk being left in the dust" (Marketing Mania, 2013). It needs to be underlined, that ultimately all activities in the creation of Buyer Persona, visualizing its Customer Journey focus mainly on maximizing or optimizing customer experience (Waqas, Hamzah, & Salleh, 2020; Barwitz & Maas, 2018) to understand their purchase behavior (Bagga & Bhatt, 2013) and gather as much data about the users as possible throughout available touchpoints (Colicev et al., 2019; Ieva & Ziliani, 2018).

Figure 3. Template for Buyer Persona analysis
Source: Own elaboration, 2021

Indeed, the digital audit and understanding the details of website visitors and their behavior on social media allows to draft a template of a buyer persona (Cf. Figure 3), which depending on the need of the brand may be created either in a very detailed or pretty broad approach. Ultimately, a defined Buyer Persona will help the R&D and sales teams for better product/offer development and enable the marketing team to visualize and understand the target audience. Working with a semi-fictional representation of the audience empowers more effective keyword search and advertisement copy creation, basing on assumptions, stereotypes, and behavior patterns. According to SEMrush research, a well-defined Buyer Persona impacts visibly the company KPIs: boosting up to 100% page views per visit, may lead to a 900% increase in website visit duration and result in a 171% spike in marketing ROI (SEMrush, 2020). These numbers may be achieved only when this fictitious representation is compiled with the data flowing from Google Analytics and insights from social media channels (Facebook, Youtube, Instagram, etc.).

The ultimate goal of Buyer Persona is to present in a concise manner profile "sales pitch", which will highlight the most typical points to understand the motivations and fears of a prospect during the purchase decision process and while ultimately buying the product. Moreover, the above-mentioned template allows emphasizing certain typical triggers and purchase pathways. Likewise, while establishing the same one shall consider Perceived Usefulness, Perceived Ease of Use, and User Acceptance of Information Technology (Davis, 1989) as factors contributing to the overall future satisfaction of using the product. Marketers utilizing the proposed template are instantly exposed to the archetypes of buyers, whether B2C (both individuals and groups) and B2B, presented organization-wise. Well-defined Buyer

Persona becomes the heart of the next cornerstone - type idea - the concept of the Digital Engagement Canvas, which will be presented below.

Bird's point of view on engagement perspective: the Digital Engagement Canvas

Having the Buyer Persona defined sets the foundations for the Aquarium Framework, as it predefines the product and tailored-made offer, becoming the company's response to the needs of buyers. Brands facilitating the PUSH approach often do not understand these desires and therefore cannot communicate products' features accurately.

Table 1. Simplified translation of Positioning vs. Communication of focal points

Customer's Information Need	Company's Positioning Focal Point	Example	Explanation
What it is?	Product		Spacious and fast digital *storage for an ultrabook*
What does it do?	Benefit		Waterproof cover for the majority of popular smartphones *prevents the device from water damage*
What does it mean?	Effect		Marshall Portable Bluetooth Speakers. *Lightweight* and *easy connection* for a hassle-free experience from a top brand in terms of *sound quality*
Why shall I care?	Motivation		Maid service with the *price below* the available market benchmark

Source: Own elaboration, 2021, based on display (Image, Text, HTML) and PLA Amazon's advertisements listed by SEMrush, 2021

As a handy comes the above juxtaposition (Cf. Table 1), compiling the expectations of customers and positioning vs. communicated focal points. Each of the examples presented contains the product, its description, and function follow by highlighted benefits that shall trigger customers to finalize their transaction.

Worth noting is the fact, that in a social media-driven world, multiple authors indicate the importance of the process and structured framework of customer engagement (Bowden, 2009; Colicev et al., 2019; De Oliveira et al., 2020; Harmeling et al., 2017; Hollebeeck & Macky, 2019; Van Doorn et al., 2010; Verhoef et al., 2010;), factors generally driving it (Brodie et al., 2017; Pansari & Kumar, 2017), with particular emphasis on the digital channels and Big Data-driven insights (Anderl et al., 2016; De Oliveira et al., 2020; Gummerus et al., 2012; McLean, & Wilson, 2019; Kunz et al, 2017; Sashi, 2012).

Understanding these four points facilitate the flow of any subsequent campaigns and marketing actions in the future, where all the engagement shall be built based on the Digital Engagement Canvas.

The below-mentioned (Cf. Figure 4) interconnected building blocks create a comprehensive strategic approach for seamless digital communication in the long term.

Figure 4. Digital Engagement Canvas
Source: Tarabasz, 2020

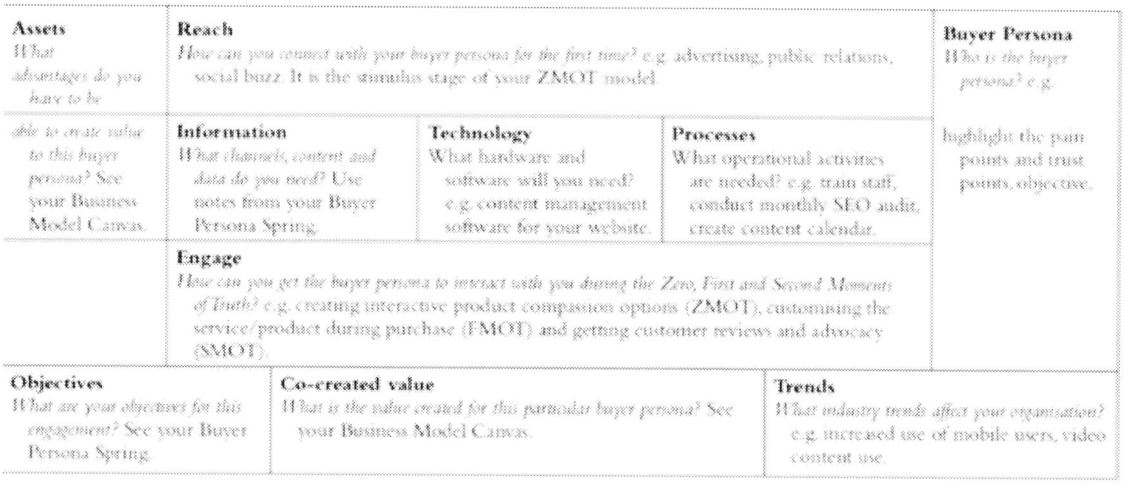

Worth noting is a fact, that many authors underline nowadays the importance of skilfully triggered customer engagement in social media (Garrido-Moreno et al., 2019; Omran, 2021; Tsiotsou, 2019), which can be achieved with a structured approach and use of the Digital Engagement Canvas, initially proposed by Visser and Richardson (2015). The starting point for the same is the definition of campaign objectives as per the SMART rule, followed by a rough idea of co-created value and an understanding of market trends. As a next step company needs to consider its assets and align with Business Model Canvas, all that to be further served as a "comprehensive package" to the desired Buyer Persona. In subsequent steps, the Reach of the campaign is defined along with a draft of Engagement across the marketing funnel, to be ensuing captured together with all the information, technology, and processes needed.

Filling the Aquarium Framework with gravel and sand: channels, tools, and content

All previously specified points were reflecting the cornerstone concepts (rocks) of the Aquarium Framework. Starting from the Buyer Persona, through USP, and relevant Business Model, to the structured strategic approach in campaign management, based on the Digital Engagement Canvas.

However, one needs to understand, that always foundations require additional building material to fill in the aquarium completely. Following this thought process, channels and tools of digital communication shall be established within various touchpoints across the entire omnichannel customer journey (Cf. Figure 5) and subsequently be filled with content.

Figure 5. Example of Omnichannel Customer Journey Framework
Source: Own elaboration, 2021

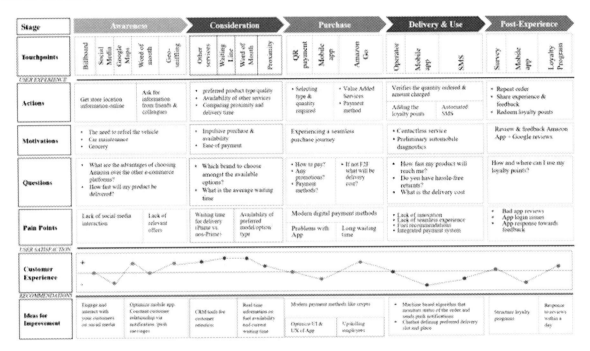

Despite the creation of a Customer Journey when defining a specific modeling language might not be an easy task (Berendes et al., 2018), when drafting it touchpoint-wise less complicated than expected. Nevertheless, the final output might be overwhelming at the first glance. Formally there is no set-up structure of defining the customer journey, as insights might come both from a qualitative and quantitative perspective and ultimately lead to particular preferences of choice (Barwitz & Maas, 2018). Graphical presentation as above is not considered mandatory, though significantly facilitates the task of the person performing it. Very often companies send a group of mystery shoppers to perform analysis across their channels, usually, it will be the task of a purchase, looking for any information, cross-checking branch opening hours, etc. With such an approach visible become, that one touchpoint might be utilized few times, each time with different expectations and different experiences. However, it can be noted that every successful Customer Journey Framework shall clearly define the points below:

Step one: consider the stage of the journey by defining at least 4 possible stages – awareness, consideration, purchase, post-purchase.
Step two: define actions, motivations, questions, pain points.
Step three: name the potential touchpoints, including both managed and unmanaged touchpoints, creating entries o the journey touchpoint-wise (column-wise).
Step four: assess the user experience, marking it each time as positive, neutral, or negative.

Step five: propose areas for improvement, usually with the use of new technologies and industry trends along with close analysis of competitors' performance.

By defining the same, foundations of strategic online presence are achieved. However, it needs to be understood, that it is only a representation of possible touchpoints, understood Buyer Persona-wise. The ultimate goal for marketers shall be, as rightly Lemon & Verhoef (2016) indicate, to analyze and understand the customer experience throughout the entire customer journey and modeling it accurately (Novak et al., 2000; Voorhees et al., 2017). The company, following the previously assumed Digital Engagement Canvas, shall start filling the channels of online communication (gravel) with the relevant content (sand), so meticulously prepared based on ongoing interactions with the stakeholders and inputs of the conducted research (water).

Setting the Technicalities – Webpage Performance & SEO

Assuming that every marketing campaign resembles a marathon, each race participant needs to undergo a throughout medical examination. Vitals shall be measured and any aberrations removed ahead of the contest. A/B testing takes this role initially (Fedorchenko & Ponomarkenko, 2019; Viser, 2021) by testing and comparing landing pages, email marketing campaigns, advertisements, logo changes, etc. Moreover, A/B testing is highly recommended by specialists in the domain for:

- Freshly established/ or about to be established websites, just starting the process of optimization.
- Web pages with a limited (and unsatisfactory low) number of visitors.
- When a limited number of conversions is visible.
- If a company is considering a significant (but gradual) revision of an existing design.

By splitting the website/social media profile traffic into equal groups of visitors being served completely different content, visible becomes the interest of one group and low engagement of the other. This exercise serves as a simple (yet very effective!) test that enables one to understand own audience, its preferences, and last, but not least triggers f behavior.

Once all the previously mentioned points are fulfilled, finally comes the time for the digital audit itself, which shall be commenced with understanding the speed of the webpage and performed with the use of **Pingdom.com** or another similar platform. This tests the performance of the website in terms of uptime, numbers of active sessions, loading time, page views, and time spent on the domain. The latter insights are being provided as well by tools like:

- **Alexa.com** (https://www.alexa.com/siteinfo)
- **SimilarWeb** (https://www.similarweb.com)
- **WebsiteGrader** powered by **Hubspot** (https://website.grader.com/)
- **SEOptimer** (https://www.seoptimer.com)
- **SEO Site Checkup** (https://seositecheckup)
- **SEMrush** (https://www.semrush.com/)

All of the below-mentioned platforms (Cf. Table 2) are (unfortunately) paid ones, though all of them have a free version/trial allowing for a discovery of the options provided. As per the list mentioned, the lower down the list, the more comprehensive the insights. However, *de gustibus non est disputandum*, therefore, selection of any of the tools/platforms shall be based on personal decision and assessment preceded with exposure to all the tools.

Table 2. Comparison of the digital audit dashboards

Alexa.com	SimilarWeb	WebsiteGrader
Good for basic website overview further requires a login in and trial version. User friendly, data is not overwhelming and presented in a user-friendly manner	Much more comprehensive than Alexa, tough it would require setting up a paid account. Is a mix of visuals and text, showcases organic traffic to the domain	This tool can be accessed for free and is mainly focused on an audit in a comprehensive manner of tiles, highlighting the strong and weak points. Good insights for "non-technical" marketers, as it sets the benchmark and accordingly grades the desired website (in green, yellow and red if the issue is critical)
SEOptimer	SEO Site Checkup	SEMrush
Initially looking overcomplicated due to amount of text, once used, definitely gain in a closer acquaintance, presenting "digestible" comments which will help while interactions with the IT department	Provides many valuable insights, more of a technical nature. Not recommended for inexperienced users, though once familiarized with, will serve forever	The most comprehensive, not too technical, user friendly. Incudes basic domain analytics, but as well keyword gap, keyword magic tool, market overview for comparison plus enables full social media/analytics accounts

Source: Own elaboration, 2021

Be Like Amazon

The main difference (apart from price, trial period, and data revealed for free) is in the dashboard set up and is a manner of personal preference. Some of the users will opt for a more visualized and less data-driven dashboard. These shall consider Alexa.com, SimilarWeb, or Website Grader due to their "infographics-led" website outline. Users are willing to focus more on technical improvements and software reflecting the same (SEOptimer, SEO Site Checkup) and of course SEMrush. Last, but not least, if software allows, the analysis shall be done in relation not only to own website but marking competitors to achieve the full picture.

Worth highlighting is the fact, that the above-mentioned software is presenting post-factum data, based on predicted traffic as a reflection of utilized keywords. The software automatically suggests competitors, based on website rank, traffic analysis, and similarities in keyword overlaps. For Amazon.ae Noon.com, eBay.com were indicated. What is interesting software takes into consideration all the similarities, therefore Carrefour and SharafDG platforms were considered. If a user wants to indicate a particular other, non previously listed domain, i.e. Alibaba.com, the same can be done easily.

Though data is often up-to-date (traffic analysis and PPC cost based on data from the previous day or last few days), still these are only certain assumptions, not real, live-tracked website traffic. This can be done with Google Analytics – providing an extremely detailed picture of own performance and allowing to align website performance with achieving own goals (sales, leads, etc.). Unfortunately, this cannot be achieved with competitive websites, as Google AdWords scripting code needs to be embedded directly into the website code (through Content Management System), which for obvious reasons cannot be performed for competitors.

At first glance amount of information might be overwhelming, therefore best to focus on one tool only and get familiarized with its capacity. As the most comprehensive and wrapped in a set of multiple options (including own detailed analytics and social media channels management). As per the current trend, these web-based platforms are allowing for benchmarking of own SEO performance versus brand's competitors, ranking wise and based on audience and utilized keywords similarities. This allows for in-depth detailed analysis of own performance and enables tracking best market practices. Moreover, tools like Website Grader, SEOptimer assign a grading similar to school assessment system (from A+ to F) which reflecting their subjective appraisal easily indicates the digital standing of the brand in terms of SEO optimization, mobile optimization, page speed, security, etc. Some of the software, like SEO Site Checkup, provide not only indicative assessment, but as well more or less detailed points for improvement, including the priority of changes to be implemented. Very often only generic things will be highlighted i.e: too long meta description, too many keywords, site speed too low, etc. However, in terms of other tools, the feedback given might be very precise: apart from highlighting the points for improvement and indicating the accurate KPIs, software with the use of Artificial Intelligence might even suggest new keywords, descriptions, best market practices. When such information overload might be overwhelming for some, others may consider it as a blessing and will gladly follow. Despite which group the marketer performing the audit will belong to, definitely such a comprehensive source of information will act as a personal assistant, especially since the majority of data, visuals, and suggestions can be easily converted into eye-catching diagrams and pre-defined cyclical reports.

Technicalities continued: customer engagement and social media listening

No digital marketing existence can be considered complete without a well-managed social media presence. Schlagwein and Prasarnphanich (2014) have been indicating rightly the way social media is managed has a clear impact on organizational performance. Moreover, it varies depending on which cultural background the company originates. Furthermore, the impact of regional presence, which needs to be adapted the global brands acting according to local customers, beliefs, and norms, plays an important role in what and how is being conveyed on social media.

Standard social media analysis shall not be narrowed down to simple Key Performance Indicators like number of followers, number of posts, or average engagement. Social media is something way more than an appealing picture wrapped with a catchy text, all combined ultimately creating "content". One needs to understand this content is a double-edged sword as it is a two-way relationship. The most successful marketers base their campaigns on engagement and user-generated content. Therefore additional KPIs shall be considered like shares, mentions, amplification rate, applause rate, and share of voice.

But in the light of this case study more important becomes not the focus on what the content is, but what impact it brings on the company's performance. Kaleynska (2015) deliberates on the importance of Business Intelligence and social media listening, clearly underlining how the crucial source of information it becomes nowadays. Moreover, she emphasizes these inputs having a significant impact on the company's data-driven decisions. By the use of social media and its listening companies may track the behavior of its users (Powell et al., 2016) and predict future trends. As rightly Schweidel and Moe (2014) indicate, social media inputs very often depend on where the content is posted, as each of the social media channels has its own, unique style and particular groups of interest, preferring a particular style of communication.

Moreover, the nature of the medium shall be taken into consideration. Social media is acting as fire and content is considered to become gasoline. Such perception proves clearly how difficult is to control and funnel down its insights without harnessing the power of technology. Useful in this regard becomes social media listening done as live tracking of brand and its hashtags. By a skillful combination of brand mentions in the positive, negative, and neutral context, and its AI-driven software can give an upfront warning. The same can prevent the need for crisis management, distinguishing the fire in its naissance stage of paracrisis (Selaković et al, 2020). Indeed better to be safe, than sorry when a small sparkle can have a truly avalanche-resembling effect. Therefore monitoring the brand in social media in an appropriate manner becomes a priority on the "to do" list of every marketer.

Social media listening tools like Meltwater, Brand24, Brandwatch, Hootsuite or Keyhole allow for constant and live monitoring of own brand, selected hashtag, keyword on long term keyword. Search triggered with the given word is then being considered in its context. Surrounded with words potentially considered positive (i.e.: love, fun, amazing, happy, excited, great experience, etc.) will lead in marking the post as green (positive) mention. On the opposite, words connotated negatively (i.e.: stupid, terrible, hate it, loss of money, etc.) will give an adverse rating. Neutral mentions, giving more balanced opinions, will be highlighted as well, but require no further action. Depending on how the alerts are set up, the social media manager may get an immediate notification in case the brand/hashtag is highlighted in the negative context. Depending on the gravity of the situation either marketing automation activity may be enabled, or the crisis management team would need to act.

Moreover, this applies not only to the own brand but can be utilized for competitive brands as well! From Author's experience the most advanced brands in this regard closely monitor every negative mention for a competitive brand and if possible, offer a free product/service to build on a former negative experience and by building on the ashes literally evoke a phoenix rising and to create brand ambassadors. Therefore, tracking of social media presence in parallel both for own and for the competitive brand seems to be a must. Last, but not least, the same mechanism will work for a positive mention, when immediate interaction on positive feedback often is coined into the state of delighting the customer and creating a future brand ambassador.

CURRENT CHALLENGES FACING THE ORGANIZATION

Being exposed to the tools of digital audit is only the beginning of the amazing, data-driven journey of challenging own competitors and raising the bar higher and higher to achieve excellence in digital performance. By default, the audit shall be performed in a benchmark format, including the company, at least one/two direct competitor(s), and one indirect competitor. Moreover, shall indicate the industry standards/average (traffic, page views, time spent on the visit, Bounce Rate, CTR (Click Through Rate), CPC (Cost Per Click), and CR (Conversion Rate). Only then the analysis becomes more complex, complete, and comprehensive. Last, but not least social media profile analysis (visits, duration, applause rate, amplification rate resulting from the content analysis). A pre-filled template is shared below (Cf. Table 2), with the last column commenting on the desired output.

Each time each factor shall be analyzed row-wise: the company, against a direct competitor(s), and indirect competitor, followed by the industry benchmark. This approach will allow for setting the expectations right and showcase if the brad is above, below, or simply meet the anticipations. Moreover, the company shall set up these reports as notifications and be able to retrieve them in no time (either report is shared via mail at the moment of its generation or is simply downloaded where the domain owner is notified about new data available. Alternatively, some platforms have a special section, where at a click of the button the desired insight is generated. This requirement comes as the need of the day, with constant as the only change in business performance.

The provided analysis gives a rough understanding of how to read the given factors/KPIs. Usually the same is done with relevant qualitative/quantitative feedback, comparing high/low performance within the given benchmark and indicating the desired improvements or direction of the proposed change.

The below-stated juxtaposition, mainly derived from SEMrush tool along with the support of SimilarWeb presents multiple touchpoints of digital audit to be performed in four different categories:

- Website-related insights
- Market Explorer study
- Advertising Analysis
- Social Media Audit

Website-related insights after highlighting the page rank (global and country-wise) and authority score, mainly focus on traffic-related analytics, presenting website traffic, the number of unique visitors (so-called unique users), the average number of pages seen per visit, visit duration along with bounce rate. These metrics allow understanding the importance of the analyzed page and the standing of benchmarked competitors. The same is being followed by organic search rate, paid traffic search with its estimated cost along with backlinks and referring domains, giving suggestions for possible websites which company may use in the future for advertising to the interested audience. Furthermore, as a part of this analysis keyword overview is presented (for Amazon.ae only), highlighting the number of listed keywords and keyword overlap, followed by keyword difficulty analysis. This part is providing more insights on existing search engine optimization opportunities, utilized later in advertising.

Table 3. Pre-filled Template for Digital Audit

No./Criteria.	**Amazon.ae** *(own brand to be analyzed)*	**Noon.com** *(a direct competitor to be analyzed)*	**Sharaf DG** *(an indirect competitor, ideal for reverse benchmarking)*	**Industry average or visible competitive performance** *Highlights performance of the analyzed company against competitors, indicates the direction for possible improvements.*
\multicolumn{5}{c}{**Website-related insights**}			
Global Rank	1522	2103	20,362	As high, as possible.
Country rank	6	27	74	As high, as possible.
Authority Score	61	55	52	The internal measure of SEMrush to showcase the importance of a domain.
Website Traffic	18.4M	14.6M	3.3M	The higher, the better.
Unique Visitors	7.5M	6.3M	1.6M	The higher, the better.
Average page/visit	7.61	3.96	3.34	Factor to be maximized.
Average Visit Duration	11:32	09:45	07:42	To reach max. Usually aligned with average page visits.
Bounce Rate	39.92%	44.74%	47.93%	This KPI shall be always minimized, though anything below 40% is considered acceptable.
Organic Search Traffic rate	2.73M	1.76	921.76K	To be maximized.
Paid Traffic Search (paid keywords/paid traffic cost)	295 / 120.08K	28 / 51.12K	44 / 36.32K	The company does not need to necessarily elevate this factor and rely on organic traffic and viral campaigns.
Backlinks	17.37M	2.82M	2.56M	The total backlinks leading the domain
Referring Domains	23.92K	4.56K	17.2K	Total number of referring domains to the analysed website
Keyword Overview				Detailed analysis of Keywords. Here done as keyword overlap and basic analysis for Amazon.ae only. Shall be conducted separately for each domain.

Continued on following page

Be Like Amazon

Table 3. Contnued

No./Criteria.	Amazon.ae *(own brand to be analyzed)*	Noon.com *(a direct competitor to be analyzed)*	Sharaf DG *(an indirect competitor, ideal for reverse benchmarking)*	**Industry average or visible competitive performance** *Highlights performance of the analyzed company against competitors, indicates the direction for possible improvements.*
	**Website-related insights**			
	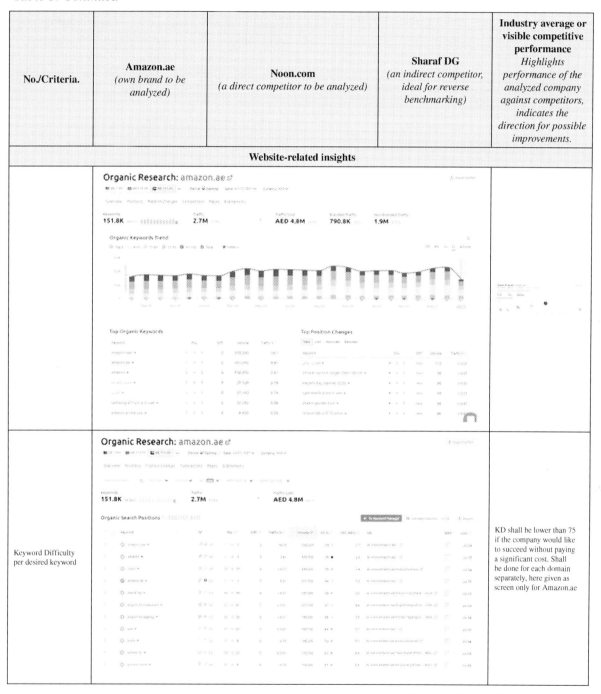			
Keyword Difficulty per desired keyword				KD shall be lower than 75 if the company would like to succeed without paying a significant cost. Shall be done for each domain separately, here given as screen only for Amazon.ae

Continued on following page

Table 3. Contnued

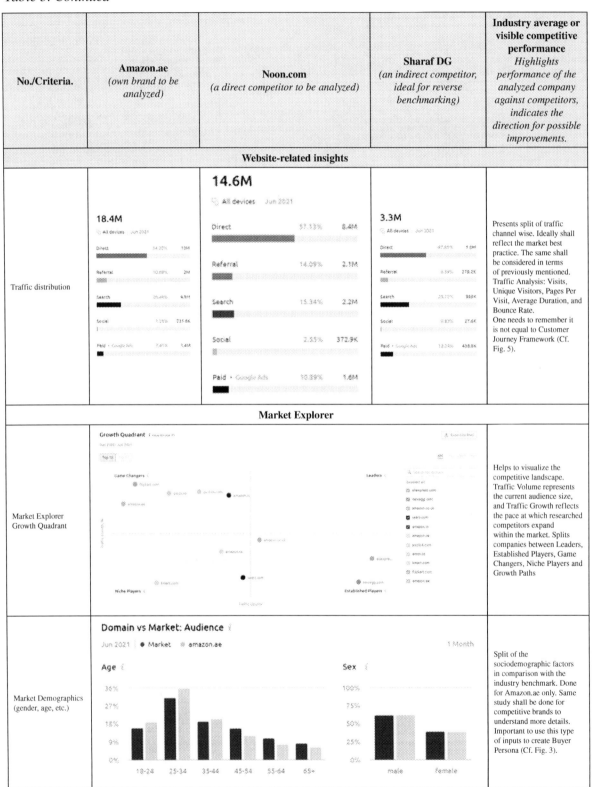

Continued on following page

Be Like Amazon

Table 3. Contnued

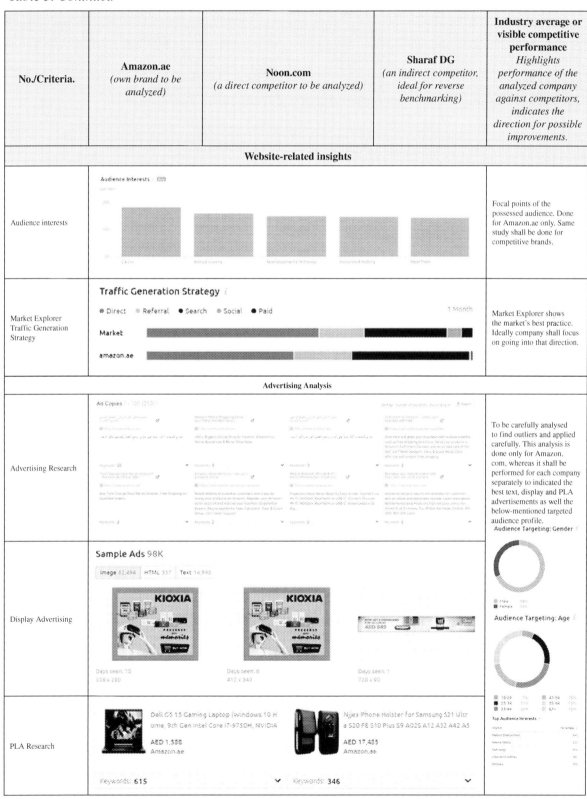

Continued on following page

Table 3. Contnued

No./Criteria.		Amazon.ae *(own brand to be analyzed)*	Noon.com *(a direct competitor to be analyzed)*	Sharaf DG *(an indirect competitor, ideal for reverse benchmarking)*	**Industry average or visible competitive performance** *Highlights performance of the analyzed company against competitors, indicates the direction for possible improvements.*
		**Website-related insights**			
		**Social Media Audit**			
Channel wise (channel, followers, number of posts, average frequency, average engagement rate, hashtags utilized and content posted. May be done separately, channel wise	*factor*	Amazon.com	Noon.com	SharafDG.com	Channel-wise detailed audit basing on social media statistics + social media listening along with posts content analysis. Figure below presents the split of audience's social media preferences (from Market Explorer, Market Demographics). Shall be performed mainly as content analysis to understand the audience preferences. In casa cells got clubbed, data is for Amazon.com only and similar analysis shall be performed for all the benchmarked companies.
	Followers	30M 482K 120K 4M 21M	817K 7K 6 266K 829	2M 3K 220 36K 160K	
	Ave. Posting Frequency per week (fb)	4	2	1	
	Engagement Rate (total)	23,796	23,612	12,915	
	Engagement overview	13,739	32,125	-18,386	-57.23%	
	Utilized hashtags	#amazonae	#noon	#sharafdg	
	Sentiment analysis				
	Example of best performing posts				

Source: Own elaboration, 2021, based on SEMrush, 2021 and SimilarWeb, 2021

The next part is **Market Explorer** analysis, providing an overview of the performance of the analyzed industry in general (in this case eCommerce marketplaces in the UAE). With Market Explorer Growth Quadrant (position 16 of Tab. 2) groups competing companies into segments of Leaders, Established Players, Game Changers, Niche Players, and Growth Paths. It is a piece of very useful information, which might serve as an eye-opener for marketers performing this analysis, as it often highlights brands usually not considered as competitors! The remaining parts of Market Explorer highlight the demographic profile of the market audience, its interest, and Traffic Generation Strategy – the same is very useful for defining Buyer Persona.

The third part presents **Advertising Analysis** performed only for Amazon.com to showcase the capacity of the software. SEMrush as a comprehensive tool allows to fetch the currently running AdWords, PLA, and display campaigns, as well enabling to "go back in time" by understanding the position taken by the company while listing for a particular keyword.

The last of the mentioned parts is related to **Social Media Audit**. Provided in the above-mentioned table, shall be always done company-wise based on selected KPIs: channel-wise number of followers, posts, average engagement, posting frequency along with sentiment analysis. Worth noting is the fact, that all the above highlighted KPIs are only the proverbial tip of an iceberg. The true challenge of digital audit and tracking the performance of competitors starts, when analyzing the data, comparing, indicating the rationale for achieved results, and proposing managerial recommendations, which shall be the main task of this chapter as a key take-away for readers, as the presented case study only highlights how achieving excellence shall be done, but not providing finalized answers, as all the data is dynamic and shall be always retrieved up-to-date.

SUGGESTIONS, RECOMMENDATIONS, AND TAKE-AWAYS

In a data-driven economy, where knowledge is power, performing marketing activities without harnessing the power of data resembles driving a car with eyes closed. The thin line between competitive intelligence and corporate espionage becomes more and more blurred nowadays. Companies shall fiercely defend their secrets and patch their systems/software/devices not to become susceptible to external attacks. At the same time they shall bear in mind, that broadly accessible sources of information like keyword analysis underlining Search Engine Optimization can become a priceless source of information both for them and their competitors. Information becomes the starting point for reaching customers faster, smarter, and more efficiently. To run a business, but not exposing own company to third-party mistakes is becoming the corporate new normal. Moreover, high search for keywords does not necessarily need to translate into leads and conversions. The beauty of long-term keywords remains dormant for many. Therefore companies shall harness the power of technology, embrace technological changes and embrace blessings given by the efforts of Artificial Intelligence. Data mining, data analysis, and data analytics shall become the everyday bread for every marketer.

In addition to the said before, in the era when everything is "wired and smart" and with the increasing role of AI for eCommerce, more and more marketers' tasks will be automated. Starting from customer segmentation, intelligent demand forecasting, smart pricing, recommendation mechanisms, and personalized products along with automated content generation, and ending with customer churn rate, lifetime value prediction, and many more.

Moreover, the business shall perceive that the boundaries between "traditional and digital" marketing have been blurred a long time back and both have the same ultimate goal – to win and retain loyal customers. But one shall see clearly that the conditions changed significantly, therefore companies do not need a digital strategy, but simply a strategy for the digital age.

Digital footprint analysis allows having a broader picture of the business, competitors, and industry trends, software performing these actions will be even capable of creating marketing content, but still, we are far from perfection, therefore there will be always space for human, compassionate marketers, but those with the new skillset of data analysis and capable of working side by side with AI.

REFERENCES

Amazon.ae. (2021). *Amazon: about us.* https://www.amazon.ae/b?node=16177380031

Andaleeb, S. S., & Hasan, K. (2016). *Strategic Marketing Management in Asia: Case Studies and Lessons across Industries.* Emerald.

Anderl, E., Schumann, J. H., & Kunz, W. (2016). Helping Firms Reduce Complexity in Multichannel Online Data: A New Taxonomy-Based Approach for Customer Journeys. *Journal of Retailing, 92*(2), 185–203. doi:10.1016/j.jretai.2015.10.001

Bagga, T., & Bhatt, M. (2013). A Study of Intrinsic and Extrinsic Factors Influencing Consumer Buying Behaviour Online. *Asia-Pacific Journal of Management Research and Innovation, 9*(1), 77–90. doi:10.1177/2319510X13483515

Barwitz, N., & Maas, P. (2018). Understanding the Omnichannel Customer Journey: Determinants of Interaction Choice. *Journal of Interactive Marketing, 43*, 116–133. doi:10.1016/j.intmar.2018.02.001

Berendes, C. I., Bartelheimer, C., Betzing, J. H., & Beverungen, D. (2018). Data-driven Customer Journey Mapping in Local High Streets: A Domain-specific Modeling Language. *Proceedings of ICIS, 1*, 218–227.

Bowden, J. L. (2009). The Process of Customer Engagement: A Conceptual Framework. *Journal of Marketing Theory and Practice, 17*(1), 63–74. doi:10.2753/MTP1069-6679170105

Brodie, R. J., Hollebeek, L. D., Jurić, B., & Ilić, A. (2011). Customer Engagement: Conceptual Domain, Fundamental Propositions, and Implications for Research. *Journal of Service Research, 14*(3), 252–271. doi:10.1177/1094670511411703

Buettner, R. (2019). *Online user behavior and digital footprints* [Unpublished habilitation dissertation]. University of Trier, Trier and Aalen, Germany.

Cameron, M. (2013). *Data is not the new oil – it's the new soil.* Marketing Magazine. https://www.marketingmag.com.au/hubs-c/data-is-not-the-new-oil-its-the-new-soil

Carlson, J., Rahman, M., Voola, R., & De Vries, N. (2018). Customer engagement behaviours in social media: Capturing innovation opportunities. *Journal of Services Marketing, 32*(1), 83–94. doi:10.1108/JSM-02-2017-0059

Cerina, R., & Duch, R. (2020). Measuring public opinion via digital footprints. *International Journal of Forecasting*, *36*(3), 987–1002. doi:10.1016/j.ijforecast.2019.10.004

Colicev, A., Kumar, A., & O'Connor, P. (2019). Modeling the relationship between firm and user generated content and the stages of the marketing funnel. *International Journal of Research in Marketing*, *36*(1), 100–116. doi:10.1016/j.ijresmar.2018.09.005

Davis, F. D. (1989). Perceived Usefulness, Perceived Ease of Use, and User Acceptance of Information Technology. *Management Information Systems Quarterly*, *13*(3), 319–340. doi:10.2307/249008

De Oliveira, S. F., Ladeira, W. J., & Pinto, D. (2020). Customer engagement in social media: A framework and meta-analysis. J. *Journal of the Academy of Marketing Science*, *48*(6), 1211–1228. doi:10.100711747-020-00731-5

Fedorchenko, A., & Ponomarenko, I. (2019). A/B-testing as an efficient tools for digital marketing. *Problems of Innovation and Investment Development*, *19*(19), 36–42. doi:10.33813/2224-1213.19.2019.4

Fielding, T., & Armstrong, R. (2020). *E-Commerce in the UAE: is it the new normal?* https://gowlingwlg.com/en/insights-resources/articles/2020/e-commerce-in-the-uae-part-one/

Garrido-Moreno, A., Lockett, N., & García-Morales, V. (2019). Social Media Use and Customer Engagement. In A. Khosrow-Pour (Ed.), *Advanced Methodologies and Technologies in Digital Marketing and Entrepreneurship* (pp. 643–655). IGI Global. doi:10.4018/978-1-5225-7766-9.ch050

Goreglyad, V. P. (2019). Digital audit in the Bank of Russia as a mechanism to improve the efficiency of business processes. *Public Administration, 21/1*(117), 64-70.

Gummerus, J., Liljander, V., Weman, E., & Pihlström, M. (2012). Customer engagement in a Facebook brand community. *Management Research Review*, *35*(9), 857–877. doi:10.1108/01409171211256578

Hall, S. J. (2021). Facing Up To Your Digital Footprint. In Inspirational Stories from English Language Classrooms (pp. 117-119). Teflin Publications.

Harmeling, C. M., Moffett, J. W., Arnold, M. J., & Carlson, B. D. (2017). Toward a theory of customer engagement marketing. *Journal of the Academy of Marketing Science*, *45*(3), 312–335. doi:10.100711747-016-0509-2

Hollebeek, L. D., & Macky, K. (2019). Digital Content Marketing's Role in Fostering Consumer Engagement, Trust, and Value: Framework, Fundamental Propositions, and Implications. *Journal of Interactive Marketing*, *45*, 27–41. doi:10.1016/j.intmar.2018.07.003

Ieva, M., & Ziliani, C. (2018). Mapping touchpoint exposure in retailing. *International Journal of Retail & Distribution Management*, *46*(3), 304–322. doi:10.1108/IJRDM-04-2017-0097

Internet World Stats. (2021). *Middle East Internet Users 2021*. https://www.internetworldstats.com

Kaleynska, T. (2015). Business Intelligence and social media listening. *Economy & Business*, *9*(1), 667–671.

Kunz, W., Aksoy, L., Bart, Y., Heinonen, K., Kabadayi, S., Ordenes, F. V., Sigala, M., Diaz, D., & Theodoulidis, B. (2017). Customer engagement in a Big Data world. *Journal of Services Marketing*, *31*(2), 161–171. doi:10.1108/JSM-10-2016-0352

Lambiotte, R. & Kosinski, M. (2014). *Tracking the Digital Footprints of Personality*. Academic Press.

Lemon, K. N., & Verhoef, P. C. (2016). Understanding Customer Experience Throughout the Customer Journey. *Journal of Marketing*, *80*(6), 69–96. doi:10.1509/jm.15.0420

Mania, M. (2013). *IBM's CEO on data, the death of segmentation and the 18-month deadline*. https://www.marketingmag.com.au/news-c/ibms-ceo-on-data-the-death-of-segmentation-and-the-18-month-deadline

McKinsey. (2020). *How COVID-19 has pushed companies over the technology tipping point—and transformed business forever*. https://www.mckinsey.com/business-functions/strategy-and-corporate-finance/our-insights/how-covid-19-has-pushed-companies-over-the-technology-tipping-point-and-transformed-business-forever

McLean, G., & Wilson, A. (2019). Shopping in the digital world: Examining customer engagement through augmented reality mobile applications. *Computers in Human Behavior*, *101*, 210–224. doi:10.1016/j.chb.2019.07.002

Micheli, M., Lutz, Ch., & Büchi, M. (2018). Digital Footprints: An Emerging Dimension of Digital Inequality. *Journal of Information Communication and Ethics in Society*, *16*(3), 242–251. doi:10.1108/JICES-02-2018-0014

Novak, T. P., Hoffman, D. L., & Yung, Y.-F. (2000). Measuring the Customer Experience in Online Environments: A Structural Modeling Approach. *Marketing Science*, *19*(1), 22–42. doi:10.1287/mksc.19.1.22.15184

Olinder, N., Tsvetkov, A., Fedyakin, K., & Zaburdaeva, K. (2020). Using Digital Footprints in Social Research: An Interdisciplinary Approach. *Wisdom*, *16*(3), 124–135. doi:10.24234/wisdom.v16i3.403

Omran, W. (2021). Customer Engagement in Social Media Brand Community. *Research Journal of Business Management*, *9*(1), 31–40.

Pansari, A., & Kumar, V. (2017). Customer engagement: The construct, antecedents, and consequences. *Journal of the Academy of Marketing Science*, *45*(3), 294–311. doi:10.100711747-016-0485-6

Polignano, M., Basile, P., Rossiello, G., de Gemmis, M., & Semerar, G. (2017). Empathic inclination from digital footprints. *Proceedings of the IEEE*, *102*(12), 1934–1939.

Powell, G., Seifert, H., Reblin, T., Burstein, P., Blowers, J., Menius, A., Painter, J., Thomas, M., Pierce, C., Rodriguez, H., Brownstein, J., Freifeld, C., Bell, H., & Dasgupta, N. (2016). Social Media Listening for Routine Post-Marketing Safety Surveillance. *Drug Safety*, *39*(5), 443–454. doi:10.100740264-015-0385-6 PMID:26798054

Rajagopal. (2016). *Sustainable Growth in Global Markets: Strategic Choices and Managerial Implications*. Palgrave Macmillan.

Sashi, C. M. (2012). Customer engagement, buyer-seller relationships, and social media. *Management Decision, 50*(2), 253–272. doi:10.1108/00251741211203551

Schlagwein, D., & Prasarnphanich, P. (2014). Social Media Around the Globe. *Journal of Organizational Computing and Electronic Commerce, 24*(2), 122–137. doi:10.1080/10919392.2014.896713

Schlegelmilch, B. B. (2016). *Global Marketing Strategy: An Executive Digest.* Springer. doi:10.1007/978-3-319-26279-6

Schweidel, D. A., & Moe, W. W. (2014). Listening in on Social Media: A Joint Model of Sentiment and Venue Format Choice. *JMR, Journal of Marketing Research, 51*(4), 387–402. doi:10.1509/jmr.12.0424

Selaković, M., Tarabasz, A., & Gallant, M. (2020). Typology of Business-Related Fake News Online: A Literature Review. *Journal of Management and Marketing Review, 5*(4), 234–243.

SEMrush. (2020). *SEMrush tutorial: How To Create a Buyer Persona.* https://www.youtube.com/watch?v=9aPAPANeMKg

SEMrush. (2021). *Traffic analytics.* https://www.semrush.com/analytics/traffic/overview/amazon.ae

SimilarWeb. (2021). *Domain overview.* https://www.similarweb.com/website/amazon.ae/

Tarabasz, A. (2020). Campaign Planning and Project Management. In A. Heinze, G. Fletcher, T. Rashid, & A. Cruz (Eds.), *Digital and Social Media Marketing: A Results-Driven Approach* (pp. 123–148). Routledge. doi:10.4324/9780429280689-9

Teng, C. C., & Maxwell, W. (2021). A size and impact analysis of digital footprints. International. *Journal of Business and Systems Research, 15*(2), 163–181. doi:10.1504/IJBSR.2021.113418

Tsiotsou, R. H. (2019). Social Media and Customer Engagement. In E. Bridges & K. Fowler (Eds.), *The Routledge Handbook of Service Research Insights and Ideas.* Routledge.

Van Doorn, J., Lemon, K. N., Mittal, V., Nass, S., Pick, D., Pirner, P., & Verhoef, P. C. (2010). Customer Engagement Behavior: Theoretical Foundations and Research Directions. *Journal of Service Research, 13*(3), 253–266. doi:10.1177/1094670510375599

Verhoef, P. C., Reinartz, W. J., & Krafft, M. (2010). Customer Engagement as a New Perspective in Customer Management. *Journal of Service Research, 13*(3), 247–252. doi:10.1177/1094670510375461

Vidal-Cabeza, D. (2015). *6 Types of Customers in the Plumbing Industry You Need to Know.* https://davevidal.com/6-types-of-customers-in-the-plumbing-industry-you-need-to-know

Visa. (2019). *The UAE eCommerce Landscape.* https://ae.visamiddleeast.com/dam/VCOM/regional/cemea/unitedarabemirates/home-page/documents/visa-white-paper-v4.pdf

Visser, J., & Richardson, J. (2015). *Digital Engagement Framework. Create value with digital engagement.* https://digitalengagementframework.com/

Visser, M. (2021). *Digital Marketing.* Tylor & Francis.

Voorhees, C. M., Fombelle, P. W., Gregoire, Y., Bone, S., Gustafsson, A., Sousa, R., & Walkowiak, T. (2017). Service encounters, experiences and the customer journey: Defining the field and a call to expand our lens. *Journal of Business Research*, *79*, 269–280. doi:10.1016/j.jbusres.2017.04.014

Waqas, M., Hamzah, Z. L. B., & Salleh, N. A. M. (2020). Customer experience: A systematic literature review and consumer culture theory-based conceptualisation. *Management Review Quarterly*, *71*(1), 135–176. doi:10.100711301-020-00182-w

We Are Social. (2021). *Digital 2021: the latest insights into the 'state of digital'*. https://wearesocial.com/blog/2021/01/digital-2021-the-latest-insights-into-the-state-of-digital

Weinstein, A. (2004). *Handbook of Market Segmentation: Strategic Targeting for Business and Technology Firms*. The Haworth Press.

Zambito, T. (2016). *State Of Buyer Personas 2016: Strong Correlation Between Effectiveness And Goals*. https://customerthink.com/state-of-buyer-personas-2016-strong-correlation-between-effectiveness-and-goals

ADDITIONAL READING

Dawar, N. (2018). Marketing in the age of Alexa. AI assistants will transform how companies and customers connect. *HBR*. https://hbr.org/2018/05/marketing-in-the-age-of-alexa

Heinze, A., Fletcher, G., Rashid, T., & Cruz, A. (2020). *Digital and social media marketing. A results-driven approach* (2nd ed.). Routledge. doi:10.4324/9780429280689

SEMrush Academy. (2021). *Courses & Certifications*. https://www.semrush.com/academy

Visser, J., & Richardson, J. (2015). *Digital Engagement Framework. Create value with digital engagement*. https://digitalengagementframework.com/

APPENDIX

Questions and Answers

1. Discuss the importance of management of the corporate digital footprint.

Skillfully managed corporate footprint provides a competitive advantage and leads to seamless customer omnichannel experience. It allows to leverage on the benefits and strong points, while decreasing the weak ones. Done as a continuous cycle of improvement swill be helpful in setting competitors aside.

2. List the concepts/frameworks helpful in conducting the digital audit/strengthening the performance of a company mentioned in the case study.

Aquarium Framework, Buyer Persona Template, Customer Omnichannel Journey, Digital Engagement Canvas, Digital footprint and Touchpoints analysis.

3. How the concept of Buyer Persona helps contemporary marketing managers?

Concept of Buyer Persona creates a semi-fictional representation of an ideal customer and facilitates both product development and marketing communication due to personalization of sociodemographic and psychographic factors.

4. In teams discuss and propose Buyer Persona for a selected brand. How B2C Buyer Persona varies from the B2B one?

This assignment can be both done individually and in Team. The group shall highlight all the building blocks and imagine challenges and pain points of Buyer Persona, usually putting themselves in their shoes. For B2B Buyer Persona participants shall draft a facilitated version of a corporate segment (company size, industry, decision makers, main focal points while selling the product and main showstoppers why the offer cannot be pitched easily.

5. Draft briefly the Digital Engagement Canvas for any selected brand.

This assignment can be both done individually and in Team. The group shall highlight all the building blocks and visualize an appealing campaign, which will involve a two-way communication and translate the same into the DEC framework.

6. Omnichannel customer journey is straightforward and linear. Debate.

Customer journey may be purely offline, online or mixed. Unless and until it is a repetitive purchase of inexpensive goods (i.e. grocery shopping round the corner) it will never be a linear one, but will involve many touchpoints across different engagement stages.

7. Name the emerging technologies and softwares that should be considered in solving the problem(s) related to the case.

Trends in Digital Technologies listed by Gartner 2020. SEMrush, SimilarWeb, SEOptimer, Alexa.com, SEOSite Checkup, SebsiteGrader, Brand24, Keyhole, Hubspot.

EPILOGUE AND LESSONS LEARNED

Case study provides a ready made pathway along with tools and assessment templates to assess and create successful digital footprint of the company, followed by Digital Engagement Canvas. It Gathers in one place a mix of 16 years of experience both in business consulting and academia.

Chapter 3
Digital Value Innovation and Strategic Management Practices of Adyar Ananda Bhavan

Shakti Chaturvedi
REVA Business School, India

Meenakshi Verma
Symbiosis International University, India

Sonal Purohit
Chandigarh University, India

Raghava Reddy Varaprasad
REVA University, India

EXECUTIVE SUMMARY

This case focuses on the strategic management practices of Adyar Ananda Bhavan (prevalently known as A2B), a quickly developing contemporary sweet chain of Chennai in South India that is currently proclaiming a target of 900 crores turnover from 2021 onwards with 8,000 employees. The case has a close theoretical association with the famous strategic management models, for instance Michael E. Porter's model, Ansoff Matrix, Blue Ocean Strategy, Balanced Scorecard, and Resource-Based View and explains how an organization can strategically grow its business through digital value-based innovation. Contending sources of data, for example print and electronic media, have been utilized to accumulate and report raw facts and figures. The authors analyzed based on insights gained from various academicians from different universities across India, some mid-level managers from industry, and some unofficial conversations with A2B staff in Bangalore. This case is planned to be utilized in the strategic management subject for both undergraduate and postgraduate courses.

DOI: 10.4018/978-1-7998-1630-0.ch003

ORGANIZATION BACKGROUND

In the seventies, a crop-growing family in Rajapalayam in South Tamil Nadu state was utterly overdrawn after an erratic typhoon shattered their farmland, making it uncultivable. Thirupathi Raja, the pinnacle of the family, was shattered after the heavy dust storm. His source of income was agriculture as he used to cultivate paddy and sugarcane in their eight-acre plot and had lately borrowed bucks to lease more plots to enlarge his farming activities. He had four siblings, all of them shared the family's battles before propelling the now well-known desserts chain, Adyar Ananda Bhavan, which was esteemed at an astounding Rs 1,800 crore two years back. When Thirupati Raja was around the age of 10, he fled from Rajapalayam to Chennai, where he first worked as an eatery cleaner of dining tables. Subsequently, he started to help in cooking and learned to make all types of desserts from a senior cook. Later, Thirupathi Raja followed his father's advice to return to Rajapalayam, stayed with the family, and began paddy and sugarcane cultivation. Over time, he decided to use the sweet-making skills he had learned as a young boy in Mumbai and commenced a new sweets shop in Rajapalayam in 1960 and titled it Guru Sweets. In the meantime, the agriculture business floated with high returns, and Thirupathi Raja purchased additional land to expand his farming activities. Unfortunately, the fanatic dust storm shattered his plans and left his family heartbroken once again now with his four grown-up children. Conquering the underlying shock, Thirupathi Raja chooses to move on to Bengaluru in the mid-1970s and re-constructed his life from scratch; he started a dessert outlet Srirampuram in Bengaluru, which gave an excellent opportunity to the family. The outlet was called Srinivasa sweets. From such a humble beginning, the family has made extraordinary progress. The family currently resides in a massive 12000 sq ft three-story house in an affluent area in South Chennai. Srinivasa Raju retains a couple of high-end cars, and his preferred one is the Volvo XC90 oil electric half-breed SUV. His folks may be no more, but he endures to treasure their memories and has sculptured their busts right at the entrance of his residence and inside the spacious drawing room of the house. The company's registration details, financial status can be found in Table 1 and Figure 1.

Table 1. A2B Financial Data

Operating Revenue	Over INR 500 cr
EBITDA	54.43%
Networth	22.84%
Debt/Equity Ratio	0.58
Return on Equity	18.59%
Total Assets	-2.70%
Fixed Assets	-8.57%
Current Assets	1.78%
Current Liabilities	-27.01%
Trade Receivables	2.99%
Trade Payables	-38.13%
Current Ratio	0.47

Source: www.tofler.in

Figure 1. Company Details
Source: www.tofler.in

REGISTERED DETAILS - ADYAR ANANDA BHAVAN SWEETS INDIA PRIVATE LIMITED
CIN
U15490TN2009PTC071449
INCORPORATION DATE / AGE
24 April, 2009 / 12 yrs
LAST REPORTED AGM DATE
30 December, 2020

AUTHORIZED CAPITAL
INR 108.0 Lacs
PAIDUP CAPITAL
INR 10.08 Lacs
INDUSTRY*
Manufacturing (Food products and beverages)

TYPE
Unlisted Private Company
CATEGORY
Company limited by Shares
SUBCATEGORY
Non-govt company

REGISTERED ADDRESS
NO: 9, MAHATMA GANDHI ROAD SHASTRI NAGAR, ADYAR CHENNAI - 600020
Tamil Nadu - India

SETTING THE STAGE

Making of a Brand

Mr. KT Raja, the founder of A2B aim's, is known as a renowned chef in the world for preparing healthy food items. As told by him, he has researched making nutrient-rich food that will give all the essential proteins, minerals, and omega-three needed for a healthy body. V Vishnu Shankar, who is his brother's son, is the director of A2B who is actively involved in taking care of the company's day-to-day activities. As we know, the food processing industry these days offers various beneficial checks that benefit both the organization and the consumers. It would ensure the selection of sanitation and quality confirmation instruments, for example, Total Quality Management (TQM) including ISO 9000, ISO 22000, Hazard Analysis and Critical Control Points (HACCP), Good Manufacturing Practices (GMP), and Good Hygienic Practices (GHP), which in turn will empower the organizations to stringent quality and cleanliness standards. In this manner, it prepares the sweet industry to ensure customers' well-being and face challenges internationally. It also enhances the product quality, design, taste, and preference to meet up with the needs of the customers across the borders and keep the business well updated to globally accepted procedures.

Adyar Ananda Bhavan has a whopping amount of turnover of Rs. 800 crore, and the count go on. A2B has also concentrated on employment generation by employing more than 8000 people. A2B was relying on worth expansion and item diversification to fuel its development. It has branches worldwide, with its outlets found even in the US, Malaysia, and Singapore. A2B café began its first cafe in Pondicherry in 2000, and now it has around 140 outlets, incorporating two in the US and one each in Malaysia and Singapore.

In 1979, Thirupthi Raja and his elder son KT Venkatesan established their first outlet in Chennai, Sri Anand Bhavan, in Washermanpet. They expanded their business by coming up with their second outlet in Chennai in 1988, and since then, they have overgrown. Sri Ananda Bhavan progressed towards becoming Adyar Anand Bhavan. In 1992, they came up with their third outlet in Purasaiwakkam, and different outlets followed with hardly a pause in between. Srinivasa Raju cited that A2B introduced a new assortment of desserts to distinguish themselves from their competitors. A2B came up with individual chefs from different places like Rajasthan, Bengal, Punjab, and UP to make the famous flavored desserts. They succeeded in attracting the customer and creating brand awareness among them the public. By 1994, their turnover whopped up to Rs 100 crore, and by the year 2000, they expanded and came up with 20 branches in Chennai and accomplished a turnover of Rs 150 crore. Consequently, over the period, they became one of the best sellers of desserts in India creating values and extending excellent service to consumers, stakeholders, and society (see Figure 1).

According to Shokuhi and Chashmi (2019), management strategies like cost differentiation, customer service, or market development can always lead to business growth. In line with this, recently, A2B has appointed Deloitte to help them raise the capital to grow (The Times of India, 2016). Before this, in the year 2000, A2B planned to enter the café business and set up A2B eateries along with Adyar Anand Bhavan sweet stalls, and it had a tremendous impact on the growth of the company. It contributed significantly to the company's top line, yet it got more footfalls to their outlets and expanded brand visibility. Around 25 Adyar Ananda Bhavan outlets are situated on national roadways in Karnataka, Tamil Nadu, and Andhra Pradesh. "Our goal is to have one outlet every 200km on every single national roadway crosswise over India," cites Srinivasa Raju.

The siblings are presently consulting with private value subsidizes Carlyle and sequoia, other than reflecting on joint endeavors, planning for the following next phase of their enterprising expedition. Apart from growing its outlet crosswise over India and the world, the family is looking after the business at a running budget hotel along highways to sell their idlis dosas and suppers and exporting frozen foods.

The managing director Srinivasa Raju at the age of 52, speaks, "A2B are still in concession with various offers and structures being fetched to the table". For the present, he states, their business is open to any course private value, vital joint endeavor accomplice, or even a first sale of stock.

A2B came up with various homegrown Indian food shackles that have become increasingly more open for raising private equity in recent years. By running themselves, they have spread across 7 kilometers. Today A2B has spread across 75 sweet outlets, 35 of them with eateries, and the strategy is to add 50 more by the end of the financial year. That would be acceptable to build an income of Rs 630 crore; Raja has faith in himself. Almost 66% of the incomes originate from his sweet business.

In 2000, foraying into cafes was a wholesome move. A2B gives its best to satisfy and fulfill the needs of the consumers and ensures the best quality savories (Adyar Anand Bhavan, 2017). The firms follow a policy of introducing a product according to the changing needs and preferences, launching the right product at the right time (with the right flavor practical bundling), and selecting suitable means to communicate the product. It also ensures easy availability of products to consumers through traditional and modern ways, and the best strategy followed by A2B is the use of a correct number of chefs.

Nevertheless, A2B became famous because of a variety of reasons. In Tamil Nadu, they provide parking facilities on the adjacent compound near to the shop. Then, of course, the wide range of sweets and savories. Innovation is likewise going about as the new empowering influence. It has prompted the rise of new plans of action, for example, cloud-based kitchens that help digital sustenance conveyance. A2B is additionally attempting to utilize this new upcoming pattern somehow.

CASE DESCRIPTION

A panel of experts was selected from industry and academia to understand the challenges and market expansion of A2B. The authors recorded their viewpoint on the digital management strategies used by A2B to expand their market. Besides this, the author has done an exhaustive study of the secondary data available for A2B market growth available in the public domain. Contending data sources, such as print and electronic media, have also been utilized to accumulate and report raw facts and figures. For instance, this case study had reviewed several blogs, newspaper stories, relevant websites, and articles published online in the context of A2B. It was a cross-sectional analysis where the authors searched various electronic databases in March 2020 and then again in June 2020 with no language restrictions. The keywords used for searching the databases were "A2B and Market Growth", "A2B and Digital Strategies", "A2B and Management Philosophies", "A2B and Business Value," and so on. The analysis was done based on insights gained from various academicians from different universities across India, some mid-level managers from industry and some unofficial conversation with A2B staff in Bangalore.

Making it Sweeter (Pricing it Right)

According to Wang et al. (2020), perceived quality influences customers to pay a little extra from their pocket for the product. In A2B, there was massive competition in the sweet market from competitors like Sarvana Bhavan, Bikaner desserts, and Sangam sweets. Kt Srinivasa Raja, who takes care of Adyar Ananda Bhavan chain of cafes, endorses a depression period for food products in the cities these days as customers' incomes have declined by 10 20% in the previous year due to the pandemic. Primarily because of rivalry from other cafes and decline in footfall, A2B has scaled down the costs of its items like idlis and the espresso by 5-10%. Despite maintaining the quality of their sweets, A2B had to decline its margins to increase the customer's footfalls (The Economic Times, 2013).

Value Creation in the Business

Value creation is the first aim of any food business entity (Sebastiani & Montagnini, 2020). Value creation can be defined as the changes in current place, time, and form based on the customer and market values (Anderson & Hanselka, 2009). In any business, to create sustainable value, customers' interests, employees (Chaturvedi et al., 2019), and investors are inextricably linked. Recognizing the value-added activities that will help the adequate investment in research, and marketing is significant. A2B tends to focus on quality and intangible drivers like digital innovation and customer relationship management to generate value for the business.

Value Players in the Business

According to Suhartanto et al. (2020), a business model consists of four interlocking elements that, taken together, create and deliver value. Those elements are customers, employees, profit, and processes. A2B never opted franchise route to make a profit in cities. Srinivasa Raju, elucidating their business model, said they either came up with their venture or had an income offering arrangement with the landlords who gave them their outlets (with no advance or rent). A2B would invest in the employees and products to improve employee commitment (Chaturvedi & Srivastava, 2015) and improve their product quality. Out of 140 outlets, around 15 outlets pursue the income sharing model, while the founders of A2B wholly own the rest. The enterprise owns around five outlets out of the remaining 130 outlets. All other outlets are operated on rented and leased premises. The creation and dissemination of A2B sweets involve four primary dealers in their value chain: suppliers, manufacturers, competitors, and ultimate end consumers (Figure 2).

Figure 2. Major Dealers in Value Chain of A2B

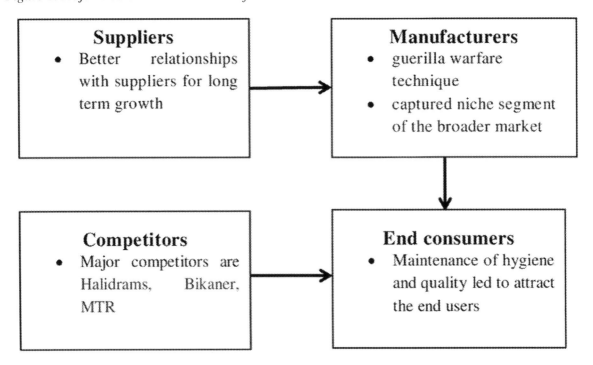

Suppliers: It has been seen that a better relationship with suppliers of resources gives any business a long-run benefit to the enterprise. It has been observed that A2B has a permanent arrangement of providers of resources like masala ingredients. With them, they have preserved a sincere relationship creating value for its suppliers.

Manufacturers: Much specialized staff like *halwais* and chefs deal with assembling sweets of A2B (Forbes India, 2019). Over the decade of five years, Adyar Anand Bhavan has timed at 15 to 20 percent compound yearly development rate with the future to come up with 60 more outlets across India. A2B follows guerilla warfare techniques to never engage in a direct fight with the local dessert manufacturers but aims to build their empire with a unique style. In this mode, they have seized a niche segment of the broader market. The roles and responsibilities are segregated among the staff to supervise the operations at A2B, which is not typical for other family-run businesses in the same space.

Competitors: Today, Haldirams, Bikaner, MTR are the major competitors of A2B in sweet fragment except that there is no real contender because there is no significant portion of marked desserts in India. If one goes to any town or village in India, they can discover many local manufacturers who sell loose sweets; thus, it is hard to compete with them in terms of pricing. Therefore, it can be said that although A2B is challenging to compete quality-wise, yet from the cost perspective, it is tough for A2B to contend with them with their entire inventory network cost, appropriation cost, retailers' edges, and so forth. This strength of maintaining quality can be called market proactiveness which has led A2B to compete effectively with its competitors (Linton & Kask, 2017; Srivastava & Chaturvedi, 2020).

End consumers: A2B saw that the values of a consumer stem from his psychological and social focal point; subsequently, it influences the demand for the product; this should be emphasized when one is setting his business. A2B attracts the customers and captures the market by maintaining hygiene and quality to the end-users at a competitive price.

Speaking further about the business model, A2B has used Michael E. Porter's five forces model for their business. Michael Porter's five forces of industry examination were progressively positive for A2B. It had a couple of barriers to entry; even though its substitutes were present in the market, A2B had a significant association with buyers and suppliers. Additionally, competitors' action was not that brutal. Similarly, the value of its resources (suppliers, employees, customers) relative to its contenders was constantly significant to drive constant differentiation from its contenders like Bikaner and Haldirams. Based on an identified market demand, opportunities existed for A2B to build its sweet business industry over the value chain (Figure 2).

Theories and Strategic Models Underpinning the Value Players

A2B used various strategic models like Porters' (1980) five force model of industry competition, Ansoff Matrix, Blue Ocean strategy, Resource Based Model and Balanced Scorecard to grow their business. We will discuss all these models and theories one by one subsequently here.

Porters Value Chain

Besanko et al. (2000) and Thompson and Stickland (1999), advocated that Porter's five force model as a powerful tool for analyzing the business scene. The central principle of Porter's aggressive viable approach is that the company is earning and surviving capacity depending on five competitive forces within the industry: the competition being too high and the risk of contenders entering the business, the force of competition among existing contenders, the danger of substitute things and services, the haggling intensity of purchasers, and the dealing intensity of suppliers (Sack & Nadim, 2002). Porters (1980) contends that organizations who breed preferable techniques over their rivals, by grasping the states of the industry better than others, may achieve manageable upper hand (i.e., an increasingly productive situation in the long haul). Porter advocated the three generic strategies of cost leadership, differentiation, and focus. Other specific examples include for instance persistently updating the product features to meet up the changing taste and preferences of the customers, utilizing advanced technology to increase revenue, redesign the product, container, trademark, design, and different advertising and marketing parts, selecting the tool for promoting the product plays a vital role in surviving in the market, discovering various innovative techniques for the usage of existing products, investigate better approaches to strengthen the business's ways, such as digital sales and warehouse sales (Figure 3).

Figure 3. Representation of the Porters five forces on A2B

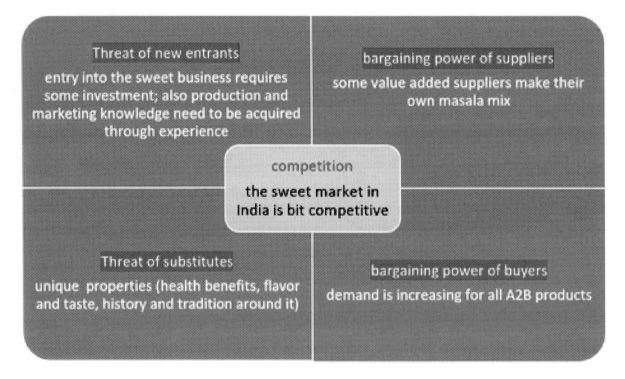

SWOT ANALYSIS OF A2B

Strengths

145 + outlets across India: A2B has been successfully able to spread its wings across 150 locations in India.

Oldest in India: It has been shining bright with over 30 years of existence in the Food Industry.

Commitment to Quality and Hygiene: It has been able to stand firm with its high degree of commitment towards Quality and Hygiene, which is the primary concern of any venture.

State of Art Technology: A2B asserts using the latest technology for cooking and preparing the savories and deserts and assuring the highest quality standards.

Taste of food: A2B is known to serve the most authentic South Indian food in our country. It makes use of homegrown spices and vegetables.

Affordable Prices: The food available at A2B maintains strict quality standards and ensures affordability to every Indian pocket.

Excellence in Retail: In addition to a long chain of restaurants; sweets, snacks, savories, ice-creams, and other confectionaries are sold at the A2B Retail.

Weaknesses

Presence only in South India: A2B boasts 145+ outlets in India, but unfortunately, all of these are concentrated in Tamil Nadu, Karnataka, and some parts of Andhra Pradesh, which leaves the entire Northern portion of our country untapped.

Perishable nature of goods: Everything comes with a minimum shelf life in this industry, right from raw material to finished goods. Much of which is wasted in transportation from warehouses to retail or vice-versa.

Time of Transportation Vehicle: Location of warehouses and retails at distant places further aggravates the problem due to the perishable nature of raw material and finished goods.

Opportunities

Business-friendly Laws: Laws such as FSSAI (Food Safety and Standards Authority of India), Shop Establishment License, Fire Safety Licence, and many more ensure the smooth functioning of A2B restaurants.

Threats

Use of Technology: Technology is very dynamic and required enormous investments for installation and maintenance. Every time a businessman invests in new technology, only to learn that it has become obsolete by the time it has been put to practice. Moreover, A2B is not immune to this. Self-Ordering Tablets, Facial recognition, etc. could be used by A2B but newer technology can anytime come up which calls for new investment.

Competition: Haldirams, Bikaner, MTR are the major competitors of A2B in sweet fragment except that there is no real contender because there is no significant portion of marked desserts in India. If one goes to any town or village in India, they can discover many local manufacturers who sell loose sweets; thus, it is hard to compete with them in terms of pricing.

Government Rules and Regulations: The Government rules and regulations are fair, but most importantly, they are challenging to adhere to always. These rules create significant problems for all the businesses to run. For example, the Covid guidelines about the opening and closing of restaurants have dug a deep hole in the pockets of these businesses (Chaturvedi & Tushar, 2021). This has directly affected the revenues of the restaurants.

A2B COMPETITOR ANALYSIS

A typical competitor analysis takes into consideration the following aspects of the competitor and self:

1. Size of the organization in terms of monetary value.
2. Market share of the competitor.
3. Items listed on the menu card (variety of dishes offered).
4. Reputation of the organization in the minds of the customers and employees.
5. Target audience.
6. A2B must carry out a thorough Competitor Analysis if it plans to maintain the same position in the field for many more years to come (Figure 4).

Figure 4. Competitor Analysis.

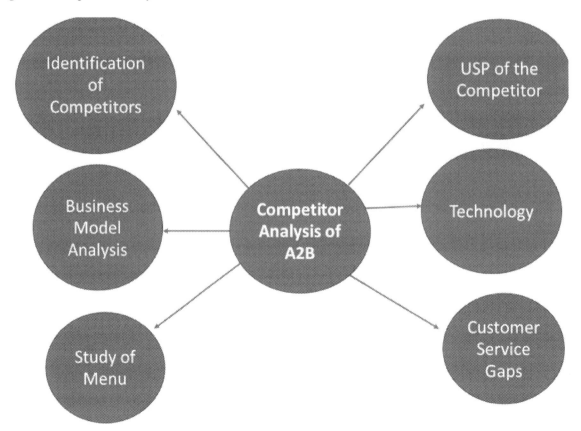

Identification of close competitors and distant competitors: Closed competitors are the ones who have similar features like the ones mentioned above (Size, Market share, menu, reputation. Target customers). A2B faces stiff competition from Bikaner and Haldiram, who are its very close competitors. Distant competitors are the ones who may not have similar features now but are in a position to become similar shortly. A2B faces foreign competition from local restaurants in AP, Karnataka.

Business Model Analysis: Every organization has trade secrets, essential suppliers, a loyal customer base, efficient cooks, and employees. A2B needs to study the business models of its competitors and try to adopt the best practices which its competitors are following, e.g., Employee safety, hygiene, quality standard, and other standard protocols. The following points must be considered by A2B:

1. Type of restaurant (fast food or traditional)
2. Additional services offered
3. Food Ordering application used
4. The theme of the restaurant
5. SWOT Analysis

Detail study of the Menu: One of the most crucial 7P is in Services Marketing is Physical Evidence, and the Menu card of any restaurant happens to satisfy this P of Services Marketing. It is imperative to study the following aspects of the competitor's menu card:

1. The size and look of the menu card do it look exquisite or are printed on glossy paper.
2. The variety of the food offered
3. Most importantly, the price of the food
4. Has the theme of the restaurant being incorporated into the menu?
5. Highest selling items on the menu

USP (Unique Selling Proposition) of the competitor: Once the competition is understood to a great extent, it is crucial to identify the organization's uniqueness. It may be in terms of a special Signature Dish, Unique ambiance, Unique items on the menu (Vegan, etc.), exceptional service quality, Master Chef, etc.

Technology in Use

1. Self-ordering tablets: this AI-based restaurant-focused technology allows consumers to browse the food menu and choose their favorite dish without involving any employee. A2B can opt for such self-ordering tablets in the future.
2. Reordering with facial recognition: a few restaurants are conducting facial recognition trial experiments that'll allow consumers to reorder last meals at self-service kiosks with the help of facial recognition. The trial was explicitly conducted on restaurants that offer a menu with numerous optional customization layers. With such a great variety of choices, the simple way to reorder encourages customers to think about coming back. A2B can also use this technology with facial recognition to help establish loyalty and make business-customer relationships lasting by providing customers a way to reorder their favorite meals quickly.
3. Entertainment available at the table: the tablets in restaurants are more than just a way to make quick orders and pay. There are numerous companies like Buzz Time that provide tablets with entertaining trivia and games to restaurants.

Customer Service gaps: Customer service is a critical aspect of the restaurant business as it functions entirely on word-of-mouth publicity. One negative expression and the entire customer base are affected. Hence it is essential to pay attention to the following:

1. Customer reviews and feedback.
2. Regular complaints about the cost of the items on the menu.
3. Identify the highest selling dish on the menu and try to build upon the existing strength.

Ansoff Matrix

Ansoff matrix is a strategic tool to identify strategic options for a business (De Waal, 2016). The matrix is propounded after the name of Igor Ansoff. This matrix depicts four growth alternatives for an organization to grow (Ansoff, 1957), which are as follows:

1. Market penetration
2. Market development
3. Product development
4. Diversification

The Ansoff matrix of A2B can be illustrated as below (Figure 5).

Figure 5. A2B Ansoff Matrix

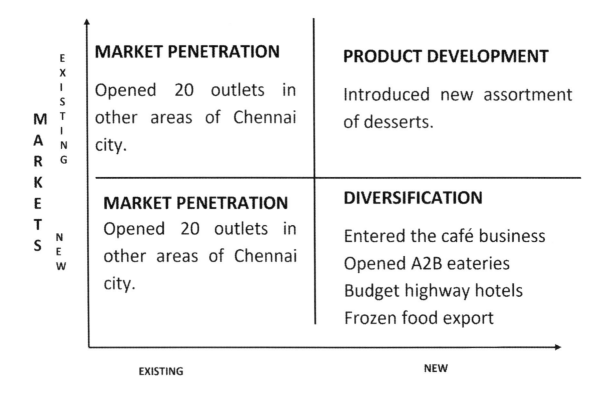

Blue Ocean

Blue Ocean Strategy is a management theory that describes the creating new market instead of competing within existing market (Carton, 2020). Kim et al. (2005) asserted that competition matters most in any business to grow. This "Blue Ocean" means making the competition irrelevant by venturing into a new market space and not competing within the existing market. In their case study, Kim et al. (2006) concluded that one Logistics provider company in South Korea was successful by using information technology (i.e., RFID-radio frequency identification), which created an uncontested market space in the electronic logistics business. Kim and Mauborgne (2005), in one of their books named 'Blue Ocean Strategy, proposed value innovation as the key for competing in the market. Value innovation is the first requirement and the sustainable way to make the competition irrelevant (Andrew 2009; Womack et al., 2007). Because of value innovation, one can minimize the cost and increase the customer value significantly. The value innovation through Blue Ocean Strategy adopted by A2B is depicted in the Figure 6.

Figure 6. A2B Blue Ocean Strategy

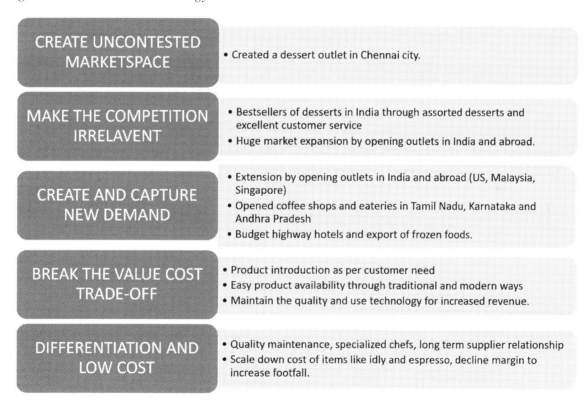

Resource Based Model

According to the resource-based view (RBV), businesses can be competitive by managing valuable resources (Rumelt 1984; Wernerfelt 1984). Wang (2014) talked about two dominant theories in early times: The Market-Based View (MBV) and the Resource-Based View (RBV). Core competencies are closely related to the resource-based view of strategy (Arnoldo & Dean, 2001). Hanningtone (2013) argues that tangible resources should be scarce, valuable non-imitable, and non-substitutable. A2B also adopted the resource Based Model in the following way (Figure 7).

Figure 7. A2B resource based view

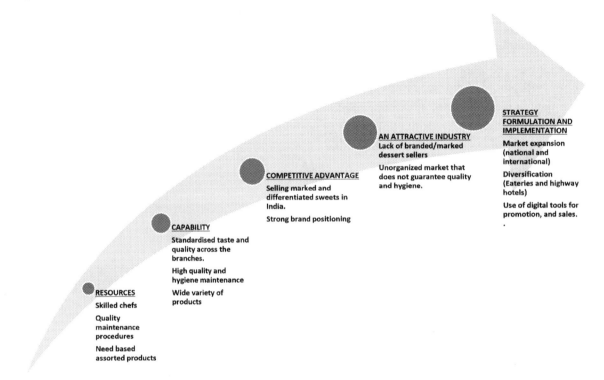

Balanced Scorecard

The balanced scorecard (BSC), initially framed by Kaplan and Norton in 1992, is an essential strategic management tool. The tool has been top-rated in past years (Hasan & Chyi 2017; Hansen & Schaltegger 2016). Quesado et al. (2018) argue that BSC is a good strategic management tool leading to organizational growth and learning. A2B adopted a balanced scorecard approach in the following way (Figure 8).

Skill & Technology – Production & Quality Mantra

A2B maintains the taste and texture of sweets uniformly maintained across all its units. This kind of consistency is because of the high standards at its manufacturing units, which boast high standards, unsurpassed hygiene, and efficient quality control mechanisms. A2B also has an unspoiled room technology that ensures the preparation of premium sweets in the most hygienic environment. Every cook is mandated to pass through the sanitization chamber and controlled temperature to assure quality and packaging. They also have a Quality control team that undertakes random checks. A2B has also set up a high-end technology bakery unit to cater to the rising demands of ice-creams, frozen desserts, and confectionary items. All these eatables are supplied to their various outlets every single day using vehicles that possess temperature controls.

Figure 8. A2B Balanced Sorecard

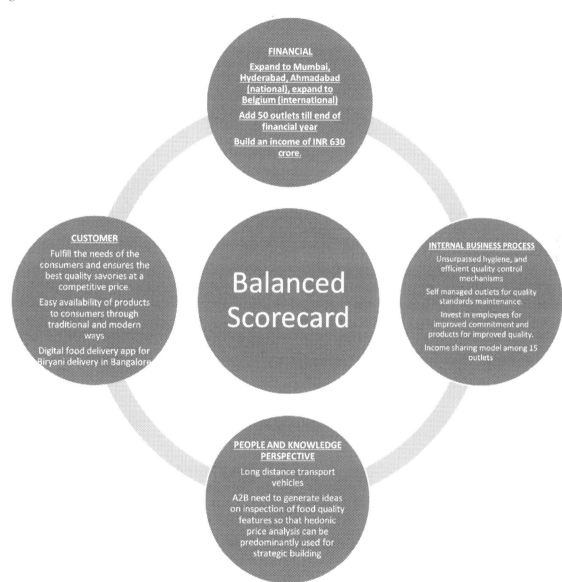

Making the best use of IoT (Internet of Things)

Quality is the key to carve a niche in any competitive market, and A2B strictly adheres to this. For instance, it procures its packaging material from Suraksha, transport vehicles from NS Rama Rao, the leading name in the travel industry, Cold storages from Themo King. To make optimal utilization of the digital technology, A2B has implemented IoT solutions across its convoy. Shortly, A2B also plans to use BharatBenz BS-VI range of vehicles to use its DSM (Driver State Monitoring) Technology. In India, A2B will be the first of its kind to use BharatBenz Technology.

Technology Components in Global Delivery

In this modern era, digital innovation plays a significant role and acts as a new empowering tool. It has encouraged expanding the new plans of action, for example, a cloud-based kitchen that helps digital food delivery (Sufi & Ahmed, 2021). A2B is very keen on utilizing this new forthcoming pattern in some way. As the end consumers needs are changing every day. A2B came up with innovation by introducing a digital food delivery app and their unique series of royal veg biryanis in Bengaluru. KT Srinivasa Raja, Managing Director of Adyar Anand Bhavan desserts and snacks, says, "A2B digital requesting app brings the flavor of the café's indulgences. This app enables one to command their preferred foodstuff and get it conveyed to their home in the briefest timeframe. Moreover, A2B has added one new to their special dry fruit biryani menu, which is accessible through a digital delivery app. Subsequently, they have come up with seven outlets in Bengaluru which will begin the biryani digital conveyance facility: BTM, HSR, BG Road, Marathahalli, Electronic City, Whitefield, and Indiranagar (The Hindu Business 2020).

Technology Supported Strategic Move

Onibonoje et al. (2021) rightly pointed out that the food sector, which is termed Food 4.0, is a significant sector to benefit tremendously from the concept and application of artificial intelligence is driving the sector into the new era of development. In line with this, A2Bs kitchen in Chennai at Ambattur is more like a factory with automated machines (artificial intelligence) making most sweets with very little human intervention. Adyar Ananda Bhavan has succeeded in the tremendous homemade Indian nutrients chains that have become comfortable raising private equity in recent years. A2B has its wide presence in two urban areas: Chennai (50 outlets) and Bengaluru (36 outlets). Bengaluru and Chennai have a centralized kitchen from where foodstuffs are prepared and delivered to the different outlets.

CURRENT CHALLENGES FACING THE ORGANIZATION

1. Shift from Paper to Digital process: like another competitor, the entire food industry and subsequently A2B also is facing many challenges in terms of the use of Digital Platforms to code their goods to ensure better operational competence.
2. Perishable nature of goods: transportation of goods with a meager shelf life has always remained a challenge for the food industry. The transportation of raw materials and the finished goods in the required conditions and temperature at the right time and right place for A2B has always been a concern.
3. Transportation vehicle: the A2B drivers are expected to drive long distances daily to transport raw materials and finished goods to the manufacturing and sales outlets. The heating of the engines in the vehicles is a prime concern which makes the drivers unhappy and gloomy.

The challenge in the future of A2B can be determined by how they allow outsiders in the next generation and deal with the passage of non-relatives into the business. The other challenge which they could face is location. The brand which is popular and preferred in one state cannot be in the same condition in other states so how they set up that brand character will be a key challenge. It bags a turnover of about Rs 800 crore and has established outlets in Singapore, Malaysia, Dallas, and New Jersey in the US. It additionally works as a South Indian café network called A2B inside its stores. A 210-seater Adyar Anand Bhavan establishment outlet is planned to open in New York, US, in a quick period.

SOLUTIONS

1. Making use of its own dairy: in order to become self-reliant A2B can make use of its own dairy for the supply of milk and semi-finished milk products. This will reduce the burden of dependency on other suppliers and ensure timely and quality supply.
2. Use of BharatBenz vehicle: as discussed before, BharatBenz shall ensure timely supply of the perishable goods in the correct manner and shall ease the unnecessary burden on the drivers.
3. Ease of production supply: the supply operations of A2B have been categorized under three heads: a) Use of small commercial vehicles for the transfer of ready-to-eat food. b) Transfer of goods from factory to the sales outlets in the city by ICV vehicles. C) Long-distance travel for the supply of milk and other essential raw materials. Deploying the use of Bharat Benz for the above-mentioned causes will definitely ensure quality and timely delivery of perishable goods across the manufacturing units and the sales outlets.

Besides this, few other important areas need our attention. The food industry is full of the intra-industry trade system, i.e., trade-in-like products post-WTO era. It also points out that there will be tough competition between national and cross boundaries companies in our home market. This competition will demand companies to work on product differentiation branding and updated quality. To stay quality efficient, firms must fathom consumers' outlook towards quality features. *Hedonic price analysis* is a methodology for buying the ingredients of sweets from the suppliers. The methodology is used for processed food products in developed nations. However, it applies to Indian food market settings. For instance, hedonic price analysis applies on a commonly used Indian processed food product-ghee. Research has explored that consumers could pay a little extra if the processed food was manufactured organically. Secondly, the flavor is a significant quality feature important for consumers. While the texture is equally relevant, it needs consensus if there is an outstanding color feature for ghee that can be used for sweets. The conclusion points out that branding offers a reputation, and dairy cooperatives may improve their brand equity to increase their sales to firms like A2B. Thirdly, another suggestion is that more significant firms like A2B need to generate ideas on inspection of food quality features so that hedonic price analysis can be predominantly used for strategic building.

RECOMMENDATIONS

As the pandemic has invaded all sorts of business across the globe, digital value-based innovations have become an indispensable part of any business. Considering the same, below are some of the recommendations for A2B to achieve operational efficiency as they go more digital in future.

Restaurant Technology

An important concern for A2B is the use of technology in their restaurants to enhance operational competence. The use of technology enables a digital platform ensuring omnichannel. Cloud computing and the use of automation have been in vogue in recent times across most sectors, and the food industry is no exception to this. Cloud-Based POS systems are now becoming very popular in terms of ease of installation, ease of use, and one-time investment. Restaurants across the globe make use of a network of computers and remote servers that are mounted on the world wide web to manage the data flow. Such a system in place ensures tamperproof and secure data.

Self-Ordering Tables

In this system, there exists no moment of truth between the customer and the staff. The restaurants are now technologically driven with no human contact. Fast food outlets like Mc Donalds already have self-ordering kiosks in place, ensuring the least human contact. Some restaurants use AI to help customers scan through the menu and order their favorite food without any human involvement. Soon A2B can make use of such kiosks to avoid any human interface.

Making use of Facial Recognition

In this system, the customers can reorder their previous menu through an inbuilt Facial Recognition kiosk enabling contactless self-service. This technology was set up on an experimental basis in certain restaurants in India which offer an ala carte. With so many varieties of food in place, such self-ordering kiosks eased the reordering process along with customer satisfaction and quick orders.

Handheld Entertainment

Many restaurants provide customers with tablets to order food. These tablets are manufactured by Buzz Time. Such handheld devices are also a source of entertainment for the customers while their order is delivered. Many online games and National Level competitions are organized on this device to keep the customer glued to the restaurant. To a very great extent, it has also helped the restaurants to gain customer loyalty.

REFERENCES

Adelakun, A. (2020). *Should Porters Five Forces have value in Businesses today. Computing for Business (BSC)*. Aston University Birmingham.

Adyar Anand Bhavan. (2017). *A2B savouries food menu*. https://www.aabsweets.in/menu-savories

Anderson, D., & Hanselka, D. (2009). *Adding value to agricultural products*. AgriLife Extension, the Texas A&M System.

Andrew, B., André van, S., & Roy, T. (2009). *Blue Ocean versus competitive strategy: Theory and Evidence*. Erasmus Research Institute of Management (ERIM).

Ansoff, I. (1957). Strategies for Diversification. *Harvard Business Review, 35*(5), 113–124.

Arnoldo, H., & Dean, W. I. I. (2001). The delta model—Discovering new sources of profitability in a networked economy. *European Management Journal, 9*(4), 379–391.

Besanko, D., Dranove, D., & Shanley, M. (2000). *The economics of strategy*. John Wiley and Sons.

Carton, G. (2020). How assemblages change when theories become performative: The case of the Blue Ocean strategy. *Organization Studies, 41*(10), 1417–1439. doi:10.1177/0170840619897197

Chaturvedi, S. (2020). Book Review: Essentials of Management by Harold Koontz and Heinz Weihrich. 10th ed. Chennai: Tata McGraw Hill Education, 2015. Journal of Education for Business, 96(1), 69-70. doi:10.1080/08832323.2020.1720572

Chaturvedi, S., & Pasipanodya, T. E. (2021). A Perspective on Reprioritizing Children's' Wellbeing Amidst COVID-19: Implications for Policymakers and Caregivers. *Frontiers in Human Dynamics, 2*, 18. doi:10.3389/fhumd.2020.615865

Chaturvedi, S., Rizvi, I. A., & Pasipanodya, E. T. (2019). How can leaders make their followers to commit to the organization? The importance of influence tactics. *Global Business Review, 20*(6), 1462–1474. doi:10.1177/0972150919846963

Chaturvedi, S., & Singh, T. (2021). Knowledge Management Initiatives for Tackling the COVID-19 Pandemic in India. *Metamorphosis, 09726225211023677*. Advance online publication. 10.1177%2F09726225211023677

Chaturvedi, S., & Srivastava, A. K. (2015). The effect of employee's organizational commitment on upward influence tactics and employees' career success: An Indian study. *International Journal of Research in Organizational Behavior and Human Resource Management, 3*(2), 41–58.

Civils Daily. (October 9, 2017). Food Processing Industry in India: Growth Drivers, FDI Policy, Investment Opportunities; Schemes Related to Food Processing Sector. https://www.civilsdaily.com/food-processing-industry-in-india-growth-drivers-fdi-policy-investment-opportunities-schemes-related-to-food-processing-sector/

Clean India Journal. (2017). Investing in food safety. Retrieved from https://www.cleanindiajournal.com/investing-in-food-safety/

De Waal, G. A. (2016). An Extended Conceptual Framework For Product-Market Innovation. *International Journal of Innovation Management, 20*(5), 1640008. doi:10.1142/S1363919616400089

Deodhar, S., & Intodia, V. (2010). *Does ghee sold by any brand smell as sweet? quality attributes and hedonic price analysis of ghee*. Working paper, IIMA.

Economic Times. (Oct 02, 2013). Eateries see steep price cuts due to growing competition and popular government schemes. https://economictimes.indiatimes.com/articleshow/23396665.cms?from=mdr&utm_source=contentofinterest&utm_medium=text&utm_campaign=cppst

Forbes India. (Feb 21, 2019). Adyar Anand bhavan. Food and folklore. https://www.forbesindia.com/article/family-business/adyar-ananda-bhavan-food-and-folklore/52605/1

Hanningtone, J. G., Miemie, S., & Elroy, E. S. (2013). Creating a sustainable competitive advantage at a high performing firm in Kenya. *African Journal of Business Management*, *7*(21), 2049–2058. doi:10.5897/ajbm2013.6974

Hansen, E. G., & Schaltegger, S. (2016). The sustainability balanced scorecard: A systematic review of architectures. *Journal of Business Ethics*, *133*(2), 193–221. doi:10.100710551-014-2340-3

Hasan, R. U., & Chyi, T. M. (2017). Practical application of Balanced Scorecard - A literature review. *Journal of Strategy and Performance Management*, *5*(3), 87–103.

India, C. C. I. (2019). CII presents award to entrepreneurs. https://www.cciindia.org/food-processing.html

Karagiannopoulos, G., Georgopoulos, N., & Nikolopoulos, K. (2005). Fathoming Porter's five forces model in the internet era. *Info*, *7*(6), 66–76. doi:10.1108/14636690510628328

Kim, W. C., & Mauborgne, R. (2005). Value innovation: A leap into the blue ocean. *The Journal of Business Strategy*, *26*(4), 22–28. doi:10.1108/02756660510608521

Kim, W. C., & Mauborgne, R. (2006). *Blue ocean strategy: How to create uncontested market space and make the competition irrelevant*. Harvard Business School Press.

KPMG. (2016). India's food service industry: Growth recipe. KPMG. https://assets.kpmg/content/dam/kpmg/in/pdf/2016/11/Indias-food-service.pdf

Linton, G., & Kask, J. (2017). Configurations of entrepreneurial orientation and competitive strategy for high performance. *Journal of Business Research*, *70*, 168–176. doi:10.1016/j.jbusres.2016.08.022

Media Ant. (2019). Advertising in Adyar Anand Bhavan. https://www.themediaant.com/nontraditional/a2b-bangalore-advertising

Porter, M. E. (1980). *Competitive strategy: techniques for analyzing industries and competitors*. The Free Press.

Porter, M. E. (1985). *Competitive Advantage: Creating and Sustaining Superior Performance*. Simon and Schuster.

Quesado, P. R., Aibar, G. B., & Lima, R. L. (2018). Advantages and contributions in the balanced scorecard implementation. *Intangible Capital*, *14*(1), 186–201. doi:10.3926/ic.1110

Rumelt, R. P. (1984). Towards a strategic theory of the firm. *Competitive Strategic Management*, *26*(3), 556–570.

Sack, A. L., & Nadim, A. (2002). Strategic Choices in a Turbulent Environment: A Case Study of Starter Corporation. *Journal of Sport Management*, *16*(1), 36–53. doi:10.1123/jsm.16.1.36

Salavou, H. (2015). Competitive strategies and their shift to the future. *European Business Review*, *27*(1), 80–99. doi:10.1108/EBR-04-2013-0073

Sebastiani, R., & Montagnini, F. (2020). Actor engagement in service ecosystems: Innovating value co-creation in food retail. In F. Musso & E. Druica (Eds.), *Handbook of research on retailing techniques for optimal consumer engagement and experiences* (pp. 400–420). IGI Global. doi:10.4018/978-1-7998-1412-2.ch018

Shokuhi, A., & Chashmi, S. (2019). Formulation of Bank Melli Iran Marketing Strategy Based on Porter's Competitive Strategy. *Journal of Business-To-Business Marketing*, 26(2), 209–215. doi:10.1080/1051712X.2019.1603421

Srivastava, A. K., & Chaturvedi, S. (2014). Negative Job Experiences and Employees Job Attitudes and Health in High-Performance Work Organizations. *Metamorphosis*, 13(2), 22–28. doi:10.1177/0972622520140205

Sufi, T., & Ahmed, S. (2021). Surviving COVID-19 Crisis by New Business Models: A Case Study of the Indian Restaurant Industry. In L. C. Carvalho, L. Reis, & C. Silveira (Eds.), *Handbook of Research on Entrepreneurship, Innovation, Sustainability, and ICTs in the Post-COVID-19 Era* (pp. 301–316). IGI Global. doi:10.4018/978-1-7998-6776-0.ch015

Suhartanto, D., Ismail, T. A. T., Leo, G., Triyuni, N. N., & Suhaeni, T. (2020). Behavioral Intention Toward Online Food Purchasing: An Analysis at Different Purchase Levels. [IJEBR]. *International Journal of E-Business Research*, 16(4), 34–50. doi:10.4018/IJEBR.2020100103

The Hindu. (2019). CII presents awards to entrepreneurs. https://www.thehindu.com/news/national/tamil-nadu/cii-presents-awards-to-entrepreneurs/article26274622.ece

The Hindu business (2020). Adyar Anand Bhavan launches delivery app. https://www.thehindubusinessline.com/companies/adyar-ananda-bhavan-launches-delivery-app/article22807346.ece

The Times of India. (2016). Ananda-bhavan-revives-plans-pe-deal-hires-banker. https://www.vccircle.com/adyar-ananda-bhavan-revives-plans-pe-deal-hires-banker/

Thompson, A. A., & Stickland, A. J. (1999). *Strategic management: Concepts and cases*. Irwin.

Trienekens, J. H., Wognum, P. M., Beulens, A. J. M., & van der Vorst, J. G. A. J. (2012). Transparency in complex dynamic food supply chains. *Advance Engineering Information*, 26(1), 55–65. doi:10.1016/j.aei.2011.07.007

Vlajic, J., van der Vorst, J. G. A. J., & Haijema, R. (2002). A framework for designing robust food supply chains. *International Journal of Production Economics*, 137(1), 176–189. doi:10.1016/j.ijpe.2011.11.026

Wang, H. (2014). *Theories for competitive advantage*. University of Wollongong.

Wang, J., Tao, J., & Chu, M. (2020). Behind the label: Chinese consumers' trust in food certification and the effect of perceived quality on purchase intention. *Food Control*, 108, 106825. doi:10.1016/j.foodcont.2019.106825

Wee, C. H. (2016). Think Tank-Beyond the Five Forces Model and Blue Ocean Strategy. *An Integrative Perspective From Sun Zi Bingfa.*, (2), 34–45.

Wernerfelt, B. (1984). A resource-based view of the firm. *Strategic Management Journal*, 5(2), 171–180. doi:10.1002mj.4250050207

Wiengarten, F., Pagell, M., & Fynes, B. (2011). Supply chain environmental investments in dynamic industries: Comparing investment and performance differences with static industries. *International Journal of Production Economics*, *135*(2), 541–551. doi:10.1016/j.ijpe.2011.03.011

Womack, J. P., Jones, D. T., & Roos, D. (2007). *The machine that changed the world: The story of lean production—Toyota's secret weapon in the global car wars that is now revolutionizing world industry*. Simon and Schuster.

ADDITIONAL READING

Cavusoglu, M. (2019). An analysis of technology applications in the restaurant industry. *Journal of Hospitality and Tourism Technology*, *10*(1), 45–72. doi:10.1108/JHTT-12-2017-0141

Hearn, G., Collie, N., Lyle, P., Choi, J. H. J., & Foth, M. (2014). Using communicative ecology theory to scope the emerging role of social media in the evolution of urban food systems. *Futures*, *62*, 202–212. doi:10.1016/j.futures.2014.04.010

Hirschberg, C., Rajko, A., Schumacher, T., & Wrulich, M. (2020). The changing market for food delivery. https://www.mckinsey.com/industries/technology-media-andtelecommunications/ our-insights/the-changing-market-for-food-delivery Güngör, D. Ö. (2019). Industry 4.0 Technologies Used in Project Management. In *Agile Approaches for Successfully Managing and Executing Projects in the Fourth Industrial Revolution* (pp. 40-63). IGI Global.

Smetana, S., Aganovic, K., & Heinz, V. (2021). Food Supply Chains as Cyber-Physical Systems: A Path for More Sustainable Personalized Nutrition. *Food Engineering Reviews*, *13*(1), 92–103. doi:10.100712393-020-09243-y

Sufi, T., & Ahmed, S. (2021). Surviving COVID-19 Crisis by New Business Models: A Case Study of the Indian Restaurant Industry. In Handbook of Research on Entrepreneurship, Innovation, Sustainability, and ICTs in the Post-COVID-19 Era (pp. 301-316). IGI Global.

Tandon, S., & Bhalla, T. (2020). Food aggregators pivot to cloud kitchens as online orders surge. https://www.livemint.com/companies/news/food-aggregators-pivot-tocloud-kitchens-as-online-orders-surge-11591730431365.html

KEY TERMS AND DEFINITIONS

Artificial Intelligence: A computer science discipline that describes the simulation of computers' intelligent behavior.

Business Models: A business model defining how an organization builds, launches, and captures value in socio-cultural and economic contexts.

Business Value Innovation: Redesigning business models wherein different value players involved in the business are redefined to improve the firm's performance.

Cloud Kitchens: Kitchens or catering units that sell food directly to customers without an attached dining facility. The food demand from customers is generated through mobile applications or websites.

Digital Innovation: Digital innovation refers to the application of digital technology to existing business problems to innovate new products or services.

Digitalization Strategies: Strategies that focus on utilizing technology to ameliorate business performance, creating new products, or restructuring current processes.

Strategic Management: It is the continuous planning, monitoring, and assessment of all requirements an organization undertakes to meet its long- and short-term objectives.

Value Chain: A value chain is a package of activities that a particular firm in a specific industry undertakes to deliver a valuable product for its end customers.

APPENDIX 1

Questions and Answers

Jot down the numerous reasons for the business growth of A2B.

The underwritten points can be utilized to foster the discussion on the causes that lead to A2B growth (refer to Table 1 also):

1. Utilizing updated technology
2. Venturing into new sweet segment.
3. Venturing into new markets.
4. Outsourcing, that is, hiring contractual workers instead of permanent workers.

According to you, which management strategies (blue ocean strategy, pricing, promotion, location) were taken up by the A2B, respectively, at each stage of the growth? Try writing specific incidences from the case to back up your answer.

1. Blue ocean strategy at the growth stage as inferred from the case:

'It bags a turnover of about Rs 800 crore and has established outlets in Singapore, Malaysia, Dallas, and New Jersey in the US.'

2. Pricing- A2B used pricing at the maturity stage while the competition increased. The following lines from case support the answer.

'Primarily because of rivalry from other cafes and decline in footfall, A2B has scaled down the costs of its items like idlis and the espresso by 5-10%. Despite maintaining the quality of their sweets, A2B had to decline its margins to increase the customer's footfalls (The Economic Times, 2013).'

3. Location- The location strategy was used at the expansion stage as indicated in case through these lines

'Around 25 Adyar Ananda Bhavan outlets are situated on national roadways in Karnataka, Tamil Nadu, and Andhra Pradesh. "Our goal is to have one outlet every 200km on every single national roadway crosswise over India," cites Srinivasa Raju.

What digital strategies were taken up by the company to stay updated in the market?

A2B came up with innovation by introducing a digital food delivery app and their unique series of royal veg biryanis in Bengaluru. KT Srinivasa Raja, Managing Director of Adyar Anand Bhavan desserts

Digital Value Innovation and Strategic Management Practices of Adyar Ananda Bhavan

and snacks, says, "A2B digital requesting app brings the flavor of the café's indulgences. This app enables one to command their preferred foodstuff and get it conveyed to their home in the briefest timeframe.

Subsequently, they have come up with seven outlets in Bengaluru which will begin the biryani digital conveyance facility: BTM, HSR, BG Road, Marathahalli, Electronic City, Whitefield, and Indiranagar (The Hindu Business 2020).

A2Bs kitchen in Chennai at Ambattur is more like a factory with automated machines (artificial intelligence) making most sweets with very little human intervention.

Jot down feasible teachings from the case and advice suitable management strategies for further market expansion of A2B overseas.

The A2B case has been taken as an exemplary example to understand the challenges of sweet business in the digital world. It brings forth several key concepts of entrepreneurship that lead to business growth. These include the use of concepts like Porter's five forces model (1980) and the value chain method (Porter 1985). The competitive advantage of the value chain is achieved by performing important value chain activities at a competitive rate with the competitors (Porter, 1985). A business leader must either have or develop some unique capabilities to achieve and sustain that position. Examples of such capabilities and resources are a dominant market share, secured supplies of scarce raw materials, or having developed more efficient linkages to suppliers and customers. Besides this, the case study also explores how the digital food industry has led to adapting to the new business model by the food service sector in India. The long range of using latest use of technology in restaurant industry will make the food business omni channel and more digital in the future.

List out Possible Learning's from the Case (answer lies in the Epilogue section)
Some of the key learning from the case are as follows

1. Use of value chain analysis for competitive advantage
2. Development of core competencies for enhanced sustainability.
3. Adaption of the business model to the market changes e.g. in this case adoption of the digital technologies for a sustainable business model.

Theory Underpinning

The model which helps distinguish the aggressive pressures within any industry condition is Porters' (1980) five force model of industry competition. The idea is also supported by Besanko, Dranove and Shanley (2000), Thompson and Stickland (1999) who advocate that Porter's five force model can be used as a powerful tool for analyzing the business scene. The central principle of Porter's aggressive viable approach is the company's earning and surviving capacity depending on five competitive forces within the industry: the competition being too high and the risk of contenders entering the business, the force of competition among existing contenders, the danger of substitute things and services, the haggling intensity of purchasers, and the dealing intensity of suppliers (Sack & Nadim, 2002). Porters (1980) contends that organizations who breed preferable techniques over their rivals, by grasping the states of the industry better than others, may achieve manageable upper hand (i.e., an increasingly productive situation in the long haul).

Porter advocated the three generic strategies of cost leadership, differentiation, and focus. Other specific examples include:

1. Persistently updating the product features so that it meets up the changing taste and preferences of the customers.
2. Utilizing advanced technology to increase revenue.
3. Redesigning the product, container, trademark, design, and different parts of advertising and marketing.
4. Selecting the tool for promoting the product plays a vital role in surviving in the market.
5. Discovering various innovative techniques for usage of existing products.
6. Investigating better approaches to strengthen the ways of doing the business such as digital sales and warehouse sales.
7. Creating a blue ocean (Wee, 2016).

Epilogue and Lessons Learned

The A2B case has been taken as an exemplary example to understand the challenges of sweet business in the digital world. It brings forth several key concepts of entrepreneurship that lead to business growth. These include the use of concepts like Porter's five forces model (Porter, 1980) and the value chain method (Porter 1985). The competitive advantage of the value chain is achieved by performing important value chain activities at a competitive rate with the competitors (Porter, 1985). A business leader must either have or develop some unique capabilities to achieve and sustain that position. Examples of such capabilities and resources are a dominant market share, secured supplies of scarce raw materials, or having developed more efficient linkages to suppliers and customers (refer to Figure 2). Besides this, the case study also explores how the digital food industry has led to adapting to the new business model by the food service sector in India. The long range of using latest use of technology in restaurant industry will make the food business omni channel and more digital in the future. Majority of consumers at present already believe that online ordering is more convenient in comparison to going out with their family. That is why, more than 80% of restaurants will adopt technology in their operations, for instance online ordering, online reservations, and restaurant analytics will be extensively involved in every restaurant operations in the near future.

Chapter 4
Consumer Perception of Brand Repositioning Through Benefit Diversification and Intensity of Use:
The Case of Pedras

Francisca Quintas Rodrigues
Faculty of Economics, University of Porto, Portugal

Beatriz Casais
https://orcid.org/0000-0002-7626-0509
School of Economics and Management & CICS.NOVA, University of Minho, Braga, Portugal

EXECUTIVE SUMMARY

A company's positioning strategy is focused on how the company wants its brand to be perceived in the market. However, the constant change of markets has led many companies to carry on repositioning strategies to deliberately change their strategic positioning, namely by widening its product or service benefits to attract a wider market audience. As product or service positioning is always defined by the consumer, there is the need to understand the extent to which each company is able to communicate its new intended positioning and actually make it perceived. This chapter presents the case of Pedras, a Portuguese brand of naturally sparkling water which ramped up its communication efforts regarding the extension of its product's benefits in order to minimize the potential gap between intended and perceived positioning. Digital communication strategies are discussed to engage young consumers.

ORGANIZATION BACKGROUND

This chapter explores the big challenge of repositioning from a product associated with elderly people and digestion functionalities to a refreshing product targeting a wider and younger market. Pedras is a

DOI: 10.4018/978-1-7998-1630-0.ch004

brand of sparkling water that is naturally carbonated; its unique profile of minerals and medicinal benefits were discovered in 1871. These attributes were admittedly seen as a competitive advantage and soon the company became an iconic brand on the Portuguese market, and eventually became the leader of the domestic sparkling water market. But these strong associations to the product extended to the whole category of sparkling water in the country, which soon after started to hamper the company's growth. These medicinal attributes became so strongly connected with the product category and the brand that it limited the other benefits associated with the type of product, even though sparkling water can have a wider range of benefits, such as refreshment.

As a result, in Portugal people used to perceive the benefits of sparkling water in association with malaise, which was a very restricted market for its potential when comparing with other countries whose consumption culture used to include sparkling water in daily meals. In this sense, in Portugal the consumption of sparkling water tended to lose significance, because it was represented mainly by elderly people. The consumption of this type of water was deeply associated with habits from the past that ceased to prevail with the evolution of society and the emergence of medicinal alternatives. The product "Água das Pedras" became a beverage suitable only for digestion or malaise-related problems, mainly associated with elderly people and with an antiquated image.

Considering the sparkling water market, in Portugal two brands stand out in terms of refreshment attributes which Pedras would later define as its intended repositioning strategy: Frize (born in 1994), and Luso Gás (born in 2014). Both brands are significantly more recent than Pedras, which arrived in the market in 1871. Therefore, these two brands achieved from the beginning a positioning more suitable for the current market than Pedras, which had to go through repositioning strategies to take the best advantage of the market throughout the years. This is attested by the fact Pedras positioning is more strongly connected with the market positioning oriented towards digestion and perceived as less modern than other sparkling water brands.

A fact to consider is that this repositioning strategy was more transversal rather than just a new communication direction, and involved the creation of new products. Regarding this topic, introductions such as Pedras Sabores (the flavored water range) should not neglect the process of consumer familiarization with a new brand, even though it is a sub-brand of a very strong brand in the market. Pedras Sabores was created as a new range brand of flavored sparkling water to compete with Frize. The sparkling water market, including flavored sparkling water, is strongly associated with digestion, with the flavored range only slightly surpassing this attribute —lifestyle-wise, the performance of flavored sparkling water is, on the other hand, very good in comparison to the other categories. In this respect, Pedras is the brand least associated with the flavored sparkling water market and with its flavored portfolio, which means that it is the brand capitalizing less on the commercial opportunities of its flavored range. Frizee brand, in turn, is more connected with the flavored range.

Repositioning is a challenge, as it involves changing consumers' mindset. In this case, repositioning involves extending the perceived benefits of the product besides other non-materialized attributes. In the case of Pedras, this repositioning is challenged by the fact that there is an enormous connection between the brand and the product category, since in Portugal Pedras designates the category of sparkling water, making it harder to disconnect from the attributes given by the market. On the other hand, Pedras brand boasts a very long history of tradition that is very dear to the Portuguese whose consumption experiences are passed on from generation to generation, including some knowledge about the product, advices on the product's medicinal benefits, along with a series of myths (which in some cases are detrimental to the acceptance of the new benefits). This heritage and importance of the brand for the general population made it an icon, which in turn remained very much untouched over the years, without incurring meaningful brand or strategy changes.

Those people who do not drink Pedras regularly usually do it for medicinal benefits. This means that people who drink Pedras every two months, for example, do it because they only perceive Pedras as suitable for periods of malaise. Regarding the positioning of Pedras Sabores functional needs and social adequacy, the emphasis is placed on the differences based on consumption profile. In this case, people who consume flavored sparkling water, even if it is not Pedras Sabores, accept its refreshing power better. This means that promoting experimentation is a very important tool in this phase to introduce the positioning to new consumers — through sampling, for example (Belch & Belch, 2003). The younger generation accepts more easily the new positioning, and therefore the fact that the brand is trying to reach this target with value propositions that are meaningful to them; it is indeed a more effective way to introduce the new message. This is also present on the positioning of Pedras in terms of lifestyle, age groups, and occupations, between retired people and students or employed people.

However, it is still a small portion of people who see Pedras in the intended way — as a modern beverage that is as refreshing as the majority of the market's offers. On the other side, there is also evidence that people are able to accept this positioning; however, they have to physically experience it in order to absorb it.

Setting the Stage

Brand managers must be aware of the perceived positioning of their products or services, as this has ultimately a direct effect on the company's results (Kostelijk & Alsem, 2020). Furthermore, if the strategic positioning is not being perceived, marketers must be able to understand what the obstacles are and adapt every marketing initiative according to those insights. Additionally, the challenge escalates with the evolution of the market, as there is a need to reposition, and therefore the professionals must be able to draw on past work to achieve future objectives. The complexity of these objectives calls for the need to go further in theory and understand what the best approaches to these strategies are, and how brand repositioning works.

However, this type of practical analysis with tools that can be used by companies to understand their standing point is scarce or not yet published (Blankson & Crawford, 2012; Zhang, Lin, & Newman, 2016). Moreover, when it comes to the specific case of diversification of benefits, repositioning strategies or consumer perception are not explored in the literature. The objective of this chapter is to analyze consumer perception about a brand's identity and attributes and how can companies use expertise and knowledge to adapt their repositioning strategy, so that consumer perception fits the intended repositioning. On this note, it is also explored the case of repositioning via diversification of the product's benefits, and how that diversification of benefits may influence repositioning strategy, and specificities to be effectively managed. To accomplish this, a case study was conducted on brand Pedras, which undertook a repositioning strategy that included diversification of benefits. Furthermore, the challenges of digital communication are also discussed, considering the importance of digital ads to reinforce the brand's new positioning in digital media, both social networks and search engines (Balça & Casais, 2021), as well as the development of content marketing strategies to reinforce customer brand engagement relationships in social media (Balio & Casais, 2020).

Consumer Perception of Brand Repositioning Through Benefit Diversification and Intensity of Use

Case Description

When brand Pedras was bought by big beverage company Unicer (present day Super Bock Group) in 2002, it became obvious the need to revitalize the brand, rejuvenate its consumers and intensify the use of the product. As the market leader, the development of the market was very much driven by the brands' efforts and, therefore, to grow the market, the brand had to educate the consumer. The strategy became to reposition the brand, without losing the luxurious heritage that gave it credibility among Portuguese consumers and distinguished it from competitors. These efforts were phased in over time in order for consumers to gradually assimilate the product's new attributes via a more complex and emotional message to connect with the consumer on a different level, beyond the strictly functional side as before. On the same year it was bought by Unicer, Pedras launched an important campaign that allowed the brand to move to a more prominent position regarding the wellbeing benefits of its water. Before, it was consumed in situations of malaise to providing well-being, and at this period the brand was still communicating functional benefits, albeit for more positive situations, such as the need to refresh and feel in balance both mentally and physically. Then, the campaign "The Power of Nature is Infinite" reinforced the product's attributes as a power of nature, educating the target consumers on the product's natural characteristics, giving more credibility to its benefits, and differentiating it from the competition.

At a later stage, the company continued to build up on the diversification of benefits, and increased its portfolio with a flavored range. The purpose of this strategy was to recruit younger consumers into this category, because due to the evolution of eating habits, this market segment became more and more receptive to sweet aliments. On the other side, this marketing drive would also increase the association of the drink with other occasions of consumption, fortifying the refreshment benefit, as it could be seen as a replacement for other flavored refreshment beverages. The second time there was an extension of product range was with the marketing of the PET (polyethylene terephthalate) bottle via a specific campaign built around the concept of the practicality of the new package and the suitability of the beverage to be consumed at time of the day. In 2008 the company focused its efforts on the association of the beverage with consumption during meals to once again intensify its consumption.

In 2009 the company felt the need to pursue a stronger and more transversal approach to the repositioning strategy and rebranded Pedras. The underlying principle was to acquire a modern and natural look that would make the brand more visually suitable for a younger target audience and to the refreshment beverage category, boasting a new logo and a new packaging.

The brand's most recent concept of communication moved to a more emotional tone and started in 2016 with a commercial ad inspired in the brand's slogan *Let the best of you shine through*. The first communication video of this campaign was a manifesto that drew a parallel with the fact that from the depths of nature comes something great as Pedras with its natural gas, as from the inner core of people also come their greater deeds. On the next year, 2017, there was a greater focus on the product, its suitability for various occasions of consumption (Pedras with coffee, after a sport activity, during a lunch or to help relax) and its natural characteristics (pure, untouchable, 100% natural). The promise of the brand is that Pedras helps people to bring out the best, by providing the physical and mental well-being on the different facets of their lives.

The association of Pedras with coffee was a result of the company's close interaction with its consumer base to learn more about their habits and preferences, which resulted in finding that this association was already being done by some people. This was a great initiative for the company to include in its diversification of benefits and occasions of consumption strategy, and to spread to a wider range of consumers, since there was already proof of acceptance.

This close proximity with the consumer has enabled the company to get meaningful inputs. This was also the case with the product line Pedras Sabores (a flavored range of Pedras), which started being marketed in 2006 via a new campaign. In that same year there was another campaign that challenged viewers to question themselves if they preferred living natural and outside experiences rather than artificial and behind-doors experiences. Still in 2016, the company realized, through market research, that people were not aware of the existence of Pedras Sabores. They had an awareness rate of almost 100% when it came to the mother brand, but most people were not aware of the existence of this line of products (even frequent consumers of regular Pedras that were the target audience for Pedras Sabores). Accordingly, in 2017 the brand launched a new campaign to get the attention of the younger generations. The slogan *Discover the other colors of Nature* continued to draw a parallel between Pedras and Nature that started a few months before with a campaign for regular Pedras, where the product would merge with images of nature as if they were one and the same, thus emphasizing the brand's natural credentials. This new slogan made a clear and strong association with the color green that people commonly associate with nature, which was also the same color associated with the sparkling water category and Pedras itself. Confident of Pedras' wide acceptance in the market and its connection with nature, people were challenged to discover other colors of nature, viz, the other colors and flavors of Pedras. The communication plan aimed at creating awareness among the target consumers by investing in the channels having more affinity to the target and through an innovative execution of the advertising materials, to be able to spark interest and retain attention (using intense colors that also worked as metaphor for flavor).

As this brief presentation of the brand's repositioning strategy and respective background proves, Pedras is a very complete case study, with a history full of milestones that where part of a wider structure for a long-term strategy. Since its successful beginning by creating strong roots on consumer perception, the brand felt the need to break free and grow beyond that market perception, with the product serving fewer benefits than its full potential. This repositioning of the brand was a long and staged process, via a transversal structure of different ways of communicating new benefits and new occasions for consumption, complemented with product line extension and rebranding. In this strategy, the diversification of benefits aimed both to intensify the consumption of Pedras (as with the communication of the association of Pedras with coffee, or the launch of Pedras PET bottle of 1 liter) and to recruit new consumers (for example, for product line Pedras Sabores).

The brand continues to be the leader of the sparkling water market, having nowadays a market share higher than 50%. But despite this factual success, the purpose of this research is to understand if this company's efforts were successful in changing consumer perception of Pedras' benefits.

CURRENT CHALLENGES FACING THE ORGANIZATION

The positioning of a brand is a constructed idea about a product, service or brand in consumers' minds that is a result of the company's efforts to deliver a differentiated promise that will create competitive advantage for its offer through differentiated benefits — which can be a combination of the product's physical attributes, service-related qualities and advertising differentiation — that fit consumer needs. The promise of added and distinctive value to the consumer defined by the positioning creates competitive advantage for the brand (Belch & Belch, 2003). Therefore, every effort from the company should be planned to reinforce the positioning that will positively differentiate the product or service. In order to accomplish this, these authors expose the need for a robust and coherent marketing plan and an aligned marketing mix. However, irrespective of the ability to execute a marketing plan where every action of the company is aligned with the positioning it needs to deliver a differentiated promise to the target audience, positioning is ultimately defined by what the consumer thinks. Therefore, sometimes there is a gap between the intended positioning, which is defined by the company, and the perceived positioning, which is the information that the target consumer actually absorbs by being in contact (or not) with the means the company uses to communicate its intended positioning (Fuchs & Diamantopoulos, 2010). In the case of a gap between the two concepts of positioning, what is perceived dictates the positioning of the product or service, as the authors explain. This gap can be the result of the company's inefficient communication strategy (Zinkhan, 1993) or it can be aggravated by target consumer characteristics such as culture, ethnicity and personal life that influence their perception. Thus, it is essential to understand the magnitude of this gap and what influences consumer perception, since the potential benefits of the repositioning only become a reality once the consumer perceives the message that the company is trying to communicate and acts accordingly (Fuchs & Diamantopoulos, 2010).

Changes in the market, the economy or the consumer force companies to change too in order to stay in the market or just to get stronger. To stay in the market, companies must constantly look for opportunities to grow, and therefore must constantly change and adapt. However, growth strategies are diverse and, according to Ansoff, can be divided into four types: market penetration, market development, product development, and diversification (Ansoff, 1957). The first case happens when the company chooses a strategy to boost its sales, both by increasing the consumption of its current consumers and by attracting consumers that use the competitors' alternatives, without changing the brand's product (Ansoff, 1957; Hussain *et al.*, 2014). This can be achieved by increasing advertising pressure (a reminder message of the brand or the situation in which its product can be used) or by resorting to other promotional tools and can even be complemented with a repositioning strategy to increase consumer use of the product and attract target audiences that are not yet customers of the brand (Craciun & Baubu, 2014; Hussain *et al.*, 2014). Additionally, the company can also strengthen its customer base via a loyalty and retention program (Craciun & Baubu, 2014). Market development is an effort to reach a new market or target (new geographical location, or other types of segments, new channels, etc.) with the same product (or with slight changes). On the other hand, the objective of product development is to stay in the same market but with a different product that will improve the company's offer to that original target market (Ansoff, 1957). Innovation is a pillar of this kind of strategy (Craciun & Baubu, 2014). Finally, there is the most extreme strategy, diversification, which implies a shift to a new market with a new product. In this last strategy, the company moves away from its comfort zone, while in the other situations there can be used synergies and economies of scale (Ansoff, 1957).

The key in any case is to innovate and differentiate, to deliver to the consumer a unique offer that cannot be replaced by competition. This is possible by working on one or more elements of the marketing mix of the product or service (Shaw, 2012). The type of the innovation that the company seeks depends on the type of strategy it is willing to adopt. Therefore, the possibilities for differentiating include not only physical changes on product/service offer, but also branding differentiation, in which a change of values, image and personality will construct a new lifestyle represented by the brand and which fits consumer interests.

The literature finds that some characteristics of companies make repositioning strategies more attractive. This is the case of big companies, since they have more power to place themselves where they want by making use of competitive advantages related with cost or quality (Riordan, 1998). Another finding of Wang and Shaver (2013) paper is that companies with a past of frequent changes of its products are more prompt to resort to repositioning than companies with a long line of classic products that remained mostly unaltered throughout the years.

On the other hand, the characteristics of consumers will also influence the decision of companies to reposition or not, as consumers, for example, might be so concentrated (in terms of needs, preferences or geographical location, for example) that there is not much space for companies to change (Wang & Shaver, 2013).

Another critical situation a company may face can be related with habits that the consumer acquired before the repositioning. Habit is a behavioral consequence of the repetition of an action from which the consumer's organism gets positive feedback (Wood & Neal, 2009). This can be indeed problematic, as it can become automatic, to the extent that the consumer acts unconsciously, repeating that action, as a result of the need to save energy for other situations that need more intellectual effort. Therefore, habits related with the old positioning can be difficult to modify (Wttenbraker et al., 1993) to fit with the new positioning the company wants the consumer to absorb.

After evaluating the feasibility of the repositioning strategy, it is imperative for the brand to align every branch of the marketing strategy (Edwing, Fowlds, & Shepherd, 1995) and construct a communication plan that is effective in replacing the old image the consumers had with the new positioning. If, at the end, consumers continue to see the product/service in the same way, then the company is not taking advantage and collecting the profit potentially generated by the repositioning, or it is not averting away from the pressures of the competition, if that was the primary reason for implementing the strategy (Jewell, 2007). This is precisely what Zhan et al. (2016) mean by the need for the company to minimize the gap between perceived and intended positioning, which might not decrease organically. This is why the authors suggest that this evolution might be faster if the company invests in educating consumers and explaining how its new repositioning fits the brand and how the product/service is aligned with the consumer's needs. To be able to accomplish this, the company must understand the tension points among its consumers that are blocking the natural evolution of their perceptions regarding the intended repositioning.

O'Donnell and Brown (2011) also call attention to the fact that, due to the limited capacity of memory storage, the most recent information has to replace past information — the so-called retroactive interference. This is why other authors have made use of this fact to find ways to use it for the advantage of companies in the case of repositioning (Jewell, 2007). Many times, a company's attempt to provide the consumer with new information regarding its product/service repositioning is blocked by the current information held by the consumer. The Interference Competition explains that when a repositioned brand has a competitor with a position similar to its previous one and both are communicating their positionings simultaneously, then the consumer will strongly connect that positioning with that specific competitor, leaving space for the company to create a new positioning on the consumer's mind (Kent & Allen, 1994). In order to strategically make use of the Interference Competition to disconnect the brand from the old attributes perceived by the consumer, the company should, if possible, align the airing of its repositioning communication strategy with the competitor's communication. On the other hand, in the case of a company with a diversified portfolio that includes another brand of the same category, the company can strategically plan the communication of both brands, so that the one not being repositioned strengthens the connection of the consumer with those attributes, and the other brand takes advantage of that situation to move away from those same attributes at the same moment (Jewell, 2007).

SOLUTIONS AND RECOMMENDATIONS

Repositioning strategies are always very challenging, as they imply a change of habits (Wttenbraker et al., 1983), and a replacement of beliefs in consumers' minds (O'Donnell & Brown, 2011). Pedras is an example of a brand whose repositioning was also challenged by an enormous connection with the market, since in Portugal Pedras gives the name to the sparkling water category, making it harder to disconnect from its attributes (Jewell, 2007). This is a sign of customer loyalty built over the years, and brands should be aware of that sign, as this means that the consumers are in the last stages of the Hierarchy of Effects Model after recognizing the product/service and its attributes, they build up a preference that is intensified as they, as consumers, get satisfied with its consumption. When brands reach this stage, the effects of previous communication are more arduous to reverse, since the consumer is very attached to the positioning (Wijaya, 2012).

Furthermore, when a brand like Pedras holds a very long history of tradition, having become very dear to its consumers, to the extent that their consumption experiences are passed on from generation to generation, consumers get used to a communication that characterizes a certain personality and attributes. Therefore, after years of stable positioning, repositioning becomes harder to implement (Wang & Shaver, 2013). These facts, as a whole, are causes of Pedras' current positioning still much digestion-oriented.

In these situations, it is determinant that brands that carried out a repositioning strategy interact with the consumer to address their standing point and act accordingly to minimize the restrains of this strategy.

One of the routes that companies can take to minimize the gap between perceived and intended positioning is portfolio management or Interference Competition (Jewell, 2007). As the case chosen shows, Portuguese sparkling water brands such as Vidago, Vimeiro or Carvalhelhos invest less on communicating new benefits and were able to be less positioned as appropriate for digestion than Pedras. This is due to the fact that the market already has a brand strongly connected with this positioning, which makes it easier for others to more easily build a new positioning. Hence, through portfolio management, a company holding more than one brand in a market should take advantage of it and enhance the old positioning perception on one brand, to allow consumers to accept the new positioning for the other brand (Jewell, 2007; Kent & Allen, 1994). On the other hand, if portfolio management is not an option, competitive interference can also be achieved if there is another brand in the market that is communicating the old positioning (Jewell, 2007). In this situation, the brand should align its new positioning communication with the other brand's communication on the old positioning.

When repositioning includes a diversification of benefits, an important part of the repositioning communication strategy should be informative, to explain how the new benefits fit consumers' routines (Zhang et al., 2016). This means that instead of a communication message that tries to make consumers accept a new attribute (and therefore drastically change their beliefs), a more contextual approach should be adopted, such as showing new and different consumption/use situations in which that attribute will be appreciated. In the case of Pedras, it proved fruitful to communicate different consumption occasions to introduce the attribute of refreshment in consumers' minds. This way, the information is not as completely disruptive for the current schema on consumer's memory, thus prompting the repositioning (O'Donnell & Brown, 2011), since it addresses moments of consumers' routine in which they can intuitively find suitability for the consumption of the product, without necessarily calling into question which benefits they associate to the product. On this stage, taking into consideration the Hierarchy of Effects Model the company should critically encourage experimentation, via promotions and sampling, since this will be crucial for the consumer to confirm product suitability for the consumption occasion, and accept the new benefit (Egede, 2013). The next stage should be to use communication techniques to create the new habit (Wood & Neal, 2009), as the Connectionist Model foresees through repetitive advertising.

Another route to revitalize a brand, when the current target seems reluctant to absorb the repositioning, is through line extension (Blasberg & Vishwanath, 2003) and targeting younger consumers (Latif et al., 2016) This way, the repositioning works as a market development strategy in which the company tries to enter new markets with diversification of benefits, without changing the product (Ansoff, 1957; Craciun & Baubu, 2014; Hussain et al., 2014). Additionally, line extension can be a complement to assess the market of the new positioned benefits via product development. Through line extension, a company can create a wider and more appropriate offer to respond to the benefits that it is comunicating (Ansoff, 1957). To illustrate this with the case of Pedras, the brand took advantage of this situation, as it diversified the benefits of regular Pedras by entering the broader market of non-alcoholic refreshment beverages, and extended its offer for this market with Pedras Sabores, as flavored still water and other similar beverages gained acceptance from the market regarding the new attributes. Indeed, the results of the investigation showed that the strategy of line extension was able to capture the brand's intended repositioning even more successfully than the mother brand. As a brand its offer moves away from the classic icon to which the old positioning is so higly associated, the new products, although much influenced by their mother brand, will somewhow benefit from a distinct consumer purchasing behavior, as the hierarchy of effects show (Smith et al., 2008), since there is the need to create awareness around the new sub-brand and go through all the following stages. Therefore, via a communication strategy designed from the beginning to convey the intended positioning, it can more easily be absorbed than regarding the original brand, since there are less associations with the sub-brand on consumers' minds. Moreover, the association of line extension with the intended positioning will also benefit the mother brand positioning (Latif et al., 2016), which in the case of Pedras was achieved through the positive (although weak) correlation between the positioning of Pedras and Pedras Sabores and the more favorable positioning of Pedras (and higher acceptance of its benefits) by consumers of Pedras Sabores.

Digital communication was important in the whole process, from content marketing in social media, to paid advertising in search engines and social media (Balça & Casais, 2020; Balio & Casais, 2020).

Another insight is that the younger respondents had a greater perception of Pedras positioning. As stated before, revitalization can also be accomplished by targeting younger people, by taking advantage of the fact that these potential consumers were not impacted for so long by the previous positioning communication, and therefore the new attributes will not contrast as much with their current beliefs (O'Donnell & Brown, 2011). As with any positioning strategy, the brand's offer must be relevant to the target in order to work, and therefore there has to be a value proposition (which can be product features appreciated by the target or differentiated advertising) recognizable by the younger segment (Belch & Belch, 2003).

The purpose of this section is to aggregate the findings of this research to address this dissertation's problem. Therefore, conclusions will be presented on how consumer perception works regarding brand repositioning strategies through benefits diversification, and how companies can coordinate their efforts to minimize the gap between intended and perceived positioning. A repositioning strategy always means a challenge, because it involves a change of consumers' beliefs about a brand.

Therefore, companies have to find ways to work around consumers' perceptions. Trying to directly and drastically change perceived previous attributes will be less effective, as it goes against human nature.

Accordingly, brands can invest in a passive approach, in which they move away from the old positioning through Interference Competition. In this case, the key is the timing in which the brand aligns its repositioning strategy with the advertising of another brand that still intends to transmit the old positioning.

A more active approach can be line extension, target rejuvenation and communication techniques to make the repositioning more effective.

On one hand, line extension may not have the repositioning limitations of the original brand, as the novelty can enable the company to create a new sub-brand that takes advantage of being new to define the best positioning from the onset, which will consequently favorably impact the positioning of the mother brand. On the other hand, innovation can have a crucial role in developing a product that best fits consumers' expectations for the market that the brand wants to reposition. Targeting a younger segment can also be a means to introduce the new positioning, since this segment is attached to the old positioing and will more easily accept the new benefits.

On the advertising aspect, communication of the new attributes should be illustrative and informative to create as much as possible a context in which the consumption of the product will make sense, rather than just proclaiming the new benefits. Then, through trial and promotions, for example, it is critical that the consumer tries the product, and that after the satisfaction stage of the hierarchy of effect mode is created a new purchasing habit resulting from repetitive advertising.

The main contributions of this study are related with the implications of the nature of consumer perception in order to make repositioning strategies more efficient. Furthermore, there are also specific contributions on the role of benefit diversification in minimizing the gap between consumer perception of the new brand attributes and the brand's intended repositioning strategy.

The previous sections presented how the purpose of diversifying a brands' benefits should be incorporated in the repositioning efforts, as well as generic guidelines to effectively manage the challenge of changing the perception of consumers on brands' positioning. To accomplish that, and given the results from the case studied, some restrainers of repositioning efficiency were addressed to detect tension points those companies face and which block the acceptance of repositioning.

REFERENCES

Ansoff, H. I. (1957). Article. *Harvard Business Review*, *35*(5), 113–124.

Balça, J., & Casais, B. (2021). Return on Investment of Display Advertising: Google Ads vs. Facebook Ads. In E. Esiyok (Ed.), *Handbook of Research on New Media Applications in Public Relations and Advertising* (pp. 1–13). IGI Global. doi:10.4018/978-1-7998-3201-0.ch001

Balio, S., & Casais, B. (2020). A Content Marketing Framework to analyze Customer Engagement on Social Media. In S. Alavi & V. Ahuja (Eds.), *Managing Social Media Practices in the Digital Economy* (pp. 45–66). IGI Global. doi:10.4018/978-1-7998-2185-4.ch003

Belch, G. E., & Belch, M. A. (2003). *Advertising and Promotion. An Integrated Marketing Communication Perspective* (6th ed.). McGraw-Hill Companies.

Blankson, C., & Crawford, J. C. (2012). Impact of positioning strategies on service firm performance. *Journal of Business Research*, *65*(3), 311–316. doi:10.1016/j.jbusres.2011.03.013

Blasberg, J., & Vishwanath, V. (2003). Making Cool Brands Hot. *Harvard Business Review*, *81*(6), 20–22.

Craciun, L., & Baubu, C. M. (2014). The Brand as Strategic Asset of the Organization. *Review of International Comparative Management*, *15*(1), 69–77.

Edwing, M. T., Fowlds, D. A., & Shepherd, I. R. (1995). Renaissance: A case study in brand revitalization and strategic realignment. *Journal of Product and Brand Management*, *4*(3), 19–26. doi:10.1108/10610429510097618

Egede, E. A. (2013). Strategic Evaluation of How Advertising Works On Product Promotions. *Developing Country Studies*, *3*(10), 139–148.

Fuchs, C., & Diamantopoulos, A. (2010). Evaluating the effectiveness of brand-positioning strategies from a consumer perspective. *European Journal of Marketing*, *44*(11-12), 1763–1786. doi:10.1108/03090561011079873

Hussain, S., Khattak, J., Rizwan, A., & Latif, M. A. (2014). Interactive Effects of Ansoff Growt Strategies and Market Environment on Firm's Growth. *British Journal of Business and Management Research*, *1*(2), 68–78.

Jewell, R. D. (2007). Establishing Effective Repositioning Communications in a Competitive Marketplace. *Journal of Marketing Communications*, *13*(4), 231–241. doi:10.1080/13527260701193325

Kent, R. J., & Allen, C. T. (1994). Competitive Interference Effects in Consumer Memory for Advertising: The Role of Brand Familiarity. *Journal of Marketing*, *58*(3), 97–105. doi:10.1177/002224299405800307

Kostelijk, E., & Alsem, K. J. (2020). *Brand positioning: Connecting marketing strategy and communications*. Routledge. doi:10.4324/9780429285820

Latif, A., Sibghatullah, A., & Siddiqui, K. A. (2016). Repositioning Horlicks in Pakistan. *Journal of Marketing Management and Consumer Behavior*, *1*(2), 44–53.

O'Donnell, E., & Brown, S. (2011). The Effect Of Memory Structure And Function On Consumers' Perception And Recall Of Marketing Messages: A Review Of The Memory Research In Marketing. *Academy of Marketing Studies Journal*, *15*(1), 71–85.

Smith, R. E., MacKenzie, S. B., Yang, X., Buchholz, L. M., & Darley, W. K. (2007). Modeling the Determinants and Effects of Creativity in Advertising. *Marketing Science*, *26*(6), 819–833. doi:10.1287/mksc.1070.0272

Thomas, S., & Kohli, C. (2009). A brand is forever! A framework for revitalizing declining and dead brands. *Business Horizons*, *52*(4), 377–386. doi:10.1016/j.bushor.2009.03.004

Wang, R. D., & Shaver, J. M. (2013). Competition-driven Repositioning. *Strategic Management Journal*, *35*(11), 1585–1604. doi:10.1002mj.2167

Wijaya, B. S. (2012). The Development of Hierarchy of Effects Model in Advertising. *International Research Journal of Business Studies*, *5*(1), 73–85. doi:10.21632/irjbs.5.1.73-85

Wood, W., & Neal, D. T. (2009). The habitual consumer. *Journal of Consumer Psychology*, *19*(4), 579–592. doi:10.1016/j.jcps.2009.08.003

Wttenbraker, J., Gibbs, B. L., & Kahle, L. R. (1983). Seat Belt Attitudes, Habits, and Behaviors: An Adaptive Amendment to the Fishbein Model. *Journal of Applied Social Psychology*, *13*(5), 406–421. doi:10.1111/j.1559-1816.1983.tb01748.x

Zahid, S., & Raja, M. N. (2014). Effect of Rebranding and Repositioning On Brand Equity Considering Brand Loyalty as a Mediating Variable. *Journal of Business and Management*, *16*(1), 58–63.

Zhang, C., Lin, Y. H., & Newman, D. G. (2016). Investigating the Effectiveness of Repositioning Strategies: The Customers' Perspective. *Journal of Travel & Tourism Marketing*, *33*(9), 1235–1250. doi:10.1080/10548408.2015.1107018

Zinkhan, G. M. (1993). Creativity in advertising. *Journal of Advertising*, *22*(2), 1–3. doi:10.1080/00913367.1993.10673398

KEY TERMS AND DEFINITIONS

Consumer Perception: Consumers' brains make a connection between different concepts and information they have absorbed, creating a schema, and if the information from the outside is not remotely aligned with their current schema, it will be automatically rejected by the consumer (O'Donnell & Brown, 2011). This is a result of selective perception, where in the presence of several alternatives of products or services, the consumer will only focus on the perceived alternatives conveyed by the message being communicated, and thus to fit their needs and interests. Nonetheless, if this information is utterly in accordance with the schema, the lack of new information will not spark the consumer's consideration. Therefore, the conclusion to withdraw from this information is that the messages communicated should not be disruptive in comparison to the schema the consumer has already formulated, but they should have added value to create the necessary attention to be able to influence new behaviors (O'Donnell & Brown, 2011).

Positioning: Positioning is present in the initial definition of the marketing strategy, where there is a study of the market, the competitors' network and the consumer (Zhang et al., 2016). Equipped with this information, the company sets a plan to differentiate itself from others, delivering a promise to consumers by transmitting a specific image and benefits to the targeted segment of the population in order to have a distinctive value in comparison with the other alternatives of the market. Positioning is the definition of how the product or service should be seen in the eyes of the target consumer in order to achieve a different placement in relation to the competition, and thus create customer-focused value.

Repositioning: Repositioning is a marketing strategy in which there is a deliberated change of a brand's positioning and therefore on how the company wants to be perceived by the target, by delivering a new proposition (Zahid & Raja, 2014). This strategy takes place when there is an added benefit from changing the company's position (Wang & Shaver, 2013; Zhang et al., 2016), which can result from a new economic or competition reality (the entry of a new player, or an existing brand that positions itself closer to the company), the emergence of new opportunities (technological innovations, customer preferences, market regulations) or simply a consequence of the natural course of the product's lifecycle. Some authors state that repositioning is the best strategy for these situations and a source of competitive advantage, as it is a tool that allows the brand to differentiate itself from the competitors (Zahid & Raja, 2014).

Revitalization: Revitalization is implemented when there is the need to rejuvenate the brand, so it is contemporary and in accordance with the tendencies of demand (Edwing et al., 1995). Latif et al., (2016) point out that this need to rejuvenate from the narrow and strict idea that people have about a product to more diversified benefits can be accomplished by reinforcing its presence among a younger target via line extensions, which will eventually bring collateral benefits even to the brand's classic products. Revitalization can be a consequence not only of deficient acceptance of the full benefits of the product, but also of pure brand decline for being old-fashioned or struggling with equity problems (Thomas & Kohli, 2009). Therefore, revitalization is linked to the need to increase consumer loyalty through reinforcement of perceived quality and recognition. This approach is adopted in companies with a long past that see themselves trapped in a positioning centered on its heritage and classic icons. This need of change must be balanced with the risk of a company losing its previous customer base by positioning itself in a segment that is too young, and completely lose its roots and authenticity, two attributes that are always a point of differentiation from the competition.

APPENDIX 1

Questions and Answers

1. What is the overall problem presented in this case?

The problem presented consists in a brand repositioning challenge via the communication of the intensity of use of a product for different functionalities in order to expand the targeted market segments.

2. What are the factors affecting the problem(s) related to this case?

The problem is affected by the fact that the brand was previously associated to elderly people and used to represent a health-related functionality. With the repositioning, young people resist accepting the brand as a product for refreshment and connected to a cool lifestyle.

3. Discuss managerial and organizational issues related to this case.

When deciding a brand's positioning and segmented target, organizations need to understand that repositioning and market development is a difficult task because brand associations created by consumers hamper the process of repositioning.

4. Based on the results of this case, what are the main digital marketing strategies that might be implemented regarding the repositioning process?

Gamification strategies in mobile apps or videogames might be developed, as well as video marketing and merchandising spots for mobile selfies and social media interaction.

5. What other marketing strategies would you recommend to face the problem?

Communication techniques such as digital marketing, advertising, and merchandising must be conducted to help the repositioning process in order to overcome the mentioned brand associations. Also, sponsorship of events targeted to young people and providing associations with contemporary lifestyles is also advised.

Epilogue and Lessons Learned

This study shows several managerial challenges, particularly that:

- Repositioning is a difficult task, for besides brand's purpose and actions, brand attitude depends on consumer perceptions and the ability to communicate the brand's essence to consumers.
- Benefit extension is a core argument to promote intensity of use and diversification of target consumers.
- Market development implies the communication of benefits for different target audiences via different arguments, which can be a difficult task when each audience aspires to a personal lifestyle and specific tribe, thus colliding with brands used by other targets, particularly from different age groups.
- The development of different lines of products for different targets may foster the process of market development.

Chapter 5
Rose–Patisserie and Coffee House:
Business Development Alternatives

Paulo Botelho Pires
https://orcid.org/0000-0003-3786-6783
Porto Business School, Portugal

António Correia Barros
Instituto Politécnico do Porto, Portugal

EXECUTIVE SUMMARY

This case traces the life of a new endeavor, starting with a small patisserie and coffeehouse and the subsequent development of the business, considering three alternatives, namely optimizing the concept, expanding through a franchise network, and building a network of company-owned stores. The story of Rui and Joana raises a wide range of issues that managers need to address. After reading and working through the case, students will be able to evaluate the product portfolio, based on actual sales data, and to evaluate and propose strategic options using classical models.

ORGANIZATION BACKGROUND

On the return to their homeland in Porto, Portugal, following a six-year journey around the world, Rui and Joana decided to open a gourmet-style patisserie and coffeehouse, certainly a reminiscence of their past and of the atmospheres they had experienced. Therefore, they decided to use all their knowledge, skills, and professional experiences, as well as an understanding of the habits and behaviours of the local market, to create this new gourmet-style patisserie and coffeehouse concept in Porto.

While Porto has many coffeehouses and patisseries, few have the combination of service quality, products, and the atmosphere they could recall from their travels. While tasting a coffee with raspberry-hibiscus fragrance and preparing for the lunchtime rush, Rui and Joana reflected on the changes the business had gone through since they first envisioned their distinctive hand-made cakes and superior

DOI: 10.4018/978-1-7998-1630-0.ch005

coffee business concept. Not even in their most enthusiastic scenarios did they imagine that it would evolve into an extremely popular shop, providing daily indulgences to their customers.

They started with a single patisserie and coffeehouse and, from the beginning, they felt that they could grow into something really big. Their dream was to expand the store, replicating the concept in multiple locations. The business progressively grew, and revenue and operating profits reached a reasonable level. Driven by the success of the first patisserie and coffeehouse in one of the most important touristic destinations in Portugal, they realized that the potential for this concept was either national or international. Given such success, they face tough decisions ahead. What should be the way forward? Should it be to consolidate and optimize the business as it was? Should it be to expand through the opening of new stores putting more capital at risk? Or would it be advisable to expand using franchisees? Rui and Joana could stay with one patisserie and coffeehouse or they could develop their business furthermore. For that purpose, there were three alternatives: 1) they could expand by opening additional stores by themselves; 2) they could sell franchises of their patisserie and coffeehouse concept; 3) they could optimize the business by improving the concept, making it more appealing, more efficient, and eliminating existing gaps.

Expanding organically by opening self-owned stores was costly, laborious, and hard to manage. They would also have to acquire resources, skills, knowledge and hire staff. An additional obstacle related to this alternative was the need to put more of their capital at risk, which they did not want to. On the other hand, it would be difficult to keep the business running smoothly and simultaneously have the time to travel to various locations around the country or abroad. Expanding through franchising was enticing. However, they only had one patisserie and coffeehouse location, business was somewhat immature and franchising management was unfamiliar to them. Rui and Joana faced the facts, and they had to be pragmatic: Franchising was one of some possible models for business development and was usually used all over the world. There is a reasonable number of factors supporting the benefit from adopting a franchising strategy instead of a growth through organic expansion strategy, namely lower capital investment, less painful consequences in the event of failure, lower risk of failure, and faster development. The main disadvantages stem from a decrease in control, the possibility of franchisees changing the original concept with the consequent negative impact on the brand and the need to have a distinctive and proved concept. But above everything else, they realized that their concept could be refined.

SETTING THE STAGE

Rose - Patisserie and Coffee House is a patisserie and coffee shop located in Porto downtown. The store has an exquisite decoration and a stylish image. The company covers two distinct economic activities. The first one is framed in NACE 5630 (beverage serving activities), while the second one is similar to the activities framed in NACE 562 (event catering and other food service activities). These two segments show idiosyncrasies, despite sharing company's resources. While the first segment is constituted by end consumers, in the second segment the customers are companies. It is also relevant to say that consumption can occur inside the store or, alternatively, customers can order the products by phone, to take-away. For these reasons, they will be subject to individual analysis.

Rose-Patisserie and Coffee House

CASE DESCRIPTION

Sales analysis

The company started its activity in October 2016. The sales figures from that date until August 2018, are shown in the table below.

Table 1. Sales by year

2016	2017	2018 (until August)	Total
€31,315	€285,794	€152,853	€469,962

The Table 1 shows that sales grew consistently for the period under review. Note that the figures for the years 2016 and 2018 are not for the whole year. Looking at the sales figures it is noticeable that the company shows a continuous growth in the period under evaluation, starting with more than 31 thousand euros in 2016, rising to 285 thousand euros in 2017. As for 2018, if in the last months the growth is 21%, it could reach 300 thousand euros. However, if the growth is lower and, in a less likely scenario, maintains the average monthly growth of 8% that has been achieved from January to August 2018, sales will reach 262 thousand euros. It should be noted that this scenario is unlikely, given the pattern shown in the last months of 2017. The Table 2 exhibits the sales data broken down by end customers and companies.

Table 2. Sales data broken down by end customers and companies

	2016	2017	2018 (until August)	Total
Companies	€1,258	€25,758	€15,174	€42,188
End customers	€30,058	€260,036	€137,678	€427,772
Total	**€31,315**	**€285,794**	**€152,852**	**€469,962**

Business customers only account for approximately 10% of total sales in 2017 and in 2018. However, breaking down the sales records into those that are ascribable to take-way and those that are not, we get a new perspective.

Table 3. Evolution of sales broken down by type consumption

	2016	2017	2018 (until August)	Total
Take-way	€11,501	€139,559	€81,882	€232,942
	37%	49%	54%	
On-site	€19,814	€146,236	€70,970	€237,019
	63%	51%	46%	
Total	€31,315	€285,794	€152,852	€469,962

Take-way sales have evolved positively from 2016 to 2018, starting at just over 11 thousand euros to over 81 thousand euros by August 2018. Moreover, it should be noted that the percentage of these sales in the company's overall sales rose from 37% in 2016 to 54% in August 2018, in 2017 reaching a near-balance, with take-way sales representing 49% of total sales (See Table 3). The monthly sales for the period under review are presented below (Table 4).

Table 4. Sale monthly evolution

	Jan	Feb	Mar	Apr	May	Jun	Jul	Aug	Sep	Oct	Nov	Dec
2016										€6,929	€10,28	€14,101
2017	€8,640	€12,997	€14,110	€14,183	€15,041	€14,782	€31,246	€29,600	€36,941	€35,204	€27,636	€45,415
2018	€13,627	€17,556	€20,082	€17,608	€21,636	€20,842	€19,114	€22,388				
2018(P)									€27,128	€32,873	€39,832	€48,265

A forecast was made for the remaining months of 2018 – September to December – considering an average monthly growth of 21%. This value was assumed because it equals the average monthly growth in the year 2017. It should be noted, however, that the average monthly growth in 2018 has been 8%, which is significantly lower than in 2017. However, the last months of the year are typically those with the highest sales figures, and for that reason, the assumption of a 21% growth seems reasonable. The data can be visualized in a monthly time series to explain the above mentioned and is illustrated in the graph below (Figure 1).

Figure 1. Monthly sales evolution

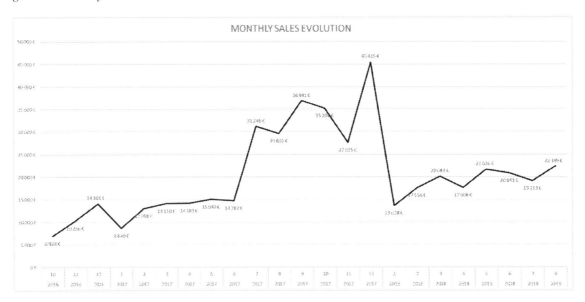

Rose-Patisserie and Coffee House

The sales pattern shows that the last months of the year are the strongest, enabling the company to maintain the desirable growth. Despite the favorable outlook, a negative pattern stands out and should be reflected upon. In 2017, sales began to grow significantly in July and remained at this level until the end of the year, however they fall in January 2018 to June 2017 levels. In 2018 this accelerated growth has not yet occurred. In 2018 a sustainable, more moderate growth has been observed. The graph below (Figure 2) displays the figures of aggregate sales per week.

Figure 2. Weekly sales evolution

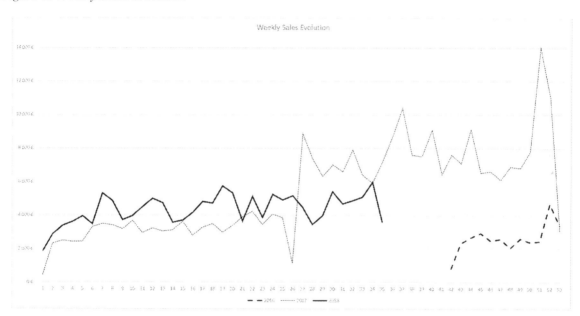

The graph corroborates the above statements and provides additional information about the sales pattern throughout the year. Three highlights stand out. The first highlight is about Christmas time, which for both 2016 and 2017 are, by far, when sales reach the highest levels. The second highlight is that, both in 2016 and in 2018, the weekly evolution of sales shows some stability, obviously removing the peaks mentioned above and other usual fluctuations. The third highlight is about the evolution of sales in 2017. In that year, sales were stable until week 25, falling abruptly in week 26, to skyrocket in week 27 and remain stable until the end of the year. Since it is impossible to compare the three years due to the absence of complete record sales for the years 2016 and 2018, one will have to wait to conclude whether the pattern of 2017 will continue into 2018 or whether it was an atypical year. The year 2018 may exhibit a major growth, a stagnation, or a residual growth.

Next, we examine sales per day of the week. Two warnings must be made before the presentation of the results. Firstly, if the company operates in two distinct segments, end consumers and companies, it is important to present and analyse the data for each segment. Alternatively, one can divide the sales records into two groups: The first group including all take-away sales records, and the other group including all the other sales records. Secondly, the estimation method for the remaining 2018 months is as follows. A new column was created, termed 2018*2, showing the 2018 data multiplied by two, which intends to be a forecast for the last 4 months of 2018. Sales figures for the months of September through December

2018 were multiplied by two, considering that in 2017 this same period represented 51% of the total sales. Thus, it is being assumed that the sales from September to December represent half of the sales for the entire year. One should note that this new form of forecast calculation will have an intermediate value between those presented above (it should be noted that whenever the term 2018*2 appears, it will be calculated according to the formula described above).

The results of this analysis were:

1. No pattern was found as for the evolution of sales by day of the week, for the three years in sales to business customers, while for the end consumers a pattern has been identified.
2. Regarding end consumers, there is an increase in sales from the beginning of the week, Monday, to the end of the week, Sunday, with emphasis on Saturday, which is always the day with the highest sales volume. Saturday accounted for almost 25% of weekly sales in 2017 and 2018.
3. As for on-site sales, there is a growth in sales from Monday to Sunday, reaching a peak on Saturday, while on Sunday there is a slight decrease, equaling Friday's sales.
4. As for take-way sales, the pattern identified above (3.) is also valid for these customers.

The same study was carried out for the evolution of sales by day of the month. No sales pattern was identified for any of the segments. The popular belief suggesting that consumers are more prone to spend after receiving their salaries does not hold. After the temporal analysis of sales, the next step is to analyze sales by product line. The data, including the column forecast 2018*2, are shown in Table 5.

Table 5. Sales by product family

	2016	2017	2018	2018*2
Drinks	€1,201	€9,029	€4,458	€8,917
	4%	3%	3%	3%
Cakes	€8,354	€60,550	€33,587	€67,174
	27%	21%	22%	22%
Coffee	€4,438	€29,525	€15,018	€30,036
	14%	10%	10%	10%
Cupcake	€7,940	€58,315	€24,175	€48,349
	25%	20%	16%	16%
Gelato	€368	€8,688	€4,856	€9,714
	1%	3%	3%	3%
Breakfast	€740	€5,526	€3,179	€6,358
	2%	2%	2%	2%
Take-way	€8,273	€114,161	€67,579	€135,158
	26%	40%	44%	44%
TOTAL	€31,315	€285,793	€152,852	€305,706

Rose-Patisserie and Coffee House

The table shows that the Take-way line has been growing since 2016, being the one with the highest sales volume, rising from 26% of total sales in 2016 to 40% in 2017 and standing for 44% in 2018.

The two other important product lines are Cakes and Cupcakes which show opposite trends compared to the Take-way line. The Cakes product line accounted for 27% of total sales in 2016, 21% in 2017 and 22% in 2018. The Cupcake line represented 25% in 2016, but evolved negatively in the following years, decreasing to 20% in 2017 and to 16% in 2018. The following chart (Figure 3) depicts this situation.

Figure 3. Sales by product family

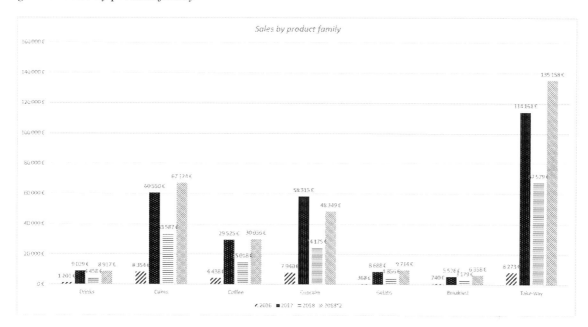

The next step is to rank product sales for the period under review, considering the data split by year and limited to the 20 products with the highest sales volume, as shown in Table 6.
The main conclusions to be drawn from the table are:

1. The first three positions – Cake 2 Levels, Cake 16, and Cake 18 – are products from the Take-way line and they will have a growth close to 40% from 2017 to 2018.
2. The product Sweet Cupcake, from the Cupcake line, ranks fourth and is expected to have a sales decrease close to 20% between 2017 and 2018.
3. The product Cake Slice, from the Cakes line, ranks fifth and is expected to have a 4% decrease in sales between 2017 and 2018.
4. The three previous points prove what had been stated concerning the sales by product line, the Take-way line leading and showing a growth trend, while the others showed a decreasing trend in importance within the company's portfolio.
5. Another product worth mentioning is CoffeeR that ranks sixth. It is anticipated a negative growth of approximately 6%, between 2017 and 2018.

6. Other products exhibiting very significant growths are Cake - Event (121%), Mini Cake (102%), and Tart slice (283%).
7. For the top 20 products with the highest sales volume, 11 will witness sales increase, while 9 will decrease.

Table 6. Top 20 products by sales volume

Rank	Products	2016	2017	2018	2018*2
1	Cake 2 Levels	€751	€18,389	€12,794	€25,589
2	Cake 16	€882	€15,715	€11,520	€23,041
3	Cake 18	€1,093	€13,831	€9,762	€19,525
4	Sweet Cupcake	€3,239	€19,406	€7,742	€15,485
5	Cake Slice	€1,978	€15,796	€7,591	€15,182
6	CoffeeR	€2,408	€15,736	€7,394	€14,788
7	Cake 14	€0	€8,693	€6,295	€12,590
8	Cake 20	€689	€10,877	€5,730	€11,461
9	6 Sweet	€1,188	€8,984	€5,617	€11,233
10	Cake 3 Levels	€0	€11,224	€4,871	€9,743
11	Cheesecake Slice	€1,154	€9,938	€4,660	€9,319
12	Mini Pavlova	€1,148	€9,260	€3,851	€7,702
13	Cake - Event	€0	€3,318	€3,667	€7,334
14	Macaron	€0	€4,048	€3,160	€6,319
15	Cake	€756	€5,041	€2,994	€5,989
16	Cake 22	€310	€5,114	€2,557	€5,113
17	Mini Cake	€37	€2,454	€2,477	€4,954
18	Tart slice	€17	€1,224	€2,344	€4,687
19	Brownie slice	€511	€4,610	€2,302	€4,604
20	Small Glass	€182	€5,140	€2,104	€4,207

The Table 7 ranks products by sales volume, keeping the same criteria.
The main conclusions to be drawn from the table are:

1. The best-selling product, CoffeeR, belongs to the Coffee line and the quantity sold more than doubles the sales of the product that ranks second. This product is expected to have a 9% decrease from 2017 to 2018.
2. The second best-selling product, Sweet Cupcake, belongs to the Cupcake line and is expected to also have a decrease in sales from 2017 to 2018, around 21%.
3. The Cake Slice product belongs to the Cakes line and ranks third and a drop of 4% from 2017 to 2018 is expected.
4. The Macaron product belongs to the Cupcake line, ranks fourth in sales volume and forecasts point to a 61% growth for the period from 2017 to 2018 (the product did not exist in 2016).

Rose-Patisserie and Coffee House

5. In the 5th position is the Cheesecake Slice, belonging to the Cakes line and, according to forecasts, will experience a drop in volume sales of 6%.
6. For the first 20 products with the highest volume sales, 11 will witness a sales increase, while for the other 9 a decrease is expected.

Table 7. Top 20 products by quantity sold

Rank	Products	2016	2017	2018	2018*2
1	CoffeeR	3,089	20,188	9,157	18,314
2	Sweet Cupcake	1,707	10,149	4,031	8,062
3	Cake Slice	847	6767	3,253	6,506
4	Macaron	0	2,654	2,142	4,284
5	Cheesecake Slice	496	4,250	2,002	4,004
6	Take-way	0	472	1,535	3,070
7	Cakepop	348	2,916	1,363	2,726
8	Mini Pavlova	399	3,222	1,346	2,692
9	Cappuccino	287	2,220	1,280	2,560
10	Tart slice	7	527	1,008	2,016
11	Brownie slice	219	1,973	988	1,976
12	Muffin	12	1,476	961	1,922
13	Mini Cake	14	930	938	1,876
14	Tea	309	1,602	806	1,612
15	Small Glass	69	1,951	798	1,596
16	Mini Cupcake	231	1,839	704	1,408
17	6 Sweet	124	934	584	1,168
18	Water 50cl	71	1,436	569	1,138
19	Decoffee	147	950	562	1,124
20	Glass of lemonade	0	697	560	1,120

A significant percentage of sales is in-store which entails physical limitations of space and service capacity, it is relevant to assess the flow of customers per hour, to uncover probable peaks, and to foresee potential bottlenecks that prevent increased sales. For this purpose, an analysis of sales broken down by year and by hour is carried out (Table 8). Given that the visitors of the store will be mainly end consumers, the analysis was focused on them.

The data in the table clearly show a sales growth trend between the first opening hour and the closing time. This pattern holds for all years. Also noteworthy:

- Sales grow until 11 am or noon, fall at 1 pm and thereafter they grow continuously until 6 pm.
- At 18 o'clock sales reach a peak, and then they start to decrease at 19 o'clock, witnessing a sharp drop at 20 o'clock.

Table 8. Hourly sales to end customers

Time	2016	2017	2018	2018*2
07:00	€0	€827	€1,093	€2,186
08:00	€80	€4,289	€800	€1,601
09:00	€672	€8,060	€2,976	€5,952
10:00	€1,634	€11,370	€7,614	€15,228
11:00	€2,146	€17,324	€12,359	€24,716
12:00	€2,179	€17,508	€10,621	€21,244
13:00	€1,621	€15,010	€7,226	€14,453
14:00	€2,412	€19,219	€9,494	€18,988
15:00	€3,556	€24,422	€12,714	€25,428
16:00	€4,042	€31,940	€15,569	€31,136
17:00	€5,045	€37,139	€19,574	€39,149
18:00	€3,780	€40,896	€21,382	€42,762
19:00	€2,471	€28,417	€14,244	€28,489
20:00	€420	€3,607	€2,033	€4,066

Figure 4. Hourly sales to end customers

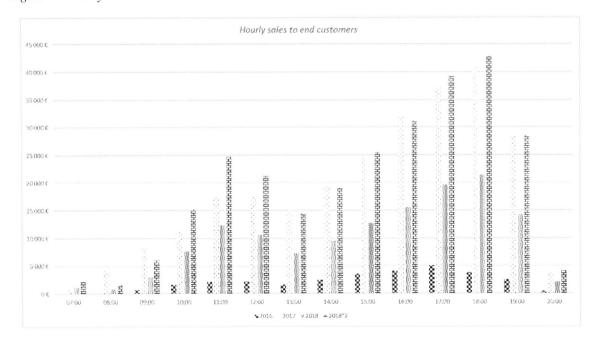

The same analysis was performed without the inclusion of the Take-way line revealing a new situation, showing that sales daily peak happens at 5 pm. The pattern is the same as described above: sales increase throughout the day, growing until 11 am, with a decrease between 12 and 1 pm, increasing again until 5 pm. From that time on the decrease is exponential. The same procedures were carried out for sales with records that have sales with the Take-way family and the results obtained are similar to those presented previously (see Figure 4).

It was also carried out an analysis of product sales per hour and which combination of products produce more sales per hour. Several products stand out exhibiting recurring sales at all hours of the day:

1. CoffeeR.
2. Sweet Cupcake.
3. Cake slice.
4. Cheesecake slice.

There are some differences in morning and afternoon consumption, implying some variation in the type of products preferred. Therefore, the results are as follows:

- Macaron´s sales are in the top five in the morning, while in the afternoon sales are less relevant.
- Cappuccino's sales are in the top five in the afternoon, while in the morning sales are less relevant.

However, CoffeeR has much more sales than the other products, in volume, and this difference is very significant. The following information about the consumption of CoffeeR is also relevant.

- More than 41,000 invoices were issued, and CoffeeR was present in more than 18,000 invoices (more than 43%);
- CoffeeR was consumed simultaneously: with Sweet Cupcake 2,330 times; with Cake Slice 2,390 times; with Cheesecake Slice 1,540 times.
- The following product combinations occurred: CoffeeR + Sweet Cupcake + Cake Slice over 330 consumptions; CoffeeR + Sweet Cupcake + Cheesecake Slice about 250 consumptions; CoffeeR + Cake Slice + Cheesecake Slice about 310 consumptions; CoffeeR + Sweet Cupcake + Cake Slice + Cheesecake Slice about 40 consumptions.

Additional information about the most consumed products is as follows:

- The Sweet Cupcake is present in approximately 7,400 invoices.
- The Cake Slice is present in approximately 6,600 invoices.
- The Cheesecake Slice is present in approximately 4,200 invoices.

Customer analysis

To assess the degree of loyalty of business customers, an analysis was carried out to identify the number of customers with repeated purchases. The Table 9 shows the number of customers with invoices issued in the period under review (in 2017, 34% of new business customers were accounted for between September and December, and this percentage is being used to gauge the potential of new business customers for 2018).

Table 9. Number of business customers

	2016	2017	2018	2018+34%
Number of customers	25	96	99	129

The data shows a sharp growth between 2016 and 2017, and a near-stagnation until August 2018. Using that percentage to extrapolate for the rest of 2018, one can say that growth could continue.

The Table 10 presents data on customers' loyalty in this segment.

Table 10. Number of loyal customers

	2016 and 2017	2016 and 2018	2017 and 2018	2016 and 2018	Total of customers
Number of loyal customers	14	10	39	9	166
Loyalty rate	15%	10%	39%	9%	

The data shows a very healthy reality, since the loyalty rate has shown a strong growth from 2016 to 2018, evolving from 15% to 39%. This shows that customers are loyal and want to maintain their business relationship with the company. The 10% figure indicates the percentage of customers who bought in 2016, did not buy in 2017 and bought again in 2018. Also important is the loyalty rate for the three years in a row, which is 9%.

As for business customers, it is also possible to assess the annual purchase frequency, i.e., how many times they have purchased per year. The data to evaluate this metric is presented in the Table 11.

Table 11. Purchase frequency for business customers

Years	\multicolumn{9}{c}{Number of times they bought per year}
	1 time	2 times	3 times	4 times	5 times	6 times	7 times	8 times	10 times
2016	19	4	2						
	76%	16%	8%						
2017	64	11	6	3	4	2	5		1
	67%	11%	6%	3%	4%	2%	5%		1%
2018	62	18	6	5	4	1	1	2	
	63%	18%	6%	5%	4%	1%	1%	2%	

Most business customers buy once, twice, or three times a year. Most customers buy once a year, followed by customers who buy twice a year, and then customers who buy three times a year. Higher frequencies are not significant. It is also important to note that the percentage of customers who buy only once a year has decreased, as opposed to customers who buy twice a year, which has increased.

CURRENT CHALLENGES FACING THE ORGANIZATION

Market segments

The owners of Rose - Patisserie and Coffee House need to define a business development strategy. Even though it is a new company, it already has proven to be a successful concept. Nevertheless, the gourmet-style patisserie and coffeehouse concept requires some improvement. Besides, Rui and Joana also want to assess what is the most suitable expansion alternative: Expansion through a network of company-owned stores or expansion through a franchisee network. Firstly, it is essential to define the market segments and the company's target market. Patisseries and coffeehouses differ from coffee shops because they are charming stores, where the attention to detail is vital, where the sophistication of the environment, decoration, equipment, tableware, and accessories must provide moments of leisure and rituals that remain in the consumers' minds. Individual consumers are the company's target market of this segment, those who come to the store (in most situations) to enjoy these moments. The availability of other services, such as ordering cakes or something similar, should be evaluated and their inclusion will depend solely on the concept that the company wants to create and communicate to the market. However, the data do not lie, and take-way sales are very important to the company's total revenues and therefore cannot be neglected. The supply of products for catering or similar events has some importance for the company. This segment differs from the previous one, even by its very definition – it comprises the activities of preparing meals or cooked dishes delivered and/or served at the place determined by the customer for a specific event – immediately implying that the facilities do not have the same requirements. The customers are companies, namely farms, resorts, hotels, restaurants, event organizers, or any type of company wanting to hold events in-house, but also final consumers who want to perform an event, party or activity that requires the supply of meals. Rose - Patisserie and Coffee House is focused solely on providing sweets, cakes, desserts, and related products.

Competitor Analysis – Pastry and Tea Houses

The competitive analysis is based on a database with information about companies operating in Portugal, by geographical location and providing some financial indicators. In 2017, Portugal had 10,972 companies under NACE 5630, located mainly in large urban centers. Almost all the companies (10,907) had operating results of up to €1,958,748; 7,462 companies had operating results up to €130 583; 1,982 companies had operating results from €130 583 up to €261 166. This means that 86.6% of the companies have operating results of up to €261,000 and that the segments with the highest value have the largest number of companies, and consequently are the most competitive. The analysis was restricted to companies that are registered as pastry, tea house or coffee shop and the market was divided into 10 initial segments, according to their operating revenues (Table 12).

Table 12. Segmentation for pastry and Tea Houses

Segments	Operating Revenue	Companies	Perc.	Segment value	Perc.
Segment 1	€0 - €254,181	815	76,70%	€80,404,298	39%
Segment 2	€254,180 - €508,361	169	15,90%	€57,675,230	28%
Segment 3	€508,361 - €762,542	41	3,90%	€25,120,823	12%
Segment 4	€762,542 - €1,016,723	15	1,40%	€12,651,251	6%
Segment 5	€1,016,723 - €1,270,904	10	0,90%	€11,185,062	5%
Segment 6	€1,270,904 - €1,525,084	5	0,50%	€7,039,880	3%
Segment 7	€1,525,084 - €1,779,265	2	0,20%	€3,230,032	2%
Segment 8	€1,779,265 - €2,033,446	3	0,30%	€5,549,757	3%
Segment 9	€2,033,446 - €2,287,627	0	0,00%	-	0%
Segment 10	€2,287,627 - €2,541,808	2	0,20%	€5,055,861	2%
		1062	100%	€207,912,194	100%

Table 13. Number of companies by region for pastry and tea shops

District	1	2	3	4	5	6	7	8	10	Total
Angra Her.	1									1
Aveiro	55	12	2		1					70
Braga	82	14	1	1	1	1		1		101
Bragança	7									7
Cast. Branc.	8	1								9
Coimbra	17	7	2		2	2				30
Évora	8	1								9
Faro	28	7	1	2						38
Funchal	3	2	1		1					7
Guarda	8									8
Horta		1								1
Leiria	34	10			1		1			46
Lisboa	352	67	21	6	4	1	1		2	454
P. Delgada	1			1						2
Portalegre	12	1								13
Porto	56	16	5	1						78
Santarém	31	4	1			1				37
Setúbal	67	12	4	3						86
V. Castelo	22	7	2	1				1		33
Vila Real	7	1	1							9
Viseu	16	6						1		23
Total	815	169	41	15	10	5	2	3	2	1062

Rose-Patisserie and Coffee House

Table 14. Value of segments by region for pastry and tea shops

District	1	2	3	4	5	6	7	Total
Angra Her.	€57,513							**€57,513**
Aveiro	€6,058,008	€4,388,193	€1,296,895		€1,046,765			**€12,789,861**
Braga	€7,816,517	€4,411,596	€652,526	€896,836	€1,232,156	€1,516,998		**€18,472,646**
Bragança	€848,091							**€848,091**
Cast. Branc.	€692,566	€291,078						**€983,645**
Coimbra	€1,857,801	€2,702,439	€1,090,830		€2,211,037	€2,853,756		**€10,715,864**
Évora	€772,956	€261,037						**€1,033,994**
Faro	€2,358,870	€2,370,711	€516,206	€1,722,935				**€6,968,721**
Funchal	€263,248	€643,832	€657,353		€1,075,216			**€2,639,650**
Guarda	€1,026,851							**€1,026,851**
Horta		€435,724						**€435,724**
Leiria	€3,745,689	€3,199,660			€1,173,221		€1,635,928	**€9,754,498**
Lisboa	€34,269,882	€22,446,496	€13,091,631	€5,004,363	€4,446,667	€1,340,085	€1,594,103	**€87,249,089**
P. Delgada	€63,787			€764,599				**€828,386**
Portalegre	€1,368,502	€393,044						**€1,761,546**
Porto	€5,697,030	€5,642,338	€3,027,556	€775,475				**€15,142,399**
Santarém	€2,714,025	€1,438,896	€567,517			€1,329,040		**€6,049,478**
Setúbal	€5,712,342	€4,067,886	€2,405,913	€2,655,694				**€14,841,835**
V. Castelo	€2,254,091	€2,345,217	€1,251,078	€831,348				**€8,476,601**
Vila Real	€1,158,925	€258,936	€563,318					**€1,981,179**
Viseu	€1,667,605	€2,378,146					-	**€5,854,624**
	€80,404,298	**€57,675,230**	**€25,120,823**	**€12,651,251**	**€11,185,062**	**€7,039,880**	**€3,230,032**	**€207,912,194**

The Table 13 reveals that Rose - Patisserie and Coffee House is in segment 1, which is the one with the highest market value with more than 80 million euros (39% of the total market), but simultaneously it is the one with the toughest competition with 815 companies, representing almost 77% of all companies. The next step evaluates the market in the different regions, broken down by the segments built above.

The data in the table above prove what was previously stated, showing a high number of companies in segments 1 and 2, strongly concentrated in the regions of Lisbon, Braga, Setúbal, and Porto. The market, by regions and broken down by segments, will now be evaluated according to the operating revenues indicator (Table 14).

The conclusions, for segments 1 and 2, reveal that the most important regions are: Lisbon, Braga, Aveiro, Porto, and Setúbal. The same analysis is accomplished for competitors that fall under NACE 56210 - provision of meals for events. There are currently 277 companies operating in Portugal under this NACE and the results are similar to the previous ones, i.e., Lisbon, Braga, Aveiro, Porto, and Setúbal clearly stand out.

Competitors Analysis – Trends and Strategies

It is also essential to evaluate the current competitors, by checking their strategies and market trends. The competitors that were evaluated are: Paul, Spirito Cupcakes, Docealto, The Sugar Bakery, Primrose Bakery, Billys Nakery NYC, Magnolia Bakery, Heavenly Desserts, Jeronymo Coffee Shops, Arcadia and Wicked Good Cupcakes, Confectionery and e Pastry Shop Pérola, Pastry Shop Montalegrense, Barca Doce Pastry Shop e Tea Room and Cheese Cake Pastry Shop. It should be noted that some of these are direct competitors, others are non-direct competitors, and some are potential future competitors. The criteria used to evaluate competitors are: 1) store location; 2) how it presents to the marketplace; 3) services portfolio; 4) target segments; 5) positioning; 6) branding; 7) style of communication; 8) product portfolio; 9) distribution; 10) price; 11) type of competitor; 12) strategy; 13) others. It can be concluded that:

- Direct competitors have an offer equal or very similar to Rose - Patisserie and Coffee House, because the concept is similar.
- Direct competitors' main products are:
  - Cakes and cupcakes; custom-made cakes; cakes and pastries for events.

In comparison with direct competitors, Rose - Patisserie and Coffee House's products such as coffee, tea, ice cream and biscuits and cookies do not have its own brand, the Rose brand. Moreover, Rose - Patisserie and Coffee House don't have specific products (conceived and designed) for companies, so called corporate gifts (e.g., party packages for companies) and products with packaging specifically for online purchase and delivery anywhere, safely (note that only one company bases its offer on this concept).

In comparison with direct competitors, Rose - Patisserie and Coffee House's offer does not include services such as training and workshops (courses on how to make cakes), party days or birthdays for children and corporate training (courses on how to make cakes for the employees).

For non-direct competitors, although the business concept is different, the most salient difference in the offer is the absence of light meals for lunch.

As for price, the competitive analysis has shown that Rose - Patisserie and Coffee House's prices are similar to its competitors.

Direct competitors with similar size have the following distribution alternatives:

- Company-owned stores (when the number of stores is small).
- Franchised stores (it is the choice of most competitors when they have a larger number of stores or intend to grow rapidly).
- Online sales.
- Food trucks.

Non-direct competitors, particularly those offering snacks, have a distribution that follows the following pattern:

- Portuguese competitors possess a network of company-owned stores.
- International market competitors use a franchising system.
  - Franchisers show a certain propensity to use private label products, be it coffees, teas, or other beverages. Other companies more often use manufacturers' brands.

Rose-Patisserie and Coffee House

Consumer Behavior Analysis

Studying and describing the consumers' buying process is always a multidimensional sequence, requiring the identification and characterization of the consumers within the target segments. In the case of Rose - Patisserie and Coffee House the following segments were identified:

1. Events for companies.
2. Events for end consumers.
3. Consumers in the store.

The first segment comprises companies that want a cake service for events, which may be recurring. In fact, companies usually have several annual events that require celebration. Products can be customized and adapted to the company's needs, from a simple cake to a more complex snack, requiring transportation, delivery, and additional services.

The second segment includes end consumers who buy cakes for celebrations, events, parties, and other circumstances, going to the store to make the payment and pick up the order, which might have been placed previously in-store, by phone, or online. In this segment, the purchase may also be recurrent, such as birthdays, Christmas parties, or otherwise occur only once, in the case of singular celebrations, such as weddings, baptisms, or similar.

The third segment includes all the consumers who go to a store to consume the products on site, either sitting at a table or at the counter, or taking them to consume elsewhere. These consumers only purchase and consume what is displayed or available at the store.

The comparison of consumers' behavior, for the three segments is portrayed in Table 15.

It should be noted that the consumer's decision-making process, i.e., how he/she chooses where to eat, necessarily depends on the offer. It should also be noted that consumers patronize traditional pastry shops, confectionery, and bakeries based on criteria that differ significantly from businesses that combine the supply of sweets and simultaneously have light meals. In the former, the predominant criteria are mainly associated with pleasure and emotions resulting from tasting sweets, while in the latter there are also criteria associated with pleasure and emotions from tasting food, not necessarily sweets. However, other more rational criteria may be used, such as the concern with a careful and balanced diet, or even more basic criteria such as the need to eat and financial criteria. This influences the decision of how the consumer selects a store and the timing of the decision, and can be summarized as follows:

1. In the morning, whether for breakfast, a morning break, or just for a coffee, the consumer can choose traditional pastry shops or bakeries that offer light meals. The determining criterion and the focus will be on the flavor of the pastries, bread, or similar.
2. At lunchtime, the consumer prefers a place that serves meals. If desserts are not gratifying, then he/she may look for a place for dessert and coffee. However, it is unlikely that the choice of a meal will be contingent on the choice of dessert.
3. Afternoon and morning patterns are similar, with more emphasis put on the time and pleasure consumers get from the taste of sweets.

Table 15. The purchasing process for the three segments

Stage	Segment 1	Segment 2	Segment 3
Consideration	Referrals from others Online Directories	Referrals from others Online Store location	Store location Physical evidence of the store (decoration, atmosphere, colors, layout, storefront, etc.)
Evaluation	Website Reviews and comments	Website Reviews and comments In-shop tasting	Physical evidence of the store (decoration, atmosphere, colors, layout, window display, etc.) and the employees
Purchase	Online Store (small business)	Store Online (major cities)	Store
Experience	The product is fundamental, but the dishes, cutlery, glasses, and napkins have a non-negligible impact (it may be controllable)	(not controllable)	The product is fundamental, but the tableware, cutlery, glasses, and napkins have a non-negligible impact (it is controllable in the store)
Advocate	Word of mouth	Word of mouth Online comments and reviews	Word of mouth Impact on other customers in the store
Bond	Preparation of the party, knowing the client and his needs beforehand Follow-up of the party	Offer something related to the celebration	Service, empathy, and professionalism are fundamental to create the relationship

Source: Edelman & Singer, 2015

Environmental conditions and context – PESTEL

The PESTEL analysis (Cadle et al., 2014; Johnson et al., 2008; Johnson et al., 2017; Lambin & Moerloose, 2012; Rothaermel, 2017) aims to identify, briefly, the macro-environmental factors (Political, Economic, Social, Technological, Environmental and Legal), that have the capacity to impact the operational and strategic activities of the organization.

- Political: it is easy to anticipate that political initiatives associated with the use of sugars will occur, such as: 1) Surcharge on products incorporating sugars; discouragement of the consumption of products containing sugars. Diabetes together with obesity already are serious health problems in Portugal and in the world.
- Economic: economic factors are not expected to have a strong influence on this market.
- Social: there is an increasing awareness and strong social pressure to reduce sugars in food. This has already happened with salt and will probably also happen with sugar. On the other hand, there is a growing trend to consume organic products, gluten-free, lactose-free, and unprocessed foods.
- Technological: technological factors are not expected to have a strong impact on the market.
- Environmental: environmental factors will most likely have no impact on the business.
- Legal: no significant legal changes are conjecturally likely to influence the market.

The PESTEL analysis did not identify factors that may cause significant disturbances in the business. Although there are some initiatives that promote a decrease in sugar consumption, in fact, in developed countries this consumption is increasing, and it is hard to foresee that in the next few years consumers will give up the pleasures associated with the consumption of sweets or even reduce this consumption. On the other hand, any political/legal initiative will have a transversal impact on the market, affecting all competitors.

Industry Analysis – Forces Driving Industry Competition (Porter's 5 Forces)

Porter's 5 Forces model (Porter, 1979, 1980, 1998) is used as a reference for external analysis of the business environment, but with a different focus from the PESTEL, because this technique carries out a structural analysis of the industry in which the firm competes, identifying the external pressures exerted on the business. The intensity of competition in an industry depends on the strength of five forces, namely: the threat of new entrants, the threat of substitutes, the bargaining power of buyers, the bargaining power of suppliers, and the rivalry among existing firms. The term "suppliers" comprises all sources of company's essential inputs. The suppliers' bargaining power in the industry under evaluation is likely to be influenced by the following conditions (Table 16).

Table 16. The bargaining power of suppliers

Condition	State
Is the market dominated by a few large suppliers, i.e. is the supply market concentrated?	No
Are there substitutes for a specific product?	Yes
Are wholesalers fragmented, so their bargaining power is low?	Yes
Are the switching costs from one supplier to another high?	No
Can the supplier integrate the chain downstream to get higher prices and margins?	No
Do intermediaries have higher profitability than suppliers?	-
Does the integration downstream provide economies of scale for the supplier?	No
Do intermediaries hinder market development (reaction to new products)?	No
Are the barriers to become an intermediary low?	No
Is volume critical for suppliers?	Yes
Are the critical raw materials for production similar?	Yes
Do raw materials have little impact on costs?	No
Are the distribution channels diversified?	Yes
Is there intense rivalry among suppliers?	Yes

This force is not expected to have strong implications for Rose - Patisserie and Coffee House's business. The bargaining power of customers determines the pressure they can impose on margins, volumes, or other contractual conditions. The customers' bargaining power is affected by the following conditions (Table 17).

Table 17. Customers' bargaining power

Condition	State
Is there concentration or do customers buy large volumes?	No
Is there a big number of intermediaries in the distribution channel?	Yes
Do intermediaries operate with high fixed costs?	Yes
Is the product undifferentiated and can it be substituted?	No
Is it simple and inexpensive to switch to an alternative product?	Yes
Are customers price sensitive?	Yes
Can customers manufacture the product themselves?	Yes
Is the product of strategic importance to the customer?	No
Is the customer aware of the production costs of the product?	No
Is there a possibility for customers to integrate upstream?	No
Is customers' dependence on intermediaries low?	Yes
Do customers require customization of the product?	No

The answers to the questions in the previous table show that the customers have no bargaining power over Rose - Patisserie and Coffee House, but there are many competitors, many alternative products, and low dependence on intermediaries. The next force, the rivalry among competitors, describes the intensity of competition among the firms in the market; a strong competition increases the pressure on prices, on margins, and consequently on the profitability of each firm in the market.

Table 18. Rivalry between competitors

Condition	State
Are there many companies competing in the same market?	Yes
Do companies have approximately the same size?	Yes
Do firms have similar strategies?	Yes
Is there differentiation among firms and products, therefore competition is not based on price?	No
Is the market growth rate low (growth of a firm is possible only at the expense of a competitor)?	Yes
Are the barriers to exit the market high?	No
Is the cost of switching from one supplier to another low?	Yes
Does the government impose limits on the competition?	No
Are fixed costs high?	Yes
Are storage costs low?	No

The evaluation of Table 18 allows to draw the conclusion that this force has a relevant impact on Rose - Patisserie and Coffee House's actions, because there are many competitors, with the same configuration and the same strategy, switching from one supplier to another has residual costs and the market growth rate is low.

The ease of a company's entry into the market increases competition. The conditions of entry and the barriers to the entry of new competitors (market shares, prices, customer loyalty, service levels, etc.) are evaluated through the critical factors shown below (Table 19).

Table 19. The competitive threat of new entrants

Condition	State
Are there economies of scale?	Yes
Are there high initial investments and fixed costs?	Yes
Are there advantages for existing companies due to the learning curve effect?	Yes
Do customers show brand loyalty?	Yes
Is the intellectual property protected (patents, licenses, etc.)?	No
Is there a shortage of important resources?	No
Do existing companies control the access to raw materials?	No
Do existing companies control distribution channels?	No
Do existing companies have privileged relationships with customers?	No
Does switching from one supplier to another have high costs for customers?	No
Do geographical factors limit competition?	No
Are there advanced technologies in use?	No
Do sunk costs limit competition?	No
Are there strong brands in the market?	No

Entering the market for pastries, confectionery and similar products always requires considerable investment and is by itself a barrier to entry for new competitors. However, all the other factors show that the barriers to entry are low. For the reasons above mentioned this force can have a determining influence on the market.

The threat from substitute products (Table 20) arises if there are alternative products with equal or better performance parameters than the traditional ones. If this happens, these substitutes (or complements) can potentially attract a significant share of the market and consequently reduce the sales volume for the existing companies.

Table 20. The threat from substitute products

Condition	State
Do customers show brand loyalty?	No
Are there close relationships with customers?	No
Are there switching costs for customers?	No
Do substitutes have a superior price/performance relation?	No
Is the number of substitutes limited?	No
Is the product differentiation substantial?	No
Do substitutes have lower quality?	No
Do the substitutes underperform or have fewer features?	No

The existence of substitute products is a force to allow for, given the data in the previous table. After performing the Porter's 5 Forces model analysis, the main conclusions to be drawn are that both suppliers and customers do not pressure the company. However, there are many competitors and they can and do exert an important pressure, having the same configuration and strategy. Furthermore, apart from the initial investments that can be substantial, there are no other barriers that stand out and prevent the entry of new competitors. Finally, the existence of substitute products is unequivocally a reality.

SWOT Analysis

SWOT analysis (**S**trengths, **W**eaknesses, **O**pportunities and **T**hreats) is a tool used to analyze strategic scenarios of a company, which aims to summarize the internal and the external analysis, identifying key elements for the company's management, knowing that Strengths and Weaknesses exist in the internal environment and Opportunities and Threats occur in the external environment (Cadle et al., 2014; Dacko, 2008; Trompenaars & Coebergh, 2015).

- Internal environment:
    - Strengths: internal advantages over competing companies.
    - Weaknesses: internal disadvantages over competing companies.
- External environment:
    - Opportunities: beneficial aspects with the potential to increase competitive advantage.
    - Threats: negative aspects with the potential to decrease competitive advantage.

For Rose - Patisserie and Coffee House it is possible to make the following SWOT analysis:

- Opportunities:
    - The concept is barely explored in Portugal.
    - Growth potential.
- Strengths
    - Different concept.
    - Good consumers' receptivity.

- - Well-defined brand.
- Threats
  - Existence of many alternative products.
  - Competition is intense.
  - Competitors have the same strategies.
  - Competitors have the same strategy.
- Weaknesses
  - The brand can limit product extension.
  - Location can limit growth.
  - No snack offerings.
  - Limited resources.
  - The concept can be improved.

Ansoff Matrix

The Ansoff matrix, also called the Product/Market matrix, is applied to identify growth opportunities by combining two axes, 'Products' and 'Markets'. Both products and markets can be 'New' or 'Existing'. Therefore, the matrix has four cells representing four strategic alternatives.

- Market penetration strategy: To sell the existing products or services to the existing or new customers in the same market (increase of market share).
- Market development strategy: To enter new markets with the existing products.
- Product development strategy: To develop new products or services for the existing customers.
- Diversification strategy: To enter new markets with new products or services.

A market penetration strategy can be adopted if sales to the existing customers have potential to grow by implementing one or more of the following actions:

- To increase the frequency of orders.
- To increase the average order value.
- To enlarge or change working hours.
- To reduce prices.
- To Increase promotions and distribution.
- Acquisition of a competitor in the same market.
- To bring in simple product refinements.

The market penetration strategy is not the most appropriate alternative for Rose - Patisserie and Coffee House, accepting that the concept's potential allows the company to opt for more aggressive strategies that will permit faster growth.

A market development strategy can be adopted if you can sell your current products to different customers, based on criteria such as:

- Different customer segments: demographics, lifestyles, perceived benefits, etc.
- Industrial buyers of a good that was previously sold only to households.

- New areas or regions of the country.
- Foreign markets.
- Organization dimension.
- Other market sectors.

Rose - Patisserie and Coffee House should use the market development strategy. Since the concept is successful in Porto, the next step will be to test it in other big cities. If the concept proves its success in other big cities, Rose - Patisserie and Coffee House will be able to expand geographically through their own stores or, alternatively, franchise the concept.

A product development strategy can be adopted if the company can sell new products in the current market, based on criteria such as:

- Investment in R&D creates additional products.
- Acquisition of the rights to produce other companies' products.
- Buying products and rebranding them.
- Joint venture with another company to distribute that company's products.
- Production costs may be lower.
- The product can be produced locally.
- Improvements in the quality of the product can be achieved.
- The product can have new packaging.

Rose - Patisserie and Coffee House should improve and complete its product portfolio, since this is a weakness in relation to the competitors. This can be done by progressively improving the concept until it reaches a stage where it is ready to be expanded. It is important to note that the brand may limit the expansion of the product line and the addition of new products may impact the brand awareness and create some dissonance. The word Patisserie inevitably creates an association with sweets and when you have products that clash with the concept, then the brand loses strength and consequently value. Still, the inclusion of snacks and private label products should be evaluated.

Diversification means that an organization tries to increase its portfolio of activities by introducing new products, in new markets. It is the riskiest strategy because it requires both product and market knowledge. Looking at the size and resources of Rose - Patisserie and Coffee House, the diversification strategy is not an option.

After applying the Ansoff matrix, the conclusions are that Rose - Patisserie, and Coffee House has the following strategic alternatives: it can use either product development or market development strategies.

SOLUTIONS AND RECOMMENDATIONS

Based on the information taken from the competitive analysis, Rose - Patisserie and Coffee House can achieve competitive advantages through:

1. Development of the gourmet-style patisserie and coffeehouse concept, with the inclusion of additional private label products, such as: Light meals for lunch; Coffee, tea, ice cream, cookies with

Rose brand (these products can be introduced gradually). This will allow the store operation to be optimized by shifting demand to off-peak times.
2. Creation of a specific offer for the corporate market (that stands for 10% of Rose - Patisserie and Coffee House's sales; currently business customers are equally addressed as end customers).
3. Improve online presence.
4. Training and workshops for individuals and organizations.

Resorting to the information above, starting with the PESTEL analysis:

1. The growing concern about the impact of sugar on health should be monitored, as institutions have already begun to ban/reduce the consumption of products containing sugar in certain places. However, an immediate impact on the market structure is not expected.
2. The trends, albeit at an early stage, point toward organic, unprocessed, gluten-free, and lactose-free foods. The consumer market for this type of product is still scarce and the products have much higher costs.

The analysis of the external environment carried out through Porter's 5 Forces model allows the following deductions:

1. The market where Rose - Patisserie and Coffee House competes, is composed by companies having essentially the same configuration and the same strategies. There are no significant barriers, besides the initial investment costs, the main force that can affect the company being the competition, its intensity and rivalry.

The SWOT analysis recommends the following adjustments:

1. To improve the concept which is barely explored.
2. To expand the business.
3. To make the concept even more different.
4. To assess the brand without compromising the development of the concept.
5. To assess the product portfolio.

The Ansoff Matrix provided the ability to gain an accurate understanding, recommending that:

1. The product portfolio should be optimized, bearing in mind that this is a current competitive disadvantage (the products that should be added were previously mentioned).
2. Rose - Patisserie and Coffee House should proceed with a market development strategy, expanding geographically, preferably to another metropolitan area in order to reinforce the concept and to improve it.

REFERENCES

Cadle, J., Paul, D., & Turner, P. (2014). *Business analysis techniques: 99 essential tools for success* (2nd ed.). BCS, The Chartered Institute for IT.

Dacko, S. G. (2008). *The advanced dictionary of marketing: putting theory to use*. Oxford University Press.

Edelman, D., & Singer, M. (2015). Competing on Customer Journeys. *Harvard Business Review*. https://hbr.org/2015/11/competing-on-customer-journeys

Johnson, G., Scholes, K., & Whittington, R. (2008). *Exploring corporate strategy: text & cases* (8th ed.). Financial Times Prentice Hall.

Johnson, G., Whittington, R., & Scholes, K. (2017). *Exploring strategy* (11th ed.). Pearson.

Lambin, J.-J., & Moerloose, C. d. (2012). *Marketing stratégique et opérationnel: du marketing à l'orientation-marché* (8th ed.). Dunod.

Porter, M. E. (1979). *How competitive forces shape strategy*. Harvard Business Review, March/April.

Porter, M. E. (1980). *Competitive strategy: techniques for analyzing industries and competitors*. Free Press.

Porter, M. E. (1998). *Competitive strategy: techniques for analyzing industries and competitors: with a new introduction*. Free Press.

Rothaermel, F. T. (2017). Strategic management (3rd ed.). McGraw-Hill Education.

Trompenaars, A., & Coebergh, P. H. (2015). *100+ management models: how to understand and apply the world's most powerful business tools*. McGraw-Hill.

ADDITIONAL READING

Chernev, A., & Kotler, P. (2014). *Strategic marketing management* (8th ed.). Cerebellum Press.

Gilligan, C., & Wilson, R. M. S. (2009). *Strategic marketing planning* (2nd ed.). Butterworth-Heinemann.

Hunt, S. D. (2015). The theoretical foundations of strategic marketing and marketing strategy: Foundational premises, R-A theory, three fundamental strategies, and societal welfare. *AMS Review, 5*(3-4), 61–77. doi:10.100713162-015-0069-5

Kaplan, R. S., & Norton, D. P. (2001). *The strategy-focused organization: how balanced scorecard companies thrive in the new business environment*. Harvard Business School Press. doi:10.11081.2001.26129cab.002

Kaplan, R. S., & Norton, D. P. (2004). *Strategy maps: converting intangible assets into tangible outcomes*. Harvard Business School Press.

Kim, W. C., & Mauborgne, R. e. (2017). The W. Chan Kim & Renée Mauborgne Blue Ocean Strategy reader. Harvard Business Review Press.

Lambin, J.-J. (1993). *Strategic marketing: a European approach*. McGraw-Hill.

Mintzberg, H., Ahlstrand, B. W., & Lampel, J. (2009). *Strategy safari: the complete guide through the wilds of strategic management* (2nd ed.). FT Prentice Hall.

KEY TERMS AND DEFINITIONS

Business Development: Involves activities and processes to create, implement and expand growth opportunities within and between organizations.

Loyalty: Consumer behavior characterized by buying from the same company, the same brand, or the same product; repeated buying from a firm due to the benefits received from those products.

Market Positioning: It is the relative position that brands, products, and services occupy in the minds of consumers.

Market Segmentation: It is the process of splitting a wide consumer or business market, usually encompassing existing and potential customers, into sub-groups of consumers (identified as segments) based on some type of common characteristics.

Marketing Mix: The marketing mix is a set of controllable variables that determine how consumers respond to the supply and consists of what the company can do to influence the demand for its supply.

Satisfaction: Emotional state arising from the purchase or use of a company's product or service; how delighted customers are with a company's products, services, and capabilities.

Strategy: Strategy is a plan, a direction, or a guide to action for the future, a path to follow from where you are to where you want to go.

APPENDIX 1

Questions and Answers

1. What is the main decision that Rose-Patisserie and Coffee House has to make?

The main decision is on how to expand the business. Three scenarios are suggested: concept optimization, expansion through company-owned stores, or franchising. However, in the current situation, the second and third scenarios are the most recommended, because only these allow the expansion of the Rose-Patisserie and Coffee House concept.

2. Bearing in mind the sales data, evaluate the strategic options for the B2B segment.

The B2B customer segment accounts for approximately 10% of the total value of sales. Although this is not negligible, it is by no means the most important segment for the company, and for this reason, the strategic focus should not be on this segment. Furthermore, the concept itself, the image, and the brand are not adjusted to this market segment, and therefore, it is necessary to evaluate if this strategy will have a positive contribution to the results or if the resources it requires do not justify the interest in developing specific strategies for this segment.

3. Identify the main problems that Rose-Patisserie and Coffee House has to solve.

Rose-Patisserie and Coffee House has several important problems to solve. The first one consists in optimizing the concept on which its business is based. Although the concept has been well accepted by customers, there is no evidence that it has reached a stage that allows for replication by expanding to other stores. Other problems are the indecision about the product portfolio, the limited management knowledge and skills to ensure the desired expansion, and a brand that may constrain the concept and its development to broader scopes.

4. How is it possible to reconcile B2B, on-site, and take-way sales?

Since Rose-Patisserie and Coffee House is dealing with different segments, it is essential to define a marketing mix for each segment. Consequently, it is possible to reconcile the segments, but changes need to be adopted to make this feasible. It should be noted, however, that the company is almost a new born company and the spreading of resources across several segments may not be the best strategic option.

5. What should be the strategy and implementation sequence for the Rose-Patisserie and Coffee House, given the strategic diagnosis provided?

It is clear from the analysis of the sales data and the models that the company has to solve the internal problems first: Improvement of the concept, definition of the brand strategy, a precise definition of the market segments, acquisition of management knowledge and skills. Despite having success with one store, at one location, this is no guarantee that the concept can gain acceptance nationally and internationally. The second step will be to open a new store in the same metropolitan area and only afterwards should there be an expansion to other more distant geographical areas. Only when this point is reached, the concept is successfully proved, the brand awareness is high, then a franchise expansion may be considered.

Epilogue and Lessons Learned

No matter how high the dreams of the entrepreneurs may be, the Rose - Patisserie and Coffee House concept has to be perfected, and only then can the expansion of the concept through a network of stores, either owned or franchised, be evaluated.

The classic marketing management process consisting of segmentation, targeting, positioning, branding, and marketing mix is crucial to the success of a strategy. Rose - Patisserie and Coffee House, like all startups, aims to have the best financial performance. However, its marketing strategy is somewhat confusing and requires a clear formulation. Currently, the company operates in B2B and B2C markets but the strategy for both is the same. The company has a store and take-way operations and although the take-way represents 50% of revenues, the strategy for this segment is neglected.

The marketing mix is a basic and elementary concept, but even nowadays it is a part of any business strategy. In the case of Rose - Patisserie and Coffee House, it is essential to define precisely the product portfolio for each segment, because customers have different needs, require different distribution and pricing, and the communication channels and messages will most likely be very distinct.

Chapter 6
THEIA:
Thermal Insulation – A Business Strategy

Paulo Botelho Pires
https://orcid.org/0000-0003-3786-6783
Porto Business School, Portugal

António Correia Barros
Politécnico do Porto, Portugal

José Duarte Santos
https://orcid.org/0000-0001-5815-4983
Polytechnic Institute of Gaya, Portugal

EXECUTIVE SUMMARY

THEIA provides technical solutions for the construction industry, specializing in materials for thermal insulation. It is positioned in the middle of the distribution channel, between manufacturers and construction companies, and the profound changes that occurred in the sector had repercussions on the company's activity, forcing it to rethink its business strategy. THEIA repositioning was studied according to a specific methodology, combining analysis techniques to assess organizations' internal capacity and the exploration of external conditioning factors. The strategic plan used financial and commercial information from THEIA and from the sector where it operates, according to the following steps: analysis of THEIA's internal situation, external positioning of THEIA in the national market, definition of strategic objectives, elaboration of scenarios and recommendations.

ORGANIZATION BACKGROUND

THEIA is a Portuguese company founded in the earlier 80s, located in the Porto region, in Portugal, and it was a pioneer in providing technical solutions for civil construction that promote the well-being and increase the user's quality of life, through the application of thermal insulation materials. The company's management held an emergency meeting to try once again to find a solution to the crisis they were ex-

DOI: 10.4018/978-1-7998-1630-0.ch006

periencing. The president of the board of directors nostalgically recalled the success he had enjoyed for many years, allowing him to grow the company, establishing it as the sector's reference company in the Portuguese thermal insulation market. The transformation of the economic structure of the market, with the entry of large manufacturers, coupled with the prolonged recessionary environment, had very negative consequences for most small and medium-sized Portuguese companies, reflected with intensity in civil construction and, consequently, throughout the distribution channel associated with this sector. THEIA is positioned in the middle of the construction sector's distribution channel, serving as an intermediary between manufacturers and retailers or/and end customers (construction companies), experiencing both upstream and downstream the effects of the crisis. It is quite clear that the distribution channel in this market, as within most sectors, has been shrinking, with direct sales from manufacturers to end customers being the norm. This practice led to the elimination of intermediaries and to the appearance of large retailers, representing multi-brands and with the capacity to transversally fulfill, the needs of both smaller retailers and end customers. The activity of companies that sell construction materials was greatly affected by the crisis that began in 2008, and it is difficult to foresee a return to the time of high growth opportunities in the sector. The financial system imposes restrictions and the country and Europe political situation, do not anticipate immediate or rapid improvements. The environmental trends required by customers and the regulations imposed by the European Union, regarding the construction sector and the building industry, follow guidelines that increasingly bet on the use of sustainable resources. It should be logical that companies anticipate, react, adapt, and adjust to this situation, because that is the only way they can succeed. THEIA is facing important challenges, but only if it faces these challenges pragmatically and straightforwardly will it be able to continue to exist as a thermal insulation solutions company.

SETTING THE STAGE

THEIA defines itself as a supplier of technical solutions for civil construction, specialized in materials for thermal insulation, aiming to improve the energy performance and comfort of buildings. THEIA is wrongly recognized in the market as a manufacturer of thermal insulation materials because for many years it had the exclusive right to sell this kind of products in the Portuguese market. The company had a continuous, strong, and solid growth until 2010, when two events occurred that affected its activity. The first is due to the 2008 economic crisis that affected the construction market, and consequently from that year on the construction of new houses decreased sharply. In fact, from that time on, the interest focused only on the housing rehabilitation. The second occurrence was due to the entry into the Portuguese construction market of large number of thermal insulation materials manufactures. From that date on THEIA lost the commercialization exclusivity from those manufacturers and its offer became less competitive. With a continuous and sharp decrease in sales, the company has been evaluating its business, redefining strategies to remain profitable, and ensure its survival.

THEIA

CASE DESCRIPTION

Company Performance

THEIA's activity is merely commercial, and operational efficiency is only achieved using the company's commercial resources, and the contraction in turnover is reflected in the sharp decrease in sales (between 2009 and 2015, it went from 6.2 million euros to 2.5 million euros).

Figure 1. Turnover between 2009 and 2015 for THEIA

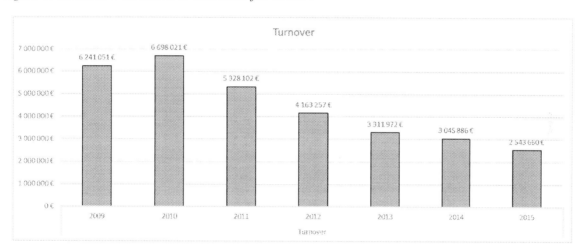

THEIA's sales have been on a downward trend since 2011, with an average annual drop of 17.2% calculated over the past five years.

Figure 2. Sales variation between 2010 and 2015 for THEIA

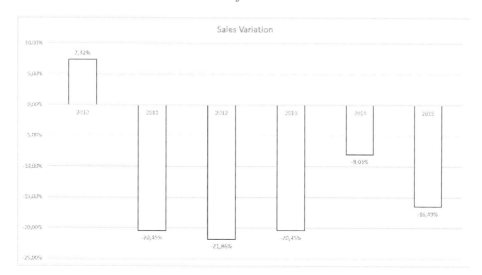

It should be emphasized that in the last two years the sales decrease rate was lower, unlike the years from 2011 to 2013, the variation surpassing -20%, with very punishing consequences for THEIA. 2014 showed a tendency contrary to the previous one, which was not maintained throughout 2015. The decrease in sales was not reversed and it has been maintained since 2011.

Assessment of Market Demand

Making use of the real estate indicators provided by the National Institute of Statistics, it is possible to determine if THEIA's sales followed the market trend. The number of housing licenses issued does not reflect a real market demand but portrays an intention to build (it must be taken into consideration that there may be a time lag between the licensing, the construction, and the buildings commercial development phase of the buildings).

Figure 3. Housing licenses issued

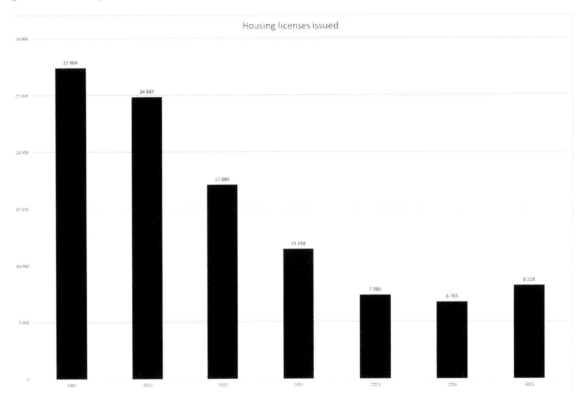

The number of licenses issued decreased significantly from 2009 to 2015, going from more than 27 thousand licenses to 8 thousand licenses. There was a considerable negative variation, reaching the minimum value in 2013. From this year on, the decreasing pattern is reversed, exhibiting positive variations and rising up to 21% in 2015. However, the number of licenses issued between 2009 and 2015, fell considerably, noting a decrease of 70%. Despite the positive variation over the last two years, that was insufficient to compensate for the tremendous rate of decline.

The number of licenses broken down by region follows the values recorded at the national level, showing that all regions experienced intense falls. In 2014, there was a recovery in Lisbon (AML), Algarve and Madeira regions. In 2015, all regions grew, except Madeira.

Table 1. Number of licenses issued per region

	2009	2010	2011	2012	2013	2014	2015
North	9 812	8 200	6 210	4 849	3 271	2 802	3 376
Center	7 044	6 961	4 461	2 989	2 060	2 034	2 267
Lisbon (AML)	4 739	4 823	2 853	1 706	728	838	1 213
Alentejo	2 020	1 707	1 242	897	579	379	525
Algarve	2 456	1 735	1 118	522	396	423	484
Azores	703	912	727	259	222	172	245
Madeira	630	509	474	216	124	137	109

The sharp decrease in licensing, verified until 2014, turned into a positive variation in the last year, but the recovery allows only slightly overcoming the values of 2013, being far below the values recorded in 2009. The regions of Lisbon, Alentejo and Azores show a positive significant variation, representing a recovery trend in 2015. Nevertheless, the number of licenses per region corroborates the national results, with all regions registering sharp drops. In 2015, the pattern was reversed, and the number of licenses grew but it was still far from the number of licenses issued in the past.

Beyond the assessment of the business intentions in the real estate market, behavior can be assessed through the analysis of the value of construction in progress, as they are leading indicators of prospects for construction materials.

Figure 4. Construction value

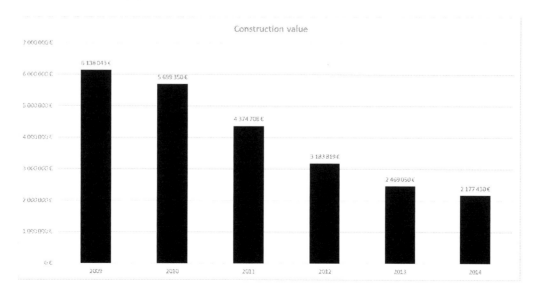

The value of construction works carried out by companies (with more than 20 people) shows a consecutive decrease in the period between 2009 and 2014. The average annual variation fell by more than 18%, unlike the number of issued licenses, showing no inversion of the trend here. The previous indicator provides a general picture of the construction sector; however, it has two limitations: The figures are at national level and it only accounts for contracts carried out by companies with more than 20 employees. To offset these restrictions, in the next section we analyze the number of new completed constructions.

Figure 5. New construction completed for housing

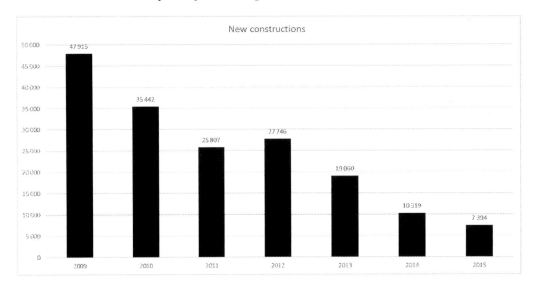

The number of new completed constructions for housing had a decrease between 2009 and 2015, going from more than 47 thousand units to approximately 7.4 thousand new constructions built. The decrease was not linear, showing a positive variation in the year 2012. The negative variations, which are generally high, stand out with average annual drops of 25% representing a decrease of more than 40 thousand completed constructions.

The new completed housing construction analysis by region confirms a sharp decrease in all geographical areas. As at the national analysis, no reversal trend occurred in 2015. The year 2012 was atypical, although with a slight increase over 2011 especially in the North, Center, Alentejo and Madeira regions.

Table 2. New construction completed for housing by region

	2009	2010	2011	2012	2013	2014	2015
North	€15,113	€12,151	€9,037	€9,785	€7,266	€4,166	€2,856
Center	€10,631	€8,646	€6,997	€7,621	€4,877	€2,924	€1,927
Lisbon (AML)	€10,711	€6,727	€4,736	€4,498	€3,496	€1,229	€1,062
Alentejo	€2,991	€2,110	€1,636	€1,701	€1,038	€604	€437
Algarve	€5,736	€3,497	€2,056	€2,852	€1,262	€963	€757
Azores	€1,169	€577	€697	€635	€600	€238	€228
Madeira	€1,564	€1,734	€648	€654	€521	€195	€127

The table corroborates the previous analyses, showing very significant negative variations for all regions. The year 2012 stands out exhibiting positive variations, while 2014, in the opposite direction, shows very strong negative variations. In general, the construction of new houses suffered a very strong contraction in all regions of the country, showing a homogeneous behavior, with no distinction between developed and developing areas).

Comparison of the Indicators

THEIA's sales performance is compared with the indicators previously presented. This comparison is made at a national level and by regions. Comparing THEIA's sales figures with the different national indicators, it is appropriate to conclude that THEIA has contracted less than the market.

Table 3. Comparison of national indicators with THEIA's sales

	2010	2011	2012	2013	2014	2015
THEIA sales variation	7%	-20%	-21%	-20%	-8%	-16%
Variation in number of licenses issued	-9%	-31%	-33%	-35%	-8%	21%
Variation in value of work carried out (€) by companies with 20 or more employees by type of work	-7%	-23%	-27%	-22%	-11%	
Variation in number of completed new construction for family housing by geographical location	-26%	-27%	7%	-31%	-45%	-28%

The average variation of THEIA was:

- Average change of THEIA's sales: -13%
- Average variation of issued licenses: -16%
- Average change of constructions value: -18%.
- Average change of new completed constructions: -25%

THEIA followed the market's trend, showing a better performance in the general indicators, and suffering a sharp contraction in sales, although less severe than the market. Comparing THEIA's sales figures with the indicators for the North region (see table 4), it is possible to conclude that THEIA had a lower contraction than the market.

Table 4. Comparison of Northern region indicators with THEIA's sales

	2010	2011	2012	2013	2014	2015
THEIA sales variation	7%	-20%	-21%	-20%	-8%	-16%
Variation in number of licenses issued in the North	-16%	-24%	-22%	-33%	-14%	20%
Variation in number of completed new construction for family housing in the North	-20%	-26%	8%	-26%	-43%	-31%

THEIA average variation was:

- Average change in THEIA sales: -13%.
- Average variation of issued licenses in the North: -15%.
- Average change of new constructions completed int the North: -23%.

Customer's Behavior

The analysis of sales by customers permits to identify which segments are the most significant for THEIA's business. The first analysis focuses on the evolution of the number of costumers, the minimum, maximum, and average annual purchase values, and a summary of the data can be found in the table.

Table 5. Characterization of customer purchases, between 2010 and 2015

	2010	2011	2012	2013	2014	2015
Number of customers	1595	1587	1430	1137	1034	879
Highest purchase volume	€164,058	€87,184	€84,067	€66,231	€81,256	€64,907
Lowest purchase volume	€2	€2	€1	-	€1	€3
Average purchase value per customer	€3,562	€3,266	€2,859	€2,683	€2,892	€2,714
Average purchase deviation per customer	€9,334	€7,599	€6,269	€6,132	€6,489	€5,723
Total	€5,681,625	€5,183,011,	€4,088,099	€3,050,876	€2,990,697	€2,385,428

For the period from 2010 to 2015, according to the table, all the variables had a successive decrease, showing different variations:

- The number of customers had a decline of 45%.
- The customer who bought the most – the largest annual customer – had a 60% drop.
- The customer average purchase dropped by 24%.

Given the range of sales values, (delimited by the maximum and minimum values), a proposition for the market segmentation is presented, based on the annual purchases. Eight segments were considered:

1. Customers who bought up to €1,000 per year.
2. Customers who bought between €1,000 and €5,000 per year.
3. Customers who bought between €5,000 and €10,000 per year.
4. Customers who bought between €10,000 and €20,000 per year.
5. Customers who bought between €20,000 and €30,000 per year.
6. Customers who bought between €30,000 and €40,000 per year.
7. Customers who bought between €40,000 and €50,000 per year.
8. Customers who bought more than €50,000 per year.

The following table exhibits the customer data for the eight segments.

Table 6. Number of customers by segment

Segment	Number of customers per segment					
	2010	2011	2012	2013	2014	2015
<€1000 and >=€0	985	931	823	666	608	520
<€5000 and >=€1000	341	390	384	303	261	224
<€10000 and >=€5000	109	129	117	102	90	74
<€20000 and >=€10000	93	89	73	35	50	39
<€30000 and >=€20000	30	20	17	17	14	15
<€40000 and >=€30000	16	12	9	9	4	4
<€50000 and >=€40000	9	4	1	1	3	2
<=Max and >=€50000	12	12	6	4	4	1

The table shows that the segments with the highest number of customers are those with the lowest annual purchase values, also exposing that, for the period under study, all segments had a decrease in the number of customers. It is also relevant to identify which segments had the sharpest decreases.

Table 7. Number of customers per segment variation

Segment	Number of customers per segment variation					
	2011	2012	2013	2014	2015	Total variation
<€1000 and >=€0	-5%	-12%	-19%	-9%	-14%	-47%
<€5000 and >=€1000	14%	-2%	-21%	-14%	-14%	-34%
<€10000 and >=€5000	18%	-9%	-13%	-12%	-18%	-32%
<€20000 and >=€10000	-4%	-18%	-52%	43%	-22%	-58%
<€30000 and >=€20000	-33%	-15%	0%	-18%	7%	-50%
<€40000 and >=€30000	-25%	-25%	0%	-56%	0%	-75%
<€50000 and >=€40000	-56%	-75%	0%	200%	-33%	-78%
<=Max and >=€50000	0%	-50%	-33%	0%	-75%	-92%

The largest variations occurred in the segments with fewer customers, corresponding to higher annual purchases. The segment with the largest number of customers, associated with lower annual purchases, stands out, with an intermediate variation. Also relevant is the analysis of the sales volume for the various segments.

Table 8. Sales volume by segment

	Sales volume by segment					
Segment	2010	2011	2012	2013	2014	2015
<€1000 and >=€0	€276,033	€267,474	€249,584	€192,065	€188,788	€156,062
<€5000 and >=€1000	€798,611	€947,287	€871,427	€676,122	€622,567	€533,133
<€10000 and >=€5000	€796,804	€923,150	€837,818	€698,477	€629,642	€493,461
<€20000 and >=€10000	€1,249,867	€1,223,917	€1,021,125	€499,553	€670,471	€549,559
<€30000 and >=€20000	€719,379	€485,651	€399,582	€399,302	€354,022	€347,622
<€40000 and >=€30000	€539,804	€417,303	€303,260	€291,644	€138,715	€149,785
<€50000 and >=€40000	€398,190	€183,791	€46,448	€47,071	€131,401	€90,899
<=Max and >=€50000	€902,938	€734,438	€358,855	€246,643	€255,089	€64,907

In accordance with the pattern already identified, there is a decrease in all customer segments. But a more insightful analysis brings out another particularity. The table reveals a change of the segments' importance hierarchy for the period under observation. Let us compare the segments' hierarchy in 2010 and 2015.

Table 9. Segment Hierarchy

Segment	Ranking position		Segment	Ranking position	
	2010	2015		2010	2015
<€1000 and >=€0	8	5	<€30000 and >=€20000	5	4
<€5000 and >=€1000	3	2	<€40000 and >=€30000	6	6
<€10000 and >=€5000	4	3	<€50000 and >=€40000	7	7
<€20000 and >=€10000	1	1	<=Max and >=€50000	2	8

The most important segment for THEIA remained the same between 2010 and 2015, comprising the customers who annually make purchases between 10 thousand euros and 20 thousand euros. The second most important segment, in 2010, became the least relevant in 2015, encompassing customers who purchased more than 50 thousand euros per year. This change is relevant because this segment went from sales of over 900 thousand euros in 2010 to approximately 65 thousand euros in 2015. On the other hand, in 2010 there was a strong heterogeneity among segments, while in 2015 there was relative homogeneity around the segment < €20,000 and ≥ €10,000. THEIA's customers in the last year were more similar to each other.

Summarizing the analysis, it can be concluded that:

- All segments, whether measured by number or value of purchases, declined.
- The segments with the largest purchase volumes were those with the strongest decreases.
- A trend towards a concentration of customers in intermediate segments is confirmed.

Customer Loyalty

Following the analysis of the evolution of segments, concerning THEIA's sales, let us now examine its behavior. Firstly, it should be noted that for the period between 2010 and 2015, THEIA had 4,430 customers and their variation is shown in table 10.

Table 10. Number of customers

	2010	2011	2012	2013	2014	2015	Total variation
Nº of customers	1595	1587	1430	1137	1034	879	-45%
Variation		-1%	-10%	-20%	-9%	-15%	

The table maintains the pattern found and described earlier, in which the number of customers had a negative variation of 100%. We now want to find out how many customers are loyal and for how many years. The table displays this information (loyalty is defined as the number of different years the customer has purchased from THEIA. For example, the column "2 Years", with a value of 593, means that in the period between 2010 and 2015, 593 customers purchased in two years.

Table 11. Number of years that customers are loyal

	6 years	5 years	4 years	3 years	2 years	1 year
Nº of customers	225	120	175	254	593	3 063

Assessing customer loyalty, it first stands out that there is a high number of customers who only buy for one year – 3,063 – which represents almost 70% of all customers (this is a negative fact). The second point is that there are 225 customers, who have bought in all the six years, characterized by long-lasting and stable relationships, with a high degree of loyalty. This fact is very positive, meaning that many customers prefer to deal continuously with THEIA, representing valuable assets. The study of the new customers evolution and the evolution of the number of customers who are loyal is carried out next.

Table 12. Number of new customers

	2010	2011	2012	2013	2014	2015	Total
Nº of customers	1595	1587	1430	1137	1034	879	
New		844	671	496	468	357	
Variation			-20%	-26%	-6%	-24%	-58%
Loyal		743	759	641	566	522	

The number of new customers, between 2011 and 2015, decreased in line with the decrease in the number of customers who made purchases. The drop in new customers was 58% for the period referred to, but the reduction considering all customers was 45%. This means that the number of new customers has had a greater reduction than that of loyal customers. The table contains data on THEIA's customer loyalty. Having previously constructed a simple loyalty indicator, we proceed now to a more advanced indicator, where the data has been transformed, allowing to take into account the number of customers who buy successively.

Table 13. Evolution of the number of new and successively loyal customers

	2010	2011	2012	2013	2014	2015
No. of customers	1595	1587	1430	1137	1034	879
New	-	844	671	496	468	357
Loyal -2	-	743	162	117	72	86
Loyal -3	-	-	526	61	48	32
Loyal -4	-	-	-	367	36	27
Loyal -5	-	-	-	-	281	24
Loyal -6	-	-	-	-	-	225

The findings are important, confirming that there is a customer base that is loyal to THEIA – they have purchased in the six years – representing 25% of all customers who have purchased in 2015. This percentage is significantly lower for customers with fewer years of loyalty (for example, customers loyal for 5 years in 2015 were 24 - representing only 11% of those loyal for 6 years).

The following table allows the comparison between the purchase amount from new customers and the purchase amount from loyal customers.

Table 14. New vs. loyal customer purchases

	New customers	Share	Loyal customers	Share
2011	€963,696	19%	€4 219,315	81%
2012	€778,219	19%	€3 309,879	81%
2013	€561,765	18%	€2 489,111	82%
2014	€540,155	18%	€2 450,542	82%
2015	€341,543	14%	€2 043,885	86%

The conclusions are clear: the amount of new customers' purchases has been decreasing, as has the share of total purchases, from 19% to 14%. The amount of loyal customers' purchases has also been decreasing, down more than 50%, but their share of total purchases has increased from 81% to 86%. No less important is the study of customers who switch from THEIA to another supplier.

Table 15. Number of customers who left

	2010	2011	2012	2013	2014	2015
They went out	745	816	788	618	584	-
Variation		10%	-3%	-22%	-6%	

It is noticeable from the table that the number of customers who stopped buying from THEIA has been decreasing, with a 20% reduction for the period 2010 to 2014. This trend is inverse to all the patterns identified previously and is a positive evidence.

Although the concept of loyalty is recognized, both theoretically and in practice, it is necessary to quantify what loyalty represents in terms of monetary value for THEIA. For that purpose, the following table was prepared, which contains the total annual value of loyal customers.

Table 16. Value of loyal customers over 6 years from 2010 to 2015

Years of loyalty	2010	2011	2012	2013	2014	2015
4 years	€693,119	€657,256	€546,591	€265,763	€201,693	€143,847
Weight in total sales	10%	12%	13%	8%	7%	6%
5 years	€540,604	€581,164	€471,399	€485,386	€354,274	€209,192
Weight in total sales	8%	11%	11%	15%	12%	8%
6 years	€2,573,017	€2,281,031	€1,860,271	€1,465,444	€1,418,164	€1,250,009
Weight in total sales	38%	43%	45%	44%	47%	49%
Total sales	€6,698,021	€5,328,102	€4,163,257	€3,311,972	€3,045,886	€2,543,660

The weight of loyal customers over 6 years is very high, starting at 38% in 2010, and approaching 50% in 2015. For loyal customers exhibiting lower loyalty rates (they bought for 4 or 5 years), their weight in sales is much lower, never exceeding 15% in a year. The evidence that THEIA has a portfolio of customers who were loyal for 6 years is extremely relevant for the design of any strategy.

Sales Analysis

The table contains the sales figures for the years 2010 and 2015, the total sales figures for that period, each district share of sales for the years 2010 and 2015, the average variation and the total variation for that period, and the decrease in value.

The analysis allows us to recognize the pattern previously identified, that is, all the districts decreased their sales between 2010 and 2015. Other inferences are also pertinent:

1. The three districts with the highest sales are Porto, Braga and Viana do Castelo, representing 75% of total sales in 2015.
2. These three districts saw their share of sales increase in comparison with the other districts.
3. These three districts are the closer ones to THEIA's facilities.

4. The following districts, usually exhibiting important sales amounts, suffered relative drops: Faro, with a reduction of over 300,000 euros – from 6% to 0%; Setúbal, with a reduction of almost 250,000 euros – from 5% to 1%; Leiria, with a reduction of approximately 200,000 euros – from 5% to 3%. Note that it is more revealing to evaluate the relative decreases by district, since THEIA's sales decreased less than the market average. This reveals which districts had important sales and which significantly decreased sales, thus affecting their contribution to the overall THEIA's sales.

Table 17. Sales by district

	2010	2015	Total 2010-2015	District share 2010	District share 2015	Average Variation	Variation	Decrease
Porto	€1,553,354	€874,966	€6,734,080	27%	37%	-10%	-44%	-€678,388
Braga	€1,548,591	€731,889	€6,474,193	27%	31%	-14%	-53%	-€816,702
V. Castelo	€306,548	€160,191	€1,155,870	5%	7%	-9%	-48%	-€146,357
Aveiro	€276,662	€121,754	€1,143,697	5%	5%	-13%	-56%	-€154,908
Lisbon	€317,576	€108,613	€1,560,104	6%	5%	-14%	-66%	-€208,963
Vila Real	€140,429	€86,465	€617,906	2%	4%	2%	-38%	-€53,964
Leiria	€283,305	€82,827	€1,136,291	5%	3%	-21%	-71%	-€200,477
Viseu	€88,764	€68,728	€674,740	2%	3%	14%	-23%	-€20,035
Setúbal	€275,456	€27,324	€674,285	5%	1%	-35%	-90%	-€248,132
Guarda	€103,349	€22,851	€349,269	2%	1%	-20%	-78%	-€80,498
Santarém	€89,245	€21,385	€364,615	2%	1%	-21%	-76%	-€67,860
Coimbra	€57,809	€15,710	€240,093	1%	1%	-18%	-73%	-€42,099
Spain	€73,130	€14,253	€364,010	1%	1%	4%	-81%	-€58,876
Bragança	€60,055	€6,167	€300,497	1%	0%	-24%	-90%	-€53,888
Faro	€348,153	€1,521	€720,980	6%	0%	-62%	-100%	-€346,632
Beja	€35,339	€288	€70,291	1%	0%	-34%	-99%	-€35,052
Madeira	€29,787	€10,377	€201,500	1%	0%	-6%	-65%	-€19,410
Others	€94,072	€30,118	€593,801	2%	1%	-	-68%	-€63,954

In general, between 2010 and 2015, there was a gradual dominance of the districts nearest to THEIA's facilities, a high decrease in the importance of the districts in the Center and South regions, and there was a concentration of sales in fewer districts.

Product Sales

As part of the analysis, it is essential to evaluate the company's product portfolio and its evolution during the research period. The table shows the evolution of sales by products, between the years 2010 and 2015.

Table 18. Product sales, between 2009 and 2015

	2010				2015			Variação	
Rank	**Products**	**Value**	**Share**	**Rank**	**Products**	**Value**	**Share**	**Difference**	**Perc.**
1	Extruded Polystyrene	€1,801,912	27%	2	Rock Wool	€592,046	23%	-€422,528,05	-42%
2	Rock Wool	€1,014,574	43%	1	Extruded Polystyrene	€531,653	44%	-€1,270,258,47	-70%
3	Asphalt Shingles	€367,385	48%	6	Mineral Wool	€320,997	57%	€69,416,86	28%
4	Expanded Polystyrene	€335,266	53%	3	Asphalt Shingles	€216,117	65%	-€151,268,35	-41%
5	Piton Screen	€297,847	58%	14	Various	€148,323	71%	€86,820,22	141%
6	Mineral Wool	€251,580	62%	5	Piton Screen	€113,259	76%	-€184,588,64	-62%
7	Under-Tile	€182,721	64%	4	Expanded Polystyrene	€107,777	80%	-€227,489,23	-68%
8	Acrylic Stone	€149,648	67%	10	Geotextile Blanket	€65,033	82%	-€44,185,64	-40%
9	Fiberglass	€124,537	68%	22	Fiberglass Net	€55,797	85%	€44,552,19	396%
10	Geotextile Blanket	€109,218	70%	13	Storm boxes	€52,234	87%	-€17,323,04	-25%
11	Profile	€104,103	72%	8	Acrylic Stone	€46,171	88%	-€103,476,69	-69%
12	Polyethylene Foams	€70,960	73%	7	Under-Tile	€42,622	90%	-€140,098,98	-77%
13	Storm boxes	€69,557	74%	17	Cement Bases	€39,603	92%	€2,336,59	6%
14	Various	€61,503	75%	9	Fiberglass	€39,464	93%	-€85,072,20	-68%
15	Cardboard tubes	€59,914	76%	15	Cardboard tubes	€38,463	95%	-€21,450,75	-36%
16	Drainage Pipes	€54,155	77%	19	Cork	€31,083	96%	€5,833,21	23%
17	Cement Bases	€37,266	77%	11	Profile	€24,417	97%	-€79,686,43	-77%
18	Fixing Accessories	€35,435	78%	18	Fixing Accessories	€17,493	98%	-€17,941,79	-51%
19	Cork	€25,249	78%	12	Polyethylene Foams	€14,518	98%	-€56,441,61	-80%
20	EPS Cornices	€18,834	78%	21	Polyethylene	€11,560	99%	-€6,110,38	-35%
21	Polyethylene	€17,670	79%	20	EPS Cornices	€11,362	99%	-€7,472,08	-40%
22	Fiberglass Net	€11,245	79%	16	Drainage Pipes	€10,701	99%	-€43,454,47	-80%

The main products had significant drops in sales and the hierarchy of products has changed, deserving some reflection. The following observations stand out:

- Extruded Polystyrene had a 70% drop going from the first position to the second.
- The mineral wool rose three positions and had a positive variation of 28%.
- The Various category rose 10 positions and a positive variation of 141%.
- The Fiberglass Net climbed 20 positions and had a positive variation of 369%.
- The two best-selling products have almost the same weight in sales. However, in 2015, sales were concentrated in a smaller number of products. Indeed, in 2010 the first 10 products accounted for 70% of the sales, while in 2015 the first 10 products are responsible for 87% of the sales.

- In 2010 the top 20 products represented 78% of the sales, but in 2015 the top 20 products represent 99% of the sales.

The table below exhibits the sales figures for customers who were loyal during the last six years, broken down by district and by product, showing the heterogeneity of loyal customers during the six years.

Table 19. Sales to loyal customers (6 years), broken down by district and product

Districts	Various	Rock Wool	Mineral Wool	Expanded Polystyrene	Extruded Polystyrene	Piton Screen	Asphalt Shingles
Aveiro	€13,439	€131,002	€22,132	€23,045	€221,560	€48,764	€37,879
Braga	€35,024	€593,235	€145,161	€261,490	€1,152,644	€178,578	€142,275
Bragança		€123			€8,472		
Coimbra		€8,033	€2,170		€4,114	€883	€4,807
Faro		€390		€510	€4,678		
Guarda		€1,290	€5,008	€14,527	€36,040	€1,954	
Madeira Island		€2,087			€118,141		
Ilha de São Miguel	€2,756	€10,764					
Ilha Terceira				€1,352	€15,930		
Leiria	€240	€177,209	€97,418	€1,181	€71,708	€87,844	€20,129
Lisboa		€44,462	€7,608	€45	€979	€56,725	€23,132
Porto	€3,395	€891,854	€165,400	€421,859	€1,478,628	€181,960	€367,931
Santarém					€5,090	€6,174	€11,666
Setúbal	€2,149	€14,249	€34,215	€440	€12,054	€879	€1,799
Viana do Castelo		€243,581	€190,959	€32,223	€100,752	€57,213	€381
Vila Real	€5,789	€48,333	€45,756	€5,831	€84,484	€1,656	€1,226
Viseu		€16,745	€9,202	€3,006	€22,504	€383	€2,068
TOTAL	€62,792	€2,183,356	€725,029	€765,509	€3,337,777	€623,013	€613,292
Relative share	1%	26%	9%	9%	40%	7%	7%

Table 19 shows the heterogeneity of loyal customers during the six years under examination. Special attention should be given to Extruded Polystyrene which accounts for 40% of total sales during the six years, considering loyal customers only. Ranking second, rock wool has 26% share.

The next table contains the number of loyal customers (6 years). Let us recall for this purpose that the number of clients who bought every year from THEIA was 255.

Table 20. Number of loyal customers (6 years) broken down by product

Product	2010	2011	2012	2013	2014	2015	Average per customer (*)
Various	20	16	6	8	6	8	1,6
Glass Fiber	67	58	54	49	45	41	3
Rock Wool	139	137	124	140	129	124	4,3
Mineral Wool	86	74	83	55	56	64	3
Geotextile Blanket	77	54	52	57	50	66	2,9
Profile	57	45	39	31	31	30	2,3
Expanded Polystyrene	115	116	106	94	82	66	3,5
Extruded Polystyrene	144	144	131	111	102	90	4,1
Fiberglass Net	9	6	6	11	37	36	1,5
Piton Screen	87	86	52	61	65	68	3
Asphalt Shingles	49	48	37	44	51	50	3

(*) Average per customer: The average number of years that customers have bought this product.

The data in the table allows several conclusions to be drawn about the purchasing behavior of customers who have bought consecutively over the past 6 years.

- The rock wool had appreciable stability, with a small oscillation. In each year, more than half of the loyal customers bought this product. On average, a customer bought rock wool 4.3 years.
- The extruded polystyrene behaved similarly to rockwool, although less regularly, showing a downward trend in the last years. This means that in recent years fewer loyal customers have been buying extruded polystyrene.
- The expanded polystyrene and mineral wool behaved similarly to extruded polystyrene.
- The asphalt shingles had a pattern similar to rock wool, although in each year only 22% of loyal customers bought this product. On average, a customer bought asphalt shingles for 3 years.
- Summarizing, customer loyalty is based primarily on two products: rock wool and extruded polystyrene.

The value of sales for loyal customers (6 years) is exhibited in the following table.

It is confirmed that for customers who have been loyal for 6 years, rock wool became the product with the highest sales volume in 2015, moving from a 19% share to 25%. Extruded polystyrene moved into 2nd place, decreasing its share from 35% to 25%. Mineral wool had a real sales growth, going from over 95 thousand euros to over 113 thousand euros, with an increase in share from 4% to 9%. Summarizing, although THEIA's customers have been loyal during the six years, their buying behavior has changed into a new pattern.

Table 21. Comparison of loyal customer sales (6 years), between 2010 and 2015

Products	2010	Share	Products	2015	Share	Perc.
Extruded Polystyrene	€869,342	35%	Rock Wool	€309,020	25%	-34%
Rock Wool	€466,371	19%	Extruded Polystyrene	€308,147	25%	-65%
Piton Screen	€176,473	7%	Mineral Wool	€113,415	9%	18%
Expanded Polystyrene	€161,334	7%	Asphalt Shingles	€88,190	7%	-37%
Asphalt Shingles	€138,981	6%	Piton Screen	€69,892	6%	-60%
Sub Roof	€98,239	4%	Expanded Polystyrene	€69,096	6%	-57%
Mineral Wool	€95,734	4%	STORM BOXES	€36,619	3%	-2%
PROFILE	€65,937	3%	Fiberglass Mesh	€34,835	3%	1632%
Geotextile Blanket	€49,671	2%	Geotextile Blanket	€32,238	3%	-35%
Formwork Tube	€46,157	2%	Under-Tile	€31,421	3%	-68%
Fiberglass	€45,495	2%	Cardboard tubes	€26,048	2%	
STORM BOXES	€37,270	2%	Cement Bases	€23,291	2%	16%
Polyethylene Foams	€35,386	1%	Fiberglass	€16,671	1%	-63%
Various	€27,525	1%	PROFILE	€16,249	1%	-75%
Sandwich Panel	€22,097	1%	Fixation Accessories	€14,254	1%	-34%
Fixing Accessories	€21,584	1%	Several	€8,165	1%	-70%
Cemented Bases	€20,106	1%	Polyethylene Foams	€7,910	1%	-78%

Competitors Analysis

The analysis of the activities developed by competitors and their pricing policies serve as guidelines for alternative scenarios and as a benchmark. Differences are established namely in the number of locations where it operates, the range of products it sells, and the services provided.

Comparing THEIA's offer regarding the four products with the highest sales (rock wool, extruded polystyrene, mineral wool and asphalt shingles) with competitors, it becomes evident that:

- Considering all the comparisons, THEIA never has the lowest price, and only in one case it does have the highest price.
- Considering all the comparisons, THEIA stands out in Polystyrene, having the largest offer and variety in this category of products in the market.

It has become clear that competitors have incorporated in their portfolio, products that are suitable for housing rehabilitation. Air conditioning and comfort, consumption control and energy use, products related to home automation, as well as new types of sustainable construction are the areas with the greatest emphasis. Is also remarkable the existence of several suppliers that can provide products and solutions that can complement, replace, or just be added to THEIA's product portfolio to increase its differentiation and competitiveness.

Distribution Channels

Traditionally, distribution channels were lengthy (manufacturer, importer or distributor, retailers, and construction companies). Each level sold only to the subsequent level. Nowadays this is not the case. Thus, it is possible for manufacturers to sell directly to end customers and to construction companies, bypassing all intermediate levels – the so-called disintermediation. The final level has access to products and materials, but also to supply conditions that equal those of intermediaries. This kind of distribution enhances difficulties to companies in the middle levels, since access to products and price are no longer differentiating factors in the decision-making process and, consequently, companies lose competitiveness if they do not add another type of value.

Customer buying process

Construction companies and building materials buyers have for decades lived in a market with very high margins, which has put off the incorporation of new methods and new technologies, as well as the optimization of processes and the adoption of good management practices. From the market analysis and from the conclusions drawn from the diagnosis and internal analysis of THEIA, it can be stated that the buying process is characterized by:

- The price is a major determinant, as a result of the economic crisis.
- There is a high degree of loyalty in the relationships between companies.
- E-commerce is beginning to be consolidated by large multinationals and implemented by medium-sized companies.
- The geographical location of the supplier can be a purchasing determinant.

CURRENT CHALLENGES FACING THE ORGANIZATION

THEIA's management must define a business strategy. All economic and financial indicators show a downward trajectory and if this trend is not reversed, it will lead to the company's bankruptcy. THEIA has not responded to the changes that have occurred in the market, namely the economic crisis and the entry of manufacturers as direct competitors. For this reason, a strategic analysis is performed, using the PESTEL, Porter's 5 Forces, SWOT and Ansoff Matrix models

PESTEL analysis

The PESTEL analysis (Cadle et al., 2014; Johnson et al., 2017; Rothaermel, 2017) intends to identify the macro-environmental factors (Political, Economic, Social, Technological, Environmental and Legal), that have the potential to impact THEIA's operational and strategic activities.

- **Political Factors**: The government actions impact on THEIA's economic activity is expected to be small; no major changes are likely to occur in the creation of interfering policies, and the same is expected to occur in the activity regulation. Changes in tax, labor or commercial law should closely follow the guidelines of recent years.

- **Economic Factors**: A slow economic growth, the difficulty for consumers to get credit, the recurrent instability of financial institutions, will continue to affect the construction sector. Economic forecasts are not favorable to the country, and economic conditions are expected to remain the same for the next few years.
- **Social factors**: The structure of the Portuguese society has changed in the last decades. The progressive population ageing, coupled with a negative birth rate in recent years, will affect the long-term demand for housing. There is also a new mindset, more concerned about sustainability, environmental protection, energy efficiency, and others.
- **Technological Factors**: Technological innovation will continue to impact the building materials sector, and new materials and products will most likely continue to appear to replace current ones.
- **Environmental Factors**: The mentality change, especially in the younger generations, will increase the demand for ecological products that aim to protect the environment, to contain climate change, and to be energy efficient and sustainable.
- **Legal Factors**: There are directives from the European Commission, which will be followed by new, stricter directives, to regulate the market where THEIA operates.

Porter's 5 Forces

Porter's 5 forces model (Porter, 1979a, 1979b, 1998a, 1998b) analyzes the intra-industry in which the company operates, identifying the external forces applied on the business and the purpose is to evaluate the forces and the underlying factors that determine them to know if the market is viable and if there are strategic positions that enable the company to defend itself from strong competitors or exploit weaknesses, judging the attractiveness to choose strategies that increase the probability of long-term survival and competitive advantage. The analysis evaluates five forces, which usually exert pressure on the company, identified as: level of competition in the industry, barriers to entry, substitute products, customers, and suppliers.

Table 22. The supplier's bargaining power

Condition	State
Is the market dominated by a few large suppliers, i.e. is the supply market concentrated?	YES
Are there substitutes for a specific product?	YES
Are wholesalers fragmented, so their bargaining power is low?	YES
Are the switching costs from one supplier to another high?	NO
Can the supplier integrate the chain downstream to get higher prices and margins?	NO
Do intermediaries have higher profitability than suppliers?	NO
Does the integration downstream provide economies of scale for the supplier?	NO
Do intermediaries hinder market development (reaction to new products)?	NO
Are the barriers to become an intermediary low?	YES
Is volume critical for suppliers?	YES
Are the critical raw materials for production similar?	NO
Do raw materials have little impact on costs?	NO
Are the distribution channels diversified?	YES
Is there intense rivalry among suppliers?	NO

THEIA

The power of suppliers lays in their ability to increase prices, reduce quality, or impose contractual conditions. In the construction materials supply sector, the existence of strong bargaining power on the part of suppliers is confirmed.

Table 23. Customers' bargaining power

Condition	State
Is there concentration or do customers buy large volumes?	NO
Is there a big number of intermediaries in the distribution channel?	YES
Do intermediaries operate with high fixed costs?	NO
Is the product undifferentiated and can it be substituted?	NO
Is it simple and inexpensive to switch to an alternative product?	YES
Are customers price sensitive?	NO
Can customers manufacture the product themselves?	NO
Is the product of strategic importance to the customer?	NO
Is the customer aware of the production costs of the product?	YES
Is there a possibility for customers to integrate upstream?	YES
Is customers' dependence on intermediaries low?	YES
Do customers require customization of the product?	NO\

It stands out from the table above that THEIA's customers have some bargaining power, mainly due to two factors: The existence of large number of intermediaries in the distribution channels, and the possibility for customers to take over distribution themselves, because they have direct access to manufacturers.

Table 24. Rivalry between competitors

Condition	State
Are there many companies competing in the same market?	YES
Do companies have approximately the same size?	NO
Do firms have similar strategies?	YES
Is there differentiation among firms and products, therefore competition is not based on price?	NO
Is the market growth rate low (growth of a firm is possible only at the expense of a competitor)?	YES
Are the barriers to exit the market high?	NO
Is the cost of switching from one supplier to another low?	YES
Does the government impose limits on the competition?	NO
Are fixed costs high?	NO
Are storage costs low?	NO

The market where THEIA operates is highly competitive, with large number of competitors with similar strategies and products, within a shrinking market.

Table 25. The competitive threat of new entrants

Condition	State
Are there economies of scale?	NO
Are there high initial investments and fixed costs?	NO
Are there advantages for existing companies due to the learning curve effect?	NO
Do customers show brand loyalty?	NO
Is the intellectual property protected (patents, licenses, etc.)?	NO
Is there a shortage of important resources?	NO
Do existing companies control the access to raw materials?	NO
Do existing companies control distribution channels?	NO
Do existing companies have privileged relationships with customers?	NO
Does switching from one supplier to another have high costs for customers?	NO
Do geographical factors limit competition?	NO
Are there advanced technologies in use?	NO
Do sunk costs limit competition?	NO
Are there strong brands in the market?	NO

It follows from the previous listing that the threat of entry of new competitors in THEIA's market will always be possible because barriers to entry are low.

Table 26. The threat of substitute products

Condition	State
Do customers show brand loyalty?	NO
Are there close relationships with customers?	NO
Are there switching costs for customers?	NO
Do substitutes have a superior price/performance relation?	NO
Is the number of substitutes limited?	YES
Is the product differentiation substantial?	NO
Do substitutes have lower quality?	NO
Do the substitutes underperform or have fewer features?	NO

It can also be concluded that the threat of substitute products is a force to be reckoned with in THEIA's strategy. Combining what was stated above, the reduction of THEIA's market conditioning forces is achieved through:

- **Supplier bargaining power**: THEIA will be able to reduce the bargaining power of suppliers through partnerships; supply chain management; supply chain training and education; decreasing dependency on suppliers or improving supplier relationships; diversification of suppliers with equivalent supplies; knowledge about suppliers' costs, processes, and methods.
    - However, the most probable situation is to have several suppliers competing against each other. All the others are not feasible.
- **Customer bargaining power**: THEIA will be able to reduce the bargaining power of customers through partnerships; managing the distribution chain; increasing loyalty; increasing incentives and add value; trying to change price-based competition by the inclusion of other factors in the buying decision making process; selling directly to the final consumer.
    - It should be emphasized that THEIA's customers have some bargaining power and so, from the options presented above, to increase incentives and to add value are the only two feasible alternatives.
- **Rivalry among competitors**: THEIA will be able to reduce rivalry between competitors by avoiding price-based competition; differentiating its product; creating a strong brand, customer loyalty or increasing switching costs; buying out competitors; focusing on market segments different from its competitors.
    - Rivalry among competitors strongly impacts in the business and none of the factors listed above can be changed by THEIA. The establishment of a strong brand and increasing customer loyalty, which were the only possibilities, have already been adjusted in time.
- **Threat of entry of competitors**: THEIA will be able to reduce the entry of new competitors through increasing economies of scale; creating a strong brand (customer loyalty as a barrier); patents, intellectual property protection; alliances with companies for products or services related to its business; engagement with suppliers; engagement with distributors; retaliation tactics; lobbying for favorable regulation.
    - The entry of new competitors cannot be limited by THEIA for the same reasons mentioned in the previous point.
- **Threat of Substitute Products**: THEIA will be able to reduce the threat of substitute products through legal actions; lobbying for favorable regulation; increasing switching costs; alliances; studying customers to learn their preferences, entering the substitute market; emphasizing differences (real or perceived).
    - Of all the items identified above, THEIA can reduce the threat of substitute products if it enters the substitute market.

In summary, THEIA can take the following actions to alleviate the opposite forces to its strategy: 1) Having multiple suppliers that compete against each other; 2) Creating incentives and adding service value when selling the product; 3) Entering the substitute market.

SWOT Analysis

SWOT informal application, while having the potential to bias analysis, provides important results for the organization and decision-maker. SWOT (Strengths, Opportunities, Weaknesses, and Threats) analysis is a tool used to perform a strategic scenario analysis of a business, which has the objective of making a synopsis of internal and external assessments, highlighting key elements for the company's administration (Grant, 2016; Hanlon & Chaffey, 2015; Johnson et al., 2017; Trompenaars & Coebergh, 2015).

- **Opportunities**:
  - Urban rehabilitation: A growing segment of the construction market, demanding for improvements in terms of comfort and energy efficiency.
  - Energy efficiency: Legal changes aimed at greater sustainability of construction systems, energy efficiency and excellence of materials, providing an opportunity for the supply of materials and solutions in line with these parameters.
  - Environmental sustainability: European Union and Portuguese State financing programs for the promotion and spreading of information on eco-innovation and sustainable policies, affecting the qualification and a potential increase in demand.
  - Products and processes innovation: Products, materials, and sustainable construction processes, more innovative and exhibiting better quality.
- **Threats**:
  - Economic crisis and uncertainty: Increased liquidity and financing difficulties, obstructing efforts to upgrade and innovate.
  - Decrease in new construction: Maturity of the domestic market and excessive offer of buildings for sale limits the future sector's growth.
  - Increased competition: A change in competition via the entry of new, very strong international competitors with more structured and dynamic commercial and marketing strategies.
  - Change in the distribution chain: Manufacturers are approaching the market directly, eliminating intermediaries and strongly reaffirming their brand strategies.
- **Strengths**:
  - Brand image and awareness in the market: Company's good image allows an easy access to new customers and new markets.
  - High customer loyalty: Allows new products introduction, boosting the launch and ensuring the success in new markets and segments.
- **Weaknesses**:
  - Lack of skills: Some of the company's key areas, such as sales and marketing, have any or limited human resources.
  - Financial weakness of the company: Resulting from successive periods with negative results.
  - Absence of positioning and strategic orientation.

Ansoff matrix

Having been developed by Igor Ansoff in 1957, recognized by many as the father of strategic management, it is applied to identify growth opportunities, combining two axes of evaluation, the Product and the Market, and for both axes, the values can assume "new" or "existing" values (Ansoff, 1965; Grant, 2016; Johnson et al., 2008; Johnson et al., 2017).

- **Market penetration strategy**: To sell existing products or services to existing in the same market (increase the market share). THEIA can adopt a market penetration strategy by implementing one or more of the following actions:

- Increase the frequency of orders; increase the average order value; increase or change the working hours; reduce prices; increasing promotions and distribution; acquisition of a competitor in the same market; bringing in simple product refinements.
    - This strategic option does not generate substantial, competitive, and sustainable added value.
- **Market development strategy**: To enter new markets with existing products. THEIA can adopt a market penetration strategy if it can sell current products to different customers, based on criteria such as:
    - Different customer segments: demographics, lifestyles, perceived benefits, etc.; find industrial buyers for a good that was previously sold only to households; new areas or regions of the country; foreign markets; other organizations sizes; other market sectors.
    - THEIA should choose this strategic option based on the criterion of new areas or regions of the country, duly identified, and described above, since company's experience can be transferred to the new market.
- **Product development strategy**: To develop new products or services for existing customers. THEIA can adopt a product development strategy if it can sell current products to different customers, based on criteria such as:
    - Investment in R&D creates additional products, acquisition of the rights to produce other companies' products, buying products and rebranding them, joint venture with another company to distribute that company's products, production costs may be lower, the product can be produced locally, improvements in the quality of the product can be achieved, the product can have new packaging.
    - THEIA should choose this strategic option based on the criteria "buying products and rebranding them", by means of a joint venture with another company owning products that need access to THEIA's distribution channels. THEIA can do so because it has two conditions that grant it superior competitiveness: 1) a strong brand in the market; 2) a highly loyal distribution channel.
- **Diversification strategy**: To enter new markets with new products or services.
    - THEIA should not choose this strategic option considering that: 1) Its current market still has development potential; 2) There are other alternatives with lower risks.

In summary, THEIA has the following strategic alternatives: Market development strategy and product development strategy.

SOLUTIONS AND RECOMMENDATIONS

In recent years, THEIA's operating structure and market position has deteriorated and diverged from the average situation of companies in the construction materials wholesale sector. Suggestions and recommendations are provided, taking into consideration the study carried out, and the results that were achieved.

Implementation of marketing and communication actions

Recognizing that THEIA's activity has the following characteristics:

- Major incidence on the marketing of products manufactured by other companies.
- Other competitors sell the same products.
- A significant part of its customers is made by building companies (selling to the public and small builders).
- Customers' loyalty is very high.
- The customers' decision-making process is influenced, among other things, by the salesperson and how the products can fulfill their needs.

It is essential to develop a set of activities to ensure that the buying decision making process can be changed to THEIA's benefit. The absence of continuous communication and other marketing actions, such as specific training to "know how to sell THEIA's products and solutions", merchandising materials visible in customers' stores, a set of regular and geographically dispersed events to help loyal customers' businesses, and a traveling road show for the same purpose, is a gap that must be filled immediately. THEIA must remove this functional weakness in its organizational structure.

Market Development

Trying to accomplish a market development strategy, the geographical areas with the greatest potential for business are identified, based on criteria such as licensed buildings, number of potential customers (building materials companies and construction companies) and the area of the region. The geographic area factor dictates the required number of salespeople. The number of licenses per km^2 (licensing density) for each region will allow to assess the number of salespeople needed.

Table 27. Licensing Density

Region	Geographic Area	Licensed buildings	Density of licensed buildings	Ranking
North	21,278km^2	3376	0,1587	2
Center	28,405km^2	2267	0,0798	4
Lisbon (AML)	2,922km^2	1213	0,4151	1
Alentejo	31,551km^2	525	0,0166	5
Algarve	5,412km^2	484	0,0894	3

THEIA commercially covers the North region. However, the location with the greatest potential for new commercial facilities will be the Lisbon (AML) area, as all indicators place this region in the lead. Ranking second, appears the North region, which is already covered by THEIA's facilities and commercial activity. Ranking third, according to the licensing criterion, is Algarve. The density of sector companies per region will give an indication of the competitiveness required to strive and to be successful, and the commercial effort required too.

Table 28. Density of construction and materials companies

Region	Construction materials companies	Density of construction material companies	Rank	Construction companies	Density of construction companies	Rank	Construction materials companies + construction companies	Density of Construction materials companies + construction companies	Rank
Norte	807	0,0379	2	2046	0,0962	2	2853	0,1341	2
Centro	889	0,0313	3	2167	0,0763	4	3056	0,1076	4
Lisboa (AML)	642	0,2197	1	2010	0,6879	1	2652	0,9076	1
Alentejo	175	0,0055	5	325	0,0103	5	500	0,0158	5
Algarve	164	0,0303	4	519	0,0959	3	683	0,1262	3

The location with the greatest potential for new commercial facilities will be the Lisbon region (AML), since all the indicators rank it first. Ranking second, according to all the indicators, is the Northern region, which is covered by THEIA's current facilities. The indicators point to the Algarve region as the third location, with two indicators ranking third and one indicator ranking fourth. If THEIA opts for an additional location in Lisbon the sales forecasts point to an increase of 72% (plus 1.6 million euros), in comparison to 2015.

Product Development

It is recommended to expand the product portfolio marketed by THEIA. The addition of a product mix that combines eco-sustainability with aspects related to rehabilitation and design, will foster the recovery of THEIA's sales volume. THEIA should gradually rethink its positioning, broadening its product base to incorporate wider characteristics of construction materials, while avoiding the narrowing that has been inflicted to it by the construction sector. The product development strategy should be based on the configurations that fit to medium and long-term market opportunities, such as: 1) The rehabilitation of buildings; 2) Energy efficiency; 3) Environmental sustainability. The implementation of the product development strategy will include the following actions.

To find alternative suppliers for the current products, allowing higher profit margins, coupled with a more diversified offer, enabling to reach other market segments and have greater independence from suppliers. The existence of European suppliers that do not have representation in Portugal is an opportunity to offer unique and superior products.

To find suppliers manufacturing substitute products for those currently marked by THEIA. This sector has been characterized by a generalized technological evolution, with the emergence of alternative products exhibiting superior specifications compared with the current products. This guideline also encompasses the possibility to represent European suppliers.

To find suppliers of products that complement THEIA's current offer. For this purpose, THEIA should adopt a positioning different from the current one, appearing as a company that offers a complete solution for the rehabilitation of buildings, energy efficiency of houses, with products that meet the environmental sustainability requirements. It should be noted that THEIA's main competitors already have made this adjustment.

This strategy requires intense commercial and marketing activity aimed to THEIA's customers, mainly to the most loyal group.

REFERENCES

Ansoff, H. I. (1965). *Corporate strategy; an analytic approach to business policy for growth and expansion*. McGraw-Hill.

Cadle, J., Paul, D., & Turner, P. (2014). Business analysis techniques: 99 essential tools for success (2nd ed.). BCS, The Chartered Institute for IT.

Grant, R. M. (2016). *Contemporary strategy analysis: text and cases* (9th ed.). Wiley.

Hanlon, A., & Chaffey, D. (2015). *Essential Marketing Models: Classic Planning Tools to inform strategy*. https://www.davidhodder.com/wp-content/uploads/2018/01/Marketing-Models.pdf

Johnson, G., Scholes, K., & Whittington, R. (2008). *Exploring corporate strategy: text & cases* (8th ed.). Financial Times Prentice Hall.

Johnson, G., Whittington, R., & Scholes, K. (2017). *Exploring strategy* (11th ed.). Pearson.

Porter, M. E. (1979a). *How competitive forces shape strategy*. Harvard Business Review.

Porter, M. E. (1979b). How competitive forces shape strategy. *Harvard Business Review*, *57*(2), 137–145. PMID:18271320

Porter, M. E. (1998a). *Competitive strategy: techniques for analyzing industries and competitors: with a new introduction*. Free Press.

Porter, M. E. (1998b). *On competition*. Harvard Business School Publishing. http://lcweb.loc.gov/catdir/toc/98007643.html

Rothaermel, F. T. (2017). *Strategic management* (3rd ed.). McGraw-Hill Education.

Trompenaars, A., & Coebergh, P. H. (2015). *100+ management models: how to understand and apply the world's most powerful business tools*. McGraw-Hill.

ADDITIONAL READING

Aaker, D. A. (2004). *Brand portfolio strategy: creating relevance, differentiation, energy, leverage, and clarity*. Free Press. Contributor biographical information

Ansoff, H. I. (1965). *Corporate strategy; an analytic approach to business policy for growth and expansion*. McGraw-Hill.

Cadle, J., Paul, D., & Turner, P. (2014). Business analysis techniques: 99 essential tools for success (2nd ed.). BCS, The Chartered Institute for IT.

Collis, D. J., & Montgomery, C. A. (1997). *Corporate strategy: resources and the scope of the firm.* McGraw-Hill/Irwin.

Drucker, P. F. (2017). *The theory of the business.* Harvard Business Review Classics.

Grant, R. M. (2016). *Contemporary strategy analysis: text and cases* (9th ed.). Wiley.

Johnson, G., Scholes, K., & Whittington, R. (2008). *Exploring corporate strategy: text & cases* (8th ed.). Financial Times Prentice Hall.

Johnson, G., Whittington, R., & Scholes, K. (2017). *Exploring strategy* (11th ed.). Pearson.

Kaplan, R. S., & Norton, D. P. (1996). *The balanced scorecard: translating strategy into action.* Harvard Business School Press.

Kaplan, R. S., & Norton, D. P. (2001). *The strategy-focused organization: how balanced scorecard companies thrive in the new business environment.* Harvard Business School Press. doi:10.11081.2001.26129cab.002

Kaplan, R. S., & Norton, D. P. (2004). *Strategy maps: converting intangible assets into tangible outcomes.* Harvard Business School Press.

Keep, W. W., Hollander, S. C., & Dickinson, R. (2008). Forces Impinging on Long-Term Business-to-Business Relationships in the United States. In D. G. B. Jones & E. H. Shaw (Eds.), *The history of marketing thought* (Vol. 2). SAGE.

Kim, W. C., & Mauborgne, R. e. (2015). Blue ocean strategy: how to create uncontested market space and make the competition irrelevant (Expanded edition). Harvard Business Review Press.

Mintzberg, H., Ahlstrand, B. W., & Lampel, J. (2009). *Strategy safari: the complete guide through the wilds of strategic management* (2nd ed.). FT Prentice Hall.

Narver, J. C., & Slater, S. F. (1990). The effect of a market orientation on business profitability. *Journal of Marketing, 54*(4), 20–35. doi:10.1177/002224299005400403

Niven, P. R. (2014). *Balanced scorecard evolution: a dynamic approach to strategy execution.* Wiley.

Porter, M. E. (1980). *Competitive strategy: techniques for analyzing industries and competitors.* Free Press. doi:10.1002/9781118915011

KEY TERMS AND DEFINITIONS

Loyalty: Consumer behavior characterized by buying from the same company, the same brand, or the same product; repeated buying from a firm due to the benefits received from those products.

Market Positioning: It is the relative position that brands, products, and services occupy in the minds of consumers.

Market Segmentation: It is the process of splitting a wide consumer or business market, usually encompassing existing and potential customers, into sub-groups of consumers (identified as segments) based on some type of common characteristics.

Marketing Mix: The marketing mix is a set of controllable variables that determine how consumers respond to the supply and consists of what the company can do to influence the demand for its supply.

Satisfaction: Emotional state arising from the purchase or use of a company's product or service; how delighted customers are with a company's products, services, and capabilities.

Strategy: Strategy is a plan, a direction, or a guide to action for the future, a path to follow from where you are to where you want to go.

APPENDIX 1

Questions and Answers

1. What main problems does THEIA currently face?

THEIA currently has several sizeable problems to deal with. The first is the sharp decline in sales that has continued since 2010. The second problem is what to do about the entry of large manufacturers of thermal insulation materials and how to deal with the entry of large distributors, whose products make up the bulk of the company's sales.

2. Does THEIA have a competitive advantage that allows it to define a business strategy strongly based on facts?

Although THEIA defines itself as a supplier of technical solutions for thermal insulation, in reality the company is just an intermediary in the distribution channel. This channel has been shortened with the entry of large manufacturers of thermal insulation materials and the entry of large distributors. All the competitive advantages and exclusivity THEIA had, disappeared. Currently, its only competitive advantage, proven through data, is a high number of loyal customers (255).

3. What are THEIA's internal problems?

THEIA admittedly has some serious internal problems. The major problem is related to the company's management itself that: 1) Weren't able to adapt to the entry of manufacturers and distributors that have changed the intra-industry balance and the distribution channel equilibrium; 2) Has not adjusted the product portfolio to the new market trends, namely to concerns of sustainability, environmental protection, energy efficiency, among others; 3) Has not outlined a strategy to limit the simultaneous impacts of the entry of new suppliers and the economic crisis.

4. Is it viable to maintain the current strategy, simply remaining as a distributor of thermal insulation materials?

It is difficult for THEIA to be competitive by remaining as an intermediary in the distribution of thermal insulation materials, competing directly with manufacturers (who probably offer better financial conditions) and with international distributors (who get better financial conditions). THEIA "missed the train", that is, it overlooked, in due course, the need to include in its portfolio products related to the rehabilitation of residential and commercial houses and to sustainability, environmental protection and energy efficiency. In fact, given the market changes, THEIA will have to search for a new position if it wants to remain viable.

5. What should be the strategy and implementation sequence for THEIA, given the strategic diagnosis provided?

The first step should be to adjust the product portfolio, to match the market trends. To reduce the power of suppliers is a must. By changing the product portfolio, THEIA will have to adjust its internal structure and to adapt to new marketing and communication strategies and policies. The second step should only occur after the consolidation of the first step and should consist of approaching other market regions. If the company chooses to open a new point of sale in the Lisbon metropolitan area, sales will increase by 1.6 million euros. For all intents and purposes, it should be clear that THEIA has to redefine its strategy and market positioning if it wants to survive.

Epilogue and Lessons Learned

This is a classic case of a company that was successful (because it had a set of agreements that guaranteed it the exclusivity of the distribution of the products encompassed, in Portugal) and this success contributed to management's inaction, erring by managing the company according to an operational perspective, instead of a strategic perspective. The company stopped in time, not adapting to the market, to trends, and to consumer needs

Porter's 5 Forces is the most popular and widely used model in strategic analysis. This case unequivocally shows the usefulness of this model by showing the vulnerability of the company to the power of the suppliers.

This case is also a plus, because it demonstrates the application of the Ansoff matrix and how it contributes to the creation of strategic scenarios. Both the product development strategy and the market development strategy are viable alternatives that should be evaluated.

It is also relevant to highlight the importance of the information systems that ensure the provision of accurate and complete information for the decision-making process. Given the context and the situation described in the case study, any formulation of an alternative strategic scenario for the company to quickly get out of the undesirable position it is in, can raise numerous objections to its real feasibility. However, the information allowed the identification of what is probably a unique and inimitable competitive advantage, which is the loyalty of 255 customers over 6 years. By itself, this guarantees some confidence in the strategic scenarios configured.

Chapter 7
The Bonduelle Group's Distribution Strategy:
Adding a Branded Retail Store?

Véronique Boulocher-Passet
University of Brighton, UK

Randall D. Harris
Texas A&M University, USA

Sabine Ruaud
EDHEC Business School, France

EXECUTIVE SUMMARY

This case study discusses the distribution strategy of the Bonduelle Group and the ability to and value of becoming a retail brand for the world's leading producer and supplier of ready-to-eat processed vegetables. In 2010, the family business opened its first flagship store named 'Bonduelle Bienvenue'. It was entirely dedicated to processed vegetables and offering a big range in the same selling space. The objective of this prototype was not to substitute the company's existing distribution network, or even to hinder it, but to complement it by providing brand visibility and enabling an increase in Bonduelle Group's market share within households. Introducing the reader to the company, the first steps of the concept store back in 2012, and the following other D2C initiatives of the group, this case aims to address the advantages and drawbacks for a food processing brand to engage in selling directly to end consumers.

ORGANIZATION BACKGROUND[1]

A family business founded in 1853 by two friends, Louis-Antoine Bonduelle-Dalle and Louis Lesaffre-Roussel, the Bonduelle Group rose in recent decades to become one of the world's largest processed vegetable companies, the global market leader in ready-to-use vegetables.

DOI: 10.4018/978-1-7998-1630-0.ch007

The Bonduelle Group's Distribution Strategy

Through its business, directly linked with the agriculture sector, through its products, a natural basis for nutrition, and through its ethics, built over generations on a foundation of essential values, the Bonduelle Group had always placed particular importance on sustainable development. Figure 1 shows the logo.

Figure 1. Bonduelle logo

For the 2019-2020 financial year[2], the Bonduelle Group reported a revenue of ca. €2.9 billion (see Figure 2) and a total growth of 2.8% and expected a revenue of €3.5 billion by 2025.

Figure 2. Bonduelle Group's consolidated revenue in million euros, years ending 30/06
Source: compiled by the authors, based upon from Bonduelle Group registration documents

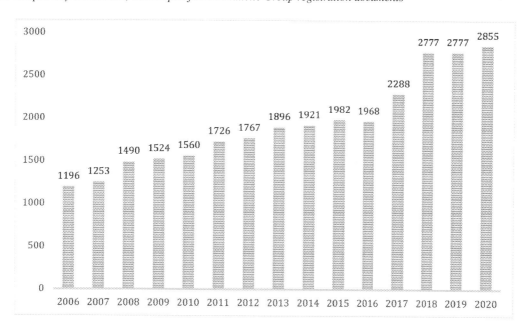

Emphasizing innovation and long-term vision, the company had diversified through both its businesses and geographic locations:

- **Diversification via businesses**: Bonduelle was established as a brand name in 1947. Operations expanded noticeably for the company in 1963 with the construction of a factory in Estrées-Mons, France. This plant, located in the northern Picardy region, would become the largest canning plant in the world. In 1968, Bonduelle entered the frozen vegetables business. In 1989, the Group acquired its main competitor at the time, Cassegrain, and then in 1997 entered the "freshly processed" vegetable business with the acquisition of Salade Minute and its four factories. This acquisition made Bonduelle the European leader in that sector. The company had an initial public offering of stock on the Secondary Stock Market in Paris in 1998, with the family retaining 52% of shares. The subsidiary Bonduelle Traiteur was created in 2003 after the acquisition of the Breton-based company Michel Caugant, specialists in delicatessen vegetable products. Finally, in 2010, Bonduelle had acquired France Champignon, the European leader in mushroom production, making mushrooms the second most popular vegetable in the Bonduelle portfolio after sweet corn.

Figure 3. Revenue breakdown by region, 2020
Source: The Bonduelle Group's shareholders journal, 2020

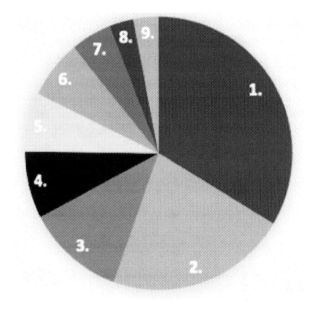

1. USA **34%**
2. France **22%**
3. Canada **12%**
4. Southern Europe **8%**
5. Germany **7%**
6. Eurasia (Russia + CIS countries) **7%**
7. Northern Europe **5%**
8. Central Europe **3%**
9. Other **3%**

- **Diversification via geographies**: The Bonduelle Group was mainly located in Western Europe, where it expanded early with the opening of the European Common Market in 1968. Bonduelle Germany was created in 1969, Bonduelle Italy in 1972 and Bonduelle Great Britain in 1973. The company achieved 50% of its sales from exports as early as 1973. Bonduelle Netherlands was created later in 1982, Bonduelle Spain in 1986, Bonduelle Portugal in 1988, and Bonduelle Denmark in 1989. Bonduelle had also gradually expanded its presence to markets with high growth potential such as Central and Eastern Europe (via the creation of Bonduelle Ceská Republika in 1991, Bonduelle Polska and Bonduelle Hungaria in 1992, Bonduelle Russia and Bonduelle Slovensko in 1994) or South America (via the creation of Bonduelle do Brasil in 1994, with opening of a production site there in 2010, and via the creation of Bonduelle Argentina in 1996). More recently, the group had consolidated its position in North America by acquiring in 2007 Aliments Carrière, the leading Canadian canned and frozen vegetables producer with its brand Arctic Gardens, enabling the group to gain access to 39.500 hectares of farmland. It had acquired four more factories (three processing plants and a packaging plant for frozen vegetables) from Allens Inc. in the USA in spring 2012. In 2015, The Bonduelle group strengthened its position in North America by acquiring the Lethbridge plant in Alberta. The strategic move secured a production capacity of 15,000 tonnes just 100 kilometres from the border between Canada and the United States.

Figure 4. Comparative revenue breakdown by region and segment in 2017 and 2018
Source: compiled by authors from the Bonduelle Group's registration documents, 2017 and 2018

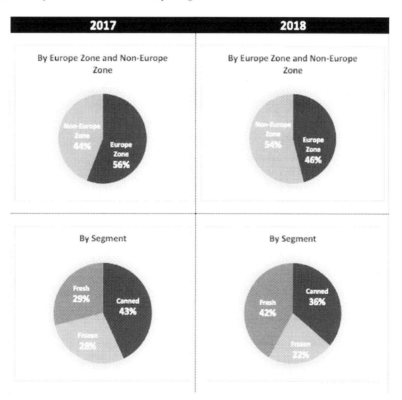

In 2017, Bonduelle entered the USA fresh market with the acquisition of Ready Pac Foods, the leader in individually portioned salads in the United States with almost 85% of the market share. The takeover brought the group 3.500 new employees and four production plants. This transaction was an important step forward in Bonduelle's strategic ambition and completely changed its profile, making the United States its number one operating country (see Figure 3) and the fresh sector its number one business segment (see Figure 4). Ready Pac Foods, renamed Bonduelle Fresh Americas, became Bonduelle's fifth business unit, devoted to the fresh market in the Americas alongside Bonduelle Americas Long Life (headquartered in Montreal) for canned and frozen products. The Bonduelle group was from then organized into three areas (Europe, Americas and Eastern Europe) shared into Business Units; some global departments supported local markets (see Figure 5). As of 2018, Europe generated circa 46% of the Group's revenues (see Figure 3), when Western Europe solely generated around 66% of the Group's revenues back in 2012.

Figure 5. The Bonduelle's Group organization
Source: www.bonduelle.com, 2021

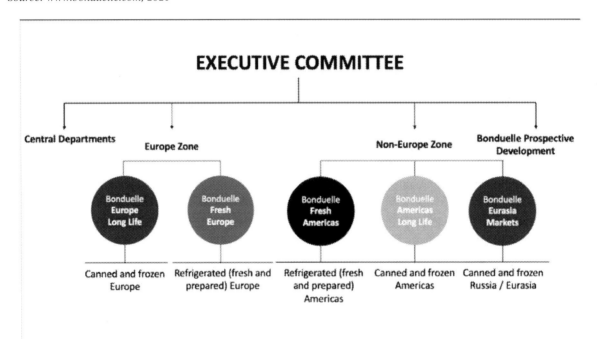

Thanks to the expansion of its operations through internal and external growth, Bonduelle had become – with one single product, the vegetable – the only multi-technology food group in canning, frozen and specialised fresh products (which included catering and pre-packed salads).

The Group's Vision, Mission and Ambition

The Bonduelle Group was a family-owned agro-industrial company. As such, it had always opted for a long-term business vision, continually investing in its agro-industrial plants and innovation to ensure its growth and independence. In 2012, the launching of VegeGo! had helped embody their core philosophy, structured around four pillars:

1. We respect the planet and our social commitments.
2. We promote our brands and develop vegetable in all forms.

3. Customer service is the focus of our organization
4. We promote equality and encourage everyone to realize their full potential.

Within a context of climate change, rapid population growth, erosion of biodiversity and depletion of natural resources, the Bonduelle Group's vision was that feeding the world sustainably was a major challenge for the entire agro-industrial chain. Since 1853, it had been motivated by a concern for People and their food. As pioneer in Corporate Social Responsibility, the Bonduelle Group regarded vegetables as key to the next food revolution and considered its mission to continually push at the boundaries of its ecosystem. The Company's ambition was to be, by 2025, the "world reference in 'well living' through vegetable products".

The Group wanted to make vegetables the future of food and become the reference of plant-based food well-being by processing vegetables in all its forms (canned, frozen, fresh, and prepared vegetables), and in so occupy the most retail shelf space possible. The Bonduelle Group participated therefore in all technologies, across all means of distribution, throughout the world, putting everything in place to favour consumption: industrial investment, quality, marketing. To become the nutritional partner of consumers, they wanted to make processed vegetables available, affordable, and tasty:

- **Availability**: like most brands, Bonduelle was facing the problem of ranking: no large or medium commercial outlet had the entire range of vegetables on its shelves due to a lack of space on the shelves; therefore, it was difficult for the consumer to visualise the breadth and depth of the offer of the four different product categories (canned, frozen products, delicatessen products and pre-packed salads) and moreover, mixing with competing brands (other national brands, private label products, discount brands, etc.). Purchased by two thirds of French households in only 1.7 shelf displays out of 4 on average, Bonduelle wanted to enable consumers to access all its products.
- **Affordability**: like fruits and vegetables, processed vegetables had the image of being expensive products, while their average selling prices was €1 to €1.30 in Europe. The Bonduelle Group's objective was to feed the greatest number of people economically, as explained by the chairman Christophe Bonduelle, interviewed in June 2012:

You do not feed the planet and its 9 billion inhabitants with organic food, what is more, organic food is a question of means and not of results. So, it is not our priority, although we produce organic food to satisfy consumer expectations. (Eco 121, 2012).

However, this did not mean that the Bonduelle Group did not care about marketing healthy products: the company was even avant-garde concerning sustainable development and practice with the cultivation of its products with ecologically intensive agriculture.

- **Taste**: the culinary know-how of the consumers was diminishing; however, there are a lot of things one can do with good produce and a bit of training to transform a standard product into a noble one. The Bonduelle Group wanted to help the consumer enjoy preparing and consuming vegetables. This required education by teaching the consumer how to cook vegetables.

The desire to offer healthy vegetables was the driving force behind the Group's commitment to improve their quality standards. Standardized nutritional labels were created, with the objective of clearly communicated nutritional value of products to consumers. Quality and creativity were the two criteria employed by the Bonduelle Group to deploy their differentiation strategy on a highly competitive market. In fact, a high level of innovation enabled the group to keep its leadership position. The Louis Bonduelle Foundation had also been created in 2004 to give a concrete expression to Bonduelle's commitment at the heart of Nutrition and encourage vegetable consumption in the world.

Trends in the Global Vegetable Market

The vegetable market was broken down into four categories:

- **fresh raw vegetables**, sold directly with no preparation stage.
- **ready-to-use processed vegetables**, which itself consisted of:
    - packaged vegetables (in cans, jars, etc.).
    - frozen vegetables.
    - and fresh-cut vegetables (pre-packaged salads and seasoned salads).

Figure 6. Vegetable consumption in all segments by value and the share of processed vegetables (in %) by region
Source: © 2020, Bonduelle. Used with permission. Bonduelle Group Registration Document

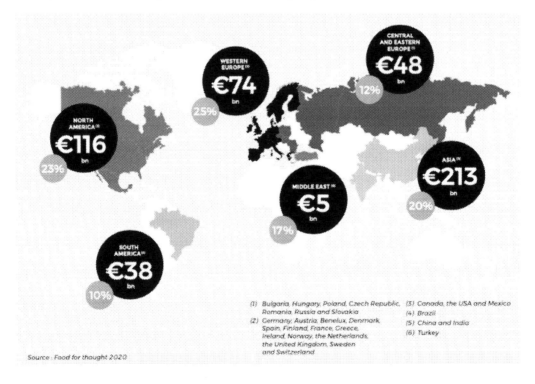

The Bonduelle Group's Distribution Strategy

In addition to those segments, the vegetable market was structured around two distribution channels according to customer type: the consumer products market, which sold vegetables directly to consumers through retailers, and the food service market, which included all commercial services in the catering segment and non-domestic food services. In this sector, where professionals expect products of consistent quality at competitive prices, the ready-to-use vegetables market generally overshadowed the fresh, raw vegetables market.

The raw vegetable category held a majority share of the market value worldwide in 2020, leaving ready-to-use processed vegetables with great potential for growth (see Figure 6).

The global vegetable processing industry was under pressure and undergoing several rapid changes. The industry was mature, with much of the global growth coming from emerging markets, there was intense competition in the industry, consumer confidence had been eroded in the wake of several food crises in Europe, and consumer behavior was undergoing a shift in developed economies. One of the most critical issues for the industry was the increased attentiveness of Western consumers to health consciousness and healthy eating.

Across the world, the vegetables market saw the share of ready-to-use vegetables increase, matching changes in lifestyles. These products met the needs of consumers seeking practical food products with optimum taste and nutritional qualities. In the space of several decades, longer commuting times, the changing role of women in the workplace, the increase in the amount of time devoted to recreational activities and new technologies designed to facilitate everyday life had had a profound impact on eating habits. Meal preparation times had shortened, and new consumption patterns had emerged, such as eating on-the-go. Ready-to-use vegetables responded to these changes by offering solutions developed through innovation. The plant-based market was also growing. Constantly better informed about the role of nutrition in health, consumers started to be hungry for plant-based, organic and locally grown food. Sensitive to innovation, they were adopting new ways of eating: meal kits, online orders, plant-based proteins or vegetarian prepared food (Bonduelle Group Registration Document, 2020).

While a global industry, market share concentration was low, with no industry player having a dominant market share on a worldwide basis in 2021 (Kanda, 2021). Given the wide variety of products this industry produced, regional differences in specific vegetable input production and dissimilar vegetable product preferences of different countries, it was difficult for a single player to control a large share of the global market for processed vegetables. Larger companies tended to dominate individual countries or regions of the world. Notable companies in this industry included Kraft Foods (U.S.), McCain Foods (Canada), The Bonduelle Group (France), and Campbell Soup Company (U.S.). The Bonduelle Group competed solely in the processed vegetable market.

The period 2019-2021 also saw an increasing online presence of processed vegetable vendors. The rise in penetration of smartphones, coupled with improved accessibility to the internet fostered the sale of processed vegetables online. E-commerce platforms gave liberty to consumers to choose from a wide range of brands. Moreover, the speedy delivery and hassle-free purchase experience encouraged more consumers to purchase processed vegetables via e-commerce channels (Businesswire.com, 2021). Store-based retailing nevertheless accounted for more than 95% of retail value (see Table 1) (Euromonitor International, 2021). Spread of the COVID-19 pandemic was expected to positively impact the growth of the global processed vegetable market. The extension of lockdown and containment efforts worldwide had led people to stock up essential food products such as processed vegetables. The growing demand was encouraging several online retail companies to deliver essential food products, including processed vegetables and thus strengthen their presence (Technavio, 2020).

Table 1. Channel Distribution for Processed Fruit and Vegetables - Retail Value RSP 2020 and Percentage Point Growth - 2015-2020

Channel	% Breakdown 2015	% Breakdown 2020
Store-Based Retailing	97.4	95.1
Grocery Retailers	91.8	89.2
Modern Grocery Retailers	76.5	76.0
Convenience Stores	4.8	4.9
Discounters	8.3	8.6
Forcount Retailers	0.4	0.3
Hypermarkets	24.9	25.4
Supermarkets	38.1	36.8
Traditional Grocery Retailers	15.3	13.1
Non-Grocery Specialists	1.9	1.9
Mixed Retailers	3.7	4.0
Non-Store Retailing	2.6	4.9
Homeshopping	0.8	0.6
E-Commerce	1.8	4,3

Source: Euromonitor International, 2021

The Group's Activities in 2020

The Bonduelle Group had secured recognised know-how in 3 main product segments: canned vegetables, the company's historical business, frozen vegetables and fresh-cut processed vegetables.

Figure 7. Breakdown of 2019-2020 revenue by segment
Source: Bonduelle Group Registration Document, 2020

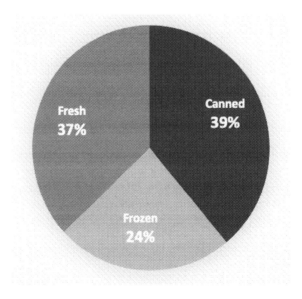

The Bonduelle Group's Distribution Strategy

In 2020, the canned vegetables business remained the Bonduelle Group's main activity and represented 39% of its revenue (see Figure 7). The Group competed in the consumer market and the out-of-home catering market under its own brands (Bonduelle, Cassegrain, Globus in Russia…), offering no less than 3,400 references, but also under many private labels. In addition, it had become the largest European producer of canned sweet corn.

Since 1968, the Bonduelle Group had also devoted a major part of its investments to developing elaborated frozen vegetables that were considered at the forefront of innovation. In just four decades, it had managed to establish itself in Europe. The frozen vegetables business represented 24% of the company's revenue (see Figure 7). Since the acquisition of Canadian Carrière, the Bonduelle Group had become the leader of this business in Canada and was present in the USA. Their most recent innovation was pre-cooked, steamed frozen products.

The fresh ready-to-eat vegetable market represented 37% of revenue for the Group (see Figure 7) and was divided into two main businesses: green salads and raw vegetables without seasoning in pre-packaged bags and seasoned delicatessen products. In the first category, the company offered many innovative and varied products: lettuce, arugula, oak leaf, mixed green salad, corn salad, curly salad, etc. The Bonduelle Traiteur division was created in 2003 and focused on seasoned delicatessen products. The unit soon became a leader in the French market. Bonduelle Traiteur's seasoned delicatessen products included a popular Tabouleh and Seasoned Carrots. The company devoted some of its production to the catering market, where products were marketed by the Bonduelle Food Service subsidiary.

Figure 8. Breakdown of 2019-2020 revenue by brand
Source: Bonduelle Group Registration Document, 2020

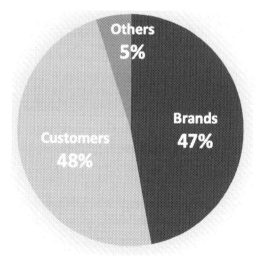

The Bonduelle brand was the primary brand for the Bonduelle Group. It was recognized by 98% of French citizens and almost as many elsewhere in Continental Europe. The Bonduelle Group had four main brand names: Bonduelle, Cassegrain (premium products in France), Arctic Gardens (vegetables processed in Canada) and Globus (canned vegetables in Russia and the Commonwealth of Independent States). Another brand, Royal Champignon, was abandoned to give greater visibility to the main brand.

The Bonduelle Group was also a major manufacturer of private label products for retailers, that represented 48% of the Bonduelle Group revenue (see Figure 8). This double positioning of their own brand and a large private label business enabled the Bonduelle Group to smooth production volumes at their facilities during crises and swings in the economic cycle. Main competitor for the Bonduelle Group remained retailers' own private-label brands. Usually positioned as a low-priced alternative of acceptable quality, private-label brands commanded a large market share in processed vegetables. Nevertheless, the Bonduelle Group considered it a strategic part of its business to also manufacture private-label products and was supplier for many leading retailers.

CASE DESCRIPTION[3]

This section of the chapter presents how an experimental retail store was developed by the Bonduelle Group to become a new direct selling distribution channel.

While the Bonduelle Group were selling their products to customers in the retail food, food service and food-manufacturing industries, using distribution channels that were traditional in the food industry, this same industry was facing a particularly complex situation: a mature market, intense competition in the industry, and the erosion of consumer confidence in the wake of successive food crises in Europe. Despite this challenging environment, or thanks to it, the Bonduelle Group's chairman, Christophe Bonduelle, was considering an initiative of strategic importance for the Group, an innovative response to changes in consumer behaviour within the food industry, namely the implementation of a brand-new distribution strategy in France, the centrepiece of which was the 'Bonduelle Bienvenue' project. Bonduelle had opened their first concept store with this name in France in December 2010. Pierre Masse, New Projects Director at Bonduelle, oversaw developing of the store and other D2C initiatives.

Pierre Masse was interested in gaining a deeper understanding of retail markets generally. After starting his career as a department manager at Auchan, a supermarket and hypermarket retailer, he was recruited as Marketing and Export Director at Michel Caugant, a company that specialized in delicatessen vegetable products. When the Michel Caugant Company was taken over by Bonduelle Group in 2003, Pierre Masse helped in the integration of the combined operations. He was not really interested in the day-to-day management of sales during his career. Rather, he was drawn toward innovative projects and market analysis. In his role as New Projects Director, he led two successive strategic missions for the company: the European launch of Bonduelle brand seasoned delicatessen products and the development of a catering service for the Group via its food service subsidiary. Pierre Masse was increasingly fascinated by trends in the development of snacking and on the go food and was interested in how the Bonduelle Group could include vegetables in more consumer meals and snacks. He thought that having a flagship store would enable the company to create a unique brand experience.

'Bonduelle Bienvenue' integrated the Group Bonduelle's products with a retail place of distribution, creating an experience that was a desirable marketing platform for all Bonduelle's products. In the rapidly changing consumer marketplace, many brands that traditionally sold to final consumers through an external retailer were attempting to grow through their own branded retail channels. Some companies were successful, and others were not. Pierre Masse was convinced that, in the future, many manufacturers would sell directly to the end consumer. The objective of this prototype store was not to substitute for the Bonduelle Group's existing distribution network, but to complement it by providing brand visibility, thus enabling an increase in Bonduelle brand recognition and market share.

Birth of a New Concept Store: The 'Bonduelle Bienvenue' Flagship Store

In early 2009, Pierre Masse started working on the creation of this store, the project took him near to two years. On December 3rd, 2010, the 1076 square foot (100 square meter) store opened in Villeneuve d'Ascq[4], in the North of France, located next to the Bonduelle Group headquarters. This all-vegetable showcase store was stocked with over 250 products from the four Bonduelle Group's product categories.

The store was named 'Bonduelle Bienvenue' to express welcome: the consumer came to Bonduelle headquarters, who welcomed them, hence "Bienvenue" in French, meaning "Welcome". This name was also chosen because it suggested openness and conviviality with a promise of simplicity, gaiety, and warmth. The intent was to create a dialogue with the customer, with a willingness on the part of Bonduelle to "unveil" the company and its values. 'Bonduelle Bienvenue' was conceived to become a real "Guest House", where consumers felt expected, welcomed, and recognized.

'Bonduelle Bienvenue' was the first all-vegetable store in France. It was segmented into different product zones using Bonduelle brand's colours (Green, Yellow and Orange), and was laid out in three sections.

The Showcase Store section was designed for vegetable lovers and enabled shoppers to enrich their relationship with the Bonduelle and related brands. These were the main product displays, labelled in Green and occupying three quarters of the store layout. This zone was designed to:

1. Discover the full range of the Group Bonduelle's branded products (canned, frozen, delicatessen and pre-packaged salad products) including more than 300 products. This included the Bonduelle and Cassegrain brands[5] as well as products sold globally, including German, Spanish and Polish products.
2. Offer a Bonus: the store carried special items, like Bonduelle steam ranges and specialty food products.
3. Provide the public with access to products that were previously reserved for professionals in the Food Service market.

An Information Zone, labelled in Yellow, enabled 'Bonduelle Bienvenue' to:

1. Present the history of the group, its culture and values, manufacturing processes, the nutritional values of its vegetables, and the Louis Bonduelle Foundation.
2. Welcome and speak to visiting groups, such as schoolchildren. The space was also useful for small meetings regarding nutrition and sustainable development.
3. Provide training for vegetable preparation: 'Bonduelle Bienvenue' provided cooking lessons and other cooking related activities. In addition to the information zone, food tastings and recipes for everyday use were offered at the front of the store. These touches, and others, helped the consumer get the best out of Bonduelle products, thus offering a unique sensory and emotional consumer experience.

A Bargain Zone, labelled in Orange, this was a clearance zone. The bargain zone offered quality products from the Bonduelle Group with a short expiration date, as well as discounted and end of line products.

The 'Bonduelle Bienvenue' store, supported by a five-person team, also included a small pilot marketing area where new packaging and recipes could be tested out with customers. 'Bonduelle Bienvenue' team members were on site to listen to customers, provide advice, and support a pleasant interaction with the Flagship Store. Customer responses to the store, collected via survey, were favourable.

The objective of 'Bonduelle Bienvenue' was to serve as the Flagship Store for the Bonduelle Group, and to test the potential for the Bonduelle retail store format. The Bonduelle Group was considering several options for the future, like adding factory outlet stores near to their rural production facilities in France or adding some flagship stores near their headquarters in different European countries. Pierre Masse stressed that 'Bonduelle Bienvenue' store was not opened to compete with supermarkets in France. Supermarkets were the main retail outlet for the company's products. The Bonduelle Group did not wish to cannibalize sales for their products from the supermarket chains. Pierre Masse emphasized that sales cannibalization was unlikely with 'Bonduelle Bienvenue' because it was located away from the centre of the city and the main shopping district of the city.

'Bonduelle Bienvenue' targeted vegetable lovers, fans of good vegetables, aficionados, and "addicts" of the Bonduelle/Cassegrain brand. Pierre Masse, when asked which customers were targeted with this store, added that the store also appealed to families concerned by the nutritional value of vegetables and those who wished to discover "fun food". He thought that the store would also be attractive to traditional customers of factory shops who were on the lookout for good bargains on quality products. Survey results after one year of opening of the store indicated it also seemed to be attractive to local consumers for their midday snacking and/or rushed evening shopping. In addition, the Bonduelle Group intended to generate new demand for their products by appealing to non-traditional markets, such as small restaurants, works councils and various civic associations in the area.

Pierre Masse saw 'Bonduelle Bienvenue' store as a complement to the Group's other retail sales outlets. The strategic intent was that the Flagship Store would enable Bonduelle customers to discover the entire range of Bonduelle products, especially Bonduelle frozen vegetables. The frozen vegetable market was dominated in most French supermarkets by private-label products. As a bonus, Bonduelle Bienvenue shoppers had access to several delicatessen products that were normally only available for Food Service sales and not the public. Bonduelle Bienvenue's goal was to increase brand recognition, generate sales and to make vegetables both the main dish and the side dish of choice for French consumers.

Development of the Marketing Strategy

Pricing: The labelled pricing at 'Bonduelle Bienvenue' was comparable to the supermarket price for the Bonduelle Group's products. Except for the Bargain Zone (Orange color zone, where prices were discounted by 50% to 66%), products sold at prices equivalent to the average regional price on the item. Shoppers benefitted from discounts based on volume. The discount policy was set as follows: buy €15 worth of products, get a 15% discount. Buy €30 of items and get a 30% discount off the purchase. The discount was calculated from the overall purchase total on the customer's receipt.

Place: 'Bonduelle Bienvenue' store was open Monday to Friday, 11am to 7pm, and on Saturdays from 10am to 6pm. Customers could place orders in advance via the store's website at http://www.bonduellebienvenue.fr (Click and Collect). Customer orders were available three hours after order and were retained for pickup for 48 hours.

Promotion: 'Bonduelle Bienvenue' opened on December 3rd, 2010. Initial promotion for the first fourteen months was word of mouth only. A promotional campaign was launched in March 2012 to

The Bonduelle Group's Distribution Strategy

promote the store. Efforts included a street marketing operation with the hand distribution of fliers in the local area around the store. A "Win your weight in Peas" promotion ran from March through April 2012. Other promotional activities included €10 vouchers on Groupon (vouchers worth €20 in the store) and sponsorship of local events. Pierre Masse was satisfied with the results of those promotional efforts in terms of new customer recruitment. In March 2012, the store had an average of 1,200 customers per month. After the "Win your weight in Peas" campaign, the store was averaging 2,000 customers per month. Pierre Masse stated that 'Bonduelle Bienvenue' tried to use different promotional channels than the supermarkets. Other promotional efforts included a monthly newsletter started in March 2012, and a Facebook page started in May 2012.

Encouraging Initial Results

The Flagship Store reached sales of 800,000 Euros in 2012. The initial results at 'Bonduelle Bienvenue' were encouraging, according to Pierre Masse. He felt confident that the store would reach breakeven within the next few years and be able to operate without the Bonduelle Group support for operating costs. Masse was frugal with start-up costs for the store, using a building from the corporate headquarters that already existed.

Market research conducted by Pierre Masse in December 2012 revealed sales in the Bargain Zone were 25% of store sales, while sales in the canned food area was 45% of store sales[6]. Frozen products were 20% of store sales and the remainder, delicatessen items and snacks, made up 10% of store sales. Further study of customer purchase behaviour suggested three types of customers at the store based upon their purchase patterns:

- **Customers with an average basket of less than €5**, "Snacking Customers" constituted approximately 35% of customers and were mainly interested in snack products: They tended to be shoppers who worked locally and came to buy their lunch. Snacking Customers spent relatively little in-store on each visit (Average Basket = €3).
- **Customers with an average basket of between €6 and €30** represented approximately 20% of customers. This shopper did not benefit from the full store discount on their purchase. They typically purchased in this range due to a lack of storage space in their home or due to a low number of persons for whom they shopped. These customers nevertheless benefitted from the 15% store discount and spent generally between €12 and €21 on each shopping trip (Average Basket = €16).
- **Customers with an average basket greater than €30** represented 40% of shoppers, predominantly mothers who were focused on health and nutrition for their families. These customers benefitted from the 30% store discount (Average Basket = €34).

Long distance shoppers at the store tended to visit with low frequency but went out with a larger purchase. Local shoppers demonstrated a higher shopping frequency but a lower average purchase. Shoppers who returned to make another purchase within one year (the re-purchase rate) was estimated by Pierre Masse at 40%. However, as there were many new customers to 'Bonduelle Bienvenue', he did not believe that this estimate reflected the real in-store return customer rate.

'Bonduelle Bienvenue' also conducted a focus group with 10 store customers in 2012. An analysis of the discussion showed that consumers were drawn to the store for the following reasons: 1. Low prices (Bargain Shopping), 2. Store Selection, especially the frozen vegetable products (as the selection was much less in a typical supermarket), 3. Delicatessen Products that were usually only available through Food Service vendors, 4. Volume Discounts, e.g., buy €15 of assorted products and get a 15% discount, or €30 = 30% discount, and 5. Availability of a dedicated sales team, who advised on meal preparation.

Results from the focus group also suggested that a typical local customer had the impression they spent 5 minutes in-store when they spent on average approximately 10 to 15 minutes. Fully three quarters of 'Bonduelle Bienvenue' customers also purchased Bonduelle products in supermarkets. Regarding their store expectations, the focus group shoppers stated they were looking for bargains, were discovering new products, and enjoyed shopping in a fun atmosphere.

From its start in 2010, it took 4 years for 'Bonduelle Bienvenue' to become profitable. The store was made a separate business unit with its own budget on July 1st, 2014. As of June 2021, 'Bonduelle Bienvenue' store in Villeneuve d'Ascq was still in operation, although having been redesigned to suppress the information zone. No additional 'Bonduelle Bienvenue' stores had been opened in France. Another experiential store named 'La Boutique l'Emotion Végétale', with a slightly different concept, had been opened in October 2018 in the suburbs of Lyon, in an industrial zone, but had not managed to attract enough customers mainly due to, according to an analysis from the company, a wrong choice of location. It was closed in 2020.

CHALLENGES FACING THE BONDUELLE GROUP

In consumer products especially, this type of branded retail initiative was not always a success. Inaugurate a concept store or open an online store did not make you a retail trader. The questions were numerous and examples of other food brands, which had engaged earlier in a branded retail strategy, various: some having been successful (Häagen-Dazs and Nespresso, for example, had made boutiques the heart of their strategy, without neglecting the multichannel, and became models of their kind), but others having failed. In the early 2000s, Lustucru, had tried to open a restaurant in the Bastille Area in Paris, and Heineken a concept store on Champs Elysées, both experiences revealed to be unprofitable.

The question facing the Bonduelle Group at the end of 2014 was how to fit the experimental store into the group's overall distribution strategy. Should the 'Bonduelle Bienvenue' experience be replicated and developed? Which role could 'Bonduelle Bienvenue' play in the overall future distribution strategy of the company? The pressing question: Was branded retail an appropriate strategy for a food company like Bonduelle?

Owning retail stores was one possible route towards D2C sales. But there were others and the Group Bonduelle wanted to multiply the D2C initiatives. In an interview within LSA, a French trade journal, Christophe Bonduelle, chairman of the Bonduelle Group, had set the tone behind the development of 'Bonduelle Bienvenue' Flagship Store as only one of many new potential direct sales modes:

We are exploring diverse marketing strategies and new distribution channels to try and generate more value, such as recently an internet website for Cassegrain or a direct sales store. This (Bonduelle Bienvenue) acts as a marketing laboratory for us. However, more generally, we are testing and exploring different distribution channels, even if this activity will always be a side activity for Bonduelle (Harel, 2014).

Thus, reflecting how the organization took into consideration important changes in consumer behaviour, that all consumer good brands were facing with the expansion of digital channels in the customer journey.

The Bonduelle Group's Distribution Strategy

In October 2014, the Bonduelle Group had started another e-commerce site selling Cassegrain premium brand. A team of 10 persons was dedicated to developing e-commerce in France and abroad. The e-boutique, beyond selling the complete range of Cassegrain canned vegetables, provided the users with recipes and videos to share, making the website a real showcase for the brand and its new products, resolutely positioned at the top of the range. In this, still at the time, embryonic food e-commerce market, experiences were currently limited to niche sites, positioned premium or local (Lentschner, 2014). The e-boutique closed on 10th June 2020, in the middle of the Covid-19 pandemic.

From January 2015, the company innovated with another channel of at home direct sales. According to Pierre Masse, home direct sales were increasing by 6 to 7% each year in France, mainly in the countryside. The concept of 'Mon Panier Secret' ('My Secret Basket') home sales was addressing this trend, with an aim to bring the company closer to consumers and communicate differently. Bonduelle ambassadors organized meetings in the form of themed culinary workshops (verrines, appetizers, pies, etc.) at hosts' homes, to learn how to cook canned and frozen vegetables differently and easily, to discover creative ways of cooking vegetables (Gore-Langton, 2017). As with Tupperware, the leading company using a direct selling approach, orders were then consolidated and delivered to the meeting location. The Bonduelle Group, which began recruiting ambassadors in its region of origin, Nord-Pas-de-Calais, had more than 150 ambassadors across France by the end of 2017 (Ylalaurencie, 2017) and was aiming at expanding its network to develop additional relays in several other regions. The Covid-19 pandemic however slowed the expansion down.

In December 2015 the company launched a Food Truck. Baptized "Les Toqués de Légumes" (The Vegetable Nuts), the Food Truck travelled across Northern France, cooking meals with Bonduelle vegetables. This innovative sales channel had been tested around the city of Lille, then moved to Lyon and Paris. The Food Truck stopped at the 'Bonduelle Bienvenue' store on some days. If successful, the Food Truck would be further developed in other regions of France.

SOLUTIONS AND RECOMMENDATIONS

The Bonduelle Group's efforts to move into branded retail are symptomatic of the wider upheaval and consolidation that has occurred in retail product markets (Urbanska, 2007). As retailers, such as supermarkets, consolidated and gained market power, many manufacturers and brands lost control of their destiny at the retail level. Retailers benefit indeed from communicating with final customers personally at their stores, right where the shopping takes place and most shopping decisions are made (Thomassen et al., 2006). Product manufacturers have therefore increasingly looked to their own branded retail efforts to mitigate their loss of control at the retail level (Ilonen et al., 2010).

The situation for the Bonduelle Group is particularly acute, given the strong market share for private label vegetable products in Europe and the Bonduelle Group's interest in the private label vegetable market. Performing a situation analysis of the Bonduelle Group enables to identify that the company both competes and collaborates with supermarkets. By using several different methods of critical analysis, readers can analyze the Bonduelle Group's internal and external environment to understand the organization's capabilities, customers, and business environment. To name a few, Porter's five forces model (Porter, 2008), SWOT and TOWS analyses (Weihrich, 1982), Value Chain Analysis (Hines & Rich, 1997) or the 5C analysis (Steenburgh and Avery, 2010) are valuable frameworks that can be used here to conduct a comprehensive analysis of the company's business to inform their strategic planning decisions.

The Bonduelle Group was a successful company with a strong brand image, moving rapidly in the direction of building a global brand. However, the firm faced a difficult industry environment, with fickle Western consumers and strong branded retail competition. Was branded retail an appropriate distribution strategy for a food producer like the Bonduelle Group? If Bonduelle had reached a brand status, could it successfully become a retail brand?

Regain Control of the Brand at the Retail Level

Yadav and Varadarajan (2005) suggested the growing power of retailers may force more manufacturers to use E-commerce to bypass channel members that devote more resources to private label brands and less shelf space to national brands. Branded retail has been found to be another appropriate direct to consumer distribution strategy for several industries, including Toys and Games (LEGO Group), Mobile Communications (Nokia), and Fashion (H&M) (Ilonen et al., 2011). While less common, the use of branded retail operations or flagship brand stores is not unprecedented in food products. In Germany, for example, national brands from the chocolate (e.g., Ritter Sport and Milka) or cereal (e.g., Kölln) categories have begun to operate flagship stores in the city centers of Berlin, Hamburg, and Munich (Nierobisch et al., 2017). Flagship Stores can also be considered one possible method to communicate with end customers and stay visible with an increasingly information overloaded consumer. The retail markets are more diverse and fragmented than ever before, presenting consumers with an overload of information and alternatives. Consumers, deluged with information from an increasingly wired and web enabled environment, face more information and consumption choices than ever before. The themed flagship brand store phenomenon may be at the cutting edge of this trend. As industries like food products consolidate, companies like the Bonduelle Group are attempting to regain control of their brand at the retail level through the flagship brand store. Building upon the in-store experience, companies are seeking to establish a connection with their consumers and build upon these emotional connections. The Bonduelle Group, through its flagship operation, is seeking to build the Bonduelle brand and merchandise it. This strategy will likely bring debate regarding the efficacy of this retail strategy for food producers. Nierobisch et al. (2017) argue it is indeed debatable whether a flagship store that creates first and foremost brand experience would generate the intensified consumer-brand relationships, improved brand cognitions, and brand loyalty desired by FMCG national brands to win the brand battle in an intensified competition. In the FMCG context, brands are less likely to evoke brand attachment, as the variety of competing offers at retail stores, coupled with the wide array of advertisements, vastly dilutes the congruity of one's self-concept with a brand's personality, especially given that consumers recognize only marginal differences at the product level (Garsvaite and Caruana, 2014). Can flagship store-fueled brand experiences enable the creation of brand equity for a processed vegetables brand? Processed vegetables are a commodity product, building a retail brand for a commodity product may not be an effective enough marketing channel. The devotion by the Bonduelle Group of exclusive space to build its brand and deepen its emotional connection to the consumer is an important retail phenomenon and mirrors the experience of other manufacturers attempting to regain control of their brand destiny at the retail level (Ilonen et al., 2011). Offering consumers an experiential retail space is custom tailored to deliver a powerful brand experience and deepen consumer connection to the brand and product. Nierobisch et al. (2017) showed in their research that flagship stores in the FMCG industry present suitable communication vehicles and marketing-tools for creating positive brand cognitions and brand-relationships with potential consumers. However, branded retail can at the moment only be regarded as a complement, and not a substitute, for the Bonduelle Group's traditional marketing sales channels.

Avoid Channel Conflict with Retail Customers

Next, the entry of the Bonduelle Group into the branded retail market is constrained by their efforts to avoid channel conflict with their other retail distribution channels. Organizing and managing a firm's channels of distribution is a mission-critical issue for a firm's marketing strategy (Frazier, 1999). Channel conflicts become even more problematic in the new era of the Internet and e-commerce (Webb, 2002). The Bonduelle Group is not alone in their attempt to preserve their classical indirect retail channels (e.g., the supermarket chains) and at the same time carefully push into direct retail sales. This is difficult without creating channel conflict. Nevertheless, some companies manage to achieve this balance, such as Danone in France developing their online presence and delivering Evian water direct to their end customers' homes. There is a need for companies in the food processing industry to reinvent their distribution models and develop direct distribution, possibly enhanced by emerging digital technologies. Potential channel conflict is likely a very sensitive topic for the Bonduelle Group. Retailers could regard the Bonduelle branded store as a potential competitor or argue that the branded store violated exclusive territorial rights to market and sell Bonduelle branded products. The Bonduelle Group has therefore several actual and potential channel conflicts with which to contend and managing them effectively would be an integral part of a successful distribution strategy for the Group. Many Flagship Stores are deliberately located near main shopping districts or heavily urban areas. Bonduelle Bienvenue was, on the contrary, deliberately located away from the centre of the city to prevent even the appearance of channel conflict. Thus, the Bonduelle Group had taken pains to ensure that the branded flagship store had not infringed upon the domain of the company's traditional retail sales channels and was positioned to be a complement to other retail channel marketing and sales efforts. A parallel can be drawn to Apple Computer. When Apple launched their Flagship Stores it had greatly upset their existing retailers. Apple had to work hard to smooth relationships with their intermediaries and justified the decision to add their own stores as a natural evolution of an already existing online sales channel. Online sales channels have also been challenging for many companies attempting to manage their channels of distribution (Webb, 2002). Opening the 'Bonduelle Bienvenue' Flagship Store could have presented a channel conflict to the Bonduelle Group's other retail market channels but appears to have been managed effectively. Nierobisch et al. (2017) insist that flagship stores are likely to enable sales in other distribution channels. Jahn et al. (2018) emphasize that experiential retail stores are complementary communication and distribution channels rather than substitutes for or threats to traditional brand outlets, retailers, or other third-party distributors. Managing this new retail channel as it further develops will nevertheless likely be an ongoing issue for the Bonduelle Group.

Use Flagship Store as an Experiential Marketing Tool

The Bonduelle Group attempted to enter the retail brand market via a Flagship Store. Can it be considered a successful operation? Flagship Stores can be very powerful marketing channel, but research in this area is still nascent. It is difficult to gain access to Flagship Stores for research purposes due to their limited number. Retail Flagship Stores appear to be an intensely ideological affair (Borghini et al., 2009). Typically, retail operations are operated and assessed upon the basis of profitability; companies, in particular family businesses, are hesitant to retain operations that do not operate at least at the breakeven point. Margins of FMCG food and grocery brands are at least three times lower than those of fashion brands or durable goods, making it harder for them to cover the costs for flagship stores. Therefore, the revenue and advertising effect for covering the costs of operating flagship stores needs to come from traditional distribution channels: the retailers (Nierobisc et al., 2017). The efficacy of the experiential retail store may be disputed within firms, and managers might face pressure to demonstrate the necessity of such stores. Especially, the moderating effects of motivational orientation and brand salience should be considered in a non-luxury retail context like that of food and grocery brands (Jahn et al., 2018).

However, flagship brand stores are more expansive in their purpose, and may require additional factors to consider in their success. Flagship Stores done well can indeed promote an engaging experience for the consumer as well as provide entertainment (Kozinets et al., 2002). This entertainment aspect of the Flagship Store is likely part of a broader societal shift toward an experience-based economy (Hollenbeck et al., 2008). Research that has been conducted on Flagship Stores suggests that they can have a stronger impact on brand attitude, brand attachment and brand equity than other types of retail formats (Dolbec and Chebat, 2013). Flagship brand stores are thus often opened to build and reinforce the brand image rather than to produce a profit. Thus, while profitability is always a consideration, the success of the operation in building and expanding the brand image is also a significant consideration. As a result, opening and operating a flagship store, particularly for manufacturers, can be complex and challenging (Kozinets et al., 2002). A successful flagship store's expense can be written off against its demonstrated long-term promotional power (ibid). In this way of thinking, flagship stores are more than a profit and loss exercise with the usual metrics of sales per square foot and foot traffic. A flagship store is all about the brand. It's about service, experience, and engagement with customers. So, it's possible to make the bold, but simple statement that, making a profit per square foot is not the point. A retail store is a huge, experiential, tactile marketing opportunity. It's where your brand comes to life, and where your sales staff engage with customers and build loyalty. With respect to building and reinforcing the brand image, the Bonduelle Group's operation seems a success. The 40% repurchase rate is one significant indicator of the success of the store's efforts toward building the brand. The length of time that consumers spent in the store itself – upwards of 10 to 15 minutes – is another. Another factor was that three quarters of customers had purchased Bonduelle products in both channels, both retail and flagship store. These points substantiate success for the flagship store in building and reinforcing the Bonduelle brand image. The new facility has achieved its marketing objectives. It clearly presents a legitimate brand, recruited new customers and has also clearly increased brand awareness. It is also reasonable to conclude that the current facility will require economic support to remain in operation in the long run. Efforts to substantially boost store sales may be hampered by the legitimate interest of management to keep the store facility outside the central urban area, and hence not present a channel conflict to the Bonduelle Group's traditional retail marketing network. Management would therefore have to regard the 'Bonduelle Bienvenue' flagship store as partially a marketing expense and not only a legitimate profit centre.

Continue Experimentation of Direct Sales Channel Initiatives

As presented earlier, additional options have been considered by the company for broadening the Bonduelle Group's direct sales channel initiatives. If selling direct to consumers is not a new idea for brands generally, the path from idea to realization has shortened considerably in the digital age, paving the way for a rise of D2C brand-building models. Digital disruption has changed (and is still changing) the world in which brands interact with their consumers. New technologies have created new markets that, in turn, have created new consumers and new competitors with new expectations, and ultimately change the way value is and should be created by brands. Gielens and Steenkamp (2019) argue that digital (dis) intermediation, in allowing manufacturers to switch or eliminate intermediaries whose added costs may exceed the value they provide, causes a seismic shift in today's marketing environment. The boundaries between brand manufacturers and retailers, between offline and online retailers, and between suppliers and consumers are increasingly blurred. Of course, retailing is a full-fledged job and not everyone can qualify for it. Certainly, few consumer products can claim to do without the shelves of hypermarkets and supermarkets, but the temptation for a company to take in hand part of its distribution is great. The reasons why to take the plunge are numerous (Dauvers, 2019): get to know end customers better, understand their expectations and the purchasing journey; control the data resulting from this customer relationship; live test new products; target new customers; offer new customer experience; develop new services; position differently; invest a new buying opportunity; promote a mode of consumption; break free from the limits of physical commerce.

If, compared to traditional channels, the direct-to-consumer experience is only a limited lever for a brand's turnover, the margin gains are not negligible, and the brand image usually improves. Direct-to-Consumer (D2C) models allow brands to directly engage with their customers using social, mobile, and digital channels. The goal is to enhance the customer journey more directly, adapt to changes in customer behaviour and differentiate the brand experience. Furthermore, over time,

Digital retailers have developed into new power players in the value chain. Making use of unique digital information that allows for mass personalization of product offerings and prices on the one hand, and recommendation and review tools on the other hand, these new digital juggernauts are increasingly pushing their private labels, thereby turning into brand competitors, rather than "mere" facilitators (Gielens & Steenkamp, 2019, p. 368)

According to Boumphrey (2020), the Covid-19 pandemic had recently accelerated the rise of online, click & collect, frictionless retail and direct-to-consumer (D2C) channels. Retail consumers shop restrictions in place during the pandemic had fast-tracked the shift to digital distribution. A turning point for e-commerce and a boost for meal kits was tempered by an adverse impact on impulse channels, as consumers were less likely to 'pop in' to buy a single chocolate bar from their local convenience store. The 'Bonduelle Bienvenue' store benefitted directly from this accelerated trend, its drive-through and click-and-collect sales, which had been anecdotical before, exploded with different lockdowns.

CONCLUSION

In the old world, retailers acted as the gatekeepers who granted access to consumers. Today, companies are finding D2C ways to get products to customers. More and more consumer-packaged goods companies are realizing the possibilities in the new world of retail. The Bonduelle Group is no exception. The future of retail will see complete integration of technologies like augmented and virtual reality, the internet of things, sensor-driven packaging and connected appliances. This will result in an exponential impact on e-commerce volumes. Brick-and-mortar stores being no longer simply a channel for the distribution of products and no longer acting as the final point in the purchase funnel, they will rather offer retailers and brands the opportunity to draw the consumer into the brand story, deliver a remarkable and immersive brand and product experience, and ultimately galvanize their relationship with consumers. By multiplying its D2C initiatives vie e-commerce website, food truck or home sales during the last decade, the Bonduelle group demonstrated the understanding of its changing environment, as well as its will to prepare for the right strategic moves when times come. How will the company navigate in the announced retail apocalypse?

REFERENCES

Borghini, S., Diamond, N., Kozinets, R., McGrath, M., Munoz, A., & Sherry, J. (2009). Why are Themed Brandstores so Powerful? Retail Brand Ideology at American Girl Place. *Journal of Retailing*, *85*(3), 363–375. doi:10.1016/j.jretai.2009.05.003

Boumphrey, S. (2020). *How will consumer markets evolve after Coronavirus?* Euromonitor International. https://go.euromonitor.com/white-paper-2020-covid-19-themes.html#download-link

Businesswire.com. (2019). *Global Processed Vegetable Market 2019-2023: Increasing Online Presence of Processed Vegetable Vendors to Boost Growth*. https://www.businesswire.com/news/home/20190714005002/en/Global-Processed-Vegetable-Market-2019-2023-Increasing-Online-Presence-of-Processed-Vegetable-Vendors-to-Boost-Growth-Technavio

Dauvers, O. (2019). *Direct to consumer 2019*. Editions Dauvers.

Dolbec, P. Y., & Chebat, J. C. (2013). The Impact of a Flagship vs. a Brand Store on Brand Attitude, Brand Attachment and Brand Equity. *Journal of Retailing*, *89*(4), 460–466. doi:10.1016/j.jretai.2013.06.003

Eco 121. (2012). *Interview with Christophe Bonduelle*. N° 22.

Euromonitor International. (2021). *Processed Fruit and Vegetables in World: Datagraphics*. Author.

Frazier, G. L. (1999). Organizing and managing channels of distribution. *Journal of the Academy of Marketing Science*, *27*(2), 226–240. doi:10.1177/0092070399272007

Garsvaite, K., & Caruana, A. (2014). Do consumers of FMCGs seek brands with congruent personalities? *Journal of Brand Management*, *21*(6), 485–494. doi:10.1057/bm.2014.17

Gielens, K., & Steenkamp, J.-B. E. M. (2019). Branding in the era of digital (dis)intermediation. *International Journal of Research in Marketing*, *36*(3), 367–384. doi:10.1016/j.ijresmar.2019.01.005

Gore-Langton, L. (2017). *Bonduelle cuts out retailers with online delivery service*. https://www.foodnavigator.com/Article/2017/01/11/Bonduelle-cuts-out-retailers-with-online-delivery-service

Harel, C. (2014). *Bonduelle s'essaie à de nouveaux territoires de chasse*. LSA N° 2336-2337.

Hines, P., & Rich, N. (1997). The seven value stream mapping tools. *International Journal of Production & Operations Management*, *17*(1), 46–64. doi:10.1108/01443579710157989

Hollenbeck, C., Peters, C., & Zinkhan, G. (2008). Retail Spectacles and Brand Meaning: Insights from a Brand Museum Case Study. *Journal of Retailing*, *84*(3), 334–353. doi:10.1016/j.jretai.2008.05.003

Ilonen, L., Wren, J., Gabrielsson, M., & Salimäki, M. (2011). The role of branded retail in manufacturers' international strategy. *International Journal of Retail & Distribution Management*, *39*(6), 414–433. doi:10.1108/09590551111137976

Jahn, S., Nierobisch, T., Toporowski, W., & Dannewald, T. (2018). Selling the extraordinary in experiential retail stores. *Journal of the Association for Consumer Research*, *3*(3), 412–424. doi:10.1086/698330

Kanda, S. (2021). *Global Fruit and Vegetable Processing: Industry Report*. IBISWorld.

Kozinets, R. V., Sherry, J. F., DeBerry-Spence, B., Duhachek, A., Nuttavuthisit, K., & Storm, D. (2002). Themed flagship brand stores in the new millennium: Theory, practice, prospects. *Journal of Retailing*, *78*(1), 17–29. doi:10.1016/S0022-4359(01)00063-X

Lentschner, K. (2014). *Bonduelle se lance dans l'e-commerce*. https://www.lefigaro.fr/societes/2014/10/01/20005-20141001ARTFIG00008-bonduelle-se-lance-dans-le-e-commerce.php

Nierobisch, T., Toporowski, W., Dannewald, T., & Jahn, S. (2017). Flagship stores for FMCG national brands: Do they improve brand cognitions and create favorable consumer reactions? *Journal of Retailing and Consumer Services*, *34*, 117–137. doi:10.1016/j.jretconser.2016.09.014

Porter, M. E. (2008). The five competitive forces that shape strategy. *Harvard Business Review*, *86*(1), 78. PMID:18271320

Steenburgh, T., & Avery, J. (2010). *Marketing Analysis Toolkit: Situation Analysis*. Harvard Business Publishing.

Technavio. (2020). *Processed Vegetable Market by Product and Geography - Forecast and Analysis 2020-2024*. http://www.technavio.com

Thomassen, L., Lincoln, K., & Aconis, A. (2006). *Retailization: Brand Survival in the Age of Retailer Power*. Kogan Page.

Yadav, M. S., & Varadarajan, P. R. (2005). Understanding product migration to the electronic marketplace: A conceptual framework. *Journal of Retailing*, *81*(2), 125–140. doi:10.1016/j.jretai.2005.03.006

Ylalaurencie. (2017). *Les légumes Bonduelle s'invitent chez vous*. https://www.bibamagazine.fr/lifestyle/les-legumes-bonduelle-sinvitent-chez-vous-9557.html

Urbanska, J. (2007). Modern Retail Distribution–The Case of Bonduelle Poland. *Advanced Logistic Systems*, *1*(1), 101–107.

Webb, K. (2002). Managing Channels of Distribution in the Age of Electronic Commerce. *Industrial Marketing Management*, *31*(2), 95–102. doi:10.1016/S0019-8501(01)00181-X

Weihrich, H. (1982). The TOWS matrix - A tool for situational analysis. *Long Range Planning*, *15*(2), 54–66. doi:10.1016/0024-6301(82)90120-0

List of Additional Sources

Here are a few selected links to YouTube videos that instructors may find useful:

Presentation of the Bonduelle Group (2 min 45 sec) (English)

https://www.youtube.com/user/GroupeBonduelle

This short video provides a quick overview of the Bonduelle group. You can start your class with this video to make sure students have a thorough understanding of the different categories of processed vegetables produced by Bonduelle Group.

Bonduelle, Inspiring you to Eat Vegetables every Day (1min 48 sec) (English)

https://www.youtube.com/watch?v=vidpdfqbvMU

The Bonduelle Group's mission and vision is presented in English, with French sub-titles. This video is a good short supplement to the first video, above.

Magasin Bonduelle Bienvenue (1 min 45 sec) (French)

https://www.youtube.com/watch?v=PsPruTQ9cT8

This short visit to the Bonduelle Bienvenue store visit can help students see the three different store zones and how they have been designed. We usually view this video in class before discussing store operations.

Bonduelle Americas Agronomy (9 min 15 sec) (English)

https://www.youtube.com/watch?v=-hDKSbZbXuQ

This video discusses daily vegetable production at Bonduelle Americas. The video gives students insights into Bonduelle's commitment to quality and sustainability. We suggest that students not familiar with agriculture and the business of growing and harvesting vegetables watch this video from home before class discussion.

Weblinks of interest to get more update registered information regarding the Bonduelle Group, its current results, and its strategy:

https://www.bonduelle.com/en/investors/bonduelle-in-brief.html

https://www.bonduelle.com/en/investors/regulated-information.html

https://www.bonduelle.com/en/group/strategy.html

https://www.bonduellebienvenue.fr

KEY TERMS AND DEFINITIONS

Bonduelle Bienvenue: Brand Name of the Bonduelle Group's Flagship Store.
Bonduelle Group: French family-run company in the agri-food industry, world-leader in ready-to-use processed vegetables.

The Bonduelle Group's Distribution Strategy

Branded Retail: Branded stores used by one manufacturer to distribute their products directly to consumers (include brick-and-mortar stores, flagship stores, pop-up stores and online stores).

Channel Conflict: Any dispute, difference or discord arising between two or more channel partners, where one partner's activities or operations affect the business of the other channel partner.

D2C (Direct-to-Consumer or Direct2Consumer): Type of Business-to-Consumer retail sales strategy where a business will sell a product directly to the customer. Selling D2C streamlines the distribution process by avoiding any middlemen (such as third-party retailers and distribution partners).

Disintermediation: Reduction in the use of intermediaries between producers and consumers.

Distribution Channel: Distribution channel is a route/method by which companies deliver products and services to customers and end users. It can be direct or indirect depending on the number of through which a good or service passes until it reaches the final buyer or the end consumer.

Distribution Strategy: The process and different channels used to make an organization's products and services available to target customers.

Family Business: A business that is owned or run by members of a single family.

Plant-Based Food: Food derived from plants (including vegetables, grains, nuts, seeds, legumes, and fruits) with no animal-source foods or artificial ingredients.

Processed Vegetables: Vegetables that are preserved using different processes like canning, freezing, packing, or seasoning.

ENDNOTES

[1] Most of this section (except otherwise mentioned source) is based upon information collected via Bonduelle's websites (www.bonduelle.com; www.bonduelle.fr), internal reports from the company (annual registration documents and shareholders' journals), as well as interviews with Pierre Masse, New Projects Director at Bonduelle.

[2] Financial year goes from 1st July of year n until 30th June of year n+1.

[3] This section is based upon field research via interviews with Pierre Masse, New Projects Director at Bonduelle.

[4] Villeneuve d'Ascq was nicknamed the "Green Technology Park" based on its activities, both academic (University of Lille and several Engineering Schools with strong research centres) and economic (several companies as well as multinationals such as Bonduelle, Cofidis and Oxylane had their headquarters there).

[5] There were no 'Bonduelle Bienvenue' branded products.

[6] This number excludes canned food sales in the Bargain Zone.

APPENDIX 1

Questions and Answers

1. What current and future trends in food retail impact the Bonduelle Group's mission, vision, and ambition?

- Growth in consumption of ready to eat products.
- New consumption patterns like eating on-the-go.
- Rise in veganism.
- Rising demand for organic vegetables and healthier products.
- Rising interest in nutrition.
- Expansion of digital channels in the customer journey.
- Growing food service market.
- Expanding in Private Labels' market share.

2. What is the overall issue presented in this case?

The Group Bonduelle's efforts to enter branded retail as a D2C new distribution strategy.
   Possible disintermediation in a traditional industry like food industry and potential for channel conflict.
   More generally, are D2C distribution strategies appropriate for a food processing company like the Bonduelle Group?

3. What are the advantages and risks for the Bonduelle Group to sell products directly to end consumers through own stores?

Advantages:

- Creates a memorable consumer experience
- Reinforces the image of the brand
- Builds a consistent relationship with customers
- Develops an emotional bond with the brand.

Risks:

- Unsuccessful execution of the store concept could detract from the firm's marketing efforts, rather than enhance
- Cost effectiveness
- Channel conflict with traditional retailers

4. How does the 'Bonduelle Bienvenue' Flagship Store compare with best practices for operating Flagship Brand Stores?

The 'Bonduelle Bienvenue' facility exhibits all the facets that previous research by Borghini, *et al.* (2009) has identified as a best practice for flagship brand stores:

- Use Physical Cues to Suggest Moral Values
- Stimulate Brand Enactment within the Retail Store
- Build a Museum
- Be Multifaceted

5. What are the pros and cons of the different D2C sales channels tested by the Bonduelle Group?

- Branded food truck. Can be quickly dispatched to local festivals, concerts, events. However, might not be successful in building the Bonduelle brand.
- Direct online sales. Easy to attempt, although scaling the effort, managing channel conflict, and developing consumer acceptance may be challenging.
- Home based direct sales. Fits well with new trends. But requires a sustained investment of time and resources.

6. Identify advantages of manufacturers using a D2C sales strategy

- Data capture and personalization.
- Expand sales despite partner limitations.
- Rapid testing and iteration of new products.
- Improve product margins.
- Smarter marketing investments.
- Valuable feedback loops.

7. Identify other D2C options that the Bonduelle Group could experiment

Pop-up stores are another popular option for retail sales. A pop-up store could be scaled up or down rapidly in response to seasonal or consumer demand.

Use of a subscription-based model could also be discussed, more customers demanding a simple and hassle-free buying experience.

What about new trends of selling through social media or marketplaces?

Epilogue and Lessons Learned

- Trends in the global vegetable market: growth and environmental responsibility.
- Despite the challenging environment, the performance achieved by the company confirms the relevance of the chosen strategic direction: to develop the group by combining external and inter-

nal growth, continuing its internationalization, and extending its plant-based product range to all distribution networks, in retail as well as in food service.
- As retailers, such as supermarkets, have consolidated and gained market power, product manufacturers have increasingly looked to their own branded retail efforts as a means to mitigate their loss of control at the retail level.
- Flagship Stores done well can promote an engaging experience for the consumer as well as provide entertainment,
- Organizing and managing a firm's channels of distribution is critical issue for a firm's marketing strategy.
- Channel conflicts become even more problematic in the new era of the internet and e-commerce.

Chapter 8
How to Build a Leading So-Called Neobank and Pursue Its Growth?
The Case of the FinTech Nickel in Europe

Jean Michel Rocchi
Sciences Po Aix, France

EXECUTIVE SUMMARY

Compte-Nickel, a brand of La Financière des Paiements Electroniques (FPE), is a FinTech founded in 2012 by Ryad Boulanouar and Hugues Le Bret. After an extremely promising start of operations in France in February 2014, the so-called neobank was acquired in 2017 by BNP Paribas, and its integration was successfully achieved thanks to good cooperation with the founders due to the preservation of its independence. Since the beginning, the key factor of its success has been an electronic terminal that allows to open a banking account in a few minutes, which is deployed in a network of partner tobacconists. In 2018, the FinTech became profitable conversely to most of its local competitors. The same year its name was shortened to Nickel, and in accordance with initial plans, development in Europe is being prepared. In December 2020, Nickel opens its doors in Spain. Will the policy of internationalization in Europe undertaken by the parent company BNP Paribas be as successful as in France?

ORGANIZATION BACKGROUND

Compte-Nickel, which was founded by a team of committed entrepreneurs, was able to invent an original business that proved to be successful. The FinTech, la financière des paiements électroniques (FPE) was created in September First 2012 by Ryad Boulanouar, Hugues Le Bret, Pierre de Perthuis and Michel Calmo. The head office is located in Charenton de le Pont in the Val de Marne, near Paris. The company is registered in the register of commerce and companies of Creteil. The profile of the two main founders is very complementary Ryad Boulanouar is an electronic engineer who already had some great technical achievements to his credit, Hugues le Bret is the former CEO of Boursorama Banque, the leading

DOI: 10.4018/978-1-7998-1630-0.ch008

online bank in France (Société Générale Group) and the former director of communication of the Société Générale. Ryad Boulanouar had registered the brand *"No Bank2*" which was to be the name of his project but he had to give it up following a meeting with the regulator the Autorité de Contrôle Prudentiel (ACP) which was categorically opposed to this name, as explained by Le Bret (2013) in a book telling the emergence of the project and the company: *"You will have a status of payment institution, but not of credit institution, you will not be a bank, and should not be assimilated to a bank..."* (No Bank, 2013, author's free translation, p. 171-172). Ryad Boulanour with tears agrees to give up his initial wish of No Bank in favor of Compte-Nickel which is accepted by the ACP. On April 15, 2013, the ACP met and informed FPE by mail a week later that it had been approved as a payment institution. Entrepreneurs who come up with radical ideas that radically transform the nature of business through innovative business models are on the periphery (e.g. FinTechs) while the large traditional banks constitute the core of the banking system. Cattani and Ferriani (2008) explain *"In addition, the benefits accrued through an individual's intermediate core/periphery position can also be observed at the team level when the same individual works in a team whose members come from both ends of the core/periphery continuum"*. As former CEO of the largest online bank Le Bret was at the core, Boulanouar at the periphery. The latest was a French citizen whose parents were Algerian. He told the newspaper *Le Monde*[1] that he had always considered himself as "a second-class citizen", and moreover because he suffered from a bank ban, a situation that he experienced as infantilizing, humiliating, making him a pariah of the banking system.

According to the theory (Cattano et al., 2017; Sgourev, 2013) if outsiders seem more efficient in providing innovation, conversely it must be emphasized that they are less likely to carry them out. The story of the emergence of the No Bank project (which became Compte-Nickel) is a good illustration of this phenomenon. Hence and as Le Bret (2013) explains, no institutional or investment fund contacted wished to participate in the financing, On February 11, 2014, the payment institution la 'Financière des paiements électroniques' (FPE), in association with the 'French Confédération des buralistes', opened the 'Compte-Nickel', a simplified low-cost payment account for the general public, available in tobacconists' shops, with no deposit or income conditions. The Confederation des Buralistes has 24,000 sales outlets in France, opened approximately 12 hours a day, 6 days a week. This unparalleled network and high availability make tobacconists the leading network of local shops in France. The tobacconists are at the same time independent traders and employees of the French State, hence it is the State that delegates the sale of tobacco to these professionals, within the framework of a monopoly. This particularity explains why the profession also sells regulated products such as tax stamps, games from the Française des Jeux and the PMU, or even products from the Post Office. This alternative banking service was initially successfully launched with around 60 tobacconists, targeting to affiliate 1,000 partner tobacconists by the end of 2014 and 100,000 customers by the same date. Most of tobacconists are primarily targeting additional revenues, while other tobacconists, particularly in rural areas, stress that this attracts new customers and that there can be synergies with the tobacconist's other activities. It can be noted that income from account openings is one shot, but conversely, income from cash deposits and withdrawals is recurring for accounts that operate regularly and satisfactorily.

SETTING THE STAGE

Nickel, which is a payment institution operating in a regulated sector, has invented a new business model that combines technological innovation and a partnership with the French confederation of tobacconists, which operates as an alternative distribution network for its services. First of all, let's go back to an element of the title that seems to be important to us and whose scope goes far beyond the mere terminological dimension: the reasons for the use of the expression "so-called neobank" which seems indispensable following the clear and very firm position taken by the Autorité de Contrôle Prudentiel et de Régulation (ACPR) formerly named ACP, the French regulator which is in charge of supervising banks (credit institutions) as well as Fintechs (and in particular, payment establishments such as Nickel or electronic money institutions as others FinTechs). Professionals must no longer use the term neobank if they do not have the status of a "credit institution" (or bank), otherwise they will be subject to sanctions, as this name would be misleading for FinTech customers who might think they are in a bank.

Box 1. The prohibition in France by the ACPR of the use of the term neobank by professionals in the Fintech ecosystem.

> *The ACPR, going against market practice, intends to reserve the term neobank for credit institutions only, i.e. banks, as the term neobank would be too close to the term bank and therefore misleading for customers. "In France, the word 'bank' corresponds to a concept defined by the Monetary and Financial Code. It is very important to maintain citizens' confidence in the banking system not to misuse this term. In this sense, a 'neobank' must first be a 'bank' in order to be able to refer to this term. While it is true that the term 'neo-bank' is commonly used, particularly in the press, to describe new players in the financial sector, it should not be forgotten that this neologism is constructed from a word that has a legal definition. Using the word 'bank' or 'credit institution' to describe a non-banking company, including payment and electronic money institutions, as well as their agents and distributors, is prohibited by law" (ACPR Review, author's translation, April 2021). The ACPR explicitly refers to Article L. 511-8 of the Monetary and Financial Code (Code Monétaire et Financier-CMF), which states that: "any company other than a credit institution or a finance company is prohibited from using a name, a corporate name, advertising or, in general, expressions that give the impression that it is authorized as a credit institution or a finance company, respectively, or from creating confusion in this respect" (Author's translation).*
>
> *In addition to clarifying the terminology, the ACPR calls on the entities concerned (payment institutions, electronic money institutions and payment service providers are mentioned) to ensure that their communications are consistent with their status and their activity. In other words, according to the French regulator, Nickel is a fintech and not a neobank.*

Credit institutions (and especially online banks) and FinTechs have one thing in common and several notable differences. The common point is that in all the countries of the Eurozone, the approval to be a bank or a FinTech is given by the European Central Bank (ECB). The practical consequence is that a *European passport* will be attached to this approval, allowing any entity approved by one of the countries of the European Economic Area (EEA) to be able to freely exercise its activity in all member countries.

The differences between the two legal regimes are very important and explain the position of the ACPR mentioned above, aiming at preventing potential clients from confusing the respective services available to them depending on the type of institution, as well as the existence (or not) of the deposit guarantee mechanism that is in force in Europe as we can see below on Table 1.

Table 1. Boursorama Banque versus Nickel

Name	Boursorama Banque	Nickel
Type of organisation	Online Bank (Bank)	FinTech
Number of customers	>2,500,000.	>2,000,000.
Parent Company	Société Générale Group	BNP Paribas Group
Legal status (ACPR-ECB)	Credit institution	Payment institution
Bank Deposit Garanty Scheme	Yes (€100,000 on deposits and €70,000 on securities, per client).	No.
Possibility to accept deposit	Yes	Yes after the opening of a cantonment account at the bank Credit Mutuel Arkéa.
Access to credit	Yes	No (Neither loan nor overdraft).
Providing means of payments	Yes	Yes
European Passport	Yes	Yes

Source: author.

Figure 1. Nickel terminal (motto ''an account for everybody and new logo)
Source: Company.

As emphasized by Kim et al. (2020): *"Unlike traditional banks, payment institutions such as Compte-Nickel cannot speculate with deposits. Funds are confined to a non-remunerated secure account to ensure that money is available at any time and protected in case of bankruptcy"*. The data needed to open an account is instantly controlled because the terminal is connected to the Internet. If everything is in order, the tobacconist checks the identity of the person who wants to open the account and activates a MasterCard from his electronic payment terminal. In return, the device prints out a statement of bank identity. Ryad Boulanouar emphasizes the ability to link the card to the customer record in real time that allows the cardholder to use his or her account immediately. *"Of course, the IT infrastructure is complex, so the FPE opted for Sab's core banking system, which had to be adapted to its specific needs, particularly in terms of real time. It also called on Crédit Mutuel Arkéa as a bank of cantonment, where money flows transit"*.[2]

CASE DESCRIPTION

Nickel had to manage two projects: the technological success of its payment system and its electronic terminal installed in tobacconists, and its successful integration into the BNP Paribas group following its acquisition.

Technology Concerns

The value proposition to customers lies in the fact that the user of the terminal, with a few simple operations taking a few minutes can leave immediately with his Mastercard and a bank account number. *"Our offer is based on a terminal installed in tobacconists: it includes a tablet on which the buyer types his personal data and a scanner with which he scans his ID and proof of address. The data is quickly checked because the terminal is connected to the Internet. If everything is correct, the tobacconist checks the identity of the person who wants to open the account and activates a MasterCard from his electronic payment terminal. In return, the device prints out a bank statement. It is the ability to link the card to the customer record in real time that allows the cardholder to use the account immediately"*[3]. Not only is the electronic terminal user friendly for clients and the bank account opening is done in a few minutes, but also it is fully automatic and hence also easy from the point of view of the tobacconist; it saves time and allows him to continue to serve his customers. He will only have to validate at the end of the account opening process which is very fast. In a complementary way, the only difficulty, but rarely raised by tobacconists, lies in the fact that some of them, having many foreign customers who do not speak French and/or cannot read French, have to help them with the account opening process which they do not master in this specific case. Nevertheless, Michel Calmo, general manager of the FPE and in charge of operations emphasizes human less functioning. The quality and reliability of the service is naturally fundamental to Nickel's future in France and abroad. On October 5, 2020[4], the company acknowledged the existence of malfunctions in its payment system, which resulted in 25,000 customers being temporarily unable to withdraw cash or pay for their purchases. The same day Nickel's statement was the following: *"The malfunctions noted today have been resolved. We would like to apologize for the inconvenience caused. Those who may have seen duplicate transactions on their accounts will be recredited as soon as possible. Sorry for not being nickel"*. In French slang 'nickel', especially among teenagers, also means perfect. The existence of technical problems was not a first, indeed the consumers association and magazine *60 million de Consommateurs* in 2018 had reported various anomalies in the operation of the accounts of Nickel customers dating back to May: delay of refunds for victims of bank card fraud, debit errors, accounts wrongly blocked.

Entrepreneurship involves the *"alertness of entrepreneurs"* (Kirzner, 1973) for the discovery, creation and lastly exploitation of opportunities (Shane & Venkataraman, 2000; Venkataraman, 1997). The founders, Boulanouar and Le Bret are willing to "banking the unbanked", targeting the forgotten of the classical banking system, notably customers with a banking ban and those who do not have a minimum or regular income, or low income individuals as students or unemployed. The nature of this technology used by Nickel (and formerly Compte-Nickel) must be discussed. According to Christensen (1997), what characterizes disruptive innovation is that they are rare and that new entrants are choosing to offer products or services that are inferior to those of the incumbents but have in return distinctive attributes such as being cheaper, more accessible, more convenient etc. Over time, these new entrants move from the low-end of the market to the high-end market. Originally, Compte-Nickel targeted exclusively the low-end market and therefore did not apply a disruptive innovation strategy in the sense of Christensen (1997). According to Benavent (2017) *"Very quickly, the value of use provided by the Nickel account was not only worth the neglected populations excluded from traditional and excluded from traditional banks, but has also extended to customers who expect more simplicity. A disruptive potential is created"*. Nevertheless, post-acquisition by BNP Paribas new strategy operated by Nickel from 2018 with the launch of the high-end Nickel Chrome card, targeting the mass affluents, seems to modify the model. If we analyze not the business model, but the technological content of the terminal, we can doubt the existence of a disruptive innovation or breakthrough; we seem to be in the presence of a *"bricolage"* described by Garud and Karnøe (2003).

Technology Components

Most of the electronic components of the Nickel terminal come from Asia but they are assembled in France; it is considered as a product manufactured in the European Union which is a source of simplification. Of course, the IT infrastructure is complex, and Compte-Nickel has chosen Sab's (a French software company acquired in 2019 by Sopra Steria, a European player) core banking system, which had to be customized to its specific needs, and notably real-time which is at the heart of his competitive advantage.

The issuance of bank cards is carried out within the framework of the partnership initially concluded with Mastercard. Moreover, the regulator having imposed a cantonment account (escrow account) to ensure the security of the depositors, it was necessary that a perfect interconnection exists with the credit institution initially chosen, the Crédit Mutuel Arkéa (a large French mutualist bank), where the money flows are managed and where the deposits are legally located.

Management and Organizational Concerns

On April 4, 2017, French bank BNP Paribas[5] announced the purchase of 95% of the shares of Financière des paiements électroniques[6], the payment institution that manages Compte-Nickel. The Confédération des buralistes remains a 5% shareholder. Compte-Nickel, which claims to have more than 540,000 customers at this date (April 2016) with a rate of 26,000 accounts opened per month, assures that it will remain independent and autonomous, with its management team remaining in place. The transaction, described in Table 2 below, which is subject to the approval of the French authorities, has been approved and Nickel will be consolidated in the accounts of BNP Paribas as of July 1, 2017.

Table 2. Compte-Nickel as of June 30, 2017 (Deal completed in July 12, 2017)

Acquisition of Compte-Nickel in France.	Objectives: differentiated service models adapted to customer needs.
• 630,000 already open for three years (of which > 61,000 in Q2 17, +41%/Q2 16). • Renewal of the exclusive partnership with the "Confédération des Buralistes de France": already 2,675 points of sale (approximately 10,000 in the future).	• Refocusing the Group's system dedicated to new banking uses: an offer that is distinct from and complementary to those of the BNP Paribas branch network and Hello Bank! • Accelerate the development of Compte-Nickel: target of 2 million accounts opened in 2020.

Source: BNP Paribas, July 28, 2017. Presentation of S1 Results (Author's translation)

Despite the fact, that several serious press sources claim a purchase price of 200 million euros, this figure seems to be wrong. The real figure is now available[7]: *"The deal, priced at €260m, was among the top 20 acquisitions in European fintech history"*. She specifies in a complementary way *"This previously-unreported figure was confirmed to Sifted by an early investor in Nickel"*. The article explains the dilemma of the should I stay or should I go for the founders: *"Yet the sale wasn't an obvious decision: Le Bret wasn't in a rush, and a handful of investors were tempted by a counteroffer to inject more venture-cash hoping to multiply Nickel's valuation again. Le Bret ultimately decided against the path, however, questioning whether rapid international expansion and haphazard product-lines would offer success"*. In Hughes Le Bret words: *"The risk was too high... I am not the man to make those aggressive strategies. I am very pragmatic"*, he told Sifted. *"If I were a poker player, I'd cash out. I'm a rational player"*.

A complementary explanation can be found in the vision carried by the other founder Ryad Boulanouar in what he called the four criteria of the oral *"charter of the Nobankers"*, indeed there is a time to develop and time to sell and withdraw when the company starts to grow and become bureaucratic. Le Bret (2013) tells about his first discussion with Ryad Boulanouar (*No Bank*, 2013, author's free translation, p. 152-153):

"- Have fun. Helping. Change. To leave. For now, we're fulfilling the first one. We're on the way to solving the second one, which concerns the daily life of all the excluded. If we are as brilliant as we seem to be, we should quickly achieve the third one and make the banks change their behavior. The fourth one follows from the three others, we have to know how to leave the place.

- I don't follow you on the fourth point. If you manage to create a momentum around your project, you will have to accompany your customers, offer them other services, and then expand internationally.

- I am not a long distance runner. I am a sprinter. I conceive, I found, I launch and pass the baton".

The company announces its new identity, "Nickel" for short, its new slogan *"the account for everybody"* ("le compte pour tous") replacing "the bankless account" ("le compte sans banque"), its new logo, reminding the "carrot" of the tobacconists who distribute its offer, but always orange (not the green of BNP Paribas), and especially a new product, the Nickel Chrome card. The new card *Nickel Chrome* is described in the following terms: *"An optional offer that responds to a strong customer demand to have access to additional insurance and services. Faithful to its values of simplicity and usefulness, Nickel has built Nickel Chrome with the ambition of making accessible to the greatest number of options hitherto reserved for the wealthiest* (Company)". The partnership with tobacconists is an illustration that the Marshallian economies of scale models works very well in the long term as shown on Table 3 below.

Table 3. Key productivity figures of FPE (Nickel)

N/Y	2015 Dec	2016 Dec	2017 Dec	2018 Dec	2019 Dec	2020 Feb	2021 Feb	2024 F
Tobacconists	1,120	2,150	2,910	4,335	5,500	5,700	6,007	10,000
Accounts	200,000	475,000	788,000	1,135,000	1,500,000	1,700,000	1,900,000	4,000,000
Employees	65	112	199	285	390	N.A.	500	N.A.

Source: Company & Press.

Since 2018, thanks to the strong increase in the number of customers and revenues, the company has become profitable as we can see below in Table 4.

Table 4. Key profitability figures of FPE (Nickel)

Indicator (€ Mi)/Year			2012	2013	2014	2015	2016	2017	2018	2019
Clients Deposits			0.00.	0.13	19.44	61.48	122.97	205.57	292.91	N.A..
Gross Banking Income			0.00	0.02	2.48	9.29	21.07	39.42	59.62.	N.A.
Net Banking Income			0.00	- 0.05	0.49	3.73	11.74	24.58	41.15	61.30
Operating Profit			- 3.36	- 5.60	- 7.77	- 6.76	- 6.23	- 2.59	1.02	6.30
Net profit (or losses)			- 3.36	-5.60	- 7.89	- 8.55	- 6.27	- 2.66	1.26	4.50

Source: Company & Press.

Nickel's profitability is anything but obvious, as the French neobank is by far the one with the most customers in the domestic market and the only one to be profitable as of December 31, 2019. The digital banking market is very competitive in France and in the same way the hexagonal online bank Fortuneo Banque is also the only online bank operating on the French market to be profitable on the same date. Nickel's success is therefore factually quite exceptional.

Table 5. Historical losses of FPE (Nickel)

Losses /Year	2012	2013	2014	2015	2016	2017
Annual Losses	-3.36	-5.60	7.77	-6.76	-6.27	-2.66
Accumulated Losses	-3.36	-8.96	16.85	-25.40	-31.67	-34.33

Source: Company & Press.

The company became profitable as of 2018, after accumulated losses for a total amount of 34.33 million euros, which constitutes a tax shield attributable to the tax result that became positive as we can see on Table 5 below.

Although Nickel is operationally relatively independent, in accounting terms it is consolidated using the full consolidation method, which is the only method permitted in the presence of total control under either French GAAP or IFRS as presented on Table 6 below.

Table 6. BNP Paribas' New digital activities as of 31 Decembre, 2020

Name	Country	Method	Control	Interest
Financière des Paiements Electroniques	France	Full consolidation	95%	95%
Financière des Paiements Electroniques Spanish Branch	Spain	Full Consolidation	95%	95%

Source: BNP Paribas Annual Report 2020, p. 133.

What interested BNP Paribas at the time of the acquisition of Compte-Nickel in April 2017 was not only its leadership as a so-called neobank in France, but a business model deemed duplicable in Europe.

CURRENT CHALLENGES FACING THE ORGANIZATION

Nickel will have to face two challenges to strengthen its leadership position in France and to assert itself as a European player. The French position will be strengthened almost automatically by the expansion of the tobacconist network, and there is little uncertainty as to whether the objectives will be achieved. The real challenge lies in the internationalization in Europe. In this case, success may be achieved but it is not guaranteed in advance. The objective of the European Union through its two directives, on payment institutions and electronic money institutions, was to fight against the overly oligopolistic nature of the European banking system. By encouraging the appearance of new players, an intermediate objective, it was a question of obtaining in the long term the final objective; a reduction in the price of products and services for the benefit of consumers. The two European directives gave fintechs that chose one or the other of these statuses the opportunity to benefit from a European passport. For example, one of these approvals obtained in France allowed them to carry out their activity in all the countries of the European Economic Area (EEA). The member countries of the EEA are the 27 countries of the European Union (Austria, Belgium, Bulgaria, Croatia, Republic of Cyprus, Czech Republic, Denmark, Estonia, Finland, France, Germany, Greece, Hungary, Ireland, Italy, Latvia, Lithuania, Luxembourg, Malta, Netherlands, Poland, Portugal, Romania, Slovakia, Slovenia, Spain, and Sweden.) as well as three other countries that are not members of this organization (Iceland, Liechtenstein, and Norway). We will see at the end of this chapter, in the section devoted to Nickel's internationalization, that the existence of this European passport attached to its payment institution license is clearly a facilitating element to carry out this strategy. The first Payment Services Directive (PSD1) was adopted in 2007. This legislation set the legal grounds for an EU single market for payments. The proposal was signed in November 2009 and became effective in December 2009. PSD1 paved the way for fintech companies choosing the "payment institution" status to enter the payments market and carry out financial transactions. Hence, before the PSD1 introduction, only banks ("credit institutions") were authorized to provide payment services. PSD2 is a revised and consolidated version of PSD1, which became effective in January 2018. PSD2 changes and improves the banking and financial services market. Newcomers have the possibility to offer their clients the opportunity of firstly consulting their accounts through *account aggregation services.*

Defining strategy is difficult, as noted by Mintzberg et al. (2009), in particular because of its duality since it is both *"a position"* and *"a perspective"*. A position means, *"namely the location of particular product in particular markets"*, and complementarily in a different perspective *"namely an organization's fundamental way of doing things"*. Nickel's internationalization covers these two aspects; selling its services in new countries, but also designing new partnerships inspired by the one at the origin of the French success while also adapting its organization. For an SME like Nickel, wanting to expand its activity abroad is anything but trivial since it will involve both adapting its organization and facing new issues related to various environments, i.e. having nothing less than the challenges that make up the daily life of multinational companies like its parent company BNP Paribas: *"One of the most influential modern organizational forms — the multinational corporation (MNC)— must simultaneously adapt to and operate within multiple societies and, hence, multiple environments… Their central management is confronted with the challenge of designing systems than retain sufficient unity and coherence to operate as a common enterprise and, at the same time, to allow sufficient latitude and flexibility to adapt to greatly varying circumstances"* (Scott, 1992, p. 138). Such new opportunities to expand revenues abroad also implies new risks and notably two. Firstly, *"the inability to transfer in other countries an existing firm specific advantage"* that can be related to the organization (Lippman & Rumelt, 1982) or to its new environment (Kogut, 1985). Secondly, *the theory of liability of foreignness* or LOF (Zaheer, 1995, p. 343) needs also to be considered: *"Whatever its source, the liability of foreignness implies that foreign firms will have lower profitability than local firms, all else being equal, and perhaps even a lower probability of survival"*. It is also important to notice that the LOF theory was identified and developed initially in the banking sector context. In other words, beyond real opportunities of additional revenues the risks in doing business abroad seem greater than in the home country. Finally, a last important point must be mentioned; according to Porter (1990, p. 53) competition in the banking sector is *not global* in nature but is on the contrary *multidomestic*: *"Competition in each nation (or small group of nations) is essentially independent. The industry is present in many nations (there is a consumer banking in Korea, one in Italy and one in the United States, for example), but competition takes place on a country-by-country basis. A bank's reputation, customer base, and physical assets in one nation, for example, have little or no impact on its success to customer banking in other nations. The international industry is a collection of essentially domestic industries, hence the term multidomestic"*.

"Nickel officially opened its branch Nickel Spain in December 2020. To support its entry into this market, Nickel concluded a unique partnership with lottery and tobacconists' associations with a national network of more than 20,000 points of sale across the country" (Nickel's Press release, 7th January 2021[8]) We will observe a model very similar to the one that prevails on the other side of the Pyrenees, namely a partnership with federations that exercise a profession regulated by the State that will act as a network distributor of Nickel services whose prices are unchanged with France at 20 euros per year.

"To serve its first Spanish customers, Nickel announces today that its local business is fully operational with 72 points of sale already active and the aim of having more than 1,000 set up by the end of the year. The local team of 30 employees in Madrid, under the responsibility of Javier Ramirez Zarzosa, CEO

Spain, aims to attract 700,000 customers and 3,000 points of sale by the end of 2024 in Spain" (Nickel's Press release, 7th January 2021).

As readers can see in Appendix 2, where the Spanish points of sale are shown, the phygital model is being rapidly deployed in the country in a manner quite similar to what had prevailed in France. In the first half of 2021, the business appears to be developing satisfactorily, with 459 points of sale already available in May 2021 in both mainland Spain and the Balearic and Canary Islands, again based on the French model, since Nickel is present both in mainland France and in some of the French overseas territories (Guadeloupe, Martinique, Guyana, Reunion), where it is also very successful.

The Spanish CEO[9] summarized in early 2021 the rationale of the opening in both countries: *"where we see strong demand in the retail banking market"* explains Nickel's CEO, within the next 5 years the FinTech is intended to open 300,000 accounts in Belgium and 450,000 in Portugal.

"Nickel aims to launch in seven European countries by 2024 and is currently studying the following four: Portugal, Belgium, Italy and Austria. In each of these countries, Nickel will focus on partnerships with networks with a strong network, such as tobacconists in France, and the launch of an offer with a local bank identification statement" (Nickel's Company statement, author's free translation, 26 November 2019).

In view of this statement, beyond 2022 for which the two openings are already planned, the new countries could be Austria and Italy. Italy seems to carry a specific risk due to the existence of Banca 5 which should be presented (see box 2 below).

Box 2. Banca 5 (formerly Banca Itb)

> *More commonly known as the bank of tobacconists it was founded by entrepreneurs, Lottomatica (the Lottery operator), Federazione italiana tabaccai (through Arianna) and Intesa Sanpaolo under the name of Banca Itb in July 2008 with the intention of creating a bank exclusively dedicated to tobacconists, to whom they would offer current accounts, overdrafts, deposits, financing, supplier payments, electronic billing and collection services and payment. At the same time, these services are also made available to citizens, since Banca Itb has stipulated agreements for the payment of postal bills, refills of telephone cards and prepaid cards, etc... In 2016, Intesa Sanpaolo decided to acquire 100% of Banca Itb for 153 million euros and renamed it Banca 5 S.p.A.. Its new name comes from the number of products it intends to offer to the unbanked segments of the population: cards, loans, accounts, insurance and services. The branchless Banca 5 is an online bank that relies on 20,000 affiliated tobacconists. An estimated number of 12 million people visit Banca 5 through the tobacconists network every year to use its services.*

More commonly known as the bank of tobacconists it was founded by entrepreneurs, Lottomatica (the Lottery operator), Federazione italiana tabaccai (through Arianna) and Intesa Sanpaolo under the name of Banca Itb in July 2008 with the intention of creating a bank exclusively dedicated to tobacconists, to whom they would offer current accounts, overdrafts, deposits, financing, supplier payments, electronic billing and collection services and payment. At the same time, these services are also made available to citizens, since Banca Itb has stipulated agreements for the payment of postal bills, refills of telephone *cards and prepaid cards, etc... In 2016, Intesa Sanpaolo decided to acquire 100% of Banca Itb for 153 million euros and renamed it Banca 5 S.p.A.. Its new name comes from the number of products it intends to offer to the unbanked segments of the population: cards, loans, accounts, insurance and services. The branchless Banca 5 is an online bank that relies on 20,000 affiliated tobacconists. An estimated number of 12 million people visit Banca 5 through the tobacconists network every year to use its services.*

While the neobank Nickel is a fintech offering only payment services, Banca 5 is a full-service bank offering all banking and even insurance services, so they are different in terms of economies of scope but also address different customers. Nevertheless, we cannot avoid asking a simple question: given the existence of this player, is there really a place for Nickel in Italy? Of course, we do not have the answer. In fact, there are two separate questions. Will Nickel take the risk of establishing itself in this country? And if so, will it be successful?

SOLUTIONS AND RECOMMENDATIONS

Our main strategic recommendation will be crystal clear *"Please change almost nothing"* i.e. to keep as much as possible the business model that has proven itself in France by simply adapting it to the new local context of the European country concerned.

Alternative Strategies are not Convincing at all: Revolut and N26 are Still Losing Money and C-Zam Closed Down

The other major European neobanks N26 (www.n26.com) and Revolut (www.revolut.com), which became online banks by obtaining a banking license, both have a purely digital strategy and are therefore in essence very different from Nickel. The aim of these two new generation online banks is to offer all services in the long term. According to its managers, Nickel does not plan to become a credit institution. The rapid growth of Revolut and N26 in many geographies at the same time is resulting in very large losses, and at this point in time despite the increase in revenue it is not clear that they are converging to breakeven. It will be necessary to keep the confidence of investors for several years, otherwise the risk of failure will become omnipresent, as shown by the current fears of investors for the survival of Monzo.

Hugues Le Bret interviewed by the journalist Isabel Woodford confides his skepticism about the business model followed by some of his most aggressive competitors until they prove their business model and *"realize the dream"* hence he explains: *"If you're not-profitable, people dream...[so] until you have sold the company, the value is theoretical"*. And he concluded: *"Maybe the value of these companies will be $5-10bn in five to 10 years. But maybe they [still] won't be profitable; And if they are not profitable, nobody-no bank, no rational insurance company- will buy them"* (*Sifted/FT*, 18 May 2020).

How to Build a Leading So-Called Neobank and Pursue Its Growth?

Box 3. C-zam's organizational death: a brief history of a complete failure

The neobank C-Zam[10] was launched on April 18, 2017 by Carrefour Banque. At the end of 2018, the bank had 131,000 activated accounts. Its business model as presented by the economic magazine Challenges is clearly a frontal attack of Compte-Nickel. It should be noted that Carrefour Banque of which C-zam is only a brand is owned 60% by Carrefour and 40% by BNP Personnal Finance. As the journalist Claire Bouleau explains in Challenges "From April 18, Carrefour customers will be able to discover in all French stores, as well as on its website Rueducommerce, the small C-zam box set. Costing 5 euros, it contains a bank card that can be activated in just 10 minutes, thanks to the associated application. All you have to do is fill out a form, scan two pieces of identification (ID card, passport, EDF bill...), activate the card and you're done. No condition of income is required" (March 23, 2017). The attack is on the availability through the 3,000 Carrefour mass distribution stores well known to the French but also and especially on the lower cost compared to Compte-Nickel. Namely, 17 euros in the first year (5 euros of a box to be purchased which contains the bank card to be activated) and bank charges of 1 euro per month, i.e. 12 euros from the 2nd year onwards, a cost lower than the 20 euros annual cost of Compte-Nickel. The advantages? 12 euros management fee per year, a free bank card, as well as free withdrawals at the 4,700 BNP Paribas and Carrefour Banque ATMs. As for the app, it updates the balance in real time, allows you to block or unblock your bank card instantly, for example in case of loss, and to recall the secret code on demand. The disadvantages? No authorized overdraft, no checkbook. Poor service quality, a bad reputation and about 30% of the boxes purchased containing a card not being activated are the main causes of the failure. Moreover, the number of customers is stagnating at around 130,000, which means that the company is not converging towards a break-even point and that shareholders must expect to finance losses for many years to come. For Carrefour parent company of Carrefour Banque, the majority shareholder, a giant in the mass retail sector where banking is not the core business, the idea of stopping is germinating. For BNP Paribas, a minority shareholder, financing the losses of a company that is a direct competitor of Nickel, which was bought out in April 2017, has become strategically insane. By mutual agreement, the shareholders put C-zam up for sale, with no takeover candidate taking action. On May 12, a definitive closure was announced for July 15, 2020. It is advised to existing clients to open an account at Nickel to replace the closed account, sometimes C-zam agrees to pay the first annual € 20 fee to Nickel. It should indeed be considered that beyond the interests of the minority shareholder BNP Paribas, due to the forced closures, Carrefour also needs to remain on good terms with the former customers of C-zam who are often regular customers of its stores. Although reliable estimates are difficult to make, it nevertheless appears that more than 10,000 C-zam customers have joined Nickel as a result of the shutdown. As C-zam lost its entire identity it must be considered as an organizational death (Sutton, 1987).

The French neobank C-zam entered into head-on competition with Compte-Nickel, the experiment ended in a bitter failure. Wanting is different from being able to do, as we can see in box 3.

TIn a press conference Hugues le Bret described the success of the so-called neobank as "unique". *"The offer was launched four and a half years ago, on February 11, 2014. We are at the very beginning of Nickel's history and growth. On August 22nd, the one millionth Nickel tobacco account was opened in Saint-Paul-lès-Dax. Reaching one million in four and a half years is something that has never been seen before in the bank's history"*, said Hugues Le Bret, co-founder of Compte Nickel, renamed Nickel

(Nickel's Press Conference, September 8, 2818). In the same conference referring to the partnership with the Confederation of Tobacconists he described[11] Nickel as *"the fourth largest banking network"* in France.

Fully Exploring the Phygital Model: France & UK a Brief Comparative Study

As explained by Rocchi (2020, p. 204), *"In France, a new word has been coined 'phygitale' which is composed of 'physique' (physical or tangible) and 'digitale' (digital or virtual)"*.

This concept describes the fact that some digital banking players (online banks, FinTech) use alternative networks that give them a physical presence, legitimacy and facilitate the opening of accounts in the face of the banking networks of traditional banking players. For example, the online banks Axa Banque and Allianz Banque use the insurance branches of their parent companies. As for Orange Bank, it can rely on the telephone stores of its majority shareholder Orange, as well as on the insurance agencies of the GAN and Groupama networks of its minority shareholder Groupama. According to its CEO, during its first years of activity, Orange Bank opened 2/3 of its accounts via agencies and only 1/3 via the Internet. Before closing its business in July 2020, C-zam relied on the 3,000 supermarkets and hypermarkets of its parent company Carrefour. Anytime, a FinTech for professionals acquired by Orange Bank in January 2021, is experimenting with account openings through Photomaton photo booths (8,000 in France and 28,500 worldwide). Finally, Ma French Bank is an online bank that gives itself visibility via the 16,000 French post offices. We have seen that Nickel for its part relies on the network of tobacconists in France and the Lottery marketers in Spain. In conclusion, various types of alternative commercial networks help the digital world to fight against the traditional banking networks.

Table 7. Main direct competitors of Nickel in France

Brand & Bank	Price	Specifics of the Offering
Eko by CA (Crédit Agricole)	€2/Month	Limited services and low-cost offering provided by a major French network bank
Enjoy by CE (Caisse d'Epargne)	€2/Month	Limited services and low-cost offering provided by a major French network bank
Ma French Bank La Banque Postale	€2/Month	Limited services and low-cost offering provided by a major French network bank
LCL Essentiel (LCL)	€2/Month	Limited services and low-cost offering provided by a major French network bank
Kapsul (Société Générale)	€2/Month	Limited services and low-cost offering provided by a major French network bank
N26 Standard (N26)	Free	Freemium version with basic services under certain conditions.
Orange Bank	Free	Freemium version with basic services uder certain conditions.
Welcome (Boursorama Banque)	Free	Freemium version with basic services under certain conditions.

We can see in the Table 7 below that the direct competitors are composed of two types: the Freemium offers of some online banks which are less expensive because they are free but restrictive in their conditions, and the low-cost offers of the big traditional banking networks which are slightly more expensive at 24 euros per year against 20 euros for Nickel.

In the UK the Paypoint network and the Post Office are the main partners for both established banks and newcomers. The Paypoint network comprising 28,200 independent local shops in the UK, 9,000 in Romania and 500 in Ireland is allowing cash payment and withdrawals. Two Challenger Banks (Monzo and Starling Bank) and two neobanks (Tide and Monese) are using these shops in the UK through a partnership. Starling Bank is using both an agreement with Paypoint and another one with the Post Office which allows both cash deposits and withdrawals in its 11,500 local post offices. Nickel's search for international partnerships is consistent with the theory, since Eden and Miller (2004) advocate using them based on the institutional and geographic distance of new markets. Lastly, the intensity of the banking competition of the targeted country must also be considered.

Ongoing Preservation of Nickel's Identity: Legal Status, Visual Identity, Values, Specific Partners and a Good Quality of Services

Nickel has the agility of an SME having less than 1,000 employees that should not be lost to the bureaucratic phenomenon that would be inherent in any absorption by the BNP Paribas Group with its approximately 200,000 employees and its numerous and burdensome processes. Moreover, Nickel as a *payment institution* (FinTech) benefits from a lighter financial regulation from the ACPR (French regulator) and ECB (Eurozone regulator) than the supervision exercised on *credit institutions* (banks) such as its parent company. Banks, at the worldwide level, are also under the supervision of the Bank of International Settlements (BIS) and notably Basel Group. It's no exaggeration to say that Nickel has remained almost entirely independent of BNP Paribas, the parent company does not appear on the logo, unlike the Group's online bank "Hello Bank! by BNP Paribas". Similarly, Nickel has kept the orange color in its visuals (BNP Paribas has green on its logo). The Orange logo in the shape of a carrot recalls the logo of the tobacconists. Nickel has kept its status as a payment institution (FinTech) and does not intend to become a credit institution (transforming itself into a bank). Of course, the medium-term expansion plan in Europe is known and has been validated by the parent company, but operationally it is managed autonomously by Nickel, which can also exploit synergies with the Group. Nickel's clientele is on average much smaller than that of its parent company, and this specificity is assumed and even asserted.

Nickel plays an inclusive social role through its four values (universality, simplicity, utility, benevolence), which express a certain voluntarism, not to say militancy.

- *Universality*: providing a bank account for everyone with limited services attached to it but at a very competitive price (low-cost model): *"with us, everyone is welcome, even those who have been banned from banking. Young or old, rich or not, party animal or early bird, etc. You are all welcome"* (French website).
- *Simplicity*: transparency and simple cost system without any hidden fee: *"At Nickel, there are no complicated options. We believe everyone should have easy access to basic banking services to simply pay and get paid"* (French website).

- *Utility*: contributing to increase the financial inclusion notably for vulnerable clients for 20 euros maximum per year: *"With no overdraft and no fees, you take back control of your money. We are the 100% useful and 0% toxic account"* (French website).
- *Benevolence*: despite the huge success, there was no increase of tariffs and the primary objective remains to help clients, especially the most fragile, in their daily lives: *"You are accompanied. Nickel is there when you need it most and fights to make your life easier"* (French website). Since its creation, Nickel has maintained excellent relations with many non-profit associations that recommend it to their members and to a fragile or vulnerable population.

When Nickel was created and developed, partnerships were formed with players that were not necessarily those chosen by its new parent company, which were not questioned, thus constituting further proof of Nickel's operational independence. For instance, at the time of its creation, Nickel concluded an agreement with Crédit Mutuel Arkéa, which was in charge of the escrow account for its customers' assets. This agreement was maintained after its acquisition by BNP Paribas, even though this banking group is a competitor of its parent company. Another example relies on the renewal of the partnership with Mastercard on 20th of October 2020. Solveig Honoré Hatton, Country Manager Mastercard France explains[12] *"Mastercard has supported Nickel since its launch in the French market in 2014 and we are proud to become Nickel's exclusive partner in Europe with the goal of accelerating its growth in France and extending its presence to 8 European countries by 2024"*. It is important to underline that Nickel cultivates its operational independence and strategic positioning, but also its technological alliances since its parent company BNP Paribas is a partner of the Visa network, the great competitor of Mastercard.

For any customer of a bank, it is essential that the bank be reliable and that it does not make recurring errors, but the consequences will be even more serious for precarious customers, as is the case for some of Nickel's customers. A double debit, a late reimbursement and even more so a blocked account can be dramatic situations for a customer with low assets and only one bank account. We have reported a few technical malfunctions that remain rare and limited and have not tarnished Nickel's image and reputation, as evidenced by its strong account opening momentum, which is also based on word of mouth and recommendation. Moreover, and this is a strong point, Nickel has been reactive and efficient in resolving the malfunctions observed, making them temporary. In Nickel's case, operational reliability is not only essential to preserve its commercial interests, it is also a moral imperative to protect the precarious. As emphazised by Ashta et al. (2021): *"Nickel began as a social enterprise with the goal of being successful while doing good, and with a long-term perspective"*.

At the end of this case study on the internalization of Nickel, it is necessary to recognize the limits of this case study linked to the fact that only one foreign entity has been opened to date. It goes without saying that in a few years' time, after the opening of 5 or 6 new foreign subsidiaries, a new assessment of the situation could be carried out and thus give rise to fruitful future research.

REFERENCES

Arner, D. W., Barberis, J., & Buckley, R. P. (2016). The evolution of FinTech: A new post-crisis paradigm? *Georgetown Journal of International Law*, *47*(4), 1272–1319.

Arslanian, H., & Fisher, F. (2019). *The Future of Finance, The Impact of Fintech, AI, and Crypto on Financial Services*. Springer. doi:10.1007/978-3-030-14533-0

Ashta A., Assadi D., & Durand N. (2021). Capture d'innovation: étude de cas d'une néo-banque à mission sociale et défis pour les pays en développement. *ISTE OpenScience*, 1–21 doi:10.21494/ISTE.OP.2021.0673

Benavent C. (2017). Disruption à l'âge des plateformes. *Économie & Management, 165*, 11-17.

Cattani, G., & Ferriani, S. (2008, November-December). A Core/Periphery Perspective on Individual Creative Performance: Social Networks and Cinematic Achievements in the Hollywood Film Industry. *Organization Science, 19*(6), 824–844. doi:10.1287/orsc.1070.0350

Cattani, G., Ferriani, S., & Lanza, A. (2017, November-December). Deconstructing the Outsider Puzzle: The Legitimation Journey of Novelty. *Organization Science, 28*(6), 965–992. doi:10.1287/orsc.2017.1161

Christensen, C. (1997). *The Innovator's Dilemma: When New Technologies Cause Great Firms to Fail*. Harvard Business Review Press.

Davis, F. D. (1986). *A technology acceptance model for empirically testing new end-user information systems: theory and results* (Doctoral Thesis). Sloan School of Management. http://dspace.mit.edu/handle/1721.1/15192

Davis, F. D. (1989). Perceived usefulness, perceived ease of use, and user acceptance of information technology. *MIS Quarterly: Management Information Systems, 13*(3), 319–339. doi:10.2307/249008

Eden, L., & Miller, S. R. (2004). Distance Matters: Liability of Foreignness, Institutional Distance and Ownership Strategy. In M. A. Hitt & J. L. C. Cheng (Eds.), *Theories of the Multinational Enterprise: Diversity, Complexity and Relevance* (pp. 187–221). Emerald Group Publishing Limited. doi:10.1016/S0747-7929(04)16010-1

Garud, R., & Karnøe, P. (2003). Bricolage versus breakthrough: Distributed and embedded agency in technology entrepreneurship. *Research Policy, 32*(2), 277–300. doi:10.1016/S0048-7333(02)00100-2

Kim W. C., Mauborgne R., & Pipino M., (2020). *Fintech: Compte-Nickel Creating New Demand in the Retail Banking Sector*. INSEAD, Case study: 01/2020-6235, 1–10.

Kirzner, I. (1973). *Competition and Entrepreneurship*. University of Chicago Press.

Kogut, B. (1985). Designing global strategies: Comparative and competitive value-added chain. *Sloan Management Review, 26*(4), 15–28.

Le Bret, H. (2013). *No Bank. L'incroyable histoire d'un entrepreneur de banlieue qui veut révolutionner la banque*. Les Arènes.

Le Bret, H. (2016). Le Compte-Nickel: un compte pour tous, sans banque. *Le Journal de l'école de Paris du Management, 6*, 24–30.

Le Bret, H. (2017). Vers un monde sans banques? [Towards a world without banks?]. In Annales des Mine- Réalités industrielles (n° 4, pp. 56–59). FFE.

Lippman, S. A., & Rumelt, R. P. (1982). Uncertain imitability: An analysis of interfirm differences in efficiency under competition. *The Bell Journal of Economics*, *13*(2), 418–439. doi:10.2307/3003464

Mintzberg, H., Ahlstrand, B., & Lampel, J. (2009). *Strategy Safari. Your complete guide through the wilds of strategic management*. FT-Prentice Hall.

Nicoletti, B. (2017). *The Future of Fintech. Integrating Finance and Technology in Financial Services*. Palgrave Macmillan.

Porter, M. (1990). *The competitive advantage of nations*. The MacMillan Press Limited. doi:10.1007/978-1-349-11336-1

Rocchi, J. M. (2020). Competition Between Neobanks and Online Banks in the French Retail Banking Market and Reactions from Universal Banks. In A. Sghari & K. Mezghani (Eds.), *Influence of FinTech on Management Transformation* (pp. 191–216). IGI Global.

Scott, W. R. (1992). *Organizations: Rational, Natural and Open Systems* (3rd ed.). Prentice-Hall.

Sgourev, S. (2013). How Paris Gave Rise to Cubism (and Picasso): Ambiguity and Fragmentation in Radical Innovation. *Organization Science*, *24*(6), 1–17. doi:10.1287/orsc.1120.0819

Shane, S., & Venkataraman, S. (2000). The promise of entrepreneurship as a field of research. *Academy of Management Review*, *25*(1), 217–226. doi:10.5465/amr.2000.2791611

Sutton, R. I. (1987). The Process of Organizational Death: Disbanding and Reconnecting. *Administrative Science Quarterly*, *32*(4), 542–569. doi:10.2307/2392883

Tardieu, H., Daly, D., Esteban-Lauzán, J., Hall, J., & Miller, G. (2020). *Deliberately Digital. Rewriting Enterprise DNA for Enduring Success*. Springer., doi:10.1007/978-3-030-37955-1

Venkataraman, S. (1997). The distinctive domain of entrepreneurship research. In J. Katz (Ed.), *Advances in Entrepreneurship: Firm Emergence and Growth* (Vol. 3, pp. 119–138). JAI Press.

Zaheer, S. (1995). Overcoming the liability of foreignness. *Academy of Management Journal*, *38*, 341–363.

KEY TERMS AND DEFINITIONS

Autorité de Contrôle Prudentiel et de Regulation (ACPR): The French regulator of banks and FinTechs in France.

Confédération des Buralistes: The French confederation of tobacconists comprises 24,000 sales outlets in the country making it the largest retailer network is a founding partner of FPE having since inception a 5% stake in the Company.

Credit Institution (or Bank): An institution that can provide the full range of banking services: receiving deposits, granting credits, and offering payment facilities.

Financière des Payments Electroniques (FPE): Company operating the services offered under the brand Nickel (formerly Compte-Nickel) both in France and Spain.

Payment Institution: A payment institution is a fintech that can provide payment services, formerly strictly reserved for bank, based on PSD1 & PSD2. Legal status of Nickel.

PSD1: The first Payment Services Directive (PSD1) which was adopted in 2007 created the status of ''payment institution''.

PSD2: The second Payment Services Directive which came into effect in 2018 is enlarging opportunities of fintech in payment services.

APPENDIX 1: THE CURRENT EXPANSION IN FRANCE

N.B. Service is also available overseas in Guadeloupe, Martinique, French Guyana, Reunion.

Figure 2. French coverage map as of August, 2021 (6203 Nickel's points of sale)
Source: https://nickel.eu/fr/points-de-vente

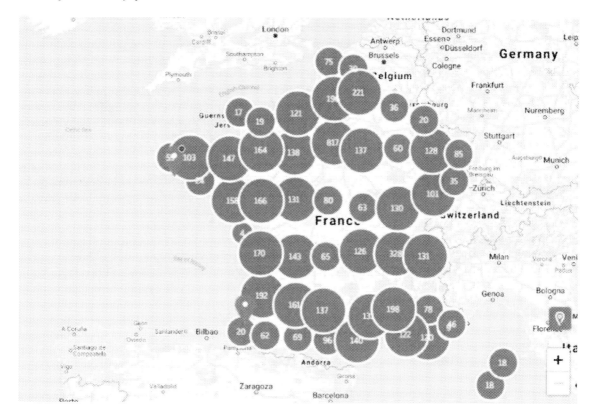

APPENDIX 2: THE CURRENT EXPANSION IN SPAIN

N.B. Service is also available in Canary Islands and Balearic Islands.

Figure 3. Spanish coverage map as of August, 2021 (593 Nickel's points of sale)
Source: https://nickel.eu/es/puntos-de-venta

APPENDIX 3

Questions and Answers

1. Why is the "phygital" business model presented in this case so powerful?

The phygital model allows to cumulate the best of both worlds, namely on the one hand, the advantages linked to digitalization and notably flexibility and availability and on the other hand, the presence through physical locations and existing customers.

In other words, when the internet meets alternative distribution networks with legitimacy, reputation and a flow of existing shops customers.

2. Why Nickel's trajectory seems inimitable?

There is only one Federation of tobacconists in France, and the first player therefore pre-empts this distribution channel, which is closed to potential competitors. All European countries do not necessarily have the same organization as in France and depending on the country, specific adaptations will have to be considered before establishing possible partnerships.

3. Discuss managerial, organizational, and technological issues and resources related to this case.

The entrepreneurial company Compte-Nickel was acquired by the multinational BNP Paribas and from then the first challenge was a successful integration. That is to say, not to lose the dynamism and agility of the acquired company, hence preserving its independence, while allowing it to create synergies with the Group if necessary.

4. What role do different players (decision-makers) play in the overall planning, implementation and management of the information technology applications?

Two of the founders, Ryad Boulanouar and Michel Calmo (still present in the company) were valuable specialists in payment systems. The existence of a proprietary, robust and reliable technology was essential to confer a technological advantage, considered transferable internationally by the new majority shareholder BNP Paribas.

5. What are the possible alternatives and pros and cons of each alternative facing the organization in dealing with the problem(s) related to the case?

There is a first strategic choice which is the model followed by the online banks (neo-banks in the sense of the ACPR) N26 and Revolut which consider that there is a *global market* of digital banking, have opted for a full digital banking, and open at the same time entities in many countries around the world, but to date these players continue to accumulate strong losses despite the fact that they each have several million customers.

Nickel thinks of the *competition as multidomestic*, opens new territories one by one, relying on partners with physical locations (phygital model), the company has been profitable for several years.

6. What is the final solution that can be recommended to the management of the organization described in the case? Provide your arguments in support of the recommended solution.

The solution is to continue the "phygital" model by adapting it to the specific environment of each new country where the Nickel's electronic terminals will be deployed.

Epilogue and Lessons Learned

Nickel links up with FinTech industry. First of all, it is necessary to recall what are FinTechs, according to Philippon's (2016) definition *"FinTech covers digital innovation and technology-enabled business model innovations in the financial sector"* (p.2). One another definition provided by Schueffel (2016) explain: *"Fintech is a new financial industry that applies technology to improve financial activities"* (p. 45).

Secondly, it is worth pointing out with Li (2011) the particular nature of the competition they exert against traditional banks (incumbent players): they are very successful specialists that each tackle a very specific parts of the banking value chain, in the case of Nickel for example payment services. Moreover, as emphasized by Arslanian and Fisher (2019) *"But payments aren't only important to incumbent financial institutions because of the fees that they generate. Payments are the starting point of the typical client's banking journey and an individual's most frequent and visceral connection with their financial institution. Consequently, they are viewed as the cornerstone of a 'sticky' relationship between banks and their customer"* (p. 32).

From a semantic point of view Tardieu et al. (2020) make a very limited use of FinTechs and prefer the expression *"digital service providers"*

Nickel's preserved independence explains the great success of its acquisition by BNP Paribas.

The pioneering spirit seems to remain intact, which is to the credit of the new management team installed by the new majority shareholder.

The first 6 months of activity of the Spanish branch of the FPE seem very promising.

Nevertheless, it is too early to assess this first 2nd country. Moreover, it should be remembered that we share Porter's (1990) view that competition in the banking sector is *multidomestic* in nature. As a result, the French success does not guarantee a positive evolution in Spain. Conversely, a possible failure in Spain would not necessarily call into question the success of subsequent launches (Portugal and Belgium).

Lessons learned 1. About entrepreneurs

When entrepreneurs define precisely how far they intend to take the business and therefore when they will sell it, things are clear from the outset. It is then necessary to respect the tacit agreement (in this case oral) between the founding shareholders. The success of the acquisition by a third party then seems greatly facilitated.

Lesson Learned 2. M&A success

We have seen that both the academic literature and that emanating from consulting firms emphasize that at least more than half of the acquisitions result in failures, this is true over time and whatever the sector considered, including the buyout of fintechs by banks. Nevertheless, every rule has exceptions.

We believe that several factors contributed to the success. The sellers experienced the sale of their business as normal at the stage of development it had reached, there was no emotional trauma. The transaction price that satisfied both parties favored the support of the sellers to the acquirer during a transition phase that took place in an optimal way. The essence of the company's identity was retained, which did not lead to any negative reactions from customers. Moreover, as a proof of success, the pace of post-acquisition account openings accelerated.

Lesson Learned 3. Progressive internationalization

Sellers and buyers shared a common vision: banking competition is multi-domestic (Porter, 1990) rather than global. As a result, a progressive internationalization was implemented, starting with countries bordering France and applying a business model very similar to that of Nickel France, but integrating the cultural specificities of each country. In other words, a strategic vision that remains attuned to common sense and the rules of prudence from an operational point of view. In this respect, there is a sharp contrast with N26 and even more so with Revolut, which believes in global competition and has set out to assault the world by establishing itself in many geographies at the same time. However, N26, using Brexit as a pretext, has withdrawn from the United Kingdom, a country where its establishment was a failure.

ENDNOTES

[1] https://www.lemonde.fr/festival/visuel/2016/06/24/ceuxquifont-ryad-boulanouar-l-inventeur-du-compte-qui-se-passe-de-banquier_4956982_4415198.html
[2] *Agéfi Hebdo*, January 9, 2014
[3] *Agéfi Hebdo*, January 9, 2014
[4] *La dépêche*, October 7, 2020.
https://www.ladepeche.fr/2020/10/07/compte-nickel-impossible-de-payer-ou-retirer-de-largent-gros-dysfonctionnements-pour-25-000-clients-9123781.php
[5] https://www.lemonde.fr/economie/article/2017/04/04/compte-nickel-tombe-dans-l-escarcelle-de-bnp-paribas_5105397_3234.html
[6] https://www.finextra.com/newsarticle/30380/bnp-paribas-to-acquire-95-stake-in-french-neo-bankcompte-nickel
[7] https://sifted.eu/articles/acquire-exit-fintech-banks/
[8] Nickel (2021). Nickel opens in Spain and continues its European growth with planned expansion into Portugal and Belgium for 2022. Press Conference January 7, https://nickel.eu/sites/default/files/CP%20Belgique%20Portugal%20Fr%20.docx_.pdf
[9] https://jornaleconomico.sapo.pt/en/noticias/fintech-francesa-nickel-chega-a-portugal-em-2022-684854
[10] https://www.challenges.fr/economie/consommation/pourquoi-carrefour-lance-le-premier-compte-courant-accessible-en-rayon_461859
[11] https://www.latribune.fr/entreprises-finance/banques-finance/avec-un-million-de-comptes-nickel-se-voit-comme-le-quatrieme-reseau-bancaire-francais-789708.html
[12] https://www.mastercard.com/news/europe/en-uk/newsroom/press-releases/en-gb/2020/october/mastercard-nickel-renew-their-partnership-to-expand-nickel-s-activities-in-france-and-europe/

Chapter 9
Purpose-Driven Marketing Wars:
Dishwashing Detergent Brands' Purpose-Driven Marketing Campaigns in Turkey

Emrah Gülmez
https://orcid.org/0000-0002-4850-9725
Anadolu University, Turkey

EXECUTIVE SUMMARY

Purpose is a definitive statement about the difference that a brand is trying to make in the world. It is becoming more and more popular every day, especially because Gen Y and Gen Z are more interested in economic, political, environmental, and social problems in the world. The interest and sensitivity of these issues have also been reflected in marketing and brand communication. In this context, purpose-driven marketing is a marketing perspective and trend that aims to connect brands with their consumers through their brand purpose. The implications of all these in the field of marketing have begun to be seen in Turkey, too. In particular, brands in the dishwashing detergent market have entered a purpose-driven marketing war with each other, so to speak. Finish, Fairy, and Pril have made purpose-driven marketing campaigns in Turkey. So, in this chapter, Water of Tomorrow by Finish, Don't Waste by Fairy, and Together at the Table by Pril campaigns are examined within the scope of purpose-driven marketing as case studies.

BACKGROUND OF DISHWASHING DETERGENT MARKET IN TURKEY

Before discussing the dishwashing detergent market in Turkey, it would be helpful to share some information about Turkey's demography that will help understand the dishwashing detergent market better.

The population residing in Turkey consists of 83 million 614 thousand 362 people in 2020, December. While the male population consists of 41 million 915 thousand 985 people, the female population

DOI: 10.4018/978-1-7998-1630-0.ch009

consists of 41 million 698 thousand 377 people. In other words, 50.1% of the total population is men, and 49.9% is women (TÜİK, 2021) (Figure 1).

Figure 1. Population of Turkey

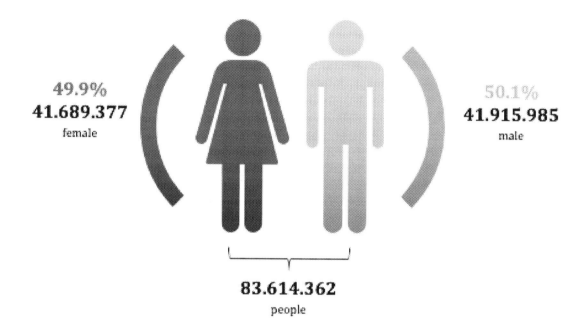

In addition, as of 2020, there are a total of 24 million 604 thousand 86 houses in Turkey. The average household size in Turkey consists of 3.3 people. In other words, an average of 3.3 people lives in each household in Turkey (TÜİK, 2021) (Figure 2). Therefore, the purpose of dishwashing detergent brands is to enter these households and be preferred and used by at least one of the 3.3 people in these households.

In this context, Turkey is an essential market for dishwashing detergent brands. Considering Turkey's population and a large number of households, the dishwashing detergent market in Turkey is a big one. Therefore, Turkey has always been an essential market for dishwashing detergent brands.

Today, the dishwashing detergent market in Turkey is growing and expanding day by day. Of course, the increasing sensitivity in hygiene and cleaning issues during the COVID-19 pandemic process significantly impacts this. However, of course, the growing market brings with it increased competition. Therefore, brands are in a tough race to get a share from each other. Before examining this tough competition among dishwashing detergent brands in Turkey, it would be helpful to get to know these brands, which will also be mentioned in this study, and examine their marketing efforts in Turkey and the world.

Figure 2. Quantity of House and Household Size of Turkey

Finish

Finish is one of the brands of Reckitt (formerly Reckitt Benckiser). Reckitt is a huge global company with more than 200 years of history. Reckitt's history begins with Thomas and Isaac Reckitt building the Maud Foster mill in 1819. Reckitt has many brands such as Airwick, Calgon, Durex, Lysol, etc., and its range provides health, hygiene, and nutrition for people in 200 countries worldwide (Reckitt Official Web Site, 2021).

As one of the brands of Reckitt, Finish says that they are the world's largest brand for automatic dishwashing products and #1 recommended dishwasher brand worldwide and have been at the forefront of automatic dishwashing for over 60 years. Finish is now sold in over 40 countries across the globe. Also, it is claimed that the line of Finish products are recommended by more brands than any other dishwashing brand (Finish Official Web Site, 2021).

Finish is a dishwasher detergent brand that offers smart solutions and innovations in everything from the hygiene of dishwashers to dishwashing since 1953. Finish introduced the first powder detergent for domestic use in 1964. In 1999, Finish launched the first tablet produced with Powerball, which is an indispensable part of the Finish tablet. Finish, which is not content with only detergent production but looking for solutions for a better future, launched the Power&Pure detergent series containing less chemicals to the market in 2014. In 2021, Finish has established a capsule detergent with Quantum Max Activblu technology, which is effective even on stains that have dried for hours without water (Finish Official Web Site, 2021).

Also, Finish's global vision is to help people achieve the cleanest possible dishes (Finish Official Web Site, 2021). In this context, Finish, which includes comments containing the satisfaction of those who use its products on its official website, used user or typical-person testimonials as a persuasion element. User or typical person testimonials involve an unknown person, presumably representing the target market, endorsing the product (Martin, et al., 2008,).

Purpose-Driven Marketing Wars

In addition, Finish has recently launched several essential advertising campaigns. One of them is #mutfaktabirlikte (#togetherinthekitchen) campaign. With this campaign, Finish draws attention to the need for women and men to work together to equality in the kitchen workforce. In addition, in the first months of 2019, Finish featured award-winning actor Feyyaz Duman in the commercial[1] it released with the hashtag #mutfaktabirlikte. In the commercial, it is told how Feyyaz Duman overcame the problems he had with the dishes as a single man, thanks to Finish Quantum. The movie ends with the brand's question, "Don't you think it's time to share the kitchen?" (Uçar, 2019).

Finish's other successful commercials are the ones for Finish Rinse Aid and Dishwasher Cleaner. Arda Türkmen, one of the famous chefs of Turkey, takes part in these commercials. The first commercial[2] is for Finish Rinse Aid, and it is released on June 2019 with the slogan, "Detergent is not enough; leave it to the experts!". In the commercial, Arda Türkmen uses Finish Rinse Aid to make the glasses come out of the dishwasher spotless (MediaCat, 2019). In the following commercial[3], Arda Türkmen appeared in front of the camera for Finish Hygiene Dishwasher Cleaner. In the commercial released on August 2020, the increasing home hygiene concern due to the effect of the COVID-19 pandemic was centered. In the commercial, Arda Türkmen, who hears that his nephew is disturbed by the smell of the dishwasher, introduces his sister who cleans machines with classical methods, to the new Finish Hygiene Dishwasher Cleaner (MediaCat, 2020).

Finish is one of the successful brands in Turkey about the usage of digital media. Its official Youtube channel Finish Türkiye that has been actively using since 2012, has 42500 subscribers as of June 2021. The total number of views of the videos on the Youtube channel is more than 138 million. (Finish Turkey Official Youtube Account, 2021). The official Instagram account, Finish Türkiye, has 353 posts and almost 25 thousand followers (Finish Turkey Official Instagram Account, 2021). In addition, Finish Türkiye, the official Twitter account that it has been using since 2012, has more than 7 thousand followers (Finish Turkey Official Twitter Account, 2021).

In addition to all of these, Finish has started a global campaign about the efficient use and non-wasting of water. This campaign, which was launched in 2019, will be discussed in detail in the following pages.

Pril

Pril is one of Henkel's brands. So, before giving information about Pril and its history, it would be helpful to mention Henkel and its marketing practices in Turkey briefly.

Henkel, which is a German company, is a nearly 150 years old organization. Its story begins in 1876 with a twenty-eight-year-old merchant who was interested in science: Fritz Henkel. On September 26, 1876, Fritz and two partners founded the company Henkel&Cie in Aachen, Germany, and marketed their first product, a universal detergent based on silicate. During the following years, the Henkel family and thousands of their employees built Henkel into a global company. (Henkel Official Web Site, 2021). Henkel, which established its first production facility abroad in Switzerland, has been operating in Turkey for many years. Henkel, which still has factories in Turkey, established Turkish Henkel in 1963 to produce textile and leather chemicals in Şişli. Then, in the same year, it opened its first facility in Turkey in Gebze. Following this facility, which operates in adhesive technologies, the first Laundry and Home Care factory was established in 1965, and the factory in Tuzla in 2001. Henkel established the first R&D department in Turkey in 1972 (Henkel Turkey Official Web Site, 2021). In 1973, Henkel launched Pril, Turkey's first liquid dishwashing detergent.

Actually, Pril was first launched in Germany in 1951 (Henkel Official Web Site, 2021). Almost a quarter of a century later, in 1973, Pril's adventure in Turkey has begun and it is launched as Turkey's first liquid dishwashing detergent. In 1993, Pril Lotion, Turkey's first dermatological dishwashing liquid, was established. Then, in 2000, Turkey's first hygienic liquid dishwashing detergent, Ultra Hygiene, was introduced to the market. Finally, in 2012, Pril Multi Perfect Gel, Turkey's first double-compartment liquid dishwasher detergent, was introduced to the market (Pril Turkey Official Web Site, 2021).

According to Nielsen sales volume data for the dishwashing liquid market for October 2019-September 2020, Pril is the most preferred dishwashing liquid in Turkey (Henkel Turkey Official Web Site, 2021). Today, Pril includes both dishwashing liquid and dishwasher detergent. Operating in Turkey for almost half a century, Pril also cares about local marketing efforts and can present products specific to Turkey. The Pril Turkey Series, which has been produced in this direction, is inspired by the beautiful scents of Turkey. The Pril Turkey Series dishwashing liquid has aromas from all over Turkey and unique to Turkey. Amasya Apple, Adana Orange, Aegean Mint, and Aydın Fig were introduced to consumers with the scents by Pril Turkey Series (Henkel Turkey Official Web Site, 2021).

Pril's commitment to consumers in Turkey is exactly as follows: "You want your family and loved ones to feel comfortable at home. Dishwashing detergent Pril allows your dishes to be cleaned easily so that you do not spend a lot of time on housework. This way, you can spend more time with yourself and your loved ones!" (Pril Turkey Official Web Site, 2021).

Pril is one of the brands that actively uses social media. Pril Türkiye, the official Instagram account, has shared 1280 posts and has more than 70 thousand followers. (Pril Turkey Official Instagram Account, 2021). In addition, Pril created its Youtube account at the beginning of 2021, has 3500 subscribers, and has more than 15 million views on Pril Türkiye Youtube channel. (Pril Turkey Official Youtube Account, 2021). Besides that, Pril doesn't have an official Twitter account

Fairy

Fairy is one of Procter&Gamble (P&G) 's brands. P&G is a major global company in consumer goods. According to Procter & Gamble's website, the Cincinnati company was founded in 1837— a year of the financial crisis in the country— by brothers-in-law William Procter and James Gamble. Procter was a candle maker, and Gamble was a soap maker. These products became the foundation of their business (Butler, 2020).

P&G, which has vast and successful brands such as Pampers, Tide, Ariel, Always, Gillette, Pantene, Ivory, reaches 5 billion consumers in approximately 70 countries with its 65 different brands (P&G Official Web Site, 2021). P&G has had a significant impact on both popular culture movements and marketing strategies and tactics. P&G's first brand, Ivory Soap, launched in 1879, sponsored a TV series, and since then, the term "soap opera" has entered the literature. Working to reach more consumers in more parts of the world, P&G is among the companies that broadcasted the first radio advertisement globally with its advertisement in 1923. Always listening to the consumers' voice, P&G established the first' market research' department in history in 1924, enabling the determination of consumers' preferences and consumption habits (Karpat, 2012).

The story of P&G entering the Turkish market goes back to 1987. Operating in the Turkish market for more than 30 years, P&G introduced Turkey to the first ready-made diaper, Prima, the first razor blade Permatik, the first shampoo Blendax, and the first hygienic pad Orkid. (Karpat, 2012).

Purpose-Driven Marketing Wars

Finally, P&G offered Fairy dishwashing liquid to the Turkish market. Consumers in Turkey loved the product, and P&G moved its Fairy production line to Turkey. As a result, the Fairy production line in Turkey is seen as the fastest production facility in the company's history. With this feature, the factory is a pioneer for other factories in the world (Karpat, 2012).

Fairy is one of the brands that actively uses social media, especially Youtube. Fairy created its official Youtube account, Fairy Türkiye, in 2011. Now, Fairy has 7500 subscribers, and has more than 8.5 million views on Fairy Türkiye Youtube channel. (Fairy Turkey Official Youtube Account, 2021). Besides that, Fairy's official Instagram account in Turkey, Fairy Türkiye, has shared 347 posts and has more than 42 thousand followers (Fairy Turkey Official Instagram Account, 2021). Besides, Fairy doesn't have an official Twitter account.

Fairy has been in the Turkish market since 2010, including dishwashing liquid and dishwasher detergent (P&G Products Official Web Site in Turkey, 2020). In 2020, according to the Ipsos Household Panel report, Fairy is the household penetration leader in the Turkish total market for dishwashing liquid and dishwasher detergent (P&G Products Official Web Site in Turkey, 2021). In 2010, when Fairy entered the Turkish market, two major brands dominated the dishwashing liquid and dishwasher detergent market in Turkey. Finish (formerly Calgonit) in dishwasher detergent and Pril in dishwashing liquid was the market leader and dominated the market. However, with the entry of Fairy, the competition in the market increased, and it is possible to say that this competition continues with all its toughness today.

Now, let's briefly examine the current competition in the dishwashing detergent market in Turkey.

Competition in Today's Market in Turkey

Today, competition is even more intense than when Fairy first entered the market. As mentioned before, with the effect of the COVID-19 pandemic process, the dishwashing detergent market in Turkey is proliferating, and the competition is increasing day by day. A recent study seems to confirm this. The Hygienic Brands Research conducted by Xsights Research and Consultancy for Marketing Türkiye magazine in November 2020 revealed how tough the competition in the market is.

In the dishwasher detergent category, where competition is high, Fairy is the most used brand with 40 percent, followed closely by Finish with 36 percent, and Migros Jel, one of the Private Label brands of Migros supermarkets, is third with 14 percent. Fairy, which did not lose first place in the most hygienic brand breakdowns, also stands out in this ranking with 43 percent, followed by Finish with a difference of only 1 percent, that is, 42 percent (Önder, 2020) (Figure 3).

When the participants are asked about their dishwashing liquid preferences, the leader does not change. However, Fairy ranks first in all dishwashing rankings as it is the most consumed dishwashing liquid with a ratio of 60 percent and the most hygienic dishwashing liquid brand with a ratio of 58 percent. Pril and Frosch follow Fairy (Önder, 2020) (Figure 4).

In the dishwashing detergent market, where competition is so intense, brands strive to differentiate themselves and become consumer's choice. On the one hand, while the competition between brands continues, brands are also looking for ways to catch up with the trends and meet the consumer on common ground. With Finish, thinking that the way to do this is to capture and understand consumers' social, economic, and environmental sensitivities, especially Gen Y and Gen Z, a new era begins for dishwashing detergent brands in Turkey: Purpose-driven marketing era.

Now, let's examine the concept of purpose-driven marketing.

Figure 3. Dishwasher Detergent Preferences of Consumers in Turkey

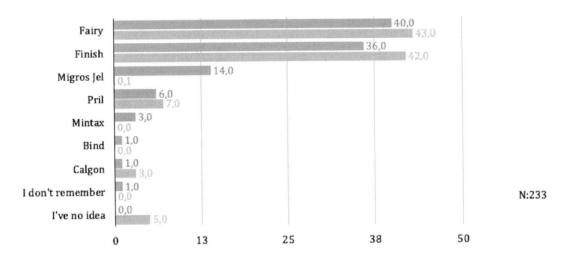

Figure 4. Dishwashing Liquid Preferences of Consumers in Turkey

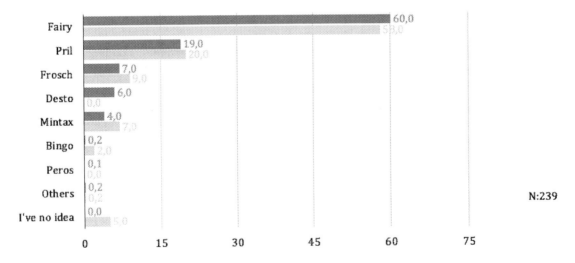

SETTING THE STAGE: RISES OF PURPOSE-DRIVEN MARKETING

Before mentioning the concept of purpose-driven marketing, it would be useful to talk about brand purpose, which is the starting point of the purpose-driven marketing concept.

The Emergence of Brand Purpose

The digitalizing world has completely changed both brands and consumers. Today, brands aim to attract consumers' attention and create a positive attitude towards them by using media, especially digital media. Brands want to build long-lasting relationships with consumers. But, consumers' expectations from brands are entirely different from twenty or maybe ten years ago. Today, consumers do not evaluate or choose a brand only with the features of its products or the prestige of using it. Consumers increasingly base their purchasing decisions on factors beyond price and product benefit in a world of nearly infinite choice. They look to how brands articulate their ideals, not simply the corporate culture, but how they aspire to benefit customers and the world (TED 2012 Ads Worth Spreading Report as cited in Hsu, 2017). Especially Gen Y and Gen Z establish a different relationship with brands than other generations. They want to know everything about a brand. And with the help of today's digital world, it is so easy. Besides that, consumers' requests for information can be about the contents of a brand's product, as well as about the sustainability and environmentalism works of that brand. Gen Y and Gen Z, which are stated to be more sensitive to social events, sustainability, and the world's future, can easily share these ideas with the whole world with the help of digital media. So, in addition to getting every piece of information, they want to know about a brand, consumers can share their knowledge with others by digital media in seconds.

So, the changing needs of consumers, new habits, social and environmental sensitivities, and way of perceiving the world compel brands to change, renew their understanding of marketing, and show more attention to consumers and the realities of the world than ever before. As Simon Sinek (2011; cited in Hsu, 2017, p. 373) said, "People don't buy what you do; they buy why you do it. And what you do simply proves what you believe.". It seems that successful brands will continue to be in consumers' lives in the future, too, by achieving this. Many current studies and researchs confirm this situation. For example, according to global marketing, communication, and media agency Havas Media Group's Meaningful Brands 2019 Research (meaningful-brands.com), people wouldn't care if 77% of brands disappeared. That means consumers say, "I don't care if that brand is out of my life tomorrow." And consumers can say this sentence for 77% of the brands they use. As another result of the Meaningful Brands Research 2019, 77% of consumers prefer to buy from companies that share their values. So, consumers expect brands to understand and empathize with them. They want brands to care about what they value and to protect those values (Meaningful Brands Research, 2019). However, another essential piece of data from Meaningful Brands Research 2019 is as follows: 55% of consumers believe companies have a more critical role than governments today in creating a better future. So, while consumers are ready to give up 77% of the brands, it can be seen that their trust in brands is more than their trust in governments in terms of having a better future. So, consumers want more interesting, more valuable, and more meaningful content/services apart from brands' usual offers. Therefore, they have expectations from brands in terms of creating a better world and future. This situation seems to be inversely proportional to the age of the consumer. In other words, as consumers get younger, their expectations from brands increase.

According to Meaningful Brands Research 2019, %63 of Boomers, %76 of Gen X, %84 of Gen Y, and %87 of Gen Z wants and expect more from brands (Meaningful Brands Research, 2019).

So, many things are changing rapidly in the world of marketing globally. But before everything else, the consumers are changing. Consumers want to meet with brands that have purposes similar to theirs. Consumers want brands to strive for the same or similar purposes as theirs. So, brands have to keep up with this change and aim to meet the consumers in the same place and for the same purposes.

So, all of these bring up the concept of brand purpose. And this consumer trend has led more brands to embrace brand purpose in marketing their products to the target audience.

The Concept of Brand Purpose

Purpose is one of the most popular concepts today. It is a definitive statement about the difference a brand is trying to make in the world (Spence & Rushing, 2009). In addition to this, Collins and Porras (2005, as cited in Spence & Rushing, 2009) define "core purpose" as an organization's fundamental reason for being. A compelling purpose reflects the importance people attach to the company's work - it taps their idealistic motivations - and gets at the deeper reasons for an organization's existence beyond just making money.

In this context, brand purpose is brand ideal, and it is an organization's inspirational and motivational reason for being, the higher-order it brings to the world (Stengel, 2011; cited in Hsu, 2017).

A brand's purpose explains why the brand exists and the impact it seeks to make in the world (Hsu, 2017). Therefore, it is a higher-order reason for a brand to exist than just making a profit. Besides the what, i.e., the company's products, and the how, i.e., resource planning such as defining structures, budgets, processes, etc., strategies include and usually start with the why (Kullnig et al., 2020).

As it can be seen, the "why" question is at the core of the brand's purpose. Of course, the main purpose of brands is to make a profit to survive, and of course, consumers are well aware of this. But especially today, consumers want an answer from a brand to this question: "Why do you exist in this world and my life?". So, it brings us to this question for a brand: "What is your purpose?".

As said before, purpose is becoming more and more popular every day because especially Gen Y and Gen Z are more interested in and aware of economic, political, environmental, and social problems in the world than other generations. The interest and sensitivity of Gen Y and Gen Z to these issues have also been reflected in marketing and brand communication. We are in a period where the reflections of Marketing 3.0 can be seen in every aspect of life, both for consumers and brands. Consumers, especially Gen Y and Gen Z, do not want brands just to produce good products or provide good service to them. It is already a must. In fact, a brand must successfully fulfill all 4P. Gen Y and Gen Z also want brands to take an active role in social, environmental, or economic problems within the framework of global values. Anyway, Kotler, Kartaja, and Setiawan (2010) call Marketing 3.0 the value-driven era, which recognizes consumers as value-driven people with minds, hearts, spirits, and potential collaborators. Also, the objective of Marketing 3.0 is to make the world a better place like Gen Y and Gen Z.

Importance of Brand Purpose

The world of brands is getting more crowded day by day, and so, competition is increasing. Nowadays, it is not easy for new brands to exist in the market compared to 20 years ago. It can be said that this situation is valid not only for new brands but also for established brands. Competition is now much more challenging for them too. For brands to differentiate themselves from their competitors and adapt to competition, they must adapt all elements of marketing management to today's conditions and consumer trends. And these upgrades, updates, and improvements need to be done in a realistic, sincere, insightful, persuasive way, not just to tick the to-do list. Because the consumer can easily understand what is truthful and what is not, who wants to draw attention to a problem to solve it, or who makes it just to keep up with trends.

As mentioned earlier, it has become more critical for a brand to create meaning in consumers' lives, especially for Gen Y and Gen Z. With identical products and lacking connection with consumers, brands are having difficulty finding a place in today's world. For this reason, brands should be able to add meaning and value to the lives of consumers. This is where brand purpose comes into play.

Consumers want sincerity and integrity. Brands that determine their brand purpose appropriately and accurately can establish sincere communication with the consumers. Therefore, brands should not see brand purpose as a trend but should internalize it to reflect it sincerely to the consumer. Because brand purpose enables brands to understand the consumer and find a place in the consumer's life. This means loyal customers for the brand. Consumers tend to prefer brands that contribute to life, create value; in other words, they have a clear brand goal. This, of course, also affects sales.

On the other hand, brand purpose is not only an essential concept for creating customer loyalty but also for internal communication, corporate culture, and employee management.

As a result of all this, brand purpose is now seen as an element of the marketing mix. Philip Kotler, a best-seller writer of marketing books, has added the purpose as a fifth to the four Ps. He explains that this is because if a company has the interest of customers, employees, and the supplier aligned to its business, then it will make everyone happy thus will improve the overall profitability of the company, and that is why, purpose should also form the core of the business (Anand, 2013). Therefore, just as brand managers strive to be holistic while shaping their brands' marketing strategies, they should also make this effort to set their purposes. Furthermore, just as all marketing mix elements need to be managed in a consistent, harmonious, and supportive way, decisions about all aspects should be made by considering the new element, the purpose. Therefore, the purpose must be reflected in all elements of the marketing mix.

In line with all these, brand purpose enables the emergence of purpose-driven marketing concept in terms of brands and marketing.

Purpose-Driven Marketing

Kotler (2011) indicates that consumers may be the primary driving force that pressures companies to change their marketing practices as consumers share Word of Mouth information through blogging, tweeting, and emailing about positive and negative behaviors of companies. He states that companies move from Marketing 1.0, the period when they view consumers choosing brands based on functionality, to Marketing 2.0, where the choice is made on emotional criteria, and now, to Marketing 3.0, with the emphasis on companies' social responsibility. Because now, consumers demand that the brand they bought have a common purpose with them, and more importantly, brands take an active role in social problems.

In this context, marketing efforts are also changing shape. It is not enough for a brand to adopt the concept of brand purpose, which is explained before; that brand must convey its purpose to consumers. So, all of these bring up the concept of purpose-driven marketing.

Purpose-driven marketing is a marketing perspective and trend aiming to connect brands with their consumers through their brand purpose. It is a type of marketing where the brand connects with its customers on causes they both believe. The brand's messaging aligns with the customer's beliefs and, in turn, that customer believes in and supports that brand.

In purpose-driven marketing, the aim is to introduce brand purpose to the consumers with specific marketing and marketing communication efforts. Therefore, for a brand to realize a purpose-driven marketing practice, it must establish a brand purpose by making strategic decisions regarding brand management.

Brands should try to create the feeling that they share the same purpose with the consumer with purpose-driven marketing practices.

Examples of Purpose-Driven Marketing Practices

Many brands have attracted the attention of consumers with purpose-driven marketing practices. And for this, it is not necessary to be a huge global brand. The important thing is to sincerely understand the consumer's insight, carry it to the brand purpose, and then implement marketing practices that can reflect the brand purpose. Being a truly global brand in today's world actually hiddens here.

Some of the examples of these brands are The Body Shop, Patagonia, and Warby Parker. For example, "Worn Wear" campaign by Patagonia (Patagonia Official Web Site, 2021), "Forever Against Animal Testing" campaign by The Body Shop (The Body Shop Official Web Site, 2021), and "Buy A Pair, Give A Pair" campaign by Warby Parker (Warby Parker Official Web Site, 2021) have carried out purpose-driven marketing practices that reflect their brand purposes.

Worn Wear by Patagonia

After the legendary campaign, "Don't Buy This Jacket", as part of its "Common Threads Initiative", Patagonia announced its experiential marketing initiative, Worn Wear Program. It started in 2017 and is still going on. Worn Wear program practices and promotes sustainability by offering free repair services, online repair tutorials, discounts for trading in used Patagonia brand apparel, and opportunities to share stories of one's adventures in repaired or long-lived garments through its micro-website, wornwear.patagonia.com. Also, they made a film about this campaign named Worn Wear – a Film About the Stories We Wear[4]. Through the Worn Wear Program, customers were encouraged to take pride in the signs of wear on their apparel by learning how to mend tears from sewing tutorials on its website. Free repairs were offered via a mobile pop-up to events across the United States and Europe. A truck equipped with sewing machines, supplies, and staff skilled in the refurbishing of clothing provided repairs to the apparel of any brand and stimulated interest in Patagonia and its initiatives (Michel et al., 2019). Besides these, there is a shopping section named Recrafted Collection on the Worn Wear website, where Patagonia puts together used clothes for sale (Patagonia Official Web Site, 2021). So, these are clothes made from other garments. There is also another section for products with some sort of flaws and defections, which is named Seconds Collection and Patagonia sells the products in this section by "Everybody Makes Mistakes" message.

Forever Against Animal Testing by The Body Shop

At Forever Against Animal Testing campaign, The Body Shop and Cruelty-Free International are working towards a worldwide ban on animal-tested cosmetics… forever (The Body Shop Official Web

Site, 2021). Forever Against Animal Testing campaign was met with an intense response and reached colossal success. On October 4, 2018, World Animal Day, The Body Shop, and Cruelty-Free International took 8.3 million signatures against cosmetic animal testing to the United Nations Headquarters in New York City to create a global framework to end animal testing while advancing the United Nations' sustainable development agenda (The Body Shop Official Web Site, 2021). The celebration of these signatures is a culmination of more than 30 years of advocacy between The Body Shop and Cruelty-Free International. The joint effort is the most ambitious campaign ever against cosmetic animal testing and serves as a model to inspire action from businesses, governments, and citizens. The petition signatures, collected from supporters worldwide in just 15 months, call on the countries of the UN to formalize an international framework to end cosmetic animal testing, everywhere and forever (The Body Shop Official Web Site, 2021).

Buy A Pair, Give A Pair by Warby Parker

And Warby Parker is a glasses brand that can be called new. Warby Parker launched a program named "Buy A Pair, Give a Pair". The reason for the realization of this program is "Almost one billion people worldwide lack access to glasses, which means that 15% of the world's population cannot effectively learn or work. To help address this problem, Warby Parker partners with non-profits like VisionSpring to ensure that a pair is distributed to someone in need for every pair of glasses sold (Warby Parker Official Web Site, 2021). To help address the problem mentioned, they work with a handful of partners worldwide to ensure that a pair of glasses is distributed to someone in need for every pair of Warby Parker glasses purchased. They employ two models (Warby Parker Official Web Site, 2021): The first one is empowering adult men and women with training opportunities to administer basic eye exams and sell glasses for ultra-affordable prices. And the second one is directly giving vision care and glasses to school-age children in their classrooms, where teachers are often the first to spot issues.

So, the implications of these changes and transformations in the field of marketing and brand communications all over the world have begun to be seen in Turkey. In particular, brands in the dishwashing detergent market have entered a purpose-driven marketing war with each other.

CASE DESCRIPTION: PURPOSE-DRIVEN MARKETING PRACTICES OF DISHWASHING DETERGENT BRANDS IN TURKEY

As mentioned before, it is possible to say that there is already a marketing war between the dishwashing detergent brands in Turkey. However, while this war has been reflected in the sales strategies, commercials, and even promotional tactics of brands, it has now taken another dimension: Purpose-driven marketing practices.

The dishwashing liquid brands, which both follow the global developments and can notice the change in Gen Y and Gen Z in Turkey, aimed to convey the goals they set to the consumers with purpose-driven marketing practices.

In addition, it should be noted that the purpose-driven marketing campaigns mentioned here are discussed with their digital practices. However, of course, some of these applications are not limited to digital practices only. In addition, conventional media were also used in these campaigns, and physical practices were also included. The digital practices realized were only one part of the campaign and were used to arouse more interest and inform.

Recent purpose-driven marketing practices by dishwashing detergent brands in Turkey are Yarının Suyu (Water of Tomorrow) by Finish, Boşa Harcama by Fairy, and Sofrada Birlikte (Together at the Table) by Pril.

The Water of Tomorrow (Yarının Suyu) by Finish

It can be said that the dishwashing detergent wars on purpose-driven marketing in Turkey have started with the Water of Tomorrow (Yarının Suyu) campaign launched by Finish in 2019 (yarininsuyu.com).

As it said before, Finish is one of Reckitt's brands. And Reckitt's brand purpose is as follows: "We exist to protect, heal and nurture in the relentless pursuit of a cleaner and healthier world. We fearlessly innovate in this pursuit across our Hygiene, Health, and Nutrition businesses" (Reckitt Official Web Site, 2021).

In this context, Finish's brand purpose is compatible with and Reckitt's brand purpose. In fact, Finish's brand intent is not only compatible with Reckitt's brand purpose but also directly supports and reinforces it. In this manner, it is possible to say that Finish's current brand purpose as follows: To prevent wasting water and thus to save water.

Finish has started the Water of Tomorrow campaign in Turkey to achieve this purpose. Actually, it should be noted that Turkey is not the only country where Finish has created a campaign to draw attention to water scarcity and to save water. It's a global project. So, Finish carries out this campaign on a global scale and has developed different campaign names or slogans and different practices for each country.

In order to draw attention to water scarcity and to encourage consumers to save water, Finish launched the campaigns below (Figure 5):

- Finish Water Waste in Australia (https://www.finishwaterwaste.com.au/) and New Zealand (https://www.finish.co.nz/finishwaterwaste/)
- Save Water Clean Clever in the UK (https://www.savewatercleanclever.co.uk/)
- Skip The Rinse in the United States (https://www.finishdishwashing.com/skip-the-rinse) and Canada (https://www.finishdishwashing.ca/en/our-values/sustainability/skip-the-rinse/)
- Finish Saves Water in South Africa (https://finishsaveswater.co.za/
- Ensemble Pour Leau in France (https://www.finishensemblepourleau.fr/)
- Stop Med At Skylle in Denmark (https://www.neophos.dk/stopmedatskylle/)
- Bez Predmyvani in Czech Republic (https://www.finishinfo.cz/bezpedmyvani/).

Finish works with National Geographic on all these campaigns. Thus, National Geographic is the main content partner for this global project of Finish. In addition, Finish carries out campaigns with different partners, although it differs from country to country. Finish is in partnership with Bosch in the Stop Med At Sylle campaign in Denmark. In the Finish Water Waste campaign, it works with Rural Aid. In the Save Water Clean Clever project, it is in partnership with Love Water and Cranfield University. Nature Conservancy and Bosch are project partners in the Skip The Rinse project in the USA. On the other hand, in Canada, the Nature Conservancy is the only partner. In Finish Saves Water campaign in South Africa, WWF is a partner. In Bez Predmyvani campaign in Czech Republic, Cesky Svaz Ochráncu Přírody-ČSOP (Czech Union for Nature Conservation) is the partner.

Purpose-Driven Marketing Wars

Figure 5. Finish's Water Scarcity Campaigns From All Over the World

In addition, Finish is running the Water of Tomorrow campaign together with National Geographic in Turkey, too. It should be reminded that National Geographic, which is the main partner of Finish in the campaigns it has carried out worldwide, is also the main partner in the Water of Tomorrow campaign in Turkey.

As already said, Finish has started the Water of Tomorrow campaign in Turkey to draw attention to the risk of Turkey's water is in danger of being poor as similar to other countries. In addition, Finish carries out projects to protect the "Water of Tomorrow" by raising awareness and mobilizing people about water consumption habits and water conservation in Turkey.

In this manner, Finish stated the manifesto of the Water of Tomorrow campaign as follows: "If we continue to waste like this, Turkey's water may run out soon. If we don't start saving today, we may not have water to save tomorrow. Today is the time to reconsider all our habits, from the shower to the dishes. Today is the day to act. To save tomorrow's water, now. Today". (Water of Tomorrow Campaign Official Web Site, 2021).

Finish officially launched the campaign on World Water Day, March 22, 2019, in Turkey (Retail Türkiye, 2019). In this sense, it is seen that even the start date of the campaign was started on a day that would serve the purpose and target of the campaign and create interest in consumers.

On the same date, along with the campaign, Finish also introduced the official campaign website, yarininsuyu.com (Figure 6). On yarininsuyu.com, Finish aims to enable people to get information about the Water of Tomorrow campaign and convey the campaign's aims to consumers. In addition, on yarininsuyu.com there is a lot of valuable informations about water conservation and water scarcity in Turkey, as well as other projects that Finish has developed within the scope of this campaign.

Figure 6. Official Website of Water of Tomorrow (Yarının Suyu) Campaign

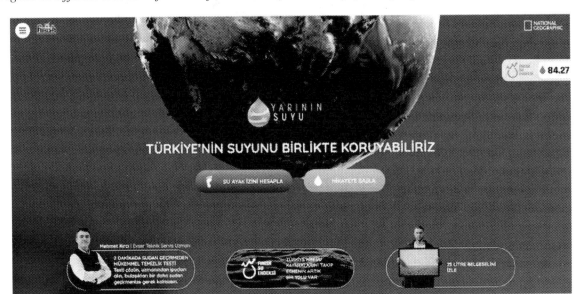

yarininsuyu.com website, which can be described as technically successful, differs from other Finish's campaign websites in the world with its user-friendly interface and interactive content. With many different contents, awareness is created for consumers about water waste and water scarcity. The contents of yarininsuyu.com website, which attracts a lot of attention from the consumer, will be given in detail in the following pages where the projects are detailed.

In addition to the campaign's official website, yarininsuyu.com, social media accounts specific to the campaign were created to raise awareness among consumers and inform them about the campaign. These social media accounts are also actively used, and promotional materials related to projects realized within the scope of the campaign such as commercials, ads, still images, and consumer-motivating messages are shared with consumers through the campaign's official social media accounts (Figure 7).

yarininsuyu, the official Twitter account of the campaign, was created in February 2019 and has 3681 followers as of June 2021, with a total of 925 tweets, 157 of which include photos or videos (Water of Tomorrow Campaign Official Twitter Account, 2021).

Purpose-Driven Marketing Wars

yarininsuyu, the official Instagram account of the campaign, shared its first post on March 20, 2019, and shared a total of 316 posts as of June 2021. In addition, it has 256000 followers as of June 2021 (Water of Tomorrow Campaign Official Instagram Account, 2021).

yarininsuyu, the official Facebook page of the campaign, created on February 12, 2019, was liked by more than 10 thousand people and followed by more than 10 thousand people as of June 2021 (Water of Tomorrow Campaign Official Facebook Account, 2021).

In addition, the films created within the scope of the campaign are broadcasted on Finish Turkey, the official Youtube channel of Finish in Turkey.

Figure 7. Official Social Media Accounts of Water of Tomorrow Campaign

There are no more women or repairmen, who we saw in the brand's commercials a few years ago, standing in front of the dishwasher and saying how wonderfully the dishwashing liquid cleans. Instead, finish has placed the water issue at the center of its communications. In addition, it tries to create awareness and behavior change in people with new sub-campaigns and projects (MediaCat, 2021).

In this context, Finish realized many sub-campaigns/projects such as Finish Water Index, Water Footprint calculation, Saving a Lake: Kuyucuk, documentaries such as 25 Liters, 25 Liters: In Pursuit of Water, and A Water Story in Water of Tomorrow campaign. And with these projects, tons of liters of water were saved and are continuing to be held. Because Finish's Water of Tomorrow Campaign is still going on as of June 2021.

Now let's briefly examine some of the sub-campaigns, works, and projects that Finish has done within the framework of the Water of Tomorrow campaign.

Promise

Finish has announced that Turkey is in danger of being water-poor and that it has launched a new campaign, Water of Tomorrow, with the commercials it has made within the framework of the Promise campaign (Figure 8). Therefore, the Promise campaign has been a launch campaign in which Finish's brand purpose is reflected and its official website, yarininsuyu.com, is announced.

In addition, in this campaign, Finish invites consumers to promise to save water. While talking about saving water in general by showing the drying lakes in Turkey in its first commercial, the brand draws attention to that 57 liters of water are wasted every time we rinse the dishes and call us to end this habit. In the second commercial, the brand invites you to try Finish Quantum, along with the same messages and promises that it will clean even dried stains without rinse and provide a perfect shine. Ads end with the question asked to consumers that 'Do you promise to stop rinsing?', for creating a desire for acting about it (CampainTR, 2019). As of June 2021, the first ad[5] has over 5 million views, and the second one[6] has over 5.5 million views.

Figure 8. Promise Ad of Water of Tomorrow Campaign

In addition, the campaign's official website, yarininsuyu.com, has a button named You Promise, Too. When this button is clicked, visitors see the Water Footprint calculation screen, which will be mentioned below.

In addition, another sub-campaign was organized in connection with the Promise campaign to see if the water-saving promise made on yarininsuyu.com is kept, to measure how much water is saved, and to encourage people to save more water: What About Bill?

Even though people were invited to save and promises were taken, the important thing was to keep this promise. To see if people kept their promises, people took pictures of their water bills and uploaded them to the official website of the whole campaign, yarininsuyu.com. A month later, they uploaded the new invoice to yarininsuyu.com and earned the same amount of Finish Quantum Max discount as they saved in a month (IABTR-Hani Fatura, 2021).

In addition, with the launch of the campaign, tips videos with various savings suggestions were shared on Facebook, Instagram, and YouTube. In addition to this, faturamatik.com, where all kinds of

Purpose-Driven Marketing Wars

bills can be paid online, was also included in the campaign. In this way, people saw how much discount they could earn by making direct savings when paying the bills. At the same time, faturamatik branches were also included in the campaign. Thus, people who paid their bills from branches were confronted both through the clerk at the counter and via SMS reaching the person (IABTR-Hani Fatura, 2021).

What About Bill, a multidimensional, successful, and cross-media project, was awarded the Silver MIXX award in the Mobilization/Community Building Campaigns category (IABTR-Hani Fatura, 2021).

Water Footprint

Everything we use, wear, buy, sell and eat takes water to make. So it can be said this is the water footprint's insight.

Figure 9. The Process of Water Footprint Calculator

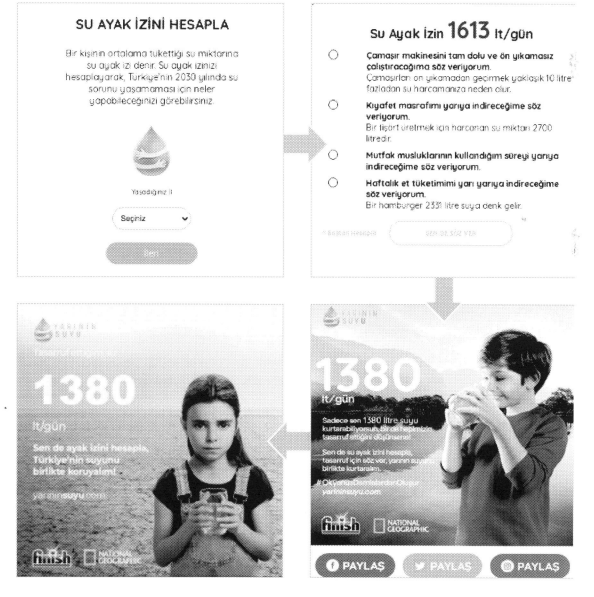

The water footprint measures the amount of water used to produce each of the goods and services we use. It can be estimated for a single process, such as growing rice, for a product, such as a pair of jeans, for the fuel we put in our car, or for an entire multi-national company. Thus, the water footprint measures humanity's appropriation of fresh water in volumes of water consumed and/or polluted (Water Footprint Network, 2011).

With the Water Footprint Calculator on the Water of Tomorrow website (Figure 9), there is a test to calculate a person's water footprint. Visitors who answer the questions in this test see how many liters of water they consume per day directly or indirectly. In other words, they can see their water footprint.

Water footprint campaign is a practice linked to the Promise campaign. The person who sees the result of the water footprint then sees how much water he/she consumes in different areas by the answers he/she gives. In addition, he/she see how much water he/she can save by reducing his/her expenditures. In other words, he/she sees how and how much he/she can reduce his/her water footprint. And eventually, he/she encounters a button that promises to reduce his/her consumptions. When he/she clicks on the Promise button, he/she sees how much water he/she can save individually and can share it on his/her social media accounts with a personalized image that appears after the click.

Finish Water Index

Finish Water Index is an index calculated by measuring the occupancy rate of dams and the trends in water consumption in agriculture, industry, and households. It is launched in October 2020, and it is a collaboration with the Industrial Development Bank of Turkey, an organization specializing in data (MediaCat, 2020).

An increase in the Finish Water Index indicates a decrease in water stress, and a decrease in the Finish Water Index reveals an increase in water stress. If the level goes below 100, it shows the presence of "Water Stress". The lower the index is below the 100 level, the higher the water stress. If the index takes the level of 70, it means that there is "Severe Water Stress". If the index goes above 100, it means that there is "no Water Stress" (Finish Water Index, 2021).

Finish Water Index, which is realized for the first time in the world and Turkey and shared with the public at the gong ceremony held in Borsa Istanbul, is created as a result of processing data from public institutions' databases and global and academic sources. Similarly, factors affecting household consumption, such as the use of dishwashers, are also included as future projections in the data revealed by the Finish Water Index (BloombergHT, 2020).

Besides, for the index to take its place in daily life, it has been ensured that the daily exchange and gold rates are right next to the news channels, newspapers, and websites. Furthermore, finish tried to show the index to people with the widgets they placed in the foreign exchange areas of various newspapers' desktop and mobile applications. Thus, people were able to see the Water Index along with the most followed financial values (IABTR-Su Endeksi, 2021).

However, on the Water of Tomorrow official website, the index value is still shared weekly, and people are invited to raise the index together with water savings.

The marketing objective of the Finish Water Index is stated as raising awareness about drought and strengthening the Finish brand perception (IABTR-Su Endeksi, 2021).

For Finish Water Index, both conventional and digital media are used. Advertisements were created to be broadcast on television, digital and social media to inform consumers about the Finish Water Index.[7][8] ve adreslerinden ulaşılabilmektedir.

Figure 10. Finish Water Index Commercial

The objective of the Finish Water Index advertisement (Figure 10) published by Finish is as follows (IABTR-Su Endeksi, 2021). With the Finish Water Index, the increase in visitors on the campaign website, yarininsuyu.com, was targeted. In addition, it was aimed to keep the water problem on the agenda and increase the rate of discussion.

With the campaign in which the gong rang for the Finish Water Index by participating in the opening of the stock market, the water index was updated weekly on tomorrowinsuyu.com, and the news websites were entered in the areas where the exchange and gold rates were included as news on TV, the press and the internet, Finish Water Index had 1.5 million TL worth earned media. Besides, the index reached 27,000,000 people on TV. It continues to reach 25,000,000 people on the web every month. With the campaign, the number of yarininsuyu.com visitors increased by 600%. The water index page was visited by 770,000 unique users in the first four months of the campaign. The rate of talking about the water problem increased by 121% compared to before the campaign. Finish's top-of-mind (TOM) score increased by 2 points (IABTR-Su Endeksi, 2021).

In addition to all these, the Finish Water Index campaign has won many awards. At the MIXX Awards organized by the Interactive Advertising Bureau (IAB), it won the Golden MIXX award in the Best of the Year category, Experimental and Innovative category, and Using Data category. It was also awarded the Silver MIXX award in the Brand Positioning/Creating Awareness category (IABTR-Su Endeksi, 2021).

The whole process, effects, and results of the Finish Water Index campaign are explained in detail in case videos [9] [10].

No Water Challange

In September 2020, Finish continued the project with a "challenge" targeting TikTok users (Figure 11). It was aimed to mobilize the masses to protect water by starting a 'challenge' that would be suitable for TikTok dynamics (IABTR- No Water Challenge, 2021).

Finish invited TikTok users to take a video of their daily activities using water without water, share it with the hashtag #nowaterchallenge and challenge their friends.

Figure 11. No Water Challange TikTok campaign

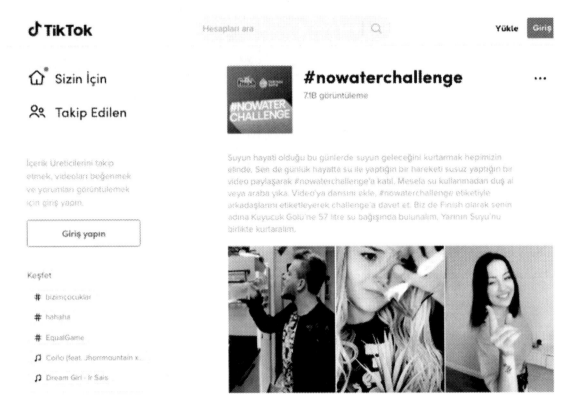

Finish announced that it would donate 57 liters of water to Lake Kuyucuk on behalf of those who participated in the movement. Also, the project was announced on TV with the editorial work with the brand spokesperson Müge Anlı (Kocasu, 2020).

Aiming to create engagement and produce more than 1,000 user-generated content videos, the campaign had 185 million views in as little as 36 hours. No water challenge campaign is created by Punch BBDO and Contentine. The music of the project belongs to Nova Norda (Kocasu, 2020).

No Water Challenge campaign won the Bronze award in Social Responsibility Communication at the Social Media Awards 2021 (Önder, 2021).

25 Liter: A Documentary

In addition to all these works, Finish also produced a documentary with National Geographic (Figure 12). The main idea of the documentary is "Imagine having to live on just 25 liters of water every day".

While the documentary 25 Liters deals with possible water scarcity in the Istanbul of the future, today it seeks ways to change this dark picture under the guidance of Turkish rock star Gökhan Özoğuz (Water of Tomorrow Campaign Official Web Site, 2021).

Purpose-Driven Marketing Wars

Figure 12. 25 Liter Poster

To announce the 25 Liter documentary on digital, draw attention to the documentary, and raise awareness of consumers about water consumption against the threat of drought, another study named News from Tomorrow was carried out.

With News from Tomorrow, it was aimed to draw attention to the water issue by teaching the concept of "Zero Day", which is the subject of the documentary. Zero-day is referred to as the day when water resources will run out. It is recommended that everyone maintain their lives with 25 Liters of water per day not to reach Zero Day. To draw attention to the 'Zero Day', raise awareness of society, and teach them what they can do about water saving, a campaign that directs them to the 25 Liter documentary was designed. On the homepage of the news sites of the Milliyet and Hürriyet newspapers, it was reported that the daily water use of the society was limited to 25 liters, with the fake news that "Zero Day has come for Istanbul". By drawing attention to the Zero Day and the depletion of water resources in Turkey in the news text, the readers were directed to the 25 Liter Documentary. In this way, the target audience group following the mainstream news channels was captured digitally, and the reading rate of the news was increased (IABTR-Yarından Haberler, 2021).

News from Tomorrow won the Bronze MIXX award in the native ads category and the Golden MIXX award in the campaign effectiveness category of the MIXX Awards (IABTR-Yarından Haberler, 2021).

Saving A Lake: 1 Million TL to Kuyucuk Lake

One of the long-running campaigns of the Water of Tomorrow project is the "Saving a Lake" project. The rescue of Lake Kuyucuk in Kars in cooperation with official institutions and scientists added a new dimension to the Water of Tomorrow campaign.

First, an advertisement was shot in Kuyucuk with a successful Turkish actor Taner Ölmez which he acts in a Turkish series Miracle Doctor. It was said, "The End of the Water is in Appearance," and the situation was shown. Immediately after, integration with the Miracle Doctor series was realized, emphasizing the importance of the lake for the local people. Cengiz, a real Kuyucuklu, was played in the series. Cengiz expressed his longing for the lake. Simultaneously with the series, the second screen application was launched with the FoxPlay app. The viewers touched the drop icon specially placed in the application where they heard the wordings determined in the Miracle Doctor. The advertiser donated to save Lake Kuyucuk on their behalf. Another mobilization was launched to save the lake. For each person following the Instagram account of Tomorrow's Water, 1 TL was donated. Users were involved, providing financing and motivation to save the lake. Necessary preparations were made to bring life water to Lake Kuyucuk by meeting with the Ministry of Agriculture and Forestry, the Governorship of Kars, and the North Nature Association (IABTR-Bir Gölü Kurtarmak, 2021).

In 2020, this rescue work yielded results, and some of the dried water in the lake was recovered. Birds who did not come to Lake Kuyucuk on the migration route of birds because the lake dried up started to come again. Finish announced this situation of birds in Lake Kuyucuk with the "Birds are Returning" campaign. A 24-hour recording consisting of the sound of birds was prepared to give the good news to the village people. It was played for one day in the village. And finally, it was ensured that life was brought to Kuyucuk Lake (IABTR-Bir Gölü Kurtarmak, 2021).

With the Saving A Lake campaign, traditional and digital channels were used simultaneously, and the situation in Lake Kuyucuk was announced to all of Turkey. People were mobilized with the campaign, which created awareness through television screens, but whose donation mechanism was built entirely on digital platforms.

Saving A Lake: Kuyucuk project won the Gold MIXX in the Non-Profit/Public Services category at the MIXX Awards (IABTR-Bir Gölü Kurtarmak, 2021).

Don't Waste (Boşa Harcama) by Fairy

Fairy was not indifferent to Finish's highly successful Water of Tomorrow campaign. However, realizing that the interests for the Water of Tomorrow campaign are not a fad and consumers really care about the environmental, social, and economic problems of the world, Fairy has started the "Don't Waste (Boşa Harcama)" project in 2020, in its 10th year in Turkey (Gıda Kurtarma Derneği Official Web Site, 2021). Fairy's partner in this project is Food Rescue Association (Gıda Kurtarma Derneği) in Turkey.

Fairy, showing the importance of sustainability, Turkish cuisine, and Turkish food culture, supports the Food Rescue Association to fight against food waste and hunger due to its 10th year in Turkey (Gıda Kurtarma Derneği Official Web Site, 2021).

Providing vital support to the fight to reduce food waste by cooperating with the Food Rescue Association, Fairy's "Don't Waste" project consists of two phases. In the first phase of the project, it is aimed to double the number of people to whom the Food Rescue Association provides monthly regular food aid. In the second phase of the project, it is desired to raise social awareness about food waste (FoodTime, 2020).

First Phase: Food Aid

In the first phase of the "Don't Waste" project, the target is to reach 330,000 people. Fairy financed logistical infrastructure support for the Food Rescue Association. With this support, it is aimed to provide food aid to 145,000 people in the Aegean Region and 185,000 people in the Mediterranean Region. Thus, the number of 330,000 people to whom the Food Rescue Association provides annual food aid doubled, and 660,000 people benefited from food support. With this work, 7 million TL worth of food will be saved every year from being wasted (NTV, 2020).

In addition, considering that the month of Ramadan is also a month of solidarity, Fairy has started extra work for Ramadan in its 10th year in Turkey. Within the scope of the "Don't Waste" project, food packages containing basic consumer goods and Fairy products were sent to 10 thousand families in need through the Food Rescue Association (Efendioğlu, 2020).

Second Phase: Social Awareness

Firstly, there is no website specially prepared for the Don't Waste campaign. In addition, there are no specially prepared social media accounts (Instagram, Twitter, or Facebook). An effort was made to raise awareness among consumers with the posts made on the official social media accounts of P&G Turkey and Fairy Turkey. In addition, communication was managed on social media using the hashtag "boşaharcama" (dontwaste in Turkish).

In addition, Fairy's "Don't Waste" project reached 50 thousand people in 24 hours with Bundle, a mobile journalism application where users consume more than 500 million content annually. The original content, prepared by Bundle Studio, reached 925 thousand people with a 3.3% CTR, received 3 million reaches, and was shared 2456 times (İçözü, 2020).

Also, a commercial was created for the announcement of the Don't Waste campaign (Figure 13). As part of its cooperation with the Food Rescue Association, Fairy released the commercial with the theme "It's yours to take care of the full plates, it's ours to clean the empty plates" (BrandAge, 2020). In addition, reminding consumers not to waste food in the commercial, Fairy gives the audience examples of the good days in the past when nothing was wasted. Fairy, which attaches importance to environmental sustainability and Turkey's food culture and says "DO NOT WASTE", reminds the audience of the value of the food for our future and hopes that our old habits will come back.

In addition, all the shootings of the commercial film, which were brought to life during the coronavirus epidemic that affected the whole world, were shot from home. It was stated that no food used in the film, which was acted upon in line with the message given by the campaign during the shooting, was wasted (Marketing Türkiye, 2020).

Figure 13. Don't Waste Campaign

However, Fairy took this initiative one step further and established the "Don't Waste Committee".

Committee of Don't Waste

Fairy Don't Waste Committee, consisting of experts in the fields of environment, food, and savings, has expanded its activities to cover not only the food field but also the protection of all environmental sustainability resources, especially water and energy (Figure 14). The Committee aims to offer solutions and options to consumers that protect the resources of Turkey and the world and to be involved in projects to increase the quality of life of the society. While promoting innovations of its products for sustainability, Fairy works with the Waste Committee to create social awareness in this area (Büyükdumlu, 2021).

Purpose-Driven Marketing Wars

Financial Literacy Pioneer Özlem Denizmen, Nature Documentarist Güven İslamoğlu, Food Writer, TV Programmer, Youtuber, Refika's Kitchen, Refika's and Börek Production Founder Refika Birgül, Environmental Engineer and Sustainability Steps Association Chairman Emrah Kurum and Economist, Influencer Saadet Algan are on the Fairy Don't Waste Committee, which was announced at the press conference.

Figure 14. Committee of Don't Waste

The Together at the Table (Sofrada Birlikte) by Pril

On the other hand, Pril, an essential player in the dishwashing detergent market, could not remain indifferent to the effectiveness of these two campaigns. Therefore, Pril has launched the Together at the Table campaign (Pril Turkey Official Web Site, 2021) and collaborated with Unicef within the framework of it. In the Together at the Table campaign (Figure 15), Pril supports UNICEF's Global Nutrition Program to reach 1 million healthy meals for children in urgent need of nutrition (Pril Turkey Official Web Site, 2021).

With every a Pril purchased, UNICEF's Global Nutrition Program, which provides basic food needs to the most vulnerable children, is supported. Pril announced this with the advertisements and public relations activities with Ceyda Düvenci, the brand spokesperson, and Danilo Zanna and Somer Sivrioğlu, famous chefs of Turkey.

Figure 15. Together at the Table Campaign

Pril's manifest for the Together at the Table campaign is as follows: We believe that the best way to bring people together is through a good meal. That's why we launched the #TOGETHERATTHETABLE campaign. Do not hesitate to be #TOGETHERATTHETABLE with your loved ones! Do not think about the future. You can easily cope with the dishes in your kitchen with the power of Pril! (Pril Turkey Official Web Site, 2021).

There is no website specially prepared for the Together at the Table campaign. In addition, there are no specially designed social media accounts (Instagram, Twitter, or Facebook). An effort was made to raise awareness among consumers with the posts made on the official social media accounts of Henkel Turkey and Pril Turkey. In addition, communication was managed on social media using the hashtag "SOFRADABİRLİKTE" (togetheratthetable in Turkish).

CHALLENGES AND SUCCESSES OF PURPOSE-DRIVEN MARKETING PRACTICES OF DISHWASHING DETERGENT BRANDS IN TURKEY

As said before, in all these purpose-driven marketing wars, Finish has been at the forefront. So Fairy and Pril followed Finish. For this reason, the work of Fairy and Pril could not go beyond the Me Too strategy.

Finish has received many awards for its projects as part of the Water of Tomorrow campaign. It has won the appreciation of both consumers and marketing and advertising professionals.

As seen from the researches Reckitt Benckiser commissioned IPSOS, the Water of Tomorrow project has started to yield results. 25 Liter Documentary, one of the first legs of the campaign, is known by 55 percent of the participants. Forty-seven percent are aware that Finish made the documentary. When 35 percent of people think of water-saving, the first brand that comes to mind is Finish. 88% of those who saw the campaign stated that they desire an effort to reduce water use. Finish managers asked the participants to keep a diary and send their water bills to them. It was determined that the water bills of these households decreased by 9 percent (Özkan, 2021).

However, commercials or projects created for the campaigns of Fairy and Pril could not reach essential awards. Campaigns that remained superficial did not enable consumers to internalize the brand purpose. Don't Waste and Together at the Table campaigns are conducted in this context and were perceived as a one-time social responsibility project rather than purpose-driven marketing practices.

SOLUTIONS AND RECOMMENDATIONS

In line with all this, it is possible to say that the winner of this war is Finish by far. Finish has attracted consumers' attention with all the projects it has carried out and has created a brand perception that cares about water and the environment.

The most crucial issue in brand purpose is to own a suitable case. Finish's brand purpose is also compatible with the brand's features. Finish has successfully reflected this harmony in purpose-driven marketing practices. Secondly, as seen from the realized projects, the brand purpose has primarily been internalized by the brand itself. This creates the perception that the brand is "sincere" in the consumer.

Today, one of the biggest requests of the Gen Y and Gen Z from brands is sincerity and authenticity. So, brands should not fall into the purpose-washing trap. Brand purpose is important not only in terms of the marketing and branding world, but also in terms of really caring about the world, acting together, and thinking about the future. Especially in today's world where environmental, social, political, and economic problems are seen in many places, brands should deal with these issues sincerely. Brands should not pretend to care about these issues. These problems should really, sincerely be cared about so that the consumer can internalize the brand and the brand does not purpose-wash with its campaign.

A purpose-led brand has to live up to its purpose. Its purpose becomes a guiding light in everything the brand does. It gives the brand immense focus and a long-term vision. It also provides a clear competitive edge against brands that focus primarily on product differentiation (Madden, 2017). A higher purpose is like a higher power. It's both inside us and outside of us. It's both the guiding north-star, ever-present yet never reachable, and it's also the glue of the organization, the thing that drives strategy and that drives every company decision. A higher purpose is about the betterment of humankind and mother earth. It's noble, just, moral, and ethical (Tate, 2016). A great purpose should manifest itself in everything a brand does: from product development to customer experience, from placement strategy to how it should conduct its marketing.

Another is its contribution to the world, as mentioned before. In this sense, Finish is on its way to becoming the next generation dishwashing detergent brand in Turkey by investing in the future instead of trying to save the day.

Another issue is the Me Too strategy. The Me Too strategy doesn't mean just copying a product. Copying an idea or a stance can also be handled within the Me Too strategy framework. And today, Gen Y and Gen Z, in particular, are more likely to respond to copying an idea than copying a product. Because consumers look for sincerity. And the way to convey this sincerity to the consumer correctly is through purpose-driven marketing practices today.

Besides all these, so, as Max Lenderman (2015) said, "purpose is the new digital." The notion of purpose will change the commercial dynamics of brands in the same way that digital transformed (and is still transforming) the way people buy and sell stuff. In other words, just like marketers had to learn to grapple with the massive implications of digital, we need to understand the profound implications of purpose which are equally transformative.

REFERENCES

Anand, N. (2013). *Kotler adds a 5th P to his set of four – Purpose*. https://www.dnaindia.com/business/report-kotler-adds-a-5th-p-to-his-set-of-four-purpose-1812393

Bez Predmyvani in Czech Republic. (2021). https://www.finishinfo.cz/bezpedmyvani/

BloombergH. T. (2020). https://www.bloomberght.com/finish-su-endeksi-kullanilabilir-su-miktarini-gosteriyor-2265599

BrandAge. (2020). https://www.thebrandage.com/fairyden-bosaharcamayalim-kampanyasi-10713

Butler, D. (2020). *History of Procter & Gamble: Timeline and Facts*. https://www.thestreet.com/personal-finance/history-of-procter-and-gamble

BüyükdumluŞ. (2021). https://pazarlamasyon.com/fairyden-surdurulebilirlik-ve-cevre-icin-anlamli-bir-adim-bosa-harcama-komitesi-calismalarina-basladi/

Campaign Türkiye. (2019). https://www.campaigntr.com/finish-yarinin-suyu-icin-soz-veriyor/

Collins, J. C., & Porras, J. I. (2005). *Built to last: Successful habits of visionary companies*. Random House.

EfendioğluK. (2020). http://sosyalup.net/fairy-ve-gida-kurtarma-derneginden-bosa-harcama-projesi/

Ensemble Pour Leau in France. (2021). https://www.finishensemblepourleau.fr/

Fairy Turkey Official Instagram Account. (2021). https://www.instagram.com/fairyturkiye/?hl=tr

Fairy Turkey Official Youtube Account. (2021). https://www.youtube.com/user/fairyturkiye/about

Finish Official Web Site. (2021). https://finish.com.tr/pages/finish-in-hikayesi

Finish Official Web Site. (2021). https://www.finishinfo.com.au/about-us/

Finish Official Web Site. (2021). https://www.finishinfo.com.au/about-us/

Finish Saves Water in South Africa. (2021). https://finishsaveswater.co.za/

Finish Turkey Official Instagram Account. (2021). https://www.instagram.com/finish_tr/

Finish Turkey Official Twitter Account. (2021). https://twitter.com/FinishTurkiye

Finish Turkey Official Youtube Account. (2021). https://www.youtube.com/c/FinishT%C3%BCrkiye/featured

Finish Water Index. (2021). https://www.yarininsuyu.com/finish-su-endeksi/

Finish Water Waste in Australia. (2021). https://www.finishwaterwaste.com.au/

Finish Water Waste in New Zealand. (2021). https://www.finish.co.nz/finishwaterwaste/

FoodTime. (2020). https://www.foodtime.com.tr/haberler/fairyden-bosa-harcama-projesi-h5680.html

Gıda Kurtarma Derneği Official Web Site. (2021). https://gktd.org/

Henkel Official Web Site. (2021). https://www.henkel.com/brands-and-businesses/pril-27222

Henkel Official Web Site. (2021). https://www.henkel.com/company/milestones-and-achievements/history

Henkel Turkey Official Web Site. (2021). https://www.henkel.com.tr/markalar-ve-isbirimleri/camasir-ve-ev-bakim/pril-648868

Henkel Turkey Official Web Site. (2021). https://www.henkel.com.tr/sirketimiz/onemli-olaylar-ve-basarilar/tarih

Henkel Turkey Official Web Site. (2021). https://www.henkel.com.tr/markalar-ve-isbirimleri/camasir-ve-ev-bakim/pril-648868

Hsu, C. K. J. (2017). Selling products by selling brand purpose. *Journal of Brand Strategy*, 5(4), 373–394.

IABTR-Bir Gölü Kurtarmak. (2021). https://iabtr.org/bir-golu-kurtarmak

IABTR-Hani Fatura. (2021). https://iabtr.org/hani-fatura

IABTR- No Water Challenge. (2021). https://iabtr.org/no-water-challenge

IABTR-Su Endeksi. (2021). https://iabtr.org/su-endeksi

IABTR-Yarından Haberler. (2021). https://iabtr.org/yarindan-haberler

İçözüT. (2020). https://webrazzi.com/2020/07/09/fairy-nin-bosa-harcama-projesi-bundle-ile-24-saat-icinde-50-bin-kisiye-ulasti/

Karpat, S. (2012). *P&G Türkiye Yönetim Kurulu Başkanı Saffet Karpat Açıklaması*. https://www.sondakika.com/haber/haber-p-g-turkiye-yonetim-kurulu-baskani-saffet-karpat-4172595/

KocasuN. A. (2020). https://mediacat.com/finish-tiktok-nowaterchallenge/

Kotler, P. (2011). Reinventing marketing to manage the environmental imperative. *Journal of Marketing*, *75*(4), 132–135.

Kotler, P., Kartajaya, H., & Setiawan, I. (2010). *Marketing 3.0: From Products to Customers to the Human Spirit*. John Wiley & Sons.

Kullnig, C., Obermüller, A., & Aichhorn, K. (2020). Improving campaign performance using purpose marketing: Case study of Run For The Oceans. *Journal of Brand Strategy*, *9*(1), 7–17.

Lenderman, M. (2015). *Cause vs. Purpose: What's the Difference?* https://sustainablebrands.com/read/product-service-design-innovation/cause-vs-purpose-what-s-the-difference

Madden, C. B. (2017). *Path to Purpose*. Sunday Lunch Pty Ltd.

Marketing Türkiye. (2020). https://www.marketingturkiye.com.tr/kampanyalar/fairynin-evden-cekilen-reklam-filmi-bosa-harcama-diyor/

Martin, B. A., Wentzel, D., & Tomczak, T. (2008). Effects of susceptibility to normative influence and type of testimonial on attitudes toward print advertising. *Journal of Advertising*, *37*(1), 29–43.

Meaningful Brands Research. (2019). https://s3.amazonaws.com/media.mediapost.com/uploads/MeaningfulBrands2019.pdf

MediaCat. (2019). https://mediacat.com/finish-ve-arda-turkmenden-isbirligi/

MediaCat. (2020). https://mediacat.com/cicek-gibi-bulasik-makineleri-icin-finish-reklami/

MediaCat. (2020). https://mediacat.com/turkiyenin-suyunu-takip-eden-endeks/

MediaCat. (2021). https://mediacat.com/2020nin-en-etkili-kampanyalari/

Michel, G. M., Feori, M., Damhorst, M. L., Lee, Y. A., & Niehm, L. S. (2019). Stories we wear: Promoting sustainability practices with the case of Patagonia. *Family and Consumer Sciences Research Journal*, *48*(2), 165–180.

NTV. (2020). https://www.ntv.com.tr/ekonomi/gida-israfina-karsi-bosa-harcama-kampanyasi,j5WjWuyhECo7_gj4bCJxQ

ÖnderN. (2020). https://www.marketingturkiye.com.tr/haberler/iste-tuketicilere-gore-turkiyenin-en-hijyenik-markalari/

ÖnderN. (2021). https://www.marketingturkiye.com.tr/haberler/iste-yilin-en-basarili-sosyal-medya-kampanyalari/

ÖzkanP. (2021). https://mediacat.com/2020nin-en-etkili-kampanyalari/4/

Patagonia Official Web Site. (2021). wornwear.patagonia.com

P&G Official Web Site. (2021). www.pg.com.tr

P&G Products Official Web Site in Turkey. (2020). https://www.kadinlarbilir.com/markalar/fairy

P&G Products Official Web Site in Turkey. (2021). https://www.kadinlarbilir.com/ev/temizlik/fairynin-neden-guvenilir-oldugu-hakkinda-daha-fazlasini-okuyun

Pril Turkey Official Instagram Account. (2021). https://www.instagram.com/prilturkiye/?hl=tr

Pril Turkey Official Web Site. (2021). https://www.pril.com.tr/tr/ana-sayfa/pril-hakkinda-her-sey/taahhudumuz.html

Pril Turkey Official Web Site. (2021). https://www.pril.com.tr/tr/ana-sayfa/sofrada-birlikte.html

Pril Turkey Official Web Site. (2021). https://www.pril.com.tr/tr/ana-sayfa/sofrada-birlikte/unicef-isbirligimiz.html

Pril Turkey Official Web Site. (2021). https://www.pril.com.tr/tr/ana-sayfa/sofradabirlikte.html

Pril Turkey Official Web Site. (2021). https://www.pril.com.tr/tr/ana-sayfa/pril-hakkinda-her-sey/tarihimiz.html

Pril Turkey Official Youtube Account. (2021). https://www.youtube.com/c/PrilT%C3%BCrkiye/about

Reckitt Official Web Site. (2021). https://www.reckitt.com/about-us/our-purpose-and-compass/

Reckitt Official Web Site. (2021). https://www.reckitt.com/brands/

Retail Türkiye. (2019). *Finish, Yarının Suyu Projesi'nin duyusunu yaptı.* https://www.retailturkiye.com/firmalardan/finish-yarinin-suyu-projesinin-duyusunu-yapti

Save Water Clean Clever in the UK. (2021). https://www.savewatercleanclever.co.uk/

Sinek, S. (2011). *Start with why: How great leaders inspire everyone to take action.* Penguin Group.

Skip The Rinse in the Canada. (2021). https://www.finishdishwashing.ca/en/our-values/sustainability/skip-the-rinse/

Skip The Rinse in the United States. (2021). https://www.finishdishwashing.com/skip-the-rinse

Spence, R. Jr, & Rushing, H. (2009). *It's Not What You Sell, It's What You Stand for: Why Every Extraordinary Business Is Driven by Purpose.* Penguin Group.

Stengel, J. (2011). *Grow: How ideals power growth and profit at the world's greatest companies.* The Crown Publishing Group.

Stop Med At Skylle in Denmark. (2021). https://www.neophos.dk/stopmedatskylle/

Tate, C. (2016). *Purpose-washing. Is it the new green-washing?* https://carolyntate.co/purpose-washing-is-it-the-new-green-washing/

TED Ads worth spreading report. (2012). https://wooshii.com/blog/author/wooshiiricardo/page/60/

The Body Shop Official Web Site. (2021). https://www.thebodyshop.com/en-gb/about-us/activism/faat/a/a00018

TÜİK. (2021). *2020 Yılı Adrese Dayalı Nüfus Kayıt Sistemi Sonuçları.* https://data.tuik.gov.tr/Bulten/Index?p=Adrese-Dayali-Nufus-Kayit-Sistemi-Sonuclari-2020-37210

TÜİK. (2021). *Nüfus ve Demografi*. https://data.tuik.gov.tr/Kategori/GetKategori?p=nufus-ve-demografi-109&dil=1

Uçar, S. (2019). *Mutfağı Paylaşma Zamanı*. https://mediacat.com/finish-mutfakta-birlikte-reklami/

Warby Parker Official Web Site. (2021). https://www.warbyparker.com/buy-a-pair-give-a-pair

Water Footprint Network. (2011). https://waterfootprint.org/en/water-footprint/what-is-water-footprint/

Water of Tomorrow Campaign Official Facebook Account. (2021). https://www.facebook.com/yarininsuyu/

Water of Tomorrow Campaign Official Instagram Account. (2021). https://www.instagram.com/yarininsuyu/

Water of Tomorrow Campaign Official Twitter Account. (2021). https://twitter.com/yarininsuyu

Water of Tomorrow Campaign Official Web Site. (2021). https://www.yarininsuyu.com/

ADDITIONAL READING

Arnett, H. (2020). The Power of a Purpose-Driven Brand (And How to Build One). https://www.blackandwhitestudios.nz/blog/purpose-driven-brand

Boitnott, J. (2020). What Is Purpose-Driven Marketing? https://www.meltwater.com/en/blog/a-sense-of-purpose-that-resonates-with-customers

Bragg Media. (2020). Is Your Business Missing Out On Purpose-Driven Marketing? https://braggmedia.com/purpose-driven-marketing/

Burn The Book. (2018). Why Brand Purpose Matters. https://www.burnthebook.co.uk/blog/why-brand-purpose-matters

Cardello, J. (2020). 4 Brands Who Mastered Purpose-Driven Marketing. https://blog.unincorporated.com/purpose-driven-marketing

Charles, K. (2021). What Is Purpose-Driven Marketing? https://www.adcouncil.org/all-articles/what-is-purpose-driven-marketing

Gregory, A. (2019). Three Great Examples of Brand Purpose. https://catalystmarketing.io/blog/three-great-examples-of-brand-purpose/

Gregory, S. (2021). Brand Purpose: How to Find Your Why With 7 Powerful Questions. https://freshsparks.com/brand-purpose/

Kramer, M. (2017). Brand purpose: The navigational code for growth. *Journal of Brand Strategy*, 6(1), 46–54. https://www.markuskramer.net/wp-content/uploads/2017/06/Kramer_JBS_V6_1.pdf

McClung, A. (2020). 5 Examples Of How Purpose-Driven Brands Are Winning. https://aaronmcclung.com/5-examples-of-how-purpose-driven-brands-are-winning/

Reiman, J. (2012). *The story of purpose: The path to creating a brighter brand, a greater company, and a lasting legacy*. John Wiley & Sons.

Setjadiningrat, J. (2019). *Building an authentic purpose-driven brand: A case study for Forestwise: Incorporating brand authenticity in the early brand development for purpose-driven brands.* https://repository.tudelft.nl/islandora/object/uuid%3A513a6a13-c8d7-47e7-94eb-8b74f6f75a6c

KEY TERMS AND DEFINITIONS

Brand Awareness: Remembering, recalling, and defining the existence of a brand in the minds of consumers.

Brand Positioning: Positioning the brand in a unique place in its target audience's mind. How the brand is positioned in the market determines how its consumers see it and what needs its products meet. Who the brand competes within its category and, finally, how much consumers will pay for its product also depends on its positioning.

Brand Purpose: The reason a brand exists for the World and consumers.

Brand Spokesperson: Mostly a celebrity who works for a brand to promote and represent it.

Me Too Strategy: A brand imitates a marketing element (4P), often successfully implemented by the market leader.

Native Ad: An advertising model in which the message that the brand wants to convey is integrated on the platform that the users are interested in and in a way that does not spoil the naturalness of the content. Native advertising generally aims to interact with the user by telling the stories of brands with entertaining content and meeting or confronting the brand in natural ways.

Purpose-Driven Marketing: The marketing activities reflect the brand purpose to consumers.

APPENDIX 1

Questions and Answers

1. What is the main object of this case?

The main object of this case is to reveal how dishwashing detergent brands in Turkey create their brand purposes and how they reflect these to their purpose-driven marketing practices. Besides, it is aimed to make a comparison between these brands. For this purpose, brand purpose and purpose-driven marketing practices of Pril, Fairy, and Finish, which are global brands operating in Turkey, were examined.

2. What is the reason for choosing and examining this case?

The main reason for choosing this case is that brand purpose is one of the concepts that will be considered the most in the future by brands. The sensitivity of Gen Y and Gen Z to the social, cultural, political, environmental, and economic situations in the world is effective in this. Brands are trying to respond to these expectations of consumers. The "dishwashing" sector is one of the sectors in Turkey where the reflections of brand purpose on purpose-driven marketing practices are seen most visible.

3. What are some of the digital technologies that should be considered in this case?

Along with digitalization, brands share their purpose-driven marketing practices with consumers through social media. Especially YouTube and Instagram are the most used social media platforms in this sense. In addition, it's vital for brands not to use social media only for their purpose-driven marketing practices carried out for brand purposes. The important thing is integrating digital and social media into purpose-driven marketing practices and making them a part of these efforts like Finish did in this case.

4. What is the main factor that makes Finish stand out more than its competitors in this case?

Finish's aim of "saving water" is directly compatible with its products as a dishwasher detergent brand. Besides, saving water is a realistic and global problem. Therefore, Finish can touch the lives of consumers from all over the world. Finish has created both awareness and a positive attitude towards the brand with its website and the practices integrating into the website. Aiming to influence today's and future consumers, Finish has succeeded in incorporating social media and digital technologies into its events.

5. What is the final solution that can be recommended to the management of brands described in the case?

Brands should set a real purpose that touches consumers' lives while determining their brand purpose. Therefore, brands today must be candidates to solve real-life problems. Brands should be sincere and realistic and reflect these in their purpose-driven marketing practices. They should use social media to promote these events and practices and interact with consumers. Brands should be consistent and approach their communication, marketing, and advertising practices holistically. In this study, the brand that achieved this best is Finish.

Epilogue and Lessons Learned

Brand purpose seems to be one of the most prominent issues in brand communication in the coming years. The biggest reason for this is the sensitivity to sociological, economic, cultural, political, and environmental problems that have changed, especially with Gen Y and Gen Z. Brands aim to place their brand purposes at the center of their brand management understanding and to bring their brand purposes to consumers through purpose-driven marketing activities. In this case, the purpose-driven marketing practices of Finish, Fairy, and Pril, which are dishwashing detergent brands operating in Turkey, were examined. It is seen that Finish has more marketing/advertising campaigns than its competitors. In addition, it is seen that all campaigns are compatible with each other and reflect Finish's brand purpose. This situation has enabled the consumer to perceive brand purpose as holistic, sincere, realistic, and consistent. As a result of all this, the most important lessons to be learned from this case are:

1- Brand purpose should be realistic. Brand purpose should be a solution to a problem that has a counterpart in the consumer's life.
2- Brands should not use digital media as a tool for introducing purpose-driven marketing practices that they have made in line with the brand's purpose. Brands should look for ways somehow to integrate digital media into their purpose-driven marketing practices. Social media, in particular, is a meaningful and valuable tool to mobilize people on issues they care about.
3- Brands should be sincere. Their brand purposes may aim to solve or draw attention to a real problem with a counterpart in the consumer. However, the important thing is that the brand can internalize it first. In other words, brands should care about that problem and convey to the consumer how much they care.

In this case, the brand that achieves all these in the best way is Finish.

ENDNOTES

[1] https://www.youtube.com/watch?v=5j7JW-dQUHA
[2] https://www.youtube.com/watch?v=9ZD2MKK5eCE
[3] https://www.youtube.com/watch?v=2R-KqsTJO4w
[4] https://youtu.be/z20CjCim8DM
[5] Finish Promise for Water of Tomorrow Ad: https://www.youtube.com/watch?v=tRPiYwKbl2M
[6] Finish Promise for Water of Tomorrow Ad2: https://www.youtube.com/watch?v=jXrioy0ChGU
[7] Finish Water Index Ad: https://www.youtube.com/watch?v=vsEM__cGgJ4
[8] Finish Water Index Ad 2: https://www.hurriyet.com.tr/ekonomi/su-bir-mucize-bu-mucizeyi-yeterince-koruyor-muyuz-41674548
[9] Finish Water Index Case Video (English): https://www.youtube.com/watch?v=Z3rDdQZYhvk
[10] Finish Water Index Case Video (Türkish): https://www.youtube.com/watch?v=2suWq-lHF8c

Chapter 10
SWOT Analysis and a Case Study at Kayseri Airport

Sabiha Annaç Göv
https://orcid.org/0000-0001-7601-559X
Gaziantep University, Turkey

EXECUTIVE SUMMARY

In this study, Kayseri Airport, which operates under Dhmi in Kayseri, is discussed within the scope of SWOT analysis. As a result, the most powerful aspect of Kayseri Airport is its proximity to the city, and the weakest dimension of Kayseri Airport is the low frequency of flights during the daytime. The outstanding features of Kayseri Airport regarding the opportunities arising from the external environment are tourism potential of the city, transport modes supporting each other, investments around the airport, supporting civil aviation nationwide, development of trade volume of the city. The most important feature of Kayseri Airport regarding the threats arising from the external environment are that it is not seen as a direct departure/destination point for international flights and distorted construction around the airport land.

ORGANIZATION BACKGROUND

The developments in the civil aviation sector, which is one of the most important developments of the 21st century and constitutes one of the most important components of the rapid and reliable transportation of modern life, is particularly noteworthy.

At the point we have reached, there are thousands of planes, thousands of airports and aviation companies, and billions of passengers are transported from one point to another, saving time comfortably and reliably with millions of flights each year (Aksoy & Dursun, 2018). It can be said that these impressive developments increase the differences between other modes of transportation that can be an alternative to aviation by making progress with each passing day.

Turkey, which shares a three-nation border in the region of nine different continents (Europe, Africa and Asia) is a country strategically placed. Rapidly increasing population, rapid urbanization, growing tourism industry and increasing regional trade in Turkey means that civil aviation in the near future would improve and the need to further develop the airport infrastructure would increase. As a reference point,

DOI: 10.4018/978-1-7998-1630-0.ch010

SWOT Analysis and a Case Study at Kayseri Airport

Turkey, in Europe outside Russia has a larger surface area than any other country. When considering the size and the growing population, the attitude of Turkey Residents of domestic and international air services are still in the positive direction (Şevkli & Diğ, 2012).

Air transport stands out as a rapidly growing sector, and privatization policies for the sector have increased the desire of enterprises to move to this sector. On the other hand, increasing competition among airline companies in terms of transporting passengers in a more comfortable, more economical and more reliable manner has led to the necessity to turn to different and modern practices in the field of aviation, that is, to create different and correct strategies (Kanbur & Karakavuz, 2017).

The aviation market has developed rapidly over the last decade, and many changes have affected the aviation market, especially after 2011. Considering traffic trends after 2008, air traffic increased by 10% from 2014 to 2017 after the interruption between 2008-2013 due to financial recession and economic recession. According to the most likely scenario of Eurocontrol, European up to about 16 million flights are expected. This increase in air traffic will put pressure on airport capacity and will direct airport operations to a situation analysis assessment (ACI, 2007).

Flight safety and aviation security are as important as strengthening civil aviation infrastructure. In this context, assign great strides in recent years at the highest level for the implementation of the ICAO standards, Turkey has become one of the countries that have made significant contributions to the development of passenger and global aviation system in the world. These developments in Turkey in 2016 was defining the international aviation rules to ensure that the ICAO Council members. In order to ensure the sustainable growth of the rapidly growing aviation sector with the liberalization steps taken in the aviation after the 2000s continued regularly. Regulations are made by the General Directorate of Civil Aviation (SGHM) within the framework of international legislation, and studies are carried out in order to realize these standards at the highest level in the auditing activities (SHGM, 2016).

While the airport management are trying to deal with the situations in today's business world, their biggest help in making decisions will be to evaluate and analyze the situation in their entirety. This situation is important for airport management as well as to develop their technologies and change their sustainable competitive environments in order to realize their strengths and weaknesses and the opportunities and threats around them. Airport management can analyze their current strengths and weaknesses in a way that can turn potential crises into opportunities and manage risks well. At the same time, it is possible for companies to analyze what is going on around them, general legal and economic conditions, to capture opportunities and to realize threats and develop strategies accordingly.

Today, it is well known that the examination of internal and external environmental conditions is an important factor for the existence and survival of an enterprise. Especially after the 1950s, with the effect of the System Approach and Contingency Approach, the environmental issue gained great importance and the environmental conditions of the enterprises and their internal factors became very effective in the strategy selection and evaluation process. Especially today, no business can be considered abstract from the national and international environment in which it takes place and their effects on its internal structure (Demirtaş, 2013).

The aim of this research is to analyze the internal and external environment of Kayseri airport strategically; to reveal its strengths and weaknesses, to identify potential threats and opportunities (SWOT analysis) and to offer recommendations in this direction. This study, which has international functions in Turkey's Kayseri airport is used for both military and civilian purposes important because it is an academic study on the current situation analysis.

SETTING THE STAGE

In the study, the relevant website and documents which are secondary data were examined and the observation method was also used. In addition to this semi-structured interview method was used. In qualitative research, analyzing data means being diverse, creative, and flexible. Each qualitative study has a number of different characteristics and requires a number of new approaches to data analysis. Therefore, the researcher should be based on the characteristics of the study and the data collected (Yıldırım & Şimşek, 2006).

Content analysis method was applied among the qualitative analysis methods. With the content analysis method, it is aimed to observe different hidden structures that cannot be seen at first glance (Kurtuluş, 2010). Both the text of the interview and the reports about Kayseri airport, etc. was subjected to content analysis. In the study content analysis method which is applied for qualitative research was used.In this study, qualitative content analysis will be used in data analysis. The reason for using this analytical approach is desire to reveal details and their approach to the topic. For this reason, it is necessary to reconstruct a text so as to create a meaningful whole of the expressions used from the documents obtained, the observations made at airport and the web sites examined.

Kayseri airport was chosen as the sample. The reason for this choice is due to the geopolitical location of the Kayseri airport. In addition to this, Kayseri Erkilet airport was chosen as the sample since the author can reach the authority of Kayseri Erkilet Airport and has opportunity to observe the airport. The strengths and weaknesses of Kayseri airport it has been presented with its opportunities and threats.

After 1999, the industrial area in the west of Kayseri started to expand. The city has expanded towards Erkilet and Airport along the transportation networks in the south and north. There is Erkilet airport in the North of the city and this situation causes construction around Erkilet (Kaya & Toroğlu, 2015). So, this distorted construction can be seen as a threat of airport.

According to interview with Airport official possibility of terror attacs can be seen as a threat. Due to Turkey's geographical location and some political problems, terrorist acts can be seen everywhere. Kayseri airport, like other airports, may be exposed to this threat. But the airport management always has measures against threats.

The 1960s and 1970s are periods in which there have been significant developments in strategic planning in enterprises. In the 1980s, the rapid development of technologies and the globalization of markets have significantly changed the competition rules of organizations. The rapid volatility of the business community has made strategic planning difficult to formulate a systematic and formal approach to strategy formulation. Rapid change requires more flexible and creative strategies. In the 1980s, the concept of strategic planning expanded to strategic management (Kandemir & Uğurluoğlu, 2017).

How strategic management issues can be applied, what needs to be done, and what kind of predictions can be made about the future of the enterprise are examined by conducting some researchers both on the enterprise and on managers and employees (Swayne et al., 2006).

According to Erdil et al. (2010), the new model defines strategic management as the processes of strategic thinking, consensus building, making this idea a strategic plan and managing strategic momentum. With the management of the strategic plan, new insights and perspectives emerge and the process of strategic thinking, planning and management is restarted. Therefore, strategic managers should become strategic thinkers with the ability to evaluate the changing environment, analyze data, question assumptions, and develop new ideas.

Furthermore, according to Baumann and Stieglitz (2013), large and small organizations can live in the same population, although they have different activities and characteristics. Newly established businesses are potentially competitors of large enterprises. Moreover, large enterprises were established as small and new organizations in this way. If we separate small businesses from the population without large and competitive enterprises, we will hinder the development of their processes, which requires a choice for the development of the population.

Although the enterprises have become obstructed in the implementation of strategic management, it has been shown that the most influential part of the result is in the formation of strategic management planning. Despite the fact that businesses are heavily engaged in the strategy development phase, the main problem in the strategic management process is experienced in the strategic implementation phase. One of the most important reasons for failure is the fact that strategies that measure how much of these strategies are realized, although the strategies that contribute to creating value to businesses are constantly changing, do not change. However, in the strategic management literature, it is seen as a necessity to have a close relationship between strategic plans and performance management (Gencer & Çetin, 2011). In short, strategic planning helps an enterprise to answer the following four key questions (Ülgen & Mirze, 2004):

- Where are we?: This question includes a comprehensive analysis of the internal and external environment in which the entity performs its activities, and examines and evaluates them.
- Where do we want to go?: The answer to this question is the mission, which means to articulate the reason for the existence of the business; a vision which is a conceptual, realistic and concise expression of the future to be achieved; principles governing the business activities; strategic goals, which can be defined as general conceptual results to which efforts and actions will be directed, and measurable results to be achieved in order to achieve the objectives are presented by putting forward tactics.
- How can we reach where we want to go?: Strategies and tactics, which are the methods to be used to achieve the objectives, are answered.
- How do we monitor and evaluate our success?: Monitoring and evaluation of the results of the monitoring and reporting of the implementation of the plan, mission, strategy and tactics, compilation of the managerial information and the evaluation of the plan and the results to be obtained. process is examined.

SWOT Analysis

SWOT analysis was explained first by Albert Humphrey in the 1960 and 70s using data from Fortune 500 companies. The problem faced by many companies was failure. As companies were failing, people started to ask question to see if there was a common theme many had failed from a lack of planning. Knowing why the planning had failed was only part of the puzzle; the companies also needed to know what could be done to change failure into success. Businesses would depend on this research to be able to analyze what was happening to their company. It was an important matter.

The research was conducted at Stanford Research Institute. The research took 10 years from 1960 to 1970. The members of the research team were Dr Otis Benepe; Marion Dosher; Albert Humphrey; Birger Lie and Robert Stewart. The extent to which the internal environment matches the external environment is expressed by the 'strategic fit', which is used to evaluate the current strategic situation of the business.

It is possible to find many definitions made in the literature by using SWOT analysis. In the study of Bayhan et al. (2017), SWOT analysis is an important analysis technique in exploiting superiority, overcoming weaknesses, evaluating opportunities and preparing for threats (Bayhan et al., 2017). In Burcu Devrim's thesis, SWOT analysis allows both the evaluation of the internal situation of the organization and the analysis of the competitors' situation of the market structure outside the organization (Devrim, 2006). According to Şengül and Bulut (2019), it is used to determine the strengths and weaknesses of an enterprise, to identify the opportunities and threats arising from the external environment, our strengths and weaknesses in the internal environment, and to provide suggestions and strategic methods in this context.

Based on the many definitions made in the literature, we can say that in aviation, businesses need to implement strategic plans in order to make the right decision and manage the future of their businesses. SWOT analysis has also been an important analysis guiding businesses at this point. A professional SWOT analysis, designed to suit the business line of the business, plays a major role in the decisions of managers. The manager should examine both the inner and outer environment of the enterprise in detail and that is, the enterprise-environment should make an interactive analysis. Each of the letters S-W-O-T in SWOT analysis has different meanings (Rankin, 2009):

- **Strengths:** They are the characteristics of an enterprise that will make it more effective than its competitors in the field it operates.
- **Weakness:** Other than the strengths of the business and weaknesses that will take it one step back from its competitors.
- **Opportunity:** These are the features that will benefit the business as a result of the analysis of the external environment and produce positive results. However, as the external environment is constantly changing, the enterprise must have sufficient experience in capturing these opportunities and gaining advantages.
- **Threats:** Restrictions on the activity of an enterprise are the factors that may cause distress caused by changes in the external environment, which may take advantage of the competitive advantage that may bring it back from its competitors.

SWOT analysis studies in the aviation sector are as follows (see Table 1).

Table 1. SWOT Analysis Studies in Aviation Sector

Turkish Airline Industry (Şevkli, et al., 2012)
Turkish Airlines (Sezgin & Yüncü, 2016)
Flag Carrier Airlines (Fett, 2009)
Airport Economy Development (Tan & Luo, 2011)
Regional Aircraft Type (Xu, 2015)
Regional Airport (Rankin, 2008)
Airport city development (Wang & Hong, 2011)
Development of Airport Logistics Strategy (Yang, 2010)
Malaysia Airline system (Jewczyn, 2010)
Airport Location Selection (Ebrahimzadeh & Izadfar, 2010)
Taiwan Air Cargo Industry (Chen & Chou, 2006)
Air China (Ahmed, Zairi, & Almarr, 2006)

SWOT Analysis and a Case Study at Kayseri Airport

SWOT analysis was done in the research. However, qualitative analysis method was used to make this analysis. Qualitative analysis it is to analyze social facts with their natural appearances in the environment they are in, and ultimately to develop a theory by using observation and interview methods and by evaluating documents. In this study, interview questions created by examining the literature and using the semi-structured interview technique were interviewed with the Kayseri airport official. Qualitative analysis can be considered as a more dynamic approach style, unlike quantitative analysis. One of the advantages of qualitative analysis is that the perspective of the individual is also effective (Yıldırım & Şimşek, 2006). Also, secondary data which are web sites, reports, literature were examined.

TOWS Analysis

TOWS Matrix as the next step of SWOT Analysis was developed by Weihrich in 1982. According to this matrix, strategies that can be implemented under four different headings have been developed. These strategies are the strengths opportunities strategy, which can be formed by developing strengths and opportunities together, the strengths threats strategy, which is formed by developing strengths and minimizing threats, the weaknesses opportunities strategy, which is formed by minimizing weaknesses and maximizing opportunities, and the strategy for reducing weaknesses and threats together which is the weaknesses threats strategy. TOWS analysis attempts to match internal factors with external factors to help identify relevant strategic options an organization can pursue. It can help an organization see how it can capitalize on opportunities, mitigate threats, overcome weaknesses, and leverage any strength (Weihrich, 1982).

CASE DESCRIPTION

A Case study at Kayseri Airport

Kayseri is a city where the tourism sector provides various benefits to the city in terms of socio-economic, socio-cultural and environmental aspects. These are benefits such as employment and income growth, cultural exchange, and environmental protection. These effects also affect airport activity. However, some features of the destination limit the contribution provided. These features are that tourism has just started to develop in the region, seasonality problem, lack of investment, promotion and marketing (Şanlıoğlu & Demirezen, 2020). Most of vacationers of Cappadocia region (very popular touristic place in Turkey) leave from Kayseri Erkilet Air terminal (Atasoy & Güllü, 2019). So, the airport is used both domestic and international flights.

The first terminal building in Kayseri was built by the Special Provincial Administration and the terminal was operated by 12 Air Transportation Main Base Command. Later, the terminal building, which was built by DLH (General Directorate of Railways, Ports and Airports), started to be used on domestic flights on November 15, 1998 and terminal operation was started by DHMİ. Until June 2007, the terminal building was used as a domestic and international line. The existing international terminal building and support buildings were officially put into service on 30 June 2007. As the old domestic terminal building was demolished and rebuilt as of 2009, the international terminal building was opened to domestic and international passengers for temporary departures and was used until the opening of our new domestic terminal. The new domestic terminal was opened on August 21, 2010 and put into service for the public (DHMI, 2019). A maintenance hangar was built by the Administration for A400M aircraft in Kayseri Airport (segaraviation.com).

Technologies in the airport industry could divide between airside and landside (Ansola et al., 2011; Augustyn & Turzyńska, 2016; Budd, 2008):

- Airside Technologies are gate management system, in-wallet scanning of travel documents or facial recognition, geolocation, tracking and managing of vehicles and people, coordination of teams and vehicles with real time information of taking-off / landing aircrafts, fuelling control system, air traffic control system, infrared de-icing, real-time operation management, radio frequency identification systems, airfield lightening system, weather monitoring system, automtaic vahicle identification and tracing sytem, self-repairing materials, self-cleaning devices.
- Landside Technologies are Real-time flight information, transport synchronization, advanced booking / payment means, intelligent passenger steering, augmented reality, sensors and digital monitoring system, automated warehouse system, biometric gate systems, real time translation, self-service kiosks, automated planning management for better use of resources like enterprise resource planning, wireless sensor networks, molecular laser scanner, wi-fi, bluetooth or imaging based flow monitoring, intelligent preventive maintenance, digital luggage tagging, self-cleaning, facial/genetics recognition, smartphone applications.

Kayseri Airport general information is as follows (see Table 2).

Table 2. Kayseri Airport general information

Location City: Kayseri
Service Year: 1998
Airport Status: Civil / Military
ICAO Code: LTAU
IATA Code: ASR
Traffic Type: Domestic / International
Terminal Building Total Size: 22.000 m2
Geographical Coordinates: 38 ° 46`13 "N, 35 ° 29`43" E

Passenger transportation data between 2007 and 2017 was given in Table 3.

Pandey and Singh (2018) identified 32 airport assessment dimensions. These dimensions are: road transport to / from the airport; distances between airport and service cities; population of service cities; basin area; airport size; support capability for aircraft maintenance; operational efficiency of ramp services; refueling aircraft; boarding gates and associated facilities; jet bridges; single terminal building; check-in facilities required; limited seating at departure; limited conveyor belt; commercial / executive lounges; limited retail and catering; air traffic congestion level; air traffic control capability; compatibility between used aircraft; runway condition and navigation aids; flexibility to provide time intervals; luggage handling efficiency; the convenience and efficiency of the CIQ procedure; ground vehicle selection for passenger transport; check-in facilities and flight information system; number of flights on the same route; incentives for LCA; airport tariff level; airport authority support attitude; low tax to users / service providers; efficient airport operations; fast airport operations; target customer and diversification.

Table 3. Passenger transportation by Kayseri Erkilet Airport

Year	Domestic	% change	international	% change	Total	% change
2017	1.886.729	%6	260.967	%29	2.147.696	%8
2016	1.781.989	%1	202.536	%6	1.984.525	%1
2015	1.756.787	%17	215.361	%4	1.972.148	%14
2014	1.501.520	%6	224.326	%3	1.725.846	%6
2013	1.414.826	%29	218.186	%6	1.633.012	%23
2012	1.096.883	%13	232.943	%9	1.329.826	%9
2011	968.942	%34	254.818	%16	1.223.760	%30
2010	720.229	%27,0	219.955	%4,0	940.184	%21,0
2009	568.106	%18,4	210.533	%8,0	778.639	%15,4
2008	479.857	%17,0	194.976	%3,0	674.833	%12,0
2007	575.473		189.833		765.306	

Source: https://www.dhmi.gov.tr/Sayfalar/FaaliyetRaporlari.aspx

It has identified 32 airport assessment dimensions. Some of these assessment dimensions stand out as criteria that passengers are not aware of at all. While adapting these dimensions for Kayseri Airport, the sub-dimensions that are noteworthy and noticed by the passengers are discussed.

SWOT Analysis of Kayseri Airport

In the adaptation of Kayseri airport to SWOT analysis, studies on airport characteristics, airport quality, airport passenger satisfaction were examined.

In order to see the current status of an airport, it is necessary to look at the status of aviation transportation in Turkey. Civil air transport activities in Turkey, especially in the context of the liberal aviation policy initiated in 2003, have entered into a very rapid development. In the last decade (2009-2018), the number of commercial flights has increased by 93%, the number of passengers carried 146% and the amount of cargo carried has increased by 232%. The total number of domestic passenger's international flights, which was 193045343 in 2017, increased by 9% to 210498164 in 2018. Domestic flights have a share of 54% in total passengers. Cappadocia airport (198%), Samsun Çarşamba (48%), Gazipaşa Alanya (46%) and Bingöl (34%) draw attention in the increase in the total number of passengers (DHMİ, 2019).

In order to see how the activity of Kayseri airport is, other airports should also be evaluated within the framework of external environment analysis. A significant portion of domestic passenger traffic was realized from Istanbul Sabiha Gökçen (20%), Istanbul Atatürk (17%), Ankara Esenboğa (13%), Izmir Adnan Menderes (9%) and Antalya (7%) Airports. In 2018, the highest total international passenger traffic was realized in Istanbul Atatürk (50%), Antalya (25%), Istanbul Sabiha Gökçen (12%), Izmir Adnan Menderes (3%) and Muğla Dalaman (3%) Airports. Kayseri airport has a lower rate compared to large and popular airports with a share of 0.3%. However, compared to airports with fewer flights, it can be said to be in good shape but not much active.

Airport official said, "An average of 50 military flights and 70 civilian flights are made daily at Kayseri airport. Having 9 parking spaces requires fast operations. When we look at 52 airport traffic, Kayseri airport ranks 10th airport". He has revealed the general activity status of Kayseri airport.

Performance measurement at airports allows airport managers to make the most appropriate decisions and can help them to take necessary precautions against unexpected changes. Furthermore, performance analysis at airports allows the comparison of the airport's current situation with other airports. With the reduction of state control over the airports, they are operated by commercial organizations and are becoming more successful in terms of efficiency and effectiveness. However, number of indicators are needed to measure efficiency and effectiveness. Thus, performance analysis is very important in terms of helping the operator attain objectives and determine new targets. With the aim of measuring the efficiency of 37 airports in Turkey in 2007, Peker and Baki used car park capacity, number of runways, airport size and number of employees as the input, and the total number of passengers and total load amount as the output. As a result of the analysis, it was reported that of the major airports, Atatürk, Antalya, Adana, Trabzon and Kayseri airports were efficient, and among the small airports, Malatya and Çardak airports were efficient (Peker & Baki, 2009). Kayseri Airport Parking capacity is quite large. There is a parking lot for approximately 420 cars.

The efficiency and productivity of the airports operating in domestic and international lines in Turkey have been examined; 2 input variables and 3 output variables were used. Input variables: number of personnel and terminal area. Output variables consisted of the number of passengers, freight traffic and total aircraft traffic. For the summer and winter periods in 2014, the performance of an airport compared to other airports was determined with the analysis made using the data envelopment analysis technique. In addition, with the efficiency value, the performance of the airports compared to the previous period was determined. The fact that the airport is fully efficient does not mean that it is at the point where it should be in terms of performance. It means that it is in the best condition of all airports. Similarly, it does not mean that the airport with the lowest efficiency is in a very bad condition. In the same way, the airport with the highest efficiency does not mean the best airport, but the airport with the highest performance. In terms of efficiency, Kayseri airport is among the airports with low efficiency both in the summer of 2014 and in the winter period (Avcı & Aktaş, 2015).

According to the operational efficiency scores, Kayseri airport was considered efficient. It is efficient for operational efficiency, because of the use of the airport in not only Kayseri province but also the settlements in their surroundings (Özsoy & Örkcü, 2021). Kayseri province has got a lot of touristic places such as Döner Kümbet, Gevher Nesibe Hospital, Seyyid Burhaneddin Hz Tomb, Forum Kayseri, Mevlana Mosque, Alaca Kumbet, Kosk Medresesi, Kayseri Clock Tower, Kayseri National Struggle Museum, Kursunlu Mosque, Cami Kebir (Grand Mosque), Atatürk Museum, Kayseri Surp Krikor Lusavoric Armenian Church, Le Bazaar D'Orient, etc. Beside city touristic places, the airport serves surroundings of the city. These surroundings are Cappadocia, Göreme, Nevşehir, Niğde, etc. Touristic places can affect airport activity and traffic.

Environmental sustainability is a factor for airport operations. According to research which conducted in Kayseri Airport in Turkey by International Civil Aviation Organization (ICAO), it is estimated that a decrease of 2 min in taxiing time causes a decrease of approximately 4% in LTO emissions. An increase of 25% in landing and take-off cycles causes an increase of around 11% in pollutant emissions. Domestic flights were responsible for 68% of the total LTO emissions from all flights at Kayseri Airport in 2010

(Yılmaz, 2017). Kayseri Erkilet Airport has a Green Foundation Certificate under the name of Green Airport and a Barrier-Free Airport Certificate under the name of Barrier-Free Airport. Many advantages are provided by following green airport criteria. With the waste water management, dirty water is aimed not to harm nature. Zero waste projects are supported with the waste management; paper, metal, glass and plastics are put into separate recycling bins and this contributes to the economy and wood-chopping is reduced. The noise management criteria aim more peaceful cities and healthier individuals. Selecting nonhazardous chemical substances used in activities carried out for de-icing of planes in cold weathers for environment contributes a more sustainable nature. With the green airport practices, sustainable city and life areas which is one of the Sustainable Development Goals have been achieved (Göv, 2019).

Weather is important parameter for safe services presented at an airport. Çınaroğlu and Unutulmaz (2019) carried out a study. The data used in the classification algorithms included 15330 days' values obtained between the years 1970 and 2012. A new data set was used to confirm the accuracy and validity of the forecasting rules attained with the former data set. For this purpose, estimations were made using the data of November 2016 and January 2017. The accuracy rates of the Kayseri Office of the Turkish State. Meteorological Service regarding these meteorological events were obtained from the forecasting and warning center authoritative. Fog event occurred on 42 days out of 61 days of observation. Fog on 40 days was correctly estimated by the obtained rules. Fog didn't occur on 19 of 61 days of observation. Of these 19 days, estimation was correct on 14 days. The fog analysis had a success rate of 89%. The accuracy rate of fog event obtained by the Kayseri Regional Office was observed as 85% for these two months. Thunderstorm event didn't occur during the 61 days of observation. The thunderstorm analysis had a success rate of 100%. The precipitation analysis had a success rate of 90.2%. The accuracy rate of precipitation event obtained by the Kayseri Regional Office was observed as 89.1% for these two months (Çınaroğlu & Unutulmaz, 2019). The manager interviewed gives the following statements about the business periods of the airport: "In winter, Erciyes is a high level of ski tourism, and in summer there is a concentration of our citizens living abroad". It can be said that the airport has a flow of passengers for different reasons both in summer and winter. The number of check-in desk at the airport, which is included in the scope of the study, is expressed as 12 on international flights and 13 on domestic flights. However, it is stated that not all of these check-in desks are actively used. It was stated that there are more flights in the summer, and there is a shortage of resources due to the fact that there are more flights in the international flights and there are airlines operating at the same hours (Bolat & Ateş, 2020).

According to the information received by the authorities "We can consider the busiest month in July. It is possible to say the first week of July as a week. To give an example in the peak period, a company always reserves 180 seats of the plane's capacity (189 seats). Plane number occupancy ratio is 95%, with 180 passengers". Kiosk devices are considered as a factor that reduces waiting times in check-in procedures. However, there is no check-in kiosk at Erkilet airport. In this context, it can be said that all check-in procedures are carried out at the check-in desk. It is stated that the arrival time of the passengers to the desks varies in domestic and international lines. The information received from the interviewer is as follows: "We open our desks 2.30 hours before international flights and 2 hours before domestic flights. We close our desks with an average of 20 minutes remaining. For the normal time, it is too late for the desk closing, but unfortunately passengers apply to the desk too late, the operations officer closes our desks late to avoid calculating again and asks the captains to close late. Passengers are often admitted to the flight when they arrive late. Assuming that the departure is at 14.00, there are times when we accept passengers at 13.55, and there are times when it is not. Assuming the flight time as 15.00, the maximum density in international flights is between 13.45. We can say that the maximum density is 14.00 in domestic lines". VIP and CIP passengers are usually different check-in desks at the airports. However, there is no separate checkin for VIP and CIP passengers due to the fact that Erkilet Airport is an airport that can be described as small in nature. It is stated that the transactions of VIP and CIP passengers are also carried out from the same check-in desks (Bolat & Ateş, 2020). As seen in this study, there are no VIP and CIP counters seperately. Also, there are no kiosks. In this sense, it can be said that the airport does not follow the technology. However, this may be due to the low number of passengers and the lack of need for self-service kiosks.

Based on the above information (secondary data, news, primary data, observation, interview) about the airport and the literature on SWOT analysis, the following SWOT analysis was created (see Table 4).

Table 4. SWOT Analysis of Kayseri Airport

	Positive (Helpful)	Negative (Harmful)
Current situation (internal origin)	**1. Strengths** • Proximity to the city center • Low air traffic jam • Fast airport operations • Landing / departure runway and navigation devices for different types of aircraft • Diversity and speed of check-in facilities • Convenience of the weather • Carbon-free airport • Green airport certification • Barrier-free airport	**2. Weaknesses** • High operating costs • High price of shopping and restaurants within the airport • Low number of flights per day • Lack of parking area for aircraft (under construction) • Inability of managers to keep pace with technological development • Inefficient airport • Lack of self service kiosks • Lack of VIP check in counter
Future possibilities (external origin)	**3. Opportunities** • Tourism potential of the city • Transport modes support each other • Investments around the airport • Supporting civil aviation nationwide • Development of trade volume of the city	**4. Threats** • Distorted construction around airport land • The climate of the city is unfavorable in winter • Preferability of other modes of transport (fast train Project) • Possibility of terror attacks

TOWS Analysis of Kayseri Airport

In this research, TOWS analysis (Table 5) was used as it makes it possible to develop strategies on how to take advantage of positive situations to eliminate the negative aspects of the current situation.

Table 5. TOWS Analysis of Kayseri Airport

	WEAKNESSES	STRENGTHS
THREATS	• **WT (mini-mini strategies)** • Highlights how weaknesses can affect business threats. • The weakest dimension of Kayseri Airport is the low flight frequency during the day. This feature poses a negative situation for the passengers to travel and causes many passengers to start their journey from other provinces.	• **ST (maxi-mini strategies)** • Examines how strengths can be used to reduce or eliminate threats to the business. • Strengths such as Low air traffic jam, Fast airport operations increase the airport's attractiveness compared to other transport systems, thereby weakening the threat of other transport systems. • Convenience of the weather can eliminate unfavourable weather of the city in winter.
OPPORTUNITIES	• **WO (mini-maxi strategies)** • Consider how opportunities will eliminate weaknesses. • The tourism potential of the city, increasing the trade volume of the city and supporting the modes of transportation with each other.	• **SO (maxi-maxi strategies)** • Focuses on how you can use your strengths to respond to potential opportunities. • Kayseri the most powerful aspect of the airport is its distance to the city. The proximity of the airport to the city is 5 km. This feature makes it easier to use the airport while at the same time saving passengers' time for pre-flight preparation.

SWOT Analysis and a Case Study at Kayseri Airport

CURRENT CHALLENGES FACING THE ORGANIZATION

According to SWOT analysis there are some negative features for Kayseri Erkilet Airport. Because of low capacity of the airport it has got some challenges. However, its capacity since 2017 some expansion works has been conducted. The passenger capacity of Kayseri Airport increases to 8 million. Kayseri, one of Turkey's fastest growing airports, is getting a new terminal. The terminal building, whose foundation was laid, will increase its annual passenger capacity to 8 million passengers per year and with its 5 bridges. The ground breaking ceremony for the new terminal building was held with the participation of Minister of Transport and Infrastructure, Minister of National Defense and General Manager of DHMI (UTIKAD, 2017). In his statement, Minister said, "We are following the increase in demand for air transportation in Kayseri. Flight traffic in Kayseri was 3197 in 2003 but it increased to over 15 thousand in 2019. The number of passengers, which was 325 thousand, exceeded 2 million 326 thousand. Since 2003, there has been a 4-fold increase in flight traffic and a six-fold increase in the number of passengers. Due to these increases, the need to build a new domestic terminal has arisen". For expansion The Turkish Air Force gave 250 thousand square meters of land to DHMI for the new terminal building of Erkilet Airport. Thus, the foundation was laid for the modern terminal building. Minister of Transport said, "We have gathered here today to lay the foundation for a terminal worthy of Kayseri residents. After combining and restoring the existing domestic and international terminal buildings, we will transform them into a larger international terminal building. Thus, Kayseri will have a renovated airport with an annual passenger capacity of 8 million. The terminal building, which is 11 thousand square meters, will be 37 thousand 190 square meters. The apron area will be expanded from 43 thousand square meters to 89 thousand 500 square meters. The aircraft parking area capacity will be increased from 9 aircraft to 15 aircraft. There will be 5 passenger bridges. The number of check-in counters will increase from 16 to 30 for domestic flights and from 12 to 16 for international flights. Vehicle parking capacity will be increased from 480 to 1141. With our new terminal, our citizens from Kayseri will be able to travel in much more comfortable and better conditions".

Akın et al. (2020) examined Kayseri province according to selected indicators competitiveness scale. The quality score of the services offered at the airport is 2,74 according to study made by Akın et al. (2020) 5 point likert selected indicators of destination competitiveness scale. So, it can be said that service quality of Kayseri airport is mid-range.

Kayseri airport's efficiency and productivity score is 71.48%. Although this airport is not active, it has been evaluated as an airport close to effective use of its resources (Öz, 2016).

SOLUTIONS AND RECOMMENDATIONS

Airport evaluation dimensions, basic dimensions and sub-dimensions of Kayseri Airport are discussed in detail. Some recommendations are presented here, as seen in the TOWS analysis.

Proximity to the city center, low air traffic jam, fast airport operations, landing / departure runway and navigation devices for different types of aircraft, diversity and speed of check-in facilities, convenience of the weather, carbon-free airport green airport sertification, barrier-free airport features are strengths of the airport.

Kayseri the most powerful aspect of the airport is its distance to the city. The proximity of the airport to the city is 5 km. This feature makes it easier to use the airport while at the same time saving passengers' time for pre-flight preparation. If you look at the examples of airports in other cities, the distance of many airports to the city center is 20-30 km, which puts the use of the airport in the background.

The weakest dimension of Kayseri Airport is the low flight frequency during the day. The total number of departures and departures from the airport, excluding special days, is around 30. This feature poses a negative situation for the passengers to travel and causes many passengers to start their journey from other provinces.

The outstanding features of Kayseri Airport regarding the opportunities arising from the external environment are more than one, but they are equally difficult. These are seen as the tourism potential of the city, increasing the trade volume of the city and supporting the modes of transportation with each other. The most important tourism potential of the city is the winter tourism of Mount Erciyes and the high number of structures such as old fortresses, inns and darüşşifa remaining from Seljuk and Ottoman times. The trade volume of the city is seen as being an organized industrial zone in the region, new commercial investments made, the existence of a free trade zone and the new project under the name of Kayseri Furniture City which will serve globally. So, features as tourism potential of the city, transport modes support each other, investments around the airport, supporting civil aviation nationwide, development of trade volume of the city were determined as opportunities of the airport.

Airport service quality dimensions were determined by Yeh and Kuo (2003) using multivariate decision making method. Five service dimensions were proposed to measure the airport service quality: comfort, processing time, convenience, courtesy of staff, visibility of routing systems and security. Comfort dimension shows the cleanliness, lighting and congestion of the waiting areas/halls and the ambiance of the airport as a whole. Processing time shows the time the passenger will spend at the airport for the journey process, customs inspection and baggage claims. Convenience (facilities) indicates the availability and accessibility of restrooms, shops, restaurants, currency exchanges, cash machines. Courtesy of staff shows the helpful and sincere behavior of the staff working at the airport. Visibility of guidance systems shows the clarity and frequency of flight information displays, directional signs indicating airport facilities. Security indicates passengers' perception of airport security measures and security facilities and equipment. So, service quality of Kayseri airport must be increased according to above dimensions.

Since the majority of tourists leave Kayseri Erkilet Airport after the holiday experience of foreign visitors visiting the Cappadocia tourism region, this airport should be made remarkable and its capacity should be increased. Since Kayseri Erkilet airport is used more actively for foreign visitors than Nevşehir Cappadocia Airport, the deficiencies should be eliminated.

Online check-in service and kiosk check-in service started to attract the attention of passengers. Thanks to such privileges, passengers lose less time. One of the biggest pluses of kiosk devices is ease of use and touch. Many airports have these devices and passengers continue to use these devices. Therefore, kiosks should be added to this airport as well.

REFERENCES

ACI. (2007). *Airport Industry Connectivity Report 2019*. ACI.

Ahmed, A. M., Zairi, M., & Almarr, K. (2006). SWOT analysis for Air China performance and its experience with quality. *Benchmarking*, *13*(1/2), 160–173. doi:10.1108/14635770610644655

Akın, M., Öztürk, Y., & Karamustafa, K. (2020). Destinasyon Rekabetçilik Analizi: Kapadokya Bölgesi Örneği. *Anatolia: Turizm Araştırmaları Dergisi, 31*(2), 161–171. doi:10.17123/atad.651245

Aksoy, C., & Dursun, Ö. O. (2018). A General Overview Of The Development Of The Civil. *Elektronik Sosyal Bilimler Dergisi, 17*(67), 1060–1076.

Ansola, G. P., De Las Morenas, J., García, A., & Otamendi, J. (2011). Distributed decision support system for airport ground handling management using WSN and MAS. *Engineering Applications of Artificial Intelligence, 25*(3), 544–553. doi:10.1016/j.engappai.2011.11.005

Atasoy, B., & Güllü, K. (2019). *Destinasyon Tercihinde Bir Motivasyon Faktörü Olarak Gastronomi* (Doctoral Dissertation). Yüksek Lisans Tezi. Erciyes Üniversitesi Sosyal Bilimler Enstitüsü.

Augustyn, S., & Turzyńska, H. (2016). *The airport tracing and handling in the near future. Scientific Research And Education In The Air Force.* Henri Coanda Air Force Academy AFASES.

Avcı, T., & Aktaş, M. (2015). Türkiye'de Faaliyet Gösteren Havalimanlarının Performanslarının Değerlendirilmesi. *Journal of Alanya Faculty of Business/Alanya Isletme Fakültesi Dergisi, 7*(3).

Baumann, O., & Stieglitz, N. (2013). *Motivating Organizational Search.* John Wiley & Sons Ltd.

Bayhan, M., Türkmen, M., & Kepe, D. (2017). Evaluation Of Denizli-Kaklik Logistics Village With SWOT Analysis. *Mehmet Akif Ersoy Üniversitesi Sosyal Bilimler Enstitüsü Dergisi, 9*(22), 555–574. doi:10.20875/makusobed.367392

Bolat, E., & Ateş, S. S. (2020). Post COVID-19 precautions management in small-scale airports: Evaluation of check-in process in Erkilet airport by simulation. *Journal of Airline and Airport Management, 10*(2), 77–86. doi:10.3926/jairm.166

Budd, L. (2008). A History Of Airport Technology. *Airports of the World, 19*, 44–51.

Chen, C. H., & Chou, S. Y. (2006). A BSC Framework for Air Cargo Terminal Design: Procedure and Case Study. *Journal of Industrial Technology, 22*(1), 1-10.

Çınaroğlu, E., & Unutulmaz, O. (2019). A data mining application of local weather forecast for Kayseri Erkilet Airport. *Politeknik Dergisi, 22*(1), 103–113.

Demirtaş, Ö. (2013). Havacilik Endüstrisinde Stratejik Yönetim. *NEÜ Sosyal Bilimler Enstitüsü Dergisi, 2*, 207–226.

Devrim, B. (2006). *Strateji Formülasyonu: SWOT Analizi.* Academic Press.

Dhmi. (2019). *Devlet Hava Meydanları İşletmesi Genel Müdürlüğü Kayseri Havalimanı.* https://kayseri.dhmi.gov.tr/Sayfalar/icerik-detay.aspx?oid=3491

Ebrahimzadeh, I., & Izadfar, E. (2009). An Analysis of the Location of Beheshti International Airport Using A Strategic Model (SWOT). *Journal of Geography and Regional Development, 7*(13), 237–260.

Erdil, O., Kalkan, A., & Alparslan, A. M. (2010). Örgütsel Ekoloji Kuramindan Stratejik Yönetim Anlayışına. *Doğuş Üniversitesi Dergisi, 12*(1), 17–31.

Fett, M. (2009). *A SWOT Analysis for the "flag-carriers": A deep insight into the aviation industry.* GRIN Verlag.

Gencer, C., & Çetin, T. (2011). Kurumsal Performans Karnesi ve Havacılık Sektöründe Bir Uygulama. *Savunma Bilimleri Dergisi, 10*(2), 105–121.

Göv, A. S. (2019). Green Airport Management Practices and Sustainability Relationship in Turkey. In *New Trends in Management Studies.* Peterlang Publishing. https://www.peterlang.com/view/9783631805947/html/ch25.xhtml

Jewczyn, N. (2010). Integrative Business Policy With a SWOT Analysis of Southwest Airlines: What Are They Doing Right in Today's Economy? *Journal of Business Leadership Today, 1*(8), 1–12.

Kanbur, E., & Karakavuz, H. (2017). Stratejik Yönetim Kapsamında Küresel Havayolu İşbirliklerinin SWOT Analizi. *Journal of Aviation, 1*(2), 74–86. doi:10.30518/jav.336347

Kandemir, A., & Uğurluoğlu, Ö. Ç. (2017). Sağlık Kurumları Yönetimi Literatüründe Stratejik Yönetim Üzerine Yürütülen. *Hacettepe Sağlık İdaresi Dergisi, 20*(1), 23–36.

Kaya, Ö., & Toroğlu, E. (2015). Monitoring urban development of Kayseri and change detection analysis. *Türk Coğrafya Dergisi, 65*, 87-96. https://dergipark.org.tr/en/pub/tcd/issue/21272/228403

Öz, Y. (2016). *Havaalanlarının etkinliklerinin yıllara göre değerlendirilmesinde veri zarflama analizinin kullanılması.* İşletme Ana Bilim Dalı Yüksek Lisans Tezi.

Özsoy, V. S., & Örkcü, H. H. (2021). Structural and operational management of Turkish airports: A bootstrap data envelopment analysis of efficiency. *Utilities Policy, 69*, 101180. doi:10.1016/j.jup.2021.101180

Pandey, M., & Singh, D. P. (2018). Evaluating the success factors for development and sustenance of low-cost regional airports in India using fuzzy multi-criteia decision making method. *Journal of Applied Economic Sciences, 3*(56), 1–14.

Peker, İ., & Baki, B. (2009). Veri zarflama analizi ile türkiye havalimanlarında bir etkinlik ölçümü uygulaması. *Çukurova Sosyal Bilimler Enstitüsü Dergisi, 15*(2), 72-88.

Rankin, W. (2008). Waco Regional Airport: A case study for strategic airport business planning. *Journal of Airport Management, 2*(4), 345–354.

Rankin, W. B. (2009). King County: A Case Study Model for Strategic Planning in College Aviation Learning. *Journal of Aviation/Aerospace Education Research, 18*(3), 19–31. doi:10.15394/jaaer.2009.1430

Şanlıoğlu, Ö., & Demirezen, B. (2020). Turizm sektörünün bölgesel kalkınma üzerindeki rolü: Kayseri iline yönelik nitel bir araştırma. *Erciyes Üniversitesi Sosyal Bilimler Enstitüsü Dergisi, 50*, 117–139.

Segar Aviation. (2021). https://segaraviation.com/page90-kayseri-havaalani-hangar-projesi-sinyal-analizi.html

Sezgin, E., & Yuncu, D. (2016). The SWOT analysis of Turkish Airlines through Skytrax quality evaluations in the global brand process. In *Development of tourism and the hospitality industry in Southeast Asia* (pp. 65–81). Springer. doi:10.1007/978-981-287-606-5_5

SHGM. (2016). *FaaliyetRaporu.* http://web.shgm.gov.tr/documents/sivilhavacilik/files/pdf/kurumsal/faaliyet/2016.pdf

Swayne, L. E., Duncan, W. J., & Ginter, P. M. (2006). *Strategic Management of Health Care Organizations.* Blackwell Publishing.

Şengül, H., & Bulut, A. (2019). Sağlik Turizmi Çerçevesinde Swot Analizi. *ESTÜDAM Halk Sağlığı Dergisi, 4*(1), 55–70.

Şevkli, M., Öztekin, A., Uysal, Ö., Torlak, G., Türkyılmaz, A., & Delen, D. (2012). Development of a fuzzy ANP based SWOT analysis for the airline industry in Turkey. *Expert Systems with Applications, 39*(1), 14–24. doi:10.1016/j.eswa.2011.06.047

Ülgen, H., & Mirze, K. (2004). *İşletmelerde Stratejik Yönetim.* Literatür Yayınları.

UTIKAD. (2017). https://www.utikad.org.tr/Detay/Sektor-Haberleri/14404/kayseri-havalimani-genisletilecek

Wang, K., & Hong, W. (2011). Competitive advantage analysis and strategy formulation of airport city development-The case of Taiwan. *Transport Policy, 18*(1), 276–288. doi:10.1016/j.tranpol.2010.08.011

Weihrich, H. (1982). The TOWS matrix— A tool for situational analysis. *Long Range Planning, 15*(2), 54–66. doi:10.1016/0024-6301(82)90120-0

Xu, H. (2015). SWOT Analysis on Chinese New Regional Jet ARJ21. In *15th COTA International Conference of Transportation* (pp. 127-138). Academic Press.

Yeh, C. H., & Kuo, Y. L. (2003). Evaluating passenger services of Asia-Pacific international airports. *Transportation Research Part E, Logistics and Transportation Review, 39*(1), 35–48. doi:10.1016/S1366-5545(00)00010-7

Yıldırım, A., & Şimşek, H. (2006). Sosyal Bilimlerde Nitel Araştırma Yöntemleri. *Journal of Theory and Practice in Education, 2*(2), 113–118.

Yılmaz, İ. (2017). Emissions from passenger aircraft at Kayseri Airport, Turkey. *Journal of Air Transport Management, 58,* 176–182. doi:10.1016/j.jairtraman.2016.11.001

ADDITIONAL READING

Bolat, E., & Ateş, S. S. (2020). Post COVID-19 precautions management in small-scale airports: Evaluation of check-in process in Erkilet airport by simulation. *Journal of Airline and Airport Management, 10*(2), 77–86. doi:10.3926/jairm.166

Budd, L. (2008). A History Of Airport Technology. *Airports of the World, 19,* 44–51.

Çınaroğlu, E., & Unutulmaz, O. (2019). A data mining application of local weather forecast for Kayseri Erkilet Airport. *Politeknik Dergisi, 22*(1), 103–113.

Demirtaş, Ö. (2013). Havacilik Endüstrisinde Stratejik Yönetim. *NEÜ Sosyal Bilimler Enstitüsü Dergisi,* 2, 207–226.

Öz, Y. (2016). *Havaalanlarının etkinliklerinin yıllara göre değerlendirilmesinde veri zarflama analizinin kullanılması.* İşletme Ana Bilim Dalı Yüksek Lisans Tezi.

Özsoy, V. S., & Örkcü, H. H. (2021). Structural and operational management of Turkish airports: A bootstrap data envelopment analysis of efficiency. *Utilities Policy,* 69, 101180. doi:10.1016/j.jup.2021.101180

Peker, İ., & Baki, B. (2009). Veri zarflama analizi ile türkiye havalimanlarında bir etkinlik ölçümü uygulaması. *Çukurova Sosyal Bilimler Enstitüsü Dergisi, 15*(2), 72-88.

Yılmaz, İ. (2017). Emissions from passenger aircraft at Kayseri Airport, Turkey. *Journal of Air Transport Management,* 58, 176–182. doi:10.1016/j.jairtraman.2016.11.001

APPENDIX 1

Questions and Answers

1. What is the overall problem presented in this case?

Expressing some deficiencies at the airport constitutes the problem of this research. Some deficiencies in following the technology and the weaknesses of the airport are the basis of the problem.

2. What are the factors affecting the problem(s) related to this case?

Investments in the airport, technological infrastructure, passenger satisfaction, the characteristics of the airport, the location of the airport, environmental factors and internal factors are the factors affecting this study.

3. Discuss managerial, organizational, and technological issues and resources related to this case.

SWOT analysis reveals the strengths and weaknesses of an organization, which are internal factors. In addition, it reveals the opportunities and threats created by the environmental factors of the organization. Swot analysis is the most important decision-making technique of strategic management. Managers often use this technique in the management and organization process. It has a very important place in the strategic management literature. This study will assist airport managers.

4. What role do different players (decision-makers) play in the overall planning, implementation and management of the information technology applications?

According to this study, the role of managers is to identify the shortcomings of the airport, to identify its strengths and weaknesses and to determine strategies and internal strategies accordingly. In addition, determining external strategies according to opportunities and threats are managerial issues. Eliminating some technical deficiencies and having technology elements such as kiosks will be good steps for information technologies.

5. What are the possible alternatives and pros and cons of each alternative facing the organization in dealing with the problem(s) related to the case?

The strengths and opportunities of the airport in order to solve the problems reveal the advantages of the airport. However, the existing weaknesses and possible threats of the airport constitute the negative aspects of the institution.

6. What are some of the emerging technologies that should be considered in solving the problem(s) related to the case?

Self-service kiosks can be seen emerging technologies for an airport management. Online check-in service and kiosk check-in service started to attract the attention of passengers. Thanks to such privileges, passengers lose less time. One of the biggest pluses of kiosk devices is ease of use and touch. Many airports have these devices and passengers continue to use these devices. Therefore, kiosks should be added to this airport as well.

7. What is the final solution that can be recommended to the management of the organization described in the case? Provide your arguments in support of the recommended solution.

Since the majority of tourists leave Kayseri Erkilet Airport after the holiday experience of foreign visitors visiting the Cappadocia tourism region, this airport should be made remarkable and its capacity should be increased. Since Kayseri Erkilet airport is used more actively for foreign visitors than Nevşehir Cappadocia Airport, the deficiencies should be eliminated. Online check-in service and kiosk check-in service started to attract the attention of passengers. Visibility of guidance systems shows the clarity and frequency of flight information displays, directional signs indicating airport facilities. Security indicates passengers' perception of airport security measures and security facilities and equipment. So Service quality of Kayseri airport must be increased according to some dimensions.

Epilogue and Lessons Learned

While the airports are trying to deal with their situations in today's business world, their biggest help in making decisions will be to evaluate and analyze the situation in their entirety. This situation is important for strategic management as well as to develop their technologies and change their sustainable competitive environments in order to realize their strengths and weaknesses and the opportunities and threats around them. Airports analyze their current strengths and weaknesses in a way that can turn potential crises into opportunities and manage risks well. At the same time, it is possible for companies to analyze what is going on around them, general legal and economic conditions, to capture opportunities and to realize threats and develop strategies accordingly.
Lessons learned are as follows:

1. The strengths and weaknesses of the airport are revealed.
2. The external environmental characteristics of the airport, consisting of opportunities and threats, were revealed.
3. By making SWOT analysis, it contributed to the airport management in making strategic planning.
4. Thanks to such privileges, passengers lose less time. One of the biggest pluses of kiosk devices is ease of use and touch. Many airports have these devices and passengers continue to use these devices. Therefore, kiosks should be added to this airport as well.
5. Service quality of Kayseri airport must be increased according to some dimensions as mentioned in the article.
6. Efficiency of the airport must be increased.

Chapter 11
The Adoption of a CRM Strategy Based on the Six-Dimensional Model:
A Case Study

José Duarte Santos
https://orcid.org/0000-0001-5815-4983
Polytechnic Institute of Gaya, Portugal

José Pita Castelo
https://orcid.org/0000-0003-3248-1139
Universidade de Vigo, Spain

EXECUTIVE SUMMARY

If the definition of CRM is not consensual, the model for incorporating or analyzing the concept within an organization is also not. In this chapter, considering the 'Six-Dimensional Model CRM Strategy', which integrates 65 critical success factors, the authors analyze how these manifest themselves in an organization. Thus, the case studied is presented and described following the six dimensions (CRM strategy formulation, relational marketing philosophy, best practices, organizational and human resources, CRM processes, CRM technology) and also synthesizes in a table how the company analyzed reacted to critical success factors.

ORGANIZATION BACKGROUND

Founded in the late 1990s, the company is a reference SME in the coding and labeling sector, with a label and label production unit, as well as the representation and distribution in Portugal of a brand of printers for this purpose. The head office and all its physical infrastructures – office, warehouse, factory, show room and technical department – are centralized in single space.

DOI: 10.4018/978-1-7998-1630-0.ch011

The company has the status of Leading SME and the status of PME Excelência (SME Excellence), both assigned by IAPMEI - Institute of Support for Small and Medium Enterprises and Innovation - in partnership with the main Portuguese banks. The first statute focuses on SMEs that pursue strategies for growth and strengthening their competitive base, selected through superior voting capacity and a broad deployment in the national territory. The second statute was created with the aim of rewarding national SMEs that are evidenced by the quality of their economic and financial performance and to recognize organizations that have been able to maintain highly competitive standards, with bets on innovation strategies and that have active contributions in the dynamics of social and economic development. The company is certified in quality management, according to ISO 9001.

The company's vision is to achieve a value-added player position, a facilitator and provider of integrated solutions that combine hardware, software and services involving any type of coding and labeling solution.

The company's business is focused on two areas, but they are interconnected. An area focused on the production and printing of labels, which may have logos, barcode reading labels, QR Code, or other elements that meet the customer's objectives. The second area is based on the marketing of printers for labels and labels, barcode readers, software and consumables (rolls for blank printers and labels). This area needs and has provided an after-sales service focused on technical support.

The customers of the first business area are mainly located in the textile industry, hygiene products and food (fruit garden, beverages). In the second area, the logistics and transport sector, agri-food and pharmaceutical industry. Customers are companies facing a B2B business.

The company started its activity in the second area described above, but currently the weight of the first has been growing, currently representing 60%, with the rest distributed by printers (25%) and barcode readers, software and consumables (15%). Forecasts point to continued sales growth in the first and stagnation in the second area.

The company has a national geographical presence (mainland and island Portugal) and the presence in international markets in a sustained manner is not foreseen in the short or medium term, although there is a residual value of 2 to 3% in the value of the invoicing corresponding to case-by-case business. However, the products resulting from printing, as they are incorporated into many products that are intended for the foreign market, the company ends up having an indirect presence, including customers who sell all their products to international markets. The company intends to focus all its attention on the domestic market, where it considers that there is still plenty of room to grow.

In relation to competition, the way it manifests itself is different in both business areas. In the first, there is high fragmentation of the market, and there is no data that can elucidate the market share. In the area of equipment, more specifically in barcode printers, there is essentially the Zebra brand that holds about 80% of the market share, and the Citizien brand that has been marketed by the company since 2004 and that went from 0% to the current 5%, and other brands with a smaller presence that compete for the remaining approximately 15%.

SETTING THE STAGE

The concept of Customer Relationship Management (CRM) is not consensual. For some authors, CRM is a tool, for others it is a set of business processes oriented to the management of customer experiences.

The Adoption of a CRM Strategy Based on the Six-Dimensional Model

Although there are different definitions of CRM, some have conceptual similarities. The number of definitions has been increasing, but we can find two trends: a narrower or broader view.

For Santos and Castelo (2018), CRM must be understood with a broad scope, "CRM is a strategy whose design is based on a formulation according to a certain model of relationship, one influenced by the benefits that one can get; and one having a philosophy with relationship marketing influences" (p. 33). So, it's not just a set of tactics, or simply a reductionist perspective of technology

There are different models on the adoption of CRM, which seek to present the elements they consider relevant to the achievement of success by the organization (Santos et al., 2020). Each model is also a reflection of how its author or authors consider the concept of CRM. Santos and Castelo (2018) studied 32 models presented by several scholars in the field of CRM and developed a model (Figure 1) composed of six dimensions – CRM strategy formulation, relational marketing philosophy, the application of best practices, organizational and human resources, CRM processes, CRM technology –, each playing its role.

Figure 1. CRM strategy adoption: the six dimensions model
Source: Santos & Castelo, 2018, p. 34.

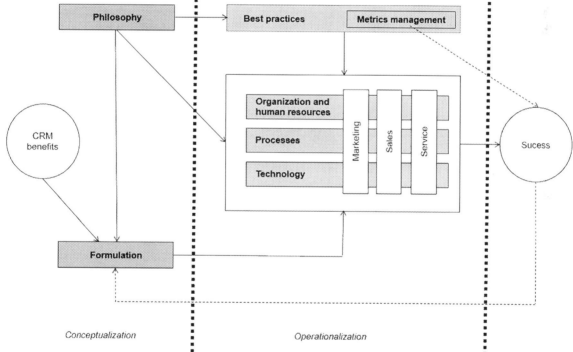

In each dimension there are several critical factors that contribute to the success of the adoption of a CRM strategy (Santos et al., 2020) and that are identified in Table 1.

Table 1. Critical success factors by dimension

Dimension	Critical Success Factors
Strategy formulation	• Adoption based on a detected issue • Covered CRM functional areas • Context and timing • Engagement and management commitment • Definition of benefits • Relationship definition (CRM vision) • Adequate investment • Strategic objectives
Relational marketing philosophy	• Customer as an asset and at the center of the organization • Creation and delivery of value • Loyalty • Customer knowledge management • Long-term customer relationship orientation • Business processes orientation • Customer satisfaction
Application of best practices	• Customer data use and analysis • LTV calculation • External consultants • Cross-selling / up-selling • Customization • Differentiation • Metrics management • Customer identification • Incremental • Innovation • Interaction • Methodology and roadmap • Customer privacy • Loyalty programs • Redesign of the business processes • Customer choice • Customer service
Organizational and human resources	• Performance evaluation • Adjustment and competencies • Commitment and employee involvement • Technological skills • Internal communication • Performance and employee motivation/satisfaction • Company size • Involvement of HR department • Organizational structure • CRM formation • Change management • CEO profile • Compensation and incentive system
CRM processes	• Process automation • Top managers involvement • Choice of interaction channels per client • Customer lifecycle management • Back and front-office integration • Multi-channel integration • Multi-functional integration • Monitoring • Single repository of information • 360° vision

Continued on following page

Table 1. Continued

Dimension	Critical Success Factors
CRM technology	• Strategy and business processes alignment • System architecture • CRM evaluation • Technological requirements definition • Top managers involvement in technology choice • Technological training • Technological integration • Supplier choice • Specialized software • Use

Source: Adapted from Santos et al., 2020.

In the adoption of a CRM strategy, it is important to identify the desired benefits as they guide the company and tend to influence the company (Santos & Castelo, 2018). These benefits presented may have interconnection, and there are benefits that arise as a result of others obtained, although not exclusively. For example, by reducing costs, the company is also achieving improved productivity although this benefit can also be achieved due to several other factors and influenced by other benefits that may have been achieved.

CASE DESCRIPTION

Strategy Formulation and Relational Marketing Philosophy

The awakening by CRM began in 2008 when attending a seminar on this topic, the general manager of the company becomes aware that the concept fits the way he wants to position himself strategically in the market. It does not arise from pressure from the environment, but rather by the need that the company feels to be closer to the customer, especially the sales force, which had a set of "traditional" performance in which it visited customers but could not respond in a timely manner to budget requests. This speed of response, for the market in question, is considered a critical success factor, as customers express the need to obtain quotes frequently for the products they need, often even continuous purchasing products.

The organization defined its vision of the relationship and framed the CRM in the strategic perspective and as a way to achieve at least one strategic goal. There is a concern about looking at what you want to benefit from CRM to be able to evaluate the results. The company also defined the immediate benefit it sought to obtain with the adoption of CRM and the following benefits.

The company chose to adopt CRM in phases, focusing on a concrete problem that it considers relevant and whose resolution is also associated with the benefit sought. This phase has implications in the functional area of CRM (sales) to be privileged in the adoption of CRM. Thus, the main initial benefit sought with CRM was the increase in the efficiency of the sales force. Then, in the next phase, the attention focused on the marketing area, seeking to increase the prospects. In parallel and in a transversal way over time, there is the objective of maintaining, preferably increase, the level of customer satisfaction and, consequently, its loyalty.

The company seeks to strengthen the relationship with the customer, providing him in the equipment area a pre-sales technical support that seeks to study the best technical alternative based on the present need, but that does not compromise future evolution. In the area of printing on labels and labels, there is also a concern to provide support in the development of products that meet the information and brand image that customers intend to transmit.

The involvement of the general management of the company is total and occurs from the first moment, and it is also the record that the entire trigger of CRM adoption occurs in a top-down aspect. It is also observed that the involvement does not occur only at the time of the formulation of the strategy, but is also present in the operational phase, as in the redesign of processes and in the choice of technology. To this much contributes the profile of the general director who comes out even more due to the size of the company (SMEs and micro, respectively) because it assumes an even more face-to-face and interventional role.

The company does not distinguish customers by their antiquity although it considers that it is easier to have a relationship with older customers because there is already greater knowledge of the reality in which they are located. However, newer customers have a greater opportunity to learn more and thus be able to meet their needs more effectively. All this knowledge is considered by the company as crucial and is available through the CRM technology used.

One of the first impacts resulting from the adoption of CRM was the increase in the loyalty rate, which has been growing and in the years 2018 and 2019 assumes values close to 100%. It was also possible to select clients, considering financial aspects and their potential.

Customer satisfaction is one of the elements that the company considers nuclear for the relationship and therefore seeks to measure it annually, applying satisfaction questionnaires since 2003, although it is only after 2008 that the questionnaire begins to integrate aspects of customer relationship evaluation.

It is verified that there is a concern by the management in providing training on the concept of CRM. In turn, employees are oriented towards the customer and consider it the best existing asset. For this, the company bets on loyalty, which it considers crucial because it turns out that there is a repurchase cycle. For this loyalty contributes the value proposition that the company seeks to present considering the specificity of its business and the differentiation it intends to obtain before its competitors, which is also one of the benefits that CRM can provide. The company assumes that the work of this loyalty is a constant of the relationship, which is seen as something that must be built in the present, seeking the best existing solution, but that does not compromise an orientation to the relationship with the client in the long term, that is, all businesses should be seen as elements of continuity in time.

The company considers customers important but also does not neglect the role that employees have in developing the relationship with the client, the need that is in providing employees with knowledge and skills at various levels, from the technician to interpersonal relationships.

The company to maintain a whole dynamic in the adoption of CRM, including the use of CRM technology, process updating, employee training and other investments that may be needed, aims to strengthen the budget between 3% to 5% every year.

Best practices

There is a constant interest in knowing more and more about the client's business so that he can help him in the best option. For example, when choosing a printer, you don't just consider what the equipment will do today but also estimate, in view of the growth of the customer's business, what the future response capacity will be.

The IDIC methodology (identify, differentiate, interact, customize) tends to be applied with a concern to identify the customer as much as possible, trying to differentiate them by their needs and value, taking advantage of all interactions to know more about the customer and customize the maximum product. All customers are perfectly identified as entities, but there is also attention to get to know all the decision-makers and other people who can contribute to strengthen the connection between the two companies. The differentiation of customers, by their needs and their value, allows the separation between the companies that make resale (which are seen as partners) and by the companies that will integrate the products in their value chain. Customization in the printing area is not only a greater value that the company can have, but a basic requirement to be able to satisfy the customer's need.

The company's innovation has always been to present the most avant-garde solutions in label and label printing, such as QR Code, augmented reality. The company also seeks to innovate in the content available in the various communication platforms it uses.

The organization seeks to boost up-selling especially when it realizes that the abnormal volume of purchases of a given consumable is the basis of oversized use of a printer, which can generate the customer's need to evolve equipment. Cross-selling tends to be absent from the perspective that a solution when it is proposed, is based on the requirements defined.

Multichannel integration is facilitated because the company communicates with the customer essentially using the phone and the Internet (e-mail, forms, landing pages, blog, social networks). This integration became easier with the change of the CRM software platform, with all recorded interactions allowing us to know what happened to the customer.

The company also gives great attention to metrics, although there is no excessive proliferating. In the sales parameters, the number of new customers that was obtained and those who remained is evaluated monthly. There is also the use of the sales funnel that allows you to keep up with the evolution of the sales cycle, and that is especially important for long-cycle businesses. The number of steps is slightly different for the two business areas. In the area of equipment there are five phases: recognition of opportunity, proposal, demonstration, negotiation and closing/loss. In the printing area, the sales cycle is shorter, and there is no demo stage, and trading in most print or consumable budgets is also absent, as customers assume that the price provided is already the best possible.

Although there is a concern about loyalty, as mentioned above, however, one of the best practices is not applicable, which is the creation of loyalty programs. However, there is demonstration equipment at special prices for partners.

The organization has used a consultant specialized in CRM and Inbound Marketing who has been making a global follow-up since the beginning of the adoption of CRM. He participates in conceptualization and in the operationalization, for example, in the definition of metrics.

Bearing in mind the need to satisfy customers, the company developed an online questionnaire to assess this satisfaction. In the key question "availability to recommend" the company scored 8.5 on a scale of 0 to 10. This value has been the same in the last two years. The company for 2021 intends to rise to 8.6.

Organization and Human Resources

The company is divided into several functional areas: the management team that consists of two persons: one with general management responsibilities and the other with financial responsibility and also of human resources. The company's sales force consists of five employees who currently rarely visit customers, only in very specific situations. It works as an inside sales team that works customers and inbound leads. The production team consists of ten people. There is also an after-sales department, related to the area of equipment marketing that seeks to ensure technical assistance. The marketing function does not exist in a dedicated way, but there is distribution of tasks by various elements of the sales area and by the general manager.

During the initial phase of the strategy, the company had a special concern in analyzing the perception of its employees in relation to the adoption of CRM, to the understanding of the new concepts underlying the CRM philosophy. Also, the process of understanding the functionalities of technology by employees, the advantages that it provides, such as the reduction of time in the execution of daily tasks, was closely monitored by the General Manager and the Director of Human Resources.

The change of culture was one of the major concerns of the company's management and the external consultant involved from the beginning. For this, awareness-raising training was carried out throughout the organization, with a special focus on the sales force. In this action, the company's CRM vision was presented, and we sought to sensitize employees to the importance of close relationship with customers.

Employee remuneration has been undergoing constant changes, with a view to improving the model. Previously, only the total value of sales was considered for the calculation of commissions, and no values per customer or sectors of activity were measured. However, metrics related to the acquisition of new customers were applied and, unlike previous years, individual objectives were changed to global objectives. There are also metrics related to customer maintenance, but for the purpose of prizes, currently, the overall goal is considered, being now for all employees and not only for sales affections, aiming to create a global motivation and boost the team spirit.

Processes

The company uses the Internet to strengthen the relationship with its customers but also to develop communication initiatives that provide new customers from the perspective of inbound marketing. Thus, it uses a message that is based essentially on informational, educational and technical content, aiming to transmit confidence and the existence of knowledge that can provide the best solution for each case. To this end, the company's website serves as a hub where users of the different social media used by the company are targeted, more specifically Facebook, YouTube, Twitter and LinkedIn.

The choice of the Internet and the phone to interact with the customer was following one of the benefits sought with the adoption of CRM and implied that the company restructured in terms of processes, trying to automate them to the maximum. However, there is awareness that it is necessary to make small adjustments in order to improve processes and adapt to the evolution of customer needs.

One of the most critical processes is the provision of budgets to customers, where the company seeks to be faster than the competition. The General Manager considers that this process is very important because when a client or potential customer asks for a proposal to supply labels or labels, the decision will be made very quickly, two to three days, a week at most. If there is a delay in the preparation and delivery of the budget to the customer, there is a risk that the customer has already decided when receive the requested information. One of the contingencies of this process is that there are on average ten product references per budget and the fact that the average daily number of budgets is fifty. Therefore, the company is studying how to create on its web platform, possibly through an extranet, an automation of this process, allowing in a self-service aspect the possibility of making simulations and getting budgets instantly. This presupposes the automatic opening of a business opportunity in CRM software so that the business can perform the follow-up and have an update of the sales funnel.

All customer information is in a single repository that can be accessed over the Internet regardless of the geographic location where the person who needs that information is.

The processes normally flow between the front and the back-office, not manifesting the existence of obstacles, functioning the company as a whole and regardless of the functions performed. This also contributes to the commitment and involvement of employees, who are manifested in the performance and motivation of employees, contributing to the involvement of the general manager and of the human resources department. The company performs employee performance evaluation using a set of previously defined and known parameters. There is also a care of the company in monitoring the processes to evaluate their performance, to optimize them but also to adjust them to meet new needs of customers and take advantage of possible technological developments.

The concern in the automation of processes is present and may eventually be the result of the use of the external consultant who sought, from the beginning, to reflect in the daily life of the organization the automation of CRM processes and that are facilitated by the use of specialized software.

Technology

The CRM technology that the company has used since 2008 is the company's on-demand software salesforce.com. The main modules used are Marketing, Sales and Service. This platform is handled primarily by the commercial area and the general manager. As mentioned above, there is no marketing department in the organization, and the various activities that the company develops are distributed by the various elements that make up the commercial area and the general manager. Thus, this module is also used by the sales area.

Recently, the company changed CRM technology, using HubSpot CRM, which also works on demand. One of the main reasons was that the company already uses tools of this platform to manage the site, SEO (Search Engine Optimization), blog, landing pages, social media, marketing automation and thus allow a greater and easier integration with CRM software. Another reason, according to the company, was the operability of HubSpot CRM software, which is more oriented to the daily life of the sales force and less focused on hierarchical reporting. The migration was used by the company to delete records from the database of companies that no longer exist and contacts that are also no longer related to the accounts in question.

As a complement to CRM software, the company uses software from another company to support billing, accounting, and human resources. This software, in addition to being used by the financial department to prepare invoices, is also used by the sales department to manage the current account of customers. The integration between the two technologies is not available in the market, but the company preferred this option because it considers that the CRM software of the ERP house software used, does not meet your needs, considering that it is mainly located in contact management.

Synthesis of Critical Success Factors Present in the Organization

Table 2 summarizes the reality of the organization for each of the critical success factors duly framed in the respective dimension.

Table 2. Critical success factors applied to the organization

Dimension	Critical Success Factors	Application
Strategy formulation	Adoption based on problem-in-between	Solving the problem of response time in the preparation of proposals.
	CRM functional areas	There is a phase-in, starting with the sales area.
	Context and moment	Does not arise by pressure from the surrounding environment.
	Management involvement and commitment	Especially the general manager but also with the participation of the human resources management that accumulates with the role of the financial director.
	Definition of benefits	Initially: increased efficiency of the sales force; increase the number of prospects. In addition, increased customer satisfaction and loyalty.
	Relationship definition (CRM vision)	All customers are likely to establish a fruitful relationship for both parties.
	Adequate investment	There is a budgeted amount that has been increasing.
	Strategic objectives	Increase customer service capacity and decrease response time to business proposal requests.
Relational marketing philosophy	Customer as an asset and in the center of the organization	Employees are aware that everything that happens within the company is designed to serve the customer.
	Value creation and delivery	A value-added player, facilitator, and provider of integrated solutions.
	Loyalty	It is a concern of the organization, reinforced by the fact that the products marketed are cyclically purchased.
	Customer knowledge management/learning organization	Knowing more about the customer provides more business opportunities, and this knowledge is shared through the platform by all employees who need it.
	Long-term customer relationship orientation	The business is seen not as an isolated sale, but as a continuation of other assets and boosters of others.
	Business process orientation	Existing processes have been designed based on certain assumptions aimed at facilitating the relationship and should therefore be followed, such as the creation of content.
	Customer satisfaction	It seeks to assess customer satisfaction, and the results are positive.
Application of best practices	Analysis and use of customer data	There is analysis and use of the elements that the company has about the customer, such as the history of purchases of consumables customers allows to evaluate whether the equipment used still has responsiveness.
	LTV calculation	There is no application of any specific formula although there is awareness of the importance of customer value throughout the relationship.
	External consultants	There is a commercial agreement with an external consultant.
	Cross-selling / up-selling	Both are applied although without a high level of incidence.
	Customization	It is considered a basic requirement for success.
	Differentiation	There is differentiation of customers, by its typology and dimension.

Continued on following page

Table 2. Continued

Dimension	Critical Success Factors	Application
	Metrics management	They exist and are permanently analyzed, especially those that allow to measure the evolution of marketing activity and sales. Automation in obtaining it is the result of the use of software.
	Customer identification	All customers or potential customers are identified.
	Incremental	The company sought to incorporate best practices,
	Innovation	Avant-garde solutions.
	Interaction	There is a constant concern about knowing more about customers, but interaction especially via the Internet is crucial to getting more qualified leads.
	Methodology and roadmap	All CRM adoption was previously planned.
	Customer privacy	There is and is total.
	Loyalty programs	There isn't,
	Redesign of business processes	There was attention to rethink all business processes, with special focus on sales processes given the benefits sought.
	Customer selection	There is a selection of clients, especially because they are associated with a particular industry sector that tends to influence their potential.
	Customer service	It is a concern and is understood as a component that is present at the time of sale.
Organizational and human resources	Performance evaluation	The company is more oriented towards global performance.
	Fit and skills	The company seeks employees to follow customer requirements in technical terms and interpersonal relationships.
	Commitment and involvement of employees	That's one of the company's concerns.
	Skills in using technology	Everyone who makes up the front office uses CRM technology.
	Internal communication	Part of the communication is written especially that which refers to technical information. Much of the communication in the sales/marketing/service area is supported by the CRM platform.
	Performance and motivation of employees	It is considered important by management because it is considered a crucial factor for an effective relationship with the client.
	Company size	The company is an SME.
	Involvement of HR department	The HR department exists although the person responsible also develops activities in the financial area.
	Organizational structure	Simple, there is some departmentalization, such as, financial area/HR, production, sales/marketing, service.
	CRM training	The presence of the General Manager in a seminar on CRM and subsequently continuing training, which is ensured by the consultant.
	Change management	It is a constant concern given that the management considers that the change is constant and therefore emerges as a flow pattern, with permanent attempts to adapt.
	Profile of the general manager	Dynamic person with an appetite to find new directions, new ways for the company to innovate.
	Remuneration and incentive system	Fixed and variable component. No great reflection of CRM metrics.

Continued on following page

Table 2. Continued

Dimension	Critical Success Factors	Application
CRM processes	Processes automation	There is a concern to automate processes as much as possible.
	Involvement of top managers	The General Manager is involved whenever there is a need to analyze and eventually redesign processes.
	Choice of customer interaction channels	The company chose to privilege contact by non-face-to-face means because it considered that it was not relevant to the client, but rather the timely response to its requests.
	Customer lifecycle management	The company seeks to act differently, such as providing institutional information in the client acquisition phase.
	Back and front office integration	It is verified, for example, in the ordering process, which is triggered by the commercial area, then moving to production and, consequently, for shipment to the customer.
	Multi-channel integration	There is, with all interactions being recorded regardless of the channel.
	Multi-functional integration	There is, especially between the sales area and after-sales service, but all contacts with the customer are centered on the sales department.
	Monitoring	There is a periodic development on the part of the consultant that suggests adjustments or changes if it deems it relevant in the department.
	Single repository of information	Almost total because there is information regarding customer billing that is not in the same repository of CRM information.
	360° single view	The whole organization may access the information deemed necessary in order to be able to follow up.
CRM technology	Alignment with business strategy and processes	It is perfectly aligned with the requirements, especially with the change introduced.
	System architecture	Use of integrated software, designed to monetize new trends in digital marketing.
	CRM system evaluation	There is a concern to have a system that responds as best as possible to the evolution of challenges, reflecting this concern in changing the system.
	Definition of technological requirements	There is a concern to have a global view of technological needs considering new forms of customer interaction.
	Involvements of top managers in the choice of technology	Yes.
	Technology training	Initial training and training throughout the year.
	Technological integration	It is not total, not existing with ERP, but it turns out that in other aspects, such as with the site, the CRM system is integrated.
	Supplier selection	It was made based on several alternatives that the external consultant presented to the company.
	Specialized software	First, they used salesforce.com (considering a reference in CRM software) and now HubSpot CRM.
	Use	There is a concern to make the most of the technology used in the three functional areas, and when it is considered that there may be alternatives that can produce results closer to the desired, the company opts for this technology.

Source: Authors

CURRENT CHALLENGES FACING THE ORGANIZATION

One of the great difficulties facing the organization is the lack of time of employees in the commercial area to perform all the tasks inherent to their area and the contributions they need to make to the marketing area, namely in the preparation of content. On the other hand, it is felt that there is a market sales potential that is not being exploited, reflecting the lack of commercial prospecting that can be developed through digital media.

On the other hand, more and more, just preparing content is not enough to attract potential leads and help existing customers to monetize existing equipment. Marketing campaigns supported by ads on social networks, especially linkedin and through Google Ads, must be developed. Video and graphic images are also not developed as it feels necessary.

The company also feels the need to differentiate its communication. Thus, in addition to the differentiation existing by the performance in two different markets – the production of labels/labels and the marketing of equipment/consumables – the company needs to communicate differently in terms of content, but also of the communication media used for those who are customers and those who are only potential customers.

Although the organization intends to focus all its attention on the domestic market, where it considers that there is still a lot of room to grow, there is a temptation of the company, the result of some international business case-by-case operations, to expand its activity, taking advantage of existing products and the services it provides, for new geographic markets and internationalize in a planned and organized way. However, there are still some doubts about when the right time is.

SOLUTIONS AND RECOMMENDATIONS

The internationalization of a company must take place in a sustained manner. This implies that the company must already have its presence fully consolidated in the domestic market before moving on to internationalization. The challenges facing the company, such as content marketing, tend to suggest that this is not the time for this step yet.

The integration of the CRM platform with internet communication initiatives is very useful and should be even more profitable. Thus, it is intended to automate more processes, integrating the results of marketing campaigns. The company should therefore continue to evolve in the CRM platform it uses, using a more complete version. Thus, it will be possible, there will be a greater profitability of leads generated through social networks and better manage relationships based on a more complete view of 360°. The company also begins to frame in a more consistent way the perspective of social media and have a strategy of Social Customer Relationship Management (SCRM).

It is also recommended that the company start to have a dedicated marketing department, which allows to develop a greater diversity of content, but also to expand the diversity, such as newsletters, press releases, white papers, brochures, how-to, case studies, e-books, webinars, short videos, longer videos. Everything must be framed in the role that content marketing plays in the various phases of the sales funnel.

The sales department, while continuing to develop content, should seek to focus more on its performance in prospecting, contribute to the distribution of content, and should develop activities at the level of Social Selling.

The development of the marketing department, a more dynamic role of the sales force in the intervention in social networks implies that the organization rethinks itself and orients itself internally in a perspective of marketing without ever losing focus on SCRM.

REFERENCES

Santos, J. D., & Castelo, J. P. (2018). The six dimensions on adoption of a CRM strategy. In I. Lee (Ed.), *Diverse Methods in Customer Relationship Marketing and Management* (pp. 17–43). IGI Global. doi:10.4018/978-1-5225-5619-0.ch002

Santos, J. D., Castelo, J. P., & Almeida, F. (2020). Critical Success Factors in a Six Dimensional Model CRM Strategy. In M. Khosrow-Pour (Ed.), *Encyclopedia of Organizational Knowledge, Administration, and Technology* (pp. 2104–2177). IGI Global. doi:10.4018/978-1-7998-3473-1.ch145

KEY TERMS AND DEFINITIONS

Best Practice Dimension: Encompasses the methods or techniques, which efficiently and effectively enables higher-level results compared to other means.

CRM: A customer-oriented strategy with two-dimensional conceptualization (formulation and relational marketing philosophy) and a four-dimensional operation (application of best practices, organizational and human resources, CRM processes, CRM technology).

CRM Dimensions: Groups a set of critical success factors that have an affinity with each other in the adoption of the CRM strategy.

CRM Strategy Formulation Dimension: Incorporates the form with CRM will be internalized by the organization.

Organizational and Human Resources Dimension: Dimension that groups the critical success factors related to how the organization is structured and aspects related to employees of the organization.

Process Dimension: Set of structured work activities that produce business results defined for customers and aiming to add value.

Relationship Marketing Philosophy Dimension: It encompasses basic aspects advocated by relational marketing that seek to support the connection to the client.

Strategy: Planned and sustained way of achieving medium/long-term objectives.

Technology Dimension: Includes factors to consider when choosing and using CRM technologies.

APPENDIX 1

Questions and Answers

1. Are the benefits of CRM reflected in the strategic formulation of CRM?

The company initially seeks to increase the efficiency of the sales force, which is one of the inherent benefits of CRM. This benefit is desired due to a problem that the company finds internally, which is the time of drafting proposals. Therefore, the adoption begins with the CRM component of the sales area, formulating as strategic objectives to increase its customer service capacity and decrease the response time to requests for commercial proposals.

2. Does CRM's strategic formulation reflect the philosophy of relational marketing?

The strategic formulation of CRM, more specifically the critical success factor 'definition of the relationship (CRM vision)', which the company intends to adopt cannot be owed away to the aspects present in relational marketing and that are mirrored in the philosophy dimension. Thus, for example, when the company states that its vision of CRM goes towards building a fruitful relationship for both parties, it is reflecting principles such as the creation and delivery of value, long-term relationship orientation and customer satisfaction (present in the philosophy dimension), the latter is also one of the benefits that the company intends to achieve.

3. Are the three functional areas of CRM supported by technology, processes, organization, and human resources?

The processes exist defined for the three functional areas of CRM, and some are also automated, supported in technology that facilitates the operation of CRM. Thus, for example, a marketing campaign developed by the company through landing page allows automatically to create leads in CRM software, which can then be worked by the commercial area.

Human resources are focused on the three areas of CRM's intervention – sales, marketing, service – and this is reflected in the way the company is organized.

4. Do best practices influence the use of technology, processes, organization and human resources?

One of the good practices adopted by the company was the use of an external consultant, which has been influencing the technology used, even recently leading to a change. It influenced the processes, for example, in the way the business opportunity is classified from the perspective of the sales cycle phase. It also provided a redesign of the structure, making it more agile and above all centered on the desired benefit with the adoption of CRM.

5. Has the strategy formulated influence the operationalization of technology, processes, organization and human resources?

The built-in technology must go against the strategy designed. In the case presented, this assumption occurs easily when they decide to change the technological supplier in order to be simpler to achieve the strategic objectives.

The processes are designed and optimized to meet the problem that has been found and that has led to the adoption of CRM.

The company through specific CRM training seeks to ensure that the organization and its human resources are better able to operationalize the strategy and reflect in their daily CRM vision.

Thus, there are critical factors in the formulation dimension that will influence critical success factors in the technology, processes, organization and human resources dimensions.

6. Does the operationalization of technology, processes, organization and human resources take into account the philosophy of relational marketing?

The chosen technology considers new forms of interaction with the customer, the need to capture more information about the customer through the Internet, the creation of content, which confirms aspects present in the philosophy dimension, such as knowledge management, guidance to business processes.

The processes are always designed bearing in mind customer satisfaction, which implies measuring it and this evaluation is carried out.

The organization and human resources mirror the philosophy of relational marketing, when considering the client as an asset and at the center of the organization, when seeking customer loyalty.

The philosophy dimension considers the client as an asset in the center of the organization and the need to seek their loyalty. These aspects are reflected, for example, in the fact that the company seeks to obtain commitment and involvement of employees, managing all the change to this new paradigm, being this management carried out in a non-incremental or transformational way, but in an attempt to continuously adjust, that is, using the flow pattern.

Epilogue and Lessons Learned

In the case presented, it is verified that the change from the transactional paradigm to the relational paradigm is possible and also the latter can and should be reinforced because its adoption is not static.

The adoption of a CRM strategy occurs in functional areas of the company that tend to be directly linked to the customer, but it is very comprehensive, presupposes the grounding on transversal elements, namely processes, organization/human resources and technology. Thus, these three dimensions also need to be rethought, adapted and continuously improved in order to be able to boost the relationship with the client.

The whole organization must be in tune. Considering the three organizational levels – strategic, tactical and operational – the integration, harmony and involvement of all is crucial to the success that is being achieved. Also, this success should be evaluated based on the intended benefits. But this evaluation should not occur only at the end, and there is the inclusion of metrics in different phases of customer interaction and at different organizational levels.

Chapter 12
How Competitive Strategies Affect Organizational Structure:
A Research in Technology Development Zones in Turkey

Muhammed Seyda Akdag
Yıldız Technical University, Turkey

Yasemin Bal
Yıldız Technical University, Turkey

EXECUTIVE SUMMARY

Organizational structures can change according to the strategy determined by the businesses. The purpose of this chapter is to extend that research by analyzing the relationship between Porter's competitive strategies and Burns and Stalker's structure types. The authors conduct their research on the enterprises in Technology Development Zones in Istanbul, Turkey. One hundred sixty of 5,506 enterprises participated in the research. Then, to search deeper, the authors conducted a qualitative research on the 25 enterprises in Technology Development Zones. Results show that, while the mechanical structure tendency is observed in the enterprises following the cost leadership strategy, the mechanical or organic structure tendency is not observed in the enterprises following the differentiation and focus strategies. Also, according to the interviews, results show that the organizational structures in the enterprises in Technology Development Zones are affected by the size of the organization or the strategic awareness level of the senior managers rather than the competitive strategies.

SETTING THE STAGE

Introduction

Due to the rapid change caused by globalization and the increase in competition conditions, it has become more important for enterprises to achieve harmony both within themselves and with the external

DOI: 10.4018/978-1-7998-1630-0.ch012

environment. Enterprises that want to achieve this harmony and survive must change their strategies and organizational structures (Pearce & Robinson, 2015). Organizational structures can change according to the strategy determined by the enterprises. For the strategies to be successful, it is especially important to design a correct organizational structure and to make it work (Drago, 1997). It has especially important effects on organizational structures because of the coordination, technical and control tasks required by the strategies (Miller, 1988). In this framework, it has always been discussed in the literature that the structural components of the organization must be compatible with the strategy to implement organizational strategies and achieve organizational goals (Miller, 1986).

This discussion is based on two fundamental assumptions that have long been accepted in business policy (Bart, 1986). One of them is that there is a relationship between business strategy and organizational structure and the second one is the assumptions that some structural adjustments are needed to realize business strategies (Bart, 1986). According to this point of view, the harmony of the structural components that are designed properly with the strategy is essential for the implementation and achievement of the strategy (Bart, 1986; Ginsberg & Venkatraman, 1985; Miller, 1986).

Although there are many studies examining the relationship between business strategy and organizational structure in the literature, it is seen that the number of studies examining the relationship between Michael Porter's generic strategies at the enterprise level and the types of organizational structure of Tom Burns and George M. Stalker are few. In this context, the main purpose of the study is to examine the findings obtained from the research in the literature in this field by examining theoretically and conceptually the relationship between M. Porter's competitive (generic) strategies and the types of structures of Burns and Stalker and to present both a conceptual model proposal and empirically analyze the model and share the results.

In this direction, firstly, the theoretical and conceptual framework of organizational strategy and organizational structure concepts are presented in the study. In the following section, studies that deal with the relationship between Porter's generic strategies and the organizational structure types of Burns and Stalker are examined and a literature review is made. In the last section, the competitive strategies and organizational structures of the enterprises considered within the scope of the research section are examined and evaluated.

Literature Review

Approaches that investigate the adaptation and change of organizations to environmental conditions are the approaches that can be considered as adaptation approaches. The theoretical framework of organizational strategies is formed within the framework of strategic management approach or organizational strategy (Kocel, 2015). The basic view of the Strategic Management approach pioneered by Chandler, Mintzberg, Porter, Miles and Snow is that organizations implement the strategies determined by the top managers to adapt to their environment. For this reason, top managers constantly monitor the environmental conditions that affect organizations and try to understand what kind of dangers or opportunities that the changes in environmental conditions bring with them. On the other hand, they decide where and how the organizations will use their resources by analyzing the strengths and weaknesses of organizations. These decisions make up the strategies of organizations (Mintzberg, 1987). Organizations create and implement various strategies to gain a competitive advantage or to maintain the advantage they hold. Organizations that cannot determine the right strategy or fail to implement it cannot adapt to their environment (Cubukcu, 2018).

How Competitive Strategies Affect Organizational Structure

Strategy is a model or plan that integrates the main goals, policies, and action sequences of an organization (Teare et al., 1998). Chandler (1962) defines strategy as determining long-term goals and objectives for the enterprise and preparing appropriate activity programs by allocating the necessary resources to achieve these goals and objectives. According to Miles and Snow (1984), strategy is a dynamic process that offers a way of harmonizing between the organization and its environment. M. Porter (1985) argues that the strategy is about choosing the set of activities in which an organization will prevail over competitors to make a sustainable difference in the market. The strategy of an organization describes the way in which it achieves its goals, given the threats and opportunities in the environment, and its resources and capabilities (Rue & Holland, 1989). An effective strategy provides an organization with a sustainable competitive advantage that leads to superior performance (Oosthuizen, 1997). However, this can only be achieved if the strategy fits correctly with the external environment and internal conditions of the organization (Nandakumar et al., 2010; Thompson & Strickland, 1996). For many years, creating strategies in organizations has been studied from many perspectives. Researchers working on creating and conceptualizing strategies are Mintzberg (1978), Miles and Snow (1978), Porter (1980), Bourgeois and Brodwin (1984), Chaffee (1985), Hrebiniak and Joyce (1985) and Nonaka (1988) (Rajaratnam & Chonko, 1995). The strategies that enterprises choose may differ due to their different strategic approaches. The strategies chosen by enterprises are classified and explained by many researchers. In the field of strategic management, researchers such as Mintzberg (1978), Miles and Snow (1978), Ansoff (1987), and Porter (1996) are major researchers who try to explain the strategies chosen by enterprises. Researchers such as Barnard (1938), March and Simon (1958), Lindblom (1959) and Ansoff (1965) contributed to the understanding of strategy in competitive approaches. Rumelt (1984) emphasized that for enterprises to gain sustainable competitive advantage, their products and resources should not be imitated, and Barney (1991) advocated the importance of implementing value creating strategies for the sustainability of competition. One of the most widely accepted methods that can be useful in determining the competitive positions of enterprises is Porter's (1985) competitive strategies. According to Porter (1985), for sustainable competition, the profitability obtained by the enterprise in a certain market compared to its competitors should be above the sector average and continue for a long time. Porter (1985) deems it necessary to constantly reveal the obstacles that make the business strategy difficult to imitate by its competitors to ensure sustainability. In addition, strategic harmony between many activities of enterprises, according to Porter (1996), is important not only for competitive advantage but also for the sustainability of this advantage (Olson et al., 2005). M. Porter (1985) states that for competitive advantage, an enterprise that has weaknesses and strengths against its competitors can have a competitive advantage in three ways. These strategies are low cost, differentiation, and focus. Porter calls these generic competitive strategies. Here, with the concept of generics, general competitive characteristics that will enable the company to be better than its competitors in its market area are meant (Dincer, 2013).

Enterprises that adopt a cost leadership strategy focus on reducing the costs and increasing the productivity of the enterprise by trying to produce the goods and services they produce in a cheaper way than the companies they compete with (Barney & Hesterly, 2012). For this reason, they attach importance to the opportunity of productive scale and for this purpose they try to reduce the cost in production, to minimize the service sales, advertisement, and R & D costs (Miller, 1988). They try to provide standardized high-capacity product at the lowest price. Therefore, they try to innovate little because innovation destroys efficiency (Miller, 1986). The main feature of this strategy typology is to ensure efficiency, to implement experience curve policies, to provide core-center control and thus to keep costs under control (Galbraith & Schendel, 1983). They emphasize profit and budget control (Miller, 1988).

It is emphasized that organizations following this strategy follow competitive methods such as ensuring operational efficiency, maintaining high inventory levels, and reducing the use of external financing (Dess & Davis, 1984). This strategy is primarily about stability, rather than taking risks or looking for new opportunities for innovation and growth. The low-cost position means that the company can lower the prices of its competitors, still offer comparable quality, and make a reasonable profit (Daft, 2007).

In the differentiation strategy, enterprises try to create a value that will be perceived as unique by the buyer by differentiating their products and services from other competitors in the sector. The enterprise may use advertising, distinctive product features, rare service, or technology to ensure that its products or services are perceived as unique. This strategy usually targets customers who are not particularly interested in price, so it can be completely profitable (Daft, 2007). The key to success for a business that adopts a differentiation strategy is focusing on quality strategy implementation, innovation, creativity, and product performance (Barney & Hesterly, 2012). Differentiation is a strategy suitable for obtaining above average returns in the sector, as it creates a sustainable position to overcome five competitive powers (Certo & Peter, 1991).

An organization that has adopted a focus strategy focuses on a specific regional market or purchasing group. The enterprise tries to achieve either a low-cost advantage or a differentiation advantage within a narrowly defined market (Daft, 2007). This strategy is used by companies that want to gain competitive advantage by using specialized knowledge and competence and want to avoid the problems of managing many businesses (Certo & Peter, 1991).

Organizational Structures

Chandler (1962) defines the structure as the design of the organization in which the strategy is applied. Changes in an organization's strategy creates new administrative problems, which requires a new or restructured structure for the successful implementation of the new strategy. Morris (1990) defines organizational structure as the framework and supporting systems surrounding the work done in an organization. Walton (1986) notes structure as the basis of organization, including hierarchical levels and areas of responsibility, roles and positions, and integration and problem-solving mechanisms. The organizational structure is the organizational form of responsibilities, duties and persons and includes the authority, hierarchy, units, departments, and coordination mechanism of the organization (Carpenter & Sanders, 2009). Organizational structure is an arrangement that shapes the interaction and responsibilities between the roles, people, and resources in an organization. It is a diagram that shows positions or titles in cascading, mostly in the form of a pyramid (Pearce & Robinson, 2015). The organizational structure is reflected in the organizational chart (Daft, 2007). It is a visual representation of the entire organization and its processes. The organizational chart enables employees to fulfill their duties, fulfill different tasks and work in different places. Organization chart is particularly useful in understanding how a company works. Covin and Slevin (1990) define organizational structure as the arrangement of authority relations, communication, and workflow within an organization. Robbins and DeCenzo (2005) argue that organizational structure plays an important role in the realization of the determined goals and the realization of strategic goals and directions. Organizational structure plays an important role in helping management achieve its goals and follow organizational strategy.

The first classification about organizational structure was made by Burns and Stalker (1961). Burns and Stalker (1961) focused on the relationship between organizational structure and the environment in his book "The Management of Innovation". We considered the structure as a process and a means of keeping the organization together so that it can determine its own destiny. Burns and Stalker (1961) proposed the theory of mechanical and organic systems of organization that provides a simple framework for understanding which organizational structures are suitable for different environmental conditions. Organizations working in dynamically changing and uncertain environments tend to need organic structures and processes, while they tend to be mechanical in more stable environments (Teare et al., 1998). The more dynamic the environment is, the more organic the organizational structure should be (Neis et al., 2016). A structure is considered mechanical to the extent that it standardizes behavior, and organic to the extent that standardization disappears (Parthasarthy & Sethi, 1992).

The framework presented by Burns and Stalker also provides a distinction between mechanical and organic forms of structure in terms of tasks, control, communication, organizational knowledge, governance, values, and prestige. The characteristics of mechanical structures include central decision making, strict adherence to formal rules and procedures, and carefully established reporting relationships, while organic structures facilitate decentralized decision making, organizational compliance and flexibility, and an emphasis on informal rules and procedures (Slevin & Covin, 1997).

A mechanical structure is a highly formal, tightly controlled, and hierarchical structure, far from participation and flexibility. In this case, organizations adopt a structure focused on vertical control, specialization, standard methods, central decision making and efficiency. However, organic structure is defined by informal, decentralized, and open communication channels (Khandwalla, 1977). There is less of a hierarchy than mechanical organizations. They focus on horizontal communication and coordination (Hatch & Cuncliffe, 2006). By its nature, organic structure provides more flexibility in the work activities of the staff (Covin & Slevin, 1990). Mechanical structures are more suitable for industries with low technical and market change. Organic structures, unlike mechanical structures, are more suitable for situations where rapid changes occur in the environment and where a minimum hierarchical order is preferred (Burns & Stalker, 1961).

Competitive Strategy and Organizational Structures

Organizations should be designed in a way to ensure the best adaptation to their conditions by developing a different organizational structure and functioning in different situations. One of the contingency factors that determine the structure and functioning of the organization is strategy. Other factors include the environment in which the organization operates, the size of the organization and the technologies used by the organization (Keskin et al., 2016).

The direction of the relationship between strategy and structure has been examined by many researchers and different opinions have been expressed. Some researchers states that the strategy should be placed in front of the structure, that is, a structure suitable for the strategy should be created. Porter (1980), one of the leading researchers, states that business strategies have an important effect on the structure. So which structure is more suitable for which competitive strategy? One of the aims of this chapter is to find the answer to this question. In this context, in this part of the study, the relationship between Porter's competitive strategies and the organizational structures of Burns and Stalker is discussed in a theoretical framework and ideally compatible strategy-structure pairings are made.

When the cost leadership strategy is evaluated, the goal is to reduce costs, cost control and efficiency (Bart, 1986). In the cost leadership strategy, mass production is required to reduce cost (Nemetz & Fry, 1988). Mass production requires standardization and formalization of work (Miller, 1988) and employee behavior (Mintzberg, 1979) because formalization reduces the variability of employee behavior and makes it easier to predict and control. Organizations that follow this strategy have lower competence composition of the workforce as jobs are standard and use less technocrats such as scientists and engineers. In low-cost leadership, the centrality of decisions is essential, and the flow of information occurs vertically (Miller, 1988). In companies that follow a cost leadership strategy, the structure is extremely rigid and programmed for efficiency (Miller, 1986). In firms that follow this strategy, bureaucratic structures dominate where decisions are central, decentralization is broad, jobs are routine and repetitive, information flow is only vertical, power stems from position, and requires specialized managerial competencies (Nemetz & Fry, 1988). Control is high in cost leadership (Nemetz & Fry, 1988). Hence, according to Govindarajan (1988) and Miller (1988), low-cost strategies are generally effective with mechanical structures (Azorín, 2012; Claver-Cortés et al., 2012).

On the other hand, in the differentiation strategy, the aim is to develop products that are perceived as unique and attractive. In this organizational strategy, emphasis is placed on creative and well-designed products, strong marketing capabilities, strong cooperation in marketing channels, a good corporate image, and the reputation and quality of the products. Since creativity and innovation are the basis of strategy, enterprises try to gain competitive advantage in this way (Miller, 1986). In organizations that adopt this strategy, the use of knowledge-intensive workforce, in other words technocrats such as engineers and scientists, are too much (Miller, 1988).

In differentiation strategy, the decentralization of decisions, autonomy and distribution of authority, horizontal and bottom-up communication and power deriving from position are the basic structural features and organizations aim to provide control (Miller, 1988). Control is low in differentiation strategy (Nemetz & Fry, 1988). In this strategy, the structure is flexible and allows interdepartmental communication (Miller, 1986). In organizations with this strategy, the structure is organic, communication is horizontal, decentralization is low in decision-making, decentralization is narrow, the source of information is power, there is autonomy and decentralization (Nemetz & Fry, 1988). Therefore, as discussed by Miller (1986), it does not seem possible to implement differentiation, which is an innovative strategy, in a mechanical structure. An innovative structure requires that decision making be decentralized, and this is only possible in organic structures (Miller, 1986). According to Govindarajan (1988) and Miller (1988), differentiation strategies are effective with organic structures (Claver-Cortés et al., 2012). In the study conducted in the Algerian organizations, it was determined that there is a significant relationship between structure and strategy, and the fit of these two parameters has an impact on the organizational effectiveness (Kerbouche et al., 2017). Sengül (2018) observed that competitive strategy and organizational design are interdependent processes in his study, in which he outlined the link between competitive strategy and organizational design by focusing on rivalry. According to Sengül, a firm's organizational design choices can affect its competitive advantage. Chinese researchers found that strategy variables, cost focus and a differentiation focus strategy were all highly significant in their impacts on organizational form in Chinese small entrepreneurial firms (Reid et al., 2020).

It would not be correct to say that there is only one structure best suited for an enterprise pursuing a focus strategy, which is Porter's (1980) last generic type. The organizational structure of the company that follows the strategy of differentiation focus and the organizational structure of the company that follows the focus on cost leadership are different from each other due to the nature of the strategy they follow. In fact, these strategies are not quite different from the main competitive strategies as the strategies they follow. The only difference between the cost leadership focus strategy and the main cost leadership strategy is that the market is narrowed according to the customer group. In this case, everything said for the cost leadership strategy is valid for the cost leadership focus strategy (Ülgen & Mirze, 2016). Therefore, it can be said that the most appropriate organizational structure for the enterprise that follows the cost leadership focus strategy is a simple mechanical organizational structure. Likewise, the differentiation focus strategy is the application of the main differentiation strategy throughout the market, focused on a specific customer group in a narrow market. Therefore, the differentiation focus strategy carries all the features of the main differentiation strategy (Ülgen & Mirze, 2016). Therefore, it can be said that the most appropriate organizational structure for the enterprise that follows the strategy of differentiation focus is the organic organizational structure, albeit in a simple way. In summary, regarding the link between competitive strategies and organizational structure, cost leadership strategies are associated with mechanical structures, while differentiation strategies are associated with organic structures.

CASE DESCRIPTION

Background of Technology Development Zones in Turkey

According to the definition of the Turkish Ministry of Industry and Technology, Technology Development Zones are academic, social, and cultural sites established to enable entrepreneurs, researchers and academicians who want to produce goods and services in the field of new or advanced technology to carry out their industrial and commercial activities near universities and to benefit from these universities (Teknopark, 2021). In Technology Development Zones, it is aimed to produce technological information, to commercialize the produced information, to increase the product quality and standard in products and production methods, to develop innovations that will increase productivity and reduce production costs, to ensure the adaptation of small and medium-sized enterprises to new and advanced technologies, to provide business opportunities for researchers and to increase the competitiveness of the industry by accelerating the entry of foreign capital to the country, which will make advanced technology investments (T.C. Sanayi ve Teknoloji Bakanlığı, 2021). As of February 2021, in Turkey, 87 Technology Development Zone has been declared by the Council of Ministers. 72 of the 87 technoparks are currently in operation, the others are under development. Most of the existing technology development zones are university-oriented technoparks. However, in addition to the technoparks established in the organized industrial zones, there are also technoparks representing the whole of the city in cooperation with the universities of the important public and industrial institutions and organizations in the province (TGBD, 2021a).

The number of companies conducting R&D studies in active technoparks has reached 6,384. Looking at the percentage distribution of companies by sectors; 37% of these companies operate in the software sector, 17% in the Computer and Communication Technologies sector, 8% in Electronics and 6% in Machinery and Equipment Manufacturing. In addition, companies from many sectors such as Medical, Energy, Chemistry, Food, Defense and Automotive are involved in R&D activities in the zones. As of February 2021, a total of 67,349 personnel has been employed in the Technology Development Zones. The number of R&D projects completed in Technology Development Zones is 39,578 and the R&D projects carried out are 10,558. The technological product exports of companies in the Technology Development Zones, which have become active, to the most developed countries of the world such as the United States, Japan, Israel, England, and Germany, reached approximately 5.7 Billion USD as of February 2021 (T.C. Sanayi ve Teknoloji Bakanlığı, 2021).

Quantitative Research

Methodology

The scope of the research consists of actively operating 5506 enterprises in 67 Technology Development Zones in Istanbul, Turkey. The reason for choosing these enterprises for research is the thought that these enterprises have certain structures and strategies in the sectors in which they operate. The research, which started in December 2019, was completed within a period of nine months, and ended in August 2020. For this reason, the study has a cross-sectional nature. The survey, prepared on organizational structures and competitive strategies, was delivered to the top managers of the referred enterprises either by e-mail or by face-to-face interviews. At each company, a manager who was familiar with business strategies and organizational structures answered the survey. Survey feedback was provided from 160 of 5506 enterprises in total.

The first data collection tool used in the research is the competitive strategies scale consisting of 18 expressions prepared for determining competitive strategies in enterprises. The scale, designed to determine the competitive strategies that enterprises follow, is the scale developed by Bal (2011), which was obtained from the studies of Dess and Davis (1984) and Nayyar (1993) and whose expressions were translated into Turkish and their suitability for our language was revised. The scale prepared to determine competitive strategies consists of 18 questions in total. The second survey form is the organizational structure survey consisting of 7 questions aimed at determining the organizational structures in enterprises. The scale used for determining the organizational structure of the enterprises is the scale obtained from the study of Covin et al. (2001). The scale was developed by the academic advisor and other two researchers by translating the expressions into Turkish and the explanatory and understandability of the survey were tested through pilot studies and interviews. The scale, prepared to determine the organicity level of the organizational structures, consists of 7 statements in total. Participants were asked to mark a frequency range ranging from 1 to 7 (the level of organicity decreases as it approaches 1, the level of organicity increases as it approaches 7) on a 7-degree Likert-type scale to determine to what extent they agree with the expressions on the scale.

Within the scope of quantitative analysis, firstly, the answers to the surveys were entered into the SPSS 22.0 program for each enterprise. Competitive strategies have been examined under the sub-details of "Differentiation Strategy", "Cost Leadership Strategy" and "Focus Strategy". According to the descriptive statistics of 154 enterprises analyzed within the scope of the research, it was determined that 49 enterprises followed differentiation strategy, 40 enterprises followed cost leadership strategy and 65 enterprises followed focus strategy. Since the main goal of enterprises operating in Technology Development Zones is to make technological innovations by focusing on a certain area and carrying out R&D activities, this result can be considered natural.

Organizational structures are examined in their "Mechanical Structure" and "Organic Structure" sub-details. According to the descriptive statistics regarding the enterprises analyzed within the scope of the research, it was evaluated that 134 enterprises had organic organization structure and 20 enterprises had mechanical organization structure. Although it is expected that enterprises operating in Technology Development Zones to have an organic structure that allows for the cooperation and expertise-based power among experts required developing innovative products, it is not considered normal for them to tend to have a large organic organization structure.

Analysis and Results

To determine whether the organizational structures of the enterprises differ according to their competitive strategies, the variables of the relationship between Porter's typology of competitive strategies and the types of organizational structure of Burns and Stalker are compared, while cost leadership strategies are associated with mechanical structures, differentiation strategies are associated with organic structures.

The dimensions of Porter's typology of competitive strategies can be listed as cost leadership, differentiation and focus strategies, and the dimensions belonging to the types of organizational structure of Burns and Stalker can be listed as mechanical and organic organizational structure. In line with these explanations, the research model is depicted in Figure 1.

Figure 1. Research Model

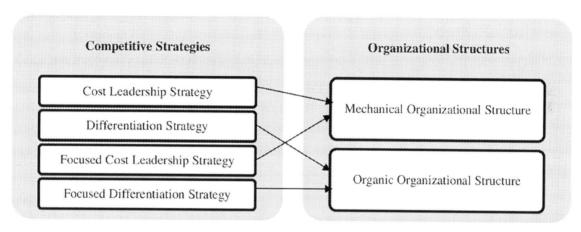

In the light of all this information, the hypotheses were formed and analyzed, respectively.

H1: There is a significant and positive relationship between the competitive strategies followed by the enterprises and their organizational structures.

The relationship between competitive strategies and organizational structures is depicted in Table 1 and the descriptive statistics for organizational structure is depicted on Table 2.

Table 1. The relationship between competitive strategies and organizational structures

	Levene's Test for Equality of Variances		t-test for Equality of Means						
	F	Sig.	t	df	Sig. (2-tailed)	Mean Difference	Std. Error Difference	95% Confidence Interval of the Difference Lower	Upper
Equal variances assumed	.012	.913	-.216	152	.829	-.01581	.07321	-.16045	.12883
Equal variances not assumed			-.212	24.697	.834	-.01581	.07463	-.16961	.13798

Table 2. Descriptive statistics for organizational structure

Organizational Structure	N	Mean	Std. Deviation
Mechanic	20	3,0215	,31235
Organic	134	3,0373	,30440

Due to the normal distribution of the data, the significance of the difference between two independent groups was measured by independent sample t-test. Since Sig. = 0.913> 0.05 in Levene's test result, it is seen that the variances are homogeneously distributed. In this context, while looking at the difference between competitive strategies and organizational structures, since sig. (2-tailed) = 0.829> 0.05, no significant difference was found between competitive strategies and organizational structures.

Looking at the averages, it is observed that the average of competitive strategy of enterprises with mechanical organization structure is 3,02, while the average of competitive strategy of enterprises with organic organization structure is 3,04. According to the data obtained from 154 enterprises within the scope of the research, the organizational structures of the enterprises do not show a significant difference according to the competitive strategies they follow.

The reasons for this result can be shown that the enterprises participating in the research have an organic organization structure to a large extent and the competitive strategy average of the enterprises with mechanical organization structure and the competitive strategy average of the enterprises with organic organization structure are close to each other. Under these circumstances, it becomes difficult to establish a meaningful relationship between the competitive strategies followed by the enterprises and their organizational structures.

H2: There is a significant and positive relationship between the cost leadership strategy followed by the enterprises and their mechanical organizational structure.

The relationship between cost leadership strategy and mechanical organization structure is depicted in Table 3 below.

Table 3. The relationship between cost leadership strategy and mechanical organizational structure

	N	Correlation	Sig.
Cost Leadership Strategy and Mechanical Organizational Structure	20	.501	.024

Since Sig = 0.024 <0.05, it was found that there was a significant relationship between cost leadership strategy and mechanical organizational structure. When the direction of this relationship is looked at, it is seen that the Pearson correlation coefficient is = 0.501 and there is a positive relationship. In this context, it has been observed that the probability of being in a mechanical organization structure has increased by 50.1% at the point where the enterprises pursue a cost leadership strategy.

Considering the studies in the literature, it is understood that the enterprises following cost leadership tend to have a mechanical organization structure. At the same time, the literature also supports that the organizational structures of small and medium-sized enterprises are closer to the mechanistic structure

How Competitive Strategies Affect Organizational Structure

(Kocyigit, 2018, p. 142). In parallel with this information, according to the data obtained from the enterprises within the scope of the research, it was seen that there is a significant relationship between cost leadership strategy and mechanical organizational structure.

H3: There is a significant and positive relationship between the differentiation strategy followed by enterprises and their organic organizational structure.

Table 4 shows information on the relationship between differentiation strategy and organic organizational structure.

Table 4. The relationship between differentiation strategy and organic organizational structure

	N	Correlation	Sig.
Differentiation Strategy and Organic Organizational Structure	134	-.018	.839

Since Sig. = 0.839 > 0.05, it was seen that there was no significant relationship between differentiation strategy and organic organizational structure.

This finding is in line with the findings of Pertusa-Ortega et al. (2008). In the research conducted on 91 small and medium sized enterprises in Alicante city located in the east of Spain, cluster analysis was performed, and the strategies applied by the enterprises were determined as cost leadership, innovation differentiation and marketing differentiation. After the organizational structures of the enterprises were divided into two groups as mechanical and organic organizational structures, it was examined whether these two organizational structures made a difference in the average of competitive strategies. As a result of the analysis, it was seen that the marketing differentiation strategy average of mechanical organizational structures was higher than organic organizations and this difference was statistically significant. On the other hand, the innovation differentiation strategy does not show a clear relationship with any organizational structure, including the organic organizational structure (Pertusa-Ortega et al., 2008). As a result of the examination, it was determined that enterprises operating in a challenging environment and implementing a differentiation strategy have mechanistic organizational structure characteristics.

As in these examples, the result of this research, which is not the same as obtained in the common literature, can be described by the unique characteristics of the enterprises established in Turkey's Technology Development Zones.

H4: There is a significant and positive relationship between the focused cost leadership strategy followed by enterprises and their mechanical organizational structure.

Table 5 shows information on the relationship between focused cost leadership strategy and mechanical organizational structure.

Table 5. The relationship between focus strategy and mechanical organizational structure

	N	Correlation	Sig.
Focus Strategy and Mechanical Organizational Structure	20	.006	.979

Since Sig. = 0.979> 0.05, it was observed that there was no significant relationship between focus strategy and mechanical organizational structure.

H5: There is a significant and positive relationship between the focused differentiation strategy followed by enterprises and their organic organizational structure.

Table 6 shows information on the relationship between focus strategy and organic organizational structure.

Table 6. The relationship between focus strategy and organic organizational structure

	N	Correlation	Sig.
Focus Strategy and Organic Organizational Structure	134	.071	.418

Since Sig. = 0.418> 0.05, it was observed that there was no significant relationship between focus strategy and organic organization structure.

According to the quantitative research results, there is no significant relationship between the focus strategy and neither the mechanical organizational structure nor the organic organizational structure. Therefore, it is possible to say that the focus strategy does not show a clear relationship with the organizational structure within the scope of this research. It is possible to say that organic structure features can be seen in some areas of the organization most causally linked to innovation in enterprises implementing the focus strategy, while the mechanistic structure features prevail in the rest of the organization. This may indicate the possible existence of hybrid structures combining organic and mechanical structural properties.

As a result, only the H2 hypothesis was accepted, and the others were rejected among the hypotheses designed regarding the competitive strategies and organizational structures in the said enterprises. It was only determined that there is a positive and significant relationship between the cost leadership strategy and the mechanical organizational structure, and no significant difference was found between other competitive strategies and organizational structure variables.

Qualitative Research

Methodology

To search deeper and understand the results gained from quantitative research, the authors conducted a qualitative research on the 25 enterprises in Technology Development Zones regarding the organizational structure, and its relationship with the competitive strategy. While preparing the interview form, the interview form prepared by Durmus (2008) to determine the dimensions of the competition strategy, organizational structure and performance indicators of food retail businesses was used. To test the validity of the research scope, pre-interviews were held with 3 senior managers from the enterprises in Technology Development Zones. The executives interviewed in line with their business policies requested that both the institution and their names be kept confidential during the research. Therefore, in this study, the names of the people and institutions interviewed were not clearly mentioned by the researcher. In this study, the reliability and validity of the interview form was provided by interviews with different experts at different time periods of the later stages of the study. After the validity of the scope of the research was ensured by pre-interviews with the relevant people and the relevant literature review, the interview form was developed and finalized during the data collection process.

The interview form was used in interviews with a total of 25 individuals, including business owners, chairmen of the board of directors, general managers, or directors, who are at the top level of the enterprises selected for the interview. The information given and the evaluations made by these managers and / or owners in different lanes (international, national and local enterprises) and different sectors (defense industry, security, aviation technologies, space, software, informatics, unmanned systems, robotics, congresses and events, food and hospitality, education, health, steel, accounting, health information systems, satellite systems, smart home technologies, lighting and electrical materials, building materials, insurance, information technology, statistics, data mining, mobile applications, autonomous system technologies, management systems, gps, gsm and bluetooth technologies) of the enterprises in the Technology Development Zones have been an important source of information in terms of guiding the research. In this study, based on the logic that competitive strategy and organizational structure, which are the basic variables of enterprises operating in Technology Development Zones, can be understood better by analyzing them at a strategic level, first, semi-structured interviews were conducted with senior managers. Thus, the information given, and the evaluations made by these people whose knowledge and experience are trusted in Technology Development Zones have become an important source of information.

Analysis and Results

Content analysis was used to evaluate the data obtained through interviews in the study. The purpose of the content analysis method applied in this context is to reveal the content of participant views objectively and systematically (Altunisik et al., 2010). Content analysis aims to examine the collected data in more detail and to reach the concepts, categories and themes that explain this data. In content analysis, the collected data are focused, and codes are extracted from the facts and events that are frequently repeated in the data set or emphasized by the participants. You can go from codes to categories and from categories to themes. In summary, codes (data) that are found to be related and like each other are combined and interpreted within the framework of certain categories (concepts) and themes (Baltaci, 2019; Bengtsson, 2016; Crabtree & William, 1999; Merriam & Grenier, 2019). All the interviews were recorded by taking notes. The records obtained were rewritten by the researcher in a textual integrity that can be analyzed. The texts prepared were examined by researchers to define the relationship between competitive strategies and organizational structure. The evaluations of the qualitative research are summarized below in Table 7.

Table 7. Summary of qualitative research results

Strategy Type	Organizational Structures and Results

Strategy Group	• According to the results of the content analysis, it was determined that the enterprises operating in Technology Development Zones cluster in many different groups in terms of their competitive strategies and organizational structures.
	• Executives of enterprises following a differentiation strategy mostly use the words "differentiation, different, original, value, innovation, innovation, improvement, development, R&D, innovation, quality, brand, image, competence, self-confidence".
	• Executives of enterprises following a cost leadership strategy mostly used the words and concepts "low cost, cost control, cost orientation, cost reduction, price, production costs, raw material costs, localization, measurability".
	• Executives of enterprises following a focus strategy mostly use the words "focus, niche, personalization, competent team" together with the words specific to the strategy they focus on.
	• Executives of enterprises following hybrid competitive strategies use common words in their main competitive strategies.
	• Executives of enterprises having a mechanical organizational structure mostly use the concepts of "hierarchy, top management, vertical communication, institutionalization, centralized".
	• Executives of enterprises having an organic organizational structure mostly use the concepts of "flattened, horizontal communication, joint decision, authorization, flexible, decentralized".
	• As a result of word analysis, the groups defined in the research include are named as
	  o mechanical organizations following the differentiation strategy,
	  o organic organizations following the differentiation strategy,
	  o mechanical organizations following the cost leadership strategy,
	  o organic organizations following the cost leadership strategy,
	  o mechanical organizations following the focus strategy,
	  o organic organizations following the focus strategy,
	  o mechanical organizations following the hybrid competitive strategy,
	  o organic organizations following the hybrid competitive strategy.

Differentiation Strategy	• According to the results of the content analysis, it was determined that the most preferred strategy among the enterprises operating in the Technology Development Zones is the differentiation strategy, and the enterprises that apply the differentiation strategy tend to have more organic organizational structure.
	• As a result of the interviews conducted within the scope of the research, when the statements of the senior executives of the enterprises following the differentiation strategy are subjected to content analysis, the following statements about their differentiation strategy are noteworthy:
	  o being generally unrivaled in their sector,
	  o differentiating their products from their competitors,
	  o adding new features by improving their existing products,
	  o making new original production studies,
	  o never leaving research, development, and innovation,
	  o adopting a cost-oriented approach by creating value,
	  o being solution-oriented,
	  o developing high value-added products,
	  o having competent human resources,
	  o giving importance to institutionalization, branding, brand awareness, company image, customer perception,
	  o being experts in their field and changing the sector.
	• According to the results of the content analysis, the main reason for the enterprises following the differentiation strategy in Technology Development Zones to operate as an organic structure is seen as being a small business or a small family business. The fact that a few family members or several partners come together and sometimes take a few employees with them to do things together and generally take decisions together ensures that such enterprises are organic.
	• According to the results of the content analysis, it is understood that the main reason for the enterprises following the differentiation strategy in Technology Development Zones to operate as mechanical structure is the size of the enterprise. As a matter of fact, in the interviews conducted with the top executives of the enterprises that belong to the mechanical organizations group following the differentiation strategy in the research, regarding the organizational structures, it is mentioned that they generally have a board of directors and an organizational chart dominated by vertical communication that extends downwards with the line of general managers, assistant general managers, presidents, managers working under this board and a hierarchical structure where decisions are taken at the top level and implemented at the lower level. Therefore, because of the analysis, it was determined that the increase in the number of employees in the enterprises following the differentiation strategy in the Technology Development Zones brought about the institutionalization in the enterprises and the mechanical organization structure tendency.

Cost Leadership Strategy	• According to the results of the content analysis, it has been determined that among the enterprises operating in the Technology Development Zones, the enterprises applying a cost leadership strategy tend to have a mechanical organizational structure.
	• As a result of the interviews conducted within the scope of the research, when the statements of the senior managers of the enterprises that follow the cost leadership strategy are subjected to content analysis, the following statements about their cost leadership strategy come to the fore:
	  o reducing costs with R&D projects,
	  o producing with equity instead of imported products,
	  o benefiting from domestic labor force,
	  o reduce raw material costs,
	  o finding alternative suppliers for imported products,
	  o reducing the prices of purchased materials, or buying imported products cheaper depending on the increase in the number of customers,
	  o reducing office costs by taking part in the technopolis.
	• According to the results of the content analysis, it can be shown that the main reason for the enterprises that follow the cost leadership strategy in Technology Development Zones to operate as a mechanical structure is the following:
	  o they are well-established, institutional enterprises with their functional structure,
	  o and they are factors that facilitate strong cost reductions through their experience.
	  o general and strategic decisions in these enterprises are made by senior managers only by acting together with technical personnel,
	  o everyone has a goal,
	  o trying to be measurable,
	  o and having an internal performance management system.
	• In the content analysis, it has been determined that some enterprises that follow a cost leadership strategy in Technology Development Zones tend to have an organic organizational structure away from hierarchy. In the research, the top managers of the enterprises that belong to the group of organic organizations following the cost leadership strategy talked about a decentralized structure in which joint decisions are made regarding organizational structures.

Continued on following page

Table 7. Continued

Strategy Type	Organizational Structures and Results

Focus Strategy	• According to the results of the content analysis, it has been determined that among the enterprises operating in the Technology Development Zones, enterprises that apply the focus strategy tend to have an organic organizational structure.
	• According to content analysis, it is seen that some enterprises in Technology Development Zones - especially startup companies - perform their activities by differentiating in the niche areas they have determined for them or by controlling costs in that area.
	• In the research, senior executives of enterprises following the focused differentiation strategy summarize their strategy-oriented efforts as:
	  o focusing on specific niche issues or projects with a qualified and competent team,
	  o and even attracting investors and promoting to the next league and branding.
	• In the research, the senior manager of the enterprise, which belongs to the group of organic organizations following focused cost leadership strategy, explains their strategy as:
	  o producing more affordable products in the market by reducing input costs.

Hybrid Strategy	• According to the results of the content analysis, it has been determined that the enterprises that apply hybrid competitive strategy among the enterprises operating in the Technology Development Zones tend to have an organic organizational structure.
	• The senior executives of the enterprises in the Technology Development Zones that belong to the group of organic organizations that implement the hybrid competitive strategy by acting flexibly defines their strategy as:
	  o being one of the firsts of the sector, respected and known brands,
	  o being either unrivaled or among the few enterprises in the work done,
	  o being the enterprise with the highest market share,
	  o always using up-to-date technologies,
	  o orienting in niche issues with the R&D dimension,
	  o having young, dynamic, competent human resources,
	  o being human-oriented, working with minimum cost,
	  o reducing costs by localization, making quality and technology-oriented production,
	  o thinking globally,
	  o keeping a regular budget,
	  o paying attention to customer requests,
	  o and branding.
	• According to the results of the content analysis, it is seen that the organic organizational structures that implement the hybrid competitive strategies among the enterprises operating in the Technology Development Zones are designed as a flat structure that is dynamic and agile, able to take quick decisions and act immediately.
	• It is understood that mechanical organizations implementing hybrid competitive strategies have a hierarchical structure consisting of the general manager reporting to the chairman of the board of directors and the managers of the departments attached to him.

According to Nayyar (1993), enterprises do not hesitate to apply to different applications day by day with the applications they carry out in order to have a strong role in developing new products / services, provide comprehensive services to their customers, create brand value, have an innovative approach in marketing, dominate distribution channels, target high-priced market segments, allocate high budget for advertising expenditures, have a strong image, to offer differentiated products / services with different features, and to be known as having superior quality. According to the literature, it has been observed that enterprises that act for this purpose follow more differentiation strategies to gain competitive advantage. Thus, according to the literature, enterprises try to earn a profit above the sector average by applying a differentiation strategy, by fulfilling their customers' expectations differently compared to their competitors and expecting customers to reward it with a higher price (Durmus, 2008).

From enterprises using new and advanced technology in Technology Development Zones, as a requirement of being in these regions, it is expected to do research and study to turn software, technology, or innovation into a commercial product / service and to provide economic development by benefiting from the scientific infrastructure and potential of a research institution or a university (Gorkemli, 2011; Keles, 2007). As a result of the content analysis, it is revealed that enterprises operating in Technology Development Zones follow the differentiation strategy more widely than the cost leadership strategy in providing competitive advantage. Since the main goal of enterprises is to make technological innovations by carrying out R&D activities, this result can be considered natural. Differentiation strategy is preferred by enterprises in Technology Development Zones because it is a strategy based on achieving competitive advantage by adding value to the products and / or services developed by the enterprises and differentiating them against competitors. Therefore, it is understood that this is the case for the enterprises participating in the research.

According to the literature, there is a low degree of centralization and formalization in enterprises applying differentiation strategy, and a flattened structure obtained by expanding management and control areas (Durmus, 2008). Procedures and rules in enterprises with an organic structure led to a flexible structure as vertical and horizontal communication is enabled. Therefore, the degree of formalization of enterprises is low (Miles & Snow, 2003). The results of the content analysis also support the literature, showing that enterprises operating in Technology Development Zones tend to have a slightly more organic organizational structure compared to the mechanical organizational structure of enterprises following the differentiation strategy.

According to the results of the content analysis, the main reason for the enterprises following the differentiation strategy in Technology Development Zones to operate as an organic structure is seen as being a small business or a small family business. The fact that a few family members or several partners come together and sometimes take a few employees with them to do things together and generally take decisions together ensures that such enterprises are organic. As a matter of fact, according to the literature, small enterprises are less mechanical and have simpler organic structures (Mintzberg, 1981). Apart from these reasons, another reason can be shown that managers have sufficient strategic awareness. Because, according to content analysis, it is understood that managers who understand that having an organic structure means the ability to move faster for them, do not prefer a gradual organizational structure in their businesses and consciously transform their business into an organic organization structure by including all enterprise employees in common decision-making mechanisms.

According to the results of the content analysis, it is understood that the main reason for the enterprises following the differentiation strategy in Technology Development Zones to operate as mechanical structure is the size of the enterprise. Size is related to the number of employees. According to the literature, large enterprises are more mechanical. As enterprises grow, they become more bureaucratic. As the age of organizations increases and grows, they transform from simple organic structures to bureaucratic ones (Mintzberg 1981). As a matter of fact, in the interviews conducted with the top executives of the enterprises that belong to the mechanical organizations group following the differentiation strategy in the research, regarding the organizational structures, it is mentioned that they generally have a board of directors and an organizational chart dominated by vertical communication that extends downwards with the line of general managers, assistant general managers, presidents, managers working under this board and a hierarchical structure where decisions are taken at the top level and implemented at the lower level. Therefore, because of the analysis, it was determined that the increase in the number of employees in the enterprises following the differentiation strategy in the Technology Development Zones brought about the institutionalization in the enterprises and the mechanical organization structure tendency.

In the research conducted on Technology Development Zones, some enterprises' R&D activities rather than differentiate from their competitors are aimed at cost-leading activities, high production / service efficiency and cost control, selling products at lower prices than competitors, controlling raw material costs and procurement process, production / service processes, reducing production / service costs.

As a result of the interviews conducted within the scope of the research, when the statements of the senior managers of the enterprises that follow the cost leadership strategy are subjected to content analysis, the following statements about their cost leadership strategy come to the fore: Reducing costs with R&D projects, producing with equity instead of imported products, benefiting from domestic labor force. reduce raw material costs, find alternative suppliers for imported products, reduce the prices of purchased materials, or buy imported products cheaper depending on the increase in the number of customers, and reduce office costs by taking part in the technopolis.

According to the literature, there is a hierarchical structure with a high degree of formalization and centralization and central control in enterprises that implement cost leadership strategy (Durmus, 2008). In the enterprises with a mechanical structure, it is stated in detail who will do the work and how. Therefore, the degree of formalization of enterprises is high (Miles & Snow, 2003). The result of the content analysis also supports the literature, showing that the data related to the cost leadership strategy of the mechanically structured enterprises are more pronounced compared to the organic structured enterprises. As a matter of fact, according to the results of the content analysis, it can be shown that the main reason for the enterprises that follow the cost leadership strategy in Technology Development Zones to operate as a mechanical structure is that they are well-established, institutional enterprises with their functional structure, and they are factors that facilitate strong cost reductions through their experience. Other reasons are that general and strategic decisions in these enterprises are made by senior managers only by acting together with technical personnel; everyone has a goal, trying to be measurable, and having an internal performance management system. This result shows that the group that applies the cost leadership strategy a little more among the enterprises operating in Technology Development Zones is the mechanically structured enterprises. In the content analysis, it has been determined that some enterprises that follow a cost leadership strategy in Technology Development Zones tend to have an organic organizational structure away from hierarchy. In the research, the top managers of the enterprises that belong to the group of organic organizations following the cost leadership strategy talked about a decentralized structure in which joint decisions are made regarding organizational structures.

In sectors where competition is fierce and the number of competing enterprises is high, enterprises may have difficulty in this competition with their skills and assets at first. To gain competitive advantage, such enterprises try to meet the expectations of the customer group with different demands by focusing on a narrow field and applying focus strategies. Thus, enterprises can strengthen their positions by overcoming the competitive disadvantage (Bowman & Johson, 1992; Durmus, 2008). According to content analysis, it is seen that some enterprises in Technology Development Zones - especially startup companies - perform their activities by differentiating in the niche areas they have determined for them or by controlling costs in that area. As a matter of fact, in the research, senior executives of enterprises following the focused differentiation strategy summarize their strategy-oriented efforts as focusing on specific niche issues or projects with a qualified and competent team, and even attracting investors and promoting to the next league and branding. In addition, enterprises that adopt a focused differentiation strategy attribute their failure to reduce costs by not making intense production enough to establish a fixed product line, establish a supply chain, and keep inventory stock.

Enterprises can also achieve competitive advantage by applying competitive strategies at the same time. That is, an enterprise can combine two or more of cost leadership or differentiation strategies, or focused cost leadership and focused differentiation strategies. According to the results of the content analysis, it has been determined that there are enterprises acting with the hybrid competitive strategy in Technology Development Zones. The most important issue in pursuing hybrid competitive strategies is that enterprises have flexibility. Developing different strategic applications in regions and times when deemed necessary mostly depends on the adaptability of the business (Hitt et al., 2005; Onur, 2007). In this way, the senior executives of the enterprises in the Technology Development Zones that belong to the group of organic organizations that implement the hybrid competitive strategy by acting flexibly defines their strategy as being one of the firsts of the sector, respected and known brands, being either unrivaled or among the few enterprises in the work done, being the enterprise with the highest market share, always using up-to-date technologies, orienting in niche issues with the R&D dimension, having young, dynamic, competent human resources, being human-oriented, working with minimum cost, reducing costs by localization, making quality and technology-oriented production, thinking globally, keeping a regular budget, paying attention to customer requests and branding. According to the results of the content analysis, it is seen that the organic organizational structures that implement the hybrid competitive strategies among the enterprises operating in the Technology Development Zones are designed as a flat structure that is dynamic and agile, able to take quick decisions and act immediately. It is understood that mechanical organizations implementing hybrid competitive strategies have a hierarchical structure consisting of the general manager reporting to the chairman of the board of directors and the managers of the departments attached to him.

CURRENT CHALLENGES FACING THE TECHNOLOGY DEVELOPMENT ZONES IN TURKEY

According to the results of this research, it is possible to summarize the life cycle of enterprises in Technology Development Zones as follows: Enterprises that establish companies in Technology Development Zones start their activities by focusing on the niche areas they have determined. In line with the different needs, wishes and expectations of customers, enterprises that carry out R&D activities in a narrow market or to produce products and services with different features, differentiate their product or service or minimize their costs. While these enterprises, which have a small number of personnel in the first place, naturally adopt the organic structure, they can turn into a mechanical structure over time as the number of personnel increases. The enterprise, which puts its business on its way, may want to go beyond the narrow market that it has determined for itself day by day and appeal to the whole market. In this case, enterprises concentrate their R&D activities to differentiate their products / services, to reduce their costs, or both. While these enterprises, which have gained the identity of big enterprise by getting rid of their small enterprise identity, evolve into a mechanical structure to control their growing enterprises, enterprises with a certain strategic awareness can shape their enterprises according to the organic structure. Therefore, because of the work carried out in Technology Development Zones, the reason why there is no relationship between competitive strategies and organizational structures can be shown that the organizational structures of the enterprises in the Technology Development Zones are affected by the size and strategic consciousness of managers rather than the competitive strategies.

The idea that if the enterprises in Technology Development Zones continue to grow, they may have centralized and evolved into a mechanical structure independent of the strategy can be considered as one of the factors that explain the results of the quantitative study. Enterprises that start as a small enterprise and reach a certain size when they do successful business may see that their organizational structure is no longer sufficient. Because when the organization gets larger, it will be difficult to manage and control. The rapid growth of the enterprise brings with it the centralization of the authority and the formalization of the decision-making process, no matter what strategy the enterprise follows. In this case there will be a tendency towards mechanical structure.

The assumption that enterprises in Technology Development Zones may not have reached a sufficient level of awareness about strategic management and strategy yet can be considered as another factor that explains the results obtained in this study. Rather than finding the most appropriate organizational structure that is suitable for their mission, vision, strategy, and goals and designing the organizational structures of enterprises with managers who do not have strategic awareness, the assumption that the enterprises may have gone to structuring according to the stage in their organizational life cycle (Greiner, 1970) is the relationship between competitive strategies and organizational structures.

SOLUTIONS AND RECOMMENDATIONS

In this study conducted in enterprises in Technology Development Zones in Turkey to examine whether organizational structures differ according to competitive strategies, it was determined that the organizational structures of enterprises do not differ according to their competitive strategies. Therefore, according to the result of this study, which determines the current situation, it is assumed that the enterprises in question have not yet reached a sufficient level of awareness and maturity in terms of both institutionalization and strategic awareness. It is anticipated that more comprehensive research to be conducted in enterprises in different sectors in the future will be useful in revealing the relationship between competitive strategies and organizational structures. This research, which is the first study on this subject in Turkey, is a preliminary study in terms of showing the way and method for future studies.

It is thought that this study will make significant contributions to both Technology Development Zones and literature. The idea that more empirical studies can be made that examine the connection between strategy and organizational structures designed with strategic awareness, which is the first step of the strategic management process, in line with business strategies, constitutes the basis for future studies in businesses in different sectors.

In order for businesses to survive in an intense competitive environment and gain a competitive advantage, it is very important for entrepreneurs and managers to have strategic awareness. Managers with the necessary strategic awareness and foresight will be more successful in creating a vision for their business and directing their employees to the target. With the detailed examination and analysis of internal and external environmental factors affecting businesses, businesses will be able to make their strategic plans more effectively and determine healthier strategies. It is obvious how important the organizational structure is in the implementation of the chosen strategy. With the selection of the right organizational structure in accordance with the strategy, businesses will be able to implement their strategies in a healthier way and be more advantageous in gaining competitive advantage. In particular, the organizational structures to be created according to the types of strategies will allow managers to manage their businesses effectively and create a competitive advantage. It is obvious that strategy-structure harmony is necessary in designing managerial processes, determining human resources practices and making decision mechanisms more effective. Today, it is even more important for businesses that implement innovative and innovation-based strategies to adopt participatory management practices that facilitate the transfer of authority, use open communication channels, consist of flexible job descriptions, and create their organizational structures in this direction. It has become a necessity for innovation enterprises operating in competitive and rapidly changing environmental conditions to take this into account. Although flexible and organic organizational structures are recommended for innovative businesses, it is seen that as businesses grow and the number of employees increases, the degree of formalization also increases and businesses begin to shift towards mechanical organizational structures. One of the main reasons for this is due to the necessity of being able to manage large structures. This is another issue that managers should consider.

It is thought that this chapter will present the perspectives of researchers, managers, and decision makers on Technology Development Zones by showing the relationship between competitive strategy and organizational structure. The results obtained in this research are expected to shed light on which issues enterprises should pay attention to between their competitive strategies and organizational structure by enabling the evaluation of Technology Development Zones. Similarly, it is possible to benefit from the design of this study in research to be conducted in technoparks and sectors in different countries.

The organizational structure and competitive strategy, which are among the basic variables specific to Technology Development Zones, and the limited number of research and measurement tools for determining the relationships between them are an indicator of the level of contribution this study to the literature. It is thought that the current theoretical discussions on the relationship between competitive strategy and organizational structure will contribute to the field by testing it with a measurement tool such as the interview form developed specifically for Technology Development Zones.

REFERENCES

Altunisik, R., Coskun, R., Bayraktaroglu, S., & Yildirim, E. (2004). *Sosyal bilimlerde araştırma yöntemleri: SPSS uygulamalı* (3rd ed.). Sakarya Kitabevi.

Ansoff, H. L. (1965). *Corporate strategy*. McGraw-Hill.

Ansoff, I. H. (1987). Strategic management of technology. *The Journal of Business Strategy*, 7(3), 28–39. doi:10.1108/eb039162

Bal, Y. (2011). *Rekabet Stratejilerinin İnsan Kaynakları Yönetimi Uygulamalarına Etkisi* [Doctoral dissertation]. Istanbul University.

Baltaci, A. (2019). Nitel Araştırma Süreci: Nitel Bir Araştırma Nasıl Yapılır? *Ahi Evran Üniversitesi Sosyal Bilimler Enstitüsü Dergisi*, 5(2), 368–388. doi:10.31592/aeusbed.598299

Barnard, C. I. (1938). *The functions of the executive*. Harvard University Press.

Barney, J. B. (1991). Firm resources and sustained competitive advantage. *Journal of Management*, 17(1), 99–120. doi:10.1177/014920639101700108

Barney, J. B., & Hesterly, W. S. (2012). *Strategic management and competitive advantage* (4th ed.). Pearson.

Bart, C. K. (1986). Product strategy and formal structure. *Strategic Management Journal*, 7(4), 293–312. doi:10.1002mj.4250070402

Barutcugil, I. (2013). *Stratejik yönetim*. Kariyer Yayincilik.

Bengtsson, M. (2016). How to Plan and Perform A Qualitative Study Using Content Analysis. *NursingPlus Open*, 2, 8–14. doi:10.1016/j.npls.2016.01.001

Bourgeois, L. J., & Brodwin, D. R. (1984). Strategic implementation: Five approaches to an elusive phenomenon. *Strategic Management Journal*, 5(3), 241–264. doi:10.1002mj.4250050305

Bowman, C., & Johnson, G. (1992). Surfacing competitive strategies. *European Management Journal*, 10(2), 210–220. doi:10.1016/0263-2373(92)90071-B

Burns, T., & Stalker, G. M. (1961). *The management of innovation*. Tavistock.

Carpenter, M. A., & Sanders, W. G. (2009). *Strategic management* (2nd ed.). Pearson.

Certo, S. C., & Peter, J. P. (1991). *Strategic management: Concepts and application*. McGraw–Hill, Inc.

Chaffee, E. E. (1985). Three models of strategy. *Academy of Management Review, 10*(1), 89–98. doi:10.5465/amr.1985.4277354

Chandler, A. D. (1962). *Strategy and structure: Chapters in the history of the American industrial enterprise*. M.I.T. Press.

Channon, D. (1973). *Strategy and structure in British Enterprise*. Harvard University Press. doi:10.1007/978-1-349-01995-3

Claver-Cortés, E., Pertusa-Ortega, E. M., & Molina-Azorín, J. F. (2012). Characteristics of organizational structure relating to hybrid competitive strategy: Implications for performance. *Journal of Business Research, 65*(7), 993–1002. doi:10.1016/j.jbusres.2011.04.012

Covin, J. G., & Dennis, P. S. (1990). New venture strategic posture, structure, and performance: An industry life cycle analysis. *Journal of Business Venturing, 5*(2), 123–135. doi:10.1016/0883-9026(90)90004-D

Covin, J. G., Slevin, D. P., & Heeley, M. B. (2001). Strategic decision making in an intuitive vs. technocratic mode: Structural and environmental considerations. *Journal of Business Research, 52*(1), 51–67. doi:10.1016/S0148-2963(99)00080-6

Crabtree, B. F., & William, L. M. (1999). *Doing Qualitative Research* (2nd ed.). Sage Publications.

Cubukcu, M. (2018). İşletmelerde uygulanan strateji tipleri ve uygulamadan örnekler. *Uluslararası Yönetim Akademisi Dergisi, 1*(2), 142–156.

Daft, R. L. (2007). *Organization theory and design*. Thomson South-Western.

Dess, G. G., & Davis, P. S. (1984). Porter's (1980) generic strategies as determinants of strategic group membership and organizational performance. *Academy of Management Journal, 27*(3), 467–488.

Dincer, O. (2013). *Stratejik yönetim ve işletme politikası* (9th ed.). Alfa Yayim.

Drago, W. A. (1997). Organization structure and strategic planning: An empirical examination. *Management Research News, 20*(6), 30–42. doi:10.1108/eb028567

Durmuş Arici, E. (2008). *Rekabet Stratejisi, Örgüt Yapısı ve Performans İlişkilerinin Gıda Perakende Sektörü Bağlamında Araştırılması* [Doctoral dissertation]. Akdeniz University.

Ertekín, İ. (2017). Classical organization theory. *Journal of Emerging Economies and Policy, 2*(2), 64–73.

Galbraith, C., & Schendel, D. (1983). An empirical analysis of strategy types. *Strategic Management Journal, 4*(2), 153–173. doi:10.1002mj.4250040206

Gibson, J. L., Ivancevich, J. M., & Donnelly, J. H. (2012). *Organizations: Behavior, structure, processes* (14th ed.). McGraw-Hill Companies, Inc.

Ginsberg, A., & Venkatraman, N. (1985). Contingency perspectives of organizational strategy: A critical review of the empirical research. *Academy of Management Review, 10*(3), 421–434. doi:10.5465/amr.1985.4278950

Gorkemli, H. N. (2011). *Bölgesel kalkınmada teknoparkların önemi ve Konya Teknokent örneği* [Doctoral dissertation]. Selcuk University.

Govindarajan, V. (1988). A contingency approach to strategy implementation at the business-unit level: Integrating administrative mechanisms with strategy. *Academy of Management Journal, 31*(4), 828–853.

Greiner, L. E., Dalton, G. W., & Lawrence, P. R. (1970). *Organization change and development*. Dorsey Press.

Hambrick, D. C., & Fredrickson, J. W. (2001). Are you sure you have a strategy? *The Academy of Management Executive, 19*(4), 48–58. doi:10.5465/ame.2001.5897655

Hatch, M. J., & Cunliffe, A. L. (2006). *Organization theory modern, symbolic, and postmodern perspectives* (2nd ed.). Oxford University Press.

Hitt, M. A., Ireland, R. D., & Hoskisson, R. E. (2005). *Strategic Management: Competitiveness and Globalization*. Thomson South-Western Publishing.

Hrebiniak, L. G., & Joyce, W. (1985). Organizational adaptation: Strategic choice and environmental determinism. *Administrative Science Quarterly, 30*(3), 336–349. doi:10.2307/2392666

Johnson, G., Whittington, R., & Scholes, K. (2011). *Exploring corporate strategy* (9th ed.). Prentice Hall.

Keles, M. K. (2007). *Türkiye'de teknokentler bir ampirik inceleme* [MSc. Thesis]. Süleyman Demirel University, Isparta, Turkey.

Kerbouche, M., Bouhelal, F., & Belmimoun, A. (2017). Organisation effectiveness under the internal factors and environment. *Les politiques Economique En Algérie, 8*(1), 33–46.

Keskin, H., Akgün, A. E., & Koçoğlu, İ. (2016). *Örgüt teorisi*. Nobel Akademik Yayincilik.

Khandwalla, P. N. (1977). *The design of organizations*. Harcourt Brace Jovanovich.

Kirk, J., & Miller, M. L. (1986). *Reliability and validity in qualitative research*. Sage Publications. doi:10.4135/9781412985659

Kocel, T. (2015). *İşletme yöneticiliği* (16th ed.). Beta Yayincilik.

Kocyigit, Y. (2018). *Firmaların örgütsel esnekliği, kullandıkları rekabet stratejileri ve algılanan rekabet üstünlüğü arasındaki etkileşim: Türkiye'nin en büyük 500 sanayi işletmesinde bir uygulama* [Doctoral dissertation]. Izmir Katip Celebi University.

Lado, A. O., & Wilson, M. C. (1994). Human resource systems and sustained competitive advantage: A competency based perspective. *Academy of Management Review, 19*(4), 699–727. doi:10.5465/amr.1994.9412190216

LeCompte, M. D., & Goetz, J. P. (1982). Problems of reliability and validity in ethnographic research. *Review of Educational Research, 52*(1), 31–60. doi:10.3102/00346543052001031

Lindblom, C. E. (1959). The science of "Muddling Through". *Public Administration Review, 19*(2), 79–88. doi:10.2307/973677

March, J. G., & Simon, H. A. (1958). *Organizations*. Wiley.

Marshall, C., & Rossman, G. B. (1994). *Designing qualitative research*. Sage Publications.

Merriam, S. B., & Robin, S. G. (2019). *Qualitative Research in Practice: Examples for Discussion and Analysis* (2nd ed.). Jossey-Bass Publishers.

Miles, M. B., & Huberman, A. M. (1994). *Qualitative data analysis: An expanded sourcebook* (2nd ed.). Sage.

Miles, R. E., & Snow, C. C. (1978). *Organizational strategy, structure, and process*. McGraw-Hill.

Miles, R. E., & Snow, C. C. (1984). Designing strategic human resource systems. *Organizational Dynamics*, *13*(1), 36–52. doi:10.1016/0090-2616(84)90030-5

Miller, D. (1986). Configurations of strategy and structure. *Strategic Management Journal*, *7*(3), 233–249. doi:10.1002mj.4250070305

Miller, D. (1988). Relating Porter's strategy to environment and structure. *Academy of Management Journal*, *31*(2), 280–308.

Miller, D. (1996). Configurations revisited. *Strategic Management Journal*, *17*(7), 505–512. doi:10.1002/(SICI)1097-0266(199607)17:7<505::AID-SMJ852>3.0.CO;2-I

Mintzberg, H. (1978). Patterns in strategy formation. *Management Science*, *24*(9), 934–948. doi:10.1287/mnsc.24.9.934

Mintzberg, H. (1979). *The structuring of organizations*. Prentice Hall.

Mintzberg, H. (1981). Organization design: Fashion or fit. *Harvard Business Review*, *59*(1), 103–116.

Mintzberg, H. (1987). The strategy concept I: Five Ps for strategy. *California Management Review*, *30*(1), 11–24. doi:10.2307/41165263

Morris, P. F. (1990). Bureaucracy, professionalization and school centred innovation strategies. *International Review of Education*, *36*(1), 21–41. doi:10.1007/BF01874975

Nandakumar, M. K., Ghobadian, A., & O'Regan, N. (2010). Business-level strategy and performance: The moderating effects of environment and structure. *Management Decision*, *48*(6), 907–939. doi:10.1108/00251741011053460

Nayyar, P. R. (1993). On the measurement of competitive strategy: Evidence from a large multiproduct U.S. firm. *Academy of Management Journal*, *36*(6), 1652–1669.

Neis, D. F., Pereira, M. F., & Maccari, E. A. (2016). Strategic planning process and organizational structure: Impacts, confluence and similarities. *Brazilian Business Review*, *14*(5), 479–492. doi:10.15728/bbr.2017.14.5.2

Nemetz, P. L., & Fry, L. W. (1988). Flexible manufacturing organizations: Implications for strategy formulation and organization design. *Academy of Management Review*, *13*(4), 627–639. doi:10.5465/amr.1988.4307510

Nonaka, I. (1988). Toward middle-up-down management: Accelerating information creation. *Sloan Management Review, 29*(3), 9–21.

Norman, G. (2010). Likert scales, levels of measurement and the 'Laws' of statistics. *Advances in Health Sciences Education: Theory and Practice, 15*(5), 625–632. doi:10.100710459-010-9222-y PMID:20146096

Odtü-Tek. (2021, March 12). *Teknokent Nedir*. http://odtuteknokent.com.tr/tr/hakkinda/teknokent-nedir#:~:text=Teknoloji%20Geli%C5%9Ftirme%20B%C3%B6lgesi%2C%20y%C3%BCksek%2Fileri,bir%20bulu%C5%9Fu%20ticari%20bir%20%C3%BCr%C3%BCn%2C

Olson, E. M., Slater, S. F., Hult, G., & Tomas, M. (2005). The performance implications of fit among business strategy, marketing organization structure and strategic behavior. *Journal of Marketing, 69*(3), 49–65. doi:10.1509/jmkg.69.3.49.66362

Onur, T. (2007). *Ayaktan sağlık hizmeti veren sağlık kuruluşu olan özel hastanelerde uygulanan rekabet stratejilerinin hasta memnuniyeti üzerine etkileri* [Master dissertation]. Maltepe University.

Oosthuizen, H. (1997). An evaluation of the relevance of the Miles & Snow strategic typology under present-day conditions of major environmental uncertainty: The emperor's new clothes or a paradigm shift? *South African Journal of Business Management, 28*(2), 63–72. doi:10.4102ajbm.v28i2.790

Parthasarthy, R. S., & Sethi, P. (1992). The impact of flexible automation on business strategy and organizational structure. *Academy of Management Review, 17*(1), 86–111. doi:10.5465/amr.1992.4279572

Patton, M. Q. (1987). *How to use qualitative methods in evaluation*. Sage Publications.

Pearce, A. J., & Robinson, R. B. (2015). *Stratejik Yonetim: Gelistirme, Uygulama ve Kontrol* (12th ed.). (M. Barca, Trans.). Nobel Yayin.

Pertusa-Ortega, E. M., Claver-Cortés, E., & Molina-Azorín, J. F. (2008). Strategy, structure, environment and performance in Spanish firms. *EuroMed Journal of Business, 3*(2), 223–239. doi:10.1108/14502190810891245

Porter, M. (1980). *Competitive strategy- Techniques for analysing industries and competitors*. Free Press.

Porter, M. (1985). *Competitive advantage: Creating and sustaining superior performance*. Free Press.

Porter, M. (1996). What is Strategy? *Harvard Business Review, 74*(6), 61–78. PMID:10158475

Rajaratnam, D., & Chonko, L. B. (1995). The effect of business strategy type on marketing organization design, product- market growth strategy, relative marketing effort, and organization performance. *Journal of Marketing Theory and Practice, 3*(3), 60–75. doi:10.1080/10696679.1995.11501696

Reid, G. C., Smith, J. A., & Xu, Z. (2020). The Impact of Strategy, Technology, Size and Business Environment on the Organizational Form of Small Firms in China. *Asian Journal of Economics. Business and Accounting, 20*(4), 15–32.

Robbins, S. P., & DeCenzo, D. A. (2005). *Fundamentals of management: Essential concepts and applications* (5th ed.). Pearson.

Rue, L. W., & Holland, P. G. (1989). *Strategic management: Concepts and experiences*. McGraw-Hill.

Rumelt, R. P. (1984). Towards a strategic theory of the firm. *Competitive Strategic Management, 26*(3), 556–570.

Salik, S. (2001). Modern yonetim yaklasimlari. *Dumlupınar Üniversitesi Sosyal Bilimler Dergisi, 5*, 1–19.

Sengul, M. (2018). Organization Design and Competitive Strategy: An Application to the Case of Divisionalization. *Advances in Strategic Management, 40*, 207–228. doi:10.1108/S0742-332220180000040007

Slevin, D. P., & Covin, J. G. (1997). Strategy formation patterns, performance, and significance of context. *Journal of Management, 23*(2), 189–209. doi:10.1177/014920639702300205

T.C. Sanayi ve Teknoloji Bakanlığı. (2021, March 12). *İstatistiki Bilgiler*. https://www.sanayi.gov.tr/istatistikler/istatistiki-bilgiler/mi0203011501

Teare, R. E., Costa, J., & Eccles, G. (1998). Relating strategy, structure, and performance. *Journal of Workplace Learning, 10*(2), 58–75. doi:10.1108/13665629810209048

Teknopark. (2021, March 12). *Teknoloji Geliştirme Bögeleri*. https://teknopark.sanayi.gov.tr/Content/Detay

TGBD. (2021a, March 12). *Dünyadaki Teknoparklar*. https://www.tgbd.org.tr/dunyadaki-teknoparklar-icerik-34

TGBD. (2021b, March 12). *Türkiye'de Teknoparklar*. https://www.tgbd.org.tr/dunyadaki-teknoparklar-icerik-35

Thompson, A. A., & Strickland, A. J. (1996). *Strategic management: Concepts & cases*. Irwin.

Tosi, H. L. (2009). *Theories of organization*. Sage Publications.

Ülgen, H., & Mirze, S. K. (2016). *İşletmelerde stratejik yönetim* (8th ed.). Beta Yayincilik.

Walker, K., Ni, N., & Dyck, B. (2015). Recipes for successful sustainability: Empirical organizational configurations for strong corporate environmental performance. *Business Strategy and the Environment, 24*(1), 40–57. doi:10.1002/bse.1805

Walton, E. J. (1986). Managers' prototypes of financial firms. *Journal of Management Studies, 23*(6), 679–698. doi:10.1111/j.1467-6486.1986.tb00442.x

Yildirim, A., & Simsek, H. (2005). *Sosyal bilimlerde nitel araştırma yöntemleri* (5th ed.). Seckin Yayincilik.

ADDITIONAL READING

Amburgey, T. L., & Dacin, T. (1994). As the Left Foot Follows the Right? The Dynamics of Strategic and Structural Change. *Academy of Management Journal, 37*(6), 1427–1452.

Amitabh, M., & Gupta, R. K. (2010). Research in Strategy-Structure Performance Construct: Review of Trends, Paradigms and Methodologies. *Journal of Management & Organization, 16*(5), 757–776. doi:10.5172/jmo.2010.16.5.744

Amoako-Gyampah, K., & Acquaah, M. (2008). Manufacturing Strategy, Competitive Strategy and Firm Performance: An Empirical Study in a Developing Economy Environment. *International Journal of Production Economics*, *111*(2), 575–592. doi:10.1016/j.ijpe.2007.02.030

Atkinson, S., Schaefer, A., & Viney, H. (2000). Organizational Structure and Effective Environmental Management. *Business Strategy and the Environment*, *9*(2), 108–120. doi:10.1002/(SICI)1099-0836(200003/04)9:2<108::AID-BSE236>3.0.CO;2-L

Beal, R. M. (2000). Competing Effectively: Environmental Scanning, Competitive Strategy, and Organizational Performance in Small Manufacturing Firms. *Journal of Small Business Management*, *38*(1), 27–47.

Çetinkaya Bozkurt, Ö., Kalkan, A., & Arman, M. (2014). The Relationship Between Structural Characteristics of Organization and Followed Business Strategy: An Application in Denizli. *Procedia: Social and Behavioral Sciences*, *150*, 222–229. doi:10.1016/j.sbspro.2014.09.041

Chatzoglou, P., Chatzoudes, D., Sarigiannidis, L., & Theriou, G. (2018). The Role of Firm-specific Factors in the Strategy-performance Relationship: Revisiting the Resource-based View of the Firm and the VRIO Framework. *Management Research Review*, *41*(1), 46–73. doi:10.1108/MRR-10-2016-0243

Eva, N., Sendjaya, S., Prajogo, D., Cavanagh, A., & Robin, M. (2018). Creating Strategic Fit: Aligning Servant Leadership with Organizational Structure and Strategy. *Personnel Review*, *47*(1), 166–186. doi:10.1108/PR-03-2016-0064

Koçyiğit, Y., & Tabak, A. (2020). The Interaction Among Organizational Flexibility, Competitive Strategy and Competitive Advantage: A Path Analytic Study1. In B. Akkaya (Ed.), *Agile Business Leadership Methods for Industry 4.0* (pp. 303–326). Emerald Publishing Limited. doi:10.1108/978-1-80043-380-920201017

Monroe Olson, E., Duray, R., Cooper, C., & Monroe Olson, K. (2016). Strategy, Structure, and Culture Within the English Premier League: An Examination of Large Clubs. *Sport, Business and Management*, *6*(1), 55–75. doi:10.1108/SBM-11-2013-0040

KEY TERMS AND DEFINITIONS

Strategic Awareness: The level of awareness that must be possessed for the effective realization of the stages of the strategic management process. The strategic management process starts with having strategic awareness.

Strategic Management: The effective and efficient use of production resources (natural resources, human resources, capital, infrastructure, raw materials, etc.) to survive the business in the long term, to gain a sustainable competitive advantage and to provide return on average profit.

Technopark: An organized research and business center where universities, research institutions and industrial organizations continue their research, development, and innovation activities in the same environment, produce value-added products, transfer information and technology between each other, and integrate academic, economic, and social structure.

APPENDIX 1

Interview Form

Section 1

The questions listed below are for determining your company's competitive strategy. For the reliability of the research, it is important that your answers to the questions are detailed.

Question 1: Do you have activities to develop new products / services or to improve existing products / services or to offer differentiated products / services with different features?

Question 2: Is the product and service quality in your company different than your competitors? If different, what are the reasons for these differences? Is your company known for its superior quality? What are the common service opportunities available to customers in your company? Are there aspects of your services that make them different from your competitors? (Innovative approach in the field of marketing, such as dominating distribution channels)

Question 3: Does your company allocate a high budget for advertising expenditures? What is the share of promotional and advertising expenditures in your company's general expenditures?

Question 4: Do you think your company has a strong image? Do you have any work on enterprise image / brand formation? If so, can you tell us about these studies? Do you think the brand has an impact on profitability?

Question 5: As senior management, is there any effort to reduce the costs of your activities in your company? Could you briefly describe these activities, if any? Do you constantly try to improve your production and service processes to reduce your costs? Does your company maintain a high level of production / service efficiency and cost control?

Question 6: Among the general policies of your company, are there any practices to set product prices lower than your competitors?

Question 7: Do you serve special geographical segments? Are special products sold? (For example, for a certain segment, customized)

Section 2

The questions below are for determining the organizational structure of your company. For the reliability of the research, it is important that your answers to the questions are detailed.

Question 1: What are your operational, strategic and administrative decision issues in your company? What are the current decision issues regarding the pre-determined standard implementation in your company? At what levels are these decisions taken?

Question 2: What is the number of management levels in your company that have management authority including general manager / owner level?

Question 3: How many departments are directly affiliated to the general manager in your company?

Question 4: Could you give information about the flow direction of the reports in your company?

Question 5: Are there written documents explaining your organizational structure in your company? If so, what are these?

APPENDIX 2

Questions and Answers

1. What is the overall problem presented in this case?

The overall problem presented in this case is to try to determine whether the organizational structures of organizations in Technology Development Zones differ according to their competitive strategies.

2. What are the factors affecting the problem(s) related to this case?

Factors affecting the organizational structure of organizations operating in Technology Development Zones are the size of the organization and the level of strategic awareness of the organizations' senior managers rather than the competitive strategies.

3. Discuss managerial, organizational, and technological issues related to this case.

Organizations from many different sectors in the field of production and service using software, hardware and Internet of Things (IoT) technologies participated in the study. In the study, it has been determined that the organizational structures of the organizations do not differ according to the technologies used by the organizations, the fields and sectors they operate. It has been understood that the organizational structure of the organizations varies according to the strategic awareness level of the organizations managers.

4. What are the possible alternatives and pros and cons of each alternative facing the organization in dealing with the problem(s) related to the case?

The main alternative facing the organization in dealing with the problem is to ensure that the organization's managers need to have a deeper knowledge of strategic management literature and practices. While the problem would be solved radically by eliminating the lack of professional management in this way, the disadvantage of this alternative is that it would take a long time.

5. What is the final solution that can be recommended to the management of the organization described in the case? Provide your arguments in support of the recommended solution.

The final solution that can be recommended to the management of the organizations described in the case is that to have managers with high strategic awareness. Because organizations in Technology Development Zones are strategically important for the future of countries and the world. It is necessary to have strategic awareness for these organizations to ensure their continuity by producing with high added value. Therefore, applications with a long-term and strategic perspective are needed.

Epilogue and Lessons Learned

In the research conducted in the organizations located in Technology Development Zones to examine whether the organizational structures differ according to the competitive strategies, it has been determined that the organizational structures of the organizations do not differ according to their competitive strategies. According to the result of this study, which determines the current situation, it is assumed that the organizations in question have not yet reached a sufficient level of awareness and maturity in terms of both institutionalization and strategic awareness. It is thought that the managers, whose strategic awareness level will have increased in the future, will lead to more meaningful studies in the organizations with the design of the organizational structures in accordance with the competitive strategies.

In our opinion, it is possible to list the lessons that can be learned from our study as follows:

- According to the result of the quantitative study, a meaningful relationship could not be established between the competitive strategies of the organizations in Technology Development Zones and their organizational structures in general. Therefore, it is understood that the managers of the organizations in question act independently of the competitive strategy while forming their organizational structures.
- As a result of the qualitative study, it has been determined that the organizational structures of the organizations in the Technology Development Zones are affected by the size of the organization. As these organizations continued to grow, they moved away from organicity and evolved into a mechanical structure by centralizing.
- As a result of the qualitative study, it was determined that the organizational structures of the organizations in the Technology Development Zones differ according to the strategic awareness level of the organizations managers. It is considered that organizations with managers who do not have strategic awareness are far away from finding the most appropriate organizational structure that can be suitable for their mission, vision, strategy and goals and designing them accordingly.

Chapter 13
The Effects of Real-Time Content Marketing on Consumer Emotions and Behaviors:
An Analysis on COVID-19 Pandemic Period

Hayat Ayar Senturk
https://orcid.org/0000-0002-8738-4603
Yildiz Technical University, Turkey

Ece Ozer Cizer
https://orcid.org/0000-0002-8597-2073
Yildiz Technical University, Turkey

Tugce Sezer
Yildiz Technical University, Turkey

EXECUTIVE SUMMARY

This study, carried out during the COVID-19 pandemic in Turkey, aimed to provide suggestions for creating a successful real-time content marketing strategy. For this purpose, data were collected from 319 participants using the online questionnaire technique. Outcomes of the analysis indicate that while positive perception toward real-time content marketing campaigns can lead to positive emotions, negative perception toward real-time content marketing campaigns can lead to negative emotions. It was also found as an important result that both positive and negative emotions affect negative consumer behavior during the pandemic period. In addition, negative emotions as a mediator variable strengthen negative consumer behavior. As a result, it can be said that real content marketing campaigns also have negative consequences on consumer behavior during pandemics. Consequently, marketing authorities should continue their real-time content marketing activities with this result in mind.

DOI: 10.4018/978-1-7998-1630-0.ch013

The Effects of Real-Time Content Marketing on Consumer Emotions and Behaviors

ORGANIZATION BACKGROUND

The structure of the market is constantly changing from the past to the present. Technological, demographic, economic developments, globalization, sustainability, and changes in consumer behavior are reshaping the market structure (Yadav et al., 2020). Enterprises conduct researches to solve the structure of the market, increase sales, and differentiate from competitors. As a result of researches, they can review and update their marketing strategies (Paul, 2019). The ease of access to technology and the internet has also caused changes in consumer behavior (Czaja & Lee, 2007). Businesses that are aware of the changes caused by technology in consumer behavior have started to digitize their marketing activities to reach their target audiences online as well as traditional marketing understanding (Ryan & Jones, 2009).

The effect of digitalization on marketing has created a new type of marketing called digital marketing (Bala & Verma, 2018). Digital marketing has made it possible for brands to reach their consumers faster and easier. It can be defined as the marketing of the goods and services of the enterprises to their consumers with the use of digital channels (Kiani, 1998). Digital marketing has become one of the most widely used marketing methods to promote and present products and services to the target audience (Yasmin et al., 2015). Digital marketing has digital marketing tools that enable it to reach consumers on digital platforms (Chaffey & Smith, 2017). The strategies used by digital marketing can include real-time marketing, content marketing, search engine optimization, affiliated marketing, viral marketing, social media platforms, email marketing, PR tools, etc. (Kumar & Singh, 2020; Lieb, 2013).

Real-time marketing is one of the marketing strategies that is frequently used in digital marketing (Tehci, 2021). Real-time marketing campaigns are used by companies competing and survive in digital market environments. Real-time marketing strengthens effective communication with the target audience through digital channels (Scott, 2011). Especially companies that seeing the positive reactions of consumers to real-time marketing campaigns frequently use these campaigns (Willemsen et al., 2018). Real-time marketing campaigns aim to create value for the consumer. With this aim, real-time marketing campaigns and content marketing started to be used together for creating value (Mazerant et al., 2021). Real-time content marketing campaigns create a snowball effect on consumers. In this way, they can influence large audiences' emotions in a short time. Besides real-time content marketing campaigns provide frequently mention the brand on social media platforms (Scott, 2011). This situation is considered a great success in terms of brand-consumer interaction. However, care should be taken when implementing real-time content marketing campaigns. Giving the right message at the right time is the most important factor that the brand should pay attention to. Consuming digital content within seconds is an inevitable reality of real-time marketing (Lu et al., 2016). For this reason, the mistakes that can be made to allow them to be noticed by the target audience instantly. As a result of right or wrong strategies, consumers' emotions, and consumer behaviors are affected positively or negatively.

Content marketing campaigns are the most widely used digital marketing tools (Nikunen, 2017). According to the research conducted by Smart Insights in 2019, businesses accept content marketing as the most effective and profitable digital marketing tool (Kotane et al., 2019). Content marketing is a strategic marketing approach that aims to communicate with the target audience by creating content suitable for the customer audience. Thus, companies attract the attention of existing and potential customers and create profitable customer actions as a result (Holliman & Rowley, 2014). This marketing tool prepares interesting, entertaining, educational, and supportive information in line with the wishes and expectations of the target audience. In this way, it strengthens brand image, the relationship between brand and target audience (Lieb, 2012). Content marketing can be implemented by any company. However, must be considered the goals of content marketing, the type of content marketing, the advertising channels, the frequency and impact of the content (Baltes, 2015).

The Covid-19 pandemic has increased the time spent at home and in front of the screen. This increase has led brands to make timely marketing campaigns with pandemic content. However, it is not known how this pandemic-themed content affects consumer emotions and behaviors. In the light of this information, this chapter aims to reveal the effects of real-time content marketing on consumer emotions and consumer behavior during the Covid-19 pandemic. Contrary to other studies in the literature (Hollebeek & Macky 2019; Kallier 2017; Mathew & Soliman 2021; Willemsen et al. 2018), in this study, a structural equation model was established in order to determine the factors that reveal negative consumer behaviors. In addition, concepts of real-time marketing and content marketing were combined as a concept called real-time content marketing. In this respect, the study differs from similar studies. Researching consumer emotions and behaviors towards real-time content marketing campaigns within the scope of the Covid-19 pandemic increases the importance of the study.

SETTING THE STAGE

Epidemics that have emerged over the ages have affected economies, societies, and living conditions in various ways (Habes et al. 2020). At the end of the year 2019, Covid-19 has spread from China to countries around the world. This virus is a major health problem that negatively affects all areas of life. The Covid-19 pandemic led to changing consumer behaviors such as shopping habits, purchase channels, and order frequency. In this way, it made digitalization a necessity. During the pandemic period, education, jobs, and shopping, etc. have become digital. In the Covid 19 pandemic, consumers have been spending most of their time at home online. So that, consumption habits have changed and traditional purchasing habits have been replaced by online environments. Researches show online demand for many product groups as well as food and personal care products has been positively affected (Deloitte, 2020).

In the Covid-19 pandemic, companies have had to intensify their digital activities to attract consumers' attention and increase their sales (Soto-Acosta, 2020). During this period, companies using effective marketing strategies were able to turn the disadvantages into advantages for the company (Kaczmarek et al., 2021). To create an effective marketing strategy, companies focused on consumer demands. By restructuring their sales strategies, companies have made more efficient online access to their target audiences. In addition, companies have invested in various digital marketing campaigns to reach more customers and increase sales during the pandemic process. In this way, they aim to pass the pandemic process positively (Arzhanova et al., 2020).

During the pandemic period, consumers began to behave more frugal with curfew restrictions (Herstatt & Tiwari, 2020). As a result of this, they developed a self-sufficient attitude that dyes the furniture in their homes, makes their bread, takes care of themselves at home. It is important that with this rapid change in the behavior of consumers, some of their behaviors can turn into permanent habits after a certain period. Because individuals who realize that they are self-sufficient will prefer to save instead of buying. This situation can create a threat for brands (Kayabaşı, 2020). Another consumer behavior expected to increase after the pandemic is online purchasing behavior. According to the research conducted by KPMG, with the new consumer models of the pandemic period, consumer models have emerged who are less confident, thriftier due to economic difficulties, more selective in purchasing decisions, and more confident online shopping than before by using online platforms (KPMG, 2020).

One of the strategies, mostly used by companies at the Covid-19 pandemic is combined real-time marketing and content marketing. Although these strategies are frequently used, the effects of these strategies on consumer behavior during the pandemic period are unknown. Therefore, the effects of the combination of real-time marketing and content marketing strategies on consumer behavior were examined in the Covid-19 pandemic.

Real-Time Marketing

Real-time marketing is a marketing strategy that strengthens effective communication with the target audience, which is presented by the companies simultaneously by collecting the issues on the same agenda with the consumers, through digital channels (Scott, 2010). In other words, "real-time marketing is systematic, multi-channel engagement, using more than one channel to communicate with the customer, based upon real-time insights" (GolinHarris, 2013). Real-time marketing is an instant marketing study that is applied by producing content on social media platforms over an event that occurs in the flow of time. An effective real-time marketing is not a work that can be done spontaneously without relying on any thought (Clow & Baack, 2016). The main goal of real-time marketing is determined to attract the attention of many users by using the intensity of talking about the topic that constitutes the agenda and to achieve success by getting the chance to interact in this way (Garner, 2013; Scott, 2010).

Real-time Marketing is used by brands for aligning their social media messages with timely moments that are highly discussed in social media. In this way, brands aim to make a meaningful connection and obtain positive consumer responses (Mazerant et al., 2021). Considering the sensitivity of people to current events, these strategic campaigns of companies allow frequent discussions among individuals and increase brand reputation. Popular real-time marketing campaigns create a snowball effect on consumers, attract attention, and thus be frequently mentioned on social media platforms. This can provide a return as a great success for the brand. However, the brand must be careful when implementing real-time marketing campaigns. Giving importance to some elements to be able to make successful campaigns will help the brand keep its communication strong. The most important factor that the brand should pay attention to is giving the right message at the right time. In real-time marketing to the effect of digitalization, the contents are consumed in a short time. For this reason, the mistakes can be noticed by the target audience instantly. To avoid mistakes, brands should carefully select the contents of their real-time marketing campaigns and presented them to the impression of the target audience with great care (Lieb, 2013).

Real-time marketing strategies are sensitive to current events (Bengtsson, & Håkansson, 2015). For this reason, the preparation of the content and its presentation to the target audience should be fast. Accordingly, the contents should provide an accurate message about current events. In addition, the consumer should be contacted before the contents are forgotten. Real-time marketing campaigns are aware of the power individuals have in social media platforms (Bolle, 2015). That's why they create content for consumers who are in constant communication with each other. Thus, real-time marketing campaigns prepared by brands quickly become known by many people. As a result, the activities that reach large masses have a positive effect contributing to the awareness of the brand. Preparing the real-time marketing strategies to be applied with strong content will increase the interest of the consumer by triggering a sense of curiosity, and thus, it will provide more interaction on social media platforms (Baran & Öymen, 2020).

The real-time marketing campaigns must take into account certain basic elements to keep communication with consumers strong, and to convey the desired message to the other party (Kallier-Tar & Wiid, 2021). All of the considerations in content marketing are also valid for real-time marketing campaigns. The reason for this is that real-time marketing campaigns are based on content. These elements can be summarized as the authenticity of the content, the correct target audience, and the right channels. On the other hand, in addition to these elements, there are other important points in creating effective content. These elements are divided into two as known topics and unknown issues while creating the content (Kerns, 2014). When a brand wants to produce content related to current events, it works regularly on this current subject to create content. Also, while preparing known events, attention is paid to the magnitude of these events. If an event is big and important, it is essential to work in a planned way. So that a list is followed to create content. These lists contain steps where topics related to daily life are presented as content (Kerns, 2014). With unknown events, the brand can have the chance to prove itself to the target audience. Studies on this subject can instantly increase the awareness of the brand. It is important to be prepared for the instant events expected to occur. Content to be prepared for sudden developed major agenda topics will result in greater opportunities (Holliman & Rowley, 2014). One should also be prepared for small events that are expected to occur. These events include social media interactions and all the events that surprise brands. To respond to such events, the brand should follow the agenda daily.

In addition to all these, Miller listed the points that companies should pay attention to produce real-time marketing campaigns effectively and efficiently (Miller, 2013; Oliver, 1998):

- Brands should communicate with their point of view.
- Brands should have planned content to be on the agenda.
- Rapid response research that emphasis on communication between consumers should be carried out.
- Rapid response research should be based on observation and listening.
- Brands must be fast to be aware of current issues.
- Strong associations should be established media agencies and platforms that will provide consumers with the opportunity to come together in digital environments.
- The idea that every current event has an end must be adopted. Therefore, real-time marketing campaigns should be planned to be completed with a satisfactory end.
- The budget for the implementation to be carried out should be adjusted in a balanced way and spread over the whole process.

Advantages and Disadvantages of Real-Time Marketing

Brands have the opportunity to communicate instantly and effectively with consumers through real-time marketing campaigns. Brands can apply these campaigns within seconds with the effect of developing technology. However, the success or failure of the application has great consequences for brands. Efficient application of real-time marketing campaigns and a good effect on the target audience provides profit for the brand. Lieb lists these achievements as follows (Lieb, 2013; Scott, 2011):

- The brand communicates instantly and effectively with consumers through real-time marketing campaigns. As a result, brand-consumer interaction increases and the brand creates good feelings on the consumer.

- Effective delivery of the right message to the right audience at the right time provides interactive communication with the consumer. The brand enables the consumer to take the participant role by using personalized messages.
- The brand implements real-time marketing campaigns in harmony with current events. Thus, it uses trend contents by brand values and gains the sympathy of the target audience.
- Thanks to the content created in line with current events, it enables the brand to be talked about more among consumers. In this way, it increases the awareness of the brand.
- Successful real-time marketing campaigns of the brand can increase the brand prestige by attracting the attention of the consumer.

While successful real-time marketing campaigns have positive results on behalf of the brand, unsuccessful campaigns can have bad results for the brand. However, this failure can have a huge impact on the brand, which is difficult to change. These negative effects are as follows (Kerns, 2014; Reece, 2010):

- The failure of the real-time marketing application prepared by the brand collects negative reactions on social media platforms, thus consumers have a negative attitude towards the brand.
- The wrong message given to consumers at the right time can cause the brand's interaction on social platforms and loss of followers.
- Real-time marketing campaigns that can be carried out at the wrong time may appear inconsistent and lead to consumers' negative responses.
- Insincerity in real-time marketing campaigns can be noticed by consumers and cause a decrease in brand value.
- The brand can be hated by the consumer because it is using items and expressions that may contradict the social structure.
- The unsuccessful real-time marketing campaigns can be criticized by the person who does not like them.

These negative effects may damage permanently the awareness and prestige of the brand. For this reason, real-time marketing campaigns should be prepared with extreme care and necessary controls.

Content Marketing

The concept of content marketing is not limited to a single definition. There are many definitions of the concept of content marketing. Kotler defined content marketing; It is defined as a marketing technique where created content, including the creation, distribution, and support of content that is relevant to a clearly defined target audience, interesting and useful to this audience, aims to communicate with customers through two-way communication (Kotler et al., 2016). Another definition was made by Goldstein. According to Goldstein, content marketing is "marketing activities carried out to create content that is relevant and valuable to customers, attracting the attention of the target audience and gaining new customers and making sales as a result." (Sarıtaş, 2018).

The main purpose of digital content marketing is to create awareness among consumers. Brands use content marketing campaigns to attract the attention of the target audience, make their products and services attractive, gain a competitive advantage against competitors, and establish effective communication. In other words, content marketing aims to build trust in consumers by influencing the target audience

(Karkar, 2016). Another aim of content marketing is to determine the product that the consumer wants, to inform the advantages of products or services without putting any pressure on it and without confusing the consumer (Karkar, 2016). It is an undeniable fact that content marketing, which has many different types, is seen as an important tool for companies to reach consumers. Thanks to content marketing, consumers have the opportunity to get information about the product, as well as follow the developments within the product and the brand. Content marketing can create value for the brand when presented to the consumer, meet the information needs, and provide content (Holliman & Rowley, 2014). A content marketing campaign is a marketing tool that does not involve purchasing pressure, and it can also provide brand loyalty with the opportunity to communicate effectively with them (Ryan & Jones, 2009). Brands use two methods when applying to content marketing campaigns to create brand loyalty. One of them is providing information that contains valuable elements to consumers to create trust in the brand. Another is creating elements that entertain the customer instantly (Lieb, 2011). Studies conducted with consumers show that the impact of both methods of content marketing has a greater impact on customers than other traditional marketing channels (Świeczak, 2012).

Companies and brands use lots of marketing tools and channels to reach target customers. Even though many marketing tools are actively used by companies, consumers are feeling overwhelmed with advertisements. For this reason, consumers have started to ignore marketing elements. Nowadays content marketing is frequently used to prevent brand ignore by consumers. Content marketing is used as an important strategy for brands to provide interesting, informative, and helpful content by awakening the sense of curiosity in the consumer (Kahraman, 2013). The purposes of content marketing are briefly as follows:

- To increase brand awareness and awareness.
- Creating positive value for the consumer.
- Increasing communication by providing trust between consumers and the brand.
- Gaining new customers by attracting the attention of the target audience.
- Creating needs for the products or services.
- Increasing the customer loyalty to the brand.

Companies and brands must follow certain steps when preparing content marketing to benefit from the increasing competition. These steps are listed below (Kotler et al., 2016):

1. Determination of purpose.
2. Determination of the target audience.
3. Determining the appropriate content.
4. Creation of the specified content.
5. Presenting the created content to the target audience.
6. Strengthening the content.
7. Evaluation of content marketing.
8. The process of improving content marketing.

Advantages and Disadvantages of Content Marketing

Content marketing enables interaction with the target customer audience. Sales increase as a result of effective communication with the customer base. However, content marketing campaigns can have some difficulties (Rowley, 2008). Some examples are finding good content ideas and taking the time to create content. The advantages of content marketing are given below (Ansari et al., 2019; Gunelius, 2011; Rowley, 2008):

- Content marketing builds brand awareness, trust, and loyalty. People who consume the content start to feel positive or negative feelings about the brand. Posting informative, well-researched content makes the company look authoritative and credible. The more trust the target audience has in the brand, the more likely they are to buy from the brand.
- By using content marketing instead of traditional advertising, the audience who avoids watching ads is reached.
- Content marketing campaigns have low costs. Unlike traditional advertisements, there are no product placement fees. Every company can run content marketing campaigns.
- Quality content increases web traffic by attracting the target audience to the brand's social media account and website. Brands can persuade customers who come to their site to sign up for them or make a purchase.
- Good content is also important to the success of many other marketing tactics such as search engine optimization, social media, and public relations. In short, content marketing supports other marketing tactics.

The disadvantages of content marketing are listed below (Gunelius, 2011; Lieb, 2012; Papagiannis, 2020; Poradova, 2020):

- Content marketing can be a long process. There is normally a period of trial and error to discover what works best before seeing results. In short, the effect of content marketing campaigns is not instant.
- Content marketing can be time-consuming. It is necessary to create content, publish it in marketing channels and analyze its impact. For these processes, it is necessary to benefit from external resources or to improve the capabilities within the company.
- It can be difficult to find ideas for effective new topics and formats. As you continue your content marketing campaigns, it will be easier to find new content. It will also be able to analyze the impact of previous content marketing campaigns.
- It is relatively easy to measure the impact of content marketing campaigns on web traffic and online conversions. However, it is more difficult to determine the impact of content on brand reputation, awareness, and loyalty.

Consumer Emotions

Emotion is a state of mental readiness that results from cognitive evaluations of events or thoughts (Bagozzi et al., 1999). In other words, a general state of arousal that people interpret through a cognitive evaluation process is defined as an emotion (Schachter & Singer, 1962). Emotions, which are a result of cognitive evaluation, differ according to the situation and the environment of the individual. In addition, emotions can result in certain actions such as behavior (Nyer, 1997). Therefore, emotions have an important place in marketing literature that studies consumer behavior.

Emotions can occur as a result of a consumption experience (Richins, 1997). At the same time, emotions can affect consumers' attitudes, product evaluations, judgments, and satisfaction (Lau-Gesk & Meyers-Levy, 2009). Especially in the context of marketing, the correct identification of emotions is extremely important in terms of establishing an effective relationship with the consumer. In the marketing literature, there are many studies emphasizing that certain emotions should be highlighted in marketing communication activities and the emotional bond between brands and consumers should be strengthened (Tosun et. al., 2019). Consumer emotions have a strong influence on the actions and behavior of individuals. They appear in consumers' behavior in the decision-making process through brand, advertising, or campaign-related stimuli. Especially in consumer behavior researches, emotional responses have been studied for understanding the impact of emotions on consumer behavior (Holbrook & Hirschman, 1982; Kujur & Singh, 2018).

Richins (1997) investigated the emotions related to the consumption of products in emotion studies in consumer behavior and identified 15 emotions, which he called the consumer emotion set. These emotions are anger, discontent, worry, sadness, fear, shame, envy, loneliness, romantic love, peacefulness, contentment, optimism, joy, excitement, and surprise. Richins (1997) stated that people most often experience these emotions during consumption. In other consumer emotion studies in the literature, it has been observed that many authors include both positive and negative emotions in their studies (Berkowitz, 2000; Diener 1999; Escadas et. al., 2019; Ruiz-Mafe et al., 2018). These researches show not only positive emotions but also negative emotions were showed up as the result of the reaction to the consumption experience. For example, negative word of mouth, avoidance of ads or products, revenge from brands are the result of negative emotions (Khatoon & Rehman, 2021). In this study, the effects of both positive and negative emotions created by real-time content marketing campaigns on consumer behavior during the Covid-19 period were investigated in order to contribute to the literature.

Consumer Behavior

A large part of human life is spent on consumption. The basis of the concept of consumption is the consumer. The consumer is defined as the people who decide to buy marketing components in line with the needs and wishes of their personal and close environment, or who have the potential to buy (Karabulut, 1989). Consumer behavior is defined as the processes by which individuals or groups select, buy, use or dispose of products, services, ideas, or experiences to satisfy needs and desires (Solomon et al., 2012). The needs and wants of each consumer are different from each other. Consumers' wants and needs are affected by demographic, psychological, social, and cultural differences. Therefore, consumer behavior also shows different characteristics.

Characteristics of Consumer Behavior

Consumers differ from each other with many features such as personal differences. Every consumer has unique behaviors, preferences and purchasing decisions. Like the environment that changes every day, human decisions can change frequently. Therefore, environmental factors are reflected on people.

Environmental factors also affect the behavior of consumers to a great extent. Main consumer behavior characteristics (Wilkie, 1986):

- Consumer behavior is the whole of the conscious or unconscious behaviors that occur to meet the wishes and desires of the consumer.
- Consumer behavior is a motivated action/behavior and creates tension unless individuals satisfy their wants and desires.
- Consumer behavior is a dynamic process in which consumers examine the before and after of this purchasing behavior as well as the time when they will make the purchase.

There are different roles for each individual in consumer behavior. While a consumer can play roles such as buyer and user, he can also play roles such as initiator, influencer and decision maker (Kotler, 2000; Verma & Kapoor, 2003).

- Initiator role: it is the person who makes a purchase recommendation by determining that it does not meet the needs and wants of a person.
- User role: it is the person who uses the product or service obtained by paying a price.
- Buyer role: it is the person who pays the necessary price for the product or service.
- Decider role: it is defined as a financial power that makes the final choice of product and service.
- Influential role: a person who voluntarily or involuntarily influences a person's purchasing process with their behavior.

Consumer Behavior in Covid-19

Multiple factors are effective on consumer behavior such as purchasing decisions. Therefore, in order to understand consumer behavior, demographic, psychological, social, and cultural factors should be examined first (Gajjar, 2013). In addition to these factors, understanding the conditions of the period in which they live is also important for understanding consumer behavior.

Today, the changes caused by the Covid-19 pandemic have also affected consumer behavior. The concept of "making stock", which was needed in times of war but was forgotten later, gained value again with the Covid-19 pandemic period. In addition, the purchasing patterns of consumers changed as well as their purchasing priorities (Erkan, 2020). The reason for these can be shown as both the curfew restrictions and the fact that people start to spend more time in their homes due to isolation. The demand for products such as canned goods, disinfectants, masks, gloves, and cologne has increased. In addition to the demand for products, there have been changes in ordering patterns. Orders are placed online with the aim of reducing contact with people. In this context, it is predicted that the Covid-19 pandemic will affect consumer behavior, not only during its current period, but also after it (Hacıalioğlu & Sağlam, 2021).

Covid-19 has brought about changes in the preferences and habits of consumers around the world. Although consumer behavior in the pandemic differed partially according to regions or cultures, it basically changed in the same direction. People have started to use their homes as workplaces, classrooms, gyms, and entertainment venues. With the increase in the time spent at home, there has been an increase in the rate of viewing visual content at home (BBC, 2020; NielsenIQ, 2020). The screen time increased during the pandemic period (Colley et al., 2020). This situation has encouraged brands to be content-oriented and to do real-time marketing campaigns. Real-time content created within the scope of the

Covid-19 pandemic evokes positive or negative emotions in consumers against the campaign. With the influence of these emotions, consumer behavior is affected in different ways by real-time content marketing campaigns. The study aims to determine the factors affecting consumer behavior and their importance in order to prevent negative consumer behaviors.

CASE DESCRIPTION

The relationships between real-time marketing-consumer behavior and content marketing-consumer behavior have been investigated in many studies in the literature. Mazerant et al. (2021) examined the mediator role of craftsmanship, originality, and meaningfulness in the relationship between real-time marketing and engagement rate. Kallier (2017) examined the influence of real-time marketing campaigns of retailers on consumer purchase behavior. Willemsen et al. (2018) studied real-time marketing strategies on sharing behavior. Mathew and Soliman (2021) examined the effect of digital content marketing on travel and tourism consumer behavior. Hollebeek and Macky (2019) studied digital content marketing's role in fostering consumers. In general, real-time marketing and content marketing have been studied in different studies in the literature. In this study, real-time marketing and content marketing are considered as real-time content marketing. Accordingly, this study aims to examine the factors affecting negative consumer behavior in the Covid-19 pandemic within the framework of real-time content marketing and emotions. This aim of study distinguishes the study from its counterparts in the literature. In this regard, the data obtained from internet users that live in Turkey by using the survey method analyzed in the Covid-19 pandemic. As a result of the analyzes carried out, contributed to the literature and recommendations have been made to marketing practitioners. In light of this information, the authors proposed hypotheses and research model were given below.

Figure 1. Research model

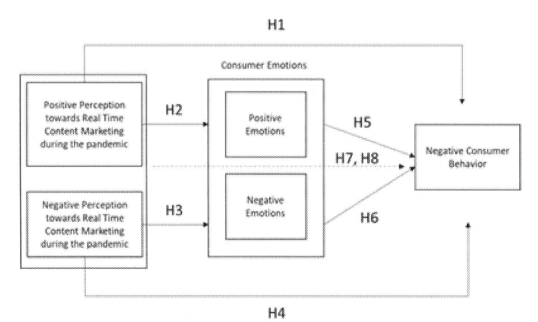

H1: There is a negative relationship between positive perception towards real-time content marketing and negative consumer behavior in the Covid-19 pandemic.

H2: There is a positive relationship between positive perception towards real-time content marketing and positive emotions in the Covid-19 pandemic.

H3: There is a positive relationship between negative perception towards real-time content marketing and negative consumer behavior in the Covid-19 pandemic.

H4: There is a positive relationship between negative perception towards real-time content marketing and negative emotions in the Covid-19 pandemic.

H5: There is a negative relationship between positive emotions and negative consumer behavior in the Covid-19 pandemic.

H6: There is a positive relationship between negative emotions and negative consumer behavior in the Covid-19 pandemic.

H7: Positive emotions mediate the relationship between positive perception towards real-time content marketing and positive emotions in the Covid-19 pandemic.

H8: Negative emotions mediate the relationship between negative perception towards real-time content marketing and positive emotions in the Covid-19 pandemic.

Sample Demographics and Questionnaire

The research questionnaire was answered by 319 volunteer participants who lived in Turkey. The study's sample selection method was chosen convenience sampling. The data collection period was from March to May 2020. The questionnaire includes 40 items of real-time content marketing perception scale, negative consumer behavior scale, and consumer emotions scale (Günaydın, 2019; Izard, 1997; Laros & Steenkamp, 2005; Müller & Christandl, 2019). The questionnaire consists of five parts. Demographic questions take part in the first part of the questionnaire. The second part has questions that measure participants' digital platform usage rate. Real-time content marketing perception scale item in the third part, consumer behavior scale in the fourth part, and consumer emotions scale in the fifth part of the questionnaire. A Five-point Likert-type scale was used in the research.

The analyzed data consisted of 168 females (52.7%), 142 males (44,5%), and 9 participants who do not want to indicate their gender (%2.8). It was observed that most participants (164) were in the 21-30 age range (51.4%). The participants' marital status was 206 single participants (64.6%) and 113 married participants (35,4%). The education level of participants showed 78.9% of the bachelor's and associate's degree levels, 16% of primary and secondary education levels, and 9.1% of master's and doctorate degrees. The majority of the participants' household income was 5000 TL and above (33.2%) and 1000 TL and below (29.8%) (Table 1).

Table 1. Demographic information

Gender	n	%
Female	168	52.7
Male	142	44.5
Unknown	9	2.8
Age		
20 and below	36	11.3
21-30	164	51.4
31-40	63	19.7
41-50	34	10.7
51 and above	22	6.9
Marital Status		
Married	113	35.4
Single	206	64.6
Education		
Primary and Secondary Education	51	16
Bachelor Degree and Associate's Degree	229	74.9
Master's Degree and Doctorate Degree	29	9.1
Household Income		
1000 TL and below	95	29.8
1000-2999 TL	68	21 3
3000-4999 TL	50	15.7
5000 TL and above	106	33.2

Digital Platforms Usage Information

Figure 2 shows participants' daily internet usage rate. According to Figure 2 majority of the participants (58%) use the internet more than four hours a day. 18,5% of participants use the internet between three-four hours. 16% of participants use the internet between two-three hours. Lastly, the minority of the participants (%7,5) use the internet for less than two hours. Figure 2 also shows which social media platform the participants use the most. According to Figure 2, Instagram is the most used (57,4%) social media platform by participants. Participants were asked do they follow brands on social media? According to answers majority of participants (57,4%) follow brands on social media. In addition, most of the participants (69,9%) answered no to the question of do you watch ads on digital platforms. According to this information, the participants avoid watching ads on digital platforms.

Figure 2. Digital platforms usage information

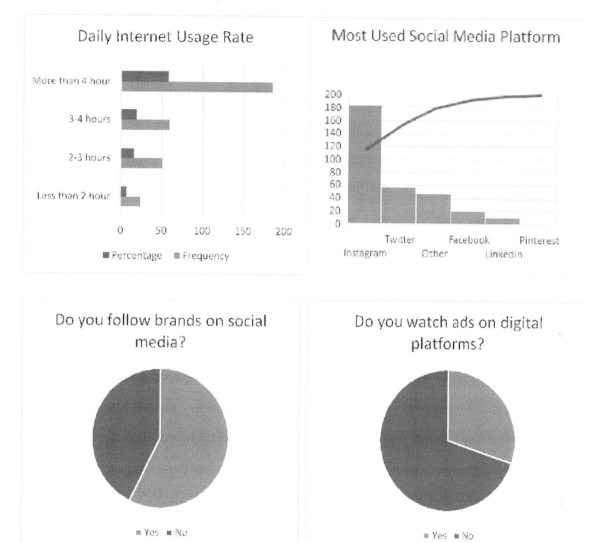

Descriptive Statistics

The data collected from participants were analyzed using the SPSS program. The frequency analysis was conducted to obtain descriptive statistics. According to Table 2 and Table 3, the participants stated that the real-time content marketing campaigns exploit the emotions of the people. In addition, they thought the real-time content marketing did not show the pandemic process in reality. According to the results, the participants said that they do not find real-time marketing sincere during the pandemic. Also, they stated that real-time content marketing does not give them a sense of happiness.

Table 2. Descriptive analysis results of positive perception towards real-time content marketing scale

Items	Mean	S.D.
I thought the content of real-time marketing campaigns exciting during the Covid-19 pandemic.	2,73	1,191
Real-time marketing campaigns in the Covid-19 pandemic aroused the feeling of happiness.	2,41	1,135
Real-time marketing campaigns in the Covid-19 pandemic were promising.	2,76	1,232
Real-time marketing campaigns in the Covid-19 pandemic were sincere.	2,49	1,221
Real-time marketing campaigns in the Covid-19 pandemic were motivating.	2,69	1,234

Table 3. Descriptive analysis results of negative perception towards real-time content marketing scale

Items	Mean	S.D.
The content of real-time marketing campaigns in the Covid-19 pandemic made me saddened.	2,81	1,339
Marketing campaigns have raised my concerns about the Covid-19 pandemic process.	2,89	1,342
Real-time marketing campaigns during the Covid-19 pandemic increased my fears by showing that bad things could happen to me and my loved ones during the pandemic.	2,88	1,358
People in real-time ads of the Covid-19 pandemic do not show the pandemic process as real.	3,48	1,317
I thought the Covid-19 pandemic real-time marketing campaigns disturbing.	2,96	1,341
Real-time ads exploit people's emotions during the Covid-19 pandemic.	3,45	1,295
I felt negative emotions about real-time marketing campaigns during the Covid-19 pandemic.	3,18	1,273

The descriptive analysis results of the negative consumer behavior scale are shown in Table 4. According to the results, the participants stated that they changed the channels to not watch the real-time marketing ads during the Covid-19 pandemic. Also, they decided to buy fewer products as a result of the real-time marketing advertisements. However, they state that they do not criticize the brand on social media. At the same time, the participants said that their attitude towards the brand is not adversely affected as a result of real-time marketing campaigns.

Table 4. Descriptive analysis results on the negative consumer behavior scale

Items	Mean	S.D.
Real-time marketing campaigns negatively affected my attitude to the brand during the Covid-19 pandemic.	2,67	1,239
Real-time marketing campaigns reduced my interest in the brand during the Covid-19 pandemic.	2,73	1,277
Real-time marketing campaigns negatively affected my purchasing decision during the Covid-19 pandemic.	2,74	1,275
I criticized real-time marketing campaigns about the Covid-19 pandemic on social media.	2,41	1,361
When I saw negative ads during the Covid-19 pandemic, I changed the channel.	3,37	1,397
Sad ads during the Covid-19 pandemic period reduced my trust in the brand.	2,86	1,320
Sad ads during the Covid-19 pandemic period negatively affected my purchase of that product.	2,92	1,326
When I saw negative ads during the Covid-19 pandemic, I stopped following the brand on social platforms.	2,77	1,397
I stopped recommending the brand to people around me as a result of negative real-time ads during the Covid-19 pandemic.	2,85	1,305
Real-time ads made me decide to buy fewer products and services.	3,01	1,315

The descriptive analysis results of the positive and negative consumer emotions scales are shown in Table 5 and Table 6. According to the results, the participants stated that the advertisements made during the pandemic period increased their anxiety and caused them to feel sadness. In addition, the participants said that the advertisements carried out during the pandemic period are not fun and do not cause them to feel peace about the process.

Table 5. Descriptive analysis results of negative consumer emotions scale

Items	Mean	S.D.
Real-time campaigns made during the Covid-19 pandemic made me fear this process.	2,91	1,220
Real-time campaigns made during the Covid-19 pandemic made me worry about this process.	3,05	1,242
Real-time campaigns during the Covid-19 pandemic made me angry about this process.	2,91	1,313
Real-time campaigns made during the Covid-19 pandemic made me sad about this process.	3,07	1,278
Real-time campaigns during the Covid-19 pandemic made me hate this process.	2,81	1,308

Table 6. Descriptive analysis results of positive consumer emotions scale

Items	Mean	S.D.
Real-time campaigns made during the Covid-19 pandemic provided me peace of mind about this process.	2,20	1,089
Real-time campaigns made during the Covid-19 pandemic gave me hope about this process.	2,43	1,125
Real-time campaigns made during the Covid-19 pandemic made me excited about this process.	2,22	1,070
Real-time campaigns made during the Covid-19 pandemic made me feel entertain about this process.	2,13	1,170

Measurement Model

The data collected from participants were analyzed using the SPSS 21 and AMOS 23. Confirmatory factor analysis (CFA) and reliability analysis were conducted to test the research model and verify the scales. The comparative fit index (CFI), the chi-squared statistic divided by the degrees of freedom (CMIN/df), the standardized root mean square residual (SRMR), the goodness of fit (GFI), and the adjusted goodness of fit index (AGFI) were used as fit statistics. The results of the analysis (CFI: 0.941; CMIN/df: 2.190; SRMR: 0.055; GFI: 0.876; AGFI: 0.844; RMSEA: 0.061) indicates that the data are suitable for the model.

Convergent validity and discriminant validity were conducted for testing constructs and variables. Composite reliability (CR) and average variance extracted (AVE) values were used for testing convergent validity and Fornell and Larcker's (1981) approach was used for testing discriminant validity.

Table 7. Convergent validity results

Items	Factor Loading	Cronbach's α	CR	AVE
Positive Perception of RTCM				
RTCM2	,865	0,91	0,91	0,66
RTCM3	,854			
RTCM5	,805			
RTCM4	,789			
RTCM1	,775			
Negative Perception of RTCM				
RTCM8	,794	0,80	0,80	0,57
RTCM7	,777			
RTCM6	,766			
Positive Emotions				
PE4	,839	0,88	0,88	0,66
PE1	,838			
PE3	,827			
PE2	,807			
Negative Emotions				
NE4	,806	0,89	0,89	0,62
NE5	,756			
NE2	,748			
NE3	,745			
NE1	,685			
Negative Consumer Behavior				
CB7	,822	0,91	0,91	0,56
CB6	,794			
CB8	,758			
CB9	,728			
CB1	,708			
CB2	,701			
CB5	,693			
CB3	,693			
KMO: 0,881 Bartlett's: 5335,092 df: 300 Sig.: 0,000)				

Firstly, exploratory factor analysis was conducted. As a result of this analysis, three items of the negative consumer behavior scale and two items of negative real-time content marketing scale were under the 0,60 limit value so that excluded. According to the results presented in Table 7, all factor loadings (FL>0.60). Cronbach's alpha values (Cronbach's alpha>0.70), CR values (CR>0.70) and AVE values (AVE>0.50) exceed the suggested values (Sekaran & Bougie, 2011; Taber, 2018). Thus, the measurement model presented adequate levels of reliability and convergent validity.

Table 8. Discriminant validity results

Factor	Mean	SD	Skew.	Kurt.	1	2	3	4	5
PRTCM	2,616	1,026	0,083	-0,723	**0,814**				
NRTCM	2,861	1,136	0,135	-0,735	-0,114	**0,756**			
PEM	2,243	0,959	0,468	-0,312	0,531	-0,055	**0,810**		
NEM	2,949	1,060	0,019	-0,474	-0,134	0,644	-0,049	**0,786**	
NCB	2,864	1,030	0,075	-0,635	-0,299	0,543	-0,044	0,650	**0,748**

Table 8 shows that the square roots of the AVE values were greater than the corresponding construct correlations; hence, the measurement model's results met the required criteria for discriminant validity (Fornell & Larcker, 1981). Besides, descriptive statistics were given in the previous frame. All variables' mean values were 2.243-2.949; standard deviation values were 0.959-1.139. Skewness and kurtosis values of all variables ranged between -1 and +1. Thus, normality was achieved (Tabachnick & Fidell, 2012).

Results

Structural model and hypothesis testing

According to the hypotheses testing results, positive perception towards real-time content marketing positively affects consumer positive emotions (β:0,531***) and negatively affects negative consumer behavior (β:-0,319***). Negative perception towards real-time content marketing positively affects consumer negative emotions (β:0,644***) and negative consumer behavior (β:0,228**). Both positive (β:0,145*) and negative emotions (β:0,482**) of consumers positively affect negative consumer behavior. Table 9 shows the proposed structural model fit indices are good that's under the suggested values (Hu and Bentler, 1999). All paths are significant (p<0.05). Thus, While H1, H2, H3, H4, and H6 hypotheses are supported.

Table 9. Path results

Hypothesis	From -> To		Standardized Estimate	Estimate	S.E.	C.R.	P	Result
H1	PRTCM	NCB	-0,319	-0,316	0,063	-5,004	***	Supported
H2	PRTCM	PE	0,531	0,496	0,061	8,185	***	Supported
H3	NRTCM	NE	0,644	0,758	0,084	9,052	***	Supported
H4	NRTCM	NCB	0,228	0,226	0,075	2,999	0,003	Supported
H5	PE	NCB	0,145	0,154	0,065	2,373	0,018	Not Supported
H6	NE	NCB	0,482	0,407	0,064	6,367	***	Supported
Model Fit Indices: CFI:0.926; CMIN/df:2.444; SRMR:0.048; GFI:0.859; AGFI:0.827; RMSEA: 0.073									

Testing Mediation Effects

Positive emotions were used as a mediator variable in the relationship between positive real-time content marketing and negative consumer behavior. Negative emotions were used as a mediator variable in the relationship between negative real-time content marketing and negative consumer behavior. For testing the mediation effects of emotions, two models were created. Model 1 includes all research variables except emotions and Model 2 includes all research variables. Table 10 shows that comparing standardized estimates values of Model 1 and Model 2. The paths of both models were significant (*p < .05). Positive emotions were used as a mediator variable in the relationship between positive real-time content marketing and negative consumer behavior. Negative emotions were used as a mediator variable in the relationship between negative real-time content marketing and negative consumer behavior. The standardized estimate value of the path that has positive emotions as a mediator increased and significance does not change (β: -0,261***; β': -0,319***). Conversely, the standardized estimate value and significance of the path that has negative emotions as a mediator decreased (β:0,535***; β':0,228**). While these results show negative emotions have a partial mediator role as positive emotions have not a mediator role (Gunzler et al., 2013). Therefore, H7 is not supported while H8 is partially supported.

Table 10. Mediation analysis

Hypothesis	Mediating Hypotheses Paths	Model 1 (Direct Relationships) Std. Estimate	Model 2 (Indirect Relationships) Std. Estimate	Result
H7	PRTCM->PE->NCB	-0.261***	-0.319***	Not Supported
H8	NRTCM->NE->NCB	0.535***	0.228**	Partial Supported

DISCUSSION AND CONCLUSION

With the worldwide danger of Covid-19 and curfews, people have started to spend more time at home. The increase in internet usage and TV watching time has provided a suitable advertising environment for brands. Brands that want to create social awareness, increase brand awareness, and their sales were also using tools such as the internet, television, etc. have taken advantage of them during the pandemic period. Brands aim to reveal positive consumer behavior by arousing various emotions in consumers with pandemic content real-time marketing activities. However, real-time content marketing campaigns of brands in some cases arouse negative emotions in consumers. As a result of negative emotions, consumers tend to show negative consumer behavior. One of the important points here is how the real-time content marketing campaign is perceived.

As a result of the analyzes performed within the scope of the study, it was determined that there is a significant and strong relationship between real-time content marketing which is perceived as positive, and positive emotions (β:0.531***). Likewise, there is a significant and strong relationship between perceived negative real-time content marketing and negative emotions (β:0.644***). These findings support other studies in the literature (Kee & Yazdanifard, 2015; Vinerean, 2017; Willemsen et al., 2018).

When negative consumer behavior and perceived positive and negative real-time content marketing relationships are examined, perceived positive real-time content marketing affects negative consumer behavior in the opposite direction (β:-0.319***), while perceived negative real-time content marketing affects negative consumer behavior positively (β:0.228**). These results parallel to literature (Chea & Luo 2008; Kuo & Wu, 2012; Verhagen & van Dolen 2011). When the relations between emotions and consumer behavior are examined, contrary to expectations, it is seen that positive emotions affect negative consumer behavior positively (β:0.145*). This finding is different from the findings of other studies in the literature (Andani & Wahyono, 2018; Duong & Khuong, 2019). On the other hand, negative emotions affect negative consumer behavior positively and quite strongly as expected (β:0,644***) (Huang & Hsieh, 2011; Koshkaki & Solhi, 2016). The mediating effect of emotions was also investigated in the study. It has been determined that negative emotions act as a mediator between perceived negative real-time content marketing and negative consumer behavior. This finding is similar to the studies in the literature (Cachero-Martínez & Vázquez-Casielles, 2021; Sherman et al., 1997).

As a result, the findings of the study in general are similar to the results of other studies in the literature. The result, which was different from the expected, was that positive emotions in consumers could also have a negative effect on consumer behavior. The excessive identification of real-time content marketing campaigns with the brand during the pandemic period creates a danger. Consumers may be inclined to show negative consumer behavior because brands remind of the disease and pandemic period. That's why real-time content marketing campaigns should be run without damaging brand positioning.

CURRENT CHALLENGES FACING THE ORGANIZATION

Today, most companies have similar technologies, due to globalization and technological developments. In this way, these companies can easily reach anywhere in the world at any time and make transactions. This situation makes work processes easier but also increases competition. As a result of this companies have started to attach importance to the marketing power that will use that technology effectively and make a difference, rather than reaching the technology. Thus, companies that want to create long-lasting brand loyalty, started to use digital marketing resources effectively and efficiently as a competitive factor. In the struggle of brands to differentiate, the combination of real-time marketing and content marketing usage has an important role. On the other hand, Covid-19 has spread all over the world from China in 2019. All countries around the world have been struggling with the Covid-19 virus. Also, the practice of social distancing and lockdown in the Covid-19 pandemic changed consumer behavior. Consumers have been spending more time at homes. As a result, there was an increase in internet usage. The consequences driven by the Covid-19 pandemic led to using a combination of real-time marketing and content marketing campaigns during the Covid-19 pandemic by companies. This combination has become the only way for brands to interact with consumers.

In this case, results show perceptions of real-time content marketing affect consumer behavior. So positive perceptions of real-time content marketing negatively and negative perceptions of real-time content marketing positively affect negative consumer behavior. In addition, this combination causes positive emotions when real-time content marketing perceived is positively, and negative emotions when real-time content marketing is perceived negatively. This finding is important because these research results show both negative and positive consumer emotions affect negative consumer behavior. Also, negative emotions have a mediator role in the relationship between negative perceptions of real-time content marketing and negative consumer behavior. In the light of these results, real-time content marketing campaigns that try to affect consumers' emotions may fail. Because consumers may don't believe that these campaigns are sincere. As a result of this, even if consumers have positive emotions, they do not show positive consumer behavior. At this point, companies face some difficulties.

SOLUTIONS AND RECOMMENDATIONS

Real-time content marketing is an effective strategy that enables brands to reach the target audience and potential customers. Brands use an existing and up-to-date topic on the agenda as a tool in real-time content marketing. Real-time content marketing is a digital communication strategy that usually does not have strict rules. However, it changes depending on the tool to be used and the content. The right time and right message are the most important factors for effective real-time marketing practice. In addition, real-time marketing has great importance for brands to evaluate the compatibility of the agenda for themselves and their target consumers. Brands should know their target consumers and followers well while using the agenda and creating their content. In addition, the interests, desires, and behaviors of the followers should be compatible with the content prepared by the brands. Brands that find the right agenda for them and present it to the target consumers and followers with the right content in real-time. In this way, they can find great opportunities to interact with users. However, improperly prepared content can create negative feelings in consumers. In such a situation, customers who feel negative about the real-time content marketing campaign will move away from the brand. With the effect of the Covid-19 pandemic, real-time content marketing campaigns had to struggle with challenges. Based on the case analysis in this chapter, some suggestions will be made to turn the difficulties faced by companies in their favor. In this direction, suggestions developed based on research findings are presented below:

- As a result of the analysis, it was found that consumers avoid watching advertisements. In addition, it is observed that the attention of the target consumers is rapidly lost in the brands' real-time content marketing campaigns. In light of this information, first of all, companies or brands might be beneficial to make improvements to regain consumer interest by making concise campaigns without overwhelming the consumers with advertisements and marketing campaigns.
- Survey results show that real-time content marketing campaigns applied during the pandemic period have negative effects on consumer perception. As a result, the extraordinary psychological state of the consumer should be taken into account while preparing real-time content advertisements.
- The fact that companies or brands stay away from activities that creating negative emotions on consumers might contribute to a more positive consumer attitude.
- Companies or brands can provide positive support to consumers overwhelmed by the global Covid-19 pandemic by offering items that can be a source of entertainment.
- Companies or brands should reduce some costs in marketing campaigns and identify areas where consumers are more effective. Thus, it can communicate more effectively with its target audience.
- Companies or brands should be more aware of the compatibility of content and real-time event.
- Companies or brands should create real-time content not only for their own needs but also for customer needs.

- Companies or brands shouldn't forget that the real-time content campaigns related to negative events might provoke consumers' emotions. These emotions may negatively affect consumer behavior.
- Companies or brands should share the real-time content that adds value for them.

REFERENCES

Andani, K., & Wahyono, W. (2018). Influence of Sales Promotion, Hedonic Shopping Motivation and Fashion Involvement Toward Impulse Buying through a Positive Emotion. *Management Analysis Journal*, 7(4), 448–457. doi:10.15294/maj.v7i4.24105

Ansari, S., Ansari, G., Ghori, M. U., & Kazi, A. G. (2019). Impact of brand awareness and social media content marketing on consumer purchase decision. *Journal of Public Value and Administrative Insight*, 2(2), 5–10. doi:10.31580/jpvai.v2i2.896

Arzhanova, K. A., Beregovskaya, T. A., & Silina, S. A. (2020). The impact of the Covid-19 pandemic on consumer behavior and companies' internet communication strategies. *Proceedings of the Research Technologies of Pandemic Coronavirus Impact (RTCOV 2020)*, 50–57. 10.2991/assehr.k.201105.010

Bagozzi, R. P., Gopinath, M., & Nyer, P. U. (1999). The role of emotions in marketing. *Journal of the Academy of Marketing Science*, 27(2), 184–206. doi:10.1177/0092070399272005

Bala, M., & Verma, D. (2018). A Critical Review of Digital Marketing. *International Journal of Management. IT & Engineering*, 8(10), 321–339.

Baltes, L. P. (2015). Content marketing-the fundamental tool of digital marketing. *Bulletin of the Transilvania University of Brasov. Economic Sciences, Series V*, 8(2), 111.

Baran, H., & Öymen, G. (2020). Gerçek zamanlı pazarlamanın markalar üzerindeki rolü "Game of Thrones" örneği. *Uluslararası Halkla İlişkiler ve Reklam Çalışmaları Dergisi*, 3(1), 80–107.

BBC. (2020). *Koronavirüs salgını tüketici alışkanlıklarını nasıl değiştiriyor?* Retrieved from https://www.bbc.com/turkce/haberler-dunya-52448919

Bolle, G. (2015). Digital content and real time marketing: Strategic challenges for the globalised football brands. In S. Chadwick, N. Chanavat, & M. Desbordes (Eds.), *Routledge Handbook of Sports Marketing* (pp. 315–330). Routledge.

Cachero-Martínez, S., & Vázquez-Casielles, R. (2021). Building consumer loyalty through e-shopping experiences: The mediating role of emotions. *Journal of Retailing and Consumer Services*, 60, 102481. doi:10.1016/j.jretconser.2021.102481

Chaffey, D., & Smith, P. R. (2017). *Digital marketing excellence: planning, optimizing, and integrating online marketing*. Taylor & Francis. doi:10.4324/9781315640341

Chea, S., & Luo, M. M. (2008). Post-adoption behaviors of e-service customers: The interplay of cognition and emotion. *International Journal of Electronic Commerce, 12*(3), 29–56. doi:10.2753/JEC1086-4415120303

Clow, K. E., & Baack, D. (2016). *Integrated Advertising, Promotion and Marketing Communications* (7th ed.). Education Limited.

Colley, R. C., Bushnik, T., & Langlois, K. (2020). Exercise and screen time during the COVID-19 pandemic. *Health Reports, 31*(6), 3–11. PMID:32672923

Czaja, S. J., & Lee, C. C. (2007). The impact of aging on access to technology. *Universal Access in the Information Society, 5*(4), 341–349. doi:10.100710209-006-0060-x

Deloitte. (2020). *Predicting the post-pandemic recovery.* Deloitte Economic-Insights. https://www2.deloitte.com/ca/en/pages/about-deloitte/articles/covid-dashboard.html

Duong, P. L., & Khuong, M. N. (2019). The Effect of In-Store Marketing on Tourists' Positive Emotion and Impulse Buying Behavior–An Empirical Study in Ho Chi Minh City, Vietnam. *International Journal of Trade. Economics and Finance, 10*(5), 119–125.

Erkan, İ. (2020). Consumers' perceptions of unity solidarity and motivation themed advertisements published in the Covid-19 period. *Gaziantep University Journal of Social Sciences, 2020*(Special Issue), 585–600. doi:10.21547/jss.788085

Escadas, M., Jalali, M. S., & Farhangmehr, M. (2019). Why bad feelings predict good behaviours: The role of positive and negative anticipated emotions on consumer ethical decision making. *Business Ethics (Oxford, England), 28*(4), 529–545. doi:10.1111/beer.12237

Fornell, C., & Larcker, D. F. (1981). Evaluating structural equation models with unobservable variables and measurement error. *JMR, Journal of Marketing Research, 18*(1), 39–50. doi:10.1177/002224378101800104

Gajjar, N. B. (2013). Factors affecting consumer behavior. *International Journal of Research in Humanities and Social Sciences, 1*(2), 10–15.

Garner, R. (2013). *Seacrh and Social: The Definitive Guide to Real-Time Content Marketing.* John WileySons.

GolinHarris. (2013). *Research: The Impact of Real-Time Marketing.* http://www.golinharris.com/#!/insights/real-timemarketing-research

Günaydın, M. (2019). *Gerçek zamanlı reklamların tüketici davranışlarına etkisi: Sosyal medya üzerine bir araştırma* [Doctoral dissertation]. Marmara University, Istanbul, Turkey.

Gunelius, S. (2011). *Content marketing for dummies.* John Wiley & Sons.

Gunzler, D., Chen, T., Wu, P., & Zhang, H. (2013). Introduction to mediation analysis with structural equation modeling. *Shanghai Jingshen Yixue, 25*(6), 390. PMID:24991183

Habes, M., Alghizzawi, M., Ali, S., Salih Alnaser, A., & Salloum, S. A. (2020). The relation among marketing ads, via digital media and mitigate (COVID-19) pandemic in Jordan. *International Journal of Advanced Science and Technology, 29*(7), 12326–12348.

Hacıalioğlu, A. B., & Sağlam, M. (2021). Covid-19 pandemi sürecinde tüketici davranışları ve e-ticaretteki değişimler. *Medya ve Kültürel Çalışmalar Dergisi, 3*(1), 16–29.

Hakanson, D., & Bengtsson, T. (2015). Real-Time Marketing Effects on Brands in Social Media. Halmstad University, International Marketing Program. Sweden: Halmstad University.

Herstatt, C., & Tiwari, R. (2020). Opportunities of frugality in the post-corona era. *International Journal of Technology Management, 83*(1-3), 15–33. doi:10.1504/IJTM.2020.109276

Hollebeek, L. D., & Macky, K. (2019). Digital content marketing's role in fostering consumer engagement, trust, and value: Framework, fundamental propositions, and implications. *Journal of Interactive Marketing, 45*, 27–41. doi:10.1016/j.intmar.2018.07.003

Holliman, G., & Rowley, J. (2014). Business to business digital content marketing: Marketers' perceptions of best practice. *Journal of Research in Interactive Marketing, 8*(4), 269–393. doi:10.1108/JRIM-02-2014-0013

Hu, L. T., & Bentler, P. M. (1999). Cutoff criteria for fit indexes in covariance structure analysis: Conventional criteria versus new alternatives. *Structural Equation Modeling, 6*(1), 1–55. doi:10.1080/10705519909540118

Huang, L. Y., & Hsieh, Y. (2011). What drives consumer impulse buying? Evidence from a retail setting in Taiwan. *Journal of International Management Studies, 6*(1), 1–8.

Izard, C. E. (1997). Emotions and facial expressions: A perspective from Differential Emotions Theory. In J. A. Russell & J. M. Fernández-Dols (Eds.), Studies in emotion and social interaction, 2nd series. The psychology of facial expression (pp. 57-77). Cambridge University Press. doi:10.1017/CBO9780511659911.005

Kaczmarek, T., Perez, K., Demir, E., & Zaremba, A. (2021). How to survive a pandemic: The corporate resiliency of travel and leisure companies to the COVID-19 outbreak. *Tourism Management, 84*, 104281. doi:10.1016/j.tourman.2020.104281

Kahraman, M. (2013). *Sosyal Medya 101 2.0 – Pazarlamacılar İçin Sosyal Medyaya Giriş*. MediaCat.

Kallier, S. M. (2017). The influence of real-time marketing campaigns of retailers on consumer purchase behavior. *International Review of Management and Marketing, 7*(3).

Kallier-Tar, S. M., & Wiid, J. A. (2021). Consumer perceptions of real-time marketing used in campaigns for retail businesses. *International Journal of Research in Business and Social Science, 10*(2), 86–105.

Karabulut, M. (1989). Tüketici Davranışı. İÜ İşletme İktisadi Enstitüsü.

Karkar, A. (2016). Değer ve güven ağlarının yükselişinde içerik pazarlaması. *International Journal of Social Sciences and Education Research, 2*(1), 275–285.

Kayabaşı, E. (2020). Covid-19'un piyasalara ve tüketici davranişlarina etkisi. *Avrasya Sosyal ve Ekonomi Araştırmaları Dergisi, 7*(5), 15–25.

Kee, A. W. A., & Yazdanifard, R. (2015). The review of content marketing as a new trend in marketing practices. *International Journal of Management. Accounting and Economics, 2*(9), 1055–1064.

Kerns, C. (2014). *Trendology/Building an Advantage Throught Data – Driven Real – Time Marketing*. Palgrave Macmillan. doi:10.1057/9781137479563

Khatoon, S., & Rehman, V. (2021). Negative emotions in consumer brand relationship: A review and future research agenda. *International Journal of Consumer Studies, 45*(4), 719–749. doi:10.1111/ijcs.12665

Kiani, G. R. (1998). Marketing Opportunities in the digital world. *Internet Research: Electronic Networking Practices and Policy, 8*(2), 185–194. doi:10.1108/10662249810211656

Koshkaki, E. R., & Solhi, S. (2016). The facilitating role of negative emotion in decision making process: A hierarchy of effects model approach. *The Journal of High Technology Management Research, 27*(2), 119–128. doi:10.1016/j.hitech.2016.10.010

Kotane, I., Znotina, D., & Hushko, S. (2019). Assessment of trends in the application of digital marketing. *Scientific Journal of Polonia University, 33*(2), 28–35. doi:10.23856/3303

Kotler, P. (2000). *Marketing Management* (10th ed.). Prentice-Hall.

Kotler, P., Kartajaya, H., & Setiawan, I. (2016). *Marketing 4.0: Moving from traditional to digital*. John Wiley & Sons Inc.

KPMG. (2020). *Pandemi sonrası yeni küresel tüketici modeli: Hesaplı, dijital, seçici*. https://home.kpmg/tr/tr/home/medya/press-releases/2020/10/pandemi-sonrasi-yeni-tuketici-modeli.html

Kujur, F., & Singh, S. (2018). Emotions as predictor for consumer engagement in YouTube advertisement. *Journal of Advances in Management Research, 15*(2), 184–197. doi:10.1108/JAMR-05-2017-0065

Kumar, P., & Singh, G. (2020). Using social media and digital marketing tools and techniques for developing brand equity with connected consumers. In S. S. Dadwal (Ed.), *Handbook of research on innovations in technology and marketing for the connected consumer* (pp. 336–355). IGI Global. doi:10.4018/978-1-7998-0131-3.ch016

Kuo, Y. F., & Wu, C. M. (2012). Satisfaction and post-purchase intentions with service recovery of online shopping websites: Perspectives on perceived justice and emotions. *International Journal of Information Management, 32*(2), 127–138. doi:10.1016/j.ijinfomgt.2011.09.001

Laros, F. J., & Steenkamp, J. B. E. (2005). Emotions in consumer behavior: A hierarchical approach. *Journal of Business Research, 58*(10), 1437–1445. doi:10.1016/j.jbusres.2003.09.013

Lau-Gesk, L., & Meyers-Levy, J. (2009). Emotional persuasion: When the valence versus the resource demands of emotions influence consumers' attitudes. *The Journal of Consumer Research, 36*(4), 585–599. doi:10.1086/605297

Lieb, R. (2011). *Marketing: Think like a publisher-how to use content to market online and in social media*. Que Publishing.

Lieb, R. (2012). *Content marketing: think like a publisher—how to use content to market online and in social media*. Que Publishing.

Lieb, R. (2013). *A market definition report. real-time marketing: The agility leverage.* https://www.slideshare.net/Altimeter/report-realtime-marketing-the-agility-to-leveragenow-by-rebecca-lieb-jessica-groopman

Lu, J., Hao, Q., & Jing, M. (2016). Consuming, sharing, and creating content: How young students use new social media in and outside school. *Computers in Human Behavior, 64,* 55–64. doi:10.1016/j.chb.2016.06.019

Mathew, V., & Soliman, M. (2021). Does digital content marketing affect tourism consumer behavior? An extension of technology acceptance model. *Journal of Consumer Behaviour, 20*(1), 61–75. doi:10.1002/cb.1854

Mazerant, K., Willemsen, L. M., Neijens, P. C., & van Noort, G. (2021). Spot-on creativity: Creativity biases and their differential effects on consumer responses in (non-) real-time marketing. *Journal of Interactive Marketing, 53,* 15–31. doi:10.1016/j.intmar.2020.06.004

Miller, M. (2013). *Real-time marketing smarts: Companies killing it with off-the-cuff content.* TopRank Marketing. https://www.toprankblog.com/2013/04/real-time-marketing-smarts/

Müller, J., & Christandl, F. (2019). Content is king–But who is the king of kings? The effect of content marketing, sponsored content & user-generated content on brand responses. *Computers in Human Behavior, 96,* 46–55. doi:10.1016/j.chb.2019.02.006

Nielsen, I. Q. (2020). *Key consumer behaviour thresholds identified as the coronavirus outbreak evolves.* https://nielseniq.com/global/en/insights/analysis/2020/key-consumerbehavior-thresholds-identified-as-the-coronavirus-outbreak-evolves-2

Nikunen, T., Saarela, M., Oikarinen, E. L., Muhos, M., & Isohella, L. (2017). Micro-enterprise's digital marketing tools for building customer relationships. *Management, 12*(2).

Nyer, P. U. (1997). A study of the relationships between cognitive appraisals and consumption emotions. *Journal of the Academy of Marketing Science, 25*(4), 296–304. doi:10.1177/0092070397254002

Papagiannis, N. (2020). *Effective SEO and content marketing: the ultimate guide for maximizing free web traffic.* John Wiley & Sons. doi:10.1002/9781119628682

Paul, J. (2019). Marketing in emerging markets: A review, theoretical synthesis and extension. *International Journal of Emerging Markets, 15*(3), 446–468. doi:10.1108/IJOEM-04-2017-0130

Poradova, M. (2020). Content marketing strategy and its impact on customers under the global market conditions. In *SHS Web of Conferences* (Vol. 74, p. 01027). EDP Sciences. 10.1051hsconf/20207401027

Reece, M. (2010). *Real-time marketing for business growth: How to use social media, measure marketing, and create a culture of execution.* Pearson Education.

Richins, M. L. (1997). Measuring emotions in the consumption experience. *The Journal of Consumer Research, 24*(2), 127–146. doi:10.1086/209499

Rowley, J. (2008). Understanding digital content marketing. *Journal of Marketing Management, 24*(5-6), 517–540. doi:10.1362/026725708X325977

Ruiz-Mafe, C., Chatzipanagiotou, K., & Curras-Perez, R. (2018). The role of emotions and conflicting online reviews on consumers' purchase intentions. *Journal of Business Research*, 89, 336–344. doi:10.1016/j.jbusres.2018.01.027

Ryan, D., & Jones, C. (2009). *Digital marketing: Marketing strategies for engaging the digital generation*. Kogan page Ltd.

Sarıtaş, A. (2018). İçerik pazarlamasına yönelik bir literatür taraması. *Sosyal Araştırmalar ve Davranış Bilimleri Dergisi*, 232–239.

Schachter, S., & Singer, J. E. (1962). Cognitive, social, and physiological determinants of emotional state. *Psychological Review*, 69(5), 379–399. doi:10.1037/h0046234 PMID:14497895

Scott, D. (2010). *Real-time marketing & PR*. John Wiley & Sons.

Scott, D. M. (2011). *Real-time marketing and PR: How to instantly engage your market, connect with customers, and create products that grow your business now*. John Wiley & Sons.

Sekaran, U., & Bougie, R. (2011). *Business Research Methods: A skill-building approach*. John Wiley& Sons Ltd.

Sherman, E., Mathur, A., & Smith, R. B. (1997). Store environment and consumer purchase behavior: Mediating role of consumer emotions. *Psychology and Marketing*, 14(4), 361–378. doi:10.1002/(SICI)1520-6793(199707)14:4<361::AID-MAR4>3.0.CO;2-7

Solomon, M., Russell-Bennett, R., & Previte, J. (2012). *Consumer behaviour*. Pearson Higher Education AU.

Soto-Acosta, P. (2020). COVID-19 pandemic: Shifting digital transformation to a high-speed gear. *Information Systems Management*, 37(4), 260–266. doi:10.1080/10580530.2020.1814461

Świeczak, W. (2012). Content marketing as an important element of marketing strategy of scientific institutions. *The Institute of Aviation*, 226(5), 133–150. doi:10.5604/05096669.1077480

Tabachnick, B. G., & Fidell, L. S. (2012). *Using Multivariate Statistics*. Pearson.

Taber, K. S. (2018). The use of Cronbach's alpha when developing and reporting research instruments in science education. *Research in Science Education*, 48(6), 1273–1296. doi:10.100711165-016-9602-2

Tehci, A. (2021). Digital Marketing in the globalization process: Examples from real-time marketing. In Y. Bayar (Ed.), *Handbook of Research on Institutional, Economic, and Social Impacts of Globalization and Liberalization* (pp. 185–200). IGI Global. doi:10.4018/978-1-7998-4459-4.ch011

Tosun, P., Sezgin, S., & Nimet, U. R. A. Y. (2019). Pazarlama biliminde duygu ve duygu durumu kavramlari için baz alinmiş teoriler. *Elektronik Sosyal Bilimler Dergisi*, 18(72), 1832–1851.

Verhagen, T., & van Dolen, W. (2011). The influence of online store beliefs on consumer online impulse buying: A model and empirical application. *Information & Management*, 48(8), 320–327. doi:10.1016/j.im.2011.08.001

Verma, D. P. S., & Kapoor, S. (2003). Dimensions of buying roles in family decision making. *IIMB Management Review*, *15*(4), 7–14.

Vinerean, S. (2017). Content marketing strategy. Definition, objectives and tactics. *Expert Journal of Marketing*, *5*(2).

Wilkie, W. (1986). *Consumer Behaviour*. John Wiley and Sons.

Willemsen, L. M., Mazerant, K., Kamphuis, A. L., & van der Veen, G. (2018). Let's Get Real (Time)! The potential of real-time marketing to catalyze the sharing of brand messages. *International Journal of Advertising*, *37*(5), 828–848. doi:10.1080/02650487.2018.1485214

Yadav, G., Luthra, S., Jakhar, S. K., Mangla, S. K., & Rai, D. P. (2020). A framework to overcome sustainable supply chain challenges through solution measures of industry 4.0 and circular economy: An automotive case. *Journal of Cleaner Production*, *254*, 120112. doi:10.1016/j.jclepro.2020.120112

Yasmin, A., Tasneem, S., & Fatema, K. (2015). Effectiveness of digital marketing in the challenging age: An empirical study. *International Journal of Management Science and Business Administration*, *1*(5), 69–80. doi:10.18775/ijmsba.1849-5664-5419.2014.15.1006

KEY TERMS AND DEFINITIONS

Consumer Behavior: It contains mental and physical actions that consumers interest in when searching for, deciding, buying, and using products and services.

Consumer Emotions: An evaluation of feelings about the experience with a brand, company, product, or service by customers.

Content Marketing: A kind of marketing focused on creating, publishing, and sharing content for targeted consumers online.

Digital Content: Digital content is any content that is a kind of digital data.

Digital Marketing: It refers to any web-based marketing practices or resources.

Digitalization: It is the use of digital technologies to improve a business model and contribute to generating new revenue and value. In short, it is the transition to a digital business.

Negative Consumer Behavior: Consumer behavior that threatens a brand, campaign, or advertisement materially and morally.

Real-Time Content Marketing: The combination of real-time marketing and content marketing.

Real-Time Marketing: A type of marketing conducted instantly to present a suitable strategy to a target customer at a particular time and place.

APPENDIX 1

Questions and Answers

1. What is the overall problem presented in this case?

The main problem presented in this case is that digital advertisements demoralize consumers by putting emotional pressure on consumers in extraordinary processes, such as pandemics. In this respect, this chapter aims to reveal the effects of real-time content marketing on consumer emotions and consumer behavior during the Covid-19 pandemic.

2. What are the variables in the proposed research model?

Main concepts are the real time content marketing, consumer emotions and consumer behaviors. According to research model, real-time content created within the scope of the Covid-19 pandemic evokes positive or negative emotions in consumers against the campaign. With the influence of these emotions, consumer behavior is affected in different ways by real-time content marketing campaigns.

3. Discuss managerial and organizational issues and resources related to this case.

In this case, one of the managerial mistakes of companies is to act without predicting the effects of their digital tools. Digital marketing tools leave a great impact on consumers, and companies use these tools without hesitation in extraordinary situations by using manipulation and sad emotions in their marketing strategies.

4. What are the findings?

Findings indicate that while positive perception toward real-time content marketing campaigns can lead to positive emotions, negative perception can lead to negative emotions. It was also found as an important result that both positive and negative emotions affect negative consumer behavior during pandemic period. In addition, negative emotions as a mediator variable strength negative consumer behavior.

5. What is the final solution that can be recommended to the management of the organization described in the case? Provide your arguments in support of the recommended solution.

Companies might be beneficial to make improvements to regain consumer interest by making concise campaigns without overwhelming the consumers with advertisements and marketing campaigns. More specifically, the extraordinary psychological state of the consumer should be taken into account while preparing real-time content advertisements.

Epilogue and Lessons Learned

Real-time content marketing campaigns created within the scope of the Covid-19 pandemic that try to affect consumers' emotions may fail. Because consumers may don't believe that these campaigns are sincere. As a result of this, even if consumers have positive emotions, they do not show positive consumer behavior. At this point, companies face some difficulties. In the long-range, for instance, it can drive the consumer away from the company/brand or reduce their purchasing behavior. On the other hand, the consumer may make negative comments against the company on social media, causing the company to be defamed with a possible lynching culture.

What will be learned from this case are:

- Although it is advantageous for companies that digital marketing is practical and easy, it should be used very carefully. While trying to reach consumers in the easiest way, unsuccessful applications can damage the reputation of the company.
- Digital marketing channels can reach consumers who are in an extraordinary mood with motivating items instead of sad content. Thus, the sympathy of the consumer towards the company can be increased.
- Digital marketing applications should reach the consumer after certain researches and thoughtful studies. If the necessary people do not pass the controls, it may take seconds to create irreversible results.
- Since digital marketing applications made through digital channels cannot be completely deleted over the internet, the people working in the relevant departments of the companies should be carefully selected. Consumers who are going through a sensitive period may have a negative attitude towards the company as their patience is running out day by day.
- The fact that companies stay away from activities that creating negative emotions on consumers might contribute to a more positive consumer attitude.
- Companies can provide positive support to consumers overwhelmed by the global Covid-19 pandemic by offering items that can be a source of entertainment.
- Companies should reduce some costs in marketing campaigns and identify areas where consumers are more effective. Thus, it can communicate more effectively with its target audience.
- Companies should be more aware of the compatibility of content and real-time event.
- Companies should create real-time content not only for their own needs but also for customer needs.
- Companies shouldn't forget that the real-time content campaigns related to negative events might provoke consumers' emotions. These emotions may negatively affect consumer behavior.
- Companies should share the real-time content that adds value for them.

Compilation of References

ACI. (2007). *Airport Industry Connectivity Report 2019*. ACI.

Adelakun, A. (2020). *Should Porters Five Forces have value in Businesses today. Computing for Business (BSC)*. Aston University Birmingham.

Adyar Anand Bhavan. (2017). *A2B savouries food menu*. https://www.aabsweets.in/menu-savories

Ahmed, A. M., Zairi, M., & Almarr, K. (2006). SWOT analysis for Air China performance and its experience with quality. *Benchmarking*, *13*(1/2), 160–173. doi:10.1108/14635770610644655

Akın, M., Öztürk, Y., & Karamustafa, K. (2020). Destinasyon Rekabetçilik Analizi: Kapadokya Bölgesi Örneği. *Anatolia: Turizm Araştırmaları Dergisi*, *31*(2), 161–171. doi:10.17123/atad.651245

Aksoy, C., & Dursun, Ö. O. (2018). A General Overview Of The Development Of The Civil. *Elektronik Sosyal Bilimler Dergisi*, *17*(67), 1060–1076.

Altunisik, R., Coskun, R., Bayraktaroglu, S., & Yildirim, E. (2004). *Sosyal bilimlerde araştırma yöntemleri: SPSS uygulamalı* (3rd ed.). Sakarya Kitabevi.

Amazon.ae. (2021). *Amazon: about us*. https://www.amazon.ae/b?node=16177380031

Anand, N. (2013). *Kotler adds a 5th P to his set of four – Purpose*. https://www.dnaindia.com/business/report-kotler-adds-a-5th-p-to-his-set-of-four-purpose-1812393

Andaleeb, S. S., & Hasan, K. (2016). *Strategic Marketing Management in Asia: Case Studies and Lessons across Industries*. Emerald.

Andani, K., & Wahyono, W. (2018). Influence of Sales Promotion, Hedonic Shopping Motivation and Fashion Involvement Toward Impulse Buying through a Positive Emotion. *Management Analysis Journal*, *7*(4), 448–457. doi:10.15294/maj.v7i4.24105

Anderl, E., Schumann, J. H., & Kunz, W. (2016). Helping Firms Reduce Complexity in Multichannel Online Data: A New Taxonomy-Based Approach for Customer Journeys. *Journal of Retailing*, *92*(2), 185–203. doi:10.1016/j.jretai.2015.10.001

Anderson, D., & Hanselka, D. (2009). *Adding value to agricultural products*. AgriLife Extension, the Texas A&M System.

Andrew, B., André van, S., & Roy, T. (2009). *Blue Ocean versus competitive strategy: Theory and Evidence*. Erasmus Research Institute of Management (ERIM).

Ansari, S., Ansari, G., Ghori, M. U., & Kazi, A. G. (2019). Impact of brand awareness and social media content marketing on consumer purchase decision. *Journal of Public Value and Administrative Insight*, *2*(2), 5–10. doi:10.31580/jpvai.v2i2.896

Compilation of References

Ansoff, H. I. (1957). Article. *Harvard Business Review*, *35*(5), 113–124.

Ansoff, H. I. (1965). *Corporate strategy; an analytic approach to business policy for growth and expansion*. McGraw-Hill.

Ansoff, H. L. (1965). *Corporate strategy*. McGraw-Hill.

Ansoff, I. (1957). Strategies for Diversification. *Harvard Business Review*, *35*(5), 113–124.

Ansoff, I. H. (1987). Strategic management of technology. *The Journal of Business Strategy*, *7*(3), 28–39. doi:10.1108/eb039162

Ansola, G. P., De Las Morenas, J., García, A., & Otamendi, J. (2011). Distributed decision support system for airport ground handling management using WSN and MAS. *Engineering Applications of Artificial Intelligence*, *25*(3), 544–553. doi:10.1016/j.engappai.2011.11.005

Arner, D. W., Barberis, J., & Buckley, R. P. (2016). The evolution of FinTech: A new post-crisis paradigm? *Georgetown Journal of International Law*, *47*(4), 1272–1319.

Arnoldo, H., & Dean, W. I. I. (2001). The delta model—Discovering new sources of profitability in a networked economy. *European Management Journal*, *9*(4), 379–391.

Arslanian, H., & Fisher, F. (2019). *The Future of Finance, The Impact of Fintech, AI, and Crypto on Financial Services*. Springer. doi:10.1007/978-3-030-14533-0

Arzhanova, K. A., Beregovskaya, T. A., & Silina, S. A. (2020). The impact of the Covid-19 pandemic on consumer behavior and companies' internet communication strategies. *Proceedings of the Research Technologies of Pandemic Coronavirus Impact (RTCOV 2020)*, 50–57. 10.2991/assehr.k.201105.010

Ashta A., Assadi D., & Durand N. (2021). Capture d'innovation: étude de cas d'une néo-banque à mission sociale et défis pour les pays en développement. *ISTE OpenScience*, 1–21 doi:10.21494/ISTE.OP.2021.0673

Atasoy, B., & Güllü, K. (2019). *Destinasyon Tercihinde Bir Motivasyon Faktörü Olarak Gastronomi* (Doctoral Dissertation). Yüksek Lisans Tezi. Erciyes Üniversitesi Sosyal Bilimler Enstitüsü.

Augustyn, S., & Turzyńska, H. (2016). *The airport tracing and handling in the near future. Scientific Research And Education In The Air Force*. Henri Coanda Air Force Academy AFASES.

Avcı, T., & Aktaş, M. (2015). Türkiye'de Faaliyet Gösteren Havalimanlarının Performanslarının Değerlendirilmesi. *Journal of Alanya Faculty of Business/Alanya Isletme Fakültesi Dergisi*, *7*(3).

Bagga, T., & Bhatt, M. (2013). A Study of Intrinsic and Extrinsic Factors Influencing Consumer Buying Behaviour Online. *Asia-Pacific Journal of Management Research and Innovation*, *9*(1), 77–90. doi:10.1177/2319510X13483515

Bagozzi, R. P., Gopinath, M., & Nyer, P. U. (1999). The role of emotions in marketing. *Journal of the Academy of Marketing Science*, *27*(2), 184–206. doi:10.1177/0092070399272005

Baker, G. (2021). *Why category leading brick and mortar retailers are likely the biggest long term Covid beneficiaries*. https://gavin-baker.medium.com/

Bal, Y. (2011). *Rekabet Stratejilerinin İnsan Kaynakları Yönetimi Uygulamalarına Etkisi* [Doctoral dissertation]. Istanbul University.

Bala, M., & Verma, D. (2018). A Critical Review of Digital Marketing. *International Journal of Management. IT & Engineering*, *8*(10), 321–339.

Balça, J., & Casais, B. (2021). Return on Investment of Display Advertising: Google Ads vs. Facebook Ads. In E. Esiyok (Ed.), *Handbook of Research on New Media Applications in Public Relations and Advertising* (pp. 1–13). IGI Global. doi:10.4018/978-1-7998-3201-0.ch001

Balio, S., & Casais, B. (2020). A Content Marketing Framework to analyze Customer Engagement on Social Media. In S. Alavi & V. Ahuja (Eds.), *Managing Social Media Practices in the Digital Economy* (pp. 45–66). IGI Global. doi:10.4018/978-1-7998-2185-4.ch003

Baltaci, A. (2019). Nitel Araştırma Süreci: Nitel Bir Araştırma Nasıl Yapılır? *Ahi Evran Üniversitesi Sosyal Bilimler Enstitüsü Dergisi, 5*(2), 368–388. doi:10.31592/aeusbed.598299

Baltes, L. P. (2015). Content marketing-the fundamental tool of digital marketing. *Bulletin of the Transilvania University of Brasov. Economic Sciences, Series V, 8*(2), 111.

Baran, H., & Öymen, G. (2020). Gerçek zamanlı pazarlamanın markalar üzerindeki rolü "Game of Thrones" örneği. *Uluslararası Halkla İlişkiler ve Reklam Çalışmaları Dergisi, 3*(1), 80–107.

Barnard, C. I. (1938). *The functions of the executive*. Harvard University Press.

Barney, J. B. (1991). Firm resources and sustained competitive advantage. *Journal of Management, 17*(1), 99–120. doi:10.1177/014920639101700108

Barney, J. B., & Hesterly, W. S. (2012). *Strategic management and competitive advantage* (4th ed.). Pearson.

Bart, C. K. (1986). Product strategy and formal structure. *Strategic Management Journal, 7*(4), 293–312. doi:10.1002mj.4250070402

Barutcugil, I. (2013). *Stratejik yönetim*. Kariyer Yayincilik.

Barwitz, N., & Maas, P. (2018). Understanding the Omnichannel Customer Journey: Determinants of Interaction Choice. *Journal of Interactive Marketing, 43*, 116–133. doi:10.1016/j.intmar.2018.02.001

Baumann, O., & Stieglitz, N. (2013). *Motivating Organizational Search*. John Wiley & Sons Ltd.

Bayhan, M., Türkmen, M., & Kepe, D. (2017). Evaluation Of Denizli-Kaklik Logistics Village With SWOT Analysis. *Mehmet Akif Ersoy Üniversitesi Sosyal Bilimler Enstitüsü Dergisi, 9*(22), 555–574. doi:10.20875/makusobed.367392

BBC. (2020). *Koronavirüs salgını tüketici alışkanlıklarını nasıl değiştiriyor?* Retrieved from https://www.bbc.com/turkce/haberler-dunya-52448919

Belch, G. E., & Belch, M. A. (2003). *Advertising and Promotion. An Integrated Marketing Communication Perspective* (6th ed.). McGraw-Hill Companies.

Benavent C. (2017). Disruption à l'âge des plateformes. *Économie & Management, 165*, 11-17.

Bengtsson, M. (2016). How to Plan and Perform A Qualitative Study Using Content Analysis. *NursingPlus Open, 2*, 8–14. doi:10.1016/j.npls.2016.01.001

Berendes, C. I., Bartelheimer, C., Betzing, J. H., & Beverungen, D. (2018). Data-driven Customer Journey Mapping in Local High Streets: A Domain-specific Modeling Language. *Proceedings of ICIS, 1*, 218–227.

Besanko, D., Dranove, D., & Shanley, M. (2000). *The economics of strategy*. John Wiley and Sons.

Bez Predmyvani in Czech Republic. (2021). https://www.finishinfo.cz/bezpedmyvani/

Compilation of References

Blankson, C., & Crawford, J. C. (2012). Impact of positioning strategies on service firm performance. *Journal of Business Research*, *65*(3), 311–316. doi:10.1016/j.jbusres.2011.03.013

Blasberg, J., & Vishwanath, V. (2003). Making Cool Brands Hot. *Harvard Business Review*, *81*(6), 20–22.

BloombergH. T. (2020). https://www.bloomberght.com/finish-su-endeksi-kullanilabilir-su-miktarini-gosteriyor-2265599

Bolat, E., & Ateş, S. S. (2020). Post COVID-19 precautions management in small-scale airports: Evaluation of check-in process in Erkilet airport by simulation. *Journal of Airline and Airport Management*, *10*(2), 77–86. doi:10.3926/jairm.166

Bolle, G. (2015). Digital content and real time marketing: Strategic challenges for the globalised football brands. In S. Chadwick, N. Chanavat, & M. Desbordes (Eds.), *Routledge Handbook of Sports Marketing* (pp. 315–330). Routledge.

Borghini, S., Diamond, N., Kozinets, R., McGrath, M., Munoz, A., & Sherry, J. (2009). Why are Themed Brandstores so Powerful? Retail Brand Ideology at American Girl Place. *Journal of Retailing*, *85*(3), 363–375. doi:10.1016/j.jretai.2009.05.003

Boumphrey, S. (2020). *How will consumer markets evolve after Coronavirus?* Euromonitor International. https://go.euromonitor.com/white-paper-2020-covid-19-themes.html#download-link

Bourgeois, L. J., & Brodwin, D. R. (1984). Strategic implementation: Five approaches to an elusive phenomenon. *Strategic Management Journal*, *5*(3), 241–264. doi:10.1002mj.4250050305

Bowden, J. L. (2009). The Process of Customer Engagement: A Conceptual Framework. *Journal of Marketing Theory and Practice*, *17*(1), 63–74. doi:10.2753/MTP1069-6679170105

Bowman, C., & Johnson, G. (1992). Surfacing competitive strategies. *European Management Journal*, *10*(2), 210–220. doi:10.1016/0263-2373(92)90071-B

BrandAge. (2020). https://www.thebrandage.com/fairyden-bosaharcamayalim-kampanyasi-10713

Brodie, R. J., Hollebeek, L. D., Jurić, B., & Ilić, A. (2011). Customer Engagement: Conceptual Domain, Fundamental Propositions, and Implications for Research. *Journal of Service Research*, *14*(3), 252–271. doi:10.1177/1094670511411703

Budd, L. (2008). A History Of Airport Technology. *Airports of the World*, *19*, 44–51.

Buettner, R. (2019). *Online user behavior and digital footprints* [Unpublished habilitation dissertation]. University of Trier, Trier and Aalen, Germany.

Burns, T., & Stalker, G. M. (1961). *The management of innovation*. Tavistock.

Businesswire.com. (2019). *Global Processed Vegetable Market 2019-2023: Increasing Online Presence of Processed Vegetable Vendors to Boost Growth*. https://www.businesswire.com/news/home/20190714005002/en/Global-Processed-Vegetable-Market-2019-2023-Increasing-Online-Presence-of-Processed-Vegetable-Vendors-to-Boost-Growth-Technavio

Butler, D. (2020). *History of Procter & Gamble: Timeline and Facts*. https://www.thestreet.com/personal-finance/history-of-procter-and-gamble

BüyükdumluŞ. (2021). https://pazarlamasyon.com/fairyden-surdurulebilirlik-ve-cevre-icin-anlamli-bir-adim-bosa-harcama-komitesi-calismalarina-basladi/

Cachero-Martínez, S., & Vázquez-Casielles, R. (2021). Building consumer loyalty through e-shopping experiences: The mediating role of emotions. *Journal of Retailing and Consumer Services*, *60*, 102481. doi:10.1016/j.jretconser.2021.102481

Cadle, J., Paul, D., & Turner, P. (2014). Business analysis techniques: 99 essential tools for success (2nd ed.). BCS, The Chartered Institute for IT.

Cameron, M. (2013). *Data is not the new oil – it's the new soil*. Marketing Magazine. https://www.marketingmag.com.au/hubs-c/data-is-not-the-new-oil-its-the-new-soil

Campaign Türkiye. (2019). https://www.campaigntr.com/finish-yarinin-suyu-icin-soz-veriyor/

Carlson, J., Rahman, M., Voola, R., & De Vries, N. (2018). Customer engagement behaviours in social media: Capturing innovation opportunities. *Journal of Services Marketing*, *32*(1), 83–94. doi:10.1108/JSM-02-2017-0059

Carton, G. (2020). How assemblages change when theories become performative: The case of the Blue Ocean strategy. *Organization Studies*, *41*(10), 1417–1439. doi:10.1177/0170840619897197

Cattani, G., & Ferriani, S. (2008, November-December). A Core/Periphery Perspective on Individual Creative Performance: Social Networks and Cinematic Achievements in the Hollywood Film Industry. *Organization Science*, *19*(6), 824–844. doi:10.1287/orsc.1070.0350

Cattani, G., Ferriani, S., & Lanza, A. (2017, November-December). Deconstructing the Outsider Puzzle: The Legitimation Journey of Novelty. *Organization Science*, *28*(6), 965–992. doi:10.1287/orsc.2017.1161

Cerina, R., & Duch, R. (2020). Measuring public opinion via digital footprints. *International Journal of Forecasting*, *36*(3), 987–1002. doi:10.1016/j.ijforecast.2019.10.004

Certo, S. C., & Peter, J. P. (1991). *Strategic management: Concepts and application*. McGraw–Hill, Inc.

Chaffee, E. E. (1985). Three models of strategy. *Academy of Management Review*, *10*(1), 89–98. doi:10.5465/amr.1985.4277354

Chaffey, D., & Smith, P. R. (2017). *Digital marketing excellence: planning, optimizing, and integrating online marketing*. Taylor & Francis. doi:10.4324/9781315640341

Chandler, A. D. (1962). *Strategy and structure: Chapters in the history of the American industrial enterprise*. M.I.T. Press.

Chanias, S., Myers, M. D., & Hess, T. (2019). Digital transformation strategy making in pre-digital organizations: The case of a financial services provider. *The Journal of Strategic Information Systems*, *28*(1), 17–33. doi:10.1016/j.jsis.2018.11.003

Channon, D. (1973). *Strategy and structure in British Enterprise*. Harvard University Press. doi:10.1007/978-1-349-01995-3

Chaturvedi, S. (2020). Book Review: Essentials of Management by Harold Koontz and Heinz Weihrich. 10th ed. Chennai: Tata McGraw Hill Education, 2015. Journal of Education for Business, 96(1), 69-70. doi:10.1080/08832323.2020.1720572

Chaturvedi, S., & Pasipanodya, T. E. (2021). A Perspective on Reprioritizing Children's' Wellbeing Amidst COVID-19: Implications for Policymakers and Caregivers. *Frontiers in Human Dynamics*, *2*, 18. doi:10.3389/fhumd.2020.615865

Chaturvedi, S., Rizvi, I. A., & Pasipanodya, E. T. (2019). How can leaders make their followers to commit to the organization? The importance of influence tactics. *Global Business Review*, *20*(6), 1462–1474. doi:10.1177/0972150919846963

Chaturvedi, S., & Singh, T. (2021). Knowledge Management Initiatives for Tackling the COVID-19 Pandemic in India. *Metamorphosis*, *09726225211023677*. Advance online publication. 10.1177%2F09726225211023677

Chaturvedi, S., & Srivastava, A. K. (2015). The effect of employee's organizational commitment on upward influence tactics and employees' career success: An Indian study. *International Journal of Research in Organizational Behavior and Human Resource Management*, *3*(2), 41–58.

Chea, S., & Luo, M. M. (2008). Post-adoption behaviors of e-service customers: The interplay of cognition and emotion. *International Journal of Electronic Commerce*, *12*(3), 29–56. doi:10.2753/JEC1086-4415120303

Chen, C. H., & Chou, S. Y. (2006). A BSC Framework for Air Cargo Terminal Design: Procedure and Case Study. *Journal of Industrial Technology, 22*(1), 1-10.

Christensen, C. (1997). *The Innovator's Dilemma: When New Technologies Cause Great Firms to Fail*. Harvard Business Review Press.

Çınaroğlu, E., & Unutulmaz, O. (2019). A data mining application of local weather forecast for Kayseri Erkilet Airport. *Politeknik Dergisi, 22*(1), 103–113.

Civils Daily. (October 9, 2017). Food Processing Industry in India: Growth Drivers, FDI Policy, Investment Opportunities; Schemes Related to Food Processing Sector. https://www.civilsdaily.com/food-processing-industry-in-india-growth-drivers-fdi-policy-investment-opportunities-schemes-related-to-food-processing-sector/

Claver-Cortés, E., Pertusa-Ortega, E. M., & Molina-Azorín, J. F. (2012). Characteristics of organizational structure relating to hybrid competitive strategy: Implications for performance. *Journal of Business Research, 65*(7), 993–1002. doi:10.1016/j.jbusres.2011.04.012

Clean India Journal. (2017). Investing in food safety. Retrieved from https://www.cleanindiajournal.com/investing-in-food-safety/

Clow, K. E., & Baack, D. (2016). *Integrated Advertising, Promotion and Marketing Communications* (7th ed.). Education Limited.

Colicev, A., Kumar, A., & O'Connor, P. (2019). Modeling the relationship between firm and user generated content and the stages of the marketing funnel. *International Journal of Research in Marketing, 36*(1), 100–116. doi:10.1016/j.ijresmar.2018.09.005

Colley, R. C., Bushnik, T., & Langlois, K. (2020). Exercise and screen time during the COVID-19 pandemic. *Health Reports, 31*(6), 3–11. PMID:32672923

Collins, J. C., & Porras, J. I. (2005). *Built to last: Successful habits of visionary companies*. Random House.

Correani, A., De Massis, A., Frattini, F., Petruzzelli, A. M., & Natalicchio, A. (2020). Implementing a Digital Strategy: Learning from the Experience of Three Digital Transformation Projects. *California Management Review, 62*(4), 37–56. doi:10.1177/0008125620934864

Covin, J. G., & Dennis, P. S. (1990). New venture strategic posture, structure, and performance: An industry life cycle analysis. *Journal of Business Venturing, 5*(2), 123–135. doi:10.1016/0883-9026(90)90004-D

Covin, J. G., Slevin, D. P., & Heeley, M. B. (2001). Strategic decision making in an intuitive vs. technocratic mode: Structural and environmental considerations. *Journal of Business Research, 52*(1), 51–67. doi:10.1016/S0148-2963(99)00080-6

Crabtree, B. F., & William, L. M. (1999). *Doing Qualitative Research* (2nd ed.). Sage Publications.

Craciun, L., & Baubu, C. M. (2014). The Brand as Strategic Asset of the Organization. *Review of International Comparative Management, 15*(1), 69–77.

Cubukcu, M. (2018). İşletmelerde uygulanan strateji tipleri ve uygulamadan örnekler. *Uluslararası Yönetim Akademisi Dergisi, 1*(2), 142–156.

Czaja, S. J., & Lee, C. C. (2007). The impact of aging on access to technology. *Universal Access in the Information Society, 5*(4), 341–349. doi:10.100710209-006-0060-x

Dacko, S. G. (2008). *The advanced dictionary of marketing: putting theory to use*. Oxford University Press.

Daft, R. L. (2007). *Organization theory and design*. Thomson South-Western.

Dauvers, O. (2019). *Direct to consumer 2019*. Editions Dauvers.

Davis, F. D. (1986). *A technology acceptance model for empirically testing new end-user information systems: theory and results* (Doctoral Thesis). Sloan School of Management. http://dspace.mit.edu/handle/1721.1/15192

Davis, F. D. (1989). Perceived Usefulness, Perceived Ease of Use, and User Acceptance of Information Technology. *Management Information Systems Quarterly, 13*(3), 319–340. doi:10.2307/249008

De Oliveira, S. F., Ladeira, W. J., & Pinto, D. (2020). Customer engagement in social media: A framework and meta-analysis. J. *Journal of the Academy of Marketing Science, 48*(6), 1211–1228. doi:10.100711747-020-00731-5

De Waal, G. A. (2016). An Extended Conceptual Framework For Product-Market Innovation. *International Journal of Innovation Management, 20*(5), 1640008. doi:10.1142/S1363919616400089

Deloitte. (2020). *Predicting the post-pandemic recovery*. Deloitte Economic-Insights. https://www2.deloitte.com/ca/en/pages/about-deloitte/articles/covid-dashboard.html

Demirtaş, Ö. (2013). Havacilik Endüstrisinde Stratejik Yönetim. *NEÜ Sosyal Bilimler Enstitüsü Dergisi, 2*, 207–226.

Deodhar, S., & Intodia, V. (2010). *Does ghee sold by any brand smell as sweet? quality attributes and hedonic price analysis of ghee*. Working paper, IIMA.

Dess, G. G., & Davis, P. S. (1984). Porter's (1980) generic strategies as determinants of strategic group membership and organizational performance. *Academy of Management Journal, 27*(3), 467–488.

Devrim, B. (2006). *Strateji Formülasyonu: SWOT Analizi*. Academic Press.

Dhmi. (2019). *Devlet Hava Meydanları İşletmesi Genel Müdürlüğü Kayseri Havalimanı*. https://kayseri.dhmi.gov.tr/Sayfalar/icerik-detay.aspx?oid=3491

Dincer, O. (2013). *Stratejik yönetim ve işletme politikası* (9th ed.). Alfa Yayim.

Dolbec, P. Y., & Chebat, J. C. (2013). The Impact of a Flagship vs. a Brand Store on Brand Attitude, Brand Attachment and Brand Equity. *Journal of Retailing, 89*(4), 460–466. doi:10.1016/j.jretai.2013.06.003

Drago, W. A. (1997). Organization structure and strategic planning: An empirical examination. *Management Research News, 20*(6), 30–42. doi:10.1108/eb028567

Duong, P. L., & Khuong, M. N. (2019). The Effect of In-Store Marketing on Tourists' Positive Emotion and Impulse Buying Behavior–An Empirical Study in Ho Chi Minh City, Vietnam. *International Journal of Trade. Economics and Finance, 10*(5), 119–125.

Durmuş Arici, E. (2008). *Rekabet Stratejisi, Örgüt Yapısı ve Performans İlişkilerinin Gıda Perakende Sektörü Bağlamında Araştırılması* [Doctoral dissertation]. Akdeniz University.

Ebrahimzadeh, I., & Izadfar, E. (2009). An Analysis of the Location of Beheshti International Airport Using A Strategic Model (SWOT). *Journal of Geography and Regional Development, 7*(13), 237–260.

Eco 121. (2012). *Interview with Christophe Bonduelle*. N° 22.

Economic Times. (Oct 02, 2013). Eateries see steep price cuts due to growing competition and popular government schemes. https://economictimes.indiatimes.com/articleshow/23396665.cms?from=mdr&utm_source=contentofinterest&utm_medium=text&utm_campaign=cppst

Compilation of References

Edelman, D., & Singer, M. (2015). Competing on Customer Journeys. *Harvard Business Review*. https://hbr.org/2015/11/competing-on-customer-journeys

Eden, L., & Miller, S. R. (2004). Distance Matters: Liability of Foreignness, Institutional Distance and Ownership Strategy. In M. A. Hitt & J. L. C. Cheng (Eds.), *Theories of the Multinational Enterprise: Diversity, Complexity and Relevance* (pp. 187–221). Emerald Group Publishing Limited. doi:10.1016/S0747-7929(04)16010-1

Edwing, M. T., Fowlds, D. A., & Shepherd, I. R. (1995). Renaissance: A case study in brand revitalization and strategic realignment. *Journal of Product and Brand Management*, 4(3), 19–26. doi:10.1108/10610429510097618

EfendioğluK. (2020). http://sosyalup.net/fairy-ve-gida-kurtarma-derneginden-bosa-harcama-projesi/

Egede, E. A. (2013). Strategic Evaluation of How Advertising Works On Product Promotions. *Developing Country Studies*, 3(10), 139–148.

Eisenhardt, K. M. (1989). Building theories from case study research. *Academy of Management Review*, 14(4), 532–550. doi:10.5465/amr.1989.4308385

Ensemble Pour Leau in France. (2021). https://www.finishensemblepourleau.fr/

Erdil, O., Kalkan, A., & Alparslan, A. M. (2010). Örgütsel Ekoloji Kuramindan Stratejik Yönetim Anlayışına. *Doğuş Üniversitesi Dergisi*, 12(1), 17–31.

Erkan, İ. (2020). Consumers' perceptions of unity solidarity and motivation themed advertisements published in the Covid-19 period. *Gaziantep University Journal of Social Sciences*, 2020(Special Issue), 585–600. doi:10.21547/jss.788085

Ertekín, İ. (2017). Classical organization theory. *Journal of Emerging Economies and Policy*, 2(2), 64–73.

Escadas, M., Jalali, M. S., & Farhangmehr, M. (2019). Why bad feelings predict good behaviours: The role of positive and negative anticipated emotions on consumer ethical decision making. *Business Ethics (Oxford, England)*, 28(4), 529–545. doi:10.1111/beer.12237

Euromonitor International. (2021). *Processed Fruit and Vegetables in World: Datagraphics*. Author.

Fagerberg, J. (2004). *Innovation: a guide to the literature*. Georgia Institute of Technology.

Fairy Turkey Official Instagram Account. (2021). https://www.instagram.com/fairyturkiye/?hl=tr

Fairy Turkey Official Youtube Account. (2021). https://www.youtube.com/user/fairyturkiye/about

Fedorchenko, A., & Ponomarenko, I. (2019). A/B-testing as an efficient tools for digital marketing. *Problems of Innovation and Investment Development*, 19(19), 36–42. doi:10.33813/2224-1213.19.2019.4

Fett, M. (2009). *A SWOT Analysis for the "flag-carriers": A deep insight into the aviation industry*. GRIN Verlag.

Fielding, T., & Armstrong, R. (2020). *E-Commerce in the UAE: is it the new normal?* https://gowlingwlg.com/en/insights-resources/articles/2020/e-commerce-in-the-uae-part-one/

Finish Official Web Site. (2021). https://finish.com.tr/pages/finish-in-hikayesi

Finish Official Web Site. (2021). https://www.finishinfo.com.au/about-us/

Finish Saves Water in South Africa. (2021). https://finishsaveswater.co.za/

Finish Turkey Official Instagram Account. (2021). https://www.instagram.com/finish_tr/

Finish Turkey Official Twitter Account. (2021). https://twitter.com/FinishTurkiye

Finish Turkey Official Youtube Account. (2021). https://www.youtube.com/c/FinishT%C3%BCrkiye/featured

Finish Water Index. (2021). https://www.yarininsuyu.com/finish-su-endeksi/

Finish Water Waste in Australia. (2021). https://www.finishwaterwaste.com.au/

Finish Water Waste in New Zealand. (2021). https://www.finish.co.nz/finishwaterwaste/

FoodTime. (2020). https://www.foodtime.com.tr/haberler/fairyden-bosa-harcama-projesi-h5680.html

Forbes India. (Feb 21, 2019). Adyar Anand bhavan. Food and folklore. https://www.forbesindia.com/article/family-business/adyar-ananda-bhavan-food-and-folklore/52605/1

Fornell, C., & Larcker, D. F. (1981). Evaluating structural equation models with unobservable variables and measurement error. *JMR, Journal of Marketing Research*, *18*(1), 39–50. doi:10.1177/002224378101800104

Frazier, G. L. (1999). Organizing and managing channels of distribution. *Journal of the Academy of Marketing Science*, *27*(2), 226–240. doi:10.1177/0092070399272007

Fuchs, C., & Diamantopoulos, A. (2010). Evaluating the effectiveness of brand-positioning strategies from a consumer perspective. *European Journal of Marketing*, *44*(11-12), 1763–1786. doi:10.1108/03090561011079873

Gajjar, N. B. (2013). Factors affecting consumer behavior. *International Journal of Research in Humanities and Social Sciences*, *1*(2), 10–15.

Galbraith, C., & Schendel, D. (1983). An empirical analysis of strategy types. *Strategic Management Journal*, *4*(2), 153–173. doi:10.1002mj.4250040206

Garner, R. (2013). *Seacrh and Social: The Definitive Guide to Real-Time Content Marketing*. John WileySons.

Garrido-Moreno, A., Lockett, N., & García-Morales, V. (2019). Social Media Use and Customer Engagement. In A. Khosrow-Pour (Ed.), *Advanced Methodologies and Technologies in Digital Marketing and Entrepreneurship* (pp. 643–655). IGI Global. doi:10.4018/978-1-5225-7766-9.ch050

Garsvaite, K., & Caruana, A. (2014). Do consumers of FMCGs seek brands with congruent personalities? *Journal of Brand Management*, *21*(6), 485–494. doi:10.1057/bm.2014.17

Garud, R., & Karnøe, P. (2003). Bricolage versus breakthrough: Distributed and embedded agency in technology entrepreneurship. *Research Policy*, *32*(2), 277–300. doi:10.1016/S0048-7333(02)00100-2

Gencer, C., & Çetin, T. (2011). Kurumsal Performans Karnesi ve Havacılık Sektöründe Bir Uygulama. *Savunma Bilimleri Dergisi*, *10*(2), 105–121.

Ghauri, P. (2004). Designing and conducting case studies in international business research. Handbook of Qualitative Research Methods for International Business, 1(1), 109–124.

Gibson, J. L., Ivancevich, J. M., & Donnelly, J. H. (2012). *Organizations: Behavior, structure, processes* (14th ed.). McGraw-Hill Companies, Inc.

Gıda Kurtarma Derneği Official Web Site. (2021). https://gktd.org/

Giddens, A. (1983). Comments on the Theory of Structuration. *Journal for the Theory of Social Behaviour*, *13*(1), 75–80. doi:10.1111/j.1468-5914.1983.tb00463.x

Gielens, K., & Steenkamp, J.-B. E. M. (2019). Branding in the era of digital (dis)intermediation. *International Journal of Research in Marketing*, *36*(3), 367–384. doi:10.1016/j.ijresmar.2019.01.005

Ginsberg, A., & Venkatraman, N. (1985). Contingency perspectives of organizational strategy: A critical review of the empirical research. *Academy of Management Review*, *10*(3), 421–434. doi:10.5465/amr.1985.4278950

GolinHarris. (2013). *Research: The Impact of Real-Time Marketing*. http://www.golinharris.com/#!/insights/real-timemarketing-research

Goreglyad, V. P. (2019). Digital audit in the Bank of Russia as a mechanism to improve the efficiency of business processes. *Public Administration*, *21/1*(117), 64-70.

Gore-Langton, L. (2017). *Bonduelle cuts out retailers with online delivery service*. https://www.foodnavigator.com/Article/2017/01/11/Bonduelle-cuts-out-retailers-with-online-delivery-service

Gorkemli, H. N. (2011). *Bölgesel kalkınmada teknoparkların önemi ve Konya Teknokent örneği* [Doctoral dissertation]. Selcuk University.

Göv, A. S. (2019). Green Airport Management Practices and Sustainability Relationship in Turkey. In *New Trends in Management Studies*. Peterlang Publishing. https://www.peterlang.com/view/9783631805947/html/ch25.xhtml

Govindarajan, V. (1988). A contingency approach to strategy implementation at the business-unit level: Integrating administrative mechanisms with strategy. *Academy of Management Journal*, *31*(4), 828–853.

Grant, R. M. (2016). *Contemporary strategy analysis: text and cases* (9th ed.). Wiley.

Greiner, L. E., Dalton, G. W., & Lawrence, P. R. (1970). *Organization change and development*. Dorsey Press.

Gummerus, J., Liljander, V., Weman, E., & Pihlström, M. (2012). Customer engagement in a Facebook brand community. *Management Research Review*, *35*(9), 857–877. doi:10.1108/01409171211256578

Günaydın, M. (2019). *Gerçek zamanlı reklamların tüketici davranışlarına etkisi: Sosyal medya üzerine bir araştırma* [Doctoral dissertation]. Marmara University, Istanbul, Turkey.

Gunelius, S. (2011). *Content marketing for dummies*. John Wiley & Sons.

Gunzler, D., Chen, T., Wu, P., & Zhang, H. (2013). Introduction to mediation analysis with structural equation modeling. *Shanghai Jingshen Yixue*, *25*(6), 390. PMID:24991183

Habes, M., Alghizzawi, M., Ali, S., Salih Alnaser, A., & Salloum, S. A. (2020). The relation among marketing ads, via digital media and mitigate (COVID-19) pandemic in Jordan. *International Journal of Advanced Science and Technology*, *29*(7), 12326–12348.

Hacıalioğlu, A. B., & Sağlam, M. (2021). Covid-19 pandemi sürecinde tüketici davranışları ve e-ticaretteki değişimler. *Medya ve Kültürel Çalışmalar Dergisi*, *3*(1), 16–29.

Hakanson, D., & Bengtsson, T. (2015). Real-Time Marketing Effects on Brands in Social Media. Halmstad University, International Marketing Program. Sweden: Halmstad University.

Hall, S. J. (2021). Facing Up To Your Digital Footprint. In *Inspirational Stories from English Language Classrooms* (pp. 117-119). Teflin Publications.

Hambrick, D. C., & Fredrickson, J. W. (2001). Are you sure you have a strategy? *The Academy of Management Executive*, *19*(4), 48–58. doi:10.5465/ame.2001.5897655

Hanlon, A., & Chaffey, D. (2015). *Essential Marketing Models: Classic Planning Tools to inform strategy*. https://www.davidhodder.com/wp-content/uploads/2018/01/Marketing-Models.pdf

Hanningtone, J. G., Miemie, S., & Elroy, E. S. (2013). Creating a sustainable competitive advantage at a high performing firm in Kenya. *African Journal of Business Management*, *7*(21), 2049–2058. doi:10.5897/ajbm2013.6974

Hansen, E. G., & Schaltegger, S. (2016). The sustainability balanced scorecard: A systematic review of architectures. *Journal of Business Ethics*, *133*(2), 193–221. doi:10.100710551-014-2340-3

Harel, C. (2014). *Bonduelle s'essaie à de nouveaux territoires de chasse*. LSA N° 2336-2337.

Harmeling, C. M., Moffett, J. W., Arnold, M. J., & Carlson, B. D. (2017). Toward a theory of customer engagement marketing. *Journal of the Academy of Marketing Science*, *45*(3), 312–335. doi:10.100711747-016-0509-2

Hasan, R. U., & Chyi, T. M. (2017). Practical application of Balanced Scorecard - A literature review. *Journal of Strategy and Performance Management*, *5*(3), 87–103.

Hatch, M. J., & Cunliffe, A. L. (2006). *Organization theory modern, symbolic, and postmodern perspectives* (2nd ed.). Oxford University Press.

Henkel Official Web Site. (2021). https://www.henkel.com/brands-and-businesses/pril-27222

Henkel Official Web Site. (2021). https://www.henkel.com/company/milestones-and-achievements/history

Henkel Turkey Official Web Site. (2021). https://www.henkel.com.tr/markalar-ve-isbirimleri/camasir-ve-ev-bakim/pril-648868

Henkel Turkey Official Web Site. (2021). https://www.henkel.com.tr/sirketimiz/onemli-olaylar-ve-basarilar/tarih

Herstatt, C., & Tiwari, R. (2020). Opportunities of frugality in the post-corona era. *International Journal of Technology Management*, *83*(1-3), 15–33. doi:10.1504/IJTM.2020.109276

Hines, P., & Rich, N. (1997). The seven value stream mapping tools. *International Journal of Production & Operations Management*, *17*(1), 46–64. doi:10.1108/01443579710157989

Hitt, M. A., Ireland, R. D., & Hoskisson, R. E. (2005). *Strategic Management: Competitiveness and Globalization*. Thomson South-Western Publishing.

Hollebeek, L. D., & Macky, K. (2019). Digital Content Marketing's Role in Fostering Consumer Engagement, Trust, and Value: Framework, Fundamental Propositions, and Implications. *Journal of Interactive Marketing*, *45*, 27–41. doi:10.1016/j.intmar.2018.07.003

Hollenbeck, C., Peters, C., & Zinkhan, G. (2008). Retail Spectacles and Brand Meaning: Insights from a Brand Museum Case Study. *Journal of Retailing*, *84*(3), 334–353. doi:10.1016/j.jretai.2008.05.003

Holliman, G., & Rowley, J. (2014). Business to business digital content marketing: Marketers' perceptions of best practice. *Journal of Research in Interactive Marketing*, *8*(4), 269–393. doi:10.1108/JRIM-02-2014-0013

Hrebiniak, L. G., & Joyce, W. (1985). Organizational adaptation: Strategic choice and environmental determinism. *Administrative Science Quarterly*, *30*(3), 336–349. doi:10.2307/2392666

Hsu, C. K. J. (2017). Selling products by selling brand purpose. *Journal of Brand Strategy*, *5*(4), 373–394.

Huang, L. Y., & Hsieh, Y. (2011). What drives consumer impulse buying? Evidence from a retail setting in Taiwan. *Journal of International Management Studies*, *6*(1), 1–8.

Hu, L. T., & Bentler, P. M. (1999). Cutoff criteria for fit indexes in covariance structure analysis: Conventional criteria versus new alternatives. *Structural Equation Modeling*, *6*(1), 1–55. doi:10.1080/10705519909540118

Compilation of References

Hussain, S., Khattak, J., Rizwan, A., & Latif, M. A. (2014). Interactive Effects of Ansoff Growt Strategies and Market Environment on Firm's Growth. *British Journal of Business and Management Research*, *1*(2), 68–78.

IABTR- No Water Challenge. (2021). https://iabtr.org/no-water-challenge

IABTR-Bir Gölü Kurtarmak. (2021). https://iabtr.org/bir-golu-kurtarmak

IABTR-Hani Fatura. (2021). https://iabtr.org/hani-fatura

IABTR-Su Endeksi. (2021). https://iabtr.org/su-endeksi

IABTR-Yarından Haberler. (2021). https://iabtr.org/yarindan-haberler

İçözüT. (2020). https://webrazzi.com/2020/07/09/fairy-nin-bosa-harcama-projesi-bundle-ile-24-saat-icinde-50-bin-kisiye-ulasti/

Ieva, M., & Ziliani, C. (2018). Mapping touchpoint exposure in retailing. *International Journal of Retail & Distribution Management*, *46*(3), 304–322. doi:10.1108/IJRDM-04-2017-0097

Ilonen, L., Wren, J., Gabrielsson, M., & Salimäki, M. (2011). The role of branded retail in manufacturers' international strategy. *International Journal of Retail & Distribution Management*, *39*(6), 414–433. doi:10.1108/09590551111137976

India, C. C. I. (2019). CII presents award to entrepreneurs. https://www.cciindia.org/food-processing.html

Internet World Stats. (2021). *Middle East Internet Users 2021*. https://www.internetworldstats.com

Izard, C. E. (1997). Emotions and facial expressions: A perspective from Differential Emotions Theory. In J. A. Russell & J. M. Fernández-Dols (Eds.), Studies in emotion and social interaction, 2nd series. The psychology of facial expression (pp. 57-77). Cambridge University Press. doi:10.1017/CBO9780511659911.005

Jahn, S., Nierobisch, T., Toporowski, W., & Dannewald, T. (2018). Selling the extraordinary in experiential retail stores. *Journal of the Association for Consumer Research*, *3*(3), 412–424. doi:10.1086/698330

Jarzabkowski, P. (2004). Strategy as practice: Recursiveness, adaptation, and practices-in-use. *Organization Studies*, *25*(4), 529–560. doi:10.1177/0170840604040675

Jewczyn, N. (2010). Integrative Business Policy With a SWOT Analysis of Southwest Airlines: What Are They Doing Right in Today's Economy? *Journal of Business Leadership Today*, *1*(8), 1–12.

Jewell, R. D. (2007). Establishing Effective Repositioning Communications in a Competitive Marketplace. *Journal of Marketing Communications*, *13*(4), 231–241. doi:10.1080/13527260701193325

Johnson, G., Scholes, K., & Whittington, R. (2008). *Exploring corporate strategy: text & cases* (8th ed.). Financial Times Prentice Hall.

Johnson, G., Whittington, R., & Scholes, K. (2011). *Exploring corporate strategy* (9th ed.). Prentice Hall.

Johnson, G., Whittington, R., & Scholes, K. (2017). *Exploring strategy* (11th ed.). Pearson.

Jones, M. R., & Karsten, H. (2008). Giddens's structuration theory and information systems research. *MIS Quarterly: Management Information Systems*, *32*(1), 127–157. doi:10.2307/25148831

Kaczmarek, T., Perez, K., Demir, E., & Zaremba, A. (2021). How to survive a pandemic: The corporate resiliency of travel and leisure companies to the COVID-19 outbreak. *Tourism Management*, *84*, 104281. doi:10.1016/j.tourman.2020.104281

Kahraman, M. (2013). *Sosyal Medya 101 2.0 – Pazarlamacılar İçin Sosyal Medyaya Giriş*. MediaCat.

Kaleynska, T. (2015). Business Intelligence and social media listening. *Economy & Business*, *9*(1), 667–671.

Kallier, S. M. (2017). The influence of real-time marketing campaigns of retailers on consumer purchase behavior. *International Review of Management and Marketing*, *7*(3).

Kallier-Tar, S. M., & Wiid, J. A. (2021). Consumer perceptions of real-time marketing used in campaigns for retail businesses. *International Journal of Research in Business and Social Science*, *10*(2), 86–105.

Kanbur, E., & Karakavuz, H. (2017). Stratejik Yönetim Kapsamında Küresel Havayolu İşbirliklerinin SWOT Analizi. *Journal of Aviation*, *1*(2), 74–86. doi:10.30518/jav.336347

Kanda, S. (2021). *Global Fruit and Vegetable Processing: Industry Report*. IBISWorld.

Kandemir, A., & Uğurluoğlu, Ö. Ç. (2017). Sağlık Kurumları Yönetimi Literatüründe Stratejik Yönetim Üzerine Yürütülen. *Hacettepe Sağlık İdaresi Dergisi*, *20*(1), 23–36.

Karabulut, M. (1989). Tüketici Davranışı. İÜ İşletme İktisadi Enstitüsü.

Karagiannopoulos, G., Georgopoulos, N., & Nikolopoulos, K. (2005). Fathoming Porter's five forces model in the internet era. *Info*, *7*(6), 66–76. doi:10.1108/14636690510628328

Karkar, A. (2016). Değer ve güven ağlarının yükselişinde içerik pazarlaması. *International Journal of Social Sciences and Education Research*, *2*(1), 275–285.

Karpat, S. (2012). *P&G Türkiye Yönetim Kurulu Başkanı Saffet Karpat Açıklaması*. https://www.sondakika.com/haber/haber-p-g-turkiye-yonetim-kurulu-baskani-saffet-karpat-4172595/

Kaya, Ö., & Toroğlu, E. (2015). Monitoring urban development of Kayseri and change detection analysis. *Türk Coğrafya Dergisi*, *65*, 87-96. https://dergipark.org.tr/en/pub/tcd/issue/21272/228403

Kayabaşı, E. (2020). Covid-19'un piyasalara ve tüketici davranişlarina etkisi. *Avrasya Sosyal ve Ekonomi Araştırmaları Dergisi*, *7*(5), 15–25.

Kee, A. W. A., & Yazdanifard, R. (2015). The review of content marketing as a new trend in marketing practices. *International Journal of Management. Accounting and Economics*, *2*(9), 1055–1064.

Keles, M. K. (2007). *Türkiye'de teknokentler bir ampirik inceleme* [MSc. Thesis]. Süleyman Demirel University, Isparta, Turkey.

Kent, R. J., & Allen, C. T. (1994). Competitive Interference Effects in Consumer Memory for Advertising: The Role of Brand Familiarity. *Journal of Marketing*, *58*(3), 97–105. doi:10.1177/002224299405800307

Kerbouche, M., Bouhelal, F., & Belmimoun, A. (2017). Organisation effectiveness under the internal factors and environment. *Les politiques Economique En Algérie*, *8*(1), 33–46.

Kerns, C. (2014). *Trendology/Building an Advantage Throught Data – Driven Real – Time Marketing*. Palgrave Macmillan. doi:10.1057/9781137479563

Keskin, H., Akgün, A. E., & Koçoğlu, İ. (2016). *Örgüt teorisi*. Nobel Akademik Yayincilik.

Khandwalla, P. N. (1977). *The design of organizations*. Harcourt Brace Jovanovich.

Khatoon, S., & Rehman, V. (2021). Negative emotions in consumer brand relationship: A review and future research agenda. *International Journal of Consumer Studies*, *45*(4), 719–749. doi:10.1111/ijcs.12665

Kiani, G. R. (1998). Marketing Opportunities in the digital world. *Internet Research: Electronic Networking Practices and Policy*, *8*(2), 185–194. doi:10.1108/10662249810211656

Kim W. C., Mauborgne R., & Pipino M., (2020). *Fintech: Compte-Nickel Creating New Demand in the Retail Banking Sector.* INSEAD, Case study: 01/2020-6235, 1–10.

Kim, W. C., & Mauborgne, R. (2005). Value innovation: A leap into the blue ocean. *The Journal of Business Strategy*, *26*(4), 22–28. doi:10.1108/02756660510608521

Kim, W. C., & Mauborgne, R. (2006). *Blue ocean strategy: How to create uncontested market space and make the competition irrelevant*. Harvard Business School Press.

Kirk, J., & Miller, M. L. (1986). *Reliability and validity in qualitative research*. Sage Publications. doi:10.4135/9781412985659

Kirzner, I. (1973). *Competition and Entrepreneurship*. University of Chicago Press.

KocasuN. A. (2020). https://mediacat.com/finish-tiktok-nowaterchallenge/

Kocel, T. (2015). *İşletme yöneticiliği* (16th ed.). Beta Yayincilik.

Kocyigit, Y. (2018). *Firmaların örgütsel esnekliği, kullandıkları rekabet stratejileri ve algılanan rekabet üstünlüğü arasındaki etkileşim: Türkiye'nin en büyük 500 sanayi işletmesinde bir uygulama* [Doctoral dissertation]. Izmir Katip Celebi University.

Kogut, B. (1985). Designing global strategies: Comparative and competitive value-added chain. *Sloan Management Review*, *26*(4), 15–28.

Koshkaki, E. R., & Solhi, S. (2016). The facilitating role of negative emotion in decision making process: A hierarchy of effects model approach. *The Journal of High Technology Management Research*, *27*(2), 119–128. doi:10.1016/j.hitech.2016.10.010

Kostelijk, E., & Alsem, K. J. (2020). *Brand positioning: Connecting marketing strategy and communications*. Routledge. doi:10.4324/9780429285820

Kotane, I., Znotina, D., & Hushko, S. (2019). Assessment of trends in the application of digital marketing. *Scientific Journal of Polonia University*, *33*(2), 28–35. doi:10.23856/3303

Kotler, P. (2000). *Marketing Management* (10th ed.). Prentice-Hall.

Kotler, P. (2011). Reinventing marketing to manage the environmental imperative. *Journal of Marketing*, *75*(4), 132–135.

Kotler, P., Kartajaya, H., & Setiawan, I. (2010). *Marketing 3.0: From Products to Customers to the Human Spirit*. John Wiley & Sons.

Kotler, P., Kartajaya, H., & Setiawan, I. (2016). *Marketing 4.0: Moving from traditional to digital*. John Wiley & Sons Inc.

Kozinets, R. V., Sherry, J. F., DeBerry-Spence, B., Duhachek, A., Nuttavuthisit, K., & Storm, D. (2002). Themed flagship brand stores in the new millennium: Theory, practice, prospects. *Journal of Retailing*, *78*(1), 17–29. doi:10.1016/S0022-4359(01)00063-X

KPMG. (2016). India's food service industry: Growth recipe. KPMG. https://assets.kpmg/content/dam/kpmg/in/pdf/2016/11/Indias-food-service.pdf

KPMG. (2020). *Pandemi sonrası yeni küresel tüketici modeli: Hesaplı, dijital, seçici*. https://home.kpmg/tr/tr/home/medya/press-releases/2020/10/pandemi-sonrasi-yeni-tuketici-modeli.html

Kujur, F., & Singh, S. (2018). Emotions as predictor for consumer engagement in YouTube advertisement. *Journal of Advances in Management Research*, *15*(2), 184–197. doi:10.1108/JAMR-05-2017-0065

Kullnig, C., Obermüller, A., & Aichhorn, K. (2020). Improving campaign performance using purpose marketing: Case study of Run For The Oceans. *Journal of Brand Strategy*, *9*(1), 7–17.

Kumar, P., & Singh, G. (2020). Using social media and digital marketing tools and techniques for developing brand equity with connected consumers. In S. S. Dadwal (Ed.), *Handbook of research on innovations in technology and marketing for the connected consumer* (pp. 336–355). IGI Global. doi:10.4018/978-1-7998-0131-3.ch016

Kumar, S., & Bhatia, M. S. (2021). Environmental dynamism, industry 4.0 and performance. *Industrial Marketing Management*, *95*, 54–64. doi:10.1016/j.indmarman.2021.03.010

Kunz, W., Aksoy, L., Bart, Y., Heinonen, K., Kabadayi, S., Ordenes, F. V., Sigala, M., Diaz, D., & Theodoulidis, B. (2017). Customer engagement in a Big Data world. *Journal of Services Marketing*, *31*(2), 161–171. doi:10.1108/JSM-10-2016-0352

Kuo, Y. F., & Wu, C. M. (2012). Satisfaction and post-purchase intentions with service recovery of online shopping websites: Perspectives on perceived justice and emotions. *International Journal of Information Management*, *32*(2), 127–138. doi:10.1016/j.ijinfomgt.2011.09.001

Lado, A. O., & Wilson, M. C. (1994). Human resource systems and sustained competitive advantage: A competency based perspective. *Academy of Management Review*, *19*(4), 699–727. doi:10.5465/amr.1994.9412190216

Lambin, J.-J., & Moerloose, C. d. (2012). *Marketing stratégique et opérationnel: du marketing à l'orientation-marché* (8th ed.). Dunod.

Lambiotte, R. & Kosinski, M. (2014). *Tracking the Digital Footprints of Personality*. Academic Press.

Laros, F. J., & Steenkamp, J. B. E. (2005). Emotions in consumer behavior: A hierarchical approach. *Journal of Business Research*, *58*(10), 1437–1445. doi:10.1016/j.jbusres.2003.09.013

Latif, A., Sibghatullah, A., & Siddiqui, K. A. (2016). Repositioning Horlicks in Pakistan. *Journal of Marketing Management and Consumer Behavior*, *1*(2), 44–53.

Lau-Gesk, L., & Meyers-Levy, J. (2009). Emotional persuasion: When the valence versus the resource demands of emotions influence consumers' attitudes. *The Journal of Consumer Research*, *36*(4), 585–599. doi:10.1086/605297

Le Bret, H. (2016). Le Compte-Nickel: un compte pour tous, sans banque. *Le Journal de l'école de Paris du Management*, *6*, 24–30.

Le Bret, H. (2017). Vers un monde sans banques? [Towards a world without banks?]. In Annales des Mine- Réalités industrielles (n° 4, pp. 56–59). FFE.

Le Bret, H. (2013). *No Bank. L'incroyable histoire d'un entrepreneur de banlieue qui veut révolutionner la banque*. Les Arènes.

LeCompte, M. D., & Goetz, J. P. (1982). Problems of reliability and validity in ethnographic research. *Review of Educational Research*, *52*(1), 31–60. doi:10.3102/00346543052001031

Lemon, K. N., & Verhoef, P. C. (2016). Understanding Customer Experience Throughout the Customer Journey. *Journal of Marketing*, *80*(6), 69–96. doi:10.1509/jm.15.0420

Lenderman, M. (2015). *Cause vs. Purpose: What's the Difference?* https://sustainablebrands.com/read/product-service-design-innovation/cause-vs-purpose-what-s-the-difference

Compilation of References

Lentschner, K. (2014). *Bonduelle se lance dans l'e-commerce*. https://www.lefigaro.fr/societes/2014/10/01/20005-20141001ARTFIG00008-bonduelle-se-lance-dans-le-e-commerce.php

Leonard-Barton, D. (1992). Core Capabilities and Core Rigidities: A Paradox in Managing New Product *Development*. *Strategic Management Journal, 13*(S1), 111–125. doi:10.1002mj.4250131009

Lieb, R. (2013). *A market definition report. real-time marketing: The agility leverage*. https://www.slideshare.net/Altimeter/report-realtime-marketing-the-agility-to-leveragenow-by-rebecca-lieb-jessica-groopman

Lieb, R. (2011). *Marketing: Think like a publisher-how to use content to market online and in social media*. Que Publishing.

Lieb, R. (2012). *Content marketing: think like a publisher—how to use content to market online and in social media*. Que Publishing.

Lindblom, C. E. (1959). The science of "Muddling Through". *Public Administration Review, 19*(2), 79–88. doi:10.2307/973677

Linton, G., & Kask, J. (2017). Configurations of entrepreneurial orientation and competitive strategy for high performance. *Journal of Business Research, 70*, 168–176. doi:10.1016/j.jbusres.2016.08.022

Lippman, S. A., & Rumelt, R. P. (1982). Uncertain imitability: An analysis of interfirm differences in efficiency under competition. *The Bell Journal of Economics, 13*(2), 418–439. doi:10.2307/3003464

Lu, J., Hao, Q., & Jing, M. (2016). Consuming, sharing, and creating content: How young students use new social media in and outside school. *Computers in Human Behavior, 64*, 55–64. doi:10.1016/j.chb.2016.06.019

Madden, C. B. (2017). *Path to Purpose*. Sunday Lunch Pty Ltd.

Mania, M. (2013). *IBM's CEO on data, the death of segmentation and the 18-month deadline*. https://www.marketingmag.com.au/news-c/ibms-ceo-on-data-the-death-of-segmentation-and-the-18-month-deadline

March, J. G. (1991). Exploration and exploitation in organization learning. *Organization Science, 2*(1), 71–87. doi:10.1287/orsc.2.1.71

March, J. G., & Simon, H. A. (1958). *Organizations*. Wiley.

Marketing Türkiye. (2020). https://www.marketingturkiye.com.tr/kampanyalar/fairynin-evden-cekilen-reklam-filmi-bosa-harcama-diyor/

Marshall, C., & Rossman, G. B. (1994). *Designing qualitative research*. Sage Publications.

Martin, B. A., Wentzel, D., & Tomczak, T. (2008). Effects of susceptibility to normative influence and type of testimonial on attitudes toward print advertising. *Journal of Advertising, 37*(1), 29–43.

Mathew, V., & Soliman, M. (2021). Does digital content marketing affect tourism consumer behavior? An extension of technology acceptance model. *Journal of Consumer Behaviour, 20*(1), 61–75. doi:10.1002/cb.1854

Mazerant, K., Willemsen, L. M., Neijens, P. C., & van Noort, G. (2021). Spot-on creativity: Creativity biases and their differential effects on consumer responses in (non-) real-time marketing. *Journal of Interactive Marketing, 53*, 15–31. doi:10.1016/j.intmar.2020.06.004

McKinsey. (2020). *How COVID-19 has pushed companies over the technology tipping point—and transformed business forever*. https://www.mckinsey.com/business-functions/strategy-and-corporate-finance/our-insights/how-covid-19-has-pushed-companies-over-the-technology-tipping-point-and-transformed-business-forever

McLean, G., & Wilson, A. (2019). Shopping in the digital world: Examining customer engagement through augmented reality mobile applications. *Computers in Human Behavior*, *101*, 210–224. doi:10.1016/j.chb.2019.07.002

Meaningful Brands Research. (2019). https://s3.amazonaws.com/media.mediapost.com/uploads/MeaningfulBrands2019.pdf

Media Ant. (2019). Advertising in Adyar Anand Bhavan. https://www.themediaant.com/nontraditional/a2b-bangalore-advertising

MediaCat. (2019). https://mediacat.com/finish-ve-arda-turkmenden-isbirligi/

MediaCat. (2020). https://mediacat.com/cicek-gibi-bulasik-makineleri-icin-finish-reklami/

MediaCat. (2020). https://mediacat.com/turkiyenin-suyunu-takip-eden-endeks/

MediaCat. (2021). https://mediacat.com/2020nin-en-etkili-kampanyalari/

Merriam, S. B., & Robin, S. G. (2019). *Qualitative Research in Practice: Examples for Discussion and Analysis* (2nd ed.). Jossey-Bass Publishers.

Michel, G. M., Feori, M., Damhorst, M. L., Lee, Y. A., & Niehm, L. S. (2019). Stories we wear: Promoting sustainability practices with the case of Patagonia. *Family and Consumer Sciences Research Journal*, *48*(2), 165–180.

Micheli, M., Lutz, Ch., & Büchi, M. (2018). Digital Footprints: An Emerging Dimension of Digital Inequality. *Journal of Information Communication and Ethics in Society*, *16*(3), 242–251. doi:10.1108/JICES-02-2018-0014

Miles, M. B., & Huberman, A. M. (1994). *Qualitative data analysis: An expanded sourcebook* (2nd ed.). Sage.

Miles, R. E., & Snow, C. C. (1978). *Organizational strategy, structure, and process*. McGraw-Hill.

Miles, R. E., & Snow, C. C. (1984). Designing strategic human resource systems. *Organizational Dynamics*, *13*(1), 36–52. doi:10.1016/0090-2616(84)90030-5

Miller, M. (2013). *Real-time marketing smarts: Companies killing it with off-the-cuff content*. TopRank Marketing. https://www.toprankblog.com/2013/04/real-time-marketing-smarts/

Miller, D. (1986). Configurations of strategy and structure. *Strategic Management Journal*, *7*(3), 233–249. doi:10.1002mj.4250070305

Miller, D. (1988). Relating Porter's strategy to environment and structure. *Academy of Management Journal*, *31*(2), 280–308.

Miller, D. (1996). Configurations revisited. *Strategic Management Journal*, *17*(7), 505–512. doi:10.1002/(SICI)1097-0266(199607)17:7<505::AID-SMJ852>3.0.CO;2-I

Miller, E. S. (1991). Of economic paradigms, puzzles, problems, and policies; or, is the economy too important to be entrusted to the economists? *Journal of Economic Issues*, *25*(4), 993–1004. doi:10.1080/00213624.1991.11505228

Mintzberg, H. (1978). Patterns in strategy formation. *Management Science*, *24*(9), 934–948. doi:10.1287/mnsc.24.9.934

Mintzberg, H. (1979). *The structuring of organizations*. Prentice Hall.

Mintzberg, H. (1981). Organization design: Fashion or fit. *Harvard Business Review*, *59*(1), 103–116.

Mintzberg, H. (1987). Crafting strategy. *Harvard Business Review*, 477–486.

Compilation of References

Mintzberg, H. (1987). The strategy concept I: Five Ps for strategy. *California Management Review*, *30*(1), 11–24. doi:10.2307/41165263

Mintzberg, H., Ahlstrand, B., & Lampel, J. (2009). *Strategy Safari. Your complete guide through the wilds of strategic management*. FT-Prentice Hall.

Mintzberg, H., Ahlstrand, B., & Lampel, J. (2010). Safari de estratégia: Um roteiro pela selva do planejamento estratégico. *The Bookman*.

Mintzberg, H., & Waters, J. A. (1985). Of strategies, deliberate and emergent. *Strategic Management Journal*, *6*(3), 257–272. doi:10.1002mj.4250060306

Morris, P. F. (1990). Bureaucracy, professionalization and school centred innovation strategies. *International Review of Education*, *36*(1), 21–41. doi:10.1007/BF01874975

Müller, J., & Christandl, F. (2019). Content is king–But who is the king of kings? The effect of content marketing, sponsored content & user-generated content on brand responses. *Computers in Human Behavior*, *96*, 46–55. doi:10.1016/j.chb.2019.02.006

Nandakumar, M. K., Ghobadian, A., & O'Regan, N. (2010). Business-level strategy and performance: The moderating effects of environment and structure. *Management Decision*, *48*(6), 907–939. doi:10.1108/00251741011053460

Nayyar, P. R. (1993). On the measurement of competitive strategy: Evidence from a large multiproduct U.S. firm. *Academy of Management Journal*, *36*(6), 1652–1669.

Neis, D. F., Pereira, M. F., & Maccari, E. A. (2016). Strategic planning process and organizational structure: Impacts, confluence and similarities. *Brazilian Business Review*, *14*(5), 479–492. doi:10.15728/bbr.2017.14.5.2

Nemetz, P. L., & Fry, L. W. (1988). Flexible manufacturing organizations: Implications for strategy formulation and organization design. *Academy of Management Review*, *13*(4), 627–639. doi:10.5465/amr.1988.4307510

Nicoletti, B. (2017). *The Future of Fintech. Integrating Finance and Technology in Financial Services*. Palgrave Macmillan.

Nielsen, I. Q. (2020). *Key consumer behaviour thresholds identified as the coronavirus outbreak evolves*. https://nielseniq.com/global/en/insights/analysis/2020/key-consumerbehavior-thresholds-identified-as-the-coronavirus-outbreak-evolves-2

Nierobisch, T., Toporowski, W., Dannewald, T., & Jahn, S. (2017). Flagship stores for FMCG national brands: Do they improve brand cognitions and create favorable consumer reactions? *Journal of Retailing and Consumer Services*, *34*, 117–137. doi:10.1016/j.jretconser.2016.09.014

Nikunen, T., Saarela, M., Oikarinen, E. L., Muhos, M., & Isohella, L. (2017). Micro-enterprise's digital marketing tools for building customer relationships. *Management*, *12*(2).

Nonaka, I. (1988). Toward middle-up-down management: Accelerating information creation. *Sloan Management Review*, *29*(3), 9–21.

Norman, G. (2010). Likert scales, levels of measurement and the 'Laws' of statistics. *Advances in Health Sciences Education: Theory and Practice*, *15*(5), 625–632. doi:10.100710459-010-9222-y PMID:20146096

Novak, J., Purta, M., Marciniak, T., Ignatowicz, K., Rozenbaum, K., & Yearwood, K. (2018). *The rise of Digital Challengers*. Digital McKinsey. https://www.mckinsey.com/~/media/McKinsey/Featured%20Insights/Europe/Central%20and%20Eastern%20Europe%20needs%20a%20new%20engine%20for%20growth/The-rise-of-Digital-Challengers.ashx

Novak, T. P., Hoffman, D. L., & Yung, Y.-F. (2000). Measuring the Customer Experience in Online Environments: A Structural Modeling Approach. *Marketing Science*, *19*(1), 22–42. doi:10.1287/mksc.19.1.22.15184

NTV. (2020). https://www.ntv.com.tr/ekonomi/gida-israfina-karsi-bosa-harcama-kampanyasi,j5WjWuyh-ECo7_gj4bCJxQ

Nyer, P. U. (1997). A study of the relationships between cognitive appraisals and consumption emotions. *Journal of the Academy of Marketing Science*, *25*(4), 296–304. doi:10.1177/0092070397254002

O'Donnell, E., & Brown, S. (2011). The Effect Of Memory Structure And Function On Consumers' Perception And Recall Of Marketing Messages: A Review Of The Memory Research In Marketing. *Academy of Marketing Studies Journal*, *15*(1), 71–85.

Odtü-Tek. (2021, March 12). *Teknokent Nedir*. http://odtuteknokent.com.tr/tr/hakkinda/teknokent-nedir#:~:text=Teknoloji%20Geli%C5%9Ftirme%20B%C3%B6lgesi%2C%20y%C3%BCksek%2Fileri,bir%20bulu%C5%9Fu%20ticari%20bir%20%C3%BCr%C3%BCn%2C

Olinder, N., Tsvetkov, A., Fedyakin, K., & Zaburdaeva, K. (2020). Using Digital Footprints in Social Research: An Interdisciplinary Approach. *Wisdom*, *16*(3), 124–135. doi:10.24234/wisdom.v16i3.403

Olson, E. M., Slater, S. F., Hult, G., & Tomas, M. (2005). The performance implications of fit among business strategy, marketing organization structure and strategic behavior. *Journal of Marketing*, *69*(3), 49–65. doi:10.1509/jmkg.69.3.49.66362

Omran, W. (2021). Customer Engagement in Social Media Brand Community. *Research Journal of Business Management*, *9*(1), 31–40.

ÖnderN. (2020). https://www.marketingturkiye.com.tr/haberler/iste-tuketicilere-gore-turkiyenin-en-hijyenik-markalari/

ÖnderN. (2021). https://www.marketingturkiye.com.tr/haberler/iste-yilin-en-basarili-sosyal-medya-kampanyalari/

Onur, T. (2007). *Ayaktan sağlık hizmeti veren sağlık kuruluşu olan özel hastanelerde uygulanan rekabet stratejilerinin hasta memnuniyeti üzerine etkileri* [Master dissertation]. Maltepe University.

Oosthuizen, H. (1997). An evaluation of the relevance of the Miles & Snow strategic typology under present-day conditions of major environmental uncertainty: The emperor's new clothes or a paradigm shift? *South African Journal of Business Management*, *28*(2), 63–72. doi:10.4102ajbm.v28i2.790

ÖzkanP. (2021). https://mediacat.com/2020nin-en-etkili-kampanyalari/4/

Özsoy, V. S., & Örkcü, H. H. (2021). Structural and operational management of Turkish airports: A bootstrap data envelopment analysis of efficiency. *Utilities Policy*, *69*, 101180. doi:10.1016/j.jup.2021.101180

Öz, Y. (2016). *Havaalanlarının etkinliklerinin yıllara göre değerlendirilmesinde veri zarflama analizinin kullanılması*. İşletme Ana Bilim Dalı Yüksek Lisans Tezi.

P&G Official Web Site. (2021). www.pg.com.tr

P&G Products Official Web Site in Turkey. (2020). https://www.kadinlarbilir.com/markalar/fairy

P&G Products Official Web Site in Turkey. (2021). https://www.kadinlarbilir.com/ev/temizlik/fairynin-neden-guvenilir-oldugu-hakkinda-daha-fazlasini-okuyun

Pandey, M., & Singh, D. P. (2018). Evaluating the success factors for development and sustenance of low-cost regional airports in India using fuzzy multi-criteia decision making method. *Journal of Applied Economic Sciences*, *3*(56), 1–14.

Pansari, A., & Kumar, V. (2017). Customer engagement: The construct, antecedents, and consequences. *Journal of the Academy of Marketing Science*, *45*(3), 294–311. doi:10.100711747-016-0485-6

Papagiannis, N. (2020). *Effective SEO and content marketing: the ultimate guide for maximizing free web traffic*. John Wiley & Sons. doi:10.1002/9781119628682

Parthasarthy, R. S., & Sethi, P. (1992). The impact of flexible automation on business strategy and organizational structure. *Academy of Management Review*, *17*(1), 86–111. doi:10.5465/amr.1992.4279572

Patagonia Official Web Site. (2021). wornwear.patagonia.com

Patton, M. Q. (1987). *How to use qualitative methods in evaluation*. Sage Publications.

Patton, M. Q. (2002). *Qualitative research & Evaluation Methods* (3rd ed.).

Paul, J. (2019). Marketing in emerging markets: A review, theoretical synthesis and extension. *International Journal of Emerging Markets*, *15*(3), 446–468. doi:10.1108/IJOEM-04-2017-0130

Pearce, A. J., & Robinson, R. B. (2015). *Stratejik Yonetim: Gelistirme, Uygulama ve Kontrol* (12th ed.). (M. Barca, Trans.). Nobel Yayin.

Peker, İ., & Baki, B. (2009). Veri zarflama analizi ile türkiye havalimanlarında bir etkinlik ölçümü uygulaması. *Çukurova Sosyal Bilimler Enstitüsü Dergisi*, *15*(2), 72-88.

Pertusa-Ortega, E. M., Claver-Cortés, E., & Molina-Azorín, J. F. (2008). Strategy, structure, environment and performance in Spanish firms. *EuroMed Journal of Business*, *3*(2), 223–239. doi:10.1108/14502190810891245

Pettigrew, A. M. (2012). Context and Action in the Transformation of the Firm. *Journal of Management Studies*, *49*(7), 1304–1328. doi:10.1111/j.1467-6486.2012.01054.x

Polignano, M., Basile, P., Rossiello, G., de Gemmis, M., & Semerar, G. (2017). Empathic inclination from digital footprints. *Proceedings of the IEEE*, *102*(12), 1934–1939.

Poradova, M. (2020). Content marketing strategy and its impact on customers under the global market conditions. In *SHS Web of Conferences* (Vol. 74, p. 01027). EDP Sciences. 10.1051hsconf/20207401027

Porter, M. E. (1998b). *On competition*. Harvard Business School Publishing. http://lcweb.loc.gov/catdir/toc/98007643.html

Porter, M. (1980). *Competitive strategy- Techniques for analysing industries and competitors*. Free Press.

Porter, M. (1985). *Competitive advantage: Creating and sustaining superior performance*. Free Press.

Porter, M. (1990). *The competitive advantage of nations*. The MacMillan Press Limited. doi:10.1007/978-1-349-11336-1

Porter, M. (1996). What is Strategy? *Harvard Business Review*, *74*(6), 61–78. PMID:10158475

Porter, M. E. (1979). *How competitive forces shape strategy*. Harvard Business Review, March/April.

Porter, M. E. (1979b). How competitive forces shape strategy. *Harvard Business Review*, *57*(2), 137–145. PMID:18271320

Porter, M. E. (1980). *Competitive strategy: techniques for analyzing industries and competitors*. The Free Press.

Porter, M. E. (1985). *Competitive Advantage: Creating and Sustaining Superior Performance*. Simon and Schuster.

Porter, M. E. (1998). *Competitive strategy: techniques for analyzing industries and competitors: with a new introduction*. Free Press.

Porter, M. E. (2008). The five competitive forces that shape strategy. *Harvard Business Review*, *86*(1), 78. PMID:18271320

Powell, G., Seifert, H., Reblin, T., Burstein, P., Blowers, J., Menius, A., Painter, J., Thomas, M., Pierce, C., Rodriguez, H., Brownstein, J., Freifeld, C., Bell, H., & Dasgupta, N. (2016). Social Media Listening for Routine Post-Marketing Safety Surveillance. *Drug Safety*, *39*(5), 443–454. doi:10.100740264-015-0385-6 PMID:26798054

Pril Turkey Official Instagram Account. (2021). https://www.instagram.com/prilturkiye/?hl=tr

Pril Turkey Official Web Site. (2021). https://www.pril.com.tr/tr/ana-sayfa/pril-hakkinda-her-sey/taahhudumuz.html

Pril Turkey Official Web Site. (2021). https://www.pril.com.tr/tr/ana-sayfa/pril-hakkinda-her-sey/tarihimiz.html

Pril Turkey Official Web Site. (2021). https://www.pril.com.tr/tr/ana-sayfa/sofradabirlikte.html

Pril Turkey Official Web Site. (2021). https://www.pril.com.tr/tr/ana-sayfa/sofrada-birlikte.html

Pril Turkey Official Web Site. (2021). https://www.pril.com.tr/tr/ana-sayfa/sofrada-birlikte/unicef-isbirligimiz.html

Pril Turkey Official Youtube Account. (2021). https://www.youtube.com/c/PrilT%C3%BCrkiye/about

Quesado, P. R., Aibar, G. B., & Lima, R. L. (2018). Advantages and contributions in the balanced scorecard implementation. *Intangible Capital*, *14*(1), 186–201. doi:10.3926/ic.1110

Rajagopal. (2016). *Sustainable Growth in Global Markets: Strategic Choices and Managerial Implications*. Palgrave Macmillan.

Rajaratnam, D., & Chonko, L. B. (1995). The effect of business strategy type on marketing organization design, product-market growth strategy, relative marketing effort, and organization performance. *Journal of Marketing Theory and Practice*, *3*(3), 60–75. doi:10.1080/10696679.1995.11501696

Rankin, W. (2008). Waco Regional Airport: A case study for strategic airport business planning. *Journal of Airport Management*, *2*(4), 345–354.

Rankin, W. B. (2009). King County: A Case Study Model for Strategic Planning in College Aviation Learning. *Journal of Aviation/Aerospace Education Research*, *18*(3), 19–31. doi:10.15394/jaaer.2009.1430

Reckitt Official Web Site. (2021). https://www.reckitt.com/about-us/our-purpose-and-compass/

Reckitt Official Web Site. (2021). https://www.reckitt.com/brands/

Reece, M. (2010). *Real-time marketing for business growth: How to use social media, measure marketing, and create a culture of execution*. Pearson Education.

Reid, G. C., Smith, J. A., & Xu, Z. (2020). The Impact of Strategy, Technology, Size and Business Environment on the Organizational Form of Small Firms in China. *Asian Journal of Economics. Business and Accounting*, *20*(4), 15–32.

Reinartz, W., Wiegand, N., & Imschloss, M. (2019). The impact of digital transformation on the retailing value chain. *International Journal of Research in Marketing*, *36*(3), 350–366. doi:10.1016/j.ijresmar.2018.12.002

Retail Türkiye. (2019). *Finish, Yarının Suyu Projesi'nin duyusunu yaptı*. https://www.retailturkiye.com/firmalardan/finish-yarinin-suyu-projesinin-duyusunu-yapti

Richard, P. J., Devinney, T. M., Yip, G. S., & Johnson, G. (2009). Measuring Organizational Performance. *Journal of Management*, *35*(3), 718–804. doi:10.1177/0149206308330560

Richins, M. L. (1997). Measuring emotions in the consumption experience. *The Journal of Consumer Research*, *24*(2), 127–146. doi:10.1086/209499

Robbins, S. P., & DeCenzo, D. A. (2005). *Fundamentals of management: Essential concepts and applications* (5th ed.). Pearson.

Compilation of References

Rocchi, J. M. (2020). Competition Between Neobanks and Online Banks in the French Retail Banking Market and Reactions from Universal Banks. In A. Sghari & K. Mezghani (Eds.), *Influence of FinTech on Management Transformation* (pp. 191–216). IGI Global.

Rothaermel, F. T. (2017). Strategic management (3rd ed.). McGraw-Hill Education.

Rothaermel, F. T. (2017). *Strategic management* (3rd ed.). McGraw-Hill Education.

Rowley, J. (2008). Understanding digital content marketing. *Journal of Marketing Management*, 24(5-6), 517–540. doi:10.1362/026725708X325977

Rue, L. W., & Holland, P. G. (1989). *Strategic management: Concepts and experiences*. McGraw-Hill.

Ruiz-Mafe, C., Chatzipanagiotou, K., & Curras-Perez, R. (2018). The role of emotions and conflicting online reviews on consumers' purchase intentions. *Journal of Business Research*, 89, 336–344. doi:10.1016/j.jbusres.2018.01.027

Rumelt, R. P. (1984). Towards a strategic theory of the firm. *Competitive Strategic Management*, 26(3), 556–570.

Ryan, D., & Jones, C. (2009). *Digital marketing: Marketing strategies for engaging the digital generation*. Kogan page Ltd.

Sack, A. L., & Nadim, A. (2002). Strategic Choices in a Turbulent Environment: A Case Study of Starter Corporation. *Journal of Sport Management*, 16(1), 36–53. doi:10.1123/jsm.16.1.36

Salavou, H. (2015). Competitive strategies and their shift to the future. *European Business Review*, 27(1), 80–99. doi:10.1108/EBR-04-2013-0073

Salik, S. (2001). Modern yonetim yaklasimlari. *Dumlupınar Üniversitesi Sosyal Bilimler Dergisi*, 5, 1–19.

Şanlıoğlu, Ö., & Demirezen, B. (2020). Turizm sektörünün bölgesel kalkınma üzerindeki rolü: Kayseri iline yönelik nitel bir araştırma. *Erciyes Üniversitesi Sosyal Bilimler Enstitüsü Dergisi*, 50, 117–139.

Santos, J. D., & Castelo, J. P. (2018). The six dimensions on adoption of a CRM strategy. In I. Lee (Ed.), *Diverse Methods in Customer Relationship Marketing and Management* (pp. 17–43). IGI Global. doi:10.4018/978-1-5225-5619-0.ch002

Santos, J. D., Castelo, J. P., & Almeida, F. (2020). Critical Success Factors in a Six Dimensional Model CRM Strategy. In M. Khosrow-Pour (Ed.), *Encyclopedia of Organizational Knowledge, Administration, and Technology* (pp. 2104–2177). IGI Global. doi:10.4018/978-1-7998-3473-1.ch145

Sarıtaş, A. (2018). İçerik pazarlamasına yönelik bir literatür taraması. *Sosyal Araştırmalar ve Davranış Bilimleri Dergisi*, 232–239.

Sashi, C. M. (2012). Customer engagement, buyer-seller relationships, and social media. *Management Decision*, 50(2), 253–272. doi:10.1108/00251741211203551

Save Water Clean Clever in the UK. (2021). https://www.savewatercleanclever.co.uk/

Schachter, S., & Singer, J. E. (1962). Cognitive, social, and physiological determinants of emotional state. *Psychological Review*, 69(5), 379–399. doi:10.1037/h0046234 PMID:14497895

Schallmo, D. R., & Williams, C. A. (2018). History of digital transformation. In D. Schallmo & C. Williams (Eds.), *Digital Transformation Now!* (pp. 3–8). Springer. doi:10.1007/978-3-319-72844-5_2

Schlagwein, D., & Prasarnphanich, P. (2014). Social Media Around the Globe. *Journal of Organizational Computing and Electronic Commerce*, 24(2), 122–137. doi:10.1080/10919392.2014.896713

Schlegelmilch, B. B. (2016). *Global Marketing Strategy: An Executive Digest*. Springer. doi:10.1007/978-3-319-26279-6

Schweidel, D. A., & Moe, W. W. (2014). Listening in on Social Media: A Joint Model of Sentiment and Venue Format Choice. *JMR, Journal of Marketing Research, 51*(4), 387–402. doi:10.1509/jmr.12.0424

Scott, D. (2010). *Real-time marketing & PR*. John Wiley & Sons.

Scott, D. M. (2011). *Real-time marketing and PR: How to instantly engage your market, connect with customers, and create products that grow your business now*. John Wiley & Sons.

Scott, W. R. (1992). *Organizations: Rational, Natural and Open Systems* (3rd ed.). Prentice-Hall.

Sebastiani, R., & Montagnini, F. (2020). Actor engagement in service ecosystems: Innovating value co-creation in food retail. In F. Musso & E. Druica (Eds.), *Handbook of research on retailing techniques for optimal consumer engagement and experiences* (pp. 400–420). IGI Global. doi:10.4018/978-1-7998-1412-2.ch018

Segar Aviation. (2021). https://segaraviation.com/page90-kayseri-havaalani-hangar-projesi-sinyal-analizi.html

Sekaran, U., & Bougie, R. (2011). *Business Research Methods: A skill-building approach*. John Wiley& Sons Ltd.

Selaković, M., Tarabasz, A., & Gallant, M. (2020). Typology of Business-Related Fake News Online: A Literature Review. *Journal of Management and Marketing Review, 5*(4), 234–243.

SEMrush. (2020). *SEMrush tutorial: How To Create a Buyer Persona*. https://www.youtube.com/watch?v=9aPAPANeMKg

SEMrush. (2021). *Traffic analytics*. https://www.semrush.com/analytics/traffic/overview/amazon.ae

Şengül, H., & Bulut, A. (2019). Sağlik Turizmi Çerçevesinde Swot Analizi. *ESTÜDAM Halk Sağlığı Dergisi, 4*(1), 55–70.

Sengul, M. (2018). Organization Design and Competitive Strategy: An Application to the Case of Divisionalization. *Advances in Strategic Management, 40*, 207–228. doi:10.1108/S0742-332220180000040007

Şevkli, M., Öztekin, A., Uysal, Ö., Torlak, G., Türkyılmaz, A., & Delen, D. (2012). Development of a fuzzy ANP based SWOT analysis for the airline industry in Turkey. *Expert Systems with Applications, 39*(1), 14–24. doi:10.1016/j.eswa.2011.06.047

Sezgin, E., & Yuncu, D. (2016). The SWOT analysis of Turkish Airlines through Skytrax quality evaluations in the global brand process. In *Development of tourism and the hospitality industry in Southeast Asia* (pp. 65–81). Springer. doi:10.1007/978-981-287-606-5_5

Sgourev, S. (2013). How Paris Gave Rise to Cubism (and Picasso): Ambiguity and Fragmentation in Radical Innovation. *Organization Science, 24*(6), 1–17. doi:10.1287/orsc.1120.0819

Shane, S., & Venkataraman, S. (2000). The promise of entrepreneurship as a field of research. *Academy of Management Review, 25*(1), 217–226. doi:10.5465/amr.2000.2791611

Sherman, E., Mathur, A., & Smith, R. B. (1997). Store environment and consumer purchase behavior: Mediating role of consumer emotions. *Psychology and Marketing, 14*(4), 361–378. doi:10.1002/(SICI)1520-6793(199707)14:4<361::AID-MAR4>3.0.CO;2-7

SHGM. (2016). *FaaliyetRaporu*. http://web.shgm.gov.tr/documents/sivilhavacilik/files/pdf/kurumsal/faaliyet/2016.pdf

Shokuhi, A., & Chashmi, S. (2019). Formulation of Bank Melli Iran Marketing Strategy Based on Porter's Competitive Strategy. *Journal of Business-To-Business Marketing, 26*(2), 209–215. doi:10.1080/1051712X.2019.1603421

SimilarWeb. (2021). *Domain overview*. https://www.similarweb.com/website/amazon.ae/

Sinek, S. (2011). *Start with why: How great leaders inspire everyone to take action*. Penguin Group.

Compilation of References

Skip The Rinse in the Canada. (2021). https://www.finishdishwashing.ca/en/our-values/sustainability/skip-the-rinse/

Skip The Rinse in the United States. (2021). https://www.finishdishwashing.com/skip-the-rinse

Slevin, D. P., & Covin, J. G. (1997). Strategy formation patterns, performance, and significance of context. *Journal of Management*, *23*(2), 189–209. doi:10.1177/014920639702300205

Smith, R. E., MacKenzie, S. B., Yang, X., Buchholz, L. M., & Darley, W. K. (2007). Modeling the Determinants and Effects of Creativity in Advertising. *Marketing Science*, *26*(6), 819–833. doi:10.1287/mksc.1070.0272

Solomon, M., Russell-Bennett, R., & Previte, J. (2012). *Consumer behaviour*. Pearson Higher Education AU.

Sopadjieva, E., Dholakia, U. M., & Benjamin, B. (2017). A Study of 46,000 Shoppers Shows That Omnichannel Retailing Works. *Harvard Business Review*. https://hbr.org/2017/01/a-study-of-46000-shoppers-shows-that-omnichannel-retailing-works

Soto-Acosta, P. (2020). COVID-19 pandemic: Shifting digital transformation to a high-speed gear. *Information Systems Management*, *37*(4), 260–266. doi:10.1080/10580530.2020.1814461

Spence, R. Jr, & Rushing, H. (2009). *It's Not What You Sell, It's What You Stand for: Why Every Extraordinary Business Is Driven by Purpose*. Penguin Group.

Srivastava, A. K., & Chaturvedi, S. (2014). Negative Job Experiences and Employees Job Attitudes and Health in High-Performance Work Organizations. *Metamorphosis*, *13*(2), 22–28. doi:10.1177/0972622520140205

Steenburgh, T., & Avery, J. (2010). *Marketing Analysis Toolkit: Situation Analysis*. Harvard Business Publishing.

Stengel, J. (2011). *Grow: How ideals power growth and profit at the world's greatest companies*. The Crown Publishing Group.

Stop Med At Skylle in Denmark. (2021). https://www.neophos.dk/stopmedatskylle/

Sufi, T., & Ahmed, S. (2021). Surviving COVID-19 Crisis by New Business Models: A Case Study of the Indian Restaurant Industry. In L. C. Carvalho, L. Reis, & C. Silveira (Eds.), *Handbook of Research on Entrepreneurship, Innovation, Sustainability, and ICTs in the Post-COVID-19 Era* (pp. 301–316). IGI Global. doi:10.4018/978-1-7998-6776-0.ch015

Suhartanto, D., Ismail, T. A. T., Leo, G., Triyuni, N. N., & Suhaeni, T. (2020). Behavioral Intention Toward Online Food Purchasing: An Analysis at Different Purchase Levels. [IJEBR]. *International Journal of E-Business Research*, *16*(4), 34–50. doi:10.4018/IJEBR.2020100103

Sutton, R. I. (1987). The Process of Organizational Death: Disbanding and Reconnecting. *Administrative Science Quarterly*, *32*(4), 542–569. doi:10.2307/2392883

Swayne, L. E., Duncan, W. J., & Ginter, P. M. (2006). *Strategic Management of Health Care Organizations*. Blackwell Publishing.

Świeczak, W. (2012). Content marketing as an important element of marketing strategy of scientific institutions. *The Institute of Aviation*, *226*(5), 133–150. doi:10.5604/05096669.1077480

T.C. Sanayi ve Teknoloji Bakanlığı. (2021, March 12). *İstatistiki Bilgiler*. https://www.sanayi.gov.tr/istatistikler/istatistiki-bilgiler/mi0203011501

Tabachnick, B. G., & Fidell, L. S. (2012). *Using Multivariate Statistics*. Pearson.

Taber, K. S. (2018). The use of Cronbach's alpha when developing and reporting research instruments in science education. *Research in Science Education*, *48*(6), 1273–1296. doi:10.100711165-016-9602-2

Tarabasz, A. (2020). Campaign Planning and Project Management. In A. Heinze, G. Fletcher, T. Rashid, & A. Cruz (Eds.), *Digital and Social Media Marketing: A Results-Driven Approach* (pp. 123–148). Routledge. doi:10.4324/9780429280689-9

Tardieu, H., Daly, D., Esteban-Lauzán, J., Hall, J., & Miller, G. (2020). *Deliberately Digital. Rewriting Enterprise DNA for Enduring Success*. Springer., doi:10.1007/978-3-030-37955-1

Tate, C. (2016). *Purpose-washing. Is it the new green-washing?* https://carolyntate.co/purpose-washing-is-it-the-new-green-washing/

Teare, R. E., Costa, J., & Eccles, G. (1998). Relating strategy, structure, and performance. *Journal of Workplace Learning*, *10*(2), 58–75. doi:10.1108/13665629810209048

Technavio. (2020). *Processed Vegetable Market by Product and Geography - Forecast and Analysis 2020-2024*. http://www.technavio.com

TED Ads worth spreading report. (2012). https://wooshii.com/blog/author/wooshiiricardo/page/60/

Tehci, A. (2021). Digital Marketing in the globalization process: Examples from real-time marketing. In Y. Bayar (Ed.), *Handbook of Research on Institutional, Economic, and Social Impacts of Globalization and Liberalization* (pp. 185–200). IGI Global. doi:10.4018/978-1-7998-4459-4.ch011

Teknopark. (2021, March 12). *Teknoloji Geliştirme Bögeleri*. https://teknopark.sanayi.gov.tr/Content/Detay

Teng, C. C., & Maxwell, W. (2021). A size and impact analysis of digital footprints. International. *Journal of Business and Systems Research*, *15*(2), 163–181. doi:10.1504/IJBSR.2021.113418

Teubner, R. A., & Stockhinger, J. (2020). Understanding information systems strategy in the digital age. *The Journal of Strategic Information Systems*, *29*(4), 101642. doi:10.1016/j.jsis.2020.101642

TGBD. (2021a, March 12). *Dünyadaki Teknoparklar*. https://www.tgbd.org.tr/dunyadaki-teknoparklar-icerik-34

TGBD. (2021b, March 12). *Türkiye'de Teknoparklar*. https://www.tgbd.org.tr/dunyadaki-teknoparklar-icerik-35

The Body Shop Official Web Site. (2021). https://www.thebodyshop.com/en-gb/about-us/activism/faat/a/a00018

The Hindu business (2020). Adyar Anand Bhavan launches delivery app. https://www.thehindubusinessline.com/companies/adyar-ananda-bhavan-launches-delivery-app/article22807346.ece

The Hindu. (2019). CII presents awards to entrepreneurs. https://www.thehindu.com/news/national/tamil-nadu/cii-presents-awards-to-entrepreneurs/article26274622.ece

The Times of India. (2016). Ananda-bhavan-revives-plans-pe-deal-hires-banker. https://www.vccircle.com/adyar-ananda-bhavan-revives-plans-pe-deal-hires-banker/

Thomas, S., & Kohli, C. (2009). A brand is forever! A framework for revitalizing declining and dead brands. *Business Horizons*, *52*(4), 377–386. doi:10.1016/j.bushor.2009.03.004

Thomassen, L., Lincoln, K., & Aconis, A. (2006). *Retailization: Brand Survival in the Age of Retailer Power*. Kogan Page.

Thompson, A. A., & Stickland, A. J. (1999). *Strategic management: Concepts and cases*. Irwin.

Thompson, A. A., & Strickland, A. J. (1996). *Strategic management: Concepts & cases*. Irwin.

Tosi, H. L. (2009). *Theories of organization*. Sage Publications.

Compilation of References

Tosun, P., Sezgin, S., & Nimet, U. R. A. Y. (2019). Pazarlama biliminde duygu ve duygu durumu kavramlari için baz alinmiş teoriler. *Elektronik Sosyal Bilimler Dergisi*, *18*(72), 1832–1851.

Trienekens, J. H., Wognum, P. M., Beulens, A. J. M., & van der Vorst, J. G. A. J. (2012). Transparency in complex dynamic food supply chains. *Advance Engineering Information*, *26*(1), 55–65. doi:10.1016/j.aei.2011.07.007

Trompenaars, A., & Coebergh, P. H. (2015). *100+ management models: how to understand and apply the world's most powerful business tools*. McGraw-Hill.

Tsiotsou, R. H. (2019). Social Media and Customer Engagement. In E. Bridges & K. Fowler (Eds.), *The Routledge Handbook of Service Research Insights and Ideas*. Routledge.

TÜİK. (2021). *2020 Yılı Adrese Dayalı Nüfus Kayıt Sistemi Sonuçları*. https://data.tuik.gov.tr/Bulten/Index?p=Adrese-Dayali-Nufus-Kayit-Sistemi-Sonuclari-2020-37210

TÜİK. (2021). *Nüfus ve Demografi*. https://data.tuik.gov.tr/Kategori/GetKategori?p=nufus-ve-demografi-109&dil=1

Uçar, S. (2019). *Mutfağı Paylaşma Zamanı*. https://mediacat.com/finish-mutfakta-birlikte-reklami/

Ülgen, H., & Mirze, K. (2004). *İşletmelerde Stratejik Yönetim*. Literatür Yayınları.

Ülgen, H., & Mirze, S. K. (2016). *İşletmelerde stratejik yönetim* (8th ed.). Beta Yayincilik.

Ulriksen, M. S., & Dadalauri, N. (2016). Single case studies and theory-testing: The knots and dots of the process-tracing method. *International Journal of Social Research Methodology*, *19*(2), 223–239. doi:10.1080/13645579.2014.979718

Urbanska, J. (2007). Modern Retail Distribution–The Case of Bonduelle Poland. *Advanced Logistic Systems*, *1*(1), 101–107.

UTIKAD. (2017). https://www.utikad.org.tr/Detay/Sektor-Haberleri/14404/kayseri-havalimani-genisletilecek

Van Doorn, J., Lemon, K. N., Mittal, V., Nass, S., Pick, D., Pirner, P., & Verhoef, P. C. (2010). Customer Engagement Behavior: Theoretical Foundations and Research Directions. *Journal of Service Research*, *13*(3), 253–266. doi:10.1177/1094670510375599

Venkataraman, S. (1997). The distinctive domain of entrepreneurship research. In J. Katz (Ed.), *Advances in Entrepreneurship: Firm Emergence and Growth* (Vol. 3, pp. 119–138). JAI Press.

Venkatraman, N., & Prescott, J. E. (1990). Environment-strategy coalignment: An empirical test of its performance implications. *Strategic Management Journal*, *11*(1), 1–23. doi:10.1002mj.4250110102

Verhagen, T., & van Dolen, W. (2011). The influence of online store beliefs on consumer online impulse buying: A model and empirical application. *Information & Management*, *48*(8), 320–327. doi:10.1016/j.im.2011.08.001

Verhoef, P. C., Broekhuizen, T., Bart, Y., Bhattacharya, A., Dong, J. Q., Fabian, N., & Haenlein, M. (2021). Digital transformation: A multidisciplinary reflection and research agenda. *Journal of Business Research*, *122*, 889–901. doi:10.1016/j.jbusres.2019.09.022

Verhoef, P. C., Reinartz, W. J., & Krafft, M. (2010). Customer Engagement as a New Perspective in Customer Management. *Journal of Service Research*, *13*(3), 247–252. doi:10.1177/1094670510375461

Verma, D. P. S., & Kapoor, S. (2003). Dimensions of buying roles in family decision making. *IIMB Management Review*, *15*(4), 7–14.

Verschuren, P. J. M. (2003). Case study as a research strategy. *International Journal of Social Research Methodology: Theory and Practice*, *6*(2), 121–139. doi:10.1080/13645570110106154

Vidal-Cabeza, D. (2015). *6 Types of Customers in the Plumbing Industry You Need to Know*. https://davevidal.com/6-types-of-customers-in-the-plumbing-industry-you-need-to-know

Vinerean, S. (2017). Content marketing strategy. Definition, objectives and tactics. *Expert Journal of Marketing, 5*(2).

Visa. (2019). *The UAE eCommerce Landscape*. https://ae.visamiddleeast.com/dam/VCOM/regional/cemea/unitedarabemirates/home-page/documents/visa-white-paper-v4.pdf

Visser, J., & Richardson, J. (2015). *Digital Engagement Framework. Create value with digital engagement*. https://digitalengagementframework.com/

Visser, M. (2021). *Digital Marketing*. Tylor & Francis.

Vlajic, J., van der Vorst, J. G. A. J., & Haijema, R. (2002). A framework for designing robust food supply chains. *International Journal of Production Economics, 137*(1), 176–189. doi:10.1016/j.ijpe.2011.11.026

Voorhees, C. M., Fombelle, P. W., Gregoire, Y., Bone, S., Gustafsson, A., Sousa, R., & Walkowiak, T. (2017). Service encounters, experiences and the customer journey: Defining the field and a call to expand our lens. *Journal of Business Research, 79*, 269–280. doi:10.1016/j.jbusres.2017.04.014

Walker, K., Ni, N., & Dyck, B. (2015). Recipes for successful sustainability: Empirical organizational configurations for strong corporate environmental performance. *Business Strategy and the Environment, 24*(1), 40–57. doi:10.1002/bse.1805

Walton, E. J. (1986). Managers' prototypes of financial firms. *Journal of Management Studies, 23*(6), 679–698. doi:10.1111/j.1467-6486.1986.tb00442.x

Wang, H. (2014). *Theories for competitive advantage*. University of Wollongong.

Wang, J., Tao, J., & Chu, M. (2020). Behind the label: Chinese consumers' trust in food certification and the effect of perceived quality on purchase intention. *Food Control, 108*, 106825. doi:10.1016/j.foodcont.2019.106825

Wang, K., & Hong, W. (2011). Competitive advantage analysis and strategy formulation of airport city development-The case of Taiwan. *Transport Policy, 18*(1), 276–288. doi:10.1016/j.tranpol.2010.08.011

Wang, R. D., & Shaver, J. M. (2013). Competition-driven Repositioning. *Strategic Management Journal, 35*(11), 1585–1604. doi:10.1002mj.2167

Waqas, M., Hamzah, Z. L. B., & Salleh, N. A. M. (2020). Customer experience: A systematic literature review and consumer culture theory-based conceptualisation. *Management Review Quarterly, 71*(1), 135–176. doi:10.100711301-020-00182-w

Warby Parker Official Web Site. (2021). https://www.warbyparker.com/buy-a-pair-give-a-pair

Water Footprint Network. (2011). https://waterfootprint.org/en/water-footprint/what-is-water-footprint/

Water of Tomorrow Campaign Official Facebook Account. (2021). https://www.facebook.com/yarininsuyu/

Water of Tomorrow Campaign Official Instagram Account. (2021). https://www.instagram.com/yarininsuyu/

Water of Tomorrow Campaign Official Twitter Account. (2021). https://twitter.com/yarininsuyu

Water of Tomorrow Campaign Official Web Site. (2021). https://www.yarininsuyu.com/

We Are Social. (2021). *Digital 2021: the latest insights into the 'state of digital'*. https://wearesocial.com/blog/2021/01/digital-2021-the-latest-insights-into-the-state-of-digital

Webb, K. (2002). Managing Channels of Distribution in the Age of Electronic Commerce. *Industrial Marketing Management*, *31*(2), 95–102. doi:10.1016/S0019-8501(01)00181-X

Wee, C. H. (2016). Think Tank-Beyond the Five Forces Model and Blue Ocean Strategy. *An Integrative Perspective FromSun Zi Bingfa.*, (2), 34–45.

Weihrich, H. (1982). The TOWS matrix - A tool for situational analysis. *Long Range Planning*, *15*(2), 54–66. doi:10.1016/0024-6301(82)90120-0

Weinstein, A. (2004). *Handbook of Market Segmentation: Strategic Targeting for Business and Technology Firms*. The Haworth Press.

Wernerfelt, B. (1984). A resource-based view of the firm. *Strategic Management Journal*, *5*(2), 171–180. doi:10.1002mj.4250050207

Whittington, R. (1996). Strategy as practice. *Long Range Planning*, *29*(5), 731–735. doi:10.1016/0024-6301(96)00068-4

Wiengarten, F., Pagell, M., & Fynes, B. (2011). Supply chain environmental investments in dynamic industries: Comparing investment and performance differences with static industries. *International Journal of Production Economics*, *135*(2), 541–551. doi:10.1016/j.ijpe.2011.03.011

Wijaya, B. S. (2012). The Development of Hierarchy of Effects Model in Advertising. *International Research Journal of Business Studies*, *5*(1), 73–85. doi:10.21632/irjbs.5.1.73-85

Wilkie, W. (1986). *Consumer Behaviour*. John Wiley and Sons.

Willemsen, L. M., Mazerant, K., Kamphuis, A. L., & van der Veen, G. (2018). Let's Get Real (Time)! The potential of real-time marketing to catalyze the sharing of brand messages. *International Journal of Advertising*, *37*(5), 828–848. doi:10.1080/02650487.2018.1485214

Womack, J. P., Jones, D. T., & Roos, D. (2007). *The machine that changed the world: The story of lean production—Toyota's secret weapon in the global car wars that is now revolutionizing world industry*. Simon and Schuster.

Wood, W., & Neal, D. T. (2009). The habitual consumer. *Journal of Consumer Psychology*, *19*(4), 579–592. doi:10.1016/j.jcps.2009.08.003

Wttenbraker, J., Gibbs, B. L., & Kahle, L. R. (1983). Seat Belt Attitudes, Habits, and Behaviors: An Adaptive Amendment to the Fishbein Model. *Journal of Applied Social Psychology*, *13*(5), 406–421. doi:10.1111/j.1559-1816.1983.tb01748.x

Xu, H. (2015). SWOT Analysis on Chinese New Regional Jet ARJ21. In *15th COTA International Conference of Transportation* (pp. 127-138). Academic Press.

Yadav, G., Luthra, S., Jakhar, S. K., Mangla, S. K., & Rai, D. P. (2020). A framework to overcome sustainable supply chain challenges through solution measures of industry 4.0 and circular economy: An automotive case. *Journal of Cleaner Production*, *254*, 120112. doi:10.1016/j.jclepro.2020.120112

Yadav, M. S., & Varadarajan, P. R. (2005). Understanding product migration to the electronic marketplace: A conceptual framework. *Journal of Retailing*, *81*(2), 125–140. doi:10.1016/j.jretai.2005.03.006

Yasmin, A., Tasneem, S., & Fatema, K. (2015). Effectiveness of digital marketing in the challenging age: An empirical study. *International Journal of Management Science and Business Administration*, *1*(5), 69–80. doi:10.18775/ijmsba.1849-5664-5419.2014.15.1006

Yeh, C. H., & Kuo, Y. L. (2003). Evaluating passenger services of Asia-Pacific international airports. *Transportation Research Part E, Logistics and Transportation Review*, *39*(1), 35–48. doi:10.1016/S1366-5545(00)00010-7

Yildirim, A., & Simsek, H. (2005). *Sosyal bilimlerde nitel araştırma yöntemleri* (5th ed.). Seckin Yayincilik.

Yıldırım, A., & Şimşek, H. (2006). Sosyal Bilimlerde Nitel Araştırma Yöntemleri. *Journal of Theory and Practice in Education*, *2*(2), 113–118.

Yılmaz, İ. (2017). Emissions from passenger aircraft at Kayseri Airport, Turkey. *Journal of Air Transport Management*, *58*, 176–182. doi:10.1016/j.jairtraman.2016.11.001

Ylalaurencie. (2017). *Les légumes Bonduelle s'invitent chez vous.* https://www.bibamagazine.fr/lifestyle/les-legumes-bonduelle-sinvitent-chez-vous-9557.html

Zaheer, S. (1995). Overcoming the liability of foreignness. *Academy of Management Journal*, *38*, 341–363.

Zahid, S., & Raja, M. N. (2014). Effect of Rebranding and Repositioning On Brand Equity Considering Brand Loyalty as a Mediating Variable. *Journal of Business and Management*, *16*(1), 58–63.

Zajac, E. J., Kraatz, M. S., & Bresser, R. K. F. (2000). Modeling the dynamics of strategic fit. *Strategic Management Journal*, *21*(4), 429–453. doi:10.1002/(SICI)1097-0266(200004)21:4<429::AID-SMJ81>3.0.CO;2-#

Zambito, T. (2016). *State Of Buyer Personas 2016: Strong Correlation Between Effectiveness And Goals.* https://customerthink.com/state-of-buyer-personas-2016-strong-correlation-between-effectiveness-and-goals

Zhang, C., Lin, Y. H., & Newman, D. G. (2016). Investigating the Effectiveness of Repositioning Strategies: The Customers' Perspective. *Journal of Travel & Tourism Marketing*, *33*(9), 1235–1250. doi:10.1080/10548408.2015.1107018

Zinkhan, G. M. (1993). Creativity in advertising. *Journal of Advertising*, *22*(2), 1–3. doi:10.1080/00913367.1993.10673398

About the Contributors

José Duarte Santos received his PhD in Management from the University of Vigo, Spain. He is also Master of Marketing and has a Bachelor's degree in Business Sciences. Between 1987 and 2002, he has played various roles in sales, marketing, and management of companies in the information technologies sector. From 2003, he has performed functions of a management and marketing consultant. Since 1999, he has been a professor in higher education in Portugal in the field of management and marketing. He is currently a professor at the Instituto Superior Politécnico Gaya (ISPGaya) and at the Instituto Superior de Contabilidade e Administração do Porto (ISCAP). He is also a researcher at the Centre for Organisational and Social Studies of Polytechnic of Porto (CEOS.PP). His current research areas include social customer relationship management and social selling.

* * *

Muhammed Seyda Akdag received his MS in Aeronautics and Astronautics Engineering from the Istanbul Technical University in 2015 and he received his Ph.D. in Business Administration from the Yıldız Technical University in 2021. He writes and presents widely on issues of aviation regulations, aircraft certification, airworthiness, quality management, safety management, strategic management, management, and organization.

Hayat Ayar Senturk is an assistant professor in Department of Business Administration at Yildiz Technical University since 2019. Her studies focus on strategic marketing, digital marketing, and consumer behaviour. Her researches has been published in several scholarly journals including in International Marketing Review, Journal of Destination Marketing & Management, Kybernetes and in numerous Turkish-language scholarly journals.

Yasemin Bal graduated from Istanbul University Faculty of Political Sciences Department of Business Administration in 2000 and Yıldız Technical University Human Resources Management master's program in 2005. She got her Ph.D. degree from Istanbul University Faculty of Business Administration Human Resources Management doctorate program in 2011, She became Assistant Professor in 2013 and Associate Professor in Strategy and Management in 2014 at Yıldız Technical University. Currently continuing her academic career as an Associate Professor at Yıldız Technical University Faculty of Economics and Administrative Sciences. Yasemin Bal has books and scientific articles in Management, Strategic Management and Human Resources Management. She has also presented several papers in national and international conferences. At the same time, she gives trainings and consultancy to private and public institutions related to her fields of work.

António Correia de Barros received his PhD in Management from the Portucalense University in 2008 and has a master's degree in marketing. Full professor of marketing.

Véronique Boulocher-Passet holds a Ph.D. in Education and Marketing from Université Charles de Gaulle in Lille, France. Prior to joining the School of Business and Law at University of Brighton, UK, she was Associate Professor at Edhec Business School in France. She has taught across a wide variety of courses at both under- and postgraduate level, and taken administrative responsibilities such as Head of Marketing or Head of International Relations. Her main teaching interests are in the area of strategic marketing, brand management, international marketing and research methods. Her publications include four textbooks on brand management, market analysis and packaging, as well as a monography on the role of colour in marketing strategy. Véronique also wrote and published many teaching case studies. She has experience of supervising Masters level dissertations in marketing and of accompanying students with consulting projects. Her main research interest is marketing education.

Beatriz Casais holds a PhD in Business and Management Studies – specialization in Marketing and Strategy by University of Porto with research in social marketing, business ethics and public health advertisement. She is currently assistant professor at University of Minho, and is vice-dean of the School of Economics and Management and head of UMinhoExec – the executive education unit of University of Minho. She has published in the Journal of Social Marketing, International Journal of Entrepreneurial Behavior & Research, Journal of Hospitality and Tourism Technology, Journal of Hospitality and Tourism Management, Tourism Management Perspectives, Journal of Fashion Marketing and Management, Place Branding and Public Diplomacy, Health Marketing Quarterly, Social Sciences, World Review of Entrepreneurship Management and Sustainable Development, RAUSP Management Journal, Corporate Communications, Review of International Business and Strategy and International Review on Public and Nonprofit Marketing, among others.

Shakti Chaturvedi is working as an Assistant Professor at REVA University Bengaluru. Before this, she has also worked with the University of Petroleum and Energy Studies Dehradun and IIM Lucknow. She has served as a reviewer for various reputed journals, for instance, Global Business Review journal indexed in ABDC published by sage, International Journal of Consumer Studies (ABDC-A), and International Journal of Innovation Science (published by Emerald). She has earned her bachelor's degree from the University of Delhi and her Doctorate from Banaras Hindu University (An Institute of Eminence). She was a recipient of UGC NET JRF and SRF for five years. She has six Scopus publications to her credits out of which two are ABDC listed.

Irene Ciccarino is an entrepreneur, consultant, teacher, and researcher interested in business strategy and the social investment market. Her research is focused on social value creation through entrepreneurship, innovation, and public policies. Currently, she is an invited professor at Polytechnic Institute of Leiria (Portugal) and a researcher of Innovation Research Group at IBMEC-RJ (Brazil). She is member of Project management Institute, Project 4NGO, European Anti-Poverty Network (EAPN), Doughnut Economics Action Lab (DEAL), and Zebras Unite Cooperative.

About the Contributors

Emrah Gülmez graduated from Anadolu University, Department of Advertising and Public Relations, in 2008. In 2009, he started to work as a Research Assistant in Anadolu University, Department of Advertising and Public Relations, and is still working there as an Assistant Professor. He received his MS in 2011 and Ph.D. in 2017 in Public Relations and Advertising from Anadolu University. He writes and presents widely on issues of advertising strategies, creativity in advertising, and brand communication and teaches Creativity in Advertising, Designing Advertising Campaign, Advertising Copywriting Practices, Digital Advertising Copywriting, and Brand Communication Management.

Randall Harris holds BA and MBA degrees from the University of Texas at Austin. He earned a Ph.D. in Strategic Management from the University of Florida in 1995. He worked as a Lecturer at the University of Florida from 1995-1996 before being appointed to the faculty of California State University, Stanislaus (CSUS) in 1996. Dr. Harris served in various roles at CSUS, including Professor of Management, Director of the Executive MBA Program, Founding Director of the Online MBA Program, and Interim Director of the MBA Program. Dr. Harris joined the faculty of Texas A&M – Corpus Christi in 2014. He was promoted to the rank of Professor in 2017 and was named Chair of the Department of Management & Marketing in 2018. An active Case Researcher, Dr. Harris is a Past President of the North American Case Research Association.

Ece Özer Çizer is a PhD student and research assistant at Yıldız Technical University. Her work focuses specifically on digital marketing.

Paulo Botelho Pires received his PhD in Management from the Portucalense University in 2004 and has a master's degree in marketing.

R. Vara Prasad is currently an Assistant Professor in the School of Management Studies at the REVA University in Bengaluru, India. Prior to his recent appointment at REVA, he was an Assistant Professor in Marketing at the Madanapalle Institute of Technology and Science (MITS), Madanapalle, India. Dr. Prasad received his undergraduate degree as well as his MBA and M. Com degrees from Sri Krishnadevaraya University, India and his Ph.D. in Consumer Behaviour from the same university. Dr Prasad published several papers in referred Journals and chapters in books and participated in a range of faculty development programmes and seminars. He also presented various academic as well as research-based papers at several national and international conferences. He has been involved in a major research project funded by ICSSR-IMPRESS on "Self Employed Women in the informal economy: Street Vendors in Andhra Pradesh". The Author is an Entrepreneurial Evangelist who nurtured many students to set up their dream enterprise. His areas of interest include Entrepreneurship, Digital Marketing, Branding and Advertisement.

Sonal Purohit is an Associate Professor at the University School of Business, Chandigarh University, India. She has eleven plus years of experience into teaching marketing subjects. She has research publications and cases in Journals of repute including Harvard Business Review. She has served as a reviewer for some of the renowned journals such as the Journal of Consumer Studies, Journal of Emerging Markets, and Journal of Financial Services Marketing. Her research interests include consumer behavior, services marketing and social entrepreneurship.

About the Contributors

Sabine Ruaud is a Professor in the Marketing Department at EDHEC Business School, where she is involved in a wide variety of teaching activities for Bachelor, Postgraduate and Executive programs. Her main academic research interest is focused on customer relationship management. Her works have been presented at American, Asian, European and French conferences and published in academic journals. She is the author of a book entitled "Le marketing relationnel: nouvelle donne du marketing" (Numilog) which received the Prize of Excellence in the Management Category from the Edhec Foundation. She has also co-authored many pedagogical books: "La couleur au cœur de la stratégie marketing" (De Boeck) awarded medals by the Academy of Commercial Sciences and by the FNEGE, "Analyse de marché" (5th edition, Vuibert), "Gestion de la marque locale et internationale" (Numilog), "Le packaging" (Numilog) and "Cas d'analyse des données en marketing" (Tec&Doc). Moreover, she teams up closely with companies to lead new projects to increase their strategic success and competitive effectiveness. Based on this work, she has developed great expertise in the area of the creation of pedagogical case studies and their use for enriching students' learning experience. They have been published in leading business texts and several of them have been nominated or won awards at French and international conferences.

Carla Silva holds a master's degree in Administration from Ibmec-RJ. She is graduated in Chemistry and also holds a post-graduation degree in Finance and People Management. She is a seasoned professional in Human Resources and has worked in the Beverage, Mining, Hospitality, and Gas transmission sectors.

Anna Tarabasz is Associate Professor Marketing, Dean Teaching and Learning, Head of Business and Humanities at Curtin University Dubai. Marketing, digital marketing and e-commerce specialist, with over 16 years of experience (out of it 14 in academia) working previously in banking, automotive and cosmetics industry. Serving as independent marketing & e-commerce consultant and key note speaker. Publishing (in English, French and Polish) chapters in monographs and articles in scientific journals (ABDC, Scopus listed, with Google h-index 6, i-10 index 5, Research Gate Index 9.87), follows a previously chosen path, focusing on digital communication, e-commerce & e-business, social media, AR, VR, MR, IoT and wearable technology along with cyber security. Served as a Visiting Professor in France (Université Joseph Fourier, Grenoble) and Kazakhstan (Zhetysu State University named after I. Zhansugurov). Member of Réseau PGV, international research group on economics and management, gathering academics from 45 universities in 11 countries. Board Member of International Board of Standards of the Institute of Certified Chartered Economists. Appointed as NAWA Expert - Polish National Agency for Academic Exchange. Member of Editorial Board of Journal of Innovations in Digital Marketing; Journal of Sustainable Marketing; International Journal of Business and Economics Research; and Management & Gouvernance. Member of the Scientific Council and Board of Reviewers of the Journal of Finance and Financial Law. Reviewer for Asia Pacific Journal of Marketing and Logistics and Reviewer for Entrepreneurial Business and Economics Review. Scientific Committee Member on multiple international conferences, conference chair and session chair, key note speaker and panelist.

Francisca Quintas Rodrigues is Master of Science in Management by the University of Porto and is brand manager at Super Bock Group, a beverage company in Portugal.

Meenakshi Verma is working as an Assistant Professor at Symbiosis International University, Nagpur. She has various case studies publications to her credit. Her two research articles currently are under the production phase of sage.

Index

A

advertisement 7, 29, 200, 204, 219, 222, 273, 324, 327
advertising 1, 5, 19, 37, 43, 58, 70, 76, 81-82, 85-88, 90, 168, 179, 200, 203, 219, 227, 230, 233-235, 274, 285, 297, 302, 307-308, 318, 322, 327
Adyar Ananda Bhavan 51-52, 54-55, 66, 74
Ansoff Matrix 51, 57, 62, 113-115, 137, 142, 149
Aquarium Framework 23, 27-28, 30-31, 49
Artificial Intelligence 8, 35, 43, 66, 72, 75, 249
Autorité de Contrôle Prudentiel et de Regulation (ACPR) 194
Aviation Management 236

B

balanced scorecard 51, 57, 64, 70, 116, 147
benefit diversification 77, 86
Best Practice Dimension 268
best practices 14, 20, 61, 175, 255, 257, 260-261, 268-269
Blue Ocean 51, 57, 63, 69-71, 74, 76, 116, 147
Bonduelle Bienvenue 150, 160-165, 167-169, 172-173, 175
Bonduelle Group 150-170, 172, 174-175
Boşa Harcama 200, 212, 223
brand awareness 3, 54, 114, 118, 168, 233, 306-307, 318, 321
Brand Management 77, 87, 170, 210, 234
brand positioning 85, 87, 219, 233, 319
brand purpose 200, 207-210, 212, 215, 227, 229, 232-235
brand spokesperson 220, 226, 233
branded retail 150, 160, 164-167, 171, 173-174, 176
business concept 91-92, 106
Business Development 16, 91-92, 103, 117, 119
business models 1, 3, 19, 61, 71-72, 178
business strategies 271-272, 275, 278, 289
Business Value Innovation 72
Buyer Persona 27-31, 43, 47, 49

C

case study 4, 14-15, 17, 19, 36, 43, 49-51, 55, 63, 70-72, 75-76, 79, 81, 87, 149-150, 170, 192-193, 230, 233, 236, 241, 249-250, 255
channel conflict 167-168, 173-175
Cloud Kitchens 72-73
competitive strategies 70, 271-273, 275-283, 287-290, 298-299
competitive strategy 51, 69-71, 116, 146-147, 275-276, 280, 282-283, 287, 289-291, 293, 295-297, 299
Compte-Nickel 177-178, 180, 182-183, 185, 189, 193-194, 197
Confédération des buralistes 178, 182, 194
consumer behavior 87, 107, 117, 147, 157, 300-303, 308-311, 314, 316-322, 324-325, 327-329
consumer emotions 300, 302, 307-308, 311, 315, 319, 326-328
consumer perception 77, 79, 81-82, 85-86, 88, 320
content marketing 45, 79, 85-86, 267, 300-308, 310-311, 313-314, 316-329
Covid 19 302
Credit Institution (or Bank) 194
CRM 255-257, 259-263, 267-270
CRM Dimensions 268
CRM Strategy Formulation Dimension 268

D

D2C 150, 160, 164, 168-170, 173-175
D2C (Direct-to-Consumer or Direct2Consumer) 173
digital audit 23, 29, 33-34, 37-38, 43, 45, 49
digital content 45, 301, 305, 310, 321, 323, 325, 327
Digital Engagement Canvas 30-31, 33, 49-50
Digital footprint analysis 23, 44
digital innovation 2, 13, 51, 56, 66, 73, 198
digital marketing 6-7, 23, 28, 35, 45, 47, 89-90, 300-

302, 319, 321, 324-329
digital transformation 1-4, 6-11, 13, 15-21, 24, 326
digital transformation strategy 1-2, 13, 17, 19-21
digitalization 2, 9, 73, 196, 234, 301-303, 327
Digitalization Strategies 73
disintermediation 137, 173-174
distribution channel 119-120, 143, 148, 160, 173, 197
distribution strategy 150, 160, 164, 166-167, 173-174

F

Fairy 200, 204-205, 212, 223-225, 227-228, 230, 233-234
family business 150, 173, 286
Financière des Payments Electroniques (FPE) 194
Finish 200, 202-203, 205, 212-216, 218-220, 222-223, 227-229, 231, 233-235

H

Hugues Le Bret 177, 188-189
human resources 4, 142, 255, 257, 261-263, 268-270, 288-289, 296

I

Imaginarium 2, 4-5, 8, 15
India 51, 54-55, 57-59, 66, 68-71, 74-76, 250
Industry Analysis 109, 119
intensity of use 77, 89-90

K

Kayseri airport 236-238, 241-244, 246-248, 251-254

L

La Financière des Placements Electroniques (FPE) 177
loyalty 61, 68, 82, 84, 88-89, 101-102, 111, 117, 129-131, 135, 137, 141-142, 144, 147, 149, 166, 168, 209, 259-261, 270, 306-307, 319, 321

M

market positioning 78, 117, 147, 149
Market Segmentation 48, 117, 126, 148
marketing mix 82, 117-118, 148, 209
Me Too strategy 227-228, 233

N

Native Ad 233

negative consumer behavior 300, 310-311, 314, 316-320, 327-328
Nickel 177-192, 194-199

O

omnichannel 2, 4, 6-9, 11-12, 15, 18-21, 26-27, 32, 44, 48-49, 68
organizational 4, 9, 11-13, 15-16, 18-21, 36, 47, 64, 69, 89, 144, 182, 186, 189, 194, 197, 249, 252, 255, 257, 268, 270-272, 274-283, 286-299, 328
Organizational and Human Resources Dimension 268
organizational strategies 271-272
organizational structures 271-272, 274-275, 278-282, 286-289, 298-299

P

pandemic period 300, 302-303, 309, 315, 318-320, 328
payment institution 178, 182, 185, 191, 195
Plant-Based Food 150, 155, 173
positioning 3, 28, 30, 77-79, 81-89, 106, 117-119, 142, 145, 147, 149, 160, 192, 219, 233, 319
Pril 200, 203-205, 212, 225-227, 231, 233-234
Process Dimension 268
processed vegetables 150, 155-158, 160, 166, 172-173
processes 3, 6, 8-10, 16, 24, 31, 45, 56, 73, 117, 137, 141-142, 161, 173, 191, 208, 238-239, 255-257, 260, 262-263, 267-270, 274-276, 286, 289, 291, 297, 307-308, 319, 328
PSD1 185-186, 195
PSD2 186, 195
purpose-driven marketing 200, 205, 207, 209-212, 227-228, 232-235

R

real-time content marketing 300-302, 308, 310-311, 313-314, 316-320, 322, 327-329
real-time marketing 300-305, 309-310, 313-314, 318-320, 322-323, 325-327
relational marketing philosophy 255, 257, 259, 268
Relationship Marketing Philosophy Dimension 268
repositioning 77-90, 119
resource-based view 51, 63-64, 71, 296
Retail Pre-Digital Firm 1
retail sector 1, 13, 19, 189
revitalization 85, 87, 89
Ryad Boulanouar 177-178, 180, 183, 197

Index

S

satisfaction 29, 68, 86, 117, 148, 202, 243, 252, 259-261, 269-270, 308, 324
SEMrush 23, 25-26, 29-30, 33, 35, 37, 42-43, 47-49
social media listening 23, 27, 35-36, 45-46
Sofrada Birlikte 200, 212, 225
strategic awareness 271, 286, 288-289, 296, 298-299
strategic formulation 10-11, 19-20, 119, 269
Strategic Management 1, 10, 17-19, 51, 64, 70-71, 73, 87, 91, 116-117, 119, 142, 146-147, 194, 236, 238-239, 251-252, 254, 271-273, 288-296, 298
Strategic marketing 44, 77, 116, 301
strategy 1-7, 10-21, 28, 43-44, 47, 51, 54-55, 57, 63-64, 69-71, 74, 77-88, 92, 103, 106, 111-119, 131, 137, 140-150, 156, 160, 162, 164, 166-167, 171-176, 182, 185-186, 188, 193-194, 227-230, 232-233, 237-239, 241, 251, 255, 257, 259-260, 262, 267-268, 270-278, 280-283, 285-297, 299-300, 302-303, 306, 320, 325-327
strategy as a practice 12, 14, 16, 19, 21
strategy as a process 1, 10, 14, 16, 19-20
strategy formulation 238, 251, 255, 257, 259, 268, 293
SWOT analysis 58, 61, 112, 115, 141, 236-237, 239-241, 243, 246-252, 254

T

technology 2-5, 9-10, 13-17, 29, 31, 36, 43, 45-46, 48, 58-59, 61, 63-66, 68, 72-76, 173, 181-182, 193-194, 197-198, 202, 246, 249, 251-253, 255, 257, 260, 262-263, 268-271, 274, 277-278, 281-283, 285-290, 294, 296, 298-299, 301, 304, 319, 322-325
Technology Development Zone 277
Technology Dimension 268
Technopark 296
Together at the Table 200, 212, 225-227
Turkey 200-206, 211-216, 218, 222-231, 233-234, 236-238, 241, 243-244, 247, 250-252, 271, 277-278, 281, 288-289, 292, 300, 310-311, 322

U

Uni.Co 2-10, 13-16, 20-21

V

value chain 1, 18-19, 56-57, 73, 75-76, 165, 169, 198, 261

W

Water of Tomorrow 200, 212-216, 218, 220, 222-223, 227, 232, 235

Y

Yarının Suyu 200, 212, 214, 231

Recommended Reference Books

IGI Global's reference books are available in three unique pricing formats:
Print Only, E-Book Only, or Print + E-Book.

Shipping fees may apply.

www.igi-global.com

ISBN: 978-1-7998-1048-3
EISBN: 978-1-7998-1049-0
© 2020; 605 pp.
List Price: US$ **285**

ISBN: 978-1-5225-8933-4
EISBN: 978-1-5225-8934-1
© 2020; 667 pp.
List Price: US$ **295**

ISBN: 978-1-7998-0357-7
EISBN: 978-1-7998-0359-1
© 2020; 451 pp.
List Price: US$ **235**

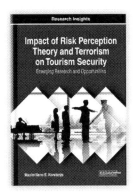

ISBN: 978-1-7998-0070-5
EISBN: 978-1-7998-0071-2
© 2020; 144 pp.
List Price: US$ **175**

ISBN: 978-1-5225-6980-0
EISBN: 978-1-5225-6981-7
© 2019; 339 pp.
List Price: US$ **235**

ISBN: 978-1-5225-5390-8
EISBN: 978-1-5225-5391-5
© 2018; 125 pp.
List Price: US$ **165**

Do you want to stay current on the latest research trends, product announcements, news, and special offers?
Join IGI Global's mailing list to receive customized recommendations, exclusive discounts, and more.
Sign up at: **www.igi-global.com/newsletters**.

Publisher of Peer-Reviewed, Timely, and Innovative Academic Research

www.igi-global.com   Sign up at www.igi-global.com/newsletters   facebook.com/igiglobal   twitter.com/igiglobal   linkedin.com/igiglobal

Ensure Quality Research is Introduced to the Academic Community

Become an Evaluator for IGI Global Authored Book Projects

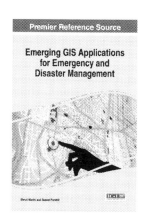 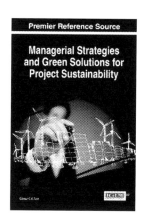  

The overall success of an authored book project is dependent on quality and timely manuscript evaluations.

Applications and Inquiries may be sent to:
development@igi-global.com

Applicants must have a doctorate (or equivalent degree) as well as publishing, research, and reviewing experience. Authored Book Evaluators are appointed for one-year terms and are expected to complete at least three evaluations per term. Upon successful completion of this term, evaluators can be considered for an additional term.

If you have a colleague that may be interested in this opportunity, we encourage you to share this information with them.

IGI Global Author Services

Providing a high-quality, affordable, and expeditious service, IGI Global's Author Services enable authors to streamline their publishing process, increase chance of acceptance, and adhere to IGI Global's publication standards.

Benefits of Author Services:

- **Professional Service:** All our editors, designers, and translators are experts in their field with years of experience and professional certifications.
- **Quality Guarantee & Certificate:** Each order is returned with a quality guarantee and certificate of professional completion.
- **Timeliness:** All editorial orders have a guaranteed return timeframe of 3-5 business days and translation orders are guaranteed in 7-10 business days.
- **Affordable Pricing:** IGI Global Author Services are competitively priced compared to other industry service providers.
- **APC Reimbursement:** IGI Global authors publishing Open Access (OA) will be able to deduct the cost of editing and other IGI Global author services from their OA APC publishing fee.

Author Services Offered:

English Language Copy Editing
Professional, native English language copy editors improve your manuscript's grammar, spelling, punctuation, terminology, semantics, consistency, flow, formatting, and more.

Scientific & Scholarly Editing
A Ph.D. level review for qualities such as originality and significance, interest to researchers, level of methodology and analysis, coverage of literature, organization, quality of writing, and strengths and weaknesses.

Figure, Table, Chart & Equation Conversions
Work with IGI Global's graphic designers before submission to enhance and design all figures and charts to IGI Global's specific standards for clarity.

Translation
Providing 70 language options, including Simplified and Traditional Chinese, Spanish, Arabic, German, French, and more.

Hear What the Experts Are Saying About IGI Global's Author Services

"Publishing with IGI Global has been *an amazing experience* for me for sharing my research. The *strong academic production* support ensures quality and timely completion." – **Prof. Margaret Niess, Oregon State University, USA**

"The service was *very fast, very thorough, and very helpful* in ensuring our chapter meets the criteria and requirements of the book's editors. I was *quite impressed and happy* with your service." – **Prof. Tom Brinthaupt, Middle Tennessee State University, USA**

Learn More or Get Started Here:

For Questions, Contact IGI Global's Customer Service Team at cust@igi-global.com or 717-533-8845

IGI Global
PUBLISHER of TIMELY KNOWLEDGE
www.igi-global.com

www.igi-global.com

Celebrating Over 30 Years of Scholarly Knowledge Creation & Dissemination

InfoSci®-Books

A Database of Nearly 6,000 Reference Books Containing Over 105,000+ Chapters Focusing on Emerging Research

GAIN ACCESS TO **THOUSANDS** OF REFERENCE BOOKS AT **A FRACTION** OF THEIR INDIVIDUAL LIST **PRICE**.

InfoSci®-Books Database

The **InfoSci®-Books** is a database of nearly 6,000 IGI Global single and multi-volume reference books, handbooks of research, and encyclopedias, encompassing groundbreaking research from prominent experts worldwide that spans over 350+ topics in 11 core subject areas including business, computer science, education, science and engineering, social sciences, and more.

Open Access Fee Waiver (Read & Publish) Initiative

For any library that invests in IGI Global's InfoSci-Books and/or InfoSci-Journals (175+ scholarly journals) databases, IGI Global will match the library's investment with a fund of equal value to go toward **subsidizing the OA article processing charges (APCs) for their students, faculty, and staff** at that institution when their work is submitted and accepted under OA into an IGI Global journal.*

INFOSCI® PLATFORM FEATURES

- Unlimited Simultaneous Access
- No DRM
- No Set-Up or Maintenance Fees
- A Guarantee of No More Than a 5% Annual Increase for Subscriptions
- Full-Text HTML and PDF Viewing Options
- Downloadable MARC Records
- COUNTER 5 Compliant Reports
- Formatted Citations With Ability to Export to RefWorks and EasyBib
- No Embargo of Content (Research is Available Months in Advance of the Print Release)

*The fund will be offered on an annual basis and expire at the end of the subscription period. The fund would renew as the subscription is renewed for each year thereafter. The open access fees will be waived after the student, faculty, or staff's paper has been vetted and accepted into an IGI Global journal and the fund can only be used toward publishing OA in an IGI Global journal. Libraries in developing countries will have the match on their investment doubled.

To Recommend or Request a Free Trial:
www.igi-global.com/infosci-books

eresources@igi-global.com • Toll Free: 1-866-342-6657 ext. 100 • Phone: 717-533-8845 x100

Publisher of Peer-Reviewed, Timely, and Innovative Academic Research Since 1988

IGI Global's Transformative Open Access (OA) Model:
How to Turn Your University Library's Database Acquisitions Into a Source of OA Funding

Well in advance of Plan S, IGI Global unveiled their OA Fee Waiver (Read & Publish) Initiative. Under this initiative, librarians who invest in IGI Global's InfoSci-Books and/or InfoSci-Journals databases will be able to subsidize their patrons' OA article processing charges (APCs) when their work is submitted and accepted (after the peer review process) into an IGI Global journal.

How Does it Work?

Step 1: **Library Invests in the InfoSci-Databases:** A library perpetually purchases or subscribes to the InfoSci-Books, InfoSci-Journals, or discipline/subject databases.

Step 2: **IGI Global Matches the Library Investment with OA Subsidies Fund:** IGI Global provides a fund to go towards subsidizing the OA APCs for the library's patrons.

Step 3: **Patron of the Library is Accepted into IGI Global Journal (After Peer Review):** When a patron's paper is accepted into an IGI Global journal, they option to have their paper published under a traditional publishing model or as OA.

Step 4: **IGI Global Will Deduct APC Cost from OA Subsidies Fund:** If the author decides to publish under OA, the OA APC fee will be deducted from the OA subsidies fund.

Step 5: **Author's Work Becomes Freely Available:** The patron's work will be freely available under CC BY copyright license, enabling them to share it freely with the academic community.

Note: This fund will be offered on an annual basis and will renew as the subscription is renewed for each year thereafter. IGI Global will manage the fund and award the APC waivers unless the librarian has a preference as to how the funds should be managed.

Hear From the Experts on This Initiative:

"I'm very happy to have been able to make one of my recent research contributions *freely available* along with having access to the *valuable resources* found within IGI Global's InfoSci-Journals database."

– **Prof. Stuart Palmer**, Deakin University, Australia

"Receiving the support from IGI Global's OA Fee Waiver Initiative *encourages me to continue my research work without any hesitation.*"

– **Prof. Wenlong Liu**, College of Economics and Management at Nanjing University of Aeronautics & Astronautics, China

For More Information, Scan the QR Code or Contact: IGI Global's Digital Resources Team at eresources@igi-global.com.

Are You Ready to Publish Your Research?

IGI Global offers book authorship and editorship opportunities across 11 subject areas, including business, computer science, education, science and engineering, social sciences, and more!

Benefits of Publishing with IGI Global:

- Free one-on-one editorial and promotional support.
- Expedited publishing timelines that can take your book from start to finish in less than one (1) year.
- Choose from a variety of formats, including: Edited and Authored References, Handbooks of Research, Encyclopedias, and Research Insights.
- Utilize IGI Global's eEditorial Discovery® submission system in support of conducting the submission and double-blind peer review process.
- IGI Global maintains a strict adherence to ethical practices due in part to our full membership with the Committee on Publication Ethics (COPE).
- Indexing potential in prestigious indices such as Scopus®, Web of Science™, PsycINFO®, and ERIC – Education Resources Information Center.
- Ability to connect your ORCID iD to your IGI Global publications.
- Earn honorariums and royalties on your full book publications as well as complimentary copies and exclusive discounts.

Join Your Colleagues from Prestigious Institutions, Including:
Australian National University, Massachusetts Institute of Technology, Johns Hopkins University, Harvard University, Tsinghua University, Columbia University in the City of New York

Learn More at: www.igi-global.com/publish
or Contact IGI Global's Aquisitions Team at: acquisition@igi-global.com

Printed in the United States
by Baker & Taylor Publisher Services